THE PELICAN HISTORY OF ART

EDITED BY NIKOLAUS PEVSNER

z6

THE ART AND ARCHITECTURE OF RUSSIA

GEORGE HEARD HAMILTON

GEORGE HEARD HAMILTON

THE ART AND ARCHITECTURE OF RUSSIA

PENGUIN BOOKS

BALTIMORE · MARYLAND

This edition first published 1954
Penguin Books Inc.
3300 Clipper Mill Road, Baltimore, Maryland

★

Copyright 1954 Penguin Books Ltd
Harmondsworth, Middlesex, England

★

Made and printed in
Great Britain

TO
MY WIFE

CONTENTS

Part One
Kievan Russia

Part Two
Icon-Painting

CONTENTS

Part Three
The Art of Muscovy

Part Four
St Petersburg

Part Five
Modern Russian Art

The Plates

LIST OF FIGURES

LIST OF PLATES

FOREWORD

THE *history of a people's art, embracing a thousand years in time and a vast continental space, is not easily or adequately encompassed in a single volume. To cover such a period, from the Chritianization of Russia in 988 to the fall of the Empire in 1917, and to consider only the more remarkable artistic manifestations, entailed a process of stringent selection, perhaps always a part of the writing of history. This account is limited to the arts of architecture, painting, and sculpture, as they have been created in the territories of European Russia by the Russian people. Within this programme the parts are not uniform, in content or chronology, but are related to the broad divisions of artistic expression as they have developed in time. The first part is concerned with architecture and painting in the oldest settlements of Kiev, Novgorod, and Suzdalia, from the later tenth century to the Mongol conquest; the second is devoted to icon painting through the fifteenth century; the third to the culture of Muscovy through the seventeenth century; the fourth treats of the architectural development of St Petersburg; and the last of more modern art, especially the development of painting, the dominant artistic manifestation in the nineteenth century. Regretfully, I have only hinted at the existence of other arts in the belief that the reader familiar with the churches and icons of medieval Russia will be in a position to understand enamels and embroideries, the most characteristic Russian contributions to the decorative arts. Peasant or folk crafts present fewer difficulties, originating as they do on a less complex cultural level; their forms and uses are comprehensible to those who have studied similar manifestations elsewhere. For those who wish further information on the decorative arts, a selected list of illustrated books has been provided in the bibliography.*

In preparing the text and in selecting the illustrations I have not sought to emphasize either the likeness or unlikeness of Russian art to similar or contemporary expressions in Western Europe. I have tried to explain the characteristic elements as they have appeared in time, and to indicate how influences from outside Russia may have helped to shape such forms. I contend, with Catherine the Great, that 'Russia is a European State', and I have tried to explain Russian art in the terms used for the study of European art. I have assumed that the reader interested in studying Russian art has some knowledge of Russian political and social history and of the principal masters and movements in European art, but that he does not read the Russian language. If he commands it, the annotation of the text will send him to my sources should he wish to amplify or to correct my argument.

This book is intended as a history of the formal structure of a national art, rather than as an exercise in criticism. I have tried to avoid impressions which could not be supported by fact, and with the facts I have tried to tell a story according to the principles of modern historical research. When the project for such a book was raised, I had thought it would be possible to verify my hypotheses by an examination of the monuments. When that expectation faded, it seemed wasteful to abandon the undertaking. I am minded now to repeat the words with which John Milton closed the preface to his Brief History of Muscovia, published in 1682:

> What was scatter'd in many volumes, and observ'd at several times by Eye-witnesses, with no cursory pains I laid together, to save the Reader a far longer travaile ... that so many things remarkable, dispers'd before, now brought under one view, might not hazard to be otherwise lost, nor the labour lost of collecting them.

My own labours in collecting these materials could not have been concluded without the unfailing assistance of the administrators and staffs of the libraries whose resources made this study possible, especially the several libraries of Columbia and Yale Universities, the Frick Art Reference Library, the Library of Congress, the New York Public Library, and the library of the Metropolitan Museum of Art. For assistance with the illustrations I am grateful to Vera Andrus, Alfred H. Barr, Jnr, Kenneth Conant, W. G. Constable, Charles C. Cunningham, Samuel Galpin, George Hann, John B. Hills, Henry La Farge, Frederic G. Ludwig, the late Elizabeth Naramore, and Warren A. Peterson. Finally, I would express my gratitude to George Vernadsky, Professor of Russian History at Yale University. Ten years ago he generously guided my first studies in Russian culture. If in the following pages the plan and purpose are mine, they would nevertheless have not been at all without his friendship and inspiration at the start.

ABBREVIATIONS

Ainalov, *Grossfürsten.*   D. V. Ainalov, *Geschichte der russischen Monumentalkunst zur Zeit des Grossfürstentums Moskau* (Berlin and Leipzig, 1933)

Ainalov, *Vormoskov.*   D. V. Ainalov, *Geschichte der russischen Monumentalkunst der vormoskovitischen Zeit* (Berlin and Leipzig, 1932)

Alpatov-Brunov   M. Alpatov and N. Brunov, *Geschichte der altrussischen Kunst* (Augsburg, 1932)

AN   *Akademiya Nauk* (Academy of Sciences)

Aplaksin   A. P. Aplaksin, *Kazanskii Sobor* (St Petersburg, 1911)

Benois   A. Benois, *Russkaya shkola zhivopisi* (St Petersburg, 1904), 10 parts

Bobrinskoi   A. A. Bobrinskoi, *Reznoi Kamen v Rossii, Sobory Vladimiro-Suzdalskoi Oblasti, XII–XIII vv.* (Moscow, 1916)

Bondarenko   I. Ye. Bondarenko, *Arkhitekturnye pamyatniki Moskvy* (Moscow, 1904–5), 3 parts

Buxton   D. R. Buxton, *Russian Mediaeval Architecture* (Cambridge, 1934)

CSRW   Central State Restoration Workshops, Moscow

Demidov   A. de Demidov, *Album du voyage pittoresque et archéologique en Russie* (Paris, 184?)

Diaghilev   S. P. Diaghilev, *Russkaya zhivopis V XVIII Veke, D. G. Levitskii* (St Petersburg, 1902)

Drevnosti, trudy kom.   Moskovskoe Arkheologicheskoe Obshchestvo, *Drevnosti, trudy kommissii po sokhraneniiu drevnykh pamyatnikov,* I–VI (1907–15)

Grabar   I. Grabar, *Istoriya russkago iskusstva* (Moscow, from 1909), 6 vols

Istor. panor.   A. I. Uspenski, *et al., Istoricheskaya panorama Sanktpeterburga i ego okrestnostei* (Moscow, 1911–14), 10 vols

Khudozh. sokrov.   *Khudozhestvennyya sokrovishcha Rossii* (1901–07)

Kondakov   N. P. Kondakov, *Russkaya ikona* (Prague, 1928–33), 4 vols

L'Art byzantin chez les slaves   G. Millet, ed., *L'Art byzantin chez les slaves* (Paris, 1930–2), 2 vols

Lukomski   G. Lukomski, *L'Architecture religieuse en Russie du XIᵉ au XVIIIᵉ siècle* (Paris, 1929)

MAO   Moskovskoe Arkheologicheskoe Obshchestvo

Meyerberg   F. Adelung, *Sammlung von Ansichten, Gebräuchen, Bildnissen, Trachten, u.s.w. welche . . . Augustin Freyherr von Meyerberg auf seinem Aufenthalt in Russland in den Jahren 1661 und 1662 hat entwerfen lassen* (St Petersburg, 1827)

MMA   Metropolitan Museum of Art, New York

Moskva   *Moskva v eya proshlom i nastoyashchem* (Moscow, 1910–?), 12 vols

Moskva; sobory   *Moskva; sobory, monastyri, i tserkvi* (Moscow, 1882–3), 4 vols

Myasoedov   V. Myasoedov, *Freski Spasa Nereditsy* (Leningrad, 1925); French ed. (Paris, 1928)

Naidenov   N. A. Naidenov, *Moskvy, snimki s vidov mestnostei* (Moscow, 1886)

Nekrasov, *Ocherki*   A. I. Nekrasov, *Ocherki po istorii drevnerusskogo zodchestva, XI–XVII veka* (Moscow, 1936)

Nicholas   Grand Duke Nicholas Mikhailovich, ed., *Russkie portrety XVIII i XIX stoletii* (St Petersburg, 1905–9), 6 vols

ABBREVIATIONS

Olearius	A. Olearius, *The Voyages and Travels of the Ambassador from the Duke of Holstein to the Great Duke of Muscovy, and the King of Persia ... Rendered into English* (London, 1662)
Prokhorov	V. Prokhorov, *Pamyatniki drevne russkago iskusstva* (Moscow, 1873)
Rzyanin	M. I. Rzyanin, *Pamyatniki russkogo zodchestva* (Moscow, 1950)
Schweinfurth	P. Schweinfurth, *Geschichte der russischen Malerei im Mittelalter* (The Hague, 1930)
S.C.R.	The Society for Cultural Relations with the U.S.S.R. (London)
Sem. Kond.	Seminarium Kondakovianum, Prague
Suslov	V. V. Suslov, *Pamyatniki drevnyago russkago zodchestva* (St Petersburg, 1895–1901), 7 parts
Thieme-Becker	U. Thieme and F. Becker, *Allgemeines Lexikon der bildenden Künstler* (Leipzig, 1907–47), 36 vols
Travels of Macarius	F. C. Belfour, tr., *The Travels of Macarius, Patriarch of Antioch; Written by his Attendant Archdeacon Paul of Aleppo, in Arabic* (London, 1829), 2 vols
Voronin	N. N. Voronin, *Pamyatniki Vladimiro-Suzdalskogo zodchestva XI–XIII vekov* (Moscow, 1945)
Zabello	S. Ya. Zabello, *et al.*, *Russkoe derevyannoe zodchestvo* (Moscow, 1942)

Varzuga

WHITE SEA

Soloveltski Is.

Kem

Arkhangelsk

Northern Dvina R.

L.LADOGA

Kizhi

L.ONEGA

Ustiug

Solvychegodsk

GULF OF FINLAND

Peterhof

BALTIC

St.Petersburg

R.Neva

Oranienbaum

Staraya Ladoga

Therapont Monastery

Reval

Tsarskoe-Selo

SEA

Gatchina

Pavlovsk

Tikhvin

WHITE LAKE

L.PEIPUS

Vologda

Novgorod

Pskov

L.ILMEN

Staraya Russa

R.Dvina

L.VALDAI

Yaroslavl

R.Volga

Rostov

Pereyaslavl-Zalesski

LITHUANIA

Trinity-Sergius

Suzdal

Nizhni-Novgorod

Monastery

Polotsk

Yuriev-

Polski

Bogoliubovo

Kazan

Zvenigorod

Moscow

Vladimir

Dyakovo-Kolomenskoe

Smolensk

Tsaritsyn

R.Oka

R.Volga

POLAND

R.Dnieper

R.Don

Chernigov

Kiev

R.Dniester

GALICIA

U K R A I N E

Odessa

Kherson

CASPIAN SEA

R.Danube

Tmutarakan

BLACK   SEA

Scale of Miles

Byzantium

0   100   200   300

xxi

PART ONE
KIEVAN RUSSIA

★

The horses neigh beyond the Sula, the glory echoes at Kiev, the trumpets blare at Novgorod, the banners stand fast at Putivl

THE TALE OF THE ARMAMENT OF IGOR
Late Twelfth Century

CHAPTER I
THE PAST OF KIEV

THE study of Russian art properly begins with the Christianization of Russia late in the tenth century. The reason for the appearance of that Christian culture may be better understood by considering the origins of the ancient Russian State. The peoples who were later to be known as Russians, and who can first be described as Eastern Slavs, are thought to have left their homeland in the Carpathian mountains and to have been living, by the third century A.D., in the territory between the Baltic and the Black Seas, and the Don and Danube rivers.[1] This vast sweep of land included the forest and steppe zones where the different natural environments went far to define later Russian culture. In the northern forests, where a living was precariously obtained by clearing the trees and working the soil with primitive instruments, trapping and hunting were the main occupations. Here lived isolated tribes and clans, principally Finns. In the South the forest gave way to the endless grass-covered plains of rich, deep soil, the so-called 'black earth'. The steppes permitted not only thriving agricultural settlements, but also the unparalleled movement of peoples in the absence of any natural barriers. Up to the limits of the forest zone swept continuous waves of nomadic peoples, pushed out of Asia by overpopulation and economic distress. The history of ancient Russia is the story of how the Slavic tribes met, countered, or accepted invasions by non-Slavic peoples from the East.

The first inhabitants of South Russia to appear in history are the Scythians of Iranian stock, known to Herodotus in the fifth century B.C. for their trade relations with the Greek colonies on the shores of the Black Sea. Judging by the objects found in their tomb-barrows, the Scythians were highly civilized and provided a lively market for luxury wares exported from Greece or manufactured in the Chersonesus.[2] In the early fourth century the Scythians were disturbed by another Iranian people, the Sarmatians. Members of one of the more important Sarmatian tribes were known as Alans, originally nomads and renowned as horsemen, who turned in time to an agricultural life and settled among the East Slavic tribes. The Caucasian Alans were called As or Os (plural,

Antes), hence the modern Ossetians. The name of one of their clans was Rukhs-As, 'the light, or brilliant Alans', which may be the origin of Ros or Rus (Russia, Russians).

From at least the third century A.D. the Antes had been living in South Russia, where they developed a high degree of social and cultural organization. They practised agriculture, animal husbandry, weaving, ceramics, and metal-working. In the sixth and seventh centuries two more tribes, the Avars and the Altaic Turks, appeared out of the East and overran South Russia. The Avars eventually passed through Pannonia, where they subjugated the peoples of that region and the Balkan Slavs as well, while the Turks settled on the steppes between the lower Volga and the Don and in the northern Caucasus. There the mixture of Turk, Hun, and Caucasian aborigine produced a new people, the Khazars, who by the middle of the seventh century had developed a prosperous state.

During the eighth and ninth centuries the Khazar state reached its greatest extent and power, and the Antes and Slavs of the lower Don and Azov region, the old As or Rus tribes, participated in the first of the empires to be established on Russian soil. Khazar power reached from the Caspian Sea and lower Volga to the Dnieper and Black Sea. The Khazars developed one of the great trade routes of history, stretching from the upper reaches of the Volga to the Caspian and on to the Near and Middle East into the lands of the Arabs.

So far we have considered only the constant movement of peoples and the passage of power in South Russia as it was determined by invasions from the East. There had been, however, considerable activity in the North. In the sixth and seventh centuries the inhabitants of Scandinavia, in particular the Swedes, had explored the eastern Baltic regions and, travelling up the Dvina, had reached the upper Volga and Oka rivers. If the history of South Russia had been written in the movement of nomadic tribes across the endless plains, the history of North Russia was similarly decided by the interminable network of waterways through the forests. At the meeting point of steppe and river, of forest and plain, of northern adventurers and nomadic hosts would be created the first essentially Russian culture.

After 825, when the Khazars were attacked by the Arabs, the Swedish-Russian chiefs defied the Khazars and established an independent Russian Kaganate with a capital presumably at Tmutarakan on the Taman Peninsula. This Kaganate took over the control of the international trade route. Scandinavian metal-work and Russian furs were transported from the northern trading-post of Staraya Russa (Old Rus, a town still in existence), down the Oka, Volga, and Don rivers to Byzantium and the East. The extent of this activity is seen in the presence in Baghdad of Russian merchants in the ninth century. When the Khazars appealed to the Byzantine Emperor for assistance, engineers were sent to build fortresses, notably that of Sarkel on the lower Don. The Khazars then controlled the Russian trade routes to the East and simultaneously broke the connexions between Taman Rus and northern Russia and, after conquering the Slavs of the Oka region, established their Magyar vassals in the area of Kiev.

The effect of the Khazar interruption of the trade route was also felt in northern Russia. Force was required to resolve the crisis which had developed in the South. But the Swedish-Russian outposts in the North, in the region of Staraya Russa and Lake Ilmen,

possessed few troops, and help was sought from abroad. Such in effect would seem to
have been the reasons for the 'calling of the Varangians from over the Sea', in the
middle of the ninth century, traditionally considered the beginning of modern Russian
history.[3]

About 856 the Norseman, Rurik, famous as an adventurer and the ruler of South Jut-
land and Friesland, arrived in northern Russia and established himself in Ladoga and
Novgorod. He showed little concern for the South, apparently because his possessions
in western Europe were in jeopardy and required his presence. Two of his followers,
Askold and Dir, ventured down the Dnieper and took Kiev in 858 under an agreement
with the Magyars. From there they reached the Taman Russians and joined in an attack
on Constantinople, apparently in protest against the assistance given the Khazars. The
attack was militarily ineffective, but it had the important consequence that the Byzantine
patriarch Photius sent missionaries after the Russians, many of whom were later baptized,
and in 867 the first Russian bishopric was established at Tmutarakan. In 873 Rurik died
and was succeeded by Oleg, who was more interested in the South. In 878 Oleg entered
Kiev, killed Askold and Dir, and declared himself an independent ruler. So, at the hands
of a Norseman, a 'Varanger', began the history of Kievan Russia.

The character of the new state was primarily military and commercial, and its independence was assured by control of the waterways linking the Baltic with the Black Sea
by way of the Gulf of Finland, the river Neva and Lake Ladoga, the river Volkhov and
Lake Ilmen, to the headwaters of the Dnieper near Smolensk, and finally down the
Dnieper to the sea, and so to Constantinople. Portages were rarely required, the most
dangerous being around the rapids which blocked the Dnieper at its furthest eastern bend
300 miles below Kiev. During the winter at the northern trading-stations were collected
quantities of the staples of Kievan trade, furs, wax, and honey, as well as slaves from the
hinterland, sometimes taken as prisoners of war. These goods were brought to Kiev,
where the traders made up their flotilla of small boats for the trip down-river in April
when the ice broke. Military protection against the hostile tribes molesting the remoter
reaches of the waterway, especially the Pechenegs, who were frequently lying in ambush
near the rapids, was provided by the Prince and his retinue of warriors, the druzhina.
Once arrived in Constantinople, the merchants spent the summer trading their goods
for fine wines and eastern silks.

With the establishment of regular mercantile relations with Constantinople the Russians were more susceptible to the influence of Christianity. In addition, many of the
Varangians may have been Christians before they reached Russia. The Greeks were not
unaware that it was to their advantage to bring the unruly merchants of Kiev under their
spiritual as well as economic influence. The chronicler relates that after the signing of the
treaty of 911 the Emperor Leo arranged for his vassals to show the Russian envoys 'the
beauties of the churches' and to instruct them in 'the true belief'.

Yet what might have been a gradual process was given sudden impetus by the appearance of an extraordinary personality, Olga, the wife and widow of Igor and the first of
the women rulers so conspicuous in Russian history. After Igor had been slain in a campaign against a Slav tribe, the Drevlianians, Olga ruled Kiev during the minority of her

son Svyatoslav. After destroying the Drevlianian threat, with clever and brutal tricks, she went to Constantinople, where she was instructed by the Patriarch and was baptized by the Emperor himself. She was unable, however, to convert Svyatoslav, who seems to have been afraid of the ridicule of his druzhina if he adopted Christianity.

It is possible that Svyatoslav's desire to rule over the whole land of Russia and even beyond made him realize that he must not yet abjure the old gods. During his personal reign, from 964 to 972, he spent most of his time campaigning, leaving the internal administration of Kiev to his mother. By 965 Svyatoslav had overcome the Khazars and occupied their chief towns, including the fortress of Sarkel on the Don and Itil at the mouth of the Volga. Immediately afterwards he turned westward, and in 967 overthrew the Bulgars on the Danube and occupied their city of Pereyaslavets, which he decided to make his permanent residence. Svyatoslav's realm was of tremendous extent, stretching from the Volga to the Danube and including the forest areas of Novgorod and the North. But this mighty empire was of short duration. In 971 Svyatoslav was defeated by the Byzantines, and on returning to Kiev perished when his army was surprised by the Pechenegs.

The history of Kievan Russia for the next 250 years is the account of the gradual dismemberment of Svyatoslav's great empire before successive waves of invasion from the East, complicated by the progressive degeneration of the political situation in a series of fratricidal civil wars among the numerous princes of the ruling house, and culminating in the fall of Kiev to the Tartars in 1240. But if politically the period lacks the epic urgency of the ninth-century Russian Kaganate or of Svyatoslav's military brilliance in the tenth century, it saw the formulation of the first specifically Russian art and architecture. These achieved definite expression in three centres of Ancient Russia: in Kiev, 'the mother of Russian cities', where Byzantine art was first introduced; in Novgorod, the northern and very ancient 'New City', where the Byzantine style was modified by distance from Byzantium and proximity to Russia's western neighbours; and in the north-eastern principality of Vladimir-Suzdal, strongly tinged with Eastern influences from the Caucasus.

In the cultural development of Kievan Russia, Christianity is an understandably dominant force. Whether or not we are to read the stories in the chronicles about the conversion of Olga and her grandson Vladimir as history or as myth, they are at least consonant with what we may believe were the actual circumstances. Not the least interesting aspect of these stories is the frequent reiteration of the beauty of Byzantine church architecture and church ritual which impressed the Russians. Here was an immediate, sensuous attraction which proved irresistible to a people which has always been noted for its love of colour, sound, and movement, whether in terms of ecclesiastical liturgy, imperial pageantry, or folk arts. In 980, according to the chronicle, after Vladimir had secured for himself the throne of Kiev by treacherously overthrowing his brother Yaropolk, he 'set up idols on the hill outside the castle'. His morals, too, were what are more usually described as pagan than Christian; according to the chronicler, he was 'insatiable in vice'. Subsequently Vladimir was visited by learned men of various faiths who expounded to him the advantages of Mohammedanism, Judaism, and of Roman and Greek

Catholicism. He was impressed by the Greek scholar who instructed him in world history according to the Old Testament, but he was still uncertain and sent emissaries into various lands to study the ritual worship of various faiths. Again the Greeks proved themselves the most adroit proselytizers. In 987 the Emperor himself took the Russian envoys into the church 'and placed them in a wide space, calling their attention to the beauty of the edifice, the chanting and the offices of the archpriest and the ministry of the deacons, while he explained to them the worship of his God'. The chronicler added: 'The Russians were astonished and in their wonder praised the Greek ceremonial'. When the envoys returned to Vladimir they reported that they had been among the Bulgarians and the Germans (Latins), and 'saw them performing many ceremonies in their temples; but we beheld no glory there'. The peerless churches of Constantinople exercised their ineluctable spell. 'Then we went on to Greece, and the Greeks led us to the edifices where they worship their God, and we knew not whether we were in heaven or on earth. For on earth there is no such splendour or such beauty, and we are at a loss how to describe it. We only know that God dwells there among men, and their service is fairer than the ceremonies of other nations. For we cannot forget that beauty.' Although he was impressed with this description of the Greek faith, Vladimir withheld his formal acquiescence until he could put such a step to political use. A year later he besieged and captured the Greek city of Kherson near the mouth of the Dnieper, which he threatened to destroy unless he were given the Emperor's sister as a wife. Basil and Constantine refused to send their sister Anna unless Vladimir were baptized, to which he agreed providing that Anna herself brought priests with her to perform the office. Vladimir was thereupon baptized in Kherson and departed for Kiev, taking with him his new wife, priests, relics, and sacred vessels for the service. In Kiev Vladimir overthrew the idols of Perun and the other gods and coerced the population into mass baptism in the Dnieper. The people of Novgorod were similarly, although more reluctantly, converted.

The consequences of Vladimir's conversion were soon felt. Many of the cultural amenities which had been unknown to pagan Russians were available to Christians. The most important, perhaps, was the new opportunity for education. Vladimir himself established schools for 'the children of the best families', probably somewhat like Charlemagne's palace schools, to assure an educated aristocracy called by birth to positions of authority in civil affairs. The Church, too, required educated men for the priesthood. With the church books brought from Constantinople, translated into Slavonic, and written in the alphabet devised by St Cyril and St Methodius for the Slavs, came the principles of Byzantine law, which are incorporated in the first Russian code, the eleventh-century *Pravda Russkaya*. With the Church came monastic institutions. The first and for long the most famous was the Kievan Monastery of the Caves, the Pecherskaya Lavra, where not only sanctity but also a high level of intellectual labour was maintained. The latter found expression in the writing of the Russian chronicles, which by the beginning of the twelfth century had grown from a mere list of yearly wonders to a systematic study of history within the framework of religious thought. And, finally, for palace, church, and monastery alike Vladimir and his successors called into existence the buildings and their decoration which constitute the first Russian art.

In Kievan Russia, where the sovereign power was vested in the family of Rurik's descendants rather than in the individual, the principle of succession led to endless and disastrous strife. Only occasionally, as with Vladimir Monomakh, grandson of Yaroslav and through his mother grandson of the Byzantine Emperor Constantine Monomachos, could an individual of unusual presence and gifts dominate the unruly family. With the decay of the central authority in Kiev, the homogeneity of Oleg's and Vladimir's river-realm declined. Barbarian raids more frequently cut the routes between Kiev and Constantinople, so that the Russians were unable to depend upon trade for a living and turned to agriculture and the exploitation of natural resources. In such a situation a new population came into being, centred in towns and depending upon the outlying regions for farm produce, grown on the estates of the wealthy boyars, a term usually understood to mean the landed proprietors among the prince's druzhina. By the middle of the twelfth century a number of local centres had emerged. In addition to Kiev and Novgorod, the Galician principality to the west, bordering on Poland, and the principality of Vladimir-Suzdal in the forests north-east of Moscow came to prominence.

As other cities and religious centres developed, different milieus were created which found distinct expression in art and architecture, as well as in political and social institutions. While Kiev continued until its downfall to stand as the political and spiritual capital of Russia, closely related to the Greek culture of Byzantium, the cities of Novgorod and of Vladimir-Suzdal were soon affected by influences from the East and West. Suzdalia succumbed to the Tartars ahead of Kiev, but before 1237 its rulers had created a princely, aristocratic environment, expressed in a series of magnificent churches and now-vanished palaces which were the wonders of the age. Through the proximity of Suzdalia to the trade-route to the Caspian, and through the marriage of its rulers to Caucasian princesses, Eastern art early appeared as a contributing factor in its art. In Novgorod, at the northern end of the trade-route, western merchants were established from a very early date, and helped to foster a commercial spirit which found political expression in the democratic institution of the town meeting or veche. The painters and architects of Novgorod absorbed Western influences and created a vigorous popular style which endured through the century of Tartar domination until the rise of Moscow in the fifteenth century.

From even this brief summary of the first millennium of Russian history certain constant factors emerge for the history of Russian culture. The first may be defined as mobility. We in the twentieth century often consider ourselves the first peoples to move widely and rapidly through the world, but the history of pre-Kievan Russia reveals a constant succession of peoples moving as widely, if not quite so swiftly, as similar groups to-day. Such a situation implies a variety of influences working in any one place through a period of time which should dispel the notion that such early cultures were fixed or rigid in their forms. Kiev itself, and before Kiev, Tmutarakan, important cities on great trade routes, attracted travellers from the whole world. To this record of the movements of peoples, whether as nations or as individuals, we must add the fact that in the tenth and eleventh centuries Russia was part of two great empires, those of the Byzantines and of the Norsemen. Through their relations with Byzantium, the Russians were in contact with an already old and still potent imperial state. Through the Varangian heritage, Kiev and Novgorod were part of that intensely mobile and brilliant civilization which the Vikings established on the coasts of northern Europe, the Mediterranean, and the Russian waterways in the tenth and eleventh centuries. Thus the Russia of Kiev and Novgorod was politically and culturally a part of Europe to a degree not again achieved to the end of the fifteenth century or even the beginning of the nineteenth or perhaps ever. To think of Kiev and Novgorod as outposts on a strange and savage frontier looking less westward to Paris and Rome than eastward into the fearful distances of Asia, is to misconstrue the historical situation. The Kievan dynasty was allied by marriage more often to the rulers of the West than it was to the Imperial family in Constantinople.[4] Indeed, Yaroslav may be considered a European sovereign through the marriages he contracted for himself and his family with the royal houses of Sweden, Norway, Denmark, Hungary, Poland, and France. His wife was a daughter of King Olaf of Sweden. Yaroslav's grandson, Vladimir Monomakh, married Harold II's daughter, Gyda of England, who had taken refuge in Sweden after the Battle of Hastings. The causes which drew Kievan Russia into the orbit of world civilization in the tenth and eleventh centuries outweighed those which might have isolated her from western European culture. Far more than her geographical situation or her acceptance of Orthodox Christianity, it was the Mongol domination from the thirteenth to the end of the fifteenth century which contributed to Russia's subsequent isolation from Europe, making of her a province of Tartary just at the time when the high medieval and early Renaissance revival of learning, discovery of scientific method, and flowering of artistic individualism brought the European nations further political differentiation and cultural interdependence. When the Great Princes of Muscovy and Tsars of Russia, Ivan III, Alexis Mikhailovich, or Peter the Great, looked to the West for political, scientific, or artistic conceptions, they found that they were separated from their contemporaries by a gulf in time more difficult to bridge than any extent in space.

7

CHAPTER 2

THE ARCHITECTURE OF KIEV
990–1240

WHEN Vladimir returned to Kiev in 989 after his conquest of Kherson and imposed conversion upon his subjects, one of his first tasks was to supply his chief cities with adequate houses of worship. Christians and Christian churches had existed before this. The chronicles in 882 record a Church of St Nicholas built by Olma over the tomb of Askold and Dir, and the Church of St Elias is mentioned in the Byzantine treaty of 945 as 'a cathedral church since many of the Varangians were Christians'. But these would certainly have been inadequate for the increased demands of the new faith. Vladimir's first act, after throwing down the idols of Perun and Volos which he had previously erected, was to build a church dedicated to St Basil, his patron, upon the site where his idols had stood. These first Kievan churches presumably were wooden structures which soon disappeared; they may have been burned in the fire which swept Kiev in 1017.[1]

Far more important was Vladimir's second church, the Cathedral of the Dormition of the Virgin (Uspenski Sobor) (Figure 1), known as the Desyatinnaya or 'Church of the (Virgin of the) Tithe' from the fact that Vladimir, in regulating the ecclesiastical institutions of Russia, dedicated to it a tithe of his income.[2] The church was founded in 989, consecrated in 996 (or 994), and rededicated by Theopomptos, the first Metropolitan, in 1039. The reasons for the rededication are unknown, but it is possible that the ceremony was required by rebuilding after a fire in 1017. The Desyatinnaya was pillaged by rebellious Kievan princes in 1169 and 1203, and was completely wrecked in 1240, when the vaults collapsed under the weight of the populace who had retreated there with their household goods during the Tartar siege. The ruins were used for building materials until the seventeenth century, when the Metropolitan Peter Mogila attempted to preserve the remaining fragments by including them in a small chapel he built in the southwest corner. After 1828, during the construction of a new church occupying some two-thirds of the original site, parts of the foundations were uncovered; they were further studied after the demolition of the nineteenth-century church in 1926. Unfortunately the first excavations were hasty, poorly reported, and subsequently spoiled, so that conclusions based upon early drawings of the foundations must be accepted with reservations. At best the evidence disclosed is scanty and contradictory, especially since the fragments of the old walls and floors have now all but disappeared. The discovery beneath these foundations of the remains of a wooden structure and of stone tombs lacking any Christian symbols suggests that Vladimir built his church on the site of a pre-Christian pagan temple.[3]

From the apparent absence at the east end of the church of piers or of a chain wall for the support of a dome it has been argued that the Desyatinnaya was a basilica with nave and aisles ending in three semi-circular, slightly horseshoe-shaped apses and that it was roofed in wood. The basilica plan, however, was out of fashion in Constantinople in the tenth century, and was not used later in Russia. Its singular appearance in Kiev in 991 would imply some influence from the West, possibly from Bulgaria, where the three-apsed basilica without domes is found in such churches as Sancta Sophia in Ochrida, founded before 1018, or from the East, from Kherson, where small churches of the basilican plan with three apses have been uncovered. Neither of these hypotheses can be dismissed, given the close relations between the Russian and Bulgarian Churches in this period. The Russian Church adapted its language – Church Slavonic – from the Bulgarian, and Vladimir built the Desyatinnaya soon after his return from Kherson accompanied by priests from that city. Yet, conversely, if the side galleries which flank

0   10   20   30   40   50 FEET

0   5   10   15 METRES

Figure 1. Kiev. Desyatinnaya

the two aisles can be considered part of the original building programme rather than additions after the fire of 1017, and the western bay a later addition, the plan closely resembles the restored plans for the Churches of St George (1037–51) and St Irene (c. 1050), which were of almost the same dimensions. Since St Irene was a five-domed church with incomplete chain walls, the Desyatinnaya may have been completed after the fire of 1017 as a vaulted five-domed cruciform church. Whatever the original covering was, it must have been supplied with masonry vaults, probably after 1017, judging by the episode in 1240 when the people took refuge on the roof.[4] Such a conclusion would seem justified given the Desyatinnaya's position as the eldest of Kiev's large masonry structures, and Vladimir's favourite church. According to the chronicle in 989: 'After he had begun to build, and the structure was completed, he adorned it with images, and entrusted it to Anastasius of Kherson. He appointed Khersonian priests to serve in it, and bestowed

9

upon this church all the images, vessels, and crosses which he had taken in that city.' Subsequently as his burial-place the church grew in veneration.

Although the Khersonian background of the Desyatinnaya is historically established, there were other influences at work in its creation. The chronicle adds that: 'with the intention of building a church dedicated to the Holy Virgin, (Vladimir) sent and imported artisans from Greece'.

Vladimir's earlier memories of the basilican churches of Kherson may later have been modified by information brought by these Greek workmen, and more particularly by the Greek priests who accompanied his Byzantine bride, the Princess Anna. Vladimir, as a Christian and the brother-in-law of the Emperor, would have considered himself closely allied with the imperial house. And he or his wife may well have had in mind the palace church in Constantinople, Basil I's Nea Ekklesia (881), as the model for their own. It is perhaps significant that the Desyatinnaya, like the Nea Ekklesia, was dedicated to the Virgin and both were in a sense personal donations. If, then, the Desyatinnaya was a cruciform rather than a basilican structure, whether originally or through modifications after 1017, as the progenitor of the later churches of southern Russia it appears in a more logical and coherent relation to Yaroslav's Sancta Sophia. Both structures thereby approach more closely a possible Byzantine prototype such as the Nea Ekklesia, which in turn inspired many Constantinopolitan and provincial churches of the tenth and early eleventh centuries.

However inadequate our attempts to recapture the original appearance of the Desyatinnaya may be, the few surviving fragments of white marble columns, carved capitals, tessellated pavements, and fresco-painting, all in the best Byzantine manner, indicate that Vladimir spared neither trouble nor money to make this church a proper monument to his new faith. As a proving ground for Russian art and architecture of the future, it must have been of the utmost significance. Whether the builders were Greeks or Russians instructed by Greeks [5] the decorators certainly came from the capital. Russian mason and painter could now learn the new techniques just as, from the Kherson and Byzantine clergy, craftsman and Christian were learning the expressive possibilities of the new religion. The workshops of the Desyatinnaya, like those later at Fontainebleau, must have been the schools where the Russians studied who were going to assist in the construction and decoration of Sancta Sophia.

Vladimir's son, Yaroslav the Wise, after overthrowing his brother, the cruel and treacherous Svyatopolk, reigned in Kiev from 1017 to 1057.[6] He continued and even amplified Vladimir's building programme, investing the city with an almost imperial splendour.

The date of the foundation of Sancta Sophia has been contested.[7] Since under the year 1036 the chronicle states that Yaroslav met and defeated the Pechenegs 'on the spot where the metropolitan Church of Sancta Sophia now stands', the mention of the church in 1037 in the list of Yaroslav's foundations has been taken to mean that it was begun in that year. Its construction would therefore have occupied the latter years of Yaroslav's reign. It happens, however, that the First Novgorod Chronicle states, in 1018, that Sancta Sophia was founded in that year. If to this is added the statement of the Kievan chronicle that in 1017 when Yaroslav occupied Kiev 'the churches were burned', the construction of Sancta Sophia must have been begun in 1018 and been carried well towards completion by 1037, when the list of Yaroslav's accomplishments was set down.[8] The earlier date may also be implied in the words of Hilarion, the first native-born Metropolitan of Russia, who in his *Discourse on Law and Grace*, a sermon preached before Yaroslav some time between 1037 and 1050, apostrophized the Prince as the successor of Vladimir, as one who had built 'a great and holy house of God ... adorned it with every beauty'.

Figure 2. Kiev. Sancta Sophia

Sancta Sophia, Yaroslav's supreme achievement, the greatest monumental religious structure in Russia and the source from which the long line of Orthodox masonry churches for the next nine centuries was to proceed, is almost as difficult to describe in its original condition as Vladimir's Desyatinnaya. While the one vanished completely, the other gradually disappeared beneath successive destruction and restoration. Damaged in the numerous sacks of Kiev, culminating in the capture of the city by the Tartars in 1240, and abandoned by its clergy during the Middle Ages, the church lay in majestic, almost forgotten, desolation until the seventeenth and eighteenth centuries, when it was internally repaired and externally reconstructed in the style of the Polish–Ukrainian Baroque. The addition of eight new domes, making a total of twenty-one, and the reconstruction of all the cupolas in an intricate baroque form gave it a bizarre appearance totally at variance with what we may conceive the original to have been. Only within the last century have the frescoes and mosaics been recovered from beneath layers of seventeenth-century whitewash, and only in the present century has anything approaching a systematic examination of the fabric begun to yield answers to the many problems it presents.

The nine-aisled plan (Figure 2) represents less the original intentions of the builders than a progressive modification and multiplication of elements developing from the basic cruciform plan with adjoining galleries, first stated in the Nea Ekklesia and modified in the Desyatinnaya. Originally Sancta Sophia had a nave and four aisles, ending in east apses with a tribune over the outer aisles. At either end of the west façade a stair tower provided access to the adjoining palaces of the Prince and Metropolitan. Surrounding the church on three sides was an open arcade upon which a gallery was later constructed and an additional one-storey arcade added to the north and south (Plate 1).[9] In the seventeenth century a gallery was added over the second, outer arcade. This gave the church a cubical appearance and accentuated the fact that the breadth had gradually become greater than the length. At the same time the domes were increased in height and number, so that the present exterior bears no relation to the original structure except on the east, where the distribution and proportions of the three central apses have been preserved. Although the chronicles contain no mention of the origin of the workmen, the construction, in *opus mixtum* composed of alternating courses of reddish quartzite, buff brick, and pink mortar, recalls contemporary Byzantine practice common in Kiev at this time.[10]

The most spectacular aspect of Sancta Sophia, that in which it departed notably from any Byzantine prototype, was its culminating arrangement of thirteen cupolas, the number signifying Christ and His twelve Apostles. These cupolas, consisting of low domes placed on high and narrow drums, were possibly suggested by a Russian precedent, worked out in a material unfamiliar to Byzantine architects. In 991 Vladimir, after imposing Christianity on the citizens of Novgorod, had founded there the Cathedral of Sancta Sophia. This wooden church was destroyed by fire in 1045, but it was conspicuous during its brief existence and in the memory of the chroniclers for its thirteen 'tops' (vierkhi). Whether these were roofs, gables, spires, or, as would seem quite unlikely, wooden cupolas, is not clear.[11] But these thirteen crowning elements may have suggested to Yaroslav, who had been Prince of Novgorod before reigning in Kiev, the possibility of surpassing the fine new masonry domes which may have been building above his father's Desyatinnaya, just as the masons were called to his new church.

If the picturesque pyramidal outline of Sancta Sophia can be related to the silhouette of its wooden predecessor in Novgorod, the church to that extent may be taken as a specifically Russian departure from Byzantine principles, and so to mark the beginning of a native architectural tradition. But the plan and organization of space upon which this silhouette was based are more difficult to explain. The church undeniably was related to Byzantine architectural tradition. A line can be traced from Sancta Sophia through such

structures as St Mary Panachrantos (the Theo-
tokos of Lips, later the Fenari-Issa, after 908)
(Figure 3), and St Theodosia (1000) to the Nea
Ekklesia (881), where the basic scheme of a
domed cruciform plan with five apses adjoined
by arcades was first promulgated. The presence
of a similar plan in the sixth-century church at
Meiafarqin in Mesopotamia and in the eleventh-
century church at Mokvi (Figure 4), in the
Caucasus may indicate the presence among the
builders of Sancta Sophia of Greek or even
Russian masons familiar with eastern Byzantine
architecture.[12] It is worth recalling that while the
chronicle specifically states that Vladimir 'sent
and imported artisans from Greece' for the Desyatinnaya, there is no mention of Yaroslav having
done so. Possibly, therefore, the gangs working

Figure 3. Constantinople. Fenari-Issa, 908

on Sancta Sophia included some of the Greek artisans come to Kiev twenty years before,
as they must have numbered among them local craftsmen trained in the shops of the
Desyatinnaya.

Within and without, the building was an evocation of Greece. The high crossing
under the central dome seemed like a courtyard surrounded by a two-storeyed portico
whence the space passed through the nave and tribunes into the outer arcades. On
the exterior the majestic breadth of the
structure, surrounded by open galleries
crowned by broad terraces, must have
seemed to Yaroslav and his courtiers fair
to rival the palaces of Tsargrad ('the
Emperor's City'), as the Russians called
Constantinople.

The interior of Sancta Sophia presented
a similar departure from, as in other respects it was a more faithful reflexion of,
Byzantine models. The many large piers,
more massive than in Greece, tended to
break up the interior space into numerous
small compartments and to accentuate
the vertical proportions. The interior was
higher and narrower than its Byzantine
prototypes, possibly owing to the necessity of providing adequate supports for
the thirteen domes. Although the total
enclosed space was actually a third that

Figure 4. Mokvi. After O. Wulff

13

of Sancta Sophia in Constantinople, the interior may not have been originally so dark, when the galleries on the sides were open. Also important for subsequent architectural development was the treatment of the external walls with rows of blind recessed windows divided by colonnettes or pilasters, and the tiled roof laid directly on the vaults in the Byzantine manner, a device suitable for a warm, dry climate but later discovered to be disastrous in the damp Russian weather. The rhythmical effect produced by the multiplication of semi-circular elements, in the windows, on the walls and drums, in the arches of the arcades, and in the undulating juncture of roof with walls, became characteristic for later architecture in the north and north-east.

By 1100 Sancta Sophia had achieved its definitive form. The construction of the outer galleries in *opus mixtum* indicates that they were completed before the end of the century. Also, the upper walls apparently threatened to collapse after the domes had been set in place. To offset this danger, six large quarter-circular buttresses were set at right angles to the walls. Since they interrupt the paintings on the gallery walls, it is obvious that they were erected after the church had been decorated, probably early in the twelfth century.

More grandiose than the Desyatinnaya or the contemporary Church of the Transfiguration at Chernigov, the pyramidal mass of Sancta Sophia, with its thirteen domes and glittering polychromatic fabric, became the first great symbolic expression in Russian architecture. Even as it proclaimed the spiritual authority of the Metropolitan of Kiev, and the magnificence of the princely court declaring its attachment to the conception of secular splendour learned in Byzantium, it established a new architectural silhouette which would become implicit in all subsequent Russian ecclesiastical architecture, however far it might appear to depart from the original Byzantine model.

Even in ruins, in the hands of the enemy, neglected by its clergy and forgotten by its own people, the church impressed the traveller with its monumental scale. At the end of the sixteenth century a German visitor, Heidenstein, secretary to Sigismund III, King of Poland, admired the western portico then still preserved with its columns of porphyry, marble, and alabaster.[13] To a seventeenth-century Dutch artist, Abraham van Westerveldt, is due the credit for revealing through his meticulous drawings how well they built who first successfully on Russian soil erected a structure of truly imperial monumentality.[14] Among van Westerveldt's drawings two are of particular interest. One shows the western façade, which was still in ruins, although the eastern end of the church, which was in better condition, had already been restored by Peter Mogila (Plate 2A). The interior of the frescoed baptistery, added in the twelfth century, can be seen beside the later south-western stair tower. In another drawing the point of view is taken from the east looking westward down the outer south aisle (Plate 2B). The buttresses inserted to support the vaults are conspicuous.

The Desyatinnaya and Sancta Sophia, with the destroyed churches of St George and St Irene,[15] form the important group of multiple-aisled churches in southern Russia. The continuous pressure on Kiev by the barbarians in the East interrupted the construction of such churches. Under the circumstances it was perhaps inevitable that a simpler plan and less elaborate structural system should have been evolved to meet the changing requirements of church building. A first indication of the new type appears in the Cathedral of the Transfiguration (Spaso-Preobrazhenski Sobor) in Chernigov (Plate 4), founded about 1017 by Mstislav of Tmutarakan, Prince of Chernigov and younger brother of Yaroslav, with whom he had disputed the Kievan succession. The church had risen 'to a point higher than a man on horseback could reach with his hand' at the time of Mstislav's death in 1034 (1036).[16] The plan represents a stage intermediary between the Desyatinnaya and St Irene. The same system of five domes over a nave and aisles where the four piers support the central dome defines the Greek cross (Figure 5). The pre-

Figure 5. Chernigov. The Transfiguration

sence at the crossing of columns rather than piers as supports for the gallery above the nave is another echo of Greek practice (Plate 3). Such columns, which are found in the Novgorod as well as the Kievan Sancta Sophia, disappear after the eleventh century. There are indications that, like Sancta Sophia and the Desyatinnaya, it had open arcades on the north and south sides. Indeed, here the specifically Russian rectangular plan was more prominent than in any of the contemporary churches of Kiev. The compromise is subtle; the length of the basilica is incorporated within the compact centrality of the domed cross by the addition of the extra bay to the east. One can, as in the Desyatinnaya and Sancta Sophia, but with more assurance, predicate an Eastern influence, probably from Asia Minor. The church at Dere Aghsy, apparently originally five-domed, is very similar to Chernigov in plan and structure.[17] And the transmission of influences to Chernigov from Asia Minor is not improbable, since Tmutarakan, at the mouth of the

Don, the appanage of Mstislav, had long been the port of entry for trade between the Eastern countries and Kievan Russia. The Cathedral of Chernigov also suffered severely in the troubled times from the end of the eleventh century, and was even more drastically rebuilt in the seventeenth century, restored in the nineteenth, and finally all but destroyed in the Second World War.

Like the Desyatinnaya, the Chernigov Transfiguration was richly decorated with marbles and frescoes, of which few traces are left. Perhaps of more significance was the treatment of the exterior walls with a series of blind arches, decoratively placed to accentuate the grouping of the various elements rather than as the expression of structure. From many points of view the church stands as an intermediary between the Desyatinnaya and Sancta Sophia, and between the latter and its provincial variants in the next century. In some respects, notably in the disposition of the central piers, the high space below the central dome, the columns supporting the tribune on the north and south sides of the crossing, and in the external arcades, we can trace the older Byzantine tradition of the Nea Ekklesia. In others, such as the reduction in depth of the apses and the relatively unencumbered space of the nave and aisles recalling the longitudinal distribution of earlier basilican plans, we see in Chernigov the beginning of the line of development which leads to the simpler churches of northern Russia in later centuries.

In Kiev itself the Church of the Dormition in the Crypt Monastery (Pecherskaya Lavra) above the river just below the city was founded by Abbot Theodosius in 1073.[18] This first and most famous monastic establishment in Russia, where the monks lived in caves dug out of the clay banks along the Dnieper, had prospered to such an extent that buildings above ground were required. The Cathedral, finished in 1075 and consecrated in 1089, was damaged by fire in 1484 and 1718, reconstructed in the baroque manner later in the eighteenth century, and almost entirely destroyed in the Second World War (Plate 5A). As with Sancta Sophia, only the eastern façade, in the distribution and proportion of the apses, provides any clue to its original appearance. The plan, so greatly simplified, resembles Chernigov, with the addition of side aisles added in the eighteenth century. Originally the church had only one dome over the crossing, supported on four masonry piers, an arrangement which soon became customary for church architecture.

The Church of the Yeletski Monastery near Chernigov, again with a modern exterior, St Basil at Ovruch, restored in 1908, and in Kiev St Michael with the Golden Roof represent progressive modifications and simplifications of the multiple plan and complex massing of the Desyatinnaya and Sancta Sophia, working towards the definitive simplified form of a cubical mass surmounted by a central cupola supported internally by pendentives on four central piers.[19] The exterior walls were frequently ornamented with arches on pilasters. While these pilasters, or more rarely colonnettes, are placed opposite the thrust of the vaults within, their purpose is decorative rather than structural, since they are too slender to serve as effective buttresses. All these churches have been so much reworked externally that the treatment of the roof and domes must remain in doubt. But if we deduce a progression from Byzantine domes of the tenth century to the twelfth- and thirteenth-century churches of Vladimir-Suzdal, where the domes and cupolas are in a better state of preservation, it would seem that the Kievan architects worked from the Byzantine flattened saucer dome on a low drum towards the slender high drum and helmet dome of the typical Russian church of the later Middle Ages.

Since Vladimir's and Yaroslav's churches were designed to make Kiev a brilliant city reminiscent of Constantinople, secular architecture of comparable dignity must have been required. Yet all such structures have vanished, leaving scarcely more than a memory. Undoubtedly such buildings were usually in wood, which was traditional in Russia for centuries to come as a material for residences, whether palatial or peasant, and so inevitably perished in the fires which regularly swept the Russian cities. In the tenth century the chronicles mention two palaces, one 'in the city', which is to say inside the citadel, and another called the castle with the hall, outside the walls.[20] The Desyatinnaya was probably a palace church; excavations have revealed two long masonry halls near it. Similarly a princely residence was built beside Sancta Sophia, with which it was connected by galleries reached from stair towers. But it is difficult to hazard even a conjecture about the appearance of these structures.

CHAPTER 3

THE ARCHITECTURE OF NOVGOROD AND PSKOV

990–1500

AT the northern terminus of the 'road between the Varangians and the Greeks', extending along both banks of the river Volkhov four miles below Lake Ilmen, was the city of Novgorod ('New Town'). In spite of its name this was a most ancient settlement which by the tenth century had already become an important centre for trade and the defence of the waterway. Although Novgorod was to endure long after Kiev had fallen to the Tartars, its prestige and power depended less on its cultural and ecclesiastical position than on its commercial relations, especially with the territories to the north and west of Russia. The townspeople not only took part in the annual collection of staple goods, furs, honey, and wax, for transportation to the south, they also maintained relations with Scandinavia and Germany through the continuation of the waterway along the Volkhov to Lake Ladoga and so down the Neva to the Gulf of Finland. To the south-west the citizens of the younger city of Pskov at the head of Lake Peipus were no less busy. From Pskov it was only a short journey overland to the Gulf of Riga, and so by water to the countries bordering the Baltic. In this way the merchants of Novgorod and Pskov early came in contact with Western culture, especially through their relations with German traders. By the middle of the twelfth century direct commerce with Bremen and Cologne was established, and in 1195 a commercial treaty was concluded between Novgorod and the Germans, Gotlanders, and 'every Latin (Roman Catholic) nation'.[1] In the city itself the district on the right bank of the river where the foreign merchants had their own shops, houses, and churches became known as the Commercial Quarter (Torgovaya Storona). Travelling along the inland waterways to the north and east, Novgorod traders subdued the Finnish tribes of the forest lands, and by the twelfth century may have penetrated as far as the Urals and beyond. Much later the members of a merchant family of Novgorod, the Stroganovs, were instrumental in effecting the discovery and exploitation of Siberia in the sixteenth and early seventeenth centuries.

Such a culture, where the success or failure of the individual depended on his own exertions quite as much as on his membership of a class or group, led very early to a separatist attitude which found expression in one of the first democratic political organizations in ancient Russia. As early as the mid eleventh century Yaroslav the Wise, who had been Prince of Novgorod before gaining Kiev, granted the city a charter, the first obtained by any Russian town. The princely rule of succession, whereby Kiev went to the eldest or most powerful of the family with Novgorod granted as an apanage to his eldest son, produced such a constant change of governments that the citizens soon were accustomed to take matters into their own hands. Their will was expressed through a general town-meeting, called the veche, known in the history of other Russian cities, but nowhere attaining such continuous and effective influence in municipal affairs as in Novgorod.

Novgorod was the only important city of Russia which escaped destruction by the Tartars, who were deterred from taking it by the flooded marshes during the unusually wet spring of 1238. It was also brilliantly defended by its famous prince, Alexander Nevski, whose title, 'of the river Neva', was bestowed for his defeat of the Swedes on the Neva in 1236. Alexander matched such military victories as this and his rout of the German Knights on Lake Peipus in 1242 with his skilful bargains with the Tartars, to whose court at Batu he had to journey no less than four times. As a result of its geographical good fortune and political astuteness, Novgorod was unmolested through the thirteenth and fourteenth centuries.

Rich, independent, and proud, Novgorod took to herself the style and title of 'Lord Novgorod the Great' and defied her enemies with the ringing challenge 'Who can stand against God and Great Novgorod?' Such boasts are dangerous; they arouse antagonism, especially when the spirit in which they are expressed seems so intractable. The end of Novgorod's long independence came in 1475, when Ivan III, determined to bring the city and its vast north-eastern possessions under the control of Muscovy, revoked the ancient charter and removed many of the leading families to Moscow. Even the great bell which in old days had been rung to summon the veche was carried off to the Kremlin. A century later the last embers of its pride were extinguished when Ivan IV, 'the Terrible', took the city in 1570 and destroyed its commercial significance with the fearful execution of some 60,000 citizens.

The architecture of Novgorod in the first period of its history derived from Kiev, and is to be understood as a provincial variant of the Kievo-Byzantine style.[2]

From the first certain factors appeared in the activity of the Novgorod builders which were constant throughout its artistic history. The historical continuity of Novgorod itself was of the first importance. Until the rise of Moscow after 1400 Novgorod remained the only great free city in Russia, maintaining constant contacts with the West through the important German trading establishments, and acting as a centre for the continuous importation and diffusion of art and influences from Constantinople. The fourteenth century, which for the rest of Russia was a period of doubt and confusion, saw the emergence at Novgorod of a style of architecture distinct in plan and structure and the development of important schools of icon and fresco-painting, at times under the direction of masters come from Greece, at others the work of local artists. Until quite recently the reputation of Novgorod, in the absence of adequate information about the history of Kiev, Vladimir-Suzdal, and Moscow, was so great that attribution to the 'Novgorod School' was sufficient to indicate work of the highest quality in painting and the minor arts. Alone of the ancient cities Novgorod had retained its complement of early medieval churches which lent it an architectural prestige, certainly in excess and somewhat to the disadvantage of other centres.

For the extent and quality of this activity the republican mercantile character of the city's traditions and institutions were in large measure responsible. The wealthier citizens, members of a powerful middle class, had not their like elsewhere in medieval

Russia as patrons of art and were the primary instigators of the city's tremendous architectural activity. In one century alone, from 1103 to 1207, the chronicles record the construction of no fewer than sixty-eight churches. For forty-one the names of the founders are preserved; fifteen were the work of private individuals or groups of merchants, while sixteen were built by the Archbishops of Novgorod. In contrast to Kiev and Suzdalia, where almost all church construction was initiated by the Prince, only ten churches in this century were so constructed.[3]

This volume of building provided unexampled opportunities for change and experiment. Unlike the princely or ecclesiastical authorities, private patrons were less inclined to follow traditional types, and since as merchants they came frequently into contact with foreign traders visiting or resident in Novgorod, they and their architects would more readily accept ideas not encountered in strictly local and inherited traditions. Quite as much as by the climate which required steep roofs for the speedy removal of accumulated snow and ice, the vertical, gabled character of later Novgorod architecture can be explained by influences reaching northern Russia from Germany, particularly from the cities of the Hanseatic League.

It is necessary also to recall that the men of Novgorod had long been noted for their carpentry, and that wooden churches stood side by side with those of brick and stone. The chronicles more often than not are silent about the material of which a given church was constructed; during the twelfth century only four wooden churches are mentioned, while nine were said to be of stone. But the frequent total destruction of large numbers of churches by fire is an indication that many more were built of wood. The presence of so much wood construction, wherein change and experiment were immediately possible, furthered the development of the characteristic Novgorod structure in the course of the thirteenth and fourteenth centuries.

Another and most considerable factor, which must be remembered in evaluating the character of this style, was the rapidity with which churches were erected in Russia. To be sure, they were never very large; only the two Cathedrals of Sancta Sophia approach the dimensions of the great buildings of Western Europe, and even they, it is worth noting, were substantially completed within twenty years. On the other hand, the smaller parish churches were erected very quickly. Of the forty-one built in Novgorod during the twelfth century for which the dates of foundation and of completion or consecration are preserved, the period of construction averaged three years. The shortest time recorded was seventy days, for the Church of the Annunciation built between 21 May and 25 August 1179, a masonry structure which survived to modern times.[4]

Such speed was possible only when plan, structure, and decorative effects had been standardized, and the history of Novgorod architecture is in large part the search for a progressive simplification which will permit such easy and rapid execution. Thus in the course of time the six-piered, five-domed plan of Kiev and Vladimir was abandoned in favour of four piers supporting a single central dome. Although three apses were retained throughout the twelfth century, they were most commonly all of equal height. The projection of the apses became less and less salient, until by the end of the twelfth century much of the space originally contained in the semi-circular apses was incorporated within the body of the church. In the fourteenth century only one apse was customary, attaining but half the height of the eastern façade.

The technical and formal evolution of architecture in Novgorod and Pskov was hastened by a change in materials. Where Kiev clung to the familiar Byzantine methods of brick and mortar, and Vladimir-Suzdal developed a splendid architecture in white stone, Novgorod soon began to use less costly materials. In any case good stone was hard to find in northern Russia. Instead the masons set odd-sized uneven blocks in thick mortar, almost in the manner of rubble, with brick for pilasters and cornices. The whole surface was then covered with stucco and given a coat of white paint. Visual appearance was very much a part of Novgorod architecture; the rough surfaces, uneven lines, and frequent departure from the vertical lend many of the smaller churches the effect of having been moulded like potter's clay, of having been 'hand-made'. Contrast was provided by the crisp accents of the brick trim laid in zig-zag and saw-tooth patterns around the cornices and drums.

Wood was early and pre-eminently the most accessible and practicable material in northern Russia. So true was this that from early days the men of Novgorod were even derided by the Kievans as 'carpenters'.[5] Wood-workers they were, for they already had to their credit the 'first truly Russian church of monumental character',[6] the Cathedral of Sancta Sophia built of oak by Vladimir's order immediately after his conversion in 988, and so contemporary with his masonry church of the Desyatinnaya in Kiev. Though the two buildings have long been destroyed (for Sancta Sophia burned in the great fire of 1045), together they illustrate the two tendencies which were for centuries paramount in Russian ecclesiastical architecture: the southern Byzantine tradition of masonry construction, closely linked spiritually and culturally with Kiev and later with Vladimir-Suzdal and Moscow; and on the other hand the northern, timber tradition, remote alike from prince and metropolitan, which came to represent the popular religious life, particularly after the tragic schism between patriarch and people in the seventeenth century. By that time the different forms evolved from masonry and timber techniques could be taken as symbols of the separatist tendencies within the Russian Church.

Vladimir's church, probably because it was the first in the north on such a scale, immediately attracted much attention. It is described as having thirteen 'tops', but whether these were roofs, gables, or spires is not known. This first church was built under the direction of Bishop Joachim, who had been sent by Vladimir to convert the people of Novgorod. Since he must have been a Greek, and so familiar with Byzantine ecclesiastical architecture, it is tempting but futile to conjecture the appearance of this remote adaptation of Byzantine liturgical requirements to local timber tradition.

The new Cathedral (Plates 6 and 7), built between 1045 and 1062 by Prince Vladimir, the son of Yaroslav the Wise, was again dedicated to Sancta Sophia, apparently to recall the great church in Constantinople rather than its only slightly elder contemporary, the church of Sancta Sophia in Kiev.[7] Since the plan of the Novgorod cathedral (Figure 6) is a simplified version of the church in Kiev, it is probable that the Greek masters whom Vladimir called to Novgorod were among those who had recently completed the Kievan Sancta Sophia. Parts of the fabric, of local grey-yellow stone alternating with courses of brick, are more typically Byzantine than others where irregular stones project from the mortar, recalling the prismatic effect of medieval gem setting. Before the exterior was stuccoed in 1151 it must have had some of the polychromatic play of light and shade seen in the Kievan churches. More important than the general resemblance to Sancta Sophia in Kiev are the divergences from Byzantine practice which prepare the way for the development of North Russian architecture. The Novgorod church has double aisles but only three apses, each outer aisle ending in a straight wall at the entrance to the apses.[8] Internally the greater bulk of the stone piers, cross-shaped in plan, divides the

Figure 6. Novgorod. Sancta Sophia

interior into even smaller cells than in Kiev, and contributes to the more insistent verticality which became characteristic of Novgorod interiors. It is important to observe that there is still the broad space beneath the central dome (Plate 5B); one bay opens out in each direction to form an equilateral cross-shaped space separated by but one column from the adjacent bays of the nave and aisles. Sancta Sophia in Novgorod still preserved, however far in the northern forest, something of that majestic Hellenic space which had been so notable in the Nea Ekklesia almost two centuries before. As early as the twelfth century, galleries and a stair-tower which were added on the south and west sides (to be completed in the nineteenth century by a gallery on the north side) emphasized the lateral extension of the structure in the manner of Sancta Sophia in Kiev.

With the addition of the bishop's palace, Novgorod obtained the nucleus of the court-church group familiar in Kiev.

Externally the church differed most from its southern prototype. There were only five main domes with a sixth over the stair-tower, although in this city we might have expected some influence from its wooden predecessor's thirteen 'tops'. Throughout the structure the tendency towards multiplicity of parts to be seen in Kiev was replaced by a desire for unity, even uniformity. This led to the elimination of much ornament, including the shallow niches on the apses characteristic of Kiev. The equal height of the three apses which reach to the cornice, the smooth wall surfaces on all four façades, and the shallow, flat pilasters contribute to this unity. Though the church retained the Byzantine rhythmical roof-line, since the roof was laid directly on the vaults, the height, the narrower windows, and the arched bands on the drums told of other than Greek influences. The latter details and the presence over the galleries above the outer aisles of quadrant vaults as buttresses for the pair of domes over each inner aisle, in the manner of French Romanesque architecture of the eleventh century, suggest that in Novgorod there were builders familiar with contemporary western European practice.[9] The greater verticality and the smaller windows, which affect the external appearance and distribute more concentrated light and shade within, may have been influenced by the existing tradition of wood construction and the colder, damper climate.

To the climate may also be due the rapid development in northern Russia of the characteristic bulbous or onion dome. Whereas the cupolas of Kiev, and later of Vladimir-Suzdal, represented only a slight modification of the flat Byzantine dome towards the helmet-shaped type, in Novgorod as early as the mid twelfth century the dome had become higher, with apex drawn upward and slightly bulging sides. Since the appearance of the bulbous dome in northern Russia antedates the Tartar occupation, its origin is not easily explained as an influence from Islamic architecture.[10] Indeed, the appearance in many widely separated regions, in the Near and Middle East, in Persia and India, of bulbous domes and of the sharply pointed ogee arch, which may be considered the section of such a dome, precludes the assumption that any single source was the model for the use of this particular form in eastern Europe. Since even masonry domes were probably evolved from earlier wooden prototypes, it is not impossible that the bulbous dome also developed more quickly in a carpentry culture, and the reasons for its appearance can be considered as much technological as aesthetic. Although frequently restored, the central twelfth-century cupola of Sancta Sophia represents an interesting intermediate stage between the flat Byzantine saucers of Kiev and the later bulbous domes of the north. It is taller, and although the sides have not begun to bulge, the apex has been drawn out. The side domes, replaced at a later date, are typical fifteenth- and sixteenth-century bulbous domes.

Although Sancta Sophia remained for long the largest and the only double-aisled church in this region, it had little influence on subsequent architecture in Novgorod. But its beauty was inseparably associated with the intransigent pride of the people. It became the symbol of civic power and independence, even as Sancta Sophia of Kiev became symbolic of the spiritual authority of the Russian church. 'Where Sancta Sophia is, there is

Novgorod,' declared Prince Mstislav in 1215, when the Tartars had already threatened the independence of Russia. Its construction seems to have absorbed the best energies of Novgorod architects for the rest of the century, and that the work was long in progress appears from the fact that the painting of the interior was only completed in 1144.

The first churches to be built in Novgorod after the turn of the century resemble Sancta Sophia only in the general tendency towards simplicity, unity, and verticality. Three in particular exhibit these aspects: the Church of St Nicholas the Wonder-Worker (1113), erected by Mstislav I in the courtyard of his palace, the Nativity of the Virgin (1117) in the St Anthony Monastery, and St George (1119–30) in the Yuriev (George) Monastery, two miles south of the city on the left bank of the Volkhov (Plate 8). The plan of each church shows the swift contraction of the multiple naves of

Figure 7. Novgorod. St George

the two Sancta Sophias into a simpler type, with nave and aisles, six piers, three apses, and a tall cupola over the crossing (Figure 7). In the latter two the addition of smaller cupolas over the western façade creates an unusually picturesque asymmetrical composition. In each the three apses are carried the full height of the structure, the walls are divided into four panels by pilasters which correspond to the position of the piers within the church, and the drums of the domes are decorated with an arched band.[11]

The name of the builder of St George has been preserved. Since the chronicle mentions him simply as 'Master Peter', without further qualification, it would seem logical to think that in him we encounter the first truly native Russian architect.[12] And since the Nativity of the Virgin so closely resembles St George, it is tempting to think of it as an earlier work of Master Peter. Pushing conjecture one step further, the Byzantine apsidal treatment of St Nicholas, again only a few years earlier than the Church of the Nativity, hints that possibly as a pupil of the Greek masters working on Sancta Sophia he may have built St Nicholas's for Mstislav as his first work.

The insistent height of these three churches, in contrast to the still lingering traces of Byzantine breadth in Sancta Sophia, gives them a cubical appearance. Here begins perhaps the most notable difference between Russian architecture and contemporary building in Western Europe. Russian church architecture moved from elaboration towards simplification, from articulation of the separate elements such as nave and aisles and choir, towards the gradual inclusion of these elements in a single mass until even the triple apses are almost submerged within the thick eastern wall. There is also a diminution in size, from Sancta Sophia of Kiev to the smaller churches of the Kievan monasteries, and from Sancta Sophia of Novgorod to the smaller churches of the Novgorod-Pskov region, until by the end of the fourteenth century the type is fixed. Again one observes as a constituent factor in Russian art the desire for conformity rather than diversity, the embracing symbol rather than the individual expression.

In the twelfth-century churches of Novgorod the growth of this type is seen in the gradual elimination of external decoration, in the broader wall-space, unbroken save for a few small windows, and in the division of the north and south walls by shallow pilasters descending from arches which express on the external walls the internal division of the church by piers and vaults. Almost always the width of the arches varies according to the distribution of the interior space, with a broad central arch representing the open space below the dome, and a narrower arch to the east corresponding to the narrow bay between the crossing and apse. Throughout the twelfth century the vaults, and consequently the arches of the external arcade, remained at the same or almost the same height, so that originally the churches of Novgorod resembled the smaller churches of Kiev and Vladimir-Suzdal. Apparently the roofs originally rested directly on the vaults, and so followed the arched curves of the cornice. The tendency of such a roof to collect snow and water caused the reconstruction of the roofs and frequently of the upper parts of the walls in later times, so that it is now difficult to judge their original appearance. Certainly the arched roofs would have mitigated somewhat the monotonous cubical appearance where the vaults have been replaced by a four-sloped roof completely unrelated to the structure as a whole.

An interesting attempt to recover the original appearance of these buildings was formerly to be seen in the restored Church of the Saviour at Nereditsa (Spas-Nereditsa, 1199) near Novgorod, once important for its complement of frescoes, but totally destroyed during the Second World War (Plate 9). In this instance the later reconstruction involved building up the walls above the arches to a uniform height as a support for the peaked roof. The removal of the later masonry and the substitution of an arched roof following the lines of the original walls provided perhaps as authentic a picture as could ever be obtained of the earlier twelfth-century churches of Novgorod.[13]

Although the pre-eminence of the Byzantine manner was asserted as late as 1199 at Nereditsa, other parish churches of the twelfth century had already departed considerably from the tradition of Sancta Sophia, still so much a part of such structures as St George in the Yuriev Monastery. These deviations from the Byzantine prototypes were perhaps in each instance minor, but taken together they make up a totality of change and experiment which led to the formation of the distinctive Novgorod type in the fourteenth century. The progressive simplification of the plan and the use of four piers instead of six affected the façades. The division of the walls by pilasters tended to follow the actual distribution of the space internally, so that the wall was divided into three unequal panels. The central one, which corresponded to the crossing, was the widest; the eastern, with the gradual reduction of the depth of the apse so that much of the altarspace was included with the church, the narrowest. The apses were also diminished in number and size. Although there were still three at Nereditsa, the side apses were more often but half the height of the central one.

Most important of all, in terms of structure and appearance, was the discovery of a new roof treatment. The flat exposed vaults of Sancta Sophia and at Nereditsa were impractical when for long months of the year ice and snow accumulated on the roof. A sharper pitch was required to dispose of such a load as quickly as possible. The solution finally obtained, and then on the basis of the four-piered plan expressed externally by a triple division of the façades, was to decrease the width and height of the side aisles. In this way on each façade the central bay was flanked by two lower ones which could be included within a single triangular gable. The roof then consisted of four equal gables surmounted by the central drum and dome. The date and place of origin of this eminently logical system are unknown, but it was undoubtedly assisted by the discovery of the quadrant arch, a western European buttressing device, which had been used above the upper chambers at the end of the aisles in Sancta Sophia, both as vaults and buttresses for the central dome.

The oldest church in Novgorod with a gabled roof is the Annunciation on Lake Myachin. It is tempting to think that the gabled system was invented on that occasion, when the church was built in seventy days, but the later reconstruction of the vaults and roof prevents absolute certainty on this point. By 1292, the date of St Nicholas na Lipne, the system was completely developed, although again the upper part of the church was spoiled by the substitution of a hipped roof for the original gables. Nevertheless, the design of St Nicholas, with a single apse, gabled roof, and severe walls relieved only by a blind arcade running immediately below the peak of the gables, indicates that throughout the thirteenth century the architects of Novgorod had constantly refined their forms.

The proportional relationships between the cubical body of the church and the cylindrical forms of apse and drum are so skilfully managed in Novgorod architecture that we must assume a considerable period of development, culminating in the fourteenth century in two important churches in the Commercial Quarter. These churches were in a sense the merchants' cathedrals, and rose in visible opposition to the older princely and episcopal Sancta Sophia within the fortified Kremlin on the other side of the river. They are St Theodore Stratilates, erected in 1361-2 by a certain Natalia, the widow of a wealthy merchant Simon Andreevich, and her son, and the Transfiguration, 1374 (Plate 10A).[14] Happily both churches have preserved to modern times their original gabled roofs, and each has the now typical Novgorod system of one apse and a single dome resting on a tall drum. The division of the walls follows the same pattern whereby four pilasters divide the wall into three panels, topped by a trefoil arch in the centre and a trefoil halved for the side panels. Internally a certain coarsening of the structure is evident in St Theodore. The piers, which rest upon very squat columns in the manner of the churches of Pskov, are joined to the lateral walls for the whole height of the building, so that the internal space develops in breadth rather than in depth, especially since a tall iconostasis was added in the sixteenth century. The Transfiguration shows greater verticality, both within and without. Except for the later cupola and small bulbous dome, it has considerably more refined proportions. In both churches the decoration of the apse by a double blind arcade, the upper containing two arches for each one in the lower, is undoubtedly due to German influence, particularly strong in Novgorod in the fourteenth century. On the Transfiguration the applied ornament of devotional crosses, in addition to the customary Novgorod brickwork on the drum, speaks of the material affluence of the Novgorod merchant-patrons. This series of substantial, massive structures concludes with the church of SS. Peter and Paul (1406), also in the Commercial Quarter, but less majestic in its proportions.

Pskov, the 'younger brother of Novgorod', was also a free city during the earlier Middle Ages and just as jealous of its liberties, but it was less wealthy and its activities were more restricted by the pressure of its enemies, the Lithuanians to the west. Consequently Pskov failed to achieve as independent a style as did Novgorod. For all that, the technical devices of the Pskov builders were to prove of great advantage in later times, and the very conservatism of the city where much older traditions were maintained than in Novgorod led to an unexpected career for its architects at the end of the fifteenth century. By 1400 they had made practicable their most important structural invention. Instead of following the developed Byzantine system of pendentives for the support of the dome, which required a very nice knowledge of stone cutting, the Pskov architects placed arches at the corners of the crossing, above and slightly in front of the barrel vaults over the nave and transept, and upon these corbelled arches, which were sometimes doubled, they placed the drums of the dome. In this way proper height was obtained for the dome, without raising the vaulted arms of the church. This small enclosed volume effectively lowered the cost of construction and prevented the loss of precious warmth in winter. By the fifteenth century they were able to place a drum and dome over a church without internal piers by throwing corbelled arches laterally across the nave. These arches eventually affected the exterior of the church. When such superimposed arches were exposed externally a decorative effect of considerable richness was obtained. This became so popular after its appearance in the later fifteenth century that often multiple rows of arches were added for effect when they were not required for support.[15]

In passing from one city to another, from an important capital to an active but much smaller trading centre, the forms became more primitive. Generally the proportions were stumpier, the walls thicker, the detail more rude. The typical Pskov system of corbelled arches, which came into frequent use in the fifteenth century, may be considered part of this system of grosser simplification. Yet in the simplicity and conservatism of such architecture there was much charm and a considerable future. A characteristic feature was the free and effective composition of the belfries, those several-storeyed constructions, pierced with arched openings, in which the bronze bells were fixed. With the simple directness of primitive art, they contribute much to the picturesque mass of the church (Plate 10B).

Conservatism and the remoteness of Pskov from Moscow were two valuable assets in its later history. Not until 1510 was the city obliged to recognize the suzerainty of Moscow, when Basil III incorporated it in his dominions; and it escaped the terrible destruction Ivan IV visited upon Novgorod. Meanwhile the ingenuity of the architects of Pskov had come to the attention of Ivan III, who summoned them to Moscow in 1480 to undertake the reconstruction of the Annunciation in the Kremlin. One may think that it was not alone their cleverness which recommended them to the Great Prince, but quite as much their knowledge of the older traditions. Since Ivan III, like his predecessors before him, was intent on asserting the continuity of the princely line and the right of Moscow to take precedence over older cities, the fact that the architects of Pskov built churches very much in the old manner worked in their favour.

CHAPTER 4

THE ARCHITECTURE OF VLADIMIR-SUZDAL

1100–1240

TOWARDS the middle of the twelfth century a third centre of architectural activity came into prominence. Derived from Kiev and not unrelated to Novgorod, and so to Western influences, the constructions of the princes of Vladimir-Suzdal were a further refinement of the earlier Byzantine style leading towards the characteristic definition at Moscow in the fifteenth century. Once again, as first at Kiev and Chernigov and later at Novgorod and Pskov, local, particular, and national factors were working upon international currents to create a peculiarly Russian style.[1]

The rapid emergence of Suzdalia as an important political and cultural centre is, like the contemporary history of Novgorod, linked to the steady economic and dynastic disintegration of the Kievan realm. Continuous nomad incursions in the south, and the consequent isolation of Russia from Constantinople, wreaked hardship on the peoples around Kiev. Seeking safety from attack, as well as security for the pursuit of a livelihood, numbers of Russians turned from trade to agriculture and ascending the river Desna from Kiev penetrated north-eastwards into the forest lands until they reached the headwaters of the Volga. In the forest clearings they could commence an agricultural existence, and the dense network of rivers and streams enabled them to maintain trade relations with both West and East. On these foundations of farming and commerce were laid the wealth of the cities of Suzdalia, of Suzdal itself and Rostov, the earliest settlements of pioneers from Kievan Russia in the tenth century, and of Vladimir, which became the capital after the middle of the twelfth century. South-westward from these cities, at a bend in the river Moskva, a tributary of the Oka, lay a small outpost established for the defence of the trade route. In the twelfth century it was scarcely more than a few cabins huddled upon a hill behind wooden ramparts. This was the site of the future city of Moscow.

The princes who ruled Suzdalia for a century and a quarter, from Vladimir Monomakh to the last ruling prince, Yuri II, who with his army was defeated by the Tartars in 1238, were men of unusual energy, intelligence, and artistic interests. Their buildings are destroyed or too rigorously restored, barren now, but once splendid with frescoes and marbles, painted and gilded within and without, and adorned with countless vessels and icons set with precious stones. Before the Mongol invasion Suzdalia rivalled Kiev in the number and splendour of its masonry structures. Only rulers of deep artistic sensibility could have created such an environment, for each church was in its own way a special foundation of the prince. They were also men of far wider culture than their heroic half-Scandinavian ancestors. Monomakh had won the reverence of all Russia for his wisdom and understanding. Vsevolod III probably knew more of the world than any

Russian prince of his generation or of that immediately before him; for, as the son of a Byzantine princess, he had been educated in Tsargrad.

The churches of Suzdalia established a new direction in ancient Russian architecture. Just as the structures of the first period were dominated by the Cathedral of Sancta Sophia, which, when transplanted to Novgorod, became the generating force there for St Nicholas, St George, and the Nativity of the Virgin, so those of Suzdalia derived from the type-church of the second Kievan building campaign, the Dormition in the Pecherskaya Lavra. The reasons are not hard to find. Not only was the Lavra church a newer, and consequently more immediately interesting building, but for Vladimir Monomakh, who was a boy when it was under construction, it must have stood in somewhat the same paternal relation as the Desyatinnaya had stood toward Yaroslav. And as the latter in his Sancta Sophia realized the aspirations of his father Vladimir, so Monomakh in his churches in Suzdal and Vladimir perfected the type established during the preceding reigns by his uncle Svyatoslav and his father Vsevolod I in the Pecherskaya Lavra.

Although nothing now remains of the buildings founded by Vladimir Monomakh, descriptions in the chronicles and a few traces uncovered in recent excavations prove their importance for the subsequent architectural history of this region. Before Monomakh here, as elsewhere in Russia, most building was in wood, and so has almost completely disappeared. Fragments of poorly preserved domestic dwellings of the eleventh and twelfth centuries seem to show that conical wooden roofs were placed over half-excavated earth foundations. Later, the artisans of Suzdal, like those of Novgorod, had a considerable reputation as wood-workers.[2] As in Kiev, so here, in contrast to this wooden architecture, derived from older pagan practice, the Christian prince asserted the power of the new spiritual order, confirmed in his political tenure, by building new churches of fine masonry. But where the first churches of Kiev and Novgorod followed the familiar Byzantine technique of brick, cement, and tile construction, here in Suzdal there were quantities of white limestone, available locally or brought by boat from Kama up the Volga, and so up the Klyazma to the very walls of the cities.

The close connexion between Kiev and the younger principality is explicitly recorded in the Kievan Paterik, according to which the 'God-fearing Vladimir (Monomakh) took the measurements of the Pecherski church (and) created a church exactly like it in height, breadth, and length in the city of Rostov. He also recorded on parchment (the place of) each picture of a feast-day, and repeated all this in the order and likeness of the example of the great church'.[3] The church in Rostov was thus erected after the plan and proportions of the Lavra Dormition, and its mural paintings followed the scheme customary in Kiev. The chronicle adds that Vladimir's son, Yuri I Dolgoruki (George 'Long-arm'), had heard from his father of the splendid Pecherski church and in his reign built a similar church in the city of Suzdal. Although Yuri at the time of the construction of the Suzdal Cathedral was but a boy, and consequently the erection of both churches may be attributed to Vladimir, the chronicler's account of their relation to the Kievan model has been confirmed by recent excavations. Beneath the foundations of the present Suzdal Cathedral (1222–5) have been found the remains of the walls of Monomakh's building. It was a monumental structure with six internal piers, a western narthex, and gallery.

The thick walls were divided by pilasters and, as the Paterik says, it was richly painted, to judge by the actual fragments of fresco found on the interior walls.[4] The technique of thin slab-shaped bricks and layers of local stone was still very close to the Kievan Byzantine practice.

After Monomakh's death in 1125 there seems to have been little building activity until late in the reign of his son and successor, Yuri Dolgoruki. Not until the year 1152 do the chronicles mention his church-building, which then became fairly intensive.[5] Before his death in 1157 Yuri had founded at least five stone churches, of which the most important was that of SS. Boris and Gleb, in the village of Kideksha, on the river Nerl below Suzdal. In addition to the churches mentioned in the chronicles, he completed and restored

0 10 20 30 40 50 FEET

0 5 10 15 METRES

Figure 8. Kideksha. SS. Boris and Gleb

the Suzdal Cathedral, broadening it on the north side by the construction of the Chapel of the Redeemer, and built the Cathedral of the Redeemer beside the ramparts of Pereyaslavl-Zalesski, later to be finished by his son Andrei. Finally, in 1157, the Church of St George rose in his new palace in Vladimir. Of these many buildings there only survived, and then much altered, the Boris and Gleb Church in Kideksha and the Transfiguration in Pereyaslavl-Zalesski. St George in Vladimir is known only from its foundations, and St George in Yuriev-Polski, as will be seen, was reconstructed at a later date.

To a degree the constructions of Yuri, and of his son and successor Andrei, are a reflexion in stone of the struggle between the prince and the boyar for control of the principality. The Church of SS. Boris and Gleb was built in the village of Kideksha, some three miles from Suzdal, within a fortified palace on the banks of the Nerl, where Yuri could remain apart from the recalcitrant nobility and people of Suzdal. The Church of

St George in Vladimir represented the next stage when Yuri transferred the seat of government from Suzdal to the smaller and less dependent city of Vladimir. His other churches, in Yuriev-Polski and Pereyaslavl, were in the nature of garrison churches in new and strongly fortified border towns.

All these buildings were small and of the type of palace church, of which the first important example was the Transfiguration in Berestovo,[6] near Kiev, built by Vladimir Monomakh. Suzdal and its dependent towns had neither the need nor the means for structures so large or costly as the cathedrals of Kiev and Novgorod. And since the future history of Russia was in a dynastic sense to proceed rather from Vladimir than from those older cities, this type of small palace church, continuing through the twelfth century in other princely centres, and ultimately receiving its final form in the churches of the Kremlin in Moscow, may be considered the culmination of the masonry church in ancient Russia.

The two extant buildings erected by Yuri demonstrate the origin of the Suzdalian type and the first step in its change from the Kievan original. In plan SS. Boris and Gleb at Kideksha (1152) (Figure 8) was a four-piered structure with one dome and three apses. The internal piers were connected by arches to pilasters on the walls, and the divisions so created were expressed externally by the device of arches resting on pilasters, familiar from the churches in Novgorod. On the exterior the church has suffered severely through the destruction of the original roof, dome, and upper part of the eastern bay, and the consequent reduction in size of the apses to half their original height (Plate 11A).

Another element of the new Suzdalian style is the clear definition on the exterior of the partitioning of the internal space. Although the architects of Russia would never attain, and apparently never desired, the rational articulation, or at least the appearance of a rational articulation of internal and external space so characteristic of medieval architecture in the West, the important steps towards it taken in the buildings of Suzdal and Vladimir may indicate the presence in these regions of Western builders, possibly reaching Russia from Galicia, where the princely churches and palaces exhibit many Western details.

Yuri's other extant church, the Cathedral of the Transfiguration at Pereyaslavl-Zalesski, finished by his son Andrei in 1158, is in a better state of preservation, having suffered only the replacement of the dome in the sixteenth century and the loss of the corbel table supported by colonnettes, which was visible until 1848. In plan it follows the four-piered, single-domed, three-apsed type of Kideksha. Again the internal piers are connected by arches with pilasters on the outer walls which are expressed similarly on the exterior. The apses rise the full height of the church, and with the original roof resting directly on the vaults, create a rhythmical composition of arches and semi-circles which may owe its origin to Kiev but here has found a distinct and harmonious expression. The fine white stone undoubtedly contributes to the aesthetic character of this, as of later Suzdalian churches. The different effect, in contrast to the churches of Novgorod and Pskov, may be noticed. In the latter regions the use of brick permitted, as it encouraged, a wider variety of proportions, greater picturesqueness, and lack of standardization. The technique of stone construction whereby the nature of the material imposed a fundamental need and consequent desire for regularity gives the churches of Vladimir-Suzdal a powerful and authoritative coherence.

If the churches of Vladimir represent the transplantation to north-eastern Russia of the Kievan style of the second period, that is to say of the later eleventh century, and the churches of Yuri, in so far as they have survived, stand for the first stage in the adaptation of the Kievan style to a new material and a new expressive need, that of an aristocratic ruler seeking to suppress the oligarchical and popular tendencies represented by the boyars and the veche, so the constructions of Andrei and of his younger brother Vsevolod III were the final realization of this particular combination of circumstances. Andrei, a man of violent impulse and determination, was more faithful to his Suzdalian inheritance than his father Yuri, who was preternaturally disposed to look towards Kiev, where his own father had ruled. Andrei remained in Suzdalia even after his capture and the sack of Kiev in 1169, appointing a deputy to rule in his stead. At home Andrei fixed his capital at Vladimir, still relatively insignificant, although fortified by Monomakh in the early twelfth century. Its secure position on the heights above the Klyazma recalled Kiev, and the resemblance was further developed by Andrei and his successors with their constructions.

Monomakh had already built one church in Vladimir, long ago destroyed, but it was the third church in stone after the cathedrals of Rostov and Suzdal to be built in this region. It was apparently a small four-piered structure, again resembling the church in Berestovo, to which he owed a special devotion as the burial church of his family. In

Figure 9. Vladimir. The Dormition

1158, the year after his accession, Andrei commenced his building programme with the construction of the Golden and Silver Gates and a new Cathedral of the Dormition in Vladimir and a new church and palace ten miles from Vladimir in the village of Bogoliubovo, whence he came in time to be known as Andrei Bogoliubski (Theophilus, 'God-fearing'). Although none of these monuments has been preserved intact, taken together they account for a noteworthy medieval building campaign, and in their time went far to define the Suzdalian style.

In Vladimir itself Andrei's new Cathedral of the Dormition of 1158–61 (Plate 12B, Figure 9) originally may have been closer to the tradition of Vladimir Monomakh's cathedrals of Rostov and Suzdal. Like them, the plan derived from the Pecherski Dormition, with its six piers, three apses, and single dome. In 1183 it was so seriously damaged by fire that an extensive reconstruction was undertaken by Andrei's brother, Vsevolod III.[7] This so changed the appearance of the building that externally and internally it must now be considered an example of late twelfth-century architecture.[8] Fragments of the original walls indicate that, like the Transfiguration at Pereyaslavl, it originally carried a corbel table at half the height of the walls, which were thicker below than above. Such windows as have been preserved were in the second storey and were deeply splayed. There were apparently galleries over the outer aisles and western bay. The exterior was adorned with reliefs, some of which were later transferred to the walls of Vsevolod's structure. Fragments of fresco on the walls of the present outer aisles seem to indicate that the exterior was also painted and gilded as the chronicles describe it.

Before the fire of 1183 the Dormition and Andrei's palace church at Bogoliubovo must have been among the most magnificent buildings in Russia, recreating in the northern woodlands the sumptuous decorative splendour, if not the monumental scale, of the Kievan churches. Andrei certainly had some such intention, for he bestowed upon the Dormition much property, including 'a tithe of the income from trade'. It was to be his Desyatinnaya.[9]

The only one of Andrei's buildings of which the present condition affords some conception of its original appearance is the Church of the Protection and Intercession of the Virgin (Pokrov Bogoroditsy) in the meadows above the river Nerl, near its confluence with the Klyazma (Plate 11B). It was erected in 1166, apparently in memory of Andrei's son Izyaslav Andreevich, who had died the year before and had been buried in the Dormition, but possibly also in commemoration of a vision of the Virgin extending her veil (pokrov) over the congregation which Andrei, like his name-saint, Andrew the Fool, had experienced.[10] Like the churches at Kideksha and Pereyaslavl, it is a four-piered, three-apsed structure with a single dome. Here, however, the small size and the thickness of the exterior walls led to a progressive unification of the structural system, so that the apses appear in plan almost as if contained within the enveloping quadrilateral mass of the walls (Figure 10).

Of all the churches of ancient Russia, the Pokrov is distinguished by its fine state of preservation, and by the harmony of its proportions. In it the low Byzantine cube acquired not only height but also grace, and an exquisite relationship was established between the various decorative elements, between column, pilaster, and corbel table, between door and window, between the arches surmounting the façades and the drum and dome, between the wall surface and the carved decoration which is the oldest preserved sculptural ornament in Suzdalia.

The plan with the sharply projecting engaged columns and splayed doors and windows inserted within the thickness of the walls suggests something of the articulation of Romanesque architecture of the twelfth century, but the triple entrances on the west, north, and south axes resemble such Eastern Byzantine churches as the Cathedral at Ani in Armenia.[11] The Pokrov thus raises once more the issue of the relative significance at this place and time of Western and Eastern influences in the development of Russian architecture. Again it is important to avoid seeking a dogmatic answer which would dispose of either influence, and so commit the history of Russian art to a one-sided development. Far as Suzdal and Vladimir may seem from present-day centres of European

Figure 10. The Pokrov on the Nerl

culture, it is well to remember that men and ideas in the Middle Ages travelled with greater ease and frequency than we are often ready to admit. Evidence of this constant interchange is provided by the statement in the chronicles that God brought to Andrei masters 'from all countries'. There was even a tradition in a chronicle now lost that Frederick Barbarossa had sent architects from Germany to Andrei in Suzdalia.[12] It is not surprising, therefore, that the doorways of the Pokrov should resemble contemporary Romanesque or Norman work in France or England. And from the West also may have come the taste for carved decoration which, like the corbel tables, is characteristic of German Romanesque architecture, familiar to the Russian princes and their builders through workmen from Galicia.

Yet the character of the carved ornament on the Vladimir-Suzdal churches, as well as the peculiarities of the plan of the Pokrov, have such close analogies with the tenth- and eleventh-century churches of the Caucasus and Armenia that one must accept the possibility that Andrei's architects, or the artisans collaborating on these structures, were

35

familiar with the plan and distribution of relief sculpture on the Armenian cathedrals. In this connexion it is important to recall that the trade relations of Vladimir-Suzdal with the East and with the Caucasus were close, and, perhaps even more significant for this period, three successive princes – Yuri I and his sons Andrei and Vsevolod III – married eastern princesses. Moreover in 1184, Queen Tamara of Georgia married Yuri, the youngest son of Andrei Bogoliubski.[13]

More important than the weight of influence accorded either the Romanesque West or the Armenian East in the development of Suzdalian architecture must be the recognition that the builders of Suzdal and Vladimir were no mere copyists, but succeeded in creating a style inimitably their own. The delicate proportions of the Pokrov, and of the other extant churches, indicate the existence of a characteristic aesthetic. The churches, although generally cubical, are not precisely square. The plans are slightly lengthened along the east–west axis, and though the height is approximately equal to the total length, the slight reduction in height of the apses lends them an additional sense of slender verticality. On the south and north façades the external arches corresponding to the internal vaults have multiple profiles and are brought to the ground on pilasters faced with engaged columns running the full height of the building. The adjustment of the width of these divisions to the internal distribution of space, whereby the central arch which corresponds to the crossing below the dome is the widest, while the western is slightly and the eastern considerably narrower, gives the structure a continual proportional variety from any point of view. If the wealth of decoration is new in Russian architecture, surpassing not only the churches of the first Suzdalian period but those of Novgorod and Kiev as well, the principles of organizing that decoration according to a two-dimensional system were characteristically Russian.

The architects of Vladimir at the end of the twelfth century, more even than those of Novgorod and Kiev, had disengaged their taste from lingering Byzantine memories and, absorbing types and techniques reaching them from East and West, had created an unmistakably Russian architecture. Merely to reflect that such progress had been achieved in the two centuries separating the foundation of the Desyatinnaya from the reconstruction of the Vladimir Cathedral, is to wonder what further developments might have occurred had not the political and spiritual history of the Russian people been so frequently and so violently diverted from a coherent course of formal evolution.

Of Andrei's palace and church at Bogoliubovo, which, to judge from contemporary accounts in the chronicles, must have been one of the most magnificent palace complexes in eastern Europe, nothing now remains but a fragment of the north stair-tower leading to the gallery within the church (Plates 12A and 15B). Here Andrei used to take visiting notables, especially foreigners and unbelievers, that they might be amazed by the splendour of this shrine of the true faith. From the excavated foundations of the church the plan, of the usual four-pier type, may be deduced.[14] Within the tower groined vaults supported on columns with carved capitals suggest the work of the foreign masters, as well as certain decorative details such as the two-storeyed blind arcades on the western façade of the tower, which are close to German Romanesque and Lombard work. In these the presence of Barbarossa's master-builders becomes more than a suspicion. The most notable aspect of Andrei's palace church was the lavish decoration. The exterior and interior were faced with jasper, and certain details were gilded. On the interior, parts of the piers, doors, and walls were gilded, and the floor of the choir was laid with gilded copper plates. When to these and the frescoes were added the icons in gold frames, it is not hard to understand why the chronicler should have remarked that 'it was hard to look at all the gold'.

When Andrei, the victim of the jealousy of the aristocracy, was assassinated in 1175, his younger brother, Vsevolod III, continued his building activities. His first important work was the rebuilding of the Dormition in Vladimir after the disastrous fire of 1183 (Plate 12B). Apparently the fabric was largely intact but so badly calcined that Vsevolod was obliged to encase it in new walls. This he did by building two-storeyed galleries on the west, south, and north. Openings were pierced in the old outer walls which now became piers between the inner and outer aisles of the new church. New and larger apses were added on the east in scale with the new building, which required some not wholly satisfactory readjustments of the eastern bays of the earlier church. In plan the new structure was surprisingly like the many-piered, multiple-celled churches of Sancta Sophia in Kiev and Novgorod, perhaps an intentional device to create for Vladimir a church reminiscent of those of the earlier Russian princely cities. The resemblance to Sancta Sophia was further accentuated by the four domes which Vsevolod placed over the corners. The resulting five-domed, double-aisled church was the largest in north-eastern Russia at this period. Internally the central dome over a broad crossing was supported by eight small pendentives, achieving the transition from square to circle, more like the squinches common in Armenia and Asia Minor than the usual broad Byzantine pendentives. The interior decoration was exceptionally rich. The walls were frescoed; on the western wall fragments of a large painting of the Last Judgement are still preserved. When it was rededicated in 1194, the new Dormition, with its frescoes, majolica tiles on the floor, gold and silver candelabra, and icons in gold frames, must have surpassed even Andrei's famous church at Bogoliubovo. Truly, as the chronicle says, 'it was like new, and great was the joy in Vladimir'.[15]

Externally the Dormition continued the tradition of the Nerl, if somewhat more elaborately, since the wall divisions now corresponded to the quintuple division of the interior. Here the corbel table on colonnettes was sunk within the thickness of the wall, but it may be that this peculiarity was due to a reworking of the exterior in the fourteenth century after damage sustained during the Mongol sack of the city. The multiple divisions of the walls, the judicious spacing of window and corbel table within each arched panel, and the fact that Vsevolod's galleries and apses were on each side somewhat lower than the walls of Andrei's church, so that the picturesque effect was obtained of a central mass rising above the peripheral constructions – all this contributes to make of the Dormition a structure elegant and refined to-day, even as it was splendid and majestic and unique in Vladimir in the twelfth century.

Vsevolod's second church, and one built wholly by him, is the Church of St Dmitri (Plate 13A), which stood in the now vanished courtyard of the palace. It was begun either in 1193, soon after a fire had ravaged the palace, or in 1194, in honour of his patron and of his son Dmitri born that year. It was apparently finished in 1197, when Vsevolod in-stalled in the church relics of St Dmitri brought from Salonika. Since the chronicle speci-fically states that Vsevolod did not summon masters from abroad, and the style of the church follows so closely that of the Pokrov, it would seem logical to assume that the same masters, or those trained by them, were still working in Vladimir throughout the later twelfth century. Like the Pokrov, this was a four-piered church with a single dome, and with an entrance on each side on axis in the Armenian manner.

If the plan and general distribution recall the Pokrov, the difference in proportions creates quite another effect, broader and more massive, suggesting that within the strict-est limitations of their style the Suzdalian architects could achieve considerable variety. The most striking contrast between St Dmitri and other churches of this group ap-pears in the lavish distribution of carved stone reliefs over the upper walls and on the drum of the dome (Plate 13B). The character of these carvings will be examined in the general discussion of sculpture, but here again it may be noted that in their arrangement and two-dimensional character these reliefs resemble those of Armenian churches. In the nineteenth century the church was drastically restored, losing in the process a two-storeyed construction at the north-west angle which may have contained remnants of one of the two stair-towers originally connecting the church with Vsevolod's palace.[16]

Vsevolod was succeeded upon his death in 1212 by a younger son, Yuri II, whose reign was disturbed by family quarrels and by the increasing threat of the Tartars. He was able, however, to accomplish one important building campaign, the reconstruction of Suzdal Cathedral (1222–33). This church, begun by Monomakh and thus scarcely a century old, had been repaired as recently as 1192, but according to the chronicles it had 'begun to collapse from its antiquity and the dome had fallen in'.[17] Unhappily even the new church has not been preserved intact. In 1445 the roof and domes were destroyed, and in 1528 the walls were demolished to the corbel table and rebuilt in brick. Consequently only the lower half of the building was preserved, but from this, the plan, and con-temporary descriptions it is apparent that the new cathedral was a noble addition to Suzdalian architecture. In 1233 it was frescoed and decorated with 'beautiful coloured marbles'.

The most remarkable feature of the church was the wealth of decorative carving and the enriched architectural details. In this respect it may have stemmed from the plastic ornament of St Dmitri in Vladimir, yet such deductions as can be made from the sur-viving parts seem to indicate that the carvings were applied without regard to the struc-tural logic maintained in the Vladimir churches by the disposition of the exterior arches and pilasters. Here at Suzdal the arches and pilasters did not correspond to the internal spatial divisions, and were in turn interrupted or broken through by the bands of decora-tive carving. It is apparent that by the beginning of the twelfth century the brief period when the exterior and interior of the building were conceived as inter-related designs had passed. Possibly under the influence of the East, two-dimensional conceptions re-sponsible for the carpeting of St Dmitri with sculpture had now grown stronger, and the façade of the church was a field for the display of virtuosity in decorative sculpture.

Such conclusions can be pronounced only hesitantly; for the succeeding monuments which might have demonstrated them are either destroyed or so radically altered as to make certainty difficult. This is the more regrettable in that the last and in some ways most remarkable monument of Suzdalian architecture presents an almost inextricable problem in reconstruction. This is the Church of St George (1229–34), built by Yuri's brother, Svyatoslav Vsevolodovich, in the capital of his apanage, Yuriev-Polski, on the site of Yuri Dolgoruki's church of 1152 (Plate 14). In 1471 the church collapsed, but was re-erected at the command of Ivan III by the Moscow architect V. D. Yermolin.[18] Most regrettably no care was taken to replace the stones in their original positions, so that at present the sculptural sequence is inextricably confused. The church must once have been much taller, if the present band of columns properly indicates half the height. In plan it had the traditional four piers, and at the sides were three porches, a now familiar feature in Suzdalian architecture. The most unusual aspect of the church was its wealth of carved detail completely covering all available wall surfaces, a sculptural treatment hitherto unknown in Russia.

Meanwhile the end of architectural activity in Suzdal had been reached. In 1228 the Tartars had inflicted their first defeat on the Russians at the battle of the river Kalka. Nine years later, in the winter of 1237, they attacked Suzdalia. Vladimir was besieged, taken, and burned. The independence and power of the principality were for ever eclipsed, and an extraordinary vital and creative architecture was untimely interrupted. These churches had been the wonder of the age. In contrast to the chronicles of Novgorod, wherein are recorded the bare facts of the date and place of the church and the name of the founder, the chronicles of Suzdal abound in expressions of enthusiasm and surprise. The eloquent descriptions of Andrei's churches have been quoted. Elsewhere the churches of Vsevolod and his successors are described as 'wonderful, astonishing, of unusual beauty'. The pride which the clergy, princes, and people took in their churches was to prove in the end an imperishable legacy. Although the continuity of Russia economically and politically would be carried on at first by Novgorod and then imperceptibly by Moscow through two centuries of Tartar domination, the churches of Vladimir preserved in their fabric the traditions of princely Russia, until the day when the new ruler of Muscovy looked to them for the inspiration and forms wherewith to embody his conception of a new dynastic power.

39

CHAPTER 5

MOSAICS AND FRESCOES IN KIEV

OUR knowledge of pre-Christian painting in Russia, like that of the earliest architecture, is handicapped by the absence of monuments and the scarcity of reliable documentary information. Probably the earlier Slavic worship of natural forces did not reach the stage of personifying the gods in human form until anthropomorphic images were introduced by the Varangians in the eighth and ninth centuries. The later idols were certainly colourful, as we learn from the description of those erected by Vladimir at Kiev before his conversion: 'On the hill outside the castle with the hall: one of Perun, made of wood with a head of silver and a mouth [beard?] of gold.'[1] But the chronicles contain few details, since their priestly and monastic authors scrupulously avoided any extended description of pagan artifacts. Philological evidence suggests the polychromatic character of earlier Russian art. From the earliest times the Slavic language contained words for such specific colours as bright blue, dark blue, red, white, whitish, black, yellow, and green.[2] Among these the trinity of white, red, and green became the characteristic and conspicuous colour scheme of Novgorodian icon-painting. Again, the Russian language has the words krasota (beauty), krasivyi (beautiful), and kraska (colour), all three related to the root of the word for 'red', krasnyi, which is also synonymous with 'beautiful'.[3] This may be taken to mean that the Slavic, pre-Christian contribution to later Russian painting lay more in a traditional attitude towards brilliant primary colours, especially red, than in any inheritance of form or technical procedure. The colour schemes of medieval painting and architectural decoration, and even much later of the folk arts of embroidery and wood-carving, demonstrate this love of brilliant hues, among which red continued for centuries to play a dominant part.

Even when allowance is made for the possible though improbable existence in pagan times of an extensive and highly developed pictorial art, the speed with which Russia embraced a new religion and within less than two centuries achieved a complete, consistent, and technically accomplished art remains remarkable. It has been truly said that in ancient Russia there were no primitives; in the pictorial arts, as in architecture, the first works were complete.[4]

A situation so unusual as this is primarily to be explained by the transference of a body of highly skilled craftsmen to the new environment. Not only the technical controls evident in the earliest pictorial works on Russian soil, but the elaborate iconographical and liturgical schemes within which they occur imply that the first artists were probably Greeks, brought from Constantinople or from one of the important regional centres of Byzantine art. Greek inscriptions in the earliest mosaics must certainly mean that the first artists were closely supervised by the Greek clergy, whether or not they themselves had come directly from Constantinople.

Just as the architectural history of Kiev is compromised by the disappearance of the Desyatinnaya, so the destruction of its interior decoration obscures the origins of Kievan painting. It is known from the chronicles that the church was richly decorated. It was even called the 'Marble Church', because of the sumptuous interior panelling in marble; externally the structure was of brick. Fragments of panels, of a marble floor inlaid with geometrical patterns of an oriental character, of mosaics, and a few precious scraps of fresco confirm the chroniclers' admiration and suggest that the Desyatinnaya first demonstrated several aspects of pictorial decoration which soon became typical for Kievan Russia. A fragment of fresco depicting the nose and right eye of a human face is typical of Byzantine art of the second Golden Age; the green underpainting is overlaid with ochre for the flesh tones, with white highlights and touches of red on the lips and cheeks.[5] The combination of mosaic and fresco is rare in Byzantium itself, but frequent in the Caucasus. This eastern source for some of the decoration of the Desyatinnaya is further substantiated by the patterns of the inlaid flooring, and is historically probable in the light of the account of Vladimir's having brought to Kiev from Kherson not only priests to establish the Christian ritual, but images, vessels, and crosses with which to adorn the new church.[6]

On the other hand, the preservation of Sancta Sophia, however partial and problematic as a result of the incessant damage and repainting of both the fabric and decoration, permits a more careful analysis of the early appearance on Russian soil of the pictorial arts. Here is to be found not only the oldest existing but in many ways the most important scheme of religious painting in ancient Russia and one of the most interesting in the entire Byzantine world. Here were established iconographic formulas which for the next millennium bound the religious art of Russia to its Greek sources, and hence proceeded the stages, however slight, for the iconographical and stylistic departures from these Byzantine models which in time became peculiarly Russian characteristics.

Chronologically the mosaics and frescoes of Sancta Sophia, which were executed between the foundation of the church in 1017 and its dedication in 1037, take their place between the early eleventh-century mosaics of the Church of St Luke in Phocis and those towards the close of the same century at Daphni. This sequence of eleventh-century Byzantine decorative schemes was derived from the now vanished ninth-century mosaics of the Nea Ekklesia and the modifications of a similar programme in the early tenth-century Church of the Holy Apostles in Constantinople. All are saturated with the nobly hieratic and profoundly religious conception of painting of the middle Byzantine period, even though a progression may be traced from the austerity at St Luke to the milder benignity and lively anecdote at Daphni, which in turn prepared the way for the Byzantine Renaissance of the thirteenth and fourteenth centuries.[7]

The iconographical order inaugurated at Sancta Sophia became customary for subsequent Russian mural painting.[8] Over the centre of this church-world, above the crossing at the juncture of the nave, apse, and side bays, was spread the great central dome, like the sky stretched spherically over the earth, and on its inner surface appeared in mosaic the representation of Christ the All-Ruler, the Pantokrator (Plate 17). His swarthy, gaunt face is not that of the human historical Christ of the Gospels familiar in Western art, but a specifically Eastern conception of the divine Christ uniting in Himself the first and second persons of the Trinity, the apocalyptic Judge who on the Last Day will open the book held in His right hand. This bust-length medallion on a gold ground is surrounded by a rainbow supported by four Archangels, whose widespread wings fill the remaining spaces on the inner surface of the dome. These awesome leaders of the heavenly host are clad in the pearl- and jewel-studded imperial Court costume of the Byzantine sovereigns, in whose likeness they hold in either hand a sphere and standard, the first emblazoned with the cross, the latter with the word Hagios (Holy), thrice repeated.

Below the Archangels the third zone embraces the drum of the dome, where between the windows stand the Apostles, and immediately below them, in the four pendentives supporting the dome, sit the Evangelists. The iconographical scheme symbolizes the omniscient character of God and the means by which the divine law was made known to man through the acts of the Apostles and the writings of the Evangelists. Immediately below these figures, and on either side of the arch separating the apse from the central crossing, stand the Archangel Gabriel and the Virgin Mary of the Annunciation, signifying the mystery of the Incarnation whereby the Word was made flesh and dwelt among men.

In the semi-dome of the apse, isolated against a radiant gold background, appears the standing figure of the Virgin Orans, raising her arms in the antique gesture of prayer. This image represents neither the Queen of Heaven nor the earlier Mother of God as she was more popularly known in the later Middle Ages, both in the East and West, but rather the Virgin as the symbol of the earthly Church interceding with her prayers for the salvation of mankind.[9] This image was venerated as the 'unbroken or indestructible wall', an allusion to the twelfth ikos of the Akathist Hymn, which commemorates the Virgin's protection of Constantinople against the siege of 626. From this association grew the legend that during the construction of Sancta Sophia the walls collapsed, except for the central apse.

On the curved wall of the apse below the Virgin are the agents and institutions whereby the Word was made known to man; the symbols of the dome have become effective on earth through action and ritual. Of the two zones into which this wall is horizontally divided, the upper represents the Liturgical Eucharist or Communion of the Apostles, commemorating the institution of the sacrament of the Lord's Supper. Following ancient Eastern precedent, Christ is presented twice, once on either side of the altar crowned with a canopy and flanked by two angels performing the office of deacons. Each Christ extends the chalice to six Apostles approaching from left to right in single file. In the lower row full-length figures of the Church Fathers, bishops, deacons, and martyrs particularly honoured in the Eastern Church complete the programme. The remaining spaces in Sancta Sophia are filled in the northern and southern aisles with scenes in fresco from the lives of Christ and the Virgin. On the western walls and vaults, opposite the Liturgical Eucharist, are episodes from the Old and New Testaments taken as prototypes or symbols of the Passion, such as the Children in the Fiery Furnace, the Sacrifice of Abraham, the Old Testament Trinity or Appearance of the Three Angels to Abraham,[10] Christ at Emmaus, the Marriage at Cana, and the Last Supper. The size of the church required an enlargement of the iconographical scheme which was ordinarily restricted in the middle Byzantine period to the twelve great Feasts: the Annunciation, Nativity, Presentation of Christ or the Purification of the Virgin, Baptism, Resurrection of Lazarus, Transfiguration, Entry into Jerusalem, Crucifixion, Resurrection, Ascension, Pentecost, and Assumption of the Virgin. The scheme of Sancta Sophia departs in another particular from custom, since the scene of the Last Judgement usually depicted on the west wall is missing. Numerous full and half-length figures of saints and medallions on the arches and piers complete the iconography.

The arrangement is coherent and systematic. From the presence of God in the heights of heaven to the ultimate salvation of his people through their knowledge of his earthly appearance and their repeated participation in the Sacraments, each part of the church received its logical expression. It is interesting to observe how this progression moves upward from the concrete, historical episodes of Christ's earthly life, painted on the flatter, uncomplicated parts of the fabric, to the tremendous pictorial demonstrations of Christian dogma on just those architectural elements which are themselves powerful, structural abstractions; the Virgin Orans on the apse, the Evangelists on the pendentives, the Pantokrator with his Archangels on the dome. As the structural system becomes more difficult or complex, so do the doctrines represented become more abstract and profound.

The poor preservation of the mosaics and frescoes of Sancta Sophia handicaps stylistic analysis. Of the Archangels, Apostles, and Evangelists on the dome and pendentives, but one of each is intact, while the saints in the apse are preserved only above the shoulders or waist. The frescoes have suffered even more than the mosaics, and after frequent repainting are now only of iconographical interest, save for some few fragments preserved under whitewash throughout the drastic nineteenth-century restorations.

In execution, as in arrangement, these mosaics and frescoes are predominantly Byzantine, executed by Greek masters working under the direction of Greek priests, or in the less important parts by Russians working from Greek models. Yet among these Greek workmen there must have been some who, whether of Eastern origin or merely acquainted with Eastern style and iconography, introduced certain elements which differ from the Court style of the eleventh century. Thus, while such figures as the Virgin of the Annunciation or the standing saints in the apse have the slender proportions and delicate outlines of Byzantine painting, and the Virgin's head is of the purest classic type in proportion and drawing, the swarthy, bearded double Christ of the Liturgical Eucharist and the vigorously realistic yet rhythmically symmetrical expressions and gestures of the Apostles show some familiarity with the recurrent trends of Eastern ascetic realism which reached Byzantine art from Syria and Anatolia. The same influence appears in the severely formal figures of the standing Fathers, whose enlarged eyes have lost the play of expression seen in antique art.[11] This important contributory source of Byzantine style is present in the pictorial decoration of Sancta Sophia in much the same degree as the Eastern elements in the plan, which, for all that it displays of the closest parallels with the conjectural plan of the Nea Ekklesia, is yet not without puzzling references to such a Caucasian church as Mokvi.

Stylistically the mosaics and frescoes of Sancta Sophia, after the earlier eleventh-century mosaics at St Luke in Phocis, are among the greatest monuments of Byzantine painting. The Kievan mosaics are representative of this second period in Byzantine art, and in their own way, in the majestic expression of the Pantokrator or the linear grace of the Virgin Annunciate, they are not inferior to any contemporary Greek work. More than any other aspect of Kievan art these mosaics witness the close ties, spiritual, cultural, and artistic, which bound the principality to Tsargrad.

Perhaps nowhere is this political and cultural affiliation more dramatically expressed than in the curious frescoes on the walls of the stair tower leading to the galleries (Plate 16). Here in 1843 was found a sequence of secular scenes such as had long been known from textual descriptions to have existed in Byzantine art.[12] These paintings, containing more than a hundred and thirty picturesque and naturalistic figures, represent the life of the Byzantine Court, its ceremonials and festivals, such as the games enacted in the hippodrome at Christmas time, including acrobats, gladiators, and wild animal hunts. Yaroslav and his nobles descending to the Cathedral might fancy themselves very much like the Emperor and his courtiers as they glanced at these depictions of imperial festivities. In spite of repeated and disastrous restorations, certain parts of these frescoes show the same oriental types and realistic expression already observed in the Eucharist, here executed in a typically Eastern technique, linear and with boldly opposed values.

If the date 1017–37 be accepted for the construction of Sancta Sophia, one may think that the Greek masters who worked upon it were the immediate successors of those who had earlier been active at the Desyatinnaya, or that they may even have been responsible for the conjectured redecoration of the Desyatinnaya immediately before the second consecration of that church in 1039. Be this so or not, the mosaics and frescoes of Sancta Sophia differ to such a degree from later work at Kiev that the masters may be said to belong to the first Kievan generation. Not until after the turn of the century is comparable work again found, and in the lapse of time between Sancta Sophia and the decoration of St Michael (after 1108), another group of masters must have come from Constantinople, bringing the later development of the Byzantine style.

Unfortunately what may have been the most important sequence of mosaics of this second generation has disappeared from the walls of the Cathedral of the Dormition in the Pecherskaya Lavra (1075–89). In 1240 the upper half of the eastern apse was destroyed by the Tartars, yet enough remained into the seventeenth century to warrant an enthusiastic description by Paul of Aleppo, Archdeacon of Antioch. That it followed the traditional scheme, already examined in Sancta Sophia, is known from the Pecherski Paterik, the monastery's own hagiographical collection. Paul added that the mosaics were: 'inlaid with gold like those in Sancta Sophia and the church in Bethlehem. A beautiful mosaic decorates the floor of the chancel'.[13] From his description it is apparent that the Pecherski church continued the scheme and splendour of the Desyatinnaya and Sancta Sophia.

Since the Church of St Michael with the Golden Roof, founded by Prince Svyatopolk in 1108 in honour of his patron saint, follows so closely in plan and structure the Pecherski church, it is tempting to think that the Greek mosaicists who had worked in the latter, or their Russian pupils who by now might have become proficient enough to rank as independent masters, may have been responsible for the decorative scheme which, again according to Paul of Aleppo's description, followed closely that in Sancta Sophia.[14]

If the programme is familiar, the extant mosaics, especially the Liturgical Eucharist (Plate 18A), seem to be the work of another generation in a quite different style. In contrast to the agitated yet stereotyped oriental Apostles in the Sancta Sophia Eucharist, the Apostles here are tall, slender figures whose draperies are composed of intricate folds with broken silhouettes, very different from the continuous contours of the earlier figures. The former pattern of arms, hands, and feet repeating identical gestures is replaced by a complex rhythmical sequence, more intricate and yet calmer, more imbued with an inner contemplative spirit than that at Sancta Sophia. The individual heads are more varied and their expressions, like the facial types, more antique and less drastically ascetic. A comparable change has taken place in the colours, which are more harmonious than the bright opposed hues in Sancta Sophia. It is clear that the masters of St Michael belonged not only to a later generation, but stood in some respects closer to the Court style in Byzantium itself. The delicate drawing and colour, the variety and subtlety of expression, are eloquent testimony of the perfection of later eleventh-century painting in Constantinople, resembling if not in detail at least in expression the slightly earlier mosaics at Daphni.[15]

With the deterioration of the frescoes of Sancta Sophia, and the loss of those at the Pecherski Church and most of those at St Michael, a perhaps excessive historical interest attaches to the remains of a frescoed interior preserved in the Church of the Holy Trinity in the St Cyril Monastery in Kiev, founded in 1140 by Prince Vsevolod. Unhappily these also have been extensively restored, but enough remains to indicate that the powerful single figures in Sancta Sophia continued to exert an influence over similar painting a century later. A departure from the familiar iconographical schemes appears in the frescoes illustrating the life of St Cyril of Alexandria (Plate 18B). If in a certain sense the broad areas of pattern and almost oppressive frontality recall mosaic technique, this indicates that after the first magnificent period of Kievan art, frescoes inevitably replaced mosaics as a less expensive substitute. The simplified linear rhythms and embracing outlines also suggest that these paintings were possibly executed by Russian painters after a Byzantine original.[16]

THE FIRST RUSSIAN SCULPTURE

GEOGRAPHICAL and historical conditions are no less significant for the development of Russian sculpture than for the other arts. At the outset, the development of sculpture was compromised by the prohibition of the Greek Church, which forbade the use of 'graven images', taken to mean carved rather than painted likenesses of the holy personages. Thus from the end of the Iconoclastic Controversy in the ninth century, and consequently at the very beginning of Christian Russia, opportunities for sculptural decoration were closed to Russian artisans by the most affluent patrons of art. Yet if Russian churches lacked monumental figure sculpture, as it was known in Western Europe, the will to create three-dimensional forms found expression in other ways. The elaborate liturgical vessels, the intricate metal frames which were fitted over icons, and the richly carved iconostases, as well as the continuous production of peasant crafts, show that throughout their history Russians have experienced an instinctive pleasure in making and using three-dimensional forms.[1]

Three factors of particular importance determined the character of Russian sculpture. There was a sculptural tradition among the Russian people even in pre-Christian times. In the century before Vladimir's conversion a mingling of the personifications of Slavic nature-worship with the deities introduced by the Varangians seems to have taken place. The Slavic god Perun, for instance, seems to have been the counterpart of the Norse Thor, and probably the images of each were not unlike. The pagan idols were of wood or stone, standing freely in space, and carved in the full round in the likeness of human figures. The Arabian traveller Ahmed ibn Fadlan, who was in Russia in 922, described the religious practices of the merchants on the lower Volga who worshipped upright pieces of wood carved with the likenesses of human faces.[2] Slightly later European accounts contain tantalizing but inconclusive glimpses of the sculpture in the last pagan sanctuaries among the western Slavs. Dietmar of Merseburg (976–1018) described a 'skilfully fashioned wooden shrine, adorned on the outside with figures of various gods and goddesses'.[3] Helmold of Bosan (c. 1200) said that the Slavs carved 'many gods with two, three, or more heads'.[4] Such deities cast their reflexions far into Christian times. Their names were perpetuated in folk-songs, even in such a sophisticated work as the late twelfth-century *Tale of the Armament of Igor*, the greatest of all ancient Russian poems. In this tale of the defeat of one of the younger princes of Kievan Russia in an expedition against the Polovtsi, the anonymous poet invoked Dazhbog, Velos, Khors, and Div, a bird of ill-omen.[5]

Since wood perished and the idols which might have survived were conscientiously destroyed by the Church, we can only estimate the character of these figures from certain stone images, such as the granite block crudely worked as a man's head which was found near Novgorod in 1893.[6] A stone post discovered in 1848 in eastern Galicia is possibly more like those described in the chronicles. Each of the four sides had been carved in the likeness of a standing male figure, with other figures and animals below.[7] Vladimir's idols in Novgorod and Kiev may have been elaborate versions of such a stone image, incrusted with precious metals. The spirited silhouette of a horse and the crouching figure of a man at the bottom of the post are not unlike similar figures on the most enigmatic of these rare pagan sculptures. On the walls of a cave at Bush in Podolia on the river Murakhva, a tributary of the Dniester, a carving in low relief depicts a man kneeling before a tree where a cock perches on one of the branches (Plate 19).[8] In his raised hands he holds a now unidentifiable object; behind him a deer stands on a small hillock. Between the cock and the deer a now illegible inscription had been cut on a small square title. The scene probably represents an act of worship, since the cock is known to have been an object of adoration in pre-Christian Russia.

Although we may consider such objects monumental in size alone, the will to create three-dimensional forms, whether carved or modelled, may take other directions, and here the history of wooden architecture in Russia must not be neglected. The builders of the earliest cities and towns were familiar with a superb sculptural material. No wooden buildings earlier than the seventeenth century are now in existence, but even in the late churches the skilful manipulation of wood and the amount of carved ornament, at the ends of beams and roofing planks, on the door and window-frames, and in the shingles on the bulbous domes, suggest an ancient craft tradition.

The condition of the Kievan churches prohibits any adequate appraisal of the earliest Russian sculpture, but such as there was must from the first have been influenced by large and important examples of antique sculpture. On his return from Kherson in 989 Vladimir I brought to Kiev 'two bronze statues and four bronze horses' which were set up behind the Desyatinnaya and, as the chronicler somewhat patronizingly added, 'the ignorant think [they] are made of wood'.[9] Fragments of stone sarcophagi discovered in the ruins of the Desyatinnaya and a sarcophagus still preserved in Sancta Sophia as the tomb of Yaroslav are so thoroughly Byzantine as to lead one to think that for the princely entombments such stone work may have been imported from Greece.[10]

The one truly flourishing and individual school in ancient Russia developed towards the middle of the twelfth century in Suzdalia.[11] In both quantity and quality this sculpture is unique in the history of Byzantine and Russian art. Its quite exceptional character is a consequence of the vigorous political and cultural policy of the princes of Vladimir, which made the region one of the most cosmopolitan artistic centres in either the European or Eastern world during the twelfth century. The elaborate decoration of the churches of Vladimir may be due to the fact that Suzdalia was remote from Kiev, and so beyond the immediate supervision of the Metropolitan.

The work of the Suzdalian school first appeared in the carved decorations which are known to have existed on the Cathedral of the Dormition built by Andrei in Vladimir and on his palace church at Bogoliubovo. But since the latter has disappeared and the reliefs on the Dormition were destroyed or severely damaged in the fire of 1183 and in subsequent restorations, it is to the Pokrov-on-the-Nerl that we must look for the first conspicuous evidence. On this church the upper parts of the triple divisions on three façades are filled with figures in relief, and the columns of the corbel tables on all four façades rest upon sculptured corbels composed of animal, plant, and purely decorative forms (Plate 20). The reliefs on the south, west, and north façades are arranged in an identical fashion. High in the centre of each central arch is a male figure, inscribed 'Tsar David', seated between confronted pairs of doves and lions. He holds a stringed instrument and raises his right hand in blessing. Below is a range of three female heads, and on either side of the window two lions recline beneath stylized trees. The side panels contain a griffin attacking an animal, perhaps a wolf, and there are two female heads below. The capitals and voussoirs of the deeply splayed portals are covered with floral designs. The triple repetition of this enthroned King David may mean that he appears as the ancestral prefiguration of Christ. The confronted lions and doves would then symbolize aspects of the soul which David charmed with his music and Christ conquered with His sacrifice.

The second important sculptural ensemble is found on the exterior of St Dmitri at Vladimir, where, in addition to the treatment of portals and corbel tables resembling the Pokrov, the wall surfaces between the columns, within the triple panels on each façade, and between the windows of the drum are filled with low relief carvings (Plate 13B). Much of the present sculpture is restored or reworked, first after a severe fire in 1719, and again in the nineteenth century in the course of a drastic restoration. Although the work of both campaigns can be distinguished from the original twelfth-century sculpture, it is more difficult to be certain that the original figures were not removed and rearranged when the windows were enlarged. As at the Pokrov, the central panel on each façade contains the figure of King David enthroned. He is surrounded by a multitude of animal and plant forms and occasional human figures arranged in confronted rows extending below him on either side of the window. There is a similar disposition in the side panels, but they seem to have suffered considerably. Among them may be found evidence of other compositions, such as two confronted flying angels (perhaps the remains of an Ascension), seated Apostles, standing saints, and groups representing the Baptism of Christ, the Sacrifice of Isaac, and the Ascension of Alexander. An enigmatic composition of a seated man holding a child on his lap and two pairs of kneeling men approaching towards him resembles the usual Adoration of the Shepherds or Magi, but the unmistakably male character of the seated figure has led to the suggestion that this is a portrait of Vsevolod III, the founder of the church, with his son Dmitri in his arms.[12]

In comparison with the figures on St Dmitri the sculpture on the Pokrov seems comparatively crude and simplified, and so may represent an earlier, more tentative stage leading towards the elaborate treatment of the later church. Similarly the iconographical programme has been considerably enriched; to the simpler prophecy of Christ's coming has been added further confirmation of His divine mission in the prophetic enactment of the Sacrifice of Isaac, and in His Ascension with the pagan parallel of the Ascension of Alexander. Likewise the floral and animal decoration has been enlarged to such a point that the whole scheme has been considered an illustration of Psalm 148, with the exhortations 'Praise ye the Lord ... Beasts, and all cattle; creeping things, and flying fowl: Kings of the earth, and all people; princes, and all judges of the earth: ... Praise ye the Lord'.

It has also been suggested that the source for many of the reliefs can be found in the old Russian popular poem, *The Book of the Holy Ghost* (*Golubinaya Kniga*), containing a theological world history in the form of questions and answers, as symmetrically posed as the confronted pairs of men and animals on St Dmitri.[13]

Application of decorative reliefs to church walls is known in the West, in such churches as Notre Dame la Grande at Poitiers, and in the East, in the church at Achtamar on Lake Van in Armenia. The latter perhaps most nearly resembles St Dmitri, although neither in East nor West were the iconographical programme and the formal arrangement so skilfully related to the structure of the church as here in Vladimir. The style of the human figures which are treated almost in the full round also resembles Romanesque sculpture, particularly in the greater projection of the heads, hands, and feet. Behind them lay a long tradition of three-dimensional carving, extending back to classical antiquity and reaching both west and east through the medium of portable Byzantine ivories. On the other hand, the floral and animal forms are most oriental, especially the pairs of animals, the peacocks whose long necks cross in opposite directions, and the lions whose confronted heads merge into one. All these are familiar in Eastern metal-work and textiles, and may have been copied from the textiles which are known to have been in Vladimir in considerable size and quantity. The chronicle, recording the great fire of 1183, mentions the loss of 'two wonderful series of fabrics which on feast days used to be hung on two cords from the Golden Gate to the Cathedral of the Dormition and from the Dormition to the archbishop's palace'.[14]

The presence of Eastern and Western elements in the sculptural programme at the Nerl and St Dmitri's is substantiated by the chronicles and by the history of Suzdalia. Since the chronicle specifically says of Prince Andrei that 'for his piety and great zeal for the Virgin, architects from all countries were brought to him by God',[15] we may presume that the princely workshops in Suzdalia included architects and craftsmen from the West as well as the East. The arrival in Suzdalia of such artisans can be postulated on the basis of dynastic and trade relations. Vsevolod's marriage to a Caucasian princess was symptomatic of the continuous trade which flourished between Suzdalia and the East along the Volga. Through the intermediation of the Bulgars of Kazan, who were settled along the middle reaches of the river and who had embraced Islam in the tenth century, articles of Persian and Turkish origin easily reached Vladimir.

The constant movement of artisans in the medieval world is no uncommon phenomenon; in 1246 the Franciscan emissary from the Pope to the Mongols, Giovanni de Plano Carpini, encountered at the Court of the Khan a Russian goldsmith 'who was greatly in the Emperor's favour'.[16]

The third and last of the important programmes in Suzdalia, if we omit the damaged carvings in the Cathedral of Suzdal, which are like the work at St Dmitri's, is the sculpture which covers the exterior surface of the Church of St George in Yuriev-Polski, the summer residence of the Vladimir princes (Plates 15A, 21, and 22A).[17] The church collapsed in the fifteenth century, and was reconstructed at the command of the Great Prince of Moscow, Ivan III, by the Moscow architect, V. D. Yermolin. Unfortunately Yermolin reduced the height of the whole structure, and with complete disregard for the sense of the sculptures replaced the stones in any order, possibly even including materials from an adjacent ruined church. The original arrangement is now inextricably confused, and only on an iconographical basis can certain portions be studied in proper sequence. Nevertheless it is apparent that once, as now, the church at Yuriev-Polski was completely covered with carved decorations; the chronicles remark that Svyatoslav 'ornamented it more than all other churches, for on the exterior of the whole church wonderful saints in carved stone were placed.[18] This arrangement is unique in the history of western architecture, and recalls such ancient Syrian systems as the fifth-century carved reliefs at Mschatta. An Eastern origin for the work at Yuriev-Polski seems plausible, and would account for the pointed arches which occur above the portals on each porch and above the heads of the standing saints.

In contrast to St Dmitri, where the human figures were submerged in a welter of plant and animal forms, the saints standing between the columns of the arcades and the figures in such scenes as the Transfiguration and deesis, which can be reconstructed from isolated fragments, are considerably more monumental. Not only are they large in comparison with the rest of the decoration, but they tend to dominate rather than to be subordinated to their architectural surroundings. Within the frames provided by columns and carved bands they show by the slightest gesture, the turn of a head or the expression of an eye, a more pronounced humanism than the stilted marionettes of St Dmitri. The difference is perhaps due to the sources from which the artists drew their iconography. Where the craftsmen of St Dmitri may have used the small illustrations in illuminated manuscripts, the sculptors of St George were thinking of the spacious frescoes of St Dmitri itself, executed probably towards the close of the 1190s. Three years after St George was completed the Tartars were at the gates of Vladimir and the brief period of its artistic pre-eminence was over. In the confusion of the occupation the artisans were probably dispersed. Perhaps one of them was the man whom Plano Carpini saw at the court of the Khan in 1246. Others may have gone westward to Galicia, where in 1259 Prince Daniel built a church of which the description in so many respects resembles the churches of Suzdalia that it is tempting to think that his architect may once have worked for Vsevolod or his successors. Certainly Daniel was aware of the value of articles of Russian workmanship for 'he ornamented the church with icons which had been brought from Kiev'. What interests us here is that 'the two entrance doors were carved of white Galician and green Cholm stone, and the designs were executed by a certain artist Avdei'. Perhaps Avdei was a fugitive from Vladimir, in which case he was the only Suzdalian sculptor whom we know by name.[19]

CHAPTER 7

FRESCOES IN VLADIMIR AND NOVGOROD

AFTER the middle of the twelfth century Kiev was no longer a dominant power politically or artistically. Successive raids by the younger princes, culminating in Andrei Bogoliubski's siege of the city in 1169, merely confirmed the fact that it could no longer be considered an effective centre, either for resistance against the nomads, whose incursions grew yearly more dangerous, or as a dynastic and cultural rallying point for the Russian people. In the north-east the princes of Suzdal were rapidly developing an almost independent state, its wealth derived from agriculture and international trade; for it lay athwart the great east–west trade route which now led down the Volga to the Caspian and by portage to the Don and thence to the Black Sea. Inevitably the pretensions of the princes of Suzdal incurred the hostility of Novgorod. As early as 1169 the Suzdalians attacked Novgorod, and were only prevented by a miracle from taking it. Which city would have been pre-eminent in the future must remain in doubt, for the Mongol advance in 1237 devastated Suzdalia. Novgorod alone maintained the consistent development of Russian painting after the deterioration of Kiev and the collapse of Suzdalia.

The earliest mural painting in Novgorod was related immediately to the Byzantine monuments of Kiev. The oldest and most important church, the Cathedral of Sancta Sophia (1045–57), although almost contemporary with Sancta Sophia in Kiev, apparently was decorated more slowly, and then in fresco rather than in more costly mosaic. Very little of the earliest painting survived damage and drastic restoration in the nineteenth century, and still less the burning of the cathedral during the Second World War.[1] Only the Pantokrator and Apostles in the dome and drum showed how closely the masters – here, too, probably Greeks – followed the Kievan types. If, indeed, they were those who had worked in the south, their presence in Novgorod and consequent absence from Kiev might account for the fact that the builders of the Dormition in the Pecherskaya Lavra were obliged to send to Constantinople for artisans. In this way the masters of the later generation who may have worked in the Lavra and whose mosaics have been preserved at St Michael reached Russia.

It is recorded that the decoration of Sancta Sophia was not finished until 1144, and to this period may be attributed the monumental figures in the chapel of St Vladimir representing SS. Constantine and Helena, depicted full-length on either side of the ever-blossoming cross. They were not only particularly fine examples of early twelfth-century Byzantine painting, but in the bold yet delicate colouring and tender gestures proved that the independent spirit of Novgorod was already at work adapting the classic proportions and imperial dignity of such figures as the Archangels at Kiev to a more naturalistic presentation.[2]

During this first period of the spread of Byzantine art in Russia, Greek masters were active not only in the north in Novgorod, but also in the north-east, in the principality of Vladimir-Suzdal. The fire in 1183 severely damaged not only the fabric of Andrei Bogoliubski's Cathedral of the Dormition in Vladimir, but also the frescoes of 1161. Fragments remaining after Vsevolod III's extensive reconstruction of the church included figures of prophets and two peacocks in an ornamental style which were recovered by the State Restoration Commission in 1918–20.[3] The position of these frescoes is particularly significant. They were found on the north exterior wall of Andrei's church (now the south or inner wall of the north aisle), and by their position indicate that Andrei's building followed the Kievan taste for exterior polychromatic decoration. Of Vsevolod's reconstruction of 1185–9 a few figures of prophets and Fathers with some traces of ornamental decoration remain. Greek inscriptions suggest the presence of Byzantine masters, which is borne out by the chronicler's pious statement that because of Andrei's great love for the Virgin, 'God sent him masters from many lands'. The Last Judgement on the west wall was repainted in 1408 by Andrei Rublev and Daniel Chorni, and will be considered in the account of their activity. From the fact that such a painting occupied this place and from the fragments of saints and prophets it can be assumed that Andrei's painters followed the usual mid-Byzantine scheme observed in the churches of Kiev.

It is almost miraculous that any frescoes in St Dmitri, painted in the last years of the twelfth century, survived until the present day.[4] In addition to the normal ravages of time, the successive 'restorations' of the nineteenth century spoiled the little that was left. Fortunately the State Restoration Commission in 1918–20 recovered fragments of a Last Judgement on the vault above the west entrance, with accompanying figures and scenes on adjacent vaults and arches which had escaped repainting in the late nineteenth century. What was left can be seen to have been executed by artists comparable in ability, in the best parts, to the mosaicists of Kiev. Considering the size of the church and the extent of the paintings which originally covered it, probably the co-operation of several masters and their assistants was required, and among the latter there may well have been Russian pupils, since several different hands may be seen at work. Thus the procession of righteous women led into Paradise by St Peter is painted in a lively and rhythmical style not unlike the Eucharist figures in the Kievan Sancta Sophia, while the Apostles seated on high thrones have a hieratic and aristocratic dignity comparable to those in St Michael. Several heads such as those of St Matthew and St Paul are among the most accomplished and spiritual achievements of Byzantine painting (Plate 23). The classic regularity of the features is in the finest tradition of Byzantine Hellenism, and the play of spiritual emotion exemplifies that mystical disturbance of classic serenity which at a later age found expression in the last great master of the Byzantine tradition, El Greco.

Behind the Apostles the rows of angel heads, some partially obscured by the lively play of intersecting haloes, can be counted one of the most gracious examples of Byzantine painting (Plate 22B). The refined Greek features, with the wide classic eyes, the long, curved nose, and small mouth, are so lightly painted that line and shade almost impalpably create the form. The painter achieved the most delicate balance between supernatural and human attributes. The frescoes of St Dmitri indicate how the Byzantine artist could create a convincing three-dimensional style without recourse to what in the West became the direct observation of Nature. Byzantine art in its noblest examples preserved from its classic heritage that subtle equilibrium between the real and ideal, between the observed and the imagined, between abstraction and naturalistic detail. This is perhaps its greatest and most characteristic achievement. The Apostles and angels of St Dmitri are proof, if proof were needed, that the best Byzantine artists would have found completely unintelligible the accusation that they were for ever immured within unchangeable abstractions.

The paintings are not all of the same quality. The Apostles and angels which we have just examined on the north side of the vault are due to the best of the artists, but even here the heads are superior to the garments. The colours, too, are more delicate than those on the south side; blues and blue-greens against gold predominate, while on the other side are murkier red, brown, and olive hues. It may be correct to say that the less technically accomplished parts were executed by Russian pupils of the Greek masters, but such apparent national distinctions may also be due only to the poor preservation of the painting.

Although Suzdalia may have claimed the best talents among the itinerant Greek masters of the later twelfth century, the very perfection of the frescoes of St Dmitri's may have been felt as a challenge as much to be avoided as to be imitated; for the course which Russian painting was to take in the following centuries was directed not by the infrequent masterpieces in Vladimir, but by the incessant activity which continued in Novgorod. Whereas Kiev disappeared for centuries from the Russian political and cultural sphere, and the cities of Suzdalia languished under Mongol vassalage, Novgorod maintained its independence and was able to continue its commercial and ecclesiastical relations with Constantinople. It is true that the confusions attending the Mongol invasion led inevitably to a certain scarcity of artistic creation during the later thirteenth century, and from this period few icons and no wall-paintings have been preserved. The more interest, therefore, attaches to the last great mural ensemble of the twelfth century, since in it may be seen the position of Novgorod painting at the end of the pre-Mongol period and some of the incipient influences which were later to become dominant.

Until the Second World War, when it was completely destroyed, the little Church of the Saviour at Nereditsa, familiarly known as the Spas-Nereditsa, in the fields some two miles from Novgorod, contained the earliest complete ensemble of wall-paintings.[5] This church was but one of many which from the twelfth to the end of the fifteenth centuries rose in the suburbs and outlying villages of Novgorod. It was built by a Prince of Novgorod, Yaroslav Vladimirovich, in 1198 and painted the following year. Abandoned in the later Middle Ages, its villagers gone, and its conventual structures destroyed, the little church had the good fortune to be ignored during the various restoration campaigns of the eighteenth and nineteenth centuries, until it was finally and carefully restored in 1904. The unusually extensive cycle of paintings covering the vaults and walls above a simulated marble dado quite reasonably attracted a degree of attention because of its completeness, but it also exhibited so many important aspects of the cultural conditions prevailing at the end of the twelfth century that its provincial character has perhaps been unduly ignored. The very fact that the frescoes represent a local variant of the dominant Byzantine trends makes them more significant for the history of Russian painting than the perfection found in St Dmitri's.[6]

The paintings reached from the dome almost to the floor of the church, and followed in the main the traditional mid-Byzantine scheme, except that in the dome itself the representation of the Ascension replaced the traditional Pantokrator (Plate 26A). At Nereditsa Christ rose in a rainbow aureole upheld by six winged angels. In the drum of the dome the dramatic movement continued in the agitated figures of the Apostles and the Virgin accompanied by two angels. These figures, like the Archangels above them, stood upon a ground, so that they seemed to move in a definite space. The Apostles were less doctrinal intermediaries between heaven and earth than companions of the corporeal, historical Saviour. In the second zone the story recovered its traditional symbolic character with the range of eight Old Testament prophets and with the Evangelists in the pendentives. These majestic, solitary figures were reminiscent of the traditional figures of the Kievan school, and indicated that the painters were still influenced by mosaic art. Indeed, the absence of anecdotal scenes at Nereditsa was in this respect the final echo of the hieratic art of Kiev.

In the apse stood the Virgin Blacherniotissa, a variant of the Virgin Orans, wearing on her breast a medallion portrait of Christ Emmanuel, again the last of the great line descending from Kiev (Plate 26B). In contrast, however, to earlier apsidal figures, which were attended only by Archangels, here there approached from either side a procession of male and female saints led by the first Russian martyrs, SS. Boris and Gleb.[7] Below the traditional Liturgical Eucharist were three rows of figures, the upper two containing the customary Fathers and other dignitaries (Plate 24), and the lower forming an unusual deesis wherein the standing figure of the tonsured Christ as High Priest was flanked by medallions of the Virgin and the Baptist. The dogmatic symbols were completed by representations on the chancel vault of the Hetimasia or empty throne of the Last Judgement prepared for Christ's second coming with the Instruments of the Passion, and of Christ as the Ancient of Days flanked by Gabriel and Michael. On the whole, the frescoes of the chief sacramental spaces of the church, the dome, apse, and chancel, complied with traditional Byzantine formulas. On the west wall was an extended depiction of the Last Judgement in two zones, with many separate and traditional scenes. The similarity of the range of seated Apostles with those in St Dmitri in Vladimir permits a conjectural restoration of the lost portions of the latter frescoes.

If the iconographical plan at Nereditsa exhibited no startling departures, except in matters of detail, or in the historical interest in such scenes as the Ascension, in just those details and in the technical execution these frescoes provided most revealing evidence of the complex sources of Russian painting in the later Middle Ages. The presence here of several different hands could easily be noted. That some of them may have been Greeks, or that the scheme was certainly devised by a priest of Greek origin or Greek training, is assumed from the programme, but other factors indicate that among these masters, of whom some may have been Russians, since many of the inscriptions are in the local Novgorod dialect, there were many who had come from the East or who had been trained elsewhere than in Constantinople. To the Constantinopolitan school we may ascribe the general iconographical plan, especially such representations as the Virgin Orans, the Hetimasia, the Archangels, and the deesis, all familiar from Kiev. The stocky figure of the Virgin was a provincial variant of the heavily proportioned Virgin in Sancta Sophia.

On the other hand, although the painting of the dome, pendentives, and apse retained the clear articulation between symbolism and structure typical of the best Byzantine work in the capital, the remainder of the church was completely covered from vault to pavement with scenes enclosed in square frames on a blue ground, which were more suggestive of the paintings in the cave churches of Cappadocia. This Eastern aspect was further substantiated in iconography and execution. Many details were closer to oriental, even Caucasian, precedent than to Constantinopolitan procedure. This was particularly evident in the Baptism of Christ, where the opportunity to portray the nude figure in a spirit evocative of classical antiquity was ignored (Plate 25A). More apparent were the anecdotal character and the realistic touches in the attendant neophytes, one of whom was removing his coat, while another swam out from the bank towards the centre of the river. Again the lack of spatial consistency whereby the figures were painted in three sizes according to their hieratic importance, the attendants smallest, the angels of middle size, the Christ and the Baptist largest of all, followed Syrian precedent.

Also, in the heads of the various saints and Apostles not only different hands but different artistic traditions might be observed. The heads of such saints as Basil the Great, John Chrysostom, Gregory the Wonder-Worker, and Nicholas the Wonder-Worker were almost transcriptions in fresco of the heads of the Fathers in Kiev. In the head of St Peter in the Ascension light and dark lines and areas created an almost sculptural effect. On the other hand, the heads of a more Eastern type and, as noted, often those of a specifically Eastern tradition, such as the ascetics and Eastern saints, were treated as severely frontal linear patterns, now approaching a summary, even sketchy impression-ism, elsewhere based on an arabesque of decorative motifs which symbolized rather than visually suggested the three-dimensional character of the forms, yet without sacrificing of the vivid realism of eastern Byzantine art (Plate 25C).[8] In addition St Rhipsime, partic-ularly venerated as the proto-martyr of the Armenian Church, was depicted in the dia-conicon. Her presence in the sanctuary leads one to wonder whether the clerical staff may not have included some Eastern priest, come to Novgorod in the train of Yaro-slav's Ossetian wife. In the heads of the first group the broad rhythmical divisions of light and shade in mosaic had been translated into a similar broadly plastic style resembling late antique illusionism (Plate 25B).

After Nereditsa a century and a half elapsed before monumental painting again ap-peared in northern Russia. This hiatus was in large part due to the disturbed times there and abroad. From 1240 the rest of Russia, with the exception of Novgorod and Pskov, was too seriously concerned with discovering a way to live under Tartar rule to under-take important schemes of public decoration, while to the south the Greek Empire itself lay for sixty years under bondage to the Western crusaders who held Constantinople from 1204 until 1261. After the recapture of Constantinople by Michael VIII in 1261, the last and one of the most brilliant periods of Byzantine art was inaugurated under the

Palaeologos dynasty. By 1303 new confidence in a revived political order had achieved remarkable artistic expression in the mosaics in the Church of the Chora Monastery in Constantinople, better known by its Turkish title as the Mosque of Kahrieh-Djami. The style which culminated in these mosaics prevailed not only in the capital itself, but throughout the Balkan peninsula, especially in Macedonia and Serbia. Hence it has come to be considered of Macedonian origin so far as it reached Northern Russia, where iconographical similarities may be observed between Serbian and Macedonian scenes and their counterparts in Novgorod. Yet the fact that the late fourteenth-century frescoes at Mistra in the Peloponnesus are in the same manner suggests that the Russian examples must have been related to Constantinople directly, as well as by the transmission of influences by itinerant masters coming north from the Balkans.

Direct connexions between Novgorod and Constantinople are in other activities historically so well attested that it would seem idle to predicate a roundabout route. The appearance of a flourishing school of fresco-painting in Novgorod and its environs soon after the middle of the fourteenth century cannot be entirely unconnected with the continuous and close relations between the clergy in Novgorod and the Patriarch in Constantinople. In 1353 emissaries sent by Bishop Moses to the Emperor John Cantacuzene and the Patriarch Philotheos returned from Constantinople and 'brought with them vestments ornamented with crosses and documents, with bestowal of great favour from the Emperor and from the Patriarch and a gold seal'.[9] From the middle years of the century there are several references to the activity of Greek painters whose influence, through their own works and the instruction they gave to their Russian pupils, may be held responsible for the revival of Russian painting after the Tartar interlude.

The impulse for much of this work can be traced to the presence of a learned and sensitive Greek, Theognostus, Metropolitan of Moscow from 1328 to 1353.[10] He had come of age in Constantinople during the first bright years of the Palaeologos Renaissance, and during his residence in Russia he continued to patronize Greek artists and to encourage their Russian pupils. Through his influence the Great Prince of Moscow, Simon Ivanovich, and his wife Anastasia also commissioned mural work. In 1344 two stone churches were decorated; the Cathedral Church of the Virgin in the Metropolitan's palace by 'Greek masters', and the palace church of the Archangel Michael by the Russian artists, 'Zacharias, Denis, Joseph, and Nicholas', commissioned by Simon Ivanovich. The following year paintings in the church of the Monastery of the Saviour were ordered by Anastasia. They were executed by 'Goitan, Simon, and Ivan, of Russian birth but pupils of the Greeks'. In 1346 the Church of St John is mentioned, making a total of four masonry churches frescoed in three years by Greek and Russian painters.

Of all this work in Moscow unfortunately no trace remains, but a group of churches in Novgorod and the vicinity preserved into the twentieth century enough of their original decoration to make possible some understanding of the character of late fourteenth-century fresco-painting in Russia. The Church of the Dormition at Volotovo was built in 1352 and painted in 1363. In the seventeenth century it was severely damaged by the Swedes. Although the frescoes were restored at that time, enough fourteenth-century work survived until the total destruction of the church in the Second World War to warrant stylistic analysis. The decorative scheme followed the typical mid-Byzantine formula. The Pantokrator brooded in the dome; beneath him were the ranks of Archangels, Prophets, and Patriarchs, the Evangelists in the pendentives, and in the apse the Virgin, here enthroned with the Child, and below her the Divine Liturgy and the Church Fathers.[11]

Familiar as this scheme may be, certain iconographical and stylistic innovations hinted that the classic serenity of the eleventh-century Byzantine concept was yielding to a more dramatic, emotional attitude towards dogma and history. The Pantokrator had lost his stern and serious expression and seemed to lean forward blessing rather than judging his people. The enthroned Virgin no longer reigned in lonely majesty in the apse, but was the focus of a double procession which included angels, prophets, Joachim and Anna, as well as the more usual saints who had appeared at Nereditsa. Taken as a whole the entire apse from dome to floor was organized as a triple series of concentric movements, from the angels and prophets moving towards the enthroned Virgin and Child, and the Apostles advancing to receive the bread and wine in actual substance from the hands of Christ, to the Church Fathers contemplating the elements symbolized in the cross and chalice on the throne. The climax, of course, was daily re-enacted in the liturgical ceremonies. In this way later Byzantine iconography enriched the dogmatic programme and accomplished that instantaneous and mystical transition from the symbolic performance to the demonstration of doctrine on the walls.

This dramatic tendency was further elaborated in the scenes from the lives of Christ and the Virgin, where there were slight but telling indications that this growing interest in what may be called the human element of the story was affected by influences reaching Novgorod through her constant commercial relations with the West. The *Noli Me Tangere*, wherein Christ appears only to Mary Magdalene, the representation of the dead Christ standing in an open tomb, and the substitution of the Vernicle (Veronica's Veil) for the Mandilion portrait are three instances of Western influence.[12]

Stylistically the frescoes were remarkable for the new manner which they announced for northern Russia, and which is best understood as the transmittal of the finest type of Palaeologos art of the last Byzantine Renaissance. Like the authors of the mosaics of the Kahrieh-Djami, these Byzantine painters had almost abandoned their taste for the isolated single figure. Even in Constantinople this was in part due to the gradual replacement of mosaic by fresco, in which complex scenes could more easily be depicted. There was a preference for narrative with small figures placed in front of landscapes or architectural settings. Unlike the earlier backgrounds, which were often merely symbols of place and time, these atmospheric landscapes and buildings in reasonably accurate perspective suggested actual situations. The use of architecture was perhaps less conspicuous at Volotovo than the treatment of landscape, but the interior of a monastic refectory included a table in correct rather than oblique perspective, and in the background a most persuasive depiction of the exterior of a building with a dome on a drum and pendentives.[13]

Even more remarkable was the treatment of landscape as a play of sharp zigzags streaking above and behind the figures in such scenes as the Nativity, the Annunciation to the Shepherds, and the Transfiguration (Plate 27A). Only along the edges were there vestiges in the form of short white dots of the earlier terraces which had stood for mountains in the eleventh and twelfth centuries. It was as if the artist, hurrying to record his visual impression of moving figures, had only glanced at the landscape beyond them and set it down as a summary contrast of light and dark.

The painter lavished his peculiar and very personal skill on his figures. Even to a standing Archangel he imparted overwhelming energy in his spacious design of the great arcs of wings and globe punctured by the broken contours of the garments (Plate 28). This search for a more complex yet unified action continued in the narrative scenes as an impressionist shorthand of extraordinary effect. The figures were quickly and slightly sketched by means of dark masses and light lines which succinctly conveyed their agitation. Gone for ever was the static equilibrium of the frescoes of St Dmitri, where tone and line are of equal value in rendering form and movement. Here the function of line was to urge the darker masses into violent movement. Only in this manner could the artist render the figure in so many positions hitherto unattempted in Byzantine painting. Palaeologos realism dictated the attitude of Mary in the Ascension twisting her head to follow the rising Christ. The shepherd standing beside the sleeping Joachim turned his back to the spectators, and in the Journey of the Magi the youth seated on the brow of a hill, like the personification of landscape in classical art, turned half round to point out the star in the sky (Plate 27B). The substitution of a visual for a conceptual aesthetic was complete.

The figures mentioned above were among the best at Volotovo, the work of an unusually gifted personality who could capture the peculiar quality of an image seen instantly and as swiftly recorded. The remaining scenes appear to have been executed by other hands and, although less competent, were treated within the same aesthetic conceptions, so that we may predicate the existence at Volotovo of a group of painters, of whom one at least must have been well acquainted with the latest developments at Constantinople.

It is tempting but imprudent to think that the leader of this atelier was the famous master, Theophanes 'the Greek' (Feofan Grek), who was working in Novgorod in 1378 in the Church of the Transfiguration.[14] If little is known of his activity in Russia, and less of his origin and early training, that little is still more than we know of his predecessors, including even the monk Alimpi of Kiev. After the frescoes of 1378 there is no reference to him until 1395, when he painted the Church of the Nativity of the Virgin in Moscow with Simon Chorni and their pupils. In 1399 he was working with his assistants in the Cathedral of St Michael in the Kremlin, and in 1405 with Prochor of Gorodets and Andrei Rublev in the Cathedral of the Annunciation. All these frescoes disappeared when the Kremlin churches were rebuilt in the late fifteenth century, so that only the frescoes in the Transfiguration in Novgorod survived to show us what his style was like.

From other sources there are precious scraps of information about the man and his career. The most extensive account is found in a letter of 1414 or 1415 from Epiphanius the Wise, the biographer of St Sergius, to another disciple of the same saint, Cyril of

Belo-ozersk, wherein Theophanes is described as the 'very excellent zoomorph, book illuminator, and painter'. Epiphanius further says that Theophanes had a special gift for architectural drawing, that he had drawn a city in a fresco in St Michael's, and that he had painted a panorama on a stone wall in the palace of Prince Vladimir Andreevich. Theophanes had also made for Epiphanius a schematic drawing of Sancta Sophia in Constantinople. Cyril had seen this several years before, and wrote to Epiphanius asking for a copy.[15] From this letter two important facts emerge: Theophanes had been to Constantinople, and he surpassed his fellow artists and attracted the admiration of his contemporaries by his ability to draw living beings. Apparently he worked swiftly, without patterns, and in full view of spectators, thereby exciting much wonder. He must have possessed an admirably sure technique, an authoritative memory, and an imaginative faculty of the highest order. With these gifts he must also have been a painter thoroughly familiar with the pictorial impressionism of the Palaeologos Renaissance. Finally, if the chronological indications are to be trusted, if he was in Novgorod in 1378, if his last work was performed in Moscow in 1405, and if he died sometime before the date of Epiphanius's letter, his birth may be placed in the decade 1330–40.

Compared with Theophanes, the painters of Volotovo seem erratic and uncertain of the success of the effects for which they strive, or perhaps of the means by which they should achieve them. Theophanes's impressionism continues the same visual appreciation of forms in light, but based upon an intimate understanding of the human body, as well as of the principles of Byzantine style. One might think Theophanes had studied ancient sculpture, so strong is the feeling that his Old Testament prophets are spiritual descendants of the late Hellenistic philosophers. The most conspicuous technical divergence from the Volotovo frescoes is the substitution of a curved for a straight line in the highlights. Although it is true that the slashing accents at Volotovo were frequently charged with dramatic and tragic sentiment, they often suggested to the eye more the flutter of drapery in the wind than the movement of substantial forms through space.

In the absence of any extensive narrative scenes we can only imagine how Theophanes would have painted movement, but his prophets show with how much care he observed the play of light over objects and distributed his highlights so that the fundamental rhythms of forms in space are suggested (Plate 29). His technique is pictorial; the masters of Volotovo were graphic artists intent on seizing with lightning speed the combination of lines which would best suit their purpose. Theophanes's colour scheme seems to revive the earth palette of antique painting. In contrast to the intense, pure colour at Volotovo, his grounds and darker areas are a flat red, upon which the modelling in a lighter red, with black outlines and white high lights, suggests the same kind of colour simplification that was appearing contemporaneously in icons. In Theophanes's work there is that perceptible echo of antiquity inseparable from the best Byzantine painting (Plate 30).

Yet Theophanes was not only an artist in the classic tradition. The intenser experience of the religious life which the East brought to Byzantium found expression in his remarkable image of St Macarius, the ascetic who claimed that he lived in the Egyptian desert for thirty years without ever eating, drinking, or sleeping as much as Nature required (Plate 31). This figure is so like a fresco of St Anthemius in the Kahrieh-Djami, that it has been suggested that Theophanes may have executed his first work in that church.[16] But the Anthemius is too assured to be the work of a beginner. The temperament which produced it, mature and spacious, could scarcely have developed the nervous energy of Theophanes. Yet he may have known this fresco, for his peculiarities are divergences rather than differences.

From Epiphanius's letter we gather that before coming to Russia, Theophanes had worked not only in Constantinople, but also in Chalcedon, Galata, and Kaffa (Theodosia) in the Crimea, and, after leaving Novgorod, in Nizhni-Novgorod and Gorodets, as well as in Moscow. But nothing remains of his frescoes except those of the Transfiguration, and icons. There perhaps some will be considered in their proper place.

Elsewhere in Novgorod, in the Churches of St Theodore Stratilates and of the Nativity of Christ in the Cemetery (na Kladbishche) and in the Church of Kovalevo near the city, are late fourteenth-century frescoes which continue the impressionist tendencies of Volotovo and Theophanes's work in the Transfiguration, but with declining technical distinction and expressive power. Apparently early in the 1380s Theophanes left Novgorod on his way to Moscow, and without his presence the Greek painters and their Russian pupils were unable to maintain the high level of his achievement. But their work, though more timid and pedestrian, at least sufficed to fill the churches of Novgorod with so many frescoes that it rivalled any Western European city of the later Middle Ages in the wealth of its pictorial embellishment.

PART TWO

ICON-PAINTING

*

All Angel-kind marvelled at thy great work of flesh-taking ; they saw the inaccessible God accessible to all as a man, dwelling with us and hearing from all : Alleluia.

THE AKATHIST HYMN

CHAPTER 8

ICON-PAINTING: CRITICISM, ICONOGRAPHY, AND TECHNIQUE

OF all the varieties of pictorial art, the religious subject on a painted panel, the icon, has become most completely identified with the conception of a specifically Russian art. The word has even seemed at times to have lost its original Greek significance and come to mean Russian, rather than generally Byzantine, panel painting. The reason for this assimilation of the word to Russian art is that far more Russian than Greek icons have been preserved and that in Russia and elsewhere in Eastern Europe the use and practice of icon-painting continued into the twentieth century, although, as the dominant manifestation of Russian pictorial expression, icon-painting was gravely compromised by the westernization of Russian art after the seventeenth century.

Familiar though the fact may be that quantities of Russian icons are still in existence, and some are even found in Western museums and private collections, the understanding of the artistic qualities of icon-painting and its historical analysis present almost insuperable difficulties for the Western observer. Even in Russia systematic study had to wait until the beginning of the present century.[1] In the course of the nineteenth century the revival of interest in the Russian past on the part of the Slavophiles inevitably drew attention to the large numbers of icons preserved in churches, and in the houses of the Old Believers who had throughout the centuries continued to collect the ancient religious pictures. Although icons at first were valued principally as examples of a historic and traditional way of life, they soon attracted the attention of connoisseurs who collected them for their rarity, technical perfection, and artistic quality. By 1914 the major historical and critical principles had been established by the study and publication of the important collections in St Petersburg and Moscow, especially those formed by N. P. Likhachev (now in the Russian Museum, Leningrad) and in Moscow by I. S. Ostroukhov (now in the Tretyakov Gallery and Historical Museum).[2] This preliminary work was reduced in value by the poor condition of almost all the icons, which were covered with layers of dirt and repaint accumulated through long years of use in churches. Although some cleaning and restoration had been done before 1917, only after the November Revolution were the true splendours of medieval Russian painting uncovered by the activity of the State Restoration Workshop in Moscow.[3] Of special interest was the recovery of a dozen icons of the twelfth and thirteenth centuries. For the first time it was possible to gain some conception of the character of icon-painting in Kievan Russia, until then merely a matter of tradition, since the oldest painted surfaces had been totally concealed beneath layers of repaint. In recent years a more coherent picture of the development of icon-painting in Russia has gradually emerged, although for the Western student the absence in Europe and America of any extensive collections of first-rate examples in public museums and the scarcity of private collections make the study of icon-painting at first hand almost impossible. In the circumstances we have to rely on the publications of the eminent Russian scholars who have devoted themselves to this work.[4]

As in the history of architecture and mural painting, the study of icons is handicapped by the difficulties caused by the successive destruction of Russian cities and the rebuilding of churches, with the usual dispersal or damage to the old furnishings. Such icons as were preserved have suffered seriously. The more revered the icon, the more frequently it was repainted or repaired if it showed signs of deterioration – a not unlikely situation in a humid climate with violent contrasts of temperature. And each repainting, often executed with little regard for preserving more than the most casual indication of the original colours and forms, was followed by frequent revarnishing, so that by the end of the nineteenth century the most famous icons venerated in the Russian sanctuaries presented a darkened surface bearing little or no relation to the original design, often buried under five or six layers of later paint.[5] And the general anonymity of medieval art meant that few icons were signed, and almost none dated. Moreover, in most cases the provenance is unclear or confused. Only by painstaking analytical comparison, constantly subject to modifications, as further icons are cleaned and unsuspected ones brought to light, can even a tentative identification of schools and manners be made. Yet even at the present stage it is possible to grasp the general outlines of a historical process.

There is, finally, one more difficulty in studying Russian icon-painting of which the Western student must be aware. His familiarity with the historical chronology and technical progression of European painting from the later Middle Ages to modern times prepares him for a similar development in Russian painting based on a gradual and continuous conquest, technically and expressively, of the world of sense impressions. In Russian and Byzantine art no such evolution occurs, and the infrequent evidences of intensive observation of the visual world are too slight to deflect painting from its inexorable pursuit of a very different kind of 'reality'. To the Western observer Russian painting often appears static, hieratic, and repetitive, whereas actually its very lack of 'progress' is only proof that its methods as well as its aims were not only different but self-sufficient.

Icon-painting, and indeed almost all Russian painting up to the end of the seventeenth century, was religious in origin and use. The secular standards of Western criticism, perceptible in European literature as early as the sixteenth century, whereby even a religious painting is examined as a work of art with definable aesthetic implications, were unknown in Russian art before the eighteenth century. The criterion of artistic beauty had nothing to do with the efficacy of the image as an aid to religious experience, although here as elsewhere in religious art the more effective the image the more it will contain those qualities of technical perfection, formal order, tonal harmony, and expressive power upon which artistic quality may be said to be based. However, the search for these elements, so conspicuous a preoccupation for the Western artist since the end of the fifteenth century, seems to have been only a secondary concern of the Russian painter. His image was intended for a specific place in a church or chapel, or alcove reserved for devotions in a private house. Until recently an icon was never studied as a historical document, or criticized as a work of art. Russian painting, in contrast to European painting, had been for centuries concerned, not with the conquest of space or of movement, but with the discovery of the mystical world which lies beyond sense experience. In its own terms it had its own schools, masters, and masterpieces, but they are impossible to assess on the basis of contemporary Western work, just as they are difficult to judge on the basis of Latin religious experience.

To understand the particular character of Russian religious painting it is necessary to consider for a moment the Byzantine art from which it originated. Early in the history of the Eastern Church the popularity of pictorial images, encouraged in large measure by enthusiastic Syrian elements, aroused the concern of more conservative Greek churchmen in Constantinople who eventually, by the end of the seventh century, considered the making and veneration of images heretical and finally succeeded in establishing this view officially. From 754 until the end of this so-called Iconoclastic Controversy in 843 an effective prohibition was in force against the manufacture and use of any painting or sculpture. The loss of art objects, of those destroyed as well as those forbidden to come into existence, was incalculable, and the effects, even after the prohibition against painting was relaxed, were enduring.

Nevertheless, with the end of the Iconoclastic Controversy and the re-establishment of images within the churches, an important position had been gained. Henceforth the icon was considered worthy of veneration as a mystical counterpart of the doctrine or person represented. In this way it had a 'reality' different from and considerably more important than any actual sensory experience on the part of those who contemplated it. The intention of the painter could never be reduced merely to the depiction of objects and situations in the world about him. His obligation was to portray as best he could events and personages whose actual presence may have been remote in space and time, but whose spiritual reality could be invoked by his skill. An icon was neither a literal representation nor an abstract symbol. The painter needed some knowledge of the world, since the persons and places he was to portray were all considered historically true, but their mystical presence prevented any too precise identification with the living world around him. Consequently the Western student must guard against considering any particular icon exclusively from any other point of view than whether or not the artist, granted his artistic means and intention, successfully complied with the demands of his craft. A history of icon-painting based on the gradual conquest of the visual world would only demonstrate spasmodic and usually unsuccessful attempts to assimilate European techniques. It could not consider some of the greatest masterpieces as anything other than 'primitive', much as the Italian painters of the thirteenth and fourteenth centuries seemed tentative to the nineteenth-century critic.

Thus to distinguish eastern from western European painting does not mean that we have to do with a school having no resemblance to European art. Russian painting, like later medieval European painting, has its source in Byzantine art, and he who is familiar with Duccio and Giotto will be in a better position to assess the qualities of Theophanes and Andrei Rublev. To say that Russian painting is different is not to say that it is unconcerned with the fundamental problems of position in space, which in turn require consideration of time, action, and sentiment. It is just that the accent, the degree of intensity, is different. Space and time are not the place here and the moment now, but taken together create an imprecise mode of duration and extension. Action and sentiment derive not from individual caprice or intention, but are related to the divine law that determined the creation of the world and its salvation by the Son of God. Feeling derives from the intimate communion between the observer and the object of his contemplation.

Russian icon-painting shares with medieval European painting the subjects and images common to both the Orthodox and Catholic Churches, but the long independent history of the Eastern Church, as well as its close connexions with the ancient sources of Christianity, early led to a different emphasis on certain subjects, and even to the use of themes unfamiliar or unusual in the West. To the traditional sources in the Old and New Testaments and in the lives of the founders of Christianity the Russians added their own local saints and interpretations of their own religious history.[6] The chief distinction is the relatively longer life of old traditions and the lack of thematic variety. In Russian painting this appears in the omission of many anecdotal or genre details which as early as the thirteenth century became conspicuous factors in religious pictures in the West.

The formal and dogmatic scheme for the interior decoration of a church, inherited from Byzantine art of the post-iconoclastic period, best serves as an indication of the fundamental character of Russian religious art. Such a scheme appeared, as we have seen, in the first great church of Sancta Sophia and was used, with only slight modifications, for such churches as received elaborate internal painting to the end of the fourteenth century.

In the usual mid-Byzantine and early Russian scheme a medallion of Christ Pantokrator was placed in the centre of the dome. Two other images of Christ are related to this. A medallion head, slightly younger but still showing the traces of ascetic experience, is known as the Mandilion or the Nerukotvornyi (Plate 37B), the 'Image Not Made with Hands', referring to a legendary contemporary portrait of Christ supposed to have been painted by Ananias for Abgar IV, King of Edessa.[7] Since the Mandilion was presumably a portrait from life, it is easily distinguished from the familiar Western image of Veronica's Veil by the absence of the crown of thorns and marks of suffering. Another popular image of Christ Emmanuel in the form of a child, somewhat aged to modern eyes, usually appears in the medallion worn by the Virgin Blacherniotissa or Znamenie ('of the Sign').

Similarly the Russian representation of the Virgin begins with the majestic images of the mid-Byzantine period, and while variations and adaptations of the major types communicate an increasing feeling of maternal love for the holy Infant, even the most intimate portrayals maintain a dignity and aloofness which the West neglected or lost in the later Middle Ages. The earliest image of the Virgin, the Byzantine Hodigitria ('She who leads'), was derived from an icon said to have been painted by St Luke and blessed by the Virgin herself.[8] It had been sent by the Empress Pulcheria from Palestine to Constantinople in the fifth century and placed in the Hodegon Monastery, where it became the Palladium of the city and Empire. The ancient painting was destroyed when the Turks conquered Constantinople, but its form is preserved in many replicas and may easily be recognized. The Virgin is always represented standing (although occasionally only the half-length figure is shown), and holds the Child on her left arm while she blesses him with her right hand. Christ is dressed in the antique tunic and mantle of an adult, holds a scroll in his left hand, and blesses the spectator with his right. Between the Mother and Son there is no play of sentiment. This austere and autocratic image is rarely encountered in Russian art. There is no extant example of it from the pre-Mongol period, but it appears occasionally in later examples, such as the fourteenth-century type of the Virgin of Tikhvin, copied from an earlier Greek original.[9] The familiar Russian variants, known by the names of the localities where particularly venerated wonder-working icons were preserved, such as the Virgins of Smolensk and of Murom, are seen to be later in date by the more sentimental relationship established between the Mother and Child. After the Hodigitria the Virgin Blacherniotissa enjoyed great popularity both in Constantinople and in Russia. This is the type of the Virgin Orans; she stands in a frontal position facing the spectator, her arms raised in the antique gesture of prayer, and on her breast she wears a medallion portrait of Christ as Emmanuel. The original of this version was the image of the Virgin in mosaic in the apse of the Church of the Blachernae in Constantinople, where was preserved the Virgin's veil. From this image and the circumstances of its veneration developed the specifically Russian scene of the Pokrov, or Miracle of the Virgin's Veil.[10]

The third most important image was the Virgin Platytera, enthroned as Queen of Heaven and holding the Christ Child on her knees. Although this image of the enthroned Virgin is found in Western iconography, the Easterners treated it with a difference, avoiding the use of royal garments in order not to compromise the supernatural character of the manifestation. In the course of time the Platytera became associated with the complex iconographical schemes of the Virgin's Assembly, and the Virgin as Queen of Angels, derived from stanzas in the ancient Akathist hymn.[11]

From the half-length representation of the Virgin Hodigitria there developed the images of mother-love known as the Eleusa (in Greek, pity or tenderness) or Umilenie in Russian. The most venerated icon of all the Russias up to modern times, the Virgin of Vladimir (Plate 32), was an early example of this type, a Constantinopolitan production of the later eleventh century. Yet, in spite of several variations in gesture, as in the manner in which the Virgin holds the Child and he embraces his Mother, the Russian artist never reached the degree of intimate human tenderness common to the Western representations of the fourteenth and fifteenth centuries. Even the Virgin of the Umi-lenie maintains her autocratic reserve. Only in the sixteenth and seventeenth centuries did the image of the Virgin nursing the Child, the Bogoroditsa Mlekopitatelnitsa, enjoy much popularity, and then as the result of Western influence.

Contrary to Western practice certain Old Testament scenes frequently occur in Russian painting, chief among them those which prefigure the Incarnation and Passion of Christ, such as the Three Children in the Fiery Furnace or Elijah fed by the Ravens. Particular importance was attached to the appearance of the Trinity to Abraham and Sarah in the form of Three Angels (Plate 53). The patriarchs and prophets of the Old Testament often accompany the image of the Pantokrator in the dome, or appear later on the iconostasis, and some were even admitted to the canon of saints, as St Elias (Elijah), to whom one of the first Christian churches in Kiev was dedicated.

Of the New Testament gospel accounts, the greatest attention was paid to the major episodes in the lives of Christ and the Virgin, particularly those illustrating the twelve principal feasts of the Christian year. These usually resembled the Western counterparts, except for the Resurrection and Assumption. The former was always depicted in the Byzantine manner as the Anastasis, known in the West as the Descent into Limbo or Harrowing of Hell. The Assumption was always represented in the Greek form of the Dormition, with the body of the Virgin stretched on a bier and attended by the sorrow-ing disciples. Behind the bier stands the invisible form of Christ, holding in his arms a small image of the Virgin's soul.

In the first period of Russian painting, from the end of the tenth to the end of the thirteenth century, these twelve feasts were usually painted in fresco on the walls of the church, illustrating the enactment of the doctrine of the Redemption through its histori-cal incidents, in contrast to and in fulfilment of the more abstract portrayal of the dogma in the images on the dome and apse. Towards the end of the fourteenth century the peculiarly Russian development in ecclesiastical decoration known as the iconostasis, or wall of pictures, came into existence. In Byzantine churches the altar-space had been separated from the rest of the church by a low barrier, at first of slabs of marble, but later treated more architecturally as an arcade.[12] In the course of time to this barrier, or to the columns of the arcade, various icons were attached, sometimes only temporarily, sometimes permanently in the form of local icons (mestnye ikony), depicting the saint or feast to which the church was dedicated or which was particularly honoured in that region. These local icons were often large, and as their number increased and it became more difficult to move them, a permanent barrier between the altar-space and the rest of the church gradually developed.

In the churches of the northern forest regions, which were almost invariably of wood, the representation of the twelve feasts on the walls was impractical in any other form than that of panel paintings, and it would appear that in the course of time icons of the twelve feasts were added to the barrier, directly above the local icons (Plate 77A). A two-fold tendency next developed. Not only did the wooden construction of the northern churches prevent the affixing to the upper parts of the building, in most cases only a flat ceiling, of the complex iconography of the Redemption which was easily portrayed in the dome, drum, and apse frescoes of masonry structures, but even in the latter the gradual increase in height of the double range of icons hid the frescoes in the apse from the view of the congregation (Plate 77B).

Upon the central doors through which only the priest and sovereign might enter the sanctuary, whence they were called Royal Doors, were painted the figures from the pendentives and apse – namely, the four Evangelists, the Annunciation, and the Divine Liturgy. Immediately above the Royal Doors and the row of local icons was set the deesis range, containing the subjects formerly painted on the dome and drum. Here Christ appeared enthroned in the centre, accompanied by the Virgin on his right and St John the Baptist on his left. Strictly speaking, these three figures account for the deesis, but to them may be joined, according to the size of the iconostasis, St Michael and St Peter on the left, St Gabriel and St Paul on the right. On either side of them could be added the Church Fathers, who had formerly appeared in a row beneath the Divine Liturgy on the apse. Above the Deesis came the icons of the Twelve Feasts, and some-times other scenes, if space were available.

The image of the Virgin which had usually occupied the central apse appeared in the third row, usually as the Blacherniotissa, flanked on either hand by Old Testament prophets, headed by David and Solomon. If the iconostasis was unusually large or elaborate, a fifth range contained the figure of the Lord God of Sabaoth, the Ancient of Days, in the form of the Trinity, with the Crucified Christ and Dove of the Holy Spirit, accompanied by cherubim and seraphim and flanked by figures of the Old Testament patriarchs. In this way the complex three-dimensional demonstration of dogma which had formerly covered the walls of the church was accommodated to a two-dimensional surface in a strictly rational and coherent order, rising from the revelation of the Word through the Evangelists and the spectacle of the Risen Christ, accompanied by the scenes of His earthly life, to the mysteries of the Incarnation and the final Origin of the Law in the apparition of the Ancient of Days half lost in the darkness overhead.[13]

The community of Byzantine and Russian saints included several who may not be familiar to the Western student. In addition to the Apostles and Evangelists, the Eastern Church honours the early Fathers, St Basil the Great, St John Chrysostom, St John of Damascus, St Gregory, St Cyril, and St Athanasius. A group of warrior saints was very popular with the laity; St George and St Dmitri, and the two Byzantine military saints, St Theodore Stratilates and St Theodore Tiron. Two female saints are interesting examples of the tendency towards abstraction which in the Greek Church is the counter-part of the Latin Church's search for a literal, naturalistic, identification of holiness with human personality. These are St Anastasia and St Paraskeva or Pyatnitsa. The former is a personification of the Resurrection, Anastasis; the latter a personification of Good Friday, Pyatnitsa being the Russian word for Friday, the fifth (pyatyi) day of the week.

To the saintly hierarchy the Russians added their own holy men and women.[14] First among them came St Vladimir, the God-Lover, and his mother St Olga, who first introduced Christianity into Russia. Then Vladimir's two younger sons, Boris and Gleb, innocent victims of the fierce family quarrels of the Rurikovichi for the succession to Kiev. Neither of these two princes, nor Vladimir himself for that matter, could be considered outstandingly virtuous, but the Russian people at once took to their hearts the pathetic stories of the defenceless Boris and Gleb, who, knowing that their elder brother Izyaslav was determined to remove them from the scene, willingly accepted death.

Subsequently the energetic founders of notable monastic establishments were canonized, including such remarkable men as St Sergius of Radonezh, St Cyril of Belo-ozersk, and SS. Zosima and Savva of the Solovetski Monastery in the White Sea. The Russians also held in affectionate esteem such fanatical 'enthusiasts' as Andrew the Fool whose vision prompted the development of the icon of the Pokrov, and St Basil the Blessed, an early sixteenth-century anchorite much admired by Ivan IV.

For the painting of religious episodes and personages it is often charged that the Eastern Church restrained the invention of the artist and hampered the development of pictorial art by insisting on the strictest adherence to established iconographic principles. The existence of pattern books for the guidance of the icon-painter has been taken to mean that the medieval artist had little or no opportunity for freedom of expression. But as it can be shown that such freedom was unnecessary, even inimical, to the process of creating icons, so the pattern books appear only when, under Western influences, the painter had begun to diverge from tradition. None are extant from the earliest period, and the later eighteenth-century examples, which are best known, are reductions of originals no earlier than the fifteenth century, if indeed as old as that.[15] Since the Greek painter Theophanes was admired in Moscow in the early fifteenth century for his ability to work from memory (that is, without a model), the later pattern books and painters' treatises were necessary disciplinary instruments in use at a time when for various reasons the artist no longer could or would follow traditional methods.

The technique of Greek and Russian icon-painting does not notably differ from that of Western medieval tempera painting. The support was always wood, of lime or imported cypress for the best and earlier Greek works, or more usually of pine for the later icons of the Russian North.[16] The wood was skilfully smoothed with an adze, and in earlier panels was much thinner than in later ones. The frame was not attached separately, but consisted of a flat raised border which was left when the centre portion of the panel had been cut back. These natural frames were at first very narrow, but gradually became so broad that in the seventeenth century they occupied half or more of the total area of small icons.

When the panel was thoroughly seasoned, it was often covered with a linen cloth upon which was laid a fine gesso ground. The design was drawn on this, often with the aid of a stencil by those painters who could not, like the celebrated Theophanes, work from memory.[17] The pigments, earth colour and mineral derivatives, were tempered with egg or wax. The latter medium resembling the ancient encaustic process produced a surface which could be smoothed and polished, and became very popular in the later elaborate works of the Moscow school.

With the systematization and even commercialization of painting in the seventeenth century, a division of labour was introduced. In the icon workshops there were masters, such as Simon Ushakov, who specialized in 'face-painting' after their assistants had completed the figures and landscape. The best works of the earlier periods, however, are indisputably by a single individual, just as the designs are personal, rather than servile copies of prescribed compositions. Only in the last period, when icon-painting had become susceptible to Western influences, was an attempt made to enforce the use of stencilled patterns.

The background of the earlier icons was gold or silver, in accordance with Greek practice, but as early as the twelfth century a ground of white or yellow ochre was substituted, which gave the icon a characteristic brightness. Later, red, rose, even green and blue grounds were used, especially in Novgorod. Flesh tones were modelled in a mixture of ochre and white lead on a dark greenish-brown ground, which was allowed to stand for the shadows. Purple and violet, ultramarine, *terra verde*, light green, and red completed the palette. Most effective colour harmonies were created by the contrast of complementaries in the modelling of garments, such as red or reddish-brown against green, set off by white highlights. In the finest icons the highlights were put in with gold leaf, mixed with lye and wax, which could be applied with a brush and then burnished. The effect was often like gold inlay. When the painting was finished it was covered with a layer of flax-seed or olive oil which temporarily brightened the colours, but after a few decades made the figures illegible. This varnished surface, further disfigured by layers of candle soot, was continuously repainted until only the subjects remained. But so highly perfected was the icon-painter's technique that the original pigments endured unchanged, and with care can still be recovered from beneath numerous layers of repaint.

The considerable darkening of the originally brilliant primary hues affected the colour schemes of icon-painting in the sixteenth and seventeenth centuries, when the Church invoked the older icons as patterns to be scrupulously imitated. The contemporary condition of the colours was also taken as sacrosanct, so that in the later icons schemes of dark olive-green and black are frequent. The more thoughtful painters of the seventeenth century objected to such unnatural colours, as we see in the complaint of Joseph Vladimirov: 'Thou demandest that in our days the painter paint lugubrious and ungainly images and thus teachest us that we should be false to the ancient Scriptures. ... Where and who found the instructions about painting the faces of the saints in dark, swarthy shades? Were all the saints dark and gaunt?'[18]

The custom of attaching metal decorations such as crowns and collars to the heads of the Virgin and Christ, which started in the fourteenth century, was gradually expanded to include stamped metal shields placed over the landscape backgrounds. Finally in the seventeenth century the metal frame (riza or oklad) became so elaborate that it covered all but the faces and hands of the figures. The bodies and other parts of the scene were represented in repoussé. In the last stage of icon-painting, in the eighteenth and nineteenth centuries, industrialized painters were limited to executing only those parts which were not covered by the frame.

CHAPTER 9

THE EARLIEST ICONS

THE historical conditions of icon-painting in Russia are like those which determined the development of architecture and of mural painting. Upon the Christianization of the land at the end of the tenth century the immediate need for religious objects was satisfied by the importation of articles of Greek manufacture, and presumably by the arrival of Greek artisans. The prestige of Kiev as the centre of religious authority understandably led to the predominant influence exerted by Greek culture over the early schools of icon-painting elsewhere in Russia, whether immediately at Novgorod or shortly afterwards in Vladimir-Suzdal.[1] Legendarily the first icons were brought from Kherson to Kiev by Vladimir. Later in the eleventh century icons were imported for the Pecherskaya Lavra, and in 1131 two icons of the Virgin were brought from Constantinople. One of these may have been the painting of the Virgin and Child (Plate 32), which in 1155 Andrei Bogoliubski took from Vishgorod to Suzdalia, and subsequently placed in his Cathedral of the Dormition in Vladimir, where, as the miraculous Virgin of Vladimir, it became the most venerated of all the ancient Russian icons.[2] In 1395 it was transferred to Moscow, where it remained on the iconostasis to the right of the Royal Doors in the later fifteenth-century Cathedral of the Dormition in the Kremlin. Its close and continuous identification with major events in Russian history, which lent it the distinction of a national palladium, began with the legendary account that the horses bearing the icon to Rostov refused to move past Vladimir, thereby sanctioning Andrei's desire to establish his centre of government in the new city of Vladimir, where he would be immune from the pressure of the powerful boyars of Rostov. Through the years the icon was frequently damaged, and just as often energetically repaired. In 1176, during the disturbances following the assassination of Andrei, and again in 1237 during the Tartar sack of Vladimir, the icon was stripped of its golden jewel-studded frame. At these times it may have lost the larger portion of its original surface. The extensive cleaning performed by the State Restoration Workshops in 1919 revealed that only the face and neck of the Virgin, the face of the Child, and inconsiderable portions of the background can be considered original.[3] Yet from these fragments and the general type of composition it is clear that what remains is a precious example of the finest Constantinopolitan painting of the late eleventh century, one of the earliest and most important examples of the Umilenie type of Virgin and Child.

The craftsmanship and conception are of the utmost certainty and elegance. In the faces the transition from contour line to modelled surface is accomplished with the greatest discretion. While the Virgin already displays such typical high Byzantine features as the narrow, pointed eyes, long nose, and small mouth and chin, there is no such insistence on either line or modelling as later led to strictly schematic renderings of the face. Over the whole a light veil of illusionism suggests rather than represents the soft play of living forms. In the Child the artist even attempted an infantile expression, very different from the aged baby who poses as Emmanuel in the usual Hodigitria. His snub-nosed, full-lipped countenance hints at the influence of classic sculpture, a suggestion borne out in the relatively lighter greenish-pink coloration of the Child in contrast to the swarthier flesh tones of the Virgin. A further illusion of living forms is seen in the interplay of glances; the Child looks up towards his mother, while the Virgin gazes directly into the eyes of the spectator. The pervading gentleness of this image not only accounts for the unreserved affection in which it was held for centuries by the Russian people, but may also be considered as in some measure responsible for the peculiar quality of affectionate tenderness which constantly reappears in later Russian religious painting.

From earliest times the fame of the icons of Kiev was so great that neighbouring princes did not hesitate to make off with important ones whenever the occasion warranted. Just as the Virgin of Vladimir was taken by Andrei Bogoliubski, so as late as the fifteenth century there are reports of the plundering of the Kievan churches. In this way, too, the style of the Kievan icons spread beyond the immediate vicinity of the older city to the provinces of the north and east. The fact that almost all the extant icons which can in one way or another be related to the earliest period of Russian icon-painting, and so to the regions of Kiev, Novgorod, and Suzdal before the Mongol invasion, were in modern times discovered in the cathedrals of the Moscow Kremlin or in towns in the neighbourhood of Moscow, may be considered as much the result of their artistic as of their dynastic prestige. They were later gathered from other parts of Russia to reinforce the pretensions of the Great Princes of Moscow as Tsars of All the Russias and of the Metropolitans of Moscow as successors to the Greek Metropolitans of Kiev.

A large icon of the Annunciation (Plate 33) in the Cathedral of the Dormition in Moscow, said to have come either from the town of Veliki Ustiug or from the George Monastery in Novgorod, may possibly be an example of later eleventh-century painting in Kiev executed by Russian masters under Greek supervision. The majestic full-length figures of the Angel and Virgin recall the Annunciation in mosaic on the triumphal arch in Sancta Sophia, although the active gestures of the latter have subsided in the icon. In spite of much damage, including the loss of large portions of paint in the lower half of the panel and the tips of the Angel's wings, enough of the drawing survives to indicate that the artist was familiar with the finest pictorial canons of the middle Byzantine period. Although, in contrast to the author of the Vladimir Virgin, he depends more on line for the description of his forms, the relation of these to later Hellenistic sculpture indicates the continuity of the Greek tradition in early Russian painting. The Russian inscriptions as well as several uncertainties in the draughtsmanship, such as the substitution of straight lines for curves in the outstretched hand of the Angel, indicate that the painter was probably a Russian rather than a Greek. An important difference may be noticed between the heads of the two figures. While the Virgin's face resembles that of the Vladimir Virgin (Plate 35) in its tenderness, and perhaps appears even more radiantly Greek in the equilibrium between line and form where the modelling of the contours of the cheek takes precedence over the linear outline of the eyes and mouth, elsewhere line is more insistent as in the Angel's head and the intricate plaiting of the gold-streaked hair (Plate 34). This difference accentuates the contrast between the almost playful glance of the Virgin, gazing straightforwardly at the spectator, and the sober, even troubled countenance of the Angel. It is as if the Virgin looked backward to the sunnier climate of Byzantium with its reminiscences of Hellas, while Gabriel anticipates the solemn definition of the Russian religious experience. With this Annunciation may be associated the head of an Archangel (Plate 36A), possibly from a destroyed deesis. The almost identical arrangement of the hair is even more linear, a tendency carried further in the drawing of the eyes and nose. The gentler, almost mollified expression shows a further, spiritual departure from the Greek model.

A large icon of the Virgin Orans (Plate 36B), later in the Kremlin Dormition, but said to have come from the Monastery of the Saviour in Yaroslavl, may also be related to the Kievan tradition. The type of standing Virgin with her arms raised in prayer and a medallion of Christ Emmanuel on her breast is familiar from the apse mosaics of Sancta Sophia, the Pecherskaya Lavra, and St Michael. Further confirmation of a Kievan origin is offered by the classical regularity of the faces of the Virgin and of the Archangels in the medallions in the upper corners. In the Archangels (Plate 37A) the play of broad planes in an embracing *chiaroscuro* is almost like a revival of ancient fresco-painting. However, certain details suggest a date later than the Sancta Sophia mosaics; the faces of Virgin, Emmanuel, and angels resemble the types of the mosaics in St Michael. The icon may be placed early in the twelfth century, and the attribution to a Russian artist, rather than a Greek, seems probable in the light of the uncertain anatomical construction. Beneath her heavy garment the Virgin's figure is incoherent and unrelated to the position of her feet, and her exaggerated height, with small arms and delicate hands, resembles the elongated figures in the St Michael mosaics. No less distinctive is the colour. The white background – an economical substitute for the silver or gold leaf of the best Greek work – acts as a foil to the massive brown and purple robes of the Virgin, accented here and there by gold ornaments and her scarlet slippers. The colours are Greek, but the range and stress are Russian, a forecast of that mastery in handling a few brilliant primary and complementary hues which became a characteristic trait of Russian painting. If this icon can be attributed to a Kievan master active in the first quarter of the twelfth century, it is tempting to see in it a work by the first recorded Russian painter.[4]

The scarcity of extant monuments makes all the more tantalizing the considerable reputation of a monk of the Pecherskaya Lavra, Alimpi, known from an extensive account of his life in the Pecherski Paterik. Since he is said to have died in 1114, it is possible that he was instructed by the second group of Greek artists who came to Kiev to decorate the Pecherski Dormition soon after 1073. Alimpi is said to have been a mosaicist himself, and may have worked after 1108 on the mosaics of St Michael, possibly executed by Russian artists trained under the Greeks who had remained as members of the Pecherski community after their work at the Lavra was finished. Alimpi's reputation was considerable in his own lifetime; Vladimir Monomakh so admired a large icon of the Virgin that he sent it from Kiev to the new church he was building in Rostov as an exact replica of the Pecherski Dormition. According to Polycarp, the author of the life of Alimpi, his icons were very large, and the Yaroslavl Virgin is almost six feet in height. Can this indeed be the icon of the Virgin which Vladimir Monomakh sent from Kiev to his new church in Rostov? Definite proof may always be wanting, but it is certainly persuasive to learn that in 1728 the more important icons in the Rostov church were removed to Yaroslavl.[5]

Another icon which may be attributed to the Kievan school of the middle or later twelfth century is the seated figure of St Dmitri, found in the town of Dmitrov near Moscow.[6] Here the cast of countenance and the general proportions of the face, although more decoratively described by complementary lines, are close to the style of the St Michael mosaics. The general type of warrior saint closely resembles the St Dmitri in St Michael and the seated posture recalls the ancient likeness of the consuls and emperors on Byzantine ivory diptychs. It is possible that such an imposing icon of St Dmitri was related to the activity of Vsevolod III in Vladimir and to his foundation of the Church of St Dmitri, his name saint, at the close of the twelfth century.

An indication that the Russian religious experience not only derived from the doctrines brought from Constantinople but was also not without its share of Eastern enthusiasm is found in another icon, tentatively attributed to the twelfth century, and also preserved in the Dormition in Moscow. The panel is worked on both sides, indicating that it was once a processional icon. On the front appears the Mandilion portrait of Christ (Plate 37B), the 'Image not Made with Hands'.[7] The hair, drawn in symmetrical parallel lines, and the precise contours of the features carry further the tendency noted in the heads of the Archangels, yet with certain expressive additions, such as the exaggerated eyes. Although we might trace this drawing back through the Archangels to the Virgin Orans, and so to the heavy-lidded figures of late antique sculpture, we should not yet have accounted for the mystical expression which supplants the late antique illusionism still apparent in the bland countenance of the Moscow Archangel. On the reverse, however, the representation of two archangels adoring the jewel-studded cross is clearly of Eastern origin (Plate 38A). The iconographical scheme derives from an early Palestinian tradition, related to the veneration of the monumental cross set up on Golgotha in the post-Constantine era. The spiritual energy of Eastern, Syrian religiosity was to find its parallels in Russia, where some of the feats of endurance by the early monks rivalled the accomplishments of the desert ascetics. That mystical energy, entering Russia through its many contacts with the East, continued to lend a particular colour to Russian religious life, and so helped to transform the aristocratic reserve of the Byzantine formulas into images of wide popular appeal.

The inscription on the drawing of the angels is in the Novgorodian dialect and must be taken as a sign of northern origin. Also the similarity in the drawing of the angels' robes to those of the angels in the frescoes at Nereditsa emphasizes the late twelfth- and early thirteenth-century date and the predominant influence exercised by monumental mural art over icon-painting during this period. The Mandilion Christ is an early and important instance of the transmission of the classic style of the Kiev mosaics to northern Russia and its transformation under the Eastern agents at Nereditsa into a linear style, so simplified in colour that the multiple harmonies of Greek painting were replaced by a broader treatment of the surface in a few tonally unvaried colours.

This tendency can be studied in another way, through the evolution of the typical Russian figure of the standing saint. Here again the mosaics in Sancta Sophia and St Michael provided Russian artists with a useful pattern for the image of the individual saint. Such an icon as the half-length St Nicholas (Plate 38B), from the Novodevichi Convent near Moscow, is almost Greek in the refinement of drawing, the careful modelling of the forms of the head, and the subdued colour scheme. Only the distortion of the face through the emphatic brow, diminished mouth and chin, and uncertain drawing of the eyes betrays the provincial hand of a Russian pupil of the Greeks. The treatment of the eyebrows as decorative lines relates this icon to the Mandilion Christ and suggests a date near 1200.

The Novodevichi St Nicholas marks an interesting transitional point in the history of Russian painting which is also seen in the icon of Christ with the Golden Hair (Plate 39A) from the Dormition in Moscow.[8] Here the same tenuous balance was established between the waning Byzantine illusionism of the Vladimir Virgin and the increasing concern of the Russian painters to transform shapes into linear patterns. Indeed, this might in some respects be considered the continuous inherent formal proposition of Russian painting. Line, with its symbolic function, its ability to suggest rather than to describe, and its power to induce through abstraction a mood of contemplation rather than observation, remained one of the basic elements of icon-painting. But simultaneously the artist was always obliged to refer his image back into the world of nature, since he had to deal not only with the reality of the spiritual life, but with the actuality which the prototype had had during its earthly existence. Again and again Russian painters would be recalled from their ecstatic meditations upon linear rhythms to the consideration of natural forms, here in the twelfth and thirteenth centuries by the authority of the Kievan mosaics, in the fourteenth and fifteenth by the charms of late Byzantine impressionism, and in the sixteenth and seventeenth centuries by sporadic but inescapable influences from the European Renaissance. In the Christ with the Golden Hair the modelling of the cheeks has become more schematic, the line of the eyebrows simpler, and the distortions of the shrunken mouth and chin even more marked than in St Nicholas. Simultaneously the decorative treatment of the hair and the insertion of coin-like gold spots on the garment and background begin to take precedence over the remnants of *chiaroscuro*.

The exact course of this tendency through the thirteenth century is difficult to follow among the few surviving examples, but an icon of St Nicholas (Plate 39B) from the Monastery of the Holy Ghost, Novgorod, represents a more consistent development of this ornamental tendency. The ease with which the contours and planes of Greek painting, still apparent in the Novodevichi St Nicholas, have been reduced to a two-dimensional formula marks the definite emergence of a Russian separatist tendency in Byzantine painting by the close of the thirteenth century. But the insistent linear pattern has not destroyed the portrait character of the image. Indeed, the Russian artist has transformed the aloof, intellectual spirituality of Greek iconography, still much a part of the Novodevichi St Nicholas, into a more popular pietism. Although the icon is badly damaged, enough of the bright contrasts of black, white, and brown against ochre remain to prove that already a distinctive Russian colour sense was at work.[9] When in the fourteenth century further waves of influence from Constantinople reached Russia, the stylistic character of late Byzantine impressionism would necessarily have to be fitted into the already well-established Russian style.

The remarkable icon of St John the Evangelist (Plate 40A), usually represented in Russian and Byzantine painting as the bearded patriarch of Patmos, with almost miniature accompanying figures of SS. George and Blaise, continues the process of decorative simplification, yet is not without reminiscences of the great mosaic schemes.[10] The unusual discrepancy in size between St John and his diminutive companions suggests the same proportional relationships which prevailed in the apses of Kiev between the standing Virgin Orans and the row of Church Fathers beneath her. In this possible formal echo of an ancient mosaic scheme we may have a replica of a Kievan product of the early twelfth century, possibly emanating from the studio of Alimpi, whom we know to have been a mosaic artist as well as an icon-painter.

CHAPTER 10

PROVINCIAL SCHOOLS OF THE THIRTEENTH
AND FOURTEENTH CENTURIES

THESE earliest icons, which may have been painted in Russia, whether by Greek or Russian artists, reveal a fundamentally pictorial attitude towards the projection of three-dimensional forms on a two-dimensional surface. Where the contour line is most prominent, as in the drawing of the eyelids of the Ustiug Virgin or in the features of St Nicholas from Novgorod, the line carefully follows the edge of the living form, and is immediately adjoined by an area of shadow, which, although simplified and in the later thirteenth century even schematic to a degree, yet in conjunction with the line acts as a modelled plane. With the relatively sober colour schemes such a system is painterly rather than graphic. The position of planes meeting at an angle in three dimensions is still held in account, and the line is not yet free to describe decorative arabesques independent of the actual position of the planes in space.

The expression of the eyes also proves the close connexion between the earliest icons and the Hellenistic traditions still alive at Constantinople. Many faces stare directly at the spectator (the Virgins of Vladimir and of Ustiug), others look towards another character in the scene (the Christ Child and Gabriel in the Annunciation at Moscow). Or, if their glance is directed neither towards the spectator nor towards another figure, the sideways glance seems to observe some presence or situation beyond the frame of the icon. This is telling evidence of a strain of Hellenistic illusionism, and the gradual elimination of this expression will be a constant factor in fourteenth- and fifteenth-century painting. In the course of time the eyes, even when turned towards the spectator, will lose the intensity of a direct look; their gaze, as if slightly out of focus, will seem directed beyond him, beyond even the circumstances of actual life, or as if turned inwards upon some private reverie. It may be taken, then, as a rough rule of thumb that the presence of a speaking glance, embracing the spectator in an immediate visual relationship, is a mark, when it occurs in later painting, of a renewal of Greek influence through the presence on Russian soil of a Greek master or of an authoritative example of Greek painting.

In the next group of icons – those which with some degree of probability may be considered fourteenth century – the effect of vast historical disturbances can be traced. The subjugation of southern and eastern Russia during the first century of Tartar rule and the interruption of relations with Constantinople, found their artistic parallels in the disruption of the Greek influence present in the icons of the twelfth and early thirteenth centuries. Again and again it appears as if the native Russian painters had been thrown on their own resources in copying or interpreting Greek originals, without the presence of Greek masters, until some time after the middle of the fourteenth century, when, with the revival of trade between Byzantium and northern Russia, masters from Greece and the Balkan peninsula brought to Novgorod and the North the latest innovations of Palaeologos style at the capital.

Since there are only the scantiest remains of painting in Russia during the later decades of the thirteenth and the early fourteenth century, the Novgorod icon of the Legend of St George (Plate 42) is of the greatest importance. The central episode representing St George victorious over the dragon was possibly derived from a late twelfth-century fresco of the same subject in the Church of St George in Staraya Ladoga, but the resemblances between the two aristocratic horsemen are only iconographical.[1] The later painter worked from a different point of view, treating his surface as a two-dimensional area upon which his figures were placed in a decorative pattern. The size of the figures follows a hierarchical rather than naturalistic canon. Naturalism is further destroyed by the cut-out design of the figures which avoids any overlapping. Yet enough of the earlier three-dimensional feeling survives in the faces of the Saint and Princess to remind us that the artist had known the Byzantine models at some remove. Around the border of the icon are fourteen scenes from the life of St George. The simplified drawing, the lack of spatial indications, and the insistent bilateral symmetry in most of the scenes accentuate the tendencies observed in the central panel. And since these characteristics, even if allowance is made for the use of a manuscript model, are common to folk art in many other times and places, we may conclude that the painter of the St George icon to some extent continued a much earlier tradition of popular painting in northern Russia. The icon was probably painted either in Novgorod or one of the subsidiary towns, since the inscriptions are in Novgorod dialect, and in the scene in the upper left corner, where St George distributes his wealth to the poor, he gives the cripple and beggar a handful of silver rods – the form of Novgorod currency in the fourteenth century.

A different expression appears in the important icon of SS. Boris and Gleb (Plate 43). This is the oldest extant panel representing the first Russian martyrs, and perhaps may be considered a replica of the icon of the same Saints which was placed near the high altar of Sancta Sophia in Constantinople, where it was seen about 1200 by Anthony, Archbishop of Novgorod: 'In Sancta Sophia, at the right ... [is] the very place where the Blessed Virgin prayed to her Son and our Lord for all Christians. On the same side there is also the large icon of SS. Boris and Gleb, which painters use as a model.'[2] Anthony's description is an eloquent testimony to the esteem in which the Greek Church held its Russian adherents, as well as to the fact that numbers of Russian pilgrims must have visited Constantinople to warrant such an organized industry. The present icon may be a copy of such a replica, for while the workmanship is certainly not Greek, the full-length standing figures have much of the monumentality of twelfth-century Byzantine painting.

In this icon there is a conflict between two modes of representation. On the one hand the painter sought to give some individual character to the two brothers, distinguishing them by the differences in age between the vigorous moustached Boris and the gentler beardless Gleb, by varying the colour-pattern of the garments from the blue cloak over a red caftan worn by Boris to the red cloak over a purple caftan worn by Gleb, and by changing the position of their right arms.[3] But such attempts at individuality and variety are overborne by the equilateral symmetry in the identical head-dresses, position of the limbs, and garments. This oriental feeling, in such contrast to the vestiges of Greek illusionism in the previous Kievan and Novgorod schools, with the two-dimensional patterning such as we saw in the St George icon, indicates a provincial or at least non-Kievan provenance. On the other hand, the princely character of the painting, so different from the rustic crudity of the George icon, urges a source near a princely Court where something of the old Byzantine ceremonial was still preserved. Such a centre might have been the Court of Vladimir-Suzdal, which, as we know from its architecture and the presence there of some of the most celebrated icons of the Kievan school, prided itself on its Kievan heritage. But at Vladimir oriental influences were also pronounced. The decorative motifs on the garments, fleurs-de-lis, palmettes, griffons, and eagles preening their feathers, are almost identical with the reliefs on the Church of St Dmitri in Vladimir, and suggest that we have here an icon which so far as the general type is concerned originated in the Suzdalian region.

An icon of St Dmitri (Plate 40B) drawing his sword has much of the same chivalric charm, that somewhat melancholy, doomed atmosphere of late Kievan knighthood which pervades the *Tale of the Armament of Igor* and seems to hover over the exploits of the Russian princes just before the Tartar invasion. Perhaps more than any other icons which have been recovered from Kievan Russia, these display a national, even if aristocratic, spirit. Although the personages depicted are saintly and the icons intentionally religious, the profounder spirit which they breathe is that of an ancient princely age.

The drawing of the faces of both icons demonstrates a stage midway between the plastic modelling of the earlier Kievan school and the emergence of a graphic Russian style in Novgorod in the course of the later fourteenth and fifteenth centuries. Over a prevailing dark-brown ground the highlights are placed in a symmetrical and highly simplified pattern. Where necessary the features are reinforced by lines which tend to substitute angles for curves. In this way line ceases to follow the curvature of a three-dimensional form and assumes an almost independent existence. As the forms flatten out on the surface, the eyes lose their expression. The typically Russian other-worldly, abstract relationship between the icon and the spectator, who no longer observes but rather contemplates the forms, grows more pronounced. In the icon of St Dmitri the highlights have lost even more of their plastic character, and have become streaks and scratches creating a design often at variance with the underlying shapes. The development of a two-dimensional, graphic, linear style is understandable when we recall that Russian painters knew little sculpture and no ancient Hellenistic painting: the two sources from which the Byzantine artist drew his continuous understanding of illusionistic form.

If we postulate at Novgorod in the first half of the fourteenth century a manner of painting which, while not without its Byzantine and Hellenistic references and its memories of the princely character of ancient Kiev, was dominated by a desire to render forms in a two-dimensional, semi-oriental manner, we shall the better assess the tremendous importance of the appearance of Greek artists in northern Russia soon after the middle of the fourteenth century. Whether they came direct from Constantinople or indirectly through Bulgaria and Serbia, they revealed to Russian eyes the Palaeologos style of the last Byzantine Renaissance. Two aspects of this style, as we know it from the early fourteenth-century mosaics in the Kahrieh-Djami and from the later paintings in the churches at Mistra, were to be of overwhelming importance for Russian icon-painting. The first was an interest in movement and scenes of dramatic action occuring in a specific place; the second, the new technique of a visual impressionism, the inevitable concomitant of the search for movement in space and placement in time. After 1350 the Russian version of Palaeologos impressionism completely transformed the earlier two-dimensional linearism into a technique capable of communicating a much wider range of spatial experience.

The relatively few icons which can with any certainty be attributed to the fourteenth century, and in which there appears some attempt to undertake the new and difficult problems of spatial composition in scenes involving several figures, also contain icono-graphical details which show their relationship to Greek painting. One of the most impressive as well as one of the largest of the early icons is a Nativity of the Virgin (Plate 41A). The Russian artist in several cases failed to understand the complexities of his original models, if indeed the pattern which he used was not already itself defective. Although the perspective construction contains several paradoxes, and St Anne lacks any support for her right elbow, the model, probably more than once removed, must have been a fourteenth-century Byzantine painting or manuscript illustration related to the mosaic scenes of the Kahrieh-Djami, which this icon resembles in the character of the architectural accessories intended to situate the event in an interior space. The intricate posture of the servant girl entering at the right has an even closer analogy with similar figures in the Byzantine mosaics. That an almost identical figure has also been found in a fourteenth-century fresco at Zarzma in the Caucasus perhaps speaks less for a direct Eastern influence than for the common source of both images in fourteenth-century Constantinopolitan painting.[4] In other ways the artist betrays his provincial origin. His conception is more blunt than serious, and he exaggerates the illusionistic play of facial expression by making his characters glare at the spectator.

In other icons the Russian painter's attempt to reproduce the illusionism of Palaeologos painting led him to replace curves with straight lines. This may be seen in the highlights on garments which as sharp streaks are prolonged beyond their place of origin until they destroy the curvature of the drapery itself. Such a tendency may be considered one of the essential characteristics of later Russian icon-painting just as that of straightening all curves. Even the most gracious curves of the innumerable angels' wings or the droop of the Virgins' heads will acquire much of their expressive effect from the presence or immediate juxtaposition of a straight line. Throughout the fourteenth century curves were never intended to describe the rounded plane of a form moving backward and out of sight, but were rather the reduction of that form to two dimensions through the association of curve and straight line.

A remarkable icon (Plate 41B) which illustrates this fusion of the ancient traditions of classic painting with Palaeologos innovations in terms of a peculiarly Russian unity is the icon of the Virgin's Assembly. The subject, found in the Christmas anthem of praise to the Virgin, resembles in several respects the Western versions of the Nativity and the Adoration of the Magi; the treatment is formal and dogmatic rather than narrative.[5] The iconographic sources are multiple. From antiquity come the personifications of Earth and the Desert; from Byzantium the processional entrances of the Magi, angels, and shepherds; from the architectural backgrounds of such Palaeologos painting as the mosaics of the Kahrieh-Djami the construction of the throne; and from the East the decorative character of the dispersed objects, the regular terracing of the mountains, and the varieties of perspective which create the angular tensions between the footstool and crib. The colouring is Russian, in its reduction of many tints within the generally uniform and sober harmony characteristic of Greek painting, to a major scale of red and green against black and white. Even more localized is the particular green, which can be attributed to the school of Pskov or to painting which seems to have originated in that city.[6]

Throughout the icon there is a stylistic compulsion to oppose curves with straight lines; the curve of the throne is so persuasive because of the vertical posts to which it is attached. The composition is a complete and unified expression with its own inner harmony and rhythms of curve, angle, and line. Sudden curves and sharp angles are counterpoints to the harsh colour accents, and the stylistic and technical elements are the equivalents of the expressive content of the painting, which with its weird association of images removes us from the comfortable domesticity of St Luke's narrative to the harsh wastes of a remote, almost hostile region.

This accent of earnest severity can be found in many icons of the later fourteenth century, perhaps a reflexion of the life of the people during those difficult times and of the consciousness of the Church that it was a bulwark against the ever-threatening waves of barbarism on the eastern frontiers. The large icon of SS. Paraskeva, Gregory the Theologian, John Chrysostom, and Basil the Great (Plate 44A) illustrates the independence won by Russian artists in these years. Content and technique combine lingering vestiges of tutelage to Greek painting with still stronger native characterizations. The gaunt St Paraskeva, the full-bearded benignant St Gregory, the more youthful and intense St John, and the placid patriarchal St Basil, are set against the decorative unification of the vestments of the three male saints in a repeated pattern of black and white. The limited but harmonious colour scheme is completed by the red-and-green garment of St Paraskeva, and the bright green ground on which the figures stand. The background in this case is gold.[7] The heads are slightly but delicately modelled in three dimensions in the best style of the Palaeologos Renaissance; the bodies are reduced to two dimensions and treated as decorative patterns. When this is compared with the best Greek work of the Palaeologos period it is clear how the Russian painter sought to counteract the plastic three-dimensional movement of the Greek figures by a decorative effect.[8] The trace of Greek modelling in the heads of the four saints shows that this was deliberate. He also created an entirely new expressive content. Where the Greek artist through his command of formal and spatial representations desired and achieved a community of feeling, the Russian painter isolated each of the saints from his fellows. Their glances are directed neither towards each other nor towards the spectator or some other point in common.

Absorbed in their own speculations, their eyes tend to lose their focus and turn inwards. The work is unmistakably Russian, and in its strong accents of black and white clearly of northern origin, perhaps of the school of Pskov which favoured such monochrome schemes.

The Pskov icon of the Four Saints indicates that by the middle of the fourteenth century the Russian artist had reached a critical point in the development of a national style. On the one hand he was constantly tempted to treat his panel as a two-dimensional design; on the other he was under the obligation to produce reasonably life-like scenes and personages. The stage reached in the Four Saints icon is too perilously balanced between two and three dimensions to be of much value for more elaborate scenes. Nor is it conceivable that from it anything could develop which would not require the sacrifice of one or the other mode. What would seem to have been needed was the invention of some system of linear description which would yet permit the introduction of slightly modelled surfaces. If this was the historical necessity, the appearance in Russia during the last two decades of the fourteenth century of an outstanding master of Palaeologos impressionism provided the solution to the dilemma.

As we have seen, the impressionism practised by Theophanes the Greek in his frescoes in the Church of the Transfiguration at Novgorod was essentially more graphic than pictorial. His method of suggesting three-dimensional forms was to reduce highlights and accents to lines rather than planes, setting them against broader areas of ground colour. This differed from the earlier system of the eleventh and twelfth centuries, where the form was modelled in tones and where line, following the curve of the plane, was inseparable, visually and conceptually, from the curved surface. Within such a system the painter of the Novgorod St Nicholas devised his compact linear structure; on its periphery the painter of the Boris and Gleb icon was still trying to suggest three-dimensional form by broadened highlights slightly curved in plane. And continuing such a system the Pskov master of the Four Saints icon created the round heads of his figures.

A minor technical device helps, on the whole, to distinguish between the plastic, illusionistic constructions of the middle Byzantine and early Russian periods and the graphic, abstract designs of later fourteenth- and fifteenth-century painting. In the earlier provincial variants lines are the counterparts of the shadowed or darkened areas; lines describe eyebrows, eyelids, edges of the nose. And the dark line is associated with the dark plane of a recessed area. In later painting line, and if not line then the edge of the adjacent plane, appears as a light, as a highlight, or as a convex area, the darker ground serving as the plane upon which the convexities are projected. This is of course not a complete reversal of the two roles, but a different, perhaps more subtle counterbalance between light and dark, dictated by an attitude towards nature which sees in terms of colour more than of plastic shape, for it is the only conceivable system whereby the brilliant juxtapositions of colour in later icon painting could still suggest form. It represents the transition from Greek vision, based upon the appreciation of plastic values trained by the apprehension of three-dimensional sculptural forms, and Russian vision, closer to oriental art in its understanding of the infinite complexities and possibilities of two-dimensional pattern, yet keeping the late antique play of light over the surface of coloured forms as the principal although not the sole modelling agent. In the activity of Theophanes the Greek, so far as it can be deduced from extant paintings attributed to him or from works of his school, this transition was accomplished and the energies of Russian painters released for another and even more remarkable period of painting.

CHAPTER II

FIFTEENTH-CENTURY PAINTING: MOSCOW

SINCE the first attempts were made in the later nineteenth century to establish a historical sequence of icon-painting, the so-called School of Novgorod has enjoyed an exceptional prestige, owing to the quite accidental circumstance that most of the surviving icons were found in the vicinity of Novgorod or in the northern territories once tributary to that city. Thus the assignment to Novgorod of every icon of good quality and the assumption that its painters enjoyed a superior mastery of technique and expression inevitably followed. But such a simplification omitted too many historical factors, and also certain necessary deductions. To accept the existence at Novgorod of an extensive icon industry it is not necessary to deny that elsewhere other shops may have been active. Moscow, while certainly inferior in size and wealth until late in the fifteenth century, was no more remote than Novgorod from those sources of Greek art which also nourished Novgorod's fresco and icon-painters. There is abundant evidence that Greek artists and Greek works of art were well known in Moscow. In 1381 Bishop Dionysius of Suzdal ordered from Constantinople two copies of the Virgin Hodigitria, which he installed in Suzdal Cathedral and in the Church of the Redeemer in Nizhni-Novgorod. Five years later Archbishop Athanasius ordered from Constantinople seven large icons for the Vysotski Monastery in Serpukhov. These must have formed part of a deesis and constitute an early example of a large iconostasis. Moscow also acquired a number of the earlier iconic treasures of ancient Russia. In 1395 the Virgin of Vladimir was brought from Vladimir to the Cathedral of the Dormition in the Kremlin, which in course of time received many ancient icons, including several discussed in an earlier chapter.[1]

In the face of the evidence it seems idle to assume that Moscow either possessed no painters at all, and so had to import all her icons from Novgorod, or that her painters were obliged to go to Novgorod to learn their trade. Nor need the fact that no important thirteenth- or fourteenth-century paintings can be attributed with absolute certainty to Moscow be taken as conclusive proof that no local school existed. Between 1380 and 1547 Moscow was several times ravaged by fire with the loss of innumerable objects of art. As late as 1547 the damage was so extensive that the Metropolitan Macarius brought icons and painters from Novgorod, but the immediate restitutions might only have supplied the slowly reviving industry with certain stylistic elements which are found in the so-called 'mixed' style of the sixteenth century.

The presence of a famous master of icon-painting in Moscow and its environs shortly after 1400 renders untenable the hypothetical dependence of Moscow upon Novgorod. The achievements of Andrei Rublev will shortly be considered in detail; it suffices to observe here that the evidence of his influence upon fifteenth-century painting, gradually merging with the nascent personality of Master Dionysius, who was active in the last half of the century, guarantees to the Moscow school a character and kind of painting unlike that practised at Novgorod.

There are other deductions to be made from the historical contrast between the two cities. For centuries Novgorod had been active as a trading centre; her political institutions and her social customs were based upon an independent, commercial, and reasonably democratic form of life. Moscow, on the other hand, from its beginnings as a frontier post facing the Tartars to the East, had of necessity been dominated by the exigencies of a military situation which demanded an autocratic, centralized form of government. When in the course of time both the ecclesiastical hierarchy and the princely authority were transferred to Moscow, this closely knit economic and military organization received the support of religious and dynastic concepts. Under these conditions it is not difficult to understand that the art of Novgorod reflected the active, intransigent, almost republican sentiments of its inhabitants, while the art of Moscow was increasingly directed towards the expression of religious authority and political power.

Three icons of the same subject may demonstrate the relative position of the two centres towards the middle of the fifteenth century. In the Dormition in the Moscow Kremlin there was preserved a Greek image of the Saviour known as the 'Christ with the Angry Eye'. The stern, even disagreeable expression recalls the earlier Byzantine conception of the Pantokrator of the type of Daphni, which had been known in Russia since the execution of the mosaics in Sancta Sophia in Kiev in the eleventh century, although this later image descends from the early fourteenth-century mosaic in the Kahrieh-Djami in Constantinople, as can be seen by comparing the garments and faces.[2] Another Christ (Plate 44B), from a deesis discovered in a storeroom of the Cathedral in Zvenigorod near Moscow, is related to this Constantinopolitan image or to one very like it. But there are deviations from the original whereby the painter, possibly Andrei Rublev or a close follower, transformed the severe majesty of the Greek original into a gentler Russian concept. The traces of an individual hand can be seen in the contraction of the mouth and chin, which emphasizes the slender proportions of the head, the elimination of the wrinkles on the brow, and the simplified treatment of the highlights. The total expression reveals such sensitivity to plastic values that one must recognize that at the beginning of the fifteenth century Moscow possessed an artist of the first quality. Far more than in the Greek icon the corporeal elements have become an almost immaterial setting for the intense spiritual revelation.

A later icon (Plate 45B), severely and schematically linear in its construction, also derives from the Moscow image, and illustrates the continuance at Novgorod of the graphic traditions of the fourteenth century. Where the Zvenigorod work is all curve and turning plane, the Novgorod icon is strictly edge. Where the one seems to move in a confined but perceptible space, the other is scored on an unyielding surface. Where the Moscow painter understood the consequences of the Greek example, the Novgorod master remained faithful to the traditional linearism.

In the face of the prevailing anonymity of most medieval painting and the scarcity of documentary evidence for the activity of individual masters, a fortunate and important source of information for defining the separatist tendencies of the schools of Novgorod and Moscow is provided by the work of the painter Theophanes the Greek. Since he is known to have worked in both cities, and paintings from his hand can with some certainty be allocated to each region, the differing use made of his methods suggests that the separate characters of Novgorod and Moscow painting were already effective. The circumstance that only frescoes by Theophanes are preserved at Novgorod and only panel paintings can be attributed to him in Moscow is a historical accident. His icons must have been known in Novgorod, and the painters of Moscow had had sufficient opportunity to study his frescoes in that city before their subsequent loss through fire and restoration in the course of the fifteenth and sixteenth centuries.

We do not know when or why Theophanes left Novgorod for Moscow, but according to the chronicle he painted the interior of the Church of the Nativity of the Virgin in Moscow with Simon Chorni and his pupils in 1395, and four years later was working, again with his pupils, in the Cathedral of St Michael in the Kremlin. None of this work has survived, but the fact that he had by this time gathered around him a group of younger artists means that he was in a position to exert considerable influence on painting in Moscow at the turn of the century. Some proof of this is supplied by the study of the iconostasis which, according to the chronicle, he executed in 1405 for the Cathedral of the Annunciation in the Kremlin. On this occasion he was assisted by the painter Prochor from Gorodets and by Andrei Rublev, who appears here for the first time in a historical document. In 1482 the fourteenth-century Annunciation was replaced by a new structure erected by masters from Pskov, but the old iconostasis was transferred to the new building. In 1547, during the great fire in the Kremlin, the panels were severely damaged, but as they were promptly repaired, the older portions were preserved intact under the oil over-paint, which was removed in the 1920s. To Theophanes himself may be ascribed the large central part of the deesis range, the enthroned Christ with the Virgin and Baptist (Plate 45A), and the figures of St Paul, St Basil the Great, and St John Chrysostom. Less authoritative but still close to the master are the figures of St Peter and the Archangel Gabriel.[3] Yet even in their present damaged condition something of the Greek spirit of Theophanes emerges. The small heads with delicate features and subtle tonal modelling justify the contemporary praise of Theophanes as a 'zoographer', that is to say one who excelled in drawing living beings.

By analogy with these panels, and especially by comparison with the Novgorod frescoes of 1378, it is possible to attribute to Theophanes the painting of the Dormition of the Virgin (Plate 46A) on the reverse of the famous icon of the Virgin of the Don (Plate 46B). This was traditionally said to have been carried by Dmitri Donskoi at the first Russian victory over the Tartars on the field of Kulikovo (1380), and was long preserved in the Cathedral of the Dormition. Here is a composition which, while following the customary Byzantine prototypes, shows in the skilful design the greatest artistic taste, as in the pathos of the group of Apostles bending over the Virgin's bier. Their bodies form the base of an arch carried above in the mandorla surrounding the figure of Christ. The discretion with which the architectural elements, the bier, and the candle have been arrayed is admirable. The tall ghostly figure of Christ emerges from the darkness like the materialization of a mystical experience. The hand of Theophanes is perhaps best seen in the painting of the Apostles' heads. Here is the careful depiction of individual facial and physical types and the accurate but incredibly swift spotting of highlights against a darker ground to achieve the maximum relief which so distinguished his Novgorod frescoes.

If the Dormition can probably be attributed to Theophanes on the excellent grounds of close technical resemblances to his Novgorod work, can he also be considered the author of the Virgin and Child on the front of the icon? At first glance the extraordinary quality of this image would seem necessarily due to the hand of a master as accomplished and renowned as Theophanes, but closer examination shows that the execution has little if anything to do with his method, as we know it in fresco and as we can conjecture it in tempera. The modelling of the faces as continuous curving surfaces and the rounded slow sweep of the linear development resemble much earlier Greek work.[4] However that may be, this icon of the Virgin of the Don was to be as important for later Russian painting as the activity of Theophanes himself, for here was not only a more modern version of the Virgin Umilenie, which Russians had known since the twelfth century in the Virgin of Vladimir, but the intimate relationship established between the more naturalistic Christ Child and his mother, who appears to be looking into his eyes, was soon taken over in fifteenth-century paintings of the theme. In this connexion the bare legs of the child are a particularly charming detail. The modelling of the legs and of the Virgin's hands, as well as of the faces, shows a concern for three-dimensional illusionism which has led to the suspicion of Western influence, possibly Italian. But if it is true that the Virgin's face with the long curved nose and almond eyes is close to those by Duccio and Simone Martini, in all probability the resemblance is best explained by the similar relation of Sienese painting to Byzantine art throughout the late thirteenth and early fourteenth century.

After the work in the Cathedral of the Annunciation no further paintings by Theophanes are recorded. His place and reputation were quickly assumed by Andrei Rublev, who had worked with him as early as 1405. The documentary sources for Andrei Rublev's life are also infrequent and fragmentary.[5] The earliest is the record of his association with Theophanes in the Cathedral of the Annunciation in 1405. From this it appears that he was already an accomplished master at work on an equal footing with the most famous painter of the day. It has been argued that Rublev underwent his early training outside the immediate sphere of Theophanes's influence, but since Theophanes is known to have been in Moscow from 1395 and may well have been there before then, it would seem unnecessary to seek other sources for Rublev's art than that of the leading Greek master of the later fourteenth century, especially since the similarities between their works are more conspicuous than the divergences. Three years later, in 1408, Rublev with a companion, Daniel Chorni, executed frescoes in the Dormition in Vladimir to replace the earlier twelfth-century paintings which had fallen into disrepair. They also painted the iconostasis in the same church. Finally, in 1425 occurs the last mention of Rublev's activity. In that year he was working with Daniel Chorni in the Trinity-Sergius Monastery near Moscow (Plate 51B).

Since Rublev seems to have died sometime between 1427 and 1430, and was presumably a man of late middle age at that time, his schooling must have occurred during the latter part of the fourteenth century, in just those years when Theophanes and other

Greek artists had brought to Russia the latest innovations of Palaeologos painting. Certain fragments of the iconostasis of the Cathedral of the Dormition in Vladimir show a sensitive understanding of late Byzantine painting, particularly the delicate impressionism combined with a very personal draughtsmanship which seems to stem from a source common to both Theophanes and Rublev (Plate 47).[6] The highlights are applied with more discretion and the spirit is far gentler and subtler, but, like Theophanes, the master of these figures understood late Palaeologos painting, with its revival of the spirit of antiquity.

The most extensive work which can be attributed to Rublev is the remains of the frescoes on the west wall of the Dormition, the repainting of which in the early fifteenth century is an indication of the reawakening of Moscow and Suzdalia after long subjection to Tartar domination. In ordering Andrei Rublev and Daniel Chorni to refresh the walls of the venerable church the Great Prince of Moscow, Basil I, called attention to the new nationalism. The fragments which emerged after the extensive restorations of 1920 consisted of portions of a Last Judgement on the west wall and adjacent vaults. Rublev's line in Vladimir seems as certain and accurate as Theophanes's in Novgorod, although treated with more lyrical expression. Indeed, Rublev's substitution of a continuous contour for the impressionist broken outlines of Novgorod was his signal contribution to Moscow painting. In the representation of the Angel and the Prophet Daniel the inclusive outlines of the Angel's figure and the ethereal floating wing have all the individuality which only an accomplished master can give.

The drawing of the angel in Vladimir is the most convincing stylistic evidence to support the assignment to Rublev of the icon of the Trinity from the Trinity-Sergius Monastery (Plate 48). Although Rublev and Chorni are known to have been at work there in 1425, the attribution of this most famous of all Russian icons must rest on the superior quality of the painting as well as on the later fifteenth-century tradition that it was Rublev's work.[7] In spite of severe and irreparable damage enough remains of the composition and colouring to indicate the traditional and progressive aspects of Rublev's art. In contrast to earlier representations where the hieratic position of the angels was opposed by the genre-like figures of Abraham and Sarah, Rublev retained only the three angels, the table with the dish containing the lamb's head, and the slightest semi-symbolical indications of place in the building, mountain, and oak of Mamre in the background. This tactful elimination of inessentials enabled the artist to concentrate on the design of the three figures. Through subtle variations on the theme of three – three figures within a triangular area, three heads, three haloes, three slender staves – Rublev achieved the most intense rhythmical movement which yet never exceeds the boundaries of the whole design. Again and again the eye returns to pass from one figure to another without any sense of fatigue. Even when the design is reduced to its simplest geometrical intervals it is apparent that Rublev marvellously mastered the expressive content of his theme, of the unity of three elements in one, indivisible and yet separate. In this way he succeeded in distinguishing the three persons of the Trinity. The centre angel symbolizes God the Father, who turns to the second person to indicate that he is prepared to send him as Messiah into the world. In accord with this he extends his hand over the dish containing the lamb's head, the symbolic sacrifice, while the angel to the left raises his hand in acceptance of the mission. Through the exercise of an instinctive pictorial imagination Rublev transformed one of the most ancient Byzantine iconographical themes, the Deliberation of the Trinity, into a new and influential image for modern times.

Close to Rublev's manner, if not indeed from the master's own hand, are the remains of a deesis discovered in a storeroom of the Cathedral in Zvenigorod. The noble St Michael (Plates 50 and 51A) resembles, in such details as the high-piled mass of hair and the delicately inclined head, the angels of the Trinity. The St Paul is close to the saints of the deesis in the Trinity Monastery. The damaged and incomplete icon of Christ, which has already been discussed, is possibly the most convincing proof of the new spirit which Rublev introduced into Russian painting. The combination of intense aristocratic dignity with an air of gentleness and compassion is peculiarly and characteristically Russian. It is as if the spirit which had inspired the anonymous master of the Boris and Gleb icon to try to impart a feeling of the meekness with which the princes accepted death had here found fulfilment in the technically more sensitive and profoundly expressive image of the Risen Christ. Traces of the same quality may be seen in the seated figure of St Mark (Plate 49), probably painted in Moscow towards the middle of the fifteenth century. Even if the composition falters under the burden of conventional architecture and accessories, the gracious drawing of the Saint's figure, and his poignant expression, prove that Rublev was still revered by a later generation.

Rublev's art, like that of any authoritative and successful artistic expression, depended not only upon the technical mastery of an individual craftsman, but upon the surrounding atmosphere of social and spiritual conditions. At the beginning of the fifteenth century the Russian Church could look back upon a strenuous past from the time, almost half a millennium ago, when Christianity was first introduced to Kiev by travellers returned from Tsargrad, through the hundred and fifty years when the Church, far more than any other Russian institution, had stood for the continuance of a national spirit during the Tartar domination, to the present, when the Metropolitan of Moscow, the spiritual successor of Kiev and Vladimir, could dream of attaining to the rank of Patriarch. The monastic establishments of the fourteenth century, in which Rublev had studied and worked, enjoyed a prosperity and stability which were soon to attract the envious attention of the Tsars. In addition to their material wealth they could number among their members, both past and present, many holy men whose lives were an inspiration to their fellow citizens. The atmosphere of confidence and piety in the Church is also that of Rublev's art. His security in the possession of his technical means is paralleled by the security of the Church in its knowledge of the means of salvation. Ahead lay the troubles between Tsar and Metropolitan in the sixteenth century which would ultimately lead to the restriction of the monasteries, the humiliation of the clergy, and the final seventeenth-century subjection of the life of the Church to a codification so severe that it provoked the great schism. The serene and harmonious quality of Rublev's art is not without its resemblances to the similar position played by Raphael's on the threshold of the sixteenth-century religious troubles in the West.

CHAPTER 12

FIFTEENTH-CENTURY PAINTING: NOVGOROD

To turn now to Novgorod and the use made there of the work of Theophanes is to move to an entirely different artistic environment. The way in which that art was understood in Novgorod can best be seen in the late fourteenth-century icon of St Elias (Plate 50B).[1] The resemblance to the prophets of Theophanes in the long, braid-like strands of hair and beard suggests the influence of the frescoes in the Church of the Transfiguration. Technically the construction of the head in terms of an overall design of linear interlaces, marked with patterned highlights which have lost the spontaneous illusionistic quality of the frescoes, is typical of Novgorod painting for the next century. And the total character of a forbidding, unearthly, superhuman manifestation of prophetic wisdom, present in Theophanes's prophets, has here, through the distortions and the small eyes, set narrowly together, from which radiate the wider circles of the head, hair, and halo, been changed to a rather peevish expression.

The style of painting in Novgorod is further discovered in the large Four-Part Icon, with scenes representing the Resurrection of Lazarus (Plate 52), the Angels of the Trinity, the Presentation, and St John the Evangelist dictating his Gospel to Prochor. Since the icon comes from the Church of St George in Novgorod, and a palaeographic examination of the inscriptions indicates a late fourteenth- or early fifteenth-century date, so well-documented a work is unusually important for the study of the Novgorod school. The representation of the Trinity permits comparison with the style of the Moscow school as seen in Rublev's only slightly later Trinity (Plate 53). The Novgorod painter shows himself at once conservative by clinging to traditional iconography and yet aware of Theophanes's work, since the position of the centre angel corresponds to the similar figure in the fresco of the Transfiguration. Nor is he so concerned as Rublev with endowing the subsidiary details with some degree of reality. His tree of Mamre is little more than a branch, and as it is placed directly behind the head of the central figure, it contributes to the symbolic rather than to the naturalistic character of the whole. Yet while the painter avoids enlarging his conception in terms of specific time and place, he retains the figures of Abraham and Sarah offering food and drink to their heavenly visitors, and thus gives his conception a genre character. The conflict between the arbitrary, almost heraldic, representation of the angels and the anecdotal treatment of the earthly figures remains unresolved in spite of the strict symmetry of the composition. The suggestion of the swing and movement of forms turning in to the third dimension which had been Rublev's supreme accomplishment, is impossible where movement is principally reduced to the left-to-right passage of forms across the picture plane. The other scenes on this icon clearly demonstrate this. In both the Resurrection of Lazarus and the Presentation movement reads from left to right, and at the right side of the picture there is not that sense of a return backward and inward which is so irresistible in

Rublev's Trinity. Iconographically the master of the Four-Part Icon preserves the traditional Early Christian and Byzantine formulas. Although they offered less promise for the future, they served Novgorod admirably in the present; for here, more than in any other centre and far more than in Moscow, may be localized the development of the narrative scene, specifically for the series of Twelve Feasts on the iconostasis. Not only are the oldest extant examples of the fifteenth and sixteenth centuries found in Novgorod, again probably the result of historical accident, but from its earliest independent beginnings Novgorod was an important source for the narrative icon. It suffices to recall the thirteenth-century icon of St George with the subsidiary scenes from the Saint's life, or the large local icon of the Nativity of the Virgin from northern Russia, which is such a remarkable essay in narrative painting.

It is thus no accident that two of the most famous icons which treat a historical or contemporary situation can be assigned to the Novgorod School. The first is perhaps the most typically Novgorodian, and may be less a religious symbol than the conjectured representation of an historical episode. The Battle between Novgorod and Suzdal (Plate 54B) is the earliest known icon to deal with an incident in strictly Russian history. In three zones it recounts the miraculous events which occurred when Novgorod was besieged by the armies of Suzdal in 1169.[2] In the course of the siege the people of Novgorod invoked the protection of their special palladium, the icon of the Virgin of the Sign (Znamenie), which in the top zone is seen being removed from its church in the Commercial Quarter and carried in procession over the bridge across the Volkhov to the Cathedral of Sancta Sophia within the Kremlin. At the entrance to the Kremlin it is received and honoured by the entire population. The second zone shows the negotiations between three men from Novgorod and three from Suzdal. But the negotiations were abruptly broken off when the Suzdalians interrupted the armistice by shooting arrows at the Virgin's icon, here seen suspended above the walls of Novgorod, behind which the army awaits the outcome of the interview. After such provocation the men of Novgorod could wait no longer. They emerged through the city gates, in the lowest zone, and, with the miraculous intervention of Russia's favourite warrior saints, George, Boris, Gleb, and Alexander Nevski, led by a warrior angel who appeared in the sky, they successfully vanquished the blasphemous Suzdalians.[3]

Although the episode recounted had occurred some three hundred years before the presumptive date of this icon, no representations earlier than the fifteenth century are known, which has led to the conclusion that this icon is to be dated towards the close of that century, at a time when the people of Novgorod, hard pressed by Moscow and already threatened with the loss of their independence, recalled the glorious past when they had been able to overcome the ancestors of their present enemies. Style and technique support these conclusions, since they indicate that it could not have been executed before 1400. Although much is traditional, such as the conventional representation of the city walls and churches in variously oblique perspectives, much also speaks of a newer interest in actuality. The details of the processional passage of the Znamenie from its own church to Sancta Sophia have a most life-like character, more so than the battle scenes below, where the opposing hosts are treated as a repetitive pattern of massed helmets and spears. No attempt was made to distinguish the armies or the groups of deputies one from the other, while the pattern of the horses' legs supplies a delicate arabesque accompaniment to the supposedly violent action. As in the battle scenes of Paolo Uccello, tradition and innovation are inextricably combined, so that what at one place appears accurate observation of the immediately actual becomes at another part of an inherited decorative pattern. Indeed, the pattern is so thoroughly imposed upon all three zones that movement is reduced to the passage of men and horses across rather than through the space. Yet the tempo of each zone has been carefully rendered, the slow processional pace of the upper zone changes in the centre of the second to a brisker walk as the deputies confront each other and the shower of arrows passes overhead. At the bottom the violent charge of one army upon another is signalled by wildly flapping flags and the movement of spears which turn down and towards the enemy, like grain before a wind.

The subject of the Intercession of the Virgin (Pokrov), which corresponds to the Virgin of the Misericord in Western iconography, is for all artistic purposes the depiction of a historical episode. In the Church of the Blachernae in Constantinople there had been preserved from early times the omphorion or veil of the Virgin, honoured as the palladium of the city and empire, whence arose the conception that as her veil had sheltered her body in life, so now she spiritually sheltered her followers.[4] In the eighth century Blessed Andrew 'the Fool' while standing near the chancel had seen a miraculous apparition of the Virgin accompanied by Apostles and the Church Fathers. Her veil, which she spread over her people, remained suspended and shining in the air some time after the Virgin herself had disappeared.

The painter of a late fifteenth- or early sixteenth-century icon of the Pokrov (Plate 54A) took pains to give his image the accent of historical authenticity.[5] For his architectural setting he chose the Cathedral of Sancta Sophia in Novgorod, itself derived from the Constantinopolitan type of Sancta Sophia in Kiev. Although the Novgorod church has only double aisles, the later additions of side galleries would easily have suggested his many-aisled basilica, shown below in an interior cross-section and above in an external elevation. This elevation is remarkably close to Sancta Sophia in Novgorod; here are the same exposed vaults, the high drums, and the swelling cupolas. Yet there is a startling indication that the painter had not mistaken the Novgorod church for its Constantinopolitan prototype; he carefully supplied the right touch of local colour by including, in the upper left corner, the colossal equestrian bronze statue of the Emperor Justinian which was one of the most conspicuous sculptures in Byzantium, and was in place as late as the fifteenth century. Lest there be any doubt in the spectator's mind as to whom the statue represented, it is carefully labelled 'Ustin'.[6]

With the stage set, the painter could proceed with his drama. In the lowest of the three tiers into which he divided his panel, he presented the interior of the church with groups of earthly personages who might actually have been present at the original miracle, or who might be thought to have attended the weekly apparition of the Virgin's image. In the centre the Cantor Romanus intones the evening service. To the left and right are seen the Emperor and the Patriarch upon their thrones. In the far right corner Andrew points out the mystic apparition to his companion, Epiphanius. In the corresponding position to the left appears the Empress with attendants. In the remaining two bays are groups of choir and clergy. The variations in gesture, pose, and number of the groups, as well as the asymmetrical distribution of closed and open bays, the latter partially shielded with drawn curtains, lend additional liveliness and veracity to the scene. Perhaps nowhere else in medieval Russian painting does one come so immediately into the presence of an actual courtly or religious ceremony. What is here portrayed has been seen and recorded with the most careful attention to just those details and movements which shall pass for life. And in this connexion it is worth observing that while the perspective drawing of the stairs leading up to the three thrones is oblique, corresponding to the point of view of the personages within the scene, the approximation of a one-point perspective in the drawing of the exterior roof of the church is a further indication of a desire for accuracy.[7]

The author's taste in the distribution of his elements appears again in the second zone, where the heavenly apparition of the Virgin, accompanied by saints and Fathers, is placed against the high white walls of the exterior of the church. The apparent discrepancy which a modern mind may feel in such an abrupt transition from the interior below to the exterior above may partially be resolved by considering the association in the painter's mind between the apparition and the actual mural treatment of the interior of such a church. Here the position of the Virgin corresponds to that of the fresco of the Virgin Orans in the apse of Sancta Sophia in Novgorod. In both cases the image is situated directly below (or behind) the central dome over the crossing. And while the painter followed standard Byzantine custom for the representation of crowds of witnesses, by arranging them in serried ranks he has again and again subtly varied the otherwise monotonous repetition of identical elements in the movement of the heads as the saints and Fathers turn towards each other, as St John the Baptist on the left reaches towards the Intercessor or as the monastic saint to the right falls on his knees in adoration. Even the overlapping of the haloes adds to this effect without distracting from the contemplative, unearthly character of the Apparition.

Above these figures the angels supporting the Virgin's Veil and the image of Christ appearing within a mandorla carried by cherubim are drawn in two dimensions and with a care for linear arabesque which separates the supernatural appearance from the lively spatial three-dimensionality of the figures on the earthly range below. The wave-like decorative pattern of the clouds beneath the Virgin's feet and the design of the angel's wings are unrivalled in fifteenth-century Russian painting (Plate 55A), and hint of the possibility of some knowledge of Chinese art having reached Novgorod through objects brought overland across Asia.

Although it is probably a historical accident that the earliest extant iconostases are found in Novgorod, certainly here during the fifteenth century the workshops must have been active in formulating the systematic character of these important church furnishings. That the Novgorod painters achieved almost a monopoly in the production of large icons for the iconostasis, particularly for the chin (the range of saints and Church Fathers approaching the central deesis), is seen in two facts. In 1547, after the burning of Moscow, the Metropolitan Macarius summoned icon-painters from Novgorod to restore the damaged icons, and in 1570, after the capitulation of Novgorod, Ivan IV brought to Moscow two large deeses which he placed in the Chapels of the Entry into Jerusalem and of the Synaxis of the Virgin in the Annunciation Cathedral.[8] Until they are cleaned it will be impossible to determine their quality, but apparently they do not greatly differ in style from fragments of other iconostases of the fifteenth and early sixteenth centuries. Such are the Enthroned Christ with the Virgin and the Baptist, and the figures of Gabriel and St Paul from a deesis (Plate 55B).[9] In contrast to the icons of action and event which we have just examined, these large figures seem strangely inert. The opportunity which Rublev might have found in the Enthroned Christ to create a three-dimensional pattern of delicately balanced forms has been neglected, and the lumpish shape of the figures betrays another aspect of Novgorodian art: the inability to articulate the body with the draperies which cover it. This same trait appeared in an exaggerated form in the seated St John of the Four-Part Icon and it recurs constantly throughout the history of the school. In the Gabriel and Paul the dangers of drastic linear simplification are readily apparent. Figures of this type were produced in such quantities in Novgorod that one can presume the existence of large workshops organized on a commercial basis.

On the other hand, for the painting of the Twelve Feasts and accompanying scenes which were placed in the row above the chin the painters of Novgorod lavished all their talents in the invention of narrative or the recreation of historical episode. Towards the end of the century, perhaps even after 1500, may be placed the masterly icon of the Entry into Jerusalem (Plate 56A).[10] If at moments it appears almost too close to the spirit of Rublev in the placing of the tree and the complex inner rhythms obtained by the two lateral groups of Apostles and Jews looking inward towards Christ, who himself turns to look back towards the Apostles, still there are unmistakable Novgorod accents. The high-piled white walls and towers are Novgorod, not Moscow, and only the masters of Novgorod could have created the busy activity of the children strewing garments before the triumphant Christ. Elsewhere, as in the drawing of the figures, the tree, and especially the mountain, the technical competence of the fifteenth century can be seen. The easy linear rhythms, the counterpoint of pattern among mountain, tree, and town, and the deft play of light and shade upon the rocky terraces were beyond the powers and experience of the painter of the Four-Part Icon.

When an icon such as the Entry into Jerusalem is described as in a 'Mixed Style', it can be taken to mean not merely that the painter, of Novgorod or Moscow, was familiar with the art of the other city, but that by the end of the century a national style was coming to the fore. That in the sixteenth century this style became localized in Moscow and acquired the special character of a hieratic and courtly art was historically inevitable. That the older manner of Novgorod was not easily disposed of is apparent in the many icons of the sixteenth century which show the continuation of the earlier manner in outlying regions. Such are the several icons from a large iconostasis illustrating the Crucifixion, Deposition, and Lamentation, which have all the marks of a provincial variant of Novgorod painting. Here is the immediate apprehension of a human situation, the direct and effectively uncomplicated design, the same attention to the emotional power of rhythmical repetition which we have found in Novgorod painting. Only in the summary and monotonous treatment of the landscape are we aware that the painter worked rather by rote than by invention, and that the model which he used was already hoary with tradition. The Deposition icon (Plate 56B) is perhaps the more successful. The continuous curves of the bodies of Christ, Nicodemus, and St Mary Magdalene are effectively arranged against the broad beam of the cross and the foil of the ladder, but even as pattern it remains so strictly two-dimensional that the forms seem fastened against a surface rather than moving through space.

When the spiritual demands were less insistent the Novgorod master could create an image often of great formal power, if not of remarkable insight. The head or bust-length icon of a single saint, of the type already noted in the late fourteenth-century St Elias, occurs again in an icon such as that of St Paraskeva (Pyatnitsa) (Plate 57A). The broad, even noble, decorative pattern is in the favourite Novgorod scheme of black against white. If ever the term icon has accurately meant a hieratic, unearthly image it is here; the Novgorod fondness for equilateral, symmetrical design takes precedence over anecdote and action. The icon of SS. Florus and Laurus (Plate 62) combines anecdote and pattern more equably. If the tendency which we have been disentangling in the history of fifteenth-century painting can be considered objective, or positive, or even perhaps materialist, it is that which confers on this otherwise abstract image a sense of authority and power. Its author was a master of his particular kind of design.

CHAPTER 13

PAINTING IN MOSCOW IN THE LATER FIFTEENTH AND SIXTEENTH CENTURIES

WHILE the Novgorod painters were developing a lively, anecdotal style, related to the dramatic narrative manner of the Palaeologos Renaissance yet coloured by the popular traditions of northern Russia and their own taste for positive facts, the painters of Moscow were working towards another end. In Novgorod the frescoes of Theophanes furnished suggestions for a more realistic technique. In Moscow the work of the same painter increased the desire for spiritual expression. However it may be, certainly the expressive gifts of Theophanes were understood and developed by Andrei Rublev, whose works left a pervading influence on later Moscow art. In such an icon as the Entry into Jerusalem the constant interplay of forms recalls clearly the similar changes rung in his Trinity.

From this principle of the rhythmic counterbalance of forms ceaselessly moving within a restricted space and so creating the effect of much greater depth than is actually present, were to come the greatest triumphs of Moscow painting. An early fifteenth-century Ascension (Plate 57B), perhaps contemporary with the work of Rublev or only slightly later, shows how even while adhering to conventional iconography the Moscow painter was aware of the possibility of movement. The strictest symmetry has been observed throughout the panel. This necessarily imposes an almost irresistible tendency towards two-dimensional design which, joined with the traditional division of the scene into heavenly and earthly zones, might easily have caused the painter to divide his panel into four more or less equal parts. Yet he treated his composition as a contrapuntal exercise. By imposing an ellipse upon a circle he suggested the spatial inter-relations which might occur when such forms are projected in three dimensions. The wider sphere formed by the apostolic congregation surrounds the elliptical central core composed of the Virgin's figure surmounted by Christ's in a mandorla borne by angels. Between the earthly and heavenly zones the angelic apparitions in the centre of the composition supply the necessary transition. Meanwhile, the contrast between the straight lines of the Virgin's figure and the circular design of the Christ above prevents the whole from degenerating into an exercise in academic design. In colour, too, the play of various olives and dark greens with red and maroon against the light ochre ground, and the contrast between the Virgin's purple omphorion and the white robes of the angels have a constant interplay analogous to the rhythmical development of the design.

This tendency is further demonstrated in a late fifteenth-century icon depicting St Varlaam of Khutyn (Plate 58) with scenes from his life. Throughout the whole panel, from the large central scene to the smaller ones along the sides, there is an ease and assurance, not only in the drawing and colour, but more significantly in the massing of the figures, landscape, and architecture within the prescribed space. In a sense such work as this can be taken to represent the fulfilment of the promises of earlier Russian painting in terms of a classic moment in that art. Within the traditional conventions of iconography and technique the artist has achieved complete technical certainty and powerful expressive control. When an enlargement of one of the smaller scenes is compared with the earlier Novgorod Resurrection of Lazarus it can be seen how the Moscow painter thought in terms of space, no matter how shallow the actual space he described. Although there are no direct references to Rublev, the lessons of that master are observed in the overall unity of each smaller composition.

The classic moment in the development of any style, within any art, is necessarily brief; for the concept of the classic as well as its formal application imply an equilibrium between form and content, between technique and style, between material and expression which is subject to disturbance when any one of the component elements, for whatever reason, becomes more insistent than another.

Evidence of such a change occurs towards the beginning of the sixteenth century in the radical re-definition of subject-matter. To the older types of icon, the narrative subjects of the Twelve Feasts, the single figures for the deesis and other ranges of the iconostasis, and the solitary devotional images of the Virgin and various saints, was added a new subject requiring not only the development of a new iconography, but also a new consideration of technique and formal properties. This is the kind of icon which presents, whether under the guise of narrative action or a devotional figure, new religious concepts of a didactic and mystical character.

The reasons for the appearance of new subjects and a new attitude towards more traditional scenes are to be found in the changed conditions prevailing both within and without the Russian Church in the course of the fifteenth century. After the fall of Constantinople in 1453 the Russian Church felt itself not only independent of but, indeed the successor to, the Greek Church, which was thought to have fallen to the enemy as a result of its lapse from orthodoxy. This feeling found expression in the theory that Moscow was 'the third Rome' (the first two, Rome and Constantinople, having failed to keep the faith).[1] The religious painting of fifteenth-century Russia was subjected to still another influence; the presence in Moscow after 1470 of Italian architects and craftsmen must inevitably have led to some familiarity on the part of the more intelligent native artists with the different iconography and means of expression of Western painting. The result of these contacts will be unquestionable in the sixteenth century. Meanwhile, the character of later fifteenth-century painting in the Moscow region is best seen by examining the work of the artist known as Master Dionysius.

Often in the history of Russian art the appearance of a new style, or a development within an existing style, depends upon the correct reading of evidence which, however complete in itself, is but a fragment of a much wider whole. As the activity and influence of Theophanes and Rublev must be deduced from mere portions of their original work, so with Master Dionysius no more survives of his work than the frescoes in the Church of the Virgin in the Therapont Monastery.[2] They are signed and dated 1500-1, but it appears from documents that Dionysius must have executed these frescoes with the help of assistants well towards the end of his career, since he is first mentioned in 1476 at work in the Monastery of St Paphnutius in Boroskovo, apparently as the assistant of an older master. In 1480 with three other painters he was called to Moscow to execute a 'deesis with Festivals and Prophets', that is to say an iconostasis, for the Cathedral of the Dormition, just completed by Aristotele Fioravanti. In the same year he repaired an icon of the Virgin Hodigitria which had been damaged by fire, and painted an iconostasis for the Cathedral in Rostov. Between 1480 and 1490 he painted a deesis for a monastery on Lake Koubenski. In 1484, with the Venerable Paissi and his own sons Theodosius and Vladimir, he painted an extensive series of icons for the Monastery of Volokolamsk. In Joseph of Volokolamsk's famous inventory of 1545 more than a hundred icons were attributed to Dionysius and his sons. Unhappily, of all this work nothing has survived which can be assigned to their hands with absolute certainty. The esteem in which his work was held as late as 1545 reflected the reputation he enjoyed in his lifetime. Bishop Vassian of Rostov, in his life of St Paphnutius Borovski, stated that Dionysius was 'the most famous of all painters of this time'. And the chronicler declared that his icons for Rostov were 'very beautiful'. In 1508 his son Theodosius is mentioned as the head of the workshop. The father was either dead or too old to continue working. From this evidence Dionysius was presumably born about 1440 and died shortly after 1500. The period of his greatest activity occurs a full generation and more after the work of Rublev and his followers, and in this respect presents a further distinct stage in the development of Moscow painting.

Although no single icon can definitely be attributed to Dionysius, the amount of work he accomplished and the high regard in which he was held could not have failed to affect later fifteenth-century panel painting. Attributions must be based on the only extant documented work, the frescoes at Therapont on the White Lake. The fact that the monastery was situated in the far north-eastern part of the territory of Novgorod has led to the identification of Dionysius and his school with the painters of Novgorod. But it would seem that in spite of its geographical situation the Therapont Monastery was more closely associated with Moscow. Its founder, St Therapont, came from Moscow, and his successors, notably the Abbot Martinian, were in frequent intercourse with the Great Princes and Tsars. Indeed, even were the documents less persuasive, the evidence of the paintings in Therapont is visually conclusive. In more than one respect they are typical of the intense spirituality and delicate coloristic grace of the Moscow school as it had developed after the time of Theophanes and Rublev.

Although the spatial arrangement of the Therapont church follows the traditional orthodox formula, the iconography departs in many respects from the schemes already seen in the earlier Novgorod churches. In place of the customary exegesis of the main tenets of Christian dogma, the painted scenes are pre-eminently illustrations of the Akathist Hymn.[3] High in the dome the Pantokrator still reigns, but no longer as the stern and brooding Ancient of Days; he is a gentle, aristocratic Saviour, very close to the Rublev type of the deesis of Zvenigorod. Below the Pantokrator, Archangels and patriarchs in the drum and Evangelists on the spandrels continue the familiar disposition. An intensification of the worship of the Virgin is witnessed in the apse and chancel, where, in addition to the enthroned Virgin and Child represented above the Liturgy of the Fathers (instead of the Divine Eucharist), the Virgin appears in the types of the Sign (Znamenie) and Intercessor (Pokrov). On the walls of the nave are scenes from the Akathist Hymn illustrating the versicles 'Rejoice' and 'Praise of the Virgin'. A further departure from traditional iconography appears in the treatment of the life of Christ and in the representations of dogmatic and doctrinal subjects. In place of the customary scenes are representations of the parables and miracles of Christ, which very rarely appear even on icons. The choice of such incidents as the Parables of the Prodigal Son of the Widow's Mite (Plate 59A), or of the Faithless Servant, for which there were few if any iconographical precedents and which therefore required the invention of new types of movement and action, indicates the growing independence of the Russian Church from traditional Greek models, as well as the painter's willingness to enlarge the restricted repertory of his art.

But what might in some respects be considered a tendency towards greater naturalism of type and action in these unfamiliar scenes is contradicted by another set of scenes: the representation of the Councils of the Church which are conventionally designed groups of patriarchs and Fathers symmetrically disposed on either side of the enthroned Emperor. In a certain sense the iconography of the Therapont church summarizes the dialectical dilemma of later Russian painting, and introduces the drama which would develop in the course of the sixteenth century. The painter was interested in new naturalistic inventions; the Church preferred traditional representations of abstract dogma. Master Dionysius succeeded in achieving a harmonious compromise, but from thesis and antithesis emerged no synthesis which was ever effective for long. Between abstract expression and naturalistic execution the gap was too wide to be bridged by less than a very great artist, perhaps by a Raphael or Michelangelo in the West, by a Rublev or Dionysius in the East. And Dionysius had no successors in this respect.

In the formal elements of technique and expression his art was a luminous and peerless solution of the programme proposed. For the sequence of scenes intended to illustrate various aspects of dogma, adoration, and exaltation he utilized a harmonious counterbalance of turquoise, pale green, and rose against darker blues and purples, the whole set off with gold in the haloes and accessories. For these harmonies his authority was Rublev and earlier fifteenth-century painting in Moscow, rather than the brilliant primary oppositions of the Novgorod tradition. The figure style of Dionysius and his sons is also both personal and characteristic of the period (Plate 59B). Although in earlier Russian painting the figure had usually tended to be tall rather than broad, the masters of Novgorod had often conveyed a sense of a massive physique beneath the long draperies. Often this effect was achieved by drawing the garments close about the body so as to emphasize the anatomy of the back and thighs. Rublev introduced a more delicate balance between the desire for slender grace and the need for expressing underlying physical structure. Although the angels of his Trinity would appear much taller were they standing figures, there is no doubt about the articulation of their bodies. In his deesis figures, even when only preserved half-length, the draperies are so disposed as to reveal more of the fundamental physical structure than in any previous Russian painting.

With Dionysius a new tendency was at work. Actually his figures are proportionally little, if at all, taller than those of his predecessors and contemporaries, but they communicate a sense of almost dematerialized buoyancy, achieved in two ways: by drastic simplifications of drawing, so thorough as to reduce the figures in many cases to flat silhouettes in colour against a lighter background, and by a new kind of composition. Since the character of the drawing prohibits any indications of depth, the figures tend, in spite of frequent overlappings, to be spread out across the picture surface, which enhances the effect of the silhouette. Indeed, it might be said that in contrast to Rublev's and earlier Novgorod compositions, which led towards a tighter inter-relationship of all the parts, the Therapont designs are discursive and disparate. The compelling need to stress the spiritual content of the parables from the gospel or the mystical enthusiasm of the Akathist subjects required and received just such a treatment. Dionysius and his sons communicate not the narrative episodes so much as the spiritual overtones of their religious content. There was never again in Russia to be painting which so perfectly established an interchange between observed nature and exalted emotion as we find in Rublev. As Russian art approached the strident troubles of the sixteenth and seventeenth centuries, the silent spaces of Dionysius's frescoes would be for ever left behind.

The reputation and extensive activity of Dionysius and his sons had considerable influence on subsequent icon-painting, but panels can be attributed to them only on the grounds of stylistic affinity with the Therapont frescoes.[4] Since these were executed late in the life of Dionysius, an icon, to be attributed to him with any certainty, should exhibit the qualities of the Therapont frescoes in a preliminary rather than a derivative way. Such is the icon of the Hexameron, or Six Days, a large panel displaying in two zones the six events commemorated in the Church week and, below, the orders of Saints.[5] In the individual scenes the loose compositions, slender figures, and impalpable atmosphere of mystical devotion seem to prepare the way for the Therapont frescoes, while the delicate colours – rose, light green, and turquoise – set against the white robes of the saints and angels are the counterparts in tempera of the frescoed hues at Therapont. Perhaps even more suggestive is the way in which the dramatic character of the narrative scenes, such as the Annunciation, Washing of the Feet, or Crucifixion, is subordinated to the processional, even mystical solemnity which prevails throughout the whole panel. Later in the century icons like the Incredulity of St Thomas (Plate 60B) still preserved something of that character.

The legacy of Dionysius was at once too personal and too refined to serve as the basis for a new school, even had the political and religious history of the sixteenth century permitted an uninterrupted succession of artistic tradition. The progressive and inescapable unification of Russia under the hegemony of the Great Prince of Moscow entailed a concentration of artistic efforts at the capital, a process assisted by a curious combination of circumstances. After the fire of 1547 so great was the need for new paintings to replace those destroyed that the Metropolitan Macarius, who had previously been Archbishop of Novgorod, not only brought to Moscow large quantities of icons, but forcibly transferred the icon-painters of Novgorod with their workshops. Thus ceased the independent character of the school of Novgorod. The presence of the Novgorod painters soon affected the character of Moscow painting, and regarding the whole sixteenth century it is difficult, if not futile, to attempt to distinguish the two manners. The term 'Mixed Style', invented to explain those icons which combine elements of technique or expression from both schools, is particularly appropriate for such sixteenth-century productions as the Vision of St Eulogius (Plate 60A).

The further development of the Moscow manner may be seen in the later sixteenth-century icon of The Entry into Jerusalem (Plate 61A).[6] When compared with the older icon of the same subject it can be seen how much of the spirituality of Rublev and Dionysius has been lost. Not only has the exquisite adjustment of the various shapes, which communicated a sense of space and processional movement, disappeared in the more vertical design, but an interest in decorative repetitions and a certain sentimental naturalism has destroyed the solemn mood of the earlier painting. The older icon was tragic with a sense of foreknowledge, the younger seems capricious and trivial. Yet there is a fine sense of decorative elegance in the chiselled terraces of the mountain and the high-piled architecture of the city gate. And in this period for the first time a specifically Russian facial type appears. The vivacious expressions of the round-headed Apostles and Jews are very different from the classic Greek types of the earlier icon. The high priest with the white head-dress in the centre of the group on the right appears so oriental that one might be persuaded that the Tartars had left descendants in Russia.

Of the many factors which had gone into the production of sixteenth-century painting, the elegance of Rublev, the pragmatic naturalism of Novgorod, or the spirituality of Dionysius, none was to prove as important an element for later painting as the kind of decorative design which is clearly of Eastern origin. So far all such tendencies towards equilateral symmetry as we have observed had been dictated either by traditional Greek iconography or by the nature of the subject, and more often than not the Russian painter had avoided absolute symmetry even in subjects which provided it. Such painting for the most part antedated the overthrow and expulsion of the Tartars, accomplished between 1480 and 1552. Possibly to the degree that the Tartars were no longer a constant threat to the security and independence of Russia, the vast reservoir of Eastern art became less distasteful and more easily assimilable. Certainly throughout the sixteenth century the presence of a taste for oriental arabesques, for the decorative effect of line divorced from form, for the repetition of identical forms, became more insistent in painting as well as in architecture. The icon of SS. Zosima and Savva (Plate 61B), the founders of the Solovetski Monastery in the White Sea, standing beside the monastic building, suggests the gradual dominance exercised by decorative aspects of design over the expressive end. It is worth noting that the icon shows a close observation of nature. The monastery was certainly familiar to the painter, if indeed he were not even resident within it, and he went to some pains to deploy a consistent perspective in his drawing of the various windows. But the desire to recreate the exact appearance of a known locality was subordinated to the decorative aspect of the whole design, for it is impossible not to feel that the architectural elements have been multiplied in order to harmonize with the flat, two-dimensional description of the island floating upright, on end as it were, surrounded by the waves of the sea.

Throughout the sixteenth century, in addition to the use of the decorative aspects of line and colour for the visual enrichment of the icon, there was a comparable development of the mystical and doctrinal elements observed in the Therapont frescoes. Such subjects had not been unknown in Greek painting, but they were comparatively rare.[7] Their appearance in numbers in Moscow was a result of the increased independence of the Russian Church, and also of the development of a technical mastery sufficient to represent the intricate symbolism such subjects required. In contrast to earlier representations of single figures or single scenes from religious history, these icons dealt with the subtleties of dogma, and the greatest ingenuity was required to find appropriate visual symbols for them. Frequently traditional and even Western iconographical themes were so combined that considerable theological knowledge is required to interpret them. Such an icon was the popular Only-Begotten Son, the Word of God, in which were combined images and symbols representing the concepts of the Creation, Redemption, and Last Judgement, including even the Western image of the Pietà.[8]

Such subjects were not introduced without difficulty. In 1551, four years after the appearance in Moscow of a large number of icons from Novgorod and Pskov, the important ecclesiastical assembly of Ivan IV's reign, the so-called Council of the Hundred Chapters (Stoglav), was convened in Moscow to consider problems of Church reform, including conditions prevailing in icon production. The Council took its name from the fact that the Tsar's queries and the Council's replies were presented in one hundred sections.[9] The Tsar's third 'question' dealt with icons and icon-painters.

The holy and venerable icons, conformable to divine rules, must reproduce the image of God, his likeness, and be faithful to the consecrated type. [According to the rules] one will paint the image of God, of the Most Pure Mother of God and that of all the intercessor saints. On this subject you have a witness in Holy Scripture. You must watch with the greatest care that the icon painters have irreproachable sentiments and practise virtue, that they instruct pupils and teach them to paint the divine images, with skill and according to the consecrated type.

In reply the Council decreed that each priest should supervise with the greatest care the icons and sacred vessels in his church. Furthermore, it was stated that 'if certain icons have suffered from the injuries of time, [the priests] will have them repaired by the painters; those which are insufficiently coated with oil must be oiled'. (The disastrous effect of this practice has already been noted.) To the question as to how the Trinity was to be indicated – whether by haloes behind the heads of the three angels or by an inscription – the answer was that 'the painters will reproduce the ancient models, those of the Greek icon painters, of Andrei Rublev and other famous painters. They will write below: The Holy Trinity. In nothing will the painters follow their own fancy.' The Council also undertook to regulate the production of icons by urging upon the bishops and priests a closer supervision of the actual process of manufacture. Not only were they to ascertain that the painter himself led a virtuous life and applied himself assiduously to his task, 'with his eyes fixed on older painters, taking for models the best icons', but they were to discourage mediocre work and punish able painters who misused their talents.

Whether or not the decisions of the Stoglav were ever operable, it is certain that the appeal to traditional types was ineffective against the newer mystical and didactic icons. At this time a celebrated controversy arose when the State Secretary Viskovati, an able and intelligent man, took exception to certain idiosyncrasies he detected in a four-part icon in the Cathedral of the Annunciation. The separate scenes represented God Resting on the Seventh Day; The Only-Begotten Son; Come, Men, and Honour the Triune God; and In the Grave is the Flesh. It is possible that these complaints were intended to annoy the priest Sylvester of the Cathedral of the Annunciation, who was Ivan IV's favourite adviser. Viskovati objected to artists painting 'according to their own under-standing and not according to sacred tradition: the same subject was treated in various ways, so that although the subjects of several icons might be identical each was painted differently: they no longer abode by the ancient custom of putting an inscription on the icon, and introduced into the painting besides sacred subjects some profane images.' [10] He condemned such visual materializations as representations of 'the invisible and flesh-less Godhead' and such realistic details as the crooked fingers of the crucified Christ.

Viskovati's criticisms were presented to a Church Council in 1554, which upheld the authenticity of the icons. Viskovati observed that in the icon Come, Men, and Honour the Triune God, 'tsars, princes, prelates, and people of the lower classes were represented as if they were alive'. The Council replied that an examination of icons of the Exaltation of the Venerable and Life-Giving Cross and of the Intercession of the Virgin showed that many people of all conditions were customarily depicted, as well as in representations of the Last Judgement. Viskovati's objections were declared heretical and he was obliged to retract.

The decision had a paradoxical effect. The departures from traditional iconography which Viskovati had noticed were indeed novelties, often due to Western influences accepted by the masters of the Pskov school, as in the figure of God the Father as an elder, or Christ surrounded by Cherubim. But the rejection of his criticism by an appeal to past authority really worked for rather than against the new. Succeeding years of the century saw a further attempt to codify and regularize traditions through the prepara-tion of manuals of iconography. The so-called 'Illuminated Original', a collection of copies in outline of established and certified patterns, scarcely served its purpose of pre-venting any deviation from authoritative models. It offered the painters too many choices, since there was still room for the inclusion of variants, and only the most servile copyists could be constrained to follow exactly the patterns set for them.[11]

PART THREE

THE ART OF MUSCOVY

*

And now that they have come into stone-built Moscow,
They have not entered the royal palace,
They have gone into the sacred cathedral,
To sing the appointed Mass.
He has blessed his beloved Son :
'God grant that the Orthodox Tsar be well,
The mighty Prince Mikhailo Feodorovich,
And that he may rule the realm of Moscow,
And all the holy Russian land!'

THE ENTRY OF THE PATRIARCH PHILARET INTO MOSCOW, 1619

CHAPTER 14

WOODEN CHURCH ARCHITECTURE

Up to now our architectural history has been principally concerned with the transmuta-
tion of foreign masonry forms and techniques. From the conversion in 988 to the establishment of the Russian Patriarchate in 1589 the most constant factors had been the continued presence of the Greek clergy, and the implicit presence in all liturgical and ecclesiastical events of the Greek heritage of the Russian Church. Despite the many modifications which prevented Sancta Sophia in Kiev from being a slavish copy of Sancta Sophia
in Constantinople, or the many differences which separate the Cathedral of the Annunciation in the Kremlin from earlier or contemporary Byzantine churches, the affiliation
of the Russian churches is clear. From Greece there had been brought and preserved the
simple logical clarity of an interior space covered with at least one central dome-shape,
directly stated on the exterior by the fundamental geometrical relation of cubical nave
to semi-circular apse to semi-spherical dome.

Russia had, however, another building tradition, one of immemorial antiquity, whose
origins can only be conjectured and whose relation to the imported systems of construction still remains enigmatic. This was the method of building in wood, the material
originally found in abundance throughout central and northern Russia north of the
steppe country. Within this area grew cities, villages, and monastic establishments which
were to be brought together as the first truly national Russian state, the Muscovy of the
period between the Tartar invasion in the early thirteenth century and the new Europeanized Russia of Peter the Great after 1700. Here were formulated many of the artistic

and philosophical conceptions which most distinguish the Russia of the post-invasion period from all that had gone before. If the Russia of Kiev certainly, and even of Novgorod partially, still preserved for the modern eye something of the serenity and geometrical clarity we tend to associate with concepts of the classical age and the masonry architecture of the antique South, the later Russia of the fourteenth and fifteenth centuries, growing up in the depths of the forests, is indelibly marked with the forms of wooden construction. To the static geometry of the cube of brick or worked stone succeeded the organic growth of the fir tree.

The successive stages in the history of wooden architecture present difficult, often insuperable obstacles to the historian who wishes to prove a neat and chronologically consecutive development.[1] It is incontestable that the peoples who inhabited the Russian land from ancient times had used wood in some form or other, and, as we have seen, the men of Novgorod upon almost their first appearance in history were derided by the Kievans as carpenters. Although wooden structures are among those first mentioned in the chronicles, the material is too perishable to allow any but the most hesitant conjectures about the appearance and construction of the earliest wooden buildings. When the Varangians arrived they must have found a thriving culture of wooden construction to which they probably added certain details of their own which are now undiscoverable.[2] Since there are, however, numerous wooden buildings, principally churches, still standing from the seventeenth and eighteenth centuries, and since from the chronicles and from the location of these structures we can deduce that a profoundly conservative attitude underlay their construction, it is not improbable that even the latest are often essentially older structures rebuilt. Thus churches of the eighteenth and even nineteenth centuries may be thought to perpetuate much earlier buildings. As evidence of this we may cite the history of the Transfiguration in Ustiug. This earliest known circular church, first mentioned in 1290, was burned in 1397 and again in 1490, and each time was rebuilt in the same form at the express wish of the inhabitants.[3] The location of most of the existing wooden churches points to a similarly conservative attitude. They are most often found in the north-east, in the former provinces of Olonets, Vologda, and Archangel, along the reaches of the Northern Dvina and its tributaries, far from the settled areas of Moscow and Novgorod and so somewhat immune from innovation. These regions after the middle of the seventeenth century were the principal refuge of the Old Believers, who clung in spite of vicious persecution to traditional religious forms.

Under these circumstances the historian is not only obliged but justified in proposing a formal development of wooden architecture based not upon the succession of documented and dated examples, but upon a progression from simpler to more complicated form. Yet even this may falsify or distort certain important factors, especially technique. Despite the fact that the most complex extant wooden church form dates from the early eighteenth century, and so succeeds by only a few years the somewhat similar decorative elaboration of the baroque churches of Moscow, the actual technical methods employed are not notably intricate, and must be assumed to have been in existence from a remote period. If we may predicate gradual complication and multiplication of the parts of the church structure, we must also assume that upon the introduction of Christianity into

Russia there already existed a technique of working in wood which permitted the most complex effects.

To the difficulty of ascertaining the probable course of formal evolution is added that of determining the precise interaction exercised upon each method by the separate development of wood and masonry construction. The striking similarity between certain sixteenth-century stone and some seventeenth-century wooden buildings has been used to assert the influence upon masonry architecture of the widely prevalent wooden forms, although this is to overlook a chronological discrepancy which can only be explained by the assumption that the late wooden forms perpetuate certain earlier prototypes. On the other hand, it can be argued that the prestige of the masonry structures in the great cities, Moscow particularly, inevitably fascinated the simpler builders of the country regions, and the later wooden buildings are then described as imitations of the forms of Court architecture.[4] Either view may be unnecessarily exclusive. Probably a certain give and take prevailed, at times preponderantly in favour of wood construction, at others of stone. Since the prevailing type of religious architecture remained the Greek cubical church, the carpenters were constantly seeking to interpret those simple static forms within the dynamic of their wooden technique, while in turn the variety and fancy achieved in wooden building were carried over by the masons into the decorative treatment of the non-structural parts of their edifices, particularly on the roof and the design of the cupolas.

The use of wood implies, then, not only possibilities for experiment and invention due to the flexible nature of the material, but also, from the circumstances under which it was used, a certain traditionalism in the repetition of familiar forms. Ease of execution and speed of construction permitted more readily than in masonry the duplication of perished shapes, and at the same time afforded a degree of experiment not always possible in brick and stone. To this paradoxical interaction of tradition upon invention we may add the further factor of the relative simplicity of structural systems in wood, again leading to the contrast between the elementary methods of construction and the elaborate, even sophisticated forms evolved.

The basic element common to all Russian wooden building is the frame of logs laid horizontally on a rectangular or polygonal plan and secured at the corners by interlocking beams, either through semi-circular or square cuts.[5] By successively reducing the length of the logs at the ends of a rectangular frame a gable was achieved. The roof was made of flat planks and laid directly on beams running lengthwise between the gables. This is the system used in the simplest form of peasant house, the izba, and from it in combination with polygonal plans and applied carved decoration were created the most complex forms. Two examples of wooden structures of the eighteenth century doubtless repeat forms long familiar to the Russian carpenter. The small storehouses (Plate 63A) demonstrate the structural method in its basic simplicity, although the forms of cutting the beam ends by circular as well as square interlocking may be seen. The large farmhouse (Plate 63B) differs from the small storehouse only in size and the quantity of applied ornament, attained by the multiplication of parts. Throughout this system a certain modular standard prevailed, based on the average length of dressed logs.[6] The introduction of interior partitions can be seen where the ends protrude as a vertical row of logs notched into the exterior wall, while the applied carved decoration, all of wood, can be seen on the edges of the roof, the window-frames, and the shaped slats of the exterior balcony. For even the apparently most elaborate buildings this structural system remained the same, the greatest possible length of the beams serving as the basic element in the design (Plate 64).[7]

Another system can be seen in a wooden belfry of the seventeenth century (Plate 65A). Here by the use of a polygonal plan a greater interior space was obtained, although the actual length of the logs is not great. Towards the top of the structure longer logs are successively introduced, so that the slight flare of the upper part serves as a projecting cornice to throw rain-water and melting snow far enough from the base of the structure to prevent rot. The conical roof is covered with vertical planks, probably replacing the original shingles, of which a few rows can still be seen near the slender drum. The ends of the slats were usually cut in a decorative pattern, often in the form of a cross.

It should also be observed that construction remained throughout an additive system of horizontal parts. Few verticals were used except as interior supports for partitions or as slanting planks on conical roofs. The only tool was the axe or adze with which the carpenters cut, shaped, and smoothed the beams. On the exterior the logs were left intact once the bark had been removed, but the interior surfaces were worked quite flat. Even into the nineteenth century the axe remained the carpenter's only tool.[8]

Until the beginning of the nineteenth century with these tools and materials were constructed not only the spectacular wooden churches, which will be examined in more detail, and the innumerable farmhouses of the peasantry scattered through the forests or clustered in tiny villages, but even whole towns and cities, including the greater part of the metropolis of Moscow itself. Few sights in Russia struck visiting foreigners more forcibly than their first glimpse of these wooden cities, so different in appearance, if not in plan, from their own towns. Thus Giles Fletcher, the English emissary to Moscow in 1588, described this wooden world:

> The streets of their cities and townes instead of paving are planked with fir trees, planed and layed even close the one to the other. Their houses are of wood without any lime or stone, built very close and warme with firre trees plained and piled one upon another. They are fastened together with dents or notches at every corner, and so clasped fast together. Betwixt the trees or timber they thrust in mosse (whereof they gather plenty in their woods) to keep out the aire. ... The greatest inconvenience of their wooden building is the aptness for firing, which happeneth very oft and in very fearful sort, by reason of the drinesse and fatnesse of the fir, that being once fired, burneth like a torch, and is hardly quenched til all be burnt up.[9]

Fletcher's description of the method of construction and of the perilous nature of the inflammable material is confirmed by many other travellers, who rarely failed to comment on the expendability of the Russian house. Guy Miege, who accompanied the Earl of Carlisle, Charles II's ambassador to Tsar Alexis Mikhailovich, wrote in 1669 that:

> Their Streets are broad enough, and from place to place there are certain Intervals left to break off and cease the fury of the Fire, but the materials of their Houses being so combustible,

they have much ado to prevent its progress. All the remedy they have, is to pull down the Houses that are next, to the end that by taking away the matter, that should nourish it, they may give the flames more room to extinguish. But this not alwaies succeeding, especially if the wind be high, it happens sometimes, that they see a great part of the Town in ashes in a very short space. ...[10]

Fortunately this material could be replaced almost as quickly as it perished. As Adam Olearius, secretary to the Embassy from the Duke of Holstein to Tsar Mikhail Feodorovich in 1636, remarked: 'Those who have their houses burnt, have this comfort withal, that they may buy houses ready built, at a market for that purpose, without the white-Wall, at a very easy rate, and have them taken down, transported, and in a short time set up in the same place where the former stood.'[11] The Russians had perfected, by the sixteenth century if not earlier, a system of prefabrication far in advance of any in Western Europe. Archdeacon Coxe described the system in some detail:

Among the curiosities of Moscow, I must not omit the market for the sale of houses. It is held in a large open space, in one of the suburbs, and exhibits *ready-made houses*, strewed on the ground. The purchaser who wants a dwelling, repairs to this spot, mentions the number of rooms he requires, examines the different timbers, which are regularly numbered, and bargains for what suit his purpose. The house is sometimes paid for on the spot, and removed by the purchaser; or the vendor contracts to transport and erect it upon the place where it is designed to stand. It may seem incredible, that a dwelling may be thus bought, removed, raised and inhabited, within the space of a week; but it will appear easily practicable by considering that these *ready-made houses* are in general merely collections of trunks of trees, tenanted and mortised at each extremity, so that nothing more is required than the labour of transporting and adjusting them.[12]

The seventeenth-century views of Moscow show the result of this system (Plate 65B). The houses are all the same size, a circumstance which doubtless led to their arrangement in parallel rows, so that the city of Moscow, so frequently burned and rebuilt, had a uniformity and regularity in certain quarters unlike that of any western European city[13] (Plate 66A).

Not only houses and churches, with other civic buildings such as palaces for the prince or governor which served the purpose of a city hall, but even walls and other fortifications were of wood, which surprised many a traveller. As Olearius remarked of Novgorod: 'The number of its steeples promises yet somewhat more great and noble, than what may now be seen; since that coming to the Citie, we see onely Walls of Wood, and Houses built with Beams lay'd one upon the other.' [14] Moscow had wooden ramparts in the seventeenth century, and Tsaritsin on the Volga, with the houses clustered behind wooden walls and towers as it appears in Olearius's view, must have been very like the usual Russian town. Until modern times such wooden walls and bastions were standing around the city of Yakutsk in farthest Siberia.[15]

Another seventeenth-century traveller, Augustin von Meyerberg, ambassador from the Emperor to the Court of Alexis Mikhailovich, had an album of drawings prepared to illustrate his account of his diplomatic mission in 1661.[16] Many of these are slight sketches of tiny villages deep in the forests. In the view of Yadrovo an elaborate wooden church rises above the wooden settlement (Plate 67B), while the view of the Iverski Monastery on an island in Lake Valdai (Plate 67A) shows the unusual scale of the single masonry church towering above the lower conventual structures enclosed by a wooden wall with wooden towers. Such was 'wooden Russia', a forest land where the people used the material for farm and city, for house and church, for street paving and eating utensils; a land where old traditions lingered centuries after they had been superseded in the metropolitan centres, where the greatest ingenuity in wood-working went hand in hand with the simplest structural methods.

That this virtuosity in the use of wood had prevailed from the earliest times is apparent in the chroniclers' account of the first church of Sancta Sophia in Novgorod, which was built of oak by Bishop Joachim and had thirteen 'upper parts' (vierkhi). Another oak church was in Rostov, then far in the interior of the forest land. It was erected in 992 by Bishop Hilarion, but burned in 1160, together with all the other churches in the city.[17] In the absence of all vestiges of these earliest wooden structures, and even of accurate descriptions, we are obliged to assume their gradual evolution from simpler to more complex forms; the first Sancta Sophia in Novgorod itself succeeded a tradition of temple and house construction in pagan Russia. Which should be considered the oldest surviving church has been a matter of dispute, but certainly the Church of St Dmitri of Salonika in Staraya Ladoga (Plate 66B), of the eighteenth century, represented the simplest form. This was the type of 'chamber' (klet) or, as one might say, 'shed' church, from the fact that the interior space consisted of one or more single rooms, each resembling the undifferentiated interiors of a peasant's izba (Figure 11). In churches of this type the largest chamber served as the nave, with smaller rooms added to the east for the apse and to the west for the porch or vestibule. Frequently the addition of a broad enclosed gallery on three sides complicated the massing of the original three chambers. With the high-pitched roofs, the wooden church gained a characteristic form, marking it at once by its angularity from the geometrical mass of stone churches. In fact, the appearance of such churches would in many cases suggest merely a lofty and impressive izba were it not for the small bulbous dome on a tall drum placed over the central element to mark the structure as the house of God. Externally the appearance of this and of almost all extant wooden churches has been changed by the flat boarding which was applied as a protective measure at the end of the nineteenth century. The loss of the original texture, so intimately a part of the technique and effect of the earlier churches, is to be deplored; for they suffer almost as much as do their masonry counterparts, where a gabled tin roof so often replaces the original covering.

The surrounding gallery, used as a vestibule in bad weather, gradually increased in size until it served as a community meeting-hall on Sundays and festivals, where the congregation, often assembled from great distances, might remain between services to take their meals if it were cold or wet. In time the galleries became so important that without them the church itself would have provided insufficient space for the congregation, as may be seen in the seventeenth-century churches of Yaroslavl (Plates 86 and 87B).

The 'shed' church, whatever may be the exact date of its appearance in Russia, is certainly the simplest solution to the problem of adapting the square Greek cross-plan to a different material and method of construction. The three internal spatial elements of nave, apse, and porch, such as had appeared at Kiev in the Church of the Redeemer at Berestovo and more frequently in the later twelfth-century churches of Vladimir-Suzdal, are present. The correspondence is, indeed, internal rather than external, for the peaked roofs, which even in the earliest churches may have been quite steep, set the church apart from all other buildings in the town. A pitched timber roof is quite unlike a stone form, and when roofs were placed above polygonal forms, such coverings be-came even more conspicuous. The tall pyramidal or 'tent' (shater) roofs above a central octagonal space are perhaps the most striking forms developed by the carpenters.

Figure 11. St Lazarus. Olonets

The origin of the octagonal church is itself a mystery. That it is of considerable anti-quity is proved by the documentary evidence for the church of 1290 at Ustiug. The form possibly represents the carpenters' attempt to re-create internally the effect of the By-zantine crossing below the central dome, although the interior was almost always covered by a low ceiling, so that the effect of a tall nave was lost. Nor can we overlook the fact that the vestiges of a large pagan temple of ancient Russia, discovered in Kiev, were oval in plan.[18] In the depths of the northern forests the population may have re-tained memories of sacred circular wooden structures far longer than in the South, and so have involuntarily willed that their new Christian temples should follow the same form. The technique of constructing a tent roof may have been evolved from roofing a polygonal, usually five-sided, chamber which was often added to a shed church in imita-tion of the semi-circular stone apse, while the construction of such an apse may have led to the ability to enlarge the central space of the church by building it as an octagon, whereby a larger enclosed space could be obtained with logs no longer than those used for a rectangular frame.

The earliest surviving example of such an octagonal church is the Nicholas Church at Panilovo, consecrated in 1600, and probably erected the previous year (Plate 68). It is the oldest of a group of such structures which includes the Church of the Vladimir Virgin in Belaya Sluda (1642), St George in Verkhnaya Toima (1672), and the Dormition in Nizhni Uftiug (Figure 12).[19] In each the octagon is adjoined by a square apse and

0   10   20   30 FEET
0   5   10 METRES

Figure 12. Nizhni Uftiug. Dormition

anteroom, the latter surrounded by a low covered porch approached by a double stairway. In the Dormition the porch has been extended to form a gallery surrounding the octagonal nave. It will be observed that though this plan is comparatively simple, since only the substitution of a central octagon for a rectangle differentiates it from the shed churches, the exterior has changed considerably. The high octagon covered with an equally tall pyramidal roof towers over the subsidiary rooms, which are covered with curious arched roofs. These bochki or 'barrels' are really part of the structure itself rather than an applied covering, and furnish another unsolved architectural riddle. It may be that they represent the carpenters' attempt to imitate the profile of the bulbous dome, in this way associating the dome concept with the covering of the whole mass, or possibly they are the wooden counterparts of the masonry zakomars, the semi-circular arches crowning the walls of the Kievan churches. If this is indeed a transposition of masonry forms into wood, it was accomplished with that remarkable simplicity which marks so many of the structural methods of Russian wooden building. All that was done was to change, progressively, the length of the logs on the end walls.

More complex forms appeared when side rooms or double chapels were added north and south of the central rectangle in addition to the eastern apse and western vestibule. When chapels were placed at the east of these side arms, a cross-shaped plan occurred which was even closer to the orthodox masonry type. While the distribution of the spaces in plan was essentially simple, the three-dimensional mass became more elaborate and accounts for many of the most picturesque and typically 'Russian' effects in wooden architecture, as in the church of SS. Florus and Laurus (1755) at Rostovskoe (Plate 69).

The addition of apses to the arms of the cross changed the original centralized plan into one whose main axis lay along the breadth rather than the length of the church. This tendency appears in the early eighteenth-century Church of the Trinity at Nenoksa (1727) (Plate 71; Figure 13). The massive tent roof was built of planks laid on vertical rafters, rather than of horizontal interlocking beams. At first glance it might seem that this structure is only a more complex version of the earlier type of octagonal church. The impressive tent roofs, rising not only over the central octagon but also above the north and south arms of the cross, testify to the affection which the people felt for these forms. But closer inspection reveals a significant modification which occurs only

Figure 13. Nenoksa

after the middle of the seventeenth century, when the reforms of the Patriarch Nikon had obliged even the carpenters to make concessions to a more 'orthodox' type; each of the octagons supporting a tent roof rises from a lower cube.

The combination of octagon, cube, and cross plan found unusually powerful expression in such churches as the Ascension at Konetsgorie (1752) and the Church of St Clement at Una. According to the parish register the latter church was erected in

1501, although a seventeenth-century date is more probable.[20] In each the plan was a simple cross, enlarged by additions to the eastern side of the north and south arms. At Una each arm was roofed with double bochki, the upper supporting a small cupola on a slender drum, and the huge tent roof, constructed according to the usual method of a gradually reduced octagon of horizontal beams, was somewhat larger than the central square. The central octagon emerged from the cross arms only at its intersection with the bochki. At Konetsgore, on the other hand, the central interior square was expressed externally as a cube adjoined by the cross arms and apses. The circumstance that the whole mass of the building was raised a storey above the ground as a protection against dampness contributes to its commanding height. In both churches the composition of masses was worked out in what might well be called inverse perspective, since it progressed from the relatively near and small, the staircase and arched openings on the landing, to the remote and large, the huge central mass of the octagon. The effect overwhelms the spectator by the apparent discrepancy in scale.

Since so far the history of the tall wooden church seems to have followed a consistent formal development based upon the interaction of function and material on technique and to have achieved a form peculiar to a specific region, the question of possible influences from abroad can again be raised. Greater verticality could perhaps have been suggested by some acquaintance with European Gothic architecture. Certainly neither from the South, from Byzantium, nor from Italy, whose monuments became familiar to Russian architects only after the arrival of the Italian master-builders and craftsmen at the Court of Ivan III in the later fifteenth century, could the Russians have derived such a taste for tall structures. Since ideas from Germany and Poland could enter Russia through Novgorod, it is interesting that most of these wooden churches have been discovered in the northern provinces which once belonged to that city. On the other hand, the gradual stabilization of relations between the Great Prince in Moscow and the Tartars which led to the opening of the Volga to Russian trade with the Near East and the Caucasus after the middle of the sixteenth century, could have hastened the arrival of influences from those regions. Not less significant, and certainly very curious, is the frequent appearance in the Russian language of architectural terms of Tartar and Turkish origin. Such a word is shater, which describes the tent form in wooden architecture.[21] Beyond the Tartars in the mountains of the Caucasus lay Georgia and Armenia, whence some three centuries earlier may have come the decorative motifs found in the churches of Vladimir-Suzdal. The Russians may well have had some knowledge of the medieval Georgian churches which frequently present, although in stone, just such a combination of tall masses subsidiary to a central cube whose pitched roofs lie just below the central polygonal or circular drum crowning the cube, which in turn is surmounted by a conical or pyramidal roof.[22] Yet, whatever may have been the influences which shaped the will of the Russian carpenters, their ultimate achievement is no deliberate imitation. The wooden church of the Russian forests, whether Gothic in its verticality or Georgian in the articulation of its parts, is, through the subtle disposition of its proportions and the brilliance of its technique, unmistakably Russian. Such is the Dormition at Varzug (1674) (Plate 72A), to modern eyes one of the most skilful examples of the octagonal tent church on the cross plan. Again the arms surround a central cube, above which rises a low octagon supporting a powerful tent roof. The transition from each cross-arm through the cube to the octagon is managed by the introduction of a second, smaller bochka above the arched roof. A third row of diminutive bochki smoothes the passage from the cube to the octagon. The proportions of this church have impressed Russian and foreign scholars alike as the most successful solution to the multiple problems presented by a structure, cross-shaped in plan, which must at one and the same time satisfy the ritual demand for a cube and the popular desire for an octagon, which could be seen as late as 1774 in the Dormition at Kondopoga (Plate 70).

A type which came closer to the new ritual legality, while at the same time answering the Russian desire for height, appeared towards the close of the seventeenth century in the so-called 'storeyed churches' (yarusnye khramy). In these structures the suggestion of placing a series of shallow cubes or octagons, or each alternately, upon a cubical mass came from the Ukraine, where such forms, in wood or masonry, had been influenced by Latin baroque churches in Poland and Galicia.[23] There a type of wooden church, square in plan, cubical in mass, and with added cubical elements above the cornice line had been developed. Essentially the plan is not unlike those of the shed churches, the central square adjoined by a rectangular porch on the west and a pentagonal apse on the east. Upon the central portion there was then placed a smaller rectangle, surmounted by a low octagon in turn carrying the slender drum and bulbous cupola. The number of churches of this type which were erected throughout the eighteenth century proves that this arrangement satisfied the church authorities. Farther north they were often more elaborate and combined with other more traditional elements. Thus the Church of St Nicholas at Berezovets (Plate 73B), erected in the first third of the eighteenth century, is in plan a cross composed of an octagon with equilateral arms roofed with large bochki. Above the octagon is a diminutive version of the church itself in the form of a central cube flanked by lower cross arms and crowned with small bulbous cupolas. Above these elements rises a miniature octagon which carries the central cupola.

The reforms of Nikon are also reflected in the 'cube churches' (kubovatye khramy), where the internal space is expressed externally through a large cubical mass. The roofing provides an ingenious solution to the desire to retain something, even if only the vaguest memory, of the silhouette of the tent roof. Hence upon the cubical mass rests what may perhaps be described as a square, flattened dome, not unlike a depressed version of the bulbous cupola which crowns the form itself. Often at the angles of this shape smaller cupolas were added to accommodate the whole to the liturgical requirements. The Church of the Virgin of Vladimir at Podporozhie (1741) (Plate 73A; Figure 14) is an intricate example of the cube type. In plan the cross is modified by the addition of three apses to the east. The bochki of the east and west arms are so large that they appear to be one axial mass, penetrated by the north and south arms and supporting the central cube. Although the clerical authorities may have been satisfied that the church fulfilled the letter of the law by wearing five domes above a cubical mass, from a distance the visual effect was much more in the spirit of the old tent churches, with their pyramidal silhouettes.

I

0   10   20   30   40   50 FEET

0   5   10   15 METRES

Figure 14. Podporozhie

The famous Church of the Transfiguration at Kizhi (1714) (Plate 74) shows how a carpenter could push his technique to its furthest limits. This church, which is to wood what St Basil in Moscow (Plate 82) is to the masonry architecture of medieval Russia, is the most frequently cited example of the Russian architects' extravagance and loss of control over materials and proportions. Yet perhaps both churches are more correctly interpreted as remarkable examples of a particular climax in the formal development of a style. At Kizhi the formal postulates are still apparent in the extraordinary contrast between the simplicity of plan and interior space and the startling three-dimensional external expression. The plan is the familiar central octagon with cross arms. Externally the arms are roofed by two superimposed bochki, and each side of the octagon by one. Four decorative bochki stand between the large and the smaller octagon which carries the central cupola. In this way the central mass seems to consist of two diminishing octagonal tiers, an influence from the storeyed churches of the South. The astonishing effect of the church is due to the additional drums and cupolas placed over each bochka, to the total of twenty-two (the eastern arm has an additional cupola).

With the church at Kizhi the traditions of ancient Russian wooden architecture were fulfilled. Beyond this it is difficult to see how a more harmonious balance between plan, structure, and decoration could be achieved. The bristling silhouette of the church, pyramidal in the tradition which can be traced back to Sancta Sophia in Kiev, achieved the same kind of aesthetic contrast with the surrounding landscape of lake and plain and woodland that the conglomeration of masonry spires at St Basil accomplished for the urban landscape of red brick walls and low wooden houses. Nor could this have been realized without that age-long practice of wooden construction, that technical mastery of the resources and possibilities of a particular material.

CHAPTER 15

ARCHITECTURE IN MOSCOW
1400–1600

TOWARDS the close of the fourteenth century the artistic and political recovery of Russia after a century and a half of Tartar domination became more perceptible. Just as the spectacular victories of Dmitri Donskoi in 1378 and 1380, even if they proved ephemeral, were a sign that the Tartars were not invincible and that better times might be ahead, so the activity of such painters as Theophanes and Andrei Rublev in Moscow after 1395 was a sign that Russia could once more create a monumental art.

The fifteenth century, which in Western Europe saw the decline of many medieval concepts and the rise of new attitudes towards life and art, was an equally decisive period in Russia. But the word Renaissance cannot be used to describe the history of both Western and Eastern civilizations at that time. In the literal sense of a revival of ancient art and letters, it would be too narrow to include the new political, intellectual, and artistic developments of Russia, and it is moreover too intimately connected with the conception of humanism. The revival of ancient learning had to wait until the seventeenth century, when the influence of Polish and Catholic scholarship affected the schools of Kiev and Moscow.[1] And fifteenth- and sixteenth-century Russian architecture entertained no memories of an antique past. For want of a better term, therefore, it is customary to speak of the period between Russia's medieval Byzantine past and her later European future as Muscovite, since the energies which directed it and the accomplishments which remain were in large part the work of the Great Princes of Moscow.

The most decisive historical situation in this period was the gradual concentration of political, economic, and industrial power in the person of the princes of the Moscow line who, as cousins to the older families of Novgorod and Suzdal, descended from Ivan Kalita ('Money Bags', 1328–41), a grandson of Alexander Nevski (1220–63), Prince of Novgorod. Since Nevski's grandfather, Vsevolod III, had been Prince of Suzdalia, and Vsevolod's grandfather, Vladimir Monomakh, Great Prince of Kiev, their descent was unimpeachable. Nevski's policy of accepting Tartar taxation in exchange for actual if not nominal independence was continued by the Princes of Moscow, who became in the fourteenth century the principal tax-gatherers for the Khans. In this way they learned such valuable lessons in the administrative organization and economic control of Central Russia that, when the Tartar power disintegrated into a number of smaller Khanates, the princes were in a position to assert their own independence with little disturbance. By the close of the sixteenth century the Russia of Kiev, distraught, magnanimous, and violent, had passed into history, and in its place had risen a new national power in the hands of the astute, patient, business-like, and violent Great Princes of Moscow.

The history of Russia during these three centuries, from 1300 to 1600, is the story of the gradual aggrandizement of Moscow. Slowly but inevitably the other Russian princes, whether sovereign or apanage, were obliged to acknowledge the suzerainty of the prince of Moscow, until, by the close of the sixteenth century, Muscovy embraced Central Russia from the White Sea to the Caspian and eastward from Novgorod and Smolensk to the Urals. In this process the gradual weakening of the Tartar overlordship, largely through internal dissension, enabled Ivan III in 1480 to dispense with the payment of tribute, and his grandson, Ivan IV, to conquer the cities and territories of Kazan and Astrakhan by victories won in 1552 and 1554. The character of the new power appears in the development of the dynastic titles. In 1337, after several decades of strife among the younger princes of the Novgorod–Vladimir line, the dignity of Great Prince (Velikii Knyaz) was confirmed by the Khan to Ivan I Kalita and his heirs in recognition of his leadership of the other princes. The older order of succession through fraternal seniority was superseded by the relatively more stable principle of succession from father to son.[2] Towards the end of the fifteenth century Ivan III, through whose marriage to Sophia Palaeologos much Byzantine ceremony and protocol had been introduced at the Moscow Court, was accustomed to sign himself Tsar (a Slavonic corruption of the Latin Caesar) by virtue of Russia's theoretical assumption of the civil and ecclesiastical traditions of the Eastern Empire, and Autocrat (in Russian Samoderzhets, 'self-ruler', a literal translation of the Greek autokrator), signifying more his independence from Tartar overlordship than the absolutism of a later age. He also adopted the spelling 'Ioann' as more aristocratic than the familiar 'Ivan'. In 1546 his grandson, Ivan IV, was the first Russian sovereign to have himself crowned as Tsar. The title of autocrat was first used officially at the coronation of the first tsar of the house of Romanov, Mikhail Feodorovich, in 1613. The final formulation of the imperial style occurred in the early eighteenth century when Peter I assumed the Western, Latinized title of Imperator.

The authority of Muscovy rested on the control of the sources of financial and industrial power in the hands of the Tsar and the ruling class. This accumulation of financial and agricultural holdings was accompanied by the appearance around the person of the sovereign of a host of courtiers, variously princes of ancient lineage, and landed aristocrats or boyars, from whose ranks were drawn such talents as were needed to run the offices of government. The boyars were obliged to supply troops in time of war, and in return for these services were gradually guaranteed the peasant labour necessary to work their lands and to raise the required military strength. Gradually the obligations of the agricultural population to the landowners became codified and hardened into the institution of serfdom whereby the peasant was the absolute property of the master. The effect upon cultural expression is perhaps best seen in the considerable supply of cheap labour for large architectural enterprises which became available in the sixteenth and seventeenth centuries. The longer and more iniquitous effects lay concealed in the increasing separation between the peasants and the landowners. The former were reduced to the status of chattels as the latter were raised to a landed aristocracy, creatures of the sovereign, fearful of absenting themselves from his presence, and so taking and spending less and less time on their estates. Consequently the middle classes who were so important in Western Europe as creators and consumers of works of art were eliminated. From the middle of the fifteenth century Russian art is increasingly two separate stories, a Court art and a folk art.

It will be recalled that although the artistic history of medieval art in Russia had centred round the church, yet in its creation participated not only the aristocracy and the clergy who built the churches of Kiev and Suzdalia, but also the wealthy merchant class in the free cities of Novgorod and Pskov who commissioned frescoes and icons. Henceforth the Church itself became gradually absorbed within the court, both figuratively and literally. Such churchmen as Joseph of Volokolamsk who energetically supported the Tsar against the Tartars maintained that it was proper for the Church to acknowledge the claims of the temporal power. Although Joseph probably had in mind the immediate end of securing to the Church control of the enormous monastic properties, the final result of such reasoning subordinated so thoroughly the spiritual to the temporal power that at the beginning of the eighteenth century Peter I could abolish the Patriarchate and assign the administration of church affairs to a government department.

With the consolidation of the national power of Moscow politically, economically, and industrially went an increasing awareness that Russia would have to take notice of the rest of the European world. As the Tartar pressure gradually decreased, the princes of Moscow more frequently turned to the West, at first in a long series of attempts to curb the power of Poland and Lithuania, and later of Sweden, and to recover for Great Russia of the central North-east the lands of White and Red Russia in the West and of Little Russia or the Ukraine in the South which had been ruled by Poland since the middle of the fourteenth century. Although the final unification of the Russian land had still to wait some time, the course of the wars and the diplomatic negotiations that they entailed brought the court at Moscow more and more into relations with Western Europe. It is true that no permanent embassies were established by foreign Powers in Moscow until the close of the seventeenth century, but the succession of diplomatic visitors accompanied by their numerous attendants could not fail to arouse the curiosity of Russians, nor to acquaint the upper class, with whom these emissaries came most often in contact, with Western manners, costumes, articles of luxury, and even works of art.

Two other important events may be noted. In 1553 the first English ships reached the White Sea and made port near the later town of Arkhangelsk. From this date commenced Russian trade with Western Europe, at first with England alone but later with France and Holland, leading in time to the establishment of merchant colonies in Moscow. Even though the Tsar might later segregate the foreign merchants in a quarter by themselves, the so-called German District (Nemetskaya Sloboda), the presence of a large group of foreigners wearing Western dress, worshipping in their own churches, and behaving with the relatively greater freedom of Europeans acted as a constant irritant to turn the Russians' attention more and more to Western matters. Concurrently the recovery in 1667 of the Ukraine, including all the Russian lands on the left (eastern) bank of the Dnieper with Kiev and its suburbs on the opposite bank, restored to Russia a large population which, although it had remained loyal and Orthodox through the long centuries of Polish and Lithuanian subjection, had been impregnated with Western and

Catholic, specifically Polish and Jesuit, ideas. However various may have been Russian reactions to these different events, ranging from the seclusion and even persecution of foreigners to the drastic reform of the Church in the seventeenth century, Russia could no longer maintain more than a pretence of being unconcerned with the affairs of the rest of the world. The reforms of Peter the Great made explicit what had already been implicit for some two centuries.

Yet the way towards the Europeanization of Russia, if the process whereby the country became less an outpost and more a participant in European affairs can be so called, was neither direct nor constant. The later conflicts in the nineteenth century between the Slavophiles and Westernizers were already foreshadowed by the alternations in political and artistic policy during the earlier period. An apparent sympathy with Western concepts would suddenly be supplanted by a revival of older national or regional tastes. If the artistic history of Russia from 1400 to 1700 appears to be an inextricable stylistic jungle, the reason is that it represents the visual realization of this continual process of rejection and acceptance, a process in the course of which more than once, by adaptation and compromise, a specifically and characteristically Russian formal tendency can be detected. The same process can be stated in terms of whether the sovereign of Moscow conceived of himself as European Prince or Russian Tsar. The architectural history of the late fourteenth and fifteenth centuries reveals how the princely and spiritual authority still vested in the forms of Suzdalian architecture was combined with the structural variety and popular character of Novgorod and Pskov traditions. The merging of these two tendencies with traditional methods of wood construction and the appearance of a number of foreign architects created the situation in which the new Muscovite style was formed. Whereas in Kievan Russia the separatist tendencies represented by the jealously independent princes had brought about the rise of such self-sufficient and characteristic centres as Chernigov, Novgorod, and Vladimir within the general Byzantine spirit of Kiev, the new architecture originating as the expression of a centralized government in Moscow was to be national and authoritative.

From its foundation, Moscow, like other Russian towns, had been built of wood, and a large proportion of its buildings were of that material until after the final disastrous fire of 1812, when new city ordinances made masonry construction obligatory. When the first stone churches were built in the thirteenth century they received special mention in the chronicles. During the reign of Ivan Kalita the Churches of the Assumption, St Michael, and the Redeemer in the Wood (Spas na Boru), all of stone, rose on the fortified hill, the Kremlin, in the heart of the city. Only of the Redeemer can one speak with any certainty; for although it was lately pulled down, sufficient photographs and drawings exist to show that at the time of its demolition the original walls stood to a height of some six feet. Although surrounded by many additions, it was clear that the Church was a simple four-piered, single-domed building with three very slightly projecting apses.[3] It may be assumed from this plan, and from the subsequent history of Moscow, that these first churches followed the Vladimirian model and that even the builders were brought from Suzdalia; for although Moscow possessed a fine white stone in the neighbourhood, it had as yet produced no skilled or experienced builders.

In the absence of any precise knowledge of the appearance of the first churches of Moscow, some indication of late fourteenth-century architectural practice is supplied by the existing monuments in Zvenigorod. The prince of this region, Yuri, the second son of Dmitri Donskoi, contested for many years the succession of his brother to the Moscow throne, which he finally occupied for the last two years of his life, in 1432–4. His intention of rivalling the prince of Moscow with a series of fine masonry buildings resulted in experiments important for subsequent architecture. Yuri's first and still best-preserved structure was the Cathedral of the Dormition in Zvenigorod (1399–1400). It is so similar to the churches of Vladimir, especially to the palace church of St Dmitri, that we can here see with our own eyes the dynastic and spiritual connexions between the two principalities. Here is the same cubical mass, four-piered plan with three apses and three entrances on axis, the triple division of the walls, and a single dome. Even the decorative details are similar: the corbel-table on the apses, the recessed portals, and the decorative frieze running along at middle height. Yet the slighter projection of these elements and the substitution of a triple band of carved ornament for the arcaded frieze in St Dmitri create a two-dimensional orientalized design, more like the last church of the Vladimirian period, St George at Yuriev-Polski. On the other hand, such details as the ogee arches over the portals and windows, and the bases, capitals, and engaged columns of the façades and doorways, presuppose some familiarity with Gothic architecture. They may be the work of Russians who had travelled in the West; for the Zvenigorod churches demonstrate a more coherent treatment of the Russian tradition than is seen in the late fifteenth-century churches of the Moscow Kremlin, where the presence of foreign architects is documented. The Western elements at Zvenigorod may have come to Muscovy by way of Serbia, where certain fourteenth-century structures exhibit similar Gothic details and even bands of ornament very close to those at Zvenigorod. In this connexion it is significant that in 1404 a Serbian architect, Lazari, constructed a bell-tower in the Moscow Kremlin.[4] The horseshoe-arches, moreover, could have come from Yuriev-Polski. Finally, the Zvenigorod church differs from such Vladimir examples as the Pokrov by the absence of any clear integration of the internal and external structural systems. There are no pilasters on the interior walls, and the decorative divisions outside do not correspond to interior bays.

Other churches built by Yuri in the next few years continued to modify the Suzdalian type with additional changes which prepared the way for the fuller development of the Moscow style at the end of the century. The Cathedral in the Monastery of St Savva in Zvenigorod (1404) shows the same treatment of the walls, with the dome displaced towards the east. The roof originally consisted of a series of superimposed arches, or kokoshniki, the expression externally of the system of corbelling the arches above the interior crossing at the base of the drum.[5] This important structural device, first worked out in Pskov and Novgorod, was unknown in Vladimir until the end of the fifteenth century. Such a combination of the traditions of Pskov and Vladimir may have been effected through the influence of wooden architecture, for the resulting pyramidal roof resembles in a general way the cone-like silhouette of the tent church, and the rows of pointed arches are very like the horseshoe-arched bochki which were so popular in wooden architecture. But where in wood the bochki made for lightness and structural flexibility, the result in masonry was otherwise. Since the stepped arches of the roof were of stone, the weight of the vaults increased until the walls became thick, sloping buttresses. The grace of Vladimir was swallowed up in the more massive proportions.

Very close to the Savva church is the Trinity in the Trinity-Sergius Monastery (1422–23).[6] The same wide horizontal band, here interrupted by broad pilasters, gives the façade a rectangular, geometric character. Internally the iconostasis has now become a permanent partition wall separating the apse from the main body of the church. The result, when the church was four-piered in plan, reduced the remaining interior space to a square with the apparent effect of spreading the interior laterally.

The dome of the Trinity is placed further east, so that the arched divisions of the exterior no longer correspond to the position of the vaults within. One may believe, therefore, that the tendency to consider the exterior a decorative scheme immediately related to the pyramidal treatment of the roof took precedence over the structural system. However illogical such a system may seem when judged by the standards of Western medieval architecture, for Russian architectural history it is of the greatest importance. Prevented as much by the relative scarcity of good building stone as encouraged by the prevalence of an ancient native tradition of wood construction wherein decorative effects were achieved with the greatest facility, the Russian architects of the sixteenth and seventeenth centuries reached their greatest triumphs through this combination of elementary structural techniques with the elaboration of decorative devices.

The culmination of this type of church occurred in the Cathedral of the Annunciation in the Kremlin (Plate 75; Figure 15) and in the St Therapont Monastery near the White Lake. The Novgorodian origin of both structures is clear. The monastery was situated in Novgorod territory, and the Annunciation was built by masters expressly summoned from Pskov. The upper part of the Therapont church has been spoiled, but the Annunciation preserves much of its original character behind the later second-storey galleries. This church, where the Tsars were christened and married, was erected between 1484 and 1489 on the site of an earlier building, the old stone foundations of which were used. It was the second major work of reconstruction undertaken by Ivan III in the Kremlin, but it owes more to the architectural past of Russia than to the new structures which were built immediately before and after it.[7] Here again the Vladimir model prevailed in a four-piered, three-apsed plan with entrances on three sides. The treatment of the exterior is close to St Dmitri, although with the five domes of the Vladimir Dormition, while the apsidal arcades clearly derive from Vladimir. In the course of the sixteenth century the church was surrounded with galleries on three sides with small chapels above them. The new type of roof, the tendency to consider the façade a separate problem in design unrelated to the internal structural system, and the enlargement of the iconostasis into a partition wall with a consequent reduction and alteration of the apparent internal volume of the church, were factors which prepared the way for the development of the national style in the new buildings erected in the Moscow Kremlin in the last quarter of the fifteenth century.

The personality of Ivan III, the Great (1462–1505), was better suited to the role of

0   10   20   30   40   50 FEET

0   5   10   15 METRES

Figure 15. Moscow. The Annunciation

European Prince than that of Russian Tsar. While he resembled his forefathers and descendants, particularly Ivan Kalita and Ivan IV, the Terrible, in his ability to amass territory for Russia and in his deliberate delaying actions against the Tartars, in other respects his conduct and character seem more like those of the contemporary merchant princes of Italy and France. Through his marriage with the Greek princess Zoë Palaeologos, the niece of the last Byzantine Emperor, Ivan III not only associated himself with the tradition of the Eastern Empire, assuming the title of Tsar and the double-headed imperial eagle as his crest, but gained direct access to Western, specifically Italian, culture. For Zoë, who took the name of Sophia when she entered the Orthodox Church, had been educated in Rome as a ward of the Pope, and thus knew something of the developing art of the Italian Renaissance. Scarcely had Sophia reached Moscow in 1472 than Ivan sent emissaries to Italy to collect information about artists and craftsmen of all kinds, and to persuade the most promising to travel to Russia. Their services were required, not only for the erection of churches and palaces within the Kremlin, but also for the instruction of Russian workmen in the hitherto unfamiliar techniques of casting cannon, coining money, and similar crafts. The result of their activity was not only the Italianate appearance of the buildings erected during the reign of Ivan III, but also a lasting acquaintance with Western architecture, which, even though known only partially and through details continually misunderstood and misapplied by local craftsmen, nevertheless through the next two centuries enabled the Russian masters to absorb more easily influences from the West.

In the later fifteenth century the buildings under construction in the Kremlin and the number of foreign craftsmen working in Moscow gave the city an aspect not unlike that of some prosperous Italian or Flemish city. Ambrogio Contarini, the Venetian Ambassador to Persia, who was in Moscow in October 1476, saw Fioravanti at work on the Cathedral of the Assumption and a Master Trifoso, 'a goldsmith from Catharo, who had made, and was engaged in making, many beautiful vases and other articles for the Duke.'[8] Contarini also mentioned the many Greeks from Constantinople who had come with Sophia, and a 'great many merchants from Germany and Poland' who frequented Moscow in the winter 'for the sole purpose of buying peltries'. Although situated on the limits of the known world, on the farthest confines of Europe towards Asia, Moscow yielded to no other northern city in the cosmopolitan character of its population. Ivan himself in contemporary descriptions seems in his cordiality and informality more like a Medici than any of his successors. Contarini's description of the Great Prince communicates something of the ease and affability of his presence, for which the spacious churches he commanded to be built were the proper expression, and which was in marked contrast to the suspicious and introspective moods of his grandson Ivan IV, who similarly created a characteristic architecture.[9]

Ivan's building programme involved nothing less than the reconstruction of the Kremlin, a task largely accomplished in his reign and finished during the sixteenth century. When he came to the throne, the Kremlin hill was covered with a mass of small structures, including the wooden residence of the prince and the churches which had gradually grown up around it. By the middle of the fifteenth century the stone church erected in 1326 by Ivan Kalita was far too small to contain even the Court, let alone to serve as the cathedral for the whole city. Ivan began by building a new cathedral of the Dormition. Within its walls a few fragments are preserved of the fourteenth-century church, and from these Soviet archaeologists have conjectured that it may have been influenced by the churches of Polotsk, notably in the single long projecting apse, and the lateral extension of the cross arms by porches which gave it somewhat the appearance of a western Romanesque structure with a transept before the choir.[10]

For the new construction two Moscow architects, Miskin and Krivtsov, were engaged and the foundations laid in 1471. But when part of the walls collapsed in the earthquake of 1472 it became apparent that more than the technical experience of the Moscow masters was needed. Even the masons of Pskov, who were called to the capital and who were known to have some acquaintance with Western building techniques, proved unequal to the task, and as a last resort a foreign architect was summoned. Ivan's agents chose Aristotele Fioravanti of Bologna, well known in northern Italy as an architect and engineer. In 1483 he had been appointed official engineer to the city of Bologna, and five years later entered the service of Galeazzo Mania Sforza in Milan. Somehow or other his popularity declined, and in 1467 he went to Hungary to build a bridge across the Danube for Matthias Corvinus. In 1475 he accepted the invitation of Prince Simeon Tolbustin to go to Russia, where he spent the remaining years of his life. From a letter written in 1476 to Galeazzo Maria Sforza it appears that he had travelled as far as the White Sea. It is said that he was invited to return to Bologna after finishing the Dormition but was prevented from leaving by Ivan.[11]

The new Cathedral of the Dormition (Plate 76; Figure 16) is an unusual and provocative building.[12] It was intended as an affirmation of dynastic and spiritual traditions and as a demonstration of progressive, for the Russians even experimental, structural techniques. For so we must interpret the programme presented to Fioravanti on his arrival at Moscow in 1474. He was told that he was to repeat the general *ordonnance* of the Dormition in Vladimir, to which his church was to be considered the mightier successor. He was also to construct a building so sound that there would be no repetition of the calamity of 1472.

Figure 16. Moscow. The Dormition

Fioravanti fulfilled both obligations. The general design of the Moscow Dormition closely follows the Vladimirian prototype. Here is the same cubical mass with plain walls divided into arched bays and ornamented by an arcade at half the height. Even the position of the windows is the same. The scheme of five domes is also retained. Fioravanti's church is so clearly based upon the Vladimir style that we have no difficulty in believing that he visited Suzdalia and carefully examined the churches there. The chronicle preserves a memory of this visit in its report that the architect, in his admiration for the churches, thought them built by his own countrymen. But Fioravanti travelled elsewhere in Russia too. The mass of the Dormition, especially the relation of the sturdy drums to the high white walls, suggests another Russian tradition – that of Novgorod. Since Fioravanti was renowned as an engineer, he probably accompanied Ivan on his campaigns against Novgorod in 1476 and 1477. The dates coincide with the slow growth of the Dormition; by the summer of 1476 the walls had risen only as far as the arcade, and the whole building was not finished until 1479. Fioravanti could thus have given them this pronounced Novgorodian character during the following summer. The plan, however, with six piers and five apses resembles, but for the two additional apses, Andrei's original Dormition rather than the present church with Vsevolod's additions. By abolishing the galleries Fioravanti established a new Russian type of unprecedented spaciousness. In other respects his plan was also novel for Russian architecture of the period. Through the position of the piers he divided the internal space into a series of compartments of equal size, whether they were roofed with vaults or domes. Disregarding the earlier Russian custom of making the aisles the same width as the apses, he widened the aisles and narrowed the apses so that each pair of apses is placed at the end of each aisle. The rationality and logical precision of such a scheme speak for his fifteenth-century Italian training and imposed a new sense of geometrical order upon Russian planning.

Fioravanti's experience as an engineer influenced his structural system. After removing the remains of the earlier walls, he enlarged and deepened the foundations, adding stumps of oak trees laid in pits. Upon these foundations rose the walls of white stone, cut in smaller blocks than had been customary in Vladimir-Suzdal. For the vaults he used light bricks, made in a kiln built to his own specifications. For further solidity and strength he bound his arches with iron tie-rods in the Italian manner. There are also accounts of his having taught the Russian masters the use of hoists for lifting and moving materials. His workshops on the Dormition were a true school of architectural construction unequalled in Russia since the first Greek masters came to Kiev in the tenth and eleventh centuries.

A peculiarity of the Dormition was the fact that the main façade on the Palace Square had to be the southern rather than the western wall. Fioravanti's solution of this problem in design contained in essence many aspects of the subsequent as well as of the past history of Russian architecture. We have already seen that in the later churches of Novgorod and Suzdal it had become customary to arrange the decorative pilasters on the external façades so that they coincided in general with the internal disposition of the vaults and arches. As time went by the displacement of the dome towards the east, and so more nearly over the altar space below, resulted in a narrower eastern bay, although if the projection of the apse were included this bay with the apse was approximately equal to the western bays.

In the early fifteenth-century Moscow churches this tendency, which for all its asymmetry at least had a certain expressive logic, was discarded in favour of a strictly symmetrical and equal treatment of the three bays, so that the displacement of the dome above such a mass produced a completely inorganic, not to say illogical arrangement, to which the projection of the apse added merely another uncoordinated element. Fioravanti's arrival at this juncture and his application to existing conditions of the logic of Italian Renaissance design may be seen on the south façade of his Dormition. In the first place, he masked the projection of the side apses by the double device of reducing their diameter and extending the south wall as a buttress some distance beyond its junction with the east wall. He then organized the remaining rectangular surface by a system of proportional relationships as accurate and coordinated as in any Italian building of the period. In contrast to the jaunty and irregular vertical divisions of the Suzdalian churches, Fioravanti's four bays, corresponding to the internal distribution of the vaults, have a solemn processional rhythm. The proportion of height to width is that of the golden section; the height of the upper windows from the ground equals the width of the two bays, etc.[13]

This complex interpenetration of old and new, of spiritual authority and modern technical practice, gives Fioravanti's measure as an architect. His skilful combination of Suzdalian plan with Novgorod volume, reorganizing the whole in terms of a modern intellectual aesthetic of abstract proportions, made it possible for him to create the first truly Renaissance building in Russia, new in its proportions, in the study of space, in the elegant uniform rhythm of bays and domes. However, to describe this church simply as an Italian building in Russian dress would be to minimize the coherent spirit which Fioravanti imparted to it. Its value becomes all the more apparent if it is compared with the next of the churches of the Kremlin to be built by a foreign architect.

Just before his death in 1505 Ivan III decided to rebuild the old Cathedral of St Michael the Archangel (Plate 78A; Figure 17). Again an Italian was summoned, this time Aloisio or Alevisio Novi, 'the New', to distinguish him from an Alevisio who had worked in Russia from 1494.[14] Alevisio's commission was to build another monumental church, destined this time to serve as the burial-place of the Tsars of the House of Rurik and of the earlier Romanovs. Again the authority of the Vladimir type determined mass and plan. But Alevisio was far less adventurous than his predecessor; his design, which resembles the Dormition in the displacement of the dome and the orientation of the entrances further towards the east, is similarly six-piered and five-domed. Otherwise the general distribution of space resembles more the Suzdalian type than the severer intellectual logic of the Dormition. Although Alevisio had to retain the entrance of the older church, which accounts for the small rooms to the north and south of his western entrance and the addition of an extra bay on the sides, he distributed his four free piers before the iconostasis so as to accentuate the breadth rather than the depth of the interior. His nave is thus wider than his aisles in harmony with the manner of earlier architecture. The thickness of his walls indicates that his structural technique was inferior to Fioravanti's. All in all St Michael in plan as well as construction appears retrogressive.

The exterior, however, is new and surprising. The walls are entirely covered with Renaissance forms; arches, pilasters, panels, and sculptural details give the church the appearance of a two-storey palace of the Italian High Renaissance. Alevisio was more a decorator than an architect, and his façades have little if any relation to interior volume or structural system, entirely unlike the fine proportions of Fioravanti's Dormition. Thus in his desire to relate the narrow windows of the Russian church to his broad wall-panels he introduces wider reveals which in many cases cannot disguise the fact that the window, an integral part of the structure, has no relation to the panel. The design of the pilasters with composite capitals and architraves, the whole carried on a high base, is as great a contradiction to the nature of the building as the scallop shells in the arches above the upper entablature which deny the existence of the internal vaults.

The building in its curiously composite and decorative character bears the same relation to Italian architecture as does an early sixteenth-century French château such as Blois. Each is the result of an attempt to apply wholesale an alien decorative pattern to a traditional structural system which had generated its own, although now rejected, method of decoration. As in Western Europe, it would be some time before the inevitable consequences of the experiment were fully understood: that the traditional style, in plan and mass as well as in technique, must be abandoned, or else a new decorative method more appropriate to the structure discovered. However fashionable the new church of St Michael may have seemed at the time, it was destined to remain without issue in Russian architecture. Unlike the Baroque churches of the seventeenth century, where such secular, palatial splendour found a happier treatment, the higher clergy and their architects soon returned to the older and more familiar type of the Dormition.

Nevertheless, St Michael added much to the repertory of Russian decoration. The bold horizontal cornice beneath the scallop shells became a favourite device, as did the use of two materials in contrasting colours. Here white stone was used for the projecting

Figure 17. Moscow. St Michael

parts, the cornices, capitals, arches, and shells, while the remainder was of red brick. Alevisio himself, before his summons to Russia, is said to have worked in Milan and Venice, which would account for the presence of such Venetian details as the group of four circular windows, one large and three small, over the main entrance. North Italian also, is the treatment of this entrance as a two-storey loggia.

The cathedrals of the Kremlin, revered because of their close association with the dynasty, and as the chief metropolitan churches of the capital, cast a long shadow over subsequent church architecture. Each of the three in its own way offered a different solution to the problem of the proper design of the Orthodox church, if not in plan and structure then in visual appearance. St Michael, the most novel, had the most obvious influence. The Cathedral of the Annunciation, especially in the treatment of the roof, was less an innovation, and so more congenial to Russian taste. However one may choose to explain the origin of the stepped arches crowning the roof, whether as the external expression of the corbelled vaults at the base of the central dome or as a decorative device

taken over from wooden architecture, the kokoshniki answered some strong formal desire and appeared with increasing frequency throughout the sixteenth and seventeenth
centuries until the reforms of Nikon in 1650.

The Cathedral of the Dormition enjoyed a different authority. As the seat of the
Metropolitan of Moscow, and so by inference the primary church in Russia, it was taken
as a model for many later urban and monastic structures. Its unbroken cubical mass
crowned by five domes was frequently copied with such slight changes that it came in
time to be considered the traditional, conservative, and basically orthodox pattern from
which no deviations were permitted. Important sixteenth-century examples are the
cathedral of the Novodevichi Convent in Moscow (1551), Sancta Sophia in Vologda
(1568–70), and the Dormition in the Trinity-Sergius Monastery (1585) (Plate 79A).

After the middle of the seventeenth century the Patriarch Nikon's insistence on the
most literal interpretations of the liturgy and the church canons led to the condemna-
tion of all but the most orthodox type of church. In this way the Dormition enjoyed a
further prolongation of its authority into the last years of the century. Perhaps the most
striking example was Nikon's own Church of the Twelve Apostles (1656), which adjoined his palace in the Kremlin (Plate 79B). Since his palace stood close beside the Tsar's,
here was visual affirmation of the political theory that Tsar and Patriarch were joint
rulers of an indissolubly autocratic and theocratic monarchy, as well as of the close personal ties which at one time existed between Alexis Mikhailovich and Nikon.[15] The
Twelve Apostles differed from the Dormition only in certain richer details, the inescapable evidence that it was a seventeenth-century structure, and in the fact that it was
raised one storey above the ground in order that the interior might be on the same level
as the main rooms of the palace.

The churches of the type descending from the Dormition were usually monastic or
cathedral structures, erected under the immediate supervision of powerful ecclesiastical
leaders who were not unaware of the necessity of maintaining friendly relations with
the authorities in Moscow. Another type of sixteenth-century church, startlingly different in appearance, arose under other conditions. These were the monumental churches
built by the ruling family or by wealthy nobles, frequently as thank-offerings or for
votive purposes. In them the spiritual authority of the Church can be seen opposed by
secular and personal taste, at variance with the hierarchy and possibly closer to popular
tradition. As a group these monuments are characterized by their central plans, octagonal
towers, and usually by their tent roofs.

Of the votive churches of this type the earliest and in many respects the finest is the
Ascension at Kolomenskoe (Plate 80A; Figure 18), the Tsar's country residence near Moscow. Built by Basil III in 1532, the church is without precedent in Russian masonry architecture. The tall, angular mass, enclosing the uncomplicated interior space, is composed of
thick walls, reinforced along the sides and in the re-entrant angles, so that the effect is that
of a powerfully buttressed support for the octagonal tower crowned with a tent roof surmounted by a small lantern and cupola. Externally the transition from the many-sided
church to the octagon is managed by the corner buttresses and the kokoshniki above each
side. The church is placed on a high basement and is reached by a gallery, originally

uncovered and approached by three flights of steps. The church demonstrates once more that peculiarly Russian characteristic, a union of opposites, here as elsewhere typified in the superposition of extremely complicated forms upon an essentially simple and logical plan. The inherent directness of the square plan internally has grown into a multi-faceted polygon in elevation. The transition to the octagon is both expressed and concealed by the buttresses and kokoshniki. The tower-like body of the church absorbs all the details in its vertical sweep, yet the whole is anchored to the ground by the broad gallery. The plan is axially symmetrical in both directions, yet any appearance of too

Figure 18. Kolomenskoe. The Ascension

rigid a balance is avoided, both by the position of the church on a gently sloping hillside, and by the stairways to the galleries which are unequally placed on three sides.

The problem of the origin of this church is very intricate. It is idle to pretend that its impressive verticality can be explained by reference to the medieval architecture of Western Europe. This had been familiar to Russian builders in one way or another since the appearance of German traders in the twelfth and thirteenth centuries in Novgorod, and, while it is true that Novgorod architects had tended to push their buildings upward rather than lengthwise, the whole cube had been made taller; no central element such as a cupola had dominated the whole building at the expense of others. Nor, despite the temptation to see in such a form some connexion, however devious and remote, with

Persian and Indian architecture, such as Hindu stupas, is it really permissible to predicate an influence upon what may be only an accidental resemblance.[16] There remains the question whether the Kolomenskoe church is not an attempt to create in brick the effect of the tall wooden churches of northern Russia in which an octagonal tower crowned with a tent roof rises over a central square. Since the earliest surviving example of such a church is that at Panilovo, built in 1599, and a closer resemblance to Kolomenskoe is not found until the Church at Varzug of 1674, chronology does not support such an hypothesis. But since the central plan was known in Russia, and neither Panilovo nor Varzug need be or can be considered the primary example of such a church, it is probable that Kolomenskoe does represent an attempt to transfer to masonry wooden forms familiar at the time of its construction. The argument may be supported by other deductions. The thick walls seem to betray some unfamiliarity with new problems of load and support. Had there been masonry precedents for Kolomenskoe, probably some other solution than the sheer weight of so much brick would have been invented to carry the octagon and roof. Secondly, the decorative details of the kokoshniki seem much more the interpretation in brick of wooden forms than a decorative device evolved from the external corbels of such a church as the Kremlin Annunciation. And finally, the wide surrounding gallery is too familiar a wooden form, and too rare in preceding masonry architecture, not to have been taken over. To assert the almost instantaneous appearance of a new form of church, at best no more than hinted at in the relatively greater height of later fourteenth- and fifteenth-century churches, and to assume that from 1532 the innumerable wooden churches in Russia were in turn derived from a few masonry buildings on the ground that the Court style would have had more prestige in the villages than would the village style in the Tsar's country palace, is to mistake the fundamental nature of materials. The tent churches of the later sixteenth and seventeenth centuries are forms too coherently evolved to have been merely called into existence by the sudden appearance of a new type of church at Court. So far as ideology is concerned we must remember that the century covered by the reigns of Ivan III, Basil III, and Ivan IV was coloured by an insistence on Russian nationality. That these tower-like churches appear first on the private estates of the dynasty and as assertions of dynastic prestige would seem sufficient warrant for the belief that the Tsars themselves, in seeking a characteristic national expression, looked to the tent churches of the popular cult. The disappearance of tent churches by fire and reconstruction in Muscovy itself, and the preservation of many later examples in remote northern villages, have arbitrarily affected the interpretation of this aspect of Russian architectural history.

The votive churches, whatever their origin, were not without some relation to the dynastic churches of the Kremlin.[17] The fine white stone Church of the Transfiguration at Ostrovo (Plate 80B) is clearly from the hand of someone familiar with St Michael and the Annunciation, as well as with the Ascension at Kolomenskoe. From the Annunciation came the tiered kokoshniki over the side-chapels and at the base of the central octagon; from St Michael certain details, such as the profiles of the pilasters and the circular windows in the side walls of the chapels. The cubic core of the main church and of the chapels is close to the Annunciation; in the chapels the walls are divided into three bays

K   129

by pilasters, in the main church they are framed by corner pilasters between which runs a blind arcade. Upon this profoundly simple and geometrical base the kokoshniki create the effect of a prodigal expenditure of decorative forms. Less elegant in its profile, and less sensitive in its proportions than Kolomenskoe, the church at Ostrovo possibly carries a step further the Russian fondness for lavish decoration. And once more it is worth observing that although in plan and structure the church is composed of few elements, and those rather rigidly placed, externally the composition is one of constantly varying dimensions, aided again by the position of the church on the gentle slope of a hill.

Another kind of tower is seen in the Decapitation of St John the Baptist at Dyakovo (Plate 81A; Figure 19), near Kolomenskoe. For long thought to have been erected in 1529 by Basil III to secure the birth of a son, it has lately been established that the documents

0   10   20   30   40   50 FEET

0   5   10   15 METRES

Figure 19. Dyakovo. The Decapitation of St John the Baptist

of 1529 referred to another church, and from the dedication of the chapels it can be adduced that the church was erected in commemoration of the coronation of Ivan IV, probably before 1547.[18] Originally the church consisted of a central octagon flanked by four smaller octagonal chapels, the five elements standing upon a high square terrace. At a later date the addition of an apse between the two eastern chapels and galleries on three sides with a belfry on the west spoiled the original composition, where a livelier diversity occurred in the relation between the large central element and the four smaller variants at its base. Except for the depressed domes with which the five elements are crowned and the presence of octagonal rather than square chapels the composition of Dyakovo resembles the slightly later church at Ostrovo. Both exhibit the same desire to construct a single, tall, tower-like mass which becomes in profile pyramidal through the addition of subsidiary shapes at its base.

If the builders of Kolomenskoe and Ostrovo knew St Michael in Moscow, but were more familiar with nearby wooden towers or tent churches, the situation was reversed at Dyakovo. Here the majority of the decorative work is a Russian version of European motifs. The curious half-columns surrounding the upper part of the tower seem to be a combination of Renaissance columns and Gothic buttresses.[19] Kolomenskoe was a wooden form translated into brick; Dyakovo is essentially and completely an expression of brick-work. Only in the considerable projection of the multiple cornices crowning the central octagon is the existence of the wooden prototypes apparent. Even the severe profiles of the kokoshniki are evidence of this feeling for the material as the dominant mode of expression, increased by the polychromatic effects in coloured tiles.

The churches at Kolomenskoe and Dyakovo were the immediate prototypes for the third and most original building. With them in mind the votive church of Ivan IV in Moscow, dedicated to the Protection and Intercession of the Virgin, but popularly known as the Cathedral of St Basil the Blessed (Vasili Blazheni) (Plates 82 and 83), appears less as a monstrosity or inexplicable curiosity than as their logical if extravagant successor. The church was intended by Ivan IV as a national votive church commemorating his conquest of the Khanates of Kazan and Astrakhan. It was erected between 1555 and 1560 by two Russian architects, Postnik and Barma. The tradition that it was built by an Italian who was then blinded by Ivan lest he create anything else like it is a later fantasy, popularized by travellers' tales in the eighteenth century as a way to account for its fantastic appearance. For the origin of the church it is perhaps of some importance that a series of separate wooden chapels was first erected. Then the central stone church was constructed and the adjacent chapels ultimately executed in masonry.[20]

Like its predecessors, St Basil enjoys a picturesque location, dominating the narrow southern side of the Red Square near the Saviour Gate of the Kremlin. Its site, like those of its prototypes, is uneven, slanting away from the Square towards the river. The tall octagonal tower of the central church, in plan and structure a repetition of the Kolomenskoe Ascension, stands upon a high terrace or platform, but is concealed externally by the towers of the four large octagonal chapels placed on the main axes and by the four smaller polygonal chapels placed in the angles between them. Once again we observe the contrast between the simplicity of the plan and the complexity of its three-dimensional expression. The principle of unity is maintained by subordinating the eight smaller towers (nine, if the belfry is included) and their cupolas in two ranks, as it were, to the central tent roof of the main church, yet within this unity the greatest freedom allows each subsidiary chapel a different height and surface treatment. The whole exhibits the widest variety of plastic expression, as can be seen by comparing any two photographs taken from different angles, and in this sense may be considered the most 'sculptural' achievement of Russian architecture. In one respect this variety is possibly more accentuated than the builders originally intended; for in the seventeenth century a small chapel and a belfry were added on the north-east, and the polychromatic decoration of the cupolas was completed. Were the cupolas identical the effect would have been closer to Dyakovo. The enclosed gallery, which was added later, conceals the articulation of the chapels so that their separation above the second storey seems unnecessarily capricious. A seventeenth century engraving made from a drawing of the church before the gallery was enclosed proves how much more coherent the original design must have been (Plate 81B).

Thus to describe St Basil as a logical outgrowth of the tendencies initiated at Kolomenskoe and Dyakovo is not to detract from its strangeness. Like the Tsar who called it into being, the church exemplifies both the continuity of a tradition, perhaps in this case a dynastic rather than a national tradition, and the extreme divergences of character within that tradition. As Ivan IV is at all times most Russian, even as he is truly terrible, so St Basil is both a part of, and a departure from, old Russian architecture. Paradoxically, it is a most particular expression of the personality of one sovereign which could have been created at no other time or place, yet conversely it is rightly considered, even

0   10   20   30   40   50 FEET

0   5   10   15 METRES

Figure 20. Moscow. St Basil

by the Russians themselves, one of the most typical examples of their national culture. As Sancta Sophia was to Kiev the symbol of the mass acceptance of Greek Christianity, so St Basil came to mean that the Russia of Muscovy had attained its own special religious and cultural expression. As we would associate Sancta Sophia with the first Greek bishops and Metropolitans of Kiev, so with St Basil we may name those passionate and mighty builders of the Moscow Church: Joseph of Volokolamsk, who fought for the closest union between the Church and the Monarchy, and Philip the Metropolitan, who dared defy even Ivan himself.

For later generations, in Russia as well as in Europe, the church became a landmark and a stumbling-block. After the seventeenth-century reforms no churches again achieved such prodigality of colour and shape, until the revival of the national style in the nineteenth century. For the eighteenth-century European traveller the church 'offered little of interest'.[21] There have even been attempts to explain its peculiar design as an influence from the East, specifically from Tartary. But surviving Mongol architecture bears little relation to St Basil, and, as we have seen, the individual forms already pre-existed in traditional wood and masonry construction. If it owes anything to the Middle or Farther East, it is only the use of rich colour which had long existed in Russian art and the complex, over-all patterning of the surfaces somewhat in the manner of textiles. Indeed, it was in ornament rather than in structural methods that the Tartars, who left few permanent buildings, influenced Russian art.[22]

The confusion and dislocation of the national political and economic life during the later years of Ivan's reign precluded any further elaborate building, nor was the short reign of his son Feodor (1584–98) any more propitious. Since this was followed by chaos and catastrophe under Boris Godunov and in the ensuing Time of Troubles, there was in effect a suspension of monumental construction until the revival of prosperity under the Tsars of the house of Romanov after 1613. Later sixteenth-century churches are small, and in the provinces frequently echo the style of the capital. Among the smaller structures, however, there emerged towards the close of the period a type which proved influential in the following century. An example is the old cathedral in the Monastery of the Virgin of the Don in Moscow (Plate 84A), built in 1593, which summarizes in miniature the architectural innovations of the sixteenth century. In spite of its small size, the plan contains many features which had grown common with the passing of time. To the central space, for instance, in this case without internal piers, were added not only the customary three apses, but also side chapels, each with an apse, the whole bound together by an enclosed gallery. Externally there is much that is familiar, however new the combination may at first appear; the cornices and lunettes of St Michael, the external massing of Ostrov, the central pyramidal effect of St Basil, as well as the full-blown cupola. In many variants this church supplied the precedent for the first churches in Moscow built under the Romanovs.

CHAPTER 16

SEVENTEENTH-CENTURY RELIGIOUS ARCHITECTURE: THE 'MOSCOW BAROQUE'

THE religious architecture of the seventeenth century reflects with unusual precision the multiple currents of thought and action present in the social and political history of the time. The slow revival of national energies after the Time of Troubles and the Polish occupation of Moscow in 1611–12 necessarily delayed the construction of monumental

| 0 | 10 | 20 | 30 | 40 | 50 FEET |
| 0 | | 5 | | 10 | 15 METRES |

Figure 21. Moscow. The Nativity of the Virgin in Putinki

buildings, although the first Romanov tsars, Mikhail Feodorovich (1613–45), and his son Alexis Mikhailovich (1645–76), felt obliged, like their predecessors in the sixteenth century, to make their contribution towards the formulation of a national Russian style. The expression of such a desire can be seen in the Church of the Nativity of the Virgin in Putinki (1649–52) (Plate 84B; Figure 21), built at the personal wish and with funds, some 800 roubles, supplied by Tsar Alexis. The church owes much to the picturesque, asymmetrical composition of Ostrov and St Basil, yet here three-dimensional variety is expressed in the plan as well as in the mass. The plan develops around a rectangle, later filled in by the low one-storey structure in the foreground of the photograph. The church actually consists of two separate chapels, each with an entrance from the court-yard. The first is a cube surmounted by triple rows of kokoshniki topped by a slender drum bearing a tent-roof with cupola. The second chapel is again square in plan, but externally it emerges as a broad rectangle crowned with three pyramidal spires on tall drums with cupolas. The two chapels are joined by a rectangular belfry, which in itself is a more elaborate version of the four other pyramidal spires. The uneven alignment of the five spires, of unequal height and carrying cupolas of different sizes, and the various rows of kokoshniki contribute to the picturesque effect. The lack of correspondence between the external massing and the disposition of the plan, and the interpenetration of each element with its neighbour, introduces a new and more exclusively visual approach to architectural design. It is as if the architect of this last of the tent-roofed churches had attempted to re-create the apparent lack of unity of St Basil without considering the fundamental logic of structure and plan which underlay it.

This irregular plan and exceedingly intricate massing appear in other Moscow churches of the period, such as the Church of the Trinity and of the Georgian Virgin (1634–54) (Plate 85). It may be noted that such churches were often built on narrow city sites along already existing streets so that to secure proper orientation the architect had to arrange the entrance either off-axis or through a chapel or belfry. Yet even churches standing in open grounds show the same multiple massing, uneven distribution of elements, and richness of surface decoration. Such is the Trinity at Ostankino (1668) (Plate 113), on the estate of Count Sheremetev near Moscow. Here accumulation and multiplication of parts reached a degree of pictorial richness unparalleled elsewhere. The principal cube is so enclosed by chapels, a two-storey gallery with adjacent vestibules and covered staircases, and an attached belfry that the total mass presents the same constant shifting of volumes in three dimensions as observed in St Basil, to which it bears some relation also in the imitation of the double flight of steps. Ostankino represents a curious moment of transition; the architect wished to retain the jagged silhouette and verticality of St Basil, but also had to adhere to the now obligatory form of a cube with the canonical five domes. And, like St Basil, his church exhibits preoccupation with the character of brick as a decorative surface. It may be said to absorb and exude the qualities of moulded and coloured brick; bricks of various shapes, sizes, and colours, laid in numerous ways, lengthwise, sidewise, in zigzags, bricks cut or moulded for some particular course. The polychromatic walls topped with gilded and painted cupolas afforded that spectacle of abundant colour which so impressed foreign visitors to Russia.

This attitude towards brick intensively felt and worked to produce the utmost variety of colour and play of light and shade over the wall surfaces is characteristic of a large group of seventeenth-century churches in Yaroslavl (Plate 87B). This ancient city, founded in the eleventh century and long an outpost of the Russian land, had known the rise and fall of fortune through the years. Long ago it had been an important centre of religious culture, and it is not uninteresting that in the library of one of its monasteries was found the manuscript of the twelfth-century *Tale of the Armament of Igor*. The city had been sacked by the Tartars in 1238, and in 1463 accepted the overlordship of Moscow. In the course of the later sixteenth and seventeenth centuries it saw a renewed increase in its fortunes, for it not only commanded the Volga, which, when the Tartars had been overthrown, became a through-waterway to the East, but it also served as an important shipping point on the route between Arkhangelsk and Moscow. So long as the trade with Western Europe reached Russia through the White Sea, Yaroslavl each year saw companies of English, French, and Dutch merchants passing on their way to the capital. Through Yaroslavl also may have passed some of the numerous western architects, stonemasons, and engineers, whose recorded presence in Russia throughout the seventeenth century is in itself sufficient explanation for the increasingly frequent appearance of western architectural details.[1] As if it had been a later and somewhat vulgar Novgorod the wealthy merchants and other trading companies of Yaroslavl vied with each other to erect sumptuous churches. From 1620 more than forty stone churches were built, many of them larger than contemporary buildings in Moscow. Even a disastrous fire in 1658 failed to halt this building activity. Most of the extant churches were built between 1660 and 1690, after which, owing to the opening of the Gulf of Finland and the foundation of St Petersburg, the trade of Yaroslavl declined and disappeared.

It is in accordance with most provincial architecture and, it may be, most architecture produced by mercantile societies, that the churches of Yaroslavl, although large, magnificent, and ingeniously decorated, are conservative in plan and structure. They return to the earlier sixteenth-century disposition of a four- or six-piered, three-apsed plan, flanked by chapels and surrounded by a wide gallery approached by porches on three sides. The Church of St John Chrysostom in Korovniki (1649–54) (Plate 86), repaired after the fire of 1658), built by wealthy merchants, the brothers Nezhdanovski, is a particularly lavish and happy fusion of eastern and western influences. The simple cubical mass of the church, wearing the canonical five domes, recalls the Kremlin type, perhaps most immediately Sancta Sophia in Vologda. But the addition of the wide gallery at the base of the walls creates a two-storeyed effect which is further worked out in terms of the arcades resting below on squat engaged columns and above on wide pilasters. In the distribution of arch and pilaster one can sense not only a distant echo of St Michael, but possibly even the presence in Yaroslavl of some more direct understanding of the European Renaissance reaching the city through foreign merchants. The elaborately framed windows in both storeys, wider below and taller above than in any Russian churches before, are hints of the new knowledge of the European Baroque which was entering Muscovy about this time from the Ukraine. The traffic of Dutch merchants in Yaroslavl may account for the extensive use of coloured tiles. The window-frames and various mouldings throughout the building are worked in this material. Although the technique is European, the decorative elements as often as not appear more oriental in origin.

The merchants and architects of Yaroslavl were obliged to accept Nikon's injunction against the use of more than three or five domes, but they were loath to forego entirely the pyramidal tent roof of ancient memory. Such a roof appears in many of the Yaroslavl churches over the side-chapels, as here in St John and in the chapel of the Deposition of Christ's Robe, which stands apart from the Church of St Elias (1647–50).[2] Tent roofs are also found above the noble belfries which are a particular feature of Yaroslavl architecture. The belfry near St John is one of the finest of its type. The powerful octagonal brick base is crowned with a delicately pierced and subtly proportioned spire whose fine profile again suggests the probability of some eastern influence reaching the city from the lower Volga (Plate 87A).

In contrast to the commercial splendours of Yaroslavl, such a city as Rostov-the-Great, on the Volga, offers the interesting picture of a fortified monastic establishment of the later seventeenth century. Rostov, too, had been founded in the eleventh century. It had been anciently the seat of the bishop serving Suzdalia. Like its neighbours it had been devastated by the Tartars, and like Yaroslavl it enjoyed a brief period of prosperity in the seventeenth century following the elevation in 1589 of the Bishop of Rostov as Metropolitan, equal to Novgorod and inferior only to Moscow. But Rostov fell into a rapid decline when Peter the Great deprived the Metropolitan of much of his revenue. The construction of the ecclesiastical Kremlin of Rostov, a group of walls, towers, and fortified churches, was due to the energy and prodigality of the Metropolitan Jonas Sysoevich (1652-91).

In the sturdy proportions of the thick walls and towers there can again be seen those archaisms so often found in provincial cities. Although they are a century and a half later than the towers and walls of the Moscow Kremlin, those of Rostov show not the slightest trace of that elegance which marked Italian designs. They seem intended to repel attacks of archers rather than of riflemen. A peculiarity of the churches of the fortified monasteries of the later seventeenth century, not only here but in the neighbouring forest-bound Monastery of SS. Boris and Gleb, is the construction of churches above the entrances (Plate 88A). In a sense this conforms to a most ancient Russian practice. In Kiev there had been churches over the Golden Gate, and over the entrance to the Pecherskaya Lavra; in Vladimir likewise a church over the Golden Gate.

At Rostov and in the nearby Boris and Gleb Monastery the composition of the mass of the churches high above the walls, flanked by twin towers with a gateway upon which is lavished an unusual amount of decoration, is most skilful. The Church of the Presentation in the Boris and Gleb Monastery surpasses the churches of Rostov in the delicate treatment of the portal and in the almost Rococo charm of the applied arcades below the roof. Whether these be considered an archaistic reminder of the arcades of Vladimir and Suzdal, or whether they be taken as a final degeneration of the early zakomars, they bridge the awkward juncture of wall and flat roof demanded by the canonical reforms after 1650.

While the churches of Yaroslavl and Rostov, although for the most part constructed after the middle of the century, continued to express certain tendencies of long standing in earlier Russian architecture, church-building at Moscow was affected by two significant developments. The first arose from the insistence of the Patriarch Nikon (elected 1652, deposed 1666) that all future church-builders renounce the pyramidal or tent roof and return to the ancient Byzantine form of a cube topped by three or five domes.[3] This arbitrary decision was only one aspect of Nikon's determination to reform the Russian Church by restoring original Greek practices. Once again paradox plays a peculiar role in Russian history. While Nikon's intentions were in one sense progressive, since he wished to purge the Russian Church of errors which had gradually crept in, and so to place it on a theological footing sound enough to withstand criticism from the Roman

Catholic countries to the West, the results were on the whole reactionary. A large minority of clergy and laymen, who came to be called the 'Old Believers', refused to accept the so-called reforms and separated themselves from the official Church, insisting that they alone were the true heirs of Orthodoxy. The schism had enduring and unhappy effects. The official Church was for ever cut off from a large number of the most sincerely religious and intelligent churchmen, and it was so weakened that it could not hope for support from any quarter but the State. How uncertain that might be was soon seen, when Peter allowed the office of patriarch to lapse after the death of Adrian in 1700. Moreover, after the reunion of the Ukraine with Great Russia in 1667, a constant stream of clergy who had been educated in the more liberal, latinized academies in Kiev began to bring to Moscow innumerable Western ideas, including first-hand knowledge of the European Baroque. Consequently in later seventeenth-century architecture can be seen a pursuit of variety and picturesqueness. The heightened accent of surprise and caprice in the break of a wall, the turn of a pilaster, the penetration of one form into another, the obscuring of one shape by the passing of another across it, the play of painted colours against carved surfaces, and the irregular massing growing out of irregular plans give such architecture a truly Baroque character.

Yet, as every action breeds its counteraction, as in Western Europe the Baroque of Bernini was countered by the classicism of Perrault and Wren, so the architecture emanating from the circle of the Patriarch Nikon may be taken as an academic reaction – academic in the sense that the designers looked to the past for rules for the present and, fearful of the play of emotion, sought to control their materials through plain surfaces, the suppression of detail, and the utmost sobriety of effect. Nikon's two most important constructions can stand as types of the academic reaction. In the Kremlin he built his own palace and patriarchal church beside the Palace of the Tsars. That new Terem of Alexis Mikhailovich, with its small rooms, broken surfaces, bright colours, and European decoration, stood for the emergence of secular, personal luxury from under the shadow of church authority. Nikon thought to restore the dignity of an older order by a close imitation of tradition. His Church of the Twelve Apostles (1656) (Plate 79B) imitates the cubical bare masses of the sixteenth-century descendants of the Moscow Dormition. The five domes on tall drums, the zakomars, and engaged arcades, all witness his desire to separate his reformed Church from the extravagant tendencies of contemporary religious architecture and to return to the ancient lineage of Kiev and Vladimir. Nikon's palace immediately adjoining the church contained rooms considerably larger than the apartments of the Tsar's new Terem. It made a deep impression on foreign visitors, especially when Nikon received the Tsar himself in the great hall.[4]

Nikon's second great church, in his Monastery of the New Jerusalem at Istra, was also a monument to his convictions (Figure 22). This was intended as a demonstration of his restored architectural style, and as an assertion of the Russian patriarch's position as actual if not titular leader of the entire Orthodox community. To prove this Nikon decided to rival the Patriarch of Jerusalem by building a replica of the most holy shrine of Christendom, the Church of the Holy Sepulchre in Jerusalem.[5] To this end he sent one of his monks, the cellarer Arseni Sukhanov, to Palestine to study the ancient structure.

Arseni returned with plans and drawings from which a model was made, and in 1658 Nikon and his architects devised a large rotunda enclosing a replica of the Holy Sepulchre at the western end of a domed, cross-plan church.[6] The church itself was more 'Greek' than the churches of Kiev and Vladimir, for the cross was expressed externally as well as in plan, the arms projecting a full storey above the corner spaces. Upon Nikon's exile in 1666 the church had risen as far as the vaults. Work was then suspended, and Tsar Alexis summoned the builders to Moscow to the Government service. Not

Figure 22. Istra. Monastery of the New Jerusalem

until 1681 was construction resumed by order of Tsar Feodor Alexeevich, and the church was finished and consecrated in 1685.

This church was Nikon's most successful attempt to revive the Greek spirit of the earliest Russian architecture. The space at the crossing rose three storeys to the drum of the dome, and the arcades and galleries were supported on columns in the manner of Sancta Sophia at Kiev and the Transfiguration at Chernigov. Beside the church rose a tall belfry of square and octagonal storeys; the base resembled the campanile in Jerusalem, but the upper part looked more like the tower of Ivan Veliki in the Kremlin. The rotunda was originally covered with a stone tent-roof, historically a paradoxical use of this earlier wooden form which Nikon himself had condemned, but which was the only structural means to cover such a large interior space. This stone tent collapsed in 1723. Thirty years later it was rebuilt, possibly by the Moscow architect K. I. Blank after designs by Bartolommeo Rastrelli. The new roof was of wood with three rows of dormer windows to lighten the walls and to illuminate the interior. At this time the iconostasis, the replica of the Holy Sepulchre in the form of a small oratory, and the interior decoration of the rotunda were redone in the Rococo taste, thereby concealing Nikon's sumptuous but restrained majolica decoration.

Nikon's building, for all his serious, even noble, purpose, remained an architectural curiosity. Nothing is more difficult than for one age wholly to recapture the spirit of another. While Nikon might revile his enemies and boast that he alone had recovered the true spirit of the Russian Church in his return to the pure Greek sources, his buildings, like those influenced by his reforms, were not wholly without contemporary feeling. The powerful verticality of the Church of the Twelve Apostles and the picturesque grandeur of the Church of the New Jerusalem belong to the new age, not to the old. But in spite of that Nikon's artificial academic revival remained an episode rather than a decisive event in the history of seventeenth-century architecture.[7]

Yet that Nikon's restrictions were frequently more honoured in the letter than in the spirit we have already seen in northern Russia, where in the wooden churches various expedients were adopted to retain the familiar and beloved pyramidal silhouettes in the form of some combination of peaked roof and cupolas. In the capital, however, it was less easy to escape ecclesiastical censure, and on the whole the churches of the second half of the century in plan and mass conform to the requirements. Their appearance, however, was profoundly affected by waves of European influence after the middle of the century. This can be seen in the treatment of the façade of the church as a series of storeys, already observed in the 'storeyed' wooden churches, as well as in the frequent and more consistent use of decorative details from Western European architecture. An example of this so-called Moscow Baroque is the late seventeenth-century church of St Nicholas of the Great Cross (Plate 88B), which was founded by a group of merchants. The tall, five-storeyed cube is approached by a flight of steps to an elegant vestibule. Although the triple division of the façades, crowned with arches, is a reminder of the traditional scheme, the treatment of the walls divided by engaged Corinthian columns supporting entablatures, the richly carved window-frames, and the scallop shells inserted in both zakomars and kokoshniki are evidence of the enthusiastic acceptance of the superficial innovations of the Baroque manner. Only the group of star-faceted cupolas on slender drums is left to remind the observer that this structure is not a secular building, but a church of the Orthodox rite.

The dynamic verticalism of the church to which the canonical cube opposed its inimical static mass was not new in Russian architecture, but towards the close of the seventeenth century this verticality received a remarkable and characteristic expression in Moscow. No sooner had the canonical reform been accepted than it was ignored, for most characteristic of the 1680s and 90s and of the early years of the eighteenth century is a group of churches arranged either as a series of superimposed storeys of different shapes, or in the form of towers. It is of no little interest that these churches, which in so many ways represent the culmination of the Muscovite style, as it had developed from Kolomenskoe and St Basil, were also founded by the sovereign, his family, or his close friends.

A small urban example of this storeyed type is the Church of the Vladimir Virgin by the Vladimir Gate in Moscow (Plate 89B), erected by Peter I in 1691–4. Upon a cubical base rests an octagonal upper storey covered with a dome-shaped roof, octagonal lantern, and cupola. The proportion of decoration to structure is admirable. The decorative elements, the window-frames, twisted colonnettes, even the spiky covering of the cupola and the spheres above the pediments, are placed with due regard for the contribution of each to the whole. The staccato silhouette would be even livelier were the outlines of the pediments not concealed by a protective tin sheet. The author of this church was undoubtedly familiar with European Baroque design, but, like his predecessors long before in Kiev and Novgorod, he transformed the alien ideas into something unmistakably his own. By 1690, when Polish Baroque ideas had been current in Moscow for almost a century, this sense of design had become idiomatic. One can see this in the photograph where the Church of the Vladimir Virgin is completely in harmony with the huge medieval Kremlin tower behind, itself a product of mixed Russian and Italian collaboration.

A most gracious as well as highly developed example of this type is the Intercession of the Virgin at Fili (Plate 89A; Figure 23), built in 1693 by Prince Lev Kirillovich Naryshkin,

Figure 23. Fili. The Intercession of the Virgin

Peter's uncle, whence the phrase 'Naryshkin Baroque' to describe the architecture of the last years of the century. The Intercession is perhaps the first Russian structure to realize on such a scale the three-dimensional spatial implications of the Western European Baroque. Like so many of its predecessors, this church combines reminiscences from the past with the most recent innovations. Its general silhouette is not unlike the tower churches of the sixteenth century, especially Ostrovo, where there occurs the same juxtaposition of lower subsidiary elements about a central tower. In another respect the wide gallery around the base recalls the gallery of the Ascension at Kolomenskoe, and the cupolas on the semi-circular projections of the first storey are reminiscent of the clustered domes of St Basil. But the spirit, like the details, is new. An elegance and ease, a captivating gaiety in the play of white stone against dark red brick, foretell that lightening of the Baroque which would be present later in the work of Russia's most truly Rococo architect, Bartolommeo Rastrelli. Indeed, much of Rastrelli's best work can be thought of as closer in spirit to the more purely Russian church at Fili than to the European eighteenth-century styles by which he was also influenced.

Fili, like its predecessors, also illustrates the fundamental simplicity of much Russian church planning. A simple square is adjoined on four sides by hemispherical ante-rooms. Externally the central cube rises one storey above the roofs of the circular projections. Upon it rests an octagon, above which a smaller open octagon serves as a belfry, and above that is a cupola on a slender octagonal drum. The carved ornaments crowning each successive storey, the crested pediments above the windows, and the crisp design of squares and points outlining the balustrades, are deftly related to the plain surfaces of the walls. Internally the space above the central nave rises through the full height of the octagon, as at Dyakovo and Kolomenskoe. As a true Baroque building the church is situated in a space through which the spectator must constantly move if he is to grasp the significance of the whole, an effect due to the divided staircases and to the tension set up at the angles of the building by the opposition of the protruding circular masses to the projecting angle of the cube and the recessed sides of the octagon.[8]

As an instance of the combination of European and older Russian forms the Intercession at Fili is a singular example of success in a field where Peter found himself beset by difficulties. It is also interesting as evidence that the world in which Peter came of age was thoroughly impregnated with European ideas. Peter's drastic 'reforms' were thus less self-generated than fostered in him from boyhood by the most advanced circles of Moscow society. A further example of these tastes is the contemporary church at Dubrovitsi (1690–1704) (Plate 90), possibly built by a foreign architect for Prince B. A. Golitsyn, Peter's tutor. Although both descend from the same type of sixteenth-century tower church, the contrast with Fili is striking, and indicates how subtle was the balance attained there and how fraught with peril was the problem for the Russian architect of adapting Western stylistic devices to older traditional forms. Dubrovitsi rather than Fili may have persuaded Peter that only by breaking entirely with tradition could Russia move forward into the future. Upon a plan much like that of Fili, although with trefoil instead of semi-circular ante-rooms, rises a three-storeyed octagonal tower finished with an open iron coronet. The church is so burdened with carved ornament, including the sculptured figures of saints, attributed to the German sculptor Konrad Osner (1669–1747), that its outlines are blurred; the separation of storeys loses definition, and the eye is surfeited with detail.

These Baroque tendencies did not disappear from Moscow when Peter attempted to turn his people westward towards Europe, the sea, and his new foundation St Petersburg, although with the growth of this city Moscow in the course of the eighteenth century came to resemble a provincial capital living on the memories of its past. An indication of the character of early eighteenth-century Moscow architecture is supplied by the remains of the famous Menshikov Tower (Plate 91). Menshikov, the childhood friend and lifelong companion and adviser of Peter, wished to build a church in the form of a tower which would out-top all rivals, including the belfry of Ivan Veliki in the Kremlin and the Sukharev Tower erected by Peter himself.[9] Menshikov entrusted the work to the Ukrainian architect Ivan Petrovich Zarudni (died 1727). The church, dedicated to the Archangel Gabriel, was in the form of a tall tower composed of octagons rising from superimposed cubes. The resemblance both to Fili and Dubrovitsi and to the earlier sixteenth-century examples was more one of general silhouette than of detail, for Zarudni embellished his structure with more robust and accurate Baroque elements. Gigantic scrolls were applied to the east and west façades in the manner of buttresses. A colossal Corinthian order of pilasters framed the corners, between which graceful projecting porches of the same order broke the severity of the walls and emphasized a new delicacy in the treatment of brick and stone. Unfortunately after 1711 Menshikov's attention was so taken up with the construction of his new palace at Oranienbaum that he lost interest in his Moscow 'tower', even though he had raised it above all its rivals. In 1723 the two upper octagons burned with the loss of elaborate musical clocks which Menshikov had imported from England. Although the church was reconstructed in 1773 the upper storeys were a meagre approximation of the original ones.[10]

With the Menshikov Tower the last great work of the period of the Moscow Baroque had been accomplished. Through the middle years of the eighteenth century the Moscow architects gradually evolved a compromise between their own fanciful centralized tower churches and the new Latin cross plan which became fashionable in St Petersburg. For a time they still kept a storeyed tower over the crossing, but this gradually subsided into a single large dome shape which absorbed the octagon and rested directly on the crossing, itself the remnant of the earlier cube. Only the bell-tower at the western end of the church preserved the storeyed effect.[11] It will be necessary later to return to Moscow to examine one or another exceptional structure, but the energies of Russia were so consumed in the creation of the splendid new city on the Neva that later Moscow architecture, like the architects themselves, is part of the currents set in motion in St Petersburg by Peter and his successors.

CHAPTER 17

SECULAR ARCHITECTURE

THE study of civil structures poses even more difficulties than that of religious architecture. Almost all domestic buildings earlier than the eighteenth century have been lost in the frequent fires which destroyed the older residential districts of most Russian towns and villages. From travellers' accounts we know that private houses were usually of wood, instantly burnt but quickly replaced from a supply of standardized materials kept in stock in the markets. The few surviving masonry structures indicate that secular buildings of the later Middle Ages, like those in Western Europe, were essentially simple and functional in plan. The Pogankin House in Pskov (Plate 92A), a merchant's residence of the late sixteenth or early seventeenth century, shows severe stout walls unadorned with any architectural detail and broken only by windows irregularly placed according to the interior arrangement and the need for light, a characteristic also of the Pskov churches of the period.[1] In plan the house consisted of a series of rooms, including large store-rooms, arranged en suite around a central courtyard, not unlike farms of the period. The most important group of surviving secular buildings are the fortifications and palaces of the Moscow Kremlin, which for political reasons were kept in better condition than the residences of even the wealthy boyars. But since repairs meant frequent rebuilding, especially after the fires of 1547 and 1571, and the Polish and French occupations of 1611 and 1812, the present Kremlin bears all the marks of the changing tastes of each successive age.[2]

Until 1367, when Dmitri Donskoi rebuilt part of the walls in stone, the fortifications of the Kremlin, like those of most Russian cities, were of wood. Only Pskov and the Kremlin in Novgorod had masonry walls (Plate 92B), and indeed the wooden walls around the city of Moscow can be seen as late as 1661 in Meyerberg's drawing (Plate 93A). In 1451, during the Tartar attack, the enemy entered through the wooden sections, a fact which persuaded Ivan III to rebuild the walls entirely in red brick. The work was commenced in 1485, under the direction of two Italian architects, Pietro Antonio Solario and Marco Ruffo, and was largely completed by 1516. Unfortunately no view of the Kremlin survives to show us the original appearance of the walls and towers, but since many visitors to Moscow commented on the Italian appearance of the fortress, we can perhaps assume that the Italian architects, with the help of Aristotele Fioravanti, created a system not unlike the contemporary fortresses of northern Italy, the Castles in Milan and Ferrara. Certainly the robust, crenellated masses of the surviving portions of the walls and towers are remarkably italianate. Solario devised an ingenious plan to bring order out of the existing confusion with a double, in part triple, system of walls and moats. These were excavated by a hydraulic engineer, Aloisio da Carcano.

During the Time of Troubles the fortifications suffered severely, and in the course of the seventeenth century the upper parts of the towers were rebuilt in a variety of styles

(Plate 94). In 1624-5 an English architect, Christopher Galloway, designed the upper part of the Gate of the Redeemer (Spasskiya Vorota) in a fantastic style combining Gothic, Renaissance, and ancient Russian motifs. In an upper storey he inserted a clock, the largest piece of mechanical apparatus to be installed publicly in Russia. It was destroyed by fire in 1654, to the grief of the Tsar and the people. Other towers were crowned with peaked and tent-shaped roofs in the Russian manner, and at the end of the century the Borovitski Tower was rebuilt as a series of diminishing square storeys in imitation of the Siumbeki Tower in Kazan, which, although ruined in 1552 and rebuilt in the seventeenth century, could be considered a rare surviving example of Tartar architecture.

After Ivan III had rebuilt the Cathedral of the Dormition, he turned to his own residence, which to his wife Sophia Palaeologos must have seemed far from adequate as a princely dwelling. At this time the palace was not a single building, but a group of small structures, principally of wood, although in some cases the foundations were of stone. The apartments of the Great Prince, his family, and the principal courtiers, were in the upper storeys. In spite of subsequent rebuilding and much alteration, the present Kremlin palaces are still a group of buildings connected by terraces and staircases surrounding the site of the oldest church of the Kremlin, the Redeemer in the Wood. The replacement of wood by stone was gradually accomplished over a long period of time. Even in 1661 many log structures could still be seen within the walls.[3] Few of Ivan III's buildings remain, except the historic Faceted Palace (Granovitaya Palata), so called from its rusticated façade, which was built by Solario and Ruffo between 1487 and 1491. This was a simple stone building, containing on the second storey a large rectangular hall, with a groined vault supported by a huge pier in the centre. The exterior walls were originally pierced by double-arched windows with smaller windows above, and two small windows and doors opening into the storerooms on the ground floor. The design was very much like such early Renaissance Italian palaces as the Palazzo Bevilacqua in Bologna or the Palazzo dei Diamanti in Ferrara. The Palace was altered in the seventeenth century, when the arched windows were replaced with square-headed openings in Renaissance frames. The importance of the Faceted Palace was due less to its architectural character than to the fact that in the vaulted hall the Tsar sat enthroned on State occasions (Plate 96A). Of all the rooms in the Kremlin it was best known abroad through the reports of the foreign ambassadors, who were here granted an audience upon their arrival in Moscow.[4] It was also the scene of many notable events in national history, such as Ivan IV's celebration of the capture of Kazan in 1552, and Peter the Great's after the victory of Poltava in 1709.

Burned and rebuilt after the fires of 1547 and 1571, the palace again suffered almost total devastation during the Polish occupation of the Kremlin. The present Terem,[5] which appears as a fantastic pavilion crowning a three-storeyed structure of Renaissance design, was built by Tsars Mikhail Feodorovich and Alexis Mikhailovich, who had to reconstruct and redecorate the residential part of the palace. Under Alexis a host of craftsmen, principally from Poland, introduced a luxury hitherto unheard of in Russia. The walls were covered with gilded leather, the ceilings ornamented with precious metals, and new kinds of conveniences, doors and cupboards, bookcases and furniture from abroad, were installed. In 1661 von Meyerberg noticed the Flemish and Persian tapestries which covered the walls of the State apartments so completely that neither the floor, walls, nor ceiling could be seen. The ceiling of the new dining-room was decorated with a painting representing 'with astronomical accuracy the solar system and the fixed stars', an indication that modern science had penetrated even the Tsar's private apartments.[6]

The English traveller, Samuel Collins, who was in Russia in 1660–9, remarked on the Tsar's taste:

> Since his Majesty has been in Poland, and seen the Princes' houses there, and ghess'd at the mode of their Kings, his thoughts are advanced, and he begins to model his Court and Edifices more stately, to furnish his rooms with Tapestry, and contrive houses of pleasure abroad.[7]

The period of the greatest magnificence of the Kremlin Palace immediately preceded its almost complete decline. During the regency of Sophia, sister of Peter the Great (1682–9), it was redecorated by her favourite, Prince Golitsyn, following a fire in 1682. Inside and out the buildings were painted and decorated, the walls were hung with tapestries, and the rooms were filled with elaborate furniture and objects in silver and gold. Much of this was of Western manufacture, and had been obtained by Golitsyn from traders in the German suburb.

With the removal of the seat of government to St Petersburg, the palaces were allowed to deteriorate to a shocking degree. Frequent fires and neglect contributed to their ruin, and they were only patched up temporarily and in a most makeshift fashion, when the sovereign visited Moscow for his coronation or marriage.

Catherine II, who had a stronger sense of Russian tradition than any of the lineal heirs of Peter the Great, ordered the palace to be kept in better repair, and even proposed transforming the whole Kremlin into a national shrine by the construction of a new colossal palace enclosing the old buildings on all sides.[8] Happily, this was never done, but the palace continued to suffer through several fires, the French occupation of 1812, the building of the new Great Palace by Ton for Nicholas I on the site of several of the older State apartments, and the somewhat drastic methods of restoration practised in the nineteenth century. The latter spoiled the most conspicuous structure in the Kremlin, Ivan Veliki ('John the Great') (Plate 95B), the tall belfry above the Church of St John, begun by Tsar Feodor Ivanovich and completed in 1600 by Boris Godunov. This and the tower and cupola above the adjacent Church of St Nicholas are noteworthy for their height, rising as they do from the highest point of ground in Moscow, but they are of little architectural interest. The upper storeys of both were destroyed in 1812 and rebuilt soon after in a flat approximation of their original appearance.

The Kremlin – the principal point of interest in Moscow – as a congeries of buildings built at various times, of different sizes and axial relationships, created a picturesque effect which could not fail to impress the foreign visitor. Often he had no other word to describe this effect than 'Eastern' or 'oriental'.[9] A view taken by the French draughtsman André Durand (1807–67), who visited Russia in 1839, proves how the Kremlin affected the romantic imagination (Plates 94, 95A, and 166B). Durand has impossibly exaggerated the height of the towers, and so accentuated the contrast of this group of buildings with anything in Western Europe.

The most important evidence for the appearance of a Russian palace of the Muscovite period is the wooden model (Plate 97B) made for Catherine II when she ordered the demolition of the dilapidated old timber palace at Kolomenskoe, on the outskirts of

Figure 24. Kolomenskoe. Palace

Moscow.[10] This had been at intervals a favourite country residence of the Great Princes and Tsars from the time of Ivan Kalita to the accession of Peter the Great. Between 1667 and 1681 it had been rebuilt by Tsar Alexis and his son Feodor Alexeevich, and had come to resemble a small village composed of many separate buildings. Indeed, to judge by the model, it was like a gigantic dictionary of all the architectural terms invented by the Russian carpenters. Bochki, kokoshniki, tent-roofs, bulbous domes, and all the variety of turned and carved woodwork have been preserved in the model. Only the original colour which lent the buildings an unworldly fairy-tale character has not been recorded, except in travellers' tales. Yet the accumulation and diversities did not produce any functional confusion. As each part was added it took its place around a rectangular courtyard divided roughly in two by a bridge-like passage on the first-storey level. Various outbuildings, including the chapel, did not disturb this harmony, so characteristic of the Russian architects' ability to create variety from the simplest elements.

Externally the most picturesque dispersion prevailed, for the rectangular structures were so situated at angles one to another that the whole conglomeration presented a constantly shifting arrangement when seen from any point. To this effect the multitudinous roof-shapes and the uneven height of the different storeys contributed not a little. Since such an assemblage afforded the greatest contrast to the regularly aligned, box-like izbas in the village streets, it is apparent that the effect achieved at Kolomenskoe was less accidental than intentional, and so may be related to the prevailing tendency to manipulate forms to achieve a play of masses moving in space, of light twisting and flickering over the agitated surfaces. The picturesque quality of the palace at Kolomenskoe was not the accidental result of a nostalgic vision of a vanished past, but a vital, creative contribution to Baroque art. The palace was to have, however, quite another history in the art of Russia. Its physical destruction together with its sentimental preservation in the model and many drawings is typical of an eighteenth-century rationalist attitude towards such clutter combined with the first stirrings of a romantic respect for the past.

By the end of Alexis's reign the Kolomenskoe Palace may have seemed old-fashioned, and more appropriate as a country house than as a truly palatial residence. It is even possible that the decision to reconstruct it may have been prompted by the desire of the first Romanov Tsars to assert the continuity of the new dynasty with their sixteenth-century predecessors. Certainly during the seventeenth century brick and stone palaces became more and more the custom. Olearius mentioned the 'very fair Palace of stone, according to the Italian architecture, for the young Prince', which he had seen in the Kremlin in 1634. But he added that 'the Great Duke (Tsar Mikhail) continues still in his wooden Palace, as being more healthy than stone structures'.[11]

Mikhail himself had been born in a 'stone structure' in Moscow, the so-called House of the Boyar Romanov, which was rediscovered and restored by order of Alexander II in 1858. Its condition was so ruinous and the restorations so drastic that now it is more interesting as an example of the revival of Russian forms in the nineteenth century than as a source for the study of earlier architecture. Similar restorations have changed the character of the other few remaining seventeenth-century palaces and town houses such as the Yusuopov Palace (formerly the Volkhov residence), and the Library in the courtyard of the Synodal Printing Office (Sinodalnaya Tipografiya).[12] A more trustworthy source for the appearance of these structures is Augustin von Meyerberg's drawing of the palace set aside for the use of the foreign embassies in Moscow, as he saw it in 1661 (Plate 97c).[13] What we can see beneath the superficial picturesqueness and the complicated mass is most important for architectural history. Here, as at Kolomenskoe, the building had grown gradually through the years as rooms were added when they were needed. The additions were of two kinds. Some of wood, one or more storeys in height, were of traditional timber construction; others were stone buildings, more elaborately designed and often influenced by European architecture. Such is the windowed gallery over an arcade in the square block beside the entrance, with quoins and a heavy cornice in the Renaissance taste. Meyerberg's attention was naturally attracted more by the unfamiliar than by the forms he knew at home, so that he exaggerated such typically Russian masonry forms as the stumpy columns and the staircases covered with tent roofs such as are known to have existed in the Kremlin at this time. Paul of Aleppo may have had some such building in mind when he wrote:

The palaces in this city are mostly new, of stone or brick; and built on the European plan, lately taught the Muscovites by the Nemtsas, or Germans. We gaped with astonishment at their beauty and the multitude of their windows, and of the sculptured pillars on every side of them; the height of their storeys, as though they were castles.[14]

The Ambassadors' Palace represents a critical period in the history of Russian architecture. In a sense we may say that in it the traditional elements, the wooden chambers and tent roofs, were gradually being relegated to the periphery, as the masonry core of the building more and more approached the European type. Many years before this Moscow had known a thoroughly European building, if we may trust the drawing of the Foreign Office (Posolski Prikaz), erected in the Kremlin in 1591, made by Erik Palmquist, a Swedish engineer in 1674. The ground-floor arcades, elaborately framed windows, and sculptured attic are so thoroughly in the Italian taste, reminding one of the sixteenth-century work of Sansovino in Venice, that the authorship of an Italian architect must be assumed. Beside it in Palmquist's drawing another building is under construction. The profiles of the bases of the tall pilasters also show considerable knowledge of European architecture.[15]

The Foreign Office was an early example of the direction which Russian architecture was to take. Towards the end of the seventeenth century the progress of Western influence in Muscovy is demonstrated in the building of the State Pharmacy (Plate 98A), later the County Office, in Moscow, on the site of the present Historical Museum.[16] This two-storey structure, in which the first Russian University was established in 1755, was a simple block-like mass broken only by a third storey over the central portion of the side façade. This in turn supported a typical late seventeenth-century tower composed of two octagons on a cube. The architectural ornament was remarkably European, especially the windows provided with columns and curved pediment, the giant order of engaged columns on tall bases, and the entablature of triglyphs and metopes running around the entire structure. Even more influential was the continuous building activity in the German Suburb (Nemetskaya Sloboda) on the eastern outskirts of Moscow. By the end of the century this region, populated entirely by foreign diplomats and merchants, was one-fifth the total size of the capital. In an early eighteenth-century engraving by Hendrik de Witt (Plate 98B) it looks more like a European town than a suburb of Moscow.[17] On one side of the river Yauza were the residences of the less affluent merchants, mostly two-storeyed brick or wooden houses standing neatly along the banks of the river. The steep gables and prim rows of trees tell of Dutch and German influence. On the opposite side of the river were the residences of the wealthier members of the community, including the palace which Peter I built in 1692 for his favourite. the Swiss adventurer François Lefort, his first experiment in modern architecture.[18] In startling contrast to the crowded conditions of Moscow and the haphazard distribution of the palaces in the Kremlin, everything here was laid out in order. The palaces and larger houses were entirely in the European manner, two- and three-storeyed buildings, rectangular in plan, fitted with large glass windows, and decorated with engaged columns, pilasters, and cornices. Even the grounds were arranged as European gardens with avenues, pavilions, orchards, fountains, pools, and even topiary effects.

The effect of the German Suburb on Russian culture turned out to be the very opposite of its purpose. The Tsars had thought to relegate the dreaded foreigners to a quarter of their own, whence their improper customs and heretical ideas could not penetrate the citadel of orthodoxy. Actually the Suburb proved so interesting to the higher nobility that it exercised an inescapable fascination over the younger generation. Here Peter learned his first lessons in European architecture; here he performed his first experiments in building; here he laid the plans for the new city he would later build by the sea.

CHAPTER 18

THE BEGINNING OF MODERN PAINTING:
MOSCOW, 1550-1700

THE Viskovati episode and the decisions of the Stoglav were not the only conspicuous incidents in the course of the long theological and political crisis which was to change the character of Russian art between 1550 and the end of the seventeenth century. So long as the State had needed the help of the Church against the Tartars, the Great Prince and the Metropolitan had shared the responsibility and authority of power. But after 1450 with the decline of the Tartar menace and the fall of Constantinople the Prince considered himself an independent sovereign, while the Metropolitan of Moscow claimed his rights as head of the only independent Orthodox Church. If the State were to remain theocratic, the Tsar must submit to the decisions of the Metropolitan and Patriarch. But after 1589 the problem changed. If the State were to become an effective political and economic expression of the destinies of the Russian people, the Church must accept the political consequences. Three spectacular events marked the difficult adjustment of these problems. In 1568 the Metropolitan Philip, who had courageously denounced Ivan IV's savage cruelty, was deposed, imprisoned, and assassinated by the Tsar's orders. At the close of the Time of Troubles in 1613, however, a new working arrangement was reached, when Mikhail, son of the Metropolitan Philaret (Feodor Romanov), was elected Tsar (1613–45). In order that his father should not suffer any loss of prestige, Philaret was consecrated Patriarch in 1620 and honoured with the title of co-Tsar, so that theoretically if not actually the theocratic State was re-established. This harmonious relationship between Tsar and Patriarch persisted into the reign of Mikhail's son, Alexis Mikhailovich (1645–76). As a young man Alexis deeply admired the Patriarch Nikon, but only so long as the priest recognized the authority of the Tsar.[1] When Nikon offended a large part of the faithful by his arrogance and stubborn insistence on correcting the church books, Alexis finally consented to the calling of the Assembly of 1666 which deposed Nikon and exiled him to a monastery. This was the last stand of the Church against the temporal power. When Peter I allowed the office of patriarch to lapse after the death of Adrian in 1700, there was no one to protest.

Throughout this period the painters of Russia were obliged to work out a new iconography and new technique with which to express a theological system of the world wherein the conflicting claims of State and Church could be approximately resolved. They could no longer 'be faithful to the consecrated type'. The saints and scenes of the older icons had referred to the historical realities of the past; the mystical and doctrinal subjects of the sixteenth and seventeenth centuries were attempts to express the realities of the immediate present, among which was the fear of heresy in the western Russian lands, where Catholic and Lutheran ideas easily entered from Poland and Germany. The search for new means of expression was also complicated by the rise of a new class of patrons. In the earlier Middle Ages there had been only one kind of painting. To be sure, it had been executed under the supervision of the Church, but it had been intended for and had been used by the whole people. After the middle of the sixteenth century there emerged public painting, intended largely as propaganda for the State, and private painting made for individuals and reflecting their own special interests.

The opportunity for a revision of artistic production occurred accidentally early in Ivan IV's personal reign when the fire of 1547 devastated Moscow. The arrival of large numbers of craftsmen from Novgorod and Pskov, and the conditions of their work, led to the organization of the first government workshops for icon-painting, which in time became an important branch of the Treasury. They were established in the Armoury (Oruzheinaya Palata), in the Kremlin, and to the leaders were assigned the conservation and execution of all old and new painting in the churches and public buildings of Moscow. So great was the demand for icons, especially after the Time of Troubles, that numerous painters from the provinces were pressed into the Government service. From the fact that the best of these painters worked exclusively for the Tsar and his family, came the terms 'Tsar's workshop' and 'Tsar's taste' for the superior icons of the earlier seventeenth century.[2]

The government workshops were in effect the first State art schools in Russia. Ancient icons and other materials were collected for the guidance of young painters who were instructed in their craft. Art became a function of government, and in this sense the decisions of the Stoglav and subsequent church councils can be considered official attempts to regularize the production of art objects and bring it more and more under the control of the central power. The Stoglav's injunction to the painters to follow prescribed models was more forcibly restated in 1658: 'he who shall paint an icon out of his imagination shall suffer endless torment'.

A further definition of the relations between art and the State could perhaps be obtained from the important fresco cycles of the later sixteenth century, if more than verbal descriptions of them now remained. After rebuilding the Kremlin palace Ivan IV had the principal State apartment, the Golden Room, painted with a series of frescoes wherein spiritual and secular symbols, spiritual and temporal powers, were strangely intermingled. The complicated cycle, probably prepared by the Priest Sylvester, commenced in an ante-room with a series of didactic pictures related to the preparation of the young Tsar for his duties. (Ivan, born in 1530, had become Tsar at the age of three.) Among the subjects were *The Wise Son is the Mother's and Father's Joy*, *The Fear of God is the Beginning of Wisdom*, and *The Heart of the Tsar is in the Hand of God*. In the hall itself a sequence of Old Testament subjects – the first time such scenes had been painted on such a scale in Russia – included ten pictures of the battles and victories of Joshua, perhaps inspired by Ivan's conquest of Kazan in 1552. These were countered by scenes from Russian history, *The Baptism of Vladimir*, *The Destruction of the Idols*, *The Deeds of Vladimir Monomakh*, *The Story of Boris and Gleb*. On the vaults and by the windows were represented the princes of the Rurik dynasty. Higher still a more religious symbolism prevailed in the painting of Christ as Emmanuel with symbols of the Evangelists and the gates of Heaven and Hell. But even here the intrusion of a secular concept of morality appeared in the allegorical figures of Virtues and Vices, an embracing cosmology of Sun, Moon, and Earth, with signs of the seasons and the elements.[3]

Such a programme, with its elaborate literary content, was not arrived at by accident; it was the expression of the Tsar's conviction that he was the head of both Church and State. Of special importance in this interpretation were the unusually extensive scenes from Russian history. No one, seeing them beside the Old Testament subjects, could doubt whence came the spiritual authority of the Russian Church. This identification of Church and State was worked out in another way in the Cathedral of the Dormition in Sviazhsk, near Kazan, where frescoes of 1558, undoubtedly the work of Moscow painters, unfold the history of the Creation and Redemption with particular attention to scenes and characters on earth, including another lengthy series of Old Testament scenes. The association of the temporal power with the world order was made clear in life-size portraits of Ivan IV and the Metropolitan Macarius among the holy personages, the first time in Russian painting that historical and contemporary personalities had occupied such prominent positions.[4]

Another series of frescoes was executed in the principal chamber of the Faceted Palace for Boris Godunov, when he was regent for Ivan's feeble son, Feodor I. Here was the same combination of biblical episodes, moralizing parables, and allegorical figures, with even more emphasis on Russian history. Nor could the political aspect be overlooked; in the midst was the representation of the reigning 'Tsar, Feodor Ivanovich sitting on a golden throne. ... At the right side of the throne stands the regent Boris Godunov ... and beside him stand the boyars. ... Above them the palace, and beside the palace the cathedral church'.[5]

While an art so expressive of centralized control was being defined in Moscow, elsewhere a new and entirely private art, likewise not immune from secular tendencies, was being developed by the so-called 'Stroganov Masters'. When Novgorod declined after 1470 many of the more energetic citizens migrated to the Novgorod territories in northeastern Russia. Here in the course of the sixteenth century the members of the Stroganov family laid the foundations of a great fortune through the exploitation of salt-mines along the tributaries of the northern Dvina. They founded towns and villages, and through their efforts Perm, Veliki Ustiug, and Solvychegodsk became for a time important commercial and cultural centres. In the latter city, where the principal members of the Stroganov family made their home, churches and palaces arose comparable to those of Novgorod or Moscow.[6] So successful were the Stroganovs that they were among the principal financiers supporting Ermak's conquest of Siberia in 1582, and during the Time of Troubles they were asked to lend money to Tsar Vasili Shuiski.

Two members of the family – the cousins Maxim Yakovlevich (c. 1550–1623) and Nikita Grigorievich (c. 1550–1619) – were unusually interested in art. They were themselves painters, and patronized the best artists they could find. Thus it is that a number of signed and dated icons from the last years of the sixteenth century and the first of the seventeenth, with inscriptions indicating that they were executed for the Stroganovs, have given rise to the supposition that there was a separate Stroganov School.[7] And since many of these icons are of the finest quality, superior to contemporary works of the Moscow School, many excellent icons of the earlier seventeenth century have without further justification been ascribed to the Stroganov painters. The fact, however, that several of the painters who worked for the Stroganovs are also known to have been active in Moscow, and even in the Tsar's workshops, indicates the danger of considering the so-called Stroganov School as much an entity as the School of Novgorod. Indeed, over a period so many different influences can be detected within the 'Stroganov' icons that the title may best be used to describe a kind of icon rather than a style of painting.

In the first place, the signed and dated icons painted for the Stroganovs themselves, and those which can be related to them, are the first examples of Russian icons executed in quantity for private persons. In their size, iconography, and technique they exemplify the tastes of wealthy and artistically sensitive individuals. These icons are small, intended to be held in the hand, of surpassing technical refinement, and depict private rather than public religious experience (Plate 100). The brilliant colours, the lavish use of gold, and the exquisite draughtsmanship are such as would appeal to patrons who intended to cherish them as works of art as well as venerate them as religious objects.

Like the Moscow painters, the Stroganov masters drew from the fund of expressive means common to the sixteenth-century followers of Dionysius, and to that extent are related to the history of painting in Moscow. The Novgorod origin of the Stroganovs themselves, and of the other families of merchants and industrialists who settled in northern Russia, perhaps accounts for the finer draughtsmanship and brighter colours. In this sense the Stroganov icons can be considered a last and brilliant product of the Novgorod schools of the Middle Ages. But since to such stylistic character they added a new interpretation of religious subjects, we must recognize that they also belong to the history of painting in central Russia in the later sixteenth century, in this time of the struggle between Tsar and Patriarch, and that they supply a most important element which had so far been neglected in the controversy, namely painting for the private client rather than for public propaganda.

Nor was their influence strictly confined to northern Russia. With the disruptions of the Time of Troubles, during which not only Moscow but Solvychegodsk itself was plundered in 1613 by the Poles, the Stroganov painters were scattered, and many found their way south. After 1613, when Tsar Mikhail Feodorovich began to repair the devastated cultural pattern of Muscovite Russia, he, like Ivan IV in 1547, was obliged to summon icon-painters from other centres, this time the North and West, and in this way many of the Stroganov masters, voluntarily or against their will, arrived in Moscow and were incorporated in the Tsar's workshops, where they were gradually absorbed into the Moscow school.

Among these painters, one of the first who found a characteristic style of his own was Prokopi Chirin, to whom may be attributed the left wing of a deesis (Plate 99A), of which the centre and right wing were painted by another well-known master, Nikifor Savin. The work of Chirin, who was active in Moscow from 1620 to about 1642, exemplifies some of the most characteristic traits of the transition period between the old styles of Novgorod and Moscow and the new painting of the Romanov period. The figure drawing is firm, the facial expression forceful, and there is clearly the intention of a devotional manner. Yet there is also a conscious aestheticism in the refinement of the drawing, in the svelte forms caressed by gold washes and in the gentleness, even gentility, of the faces. All these modifications of the older religious painting became more marked in one of the most familiar types of early seventeenth-century icon, the one depicting a saint standing in an attitude of prayer. In the first place the three-quarter position of the saint immediately established a spatial relationship between the figure and its surroundings which was further developed in the landscape backgrounds. And to this interest in a specific place and time was added a new concern with the introspective psychological experience of the figure itself. This is seen even in the portrait-like faces. Each saint was no longer an impersonal means through which the worshipper gained access to divinity, but was himself actively engaged in worship, and subject to the same doubts and hesitations as the spectator. In this way a more humanistic spirit entered icon-painting, undoubtedly influenced by innumerable currents of Western art and thought which reached Russia after the introduction of printing in 1552 and the importation and publication of religious books. It is also worth recalling that the region of the Northern Dvina, where the first Stroganov icons were created and where many of the elements of this style were developed, lay along the main trade route between Moscow and Arkhangelsk on the White Sea, the port of entry for foreign traders.

The icon of SS. Vasili Blazhenni and Artemius of Verkoli (Plate 99B) was painted for a member of the Stroganov family towards the turn of the century, and has the characteristically precious technique and refined expression. The saints themselves are also typical of a private attitude towards religion, for they were relatively new to iconography. Vasili Blazhenni, an 'enthusiast' and ascetic, spurned the comforts of civilization. His unclothed figure offered Russian artists one of their few opportunities to paint the nude.

The landscape of this icon, with the views of Moscow and Verkoli, is another proof of the new naturalism growing up within the strictest observance of iconic rules. Although the mountains are still shelf-like terraces, the plants which grow along the ridges are drawn with considerable sympathy for nature and for the infinite variations in the shapes of living things. Yet there is also a feeling for their arrangement as a decorative pattern, seen for instance in the sky, where the clouds, themselves evidence of a new understanding of weather and time, are represented as tight shell-like scrolls. The decorative element in these icons, taken together with the abundance of gold and the miniature technique, suggests that some new oriental influences entered Russian painting at this time. This would not have been unlikely. Although books and pictures were gradually filtering in from the West, from 1550 to 1667, the East was yet far more accessible. Poland and Lithuania still blocked Russian expansion to the West and were engaged in war with Moscow. An icon of St Alexis (Plate 101), the fourteenth-century Metropolitan of Moscow, illustrates how East and West met in Russian painting. The decorative pattern woven in the garments, the gold-washed mountains and the swirling clouds compel one to believe that the painter had some knowledge of Oriental art, that somehow a Chinese painting of the Sung Dynasty had reached Russia by the overland route from the East. Yet much about the icon tells of the westernizing tendencies of these years, the stooping figure of the aged Metropolitan, his expression so full of pathos and an intensity impossible to realize within the older canons of painting.

It should be noted that many of the so-called Stroganov icons, while small and square and executed with scrupulous attention to the smallest detail, are nevertheless not at all crowded. An appropriate balance between the infinitely small and the design as a whole was maintained until the middle of the century, when the concern of the Moscow School for complicated literary and doctrinal subjects overwhelmed the earlier and simpler compositions. The result was a kind of painting which fascinates by the multiplicity of its parts, but which nevertheless has lost much of the earlier power to persuade on other than purely technical grounds. The complicated iconography of such subjects as the Creed or the Lord's Prayer (Plates 102 and 103) supplied the skilled but more pedestrian painters with unheard-of opportunities to demonstrate their virtuosity. Visitors to Russia have never failed to wonder at such icons.[8]

This addiction to small detail was one solution to the dilemma confronting the Russian painter in the middle of the seventeenth century, the problem of how to express in terms of icons the enormous resources of the world of experience and imagination, which the enlarged iconographical programmes of the Church as well as the expanding intellectual horizons of Russia revealed to him. He might try to encompass this wealth of sensation and idea within his traditional technique, or, foregoing the attempt to express in one painting the whole world, he might concentrate on one aspect of it and exploit his visual impressions in the Western manner. He stood to lose as much as he could hope to gain, for in the opposition of the irreconcilable elements of old forms and new content of ancient themes and new tastes, both the old religious conceptions and the traditional technique were destroyed (Plates 100 and 104).

One master of considerable ability almost succeeded in making the new technical methods compatible with the older iconic subjects, but the narrow margin of his failure is only another indication that such reconciliation was impossible. Simon Ushakov (1626–86) at the age of twenty-two joined the Tsar's painters, and for sixteen years he worked for the Treasury, where he painted frescoes and banners as well as icons, drew maps, plans, and made designs for gold and silver instruments, coins and rifles.[9] His 'pictures on paper' are the earliest Russian prints which show an understanding of the Western techniques of copper-plate engraving. Ushakov's early works are not far removed from the miniature-like technique and careful polish of the later Stroganov painters (Plate 106). His mastery of this manner was demonstrated on a notable scale in the large icon of the Annunciation with Twelve Scenes from the Akathist Hymn, which he and two other painters executed in 1659 for the Church of the Virgin of Georgia in Moscow.[10] According to the inscription, 'the background and figures of this icon are painted by Yakov Kazanets, the details by Gavrilo Kondratev, but all the faces of the icon are painted by Simon Ushakov in 1659'. As one might expect from the collaboration of three artists, the work is eclectic, combining the detailed manner of the Stroganov school with an orientalizing, decorative feeling for pattern in the architectural silhouettes and landscape. Only the use of many European Renaissance architectural forms and the large scale of the central figures suggest that Ushakov was a man who had been seriously studying such Western painting as might have come his way.

Ushakov's understanding of Western painting appears to advantage in his celebrated images of the Vernicle (Plate 105), the form which the ancient icon of the Mandilion now usually received. Here is a reasonably successful interpretation of European painting, interestingly enough not of the contemporary Baroque art of Italy or France, but of the now archaic style of Flanders, Germany, and Holland in the early sixteenth century. Only the somewhat more lively play of light over the features might suggest that such icons were painted in the last quarter of the seventeenth century. But by the time Ushakov had mastered this style he was confronted with another obstacle; the contemporary direction of European painting was to a very great degree determined by the implications of oil technique. In tempera Ushakov remained at a stage similar to that reached by Memling or Massys a century and a half before. How Ushakov came to study models already old in his own time, and why he was to all intents and purposes ignorant of contemporary oil practice, must remain a mystery. We can only conjecture that in the German suburb of Moscow he must have seen some earlier religious paintings, treasured by the merchants and commercial agents who had come to Russia.

The relatively naturalistic image of Ushakov's Christ, much more a painting than an icon, is but the best known of many images which in their time met with the most vigorous objection from the higher clergy. In the polemical writing of the seventeenth century it is sometimes hard to tell whether the authors inveigh more against the content or the technique of icons in the new and foreign manner. In the mild and human features of Ushakov's Christ, however, we can feel something of that loss of earlier spiritual abstraction to which the Archpriest Avvakum took such violent exception when he attacked the westernizing painters:

> By God's will much unseemly foreign painting has spread over our Russian land. They paint the image of Our Saviour Emmanuel with a puffy face, and red lips, curly hair, fat arms and muscles, and stout legs and thighs. And all this is done for carnal reasons, because the heretics love sensuality and do not care for higher things.[11]

The defence of modern technique and modes of expression was eloquently set forth by a friend of Ushakov's, one Joseph Vladimirov, a painter of the new persuasion. He protested in a letter to Ushakov against the attitude of a Serbian priest who had denounced as unacceptable one of Ushakov's icons of St Mary Magdalene:

> Canst thou possibly say that only Russians are capable of painting icons, that only icons of Russian painting should be venerated, and that those of other lands should neither be accepted nor honoured? Ask thy father or the elders, and they will tell thee that in all our Christian Russian churches the church plate, chasubles, omophoria, altar cloths and palls, ornamental and gold cloths, precious stones and pearls – all these thou receivest from the foreigners and bringest them into church to adorn the altar and icons with no thought of their being good or bad.[12]

Avvakum's criticism could not stay the tide, nor could Nikon himself, who condemned such icons less for their technique than for their departure from standard iconography. Archdeacon Paul has left an interesting account of a service held by Nikon in the presence of the Tsar and the Patriarch Macarius at which Nikon formally denounced the icons in the new style and dashed them to the floor with such force that they were smashed to pieces.[13] On another occasion he commanded that the eyes of such icons should be gouged out and that after they had been carried in procession before the people they should be burned. At this point the Tsar, who on other occasions had cause to disagree with the intransigent Patriarch, is said to have taken Nikon by the arm and quietly urged that the icons be buried rather than burned.

Alexis's mild remonstrance was characteristic of the man, of his tastes, and of his times. Between his reign (1645–76) and his father's (1613–45) runs the borderline between medieval and modern Russia. In the earlier seventeenth century there were some who had been through the Time of Troubles and so had come into contact with Western matters. But they were still few, and they could not by themselves combat the established way of life. This was the case with the Tsar's uncle, Nikita Ioannovich Romanov, who was 'very rich, and took a fancy to the French mode. He had a particular affection for Strangers (and went) in the French and Polish modes in his cloaths'.[14]

Mikhail Feodorovich himself, but recently seated on the throne, was aware that he must establish some continuity between his dynasty and the earlier Rurikvichi, to whom he was related only in a roundabout way by marriage.[15] More than his uncle or his son he was conscious of tradition, and the important works of his reign were designed to guarantee the historical continuity of Russian culture. Thus for the redecoration of the Dormition in the Kremlin (1642–4), five elderly icon masters supervised a team of a hundred painters in covering the walls and vaults with a thoroughly conventional decorative scheme.[16]

Alexis stood between the old and the new worlds, and accepted the best of both. The major political effort of his reign was devoted to finding a modus vivendi with the hereditary enemy, Poland, culminating in the recovery of Kiev in 1667. After that date a flood of contemporary Western influence moved on Moscow, brought by the southern clergy, who had been educated in the liberal, latinized schools of Kiev. They introduced quantities of books and encouraged the development of printing. In 1669 the brilliant statesman of the reign, Ordyn-Nashchokin, imported eighty-two Latin books. Artamon Matveev, Alexis's friend and counsellor, read Latin and Greek and had the works of Homer, Aristotle, and Vergil in his library. The Tsar, and Nikon before this, had many Latin books. This interest in a learning far wider than the old church books had been able to provide culminated in 1689 in the foundation of the Slavonic–Greek–Latin Academy in Moscow, intended as its name indicates to acquaint Russian students with their twofold cultural heritage of eastern and western thought.

The Tsar and his friends pursued the same course in artistic matters. For the redecoration of the Kremlin Palace Alexis imported tapestries and paintings of secular subjects. Archdeacon Paul admired the colours of a marble pavement and the 'elegant and beautiful ornaments' which a wealthy merchant had brought from Germany for a church he had founded. Paul also had this to say about the houses of the richer citizens, an interesting glimpse of a kind of decorative painting which could scarcely have been supplied by native painters:

We gaped with astonishment at the beauty of their decorations, their solidity and skilful management, their elegance ... and the manifold variety of the painting, in oil colours, both of their interior and exterior walls, which you might suppose were covered with slabs of real variegated marble, or with minute mosaic.[17]

During the Time of Troubles foreign portraits and possibly even portrait painters appeared in Russia in some quantity, as can be seen from the numerous likenesses of the Pretender Dmitri and his Polish betrothed, Marina, which were circulated for political purposes.[18] Under the first Romanovs the taste for portraits increased; Tsars Mikhail and Alexis are the first Russian sovereigns whose likenesses, as they have come down in Russian and European engravings after lost originals, convince us that the artist had seen the living men. Indeed, we know that in 1671 Alexis sat for his portrait, and that other painters of this time worked from the living model.[19]

So far as the development of secular painting was concerned, portraiture was as important a branch of official activity as decorative painting, and the first foreign artists of Alexis's reign to be officially engaged in the Government service were obliged to practise both kinds. One of the first was Hans Detterson, who had entered Russian service in the last years of Tsar Mikhail's reign at the magnificent salary of twenty roubles a month, a considerable sum when many of the Tsar's artists were sending annual complaints to the Treasury about their niggardly wages. A condition of Detterson's employment was that he should teach Russian pupils, two of whom, Isaak Abramov and Flor Stepanov, helped him in painting ceilings and other decorative work. In 1650 Detterson declared to the Treasury that his pupils had learned enough and that if they studied with him only two years more they would be able to paint as well as he. Detterson died in 1655, and in the following year Stanislaus Loputski, a Polish decorator, succeeded to the position of chief instructor in Western technique. He, too, was a jack-of-many-trades, although he seems to have specialized in map-making. That he did not or could not offer a full curriculum in the Western method is seen in the petition of two of his pupils that they be allowed to leave Loputski and study with Daniel Vuchters, a Dutch painter. According to the latter's statement to the Treasury, he had been in the service of 'many monarchs and sovereigns' who had admired his work, and then had been for some time settled in Moscow, where he had married. In the absence of any documented work, it is hard to say whether any of these painters were men of particular ability, although a competent portrait of Nikon surrounded by the clergy of his Monastery of the New Jerusalem was painted with considerable knowledge of Dutch realism and communicated something of Nikon's almost unbearable arrogance.[20]

These men and several after them in the later years of the century seem to have reached Moscow by chance, rather than to have been specially selected for their abilities by the Tsar's agents, as were the Italian artists who worked for Ivan III. Russia may have meant for them a last opportunity to redeem a mediocre talent squandered in years of itinerant activity in Europe, where abler painters deprived them of a living. Certain it is that individually they left almost nothing behind them, and their influence upon younger Russian artists must have been more a matter of encouragement than of example. Until Russian painters could study abroad, or until a master of superior ability could be induced to come to them, they would remain in the trap which had snared Simon Ushakov.

The difficulties of their position and their last brilliant efforts to resolve the antagonism between medieval techniques and modern means of expression are found in the remarkable fresco cycles in the prosperous ecclesiastical and commercial centres east of Moscow. In the Volga cities of Rostov, Vologda, Kostroma, and Yaroslavl there flourished, in the period of political tension and partisan turmoil following the death of Alexis, groups of fresco-painters who wrote the final chapter in the history of old Russian painting.[21] Differences may be noted between different places; the frescoes of Rostov, for instance, are on the whole more conservative in subject and treatment than those of Yaroslavl. Rostov was dominated by its Metropolitan; Yaroslavl was the creation of wealthy merchants. Yet among them all there is a certain community of technical means and expressive intentions. Like the work of the contemporary painters in Moscow, these frescoes, which completely cover the walls of the churches and their surrounding galleries, shared the general seventeenth-century concern for overcrowding with scenes and figures, for bright colours, and fantastic architectural settings. To all this was added a lively curiosity in Western costumes and accessories. For the latter the painters were deeply indebted to a handy compendium of iconographical information, the famous illustrated Bible of Johannes Piscator (N. J. Visscher) (Plate 107B), published in 1650.[22] This collection of almost three hundred engravings illustrating the Old Testament, the Gospels, the Lord's Prayer, and the Apocalypse was so popular that in 1674 a second edition was required. As early as 1673 the influence of Piscator's subjects can be seen in a fresco of Joseph and Potiphar's wife in the Church of St Nicholas in Yaroslavl. In the 1680s and 90s subjects from Piscator dominate the decoration of the Yaroslavl churches (Plate 107A).

It might be thought that in some such way as this Russian painting would gradually be led towards a completer understanding of Western art.[23] But this could not be. Beyond all questions of technical incompatibility – and these were almost insurmountable given the Russians' ignorance of oil-painting – the expressive ends were too divergent. Piscator's illustrators used, for the most part, the forms of Northern European Mannerism, enlarged here and there by the broader energies of the early Baroque. Such an expression, stylistically mature, formally sophisticated, and inherently materialistic, bore no relation to the iconographical and formal requirements of Russian church painting. Yet even if the Russian painters of the later seventeenth century had been more familiar with contemporary European painting, one may still doubt whether they would have found it as useful as Piscator's compendium, by then quite out of fashion in the West. The abrupt perspectives of the high-piled architecture, the accumulation of elaborate decorative detail, and the intricate contrapposto of the flattened figures were just those elements in previous European painting which responded to the visual habits and emotional necessities of the iconic artists. Not Rembrandt or Le Brun, the immediate contemporaries of Ushakov and the Volga artists, but rather the Flemish Mannerists at second hand provided plausible if often inappropriate solutions to their specific spiritual and technical problems. After the seventeenth century religious and secular painting were obliged to go their own ways. For the fashionable circles of Moscow and St Petersburg religious art adopted the Western manner, until its productions became indistinguishable from the adulterated eighteenth-century Baroque painting in the West. In out-of-the-way places, where such were left, principally amongst the Old Believers, it continued in the form of traditional icon painting in tempera. However, this was only a reprieve and led but to the tired repetition of old themes, fatally weakened by the withdrawal of support from the wealthier and more influential parties of Church and State.[24]

PART FOUR

ST PETERSBURG

*

I am at length going to give you some account of this new city, of this great window lately opened in the North, thro' which Russia looks into Europe.

COUNT FRANCESCO ALGAROTTI, 30 JUNE 1739

CHAPTER 19

PETER'S BAROQUE: 1703–1741

PETER THE GREAT'S return in 1697 from his first visit to Western Europe marks the beginning of a spectacular change in Russian art. Although it is true that throughout the seventeenth century Russia had become better acquainted with Europe, Russian culture in general had remained profoundly traditional. The close ties between Tsar and Patriarch had strengthened the policy of closing the frontiers to all but a few travellers, and foreign merchants were confined upon their arrival in Moscow in a separate district, so that their Catholic and Protestant heresies, and their liberal political ideas, should not infect the Russian people. Yet in less than a century the point of view of the Russian upper classes had changed from the terror lest they be mistaken for foreigners to the fear that they might not be. Little more than a generation separated Nikita Ioannovich Romanov, the first of his family to wear Western clothes, from Peter, who always dressed in the French fashion in a short coat, boots, and breeches, instead of the full-length Russian kaftan with long sleeves.

Peter's decision to open his country to Western influence was based upon three considerations: the creation of a government which could negotiate on an equal basis with European powers, free and frequent trade with the West, and a social order capable of understanding Western ideas and making them effective for the national life. In this sense Peter's reforms amounted to a revolution in Russian life, and it is understandable why his more conservative subjects should have looked upon him as the anti-Christ, or a false Tsar. The wonder is not so much that his intentions and actions met with resistance, nor that in encountering obstacles Peter should have grown violent and cruel, but rather that in the short space of a quarter-century he should have accomplished so much. In spite of several attempts by his immediate followers to restore the old order, his work endured, and for the next two centuries imperial Russia was once again what it had been in the days of princely Kiev, a member of the European family of nations.

It may be quite convincingly argued that Peter merely brought to a head currents which were irresistible anyway and would inevitably have opened Russia to the West.

Nevertheless, the city of St Petersburg, which he founded as a practical and symbolic demonstration of his political and social concepts, and which so dramatically summarized
the Russia which he bequeathed to his successors, remains an unsurpassed achievement.
No other eighteenth-century city grew so fast within so short a time. The barren marsh
of 1703 was a world metropolis a century later. The measure of Russia's participation in
European affairs can be taken by the fact that a hundred years after Peter's victory over
Charles XII, which secured for Russia the Swedish-held coast of the Gulf of Finland, the
armies of Alexander I were engaged in their titanic struggle against Napoleon. It is true
that Napoleon had occupied Moscow, exactly two centuries after a similar occupation
by the Poles, but in the end Poland was destroyed and the victorious Russians entered
Paris.

St Petersburg was the principal focus for the artistic reforms undertaken by Peter and
his successors. Here the innumerable small decisions which followed the great decision to
build such a city, resumed, as in a microcosm, the whole history of European art of the
seventeenth and eighteenth centuries. In this sense the dynastic history of the period is of
some importance. The eighteenth century in Russia was to an extraordinary extent a
period of feminine rule, as seems to befit a century in which women played such a prominent part. Another nation, also – Austria – knew a great sovereign in Maria Theresa;
but the succession of talented women on the Russian throne remains unique, especially
since the strongest female personalities alternated with the weakest male remnants of
Peter's line. The tradition of feminine rule had commenced in Peter's minority with the
regency of his older half-sister Sophia. Peter was succeeded by his second wife, Catherine
I (1725–7), but her brief rule was merely a prelude to the political struggles which followed during the three-year reign of Peter's grandson, Peter II (1727–30), the child of
the miserable Tsarevich Alexis Petrovich. During this time reactionary elements in Russian society almost succeeded in re-establishing the Court in Moscow. The next Empress,
Anna Ioannovna (1730–40), the daughter of Peter's older half-brother, Ivan V, had been
brought up in Germany. She returned to St Petersburg, and for ten melancholy years
the Court and country languished under her German favourites. Again a woman's reign
was followed by a few months' occupancy of the throne by a male heir, Ivan VI, the
infant son of Peter's great-niece Anna, wife of Anton Ulrich of Brunswick-Lüneburg.
Since Ivan was only a baby, there was the prospect of a long regency under his mother,
Anna Leopoldovna. The younger courtiers and army officers could not endure another
German rule, and supported the *coup d'état* by which Peter's younger daughter Elizabeth
ascended the throne (1741–62). She named as heir her nephew, Peter III (1762), Peter's
grandson by his older daughter Anne. This Peter, too, had been born and reared in Ger-
many. He hated Russia and was a devoted admirer of Frederick the Great. But if Elizabeth felt obliged to select this foolish young man, because he was her father's last legitimate male descendant, she was more fortunate in her choice of his bride. The German
Princess, Sophie of Anhalt-Zerbst, was married to Peter in 1744. As the Grand Duchess
Catherine, she learned much in eighteen years about her husband, and even more about
Russia.[1] In June 1762, less than six months after Peter's accession, she swept him aside and
began her long and brilliant reign as Catherine II (1762–96). To complete this bewilder-

ing succession of men and women her son, Paul I (1796–1801), was assassinated, after five years of insane cruelty, during a palace revolution.

The work initiated by Peter was carried on by two women who seem, in contrast to their funereal male relatives and predecessors, essentially European, not only in terms of the works of art which they liked and the artists whom they employed, but also in their conception of themselves as empresses. Elizabeth's great good nature and spontaneous gaiety enlivened the simple, even dowdy city of her father and cousin Anna with the intricate graces of Italian Rococo architecture. Catherine II preferred a soberer style which became increasingly severe with time and prepared the final triumph of Russian Neo-Classicism in the reigns of her grandsons Alexander I (1801–25) and Nicholas I (1825–55). But, all the same, Elizabeth and Catherine were always conscious of their position as Tsaritsas of Russia, and the art which they sponsored, although impregnated with European influences and largely created by Europeans, is as much national as the contemporary architectures of Germany, France, or England, likewise created by artists of other countries within the general stylistic framework of the eighteenth century, are recognizably national. Even when a building looks much like contemporary work elsewhere and the Russian accent seems less stressed, we must remember that in the eighteenth century the greater ease of communication, the wide distribution of printed works on architecture, and the more universal training of the architects made them work in a more international style. For all that, the greatest monuments of Russian Classicism are distinctly Russian, and are among the most significant achievements of that phase of European architecture in any country.

Analogies come to mind in other arts. In the nineteenth century the Russians did not invent the forms of narrative poem, novel, symphony, or opera; but Pushkin and Tolstoi, Tchaikovsky and Moussorgsky used the technical means common to European art to create forms inimitably Russian which we number among the masterpieces of world literature and music. The task of the art historian is twofold: to relate Russian artistic expression to its sources in the general European cultural situation, and to indicate the specifically Russian contributions made by Russian artists, and by foreign artists employed by Russians.

It cannot be denied that this contribution was achieved at a heavy cost to Russian tradition. Henceforth the artistic energies of the nation were to be concentrated in St Petersburg, and in the nineteenth century, to a lesser extent, in Moscow, to the detriment of a living folk culture. In ancient Russia the arts had been the arts of all the people, only directed by the Church in the case of the more important monumental work, but even then by a Church to which the great majority of the people subscribed. With rare exceptions the builders of Russian churches, the painters of icons, and the manufacturers who were also the designers of the works of industrial art – all these had come from the people. After the establishment of St Petersburg as the capital, the Russians were usually students of foreign artists. Such a state of affairs inevitably alienated the people from the arts of the Court, which they could neither create nor comprehend. The loss of cultural unity eventually reached the proportions of a national tragedy, until an embittered populace took a terrible revenge upon the upper classes for having deprived them of a right and proper part in the economic, political, and cultural life of the nation.

The history of St Petersburg may be studied in three principal phases, comprising the time from its foundation in 1703 until almost a century and a quarter later, towards the close of the reign of Alexander I, when it had achieved its definitive form as a great capital and as one of the most remarkable expressions of eighteenth-century classicism in plan, form, and detail.[2] Of these the first covers the active participation of Peter and Prince Menshikov in the foundation and first constructions of the city, and continues through the reigns of Peter's immediate successors, his widow Catherine I, and his niece Anna Ioannovna. This period of the first thirty-five years of the city's life is one of experiment, hesitation, and tentative search for the ultimate direction which the city would take. In the beginning there was not even a plan, and the final growth of the city on the mainland was less a matter of choice than of necessity. By the 1730s it was apparent that the centre of population had shifted from the islands to the land side, and the main direction was fixed, when Anna rebuilt the Winter Palace, thereby closing an era of utilitarian building. The reign of Elizabeth Petrovna marks the second period. For twenty years practical interests were submerged in her insatiable love of pleasure. All construction was in the hands of her favourite architect, the Italian-born Count Bartolommeo Rastrelli, and most of his buildings were palaces. St Petersburg added the attributes of an imperial residence to its maritime, military, and commercial establishments. During the third period, which includes the reigns of Catherine II and her grandson, the city received its final classic definition, more as the centre of government than as a port, fortress, or residence. New palaces were chiefly in the suburbs; within the city rose Government offices and ministries as demonstrations of autocratic power. Under Nicholas I (1825-55) the jealous watch which the sovereigns had kept over the development of their city was relaxed and, as with the loosing of the waters of the Neva each spring, a flood of eclecticism was released which threatened to destroy St Petersburg's classic beauty. Only after 1900, through the work of such organizations as the Society of Artist-Architects, was antiquarian interest organized and an effort made to preserve what was left, if not to recapture what had disappeared.[3]

One of the most consistent aspects of this long development was the gradual progression from utilitarian towards symbolic values. Since the architects were usually men of ability, often of genius, and the sovereigns were by and large men and women of taste, it is remarkable how rarely, save perhaps for the Rococo extravagances of Elizabeth, architectural history departed from this course. The explanation must be sought in a number of historical and personal factors, not least of which was the extraordinary way successive strong rulers dispossessed weaker ones whose reigns, sanctioned in other countries by tradition or law, might have countenanced stylistic deviations. Thus Peter II's brief sojourn in Moscow, the prospect of a long German regency for the infant Ivan VI, the possibility of a lifetime of military subservience to Peter III, were quickly eliminated by the decisions of Anna, Elizabeth, and Catherine. Even the foolish Paul, whose architectural excesses threatened for a time to wreck much of his mother's noblest work, was put out of the way after five years. Architectural continuity was thus assured, particularly as the stable reigns of the three Empresses and of Alexander I covered ten, twenty, thirty-four, and twenty-four years respectively.

It might be thought that in thus first of all concentrating on the dynastic succession one were neglecting more significant aspects of architectural history. But Russian architecture from 1703 to the middle of the nineteenth century is pre-eminently an account of the interest and participation of the rulers in the embellishment of their capital, somewhat to the neglect of other cities, which were reduced during this period to a provincial status. This dynastic succession is paralleled by the extraordinary progression of style in the hands of a company of architects, of varying talents and different nationalities. Within each period both foreigners and Russians, the former predominantly Italian, German, and French, worked together to create a new and monumental Russian style. This remarkable homogeneity of expression was largely the result of the frequent participation of Russians in European affairs, artistic and social as well as political and economic. This was assisted by the educational systems in Europe as well as in Russia during the eighteenth century. The growing power of the academies with their planned programmes, competitive examinations, and awards of prizes, and the numerous architectural publications tended to draw the different national traditions into a single body of theory and practice. The final seal of authority was conferred by the international prestige of antiquity. The excavations of Herculaneum and Pompeii and the theoretical justification for the superiority of classical art which was spread throughout Europe by the doctrines of Winckelmann and other archaeologists provided an international unanimity of opinion the like of which the world had not seen since the Middle Ages. How universal this attitude was can be seen by comparing late eighteenth- and early nineteenth-century architecture from widely scattered parts of the Western world. The startling similarity between Bazhenov's Kamenni Ostrov Palace (1765) and James Hoban's White House in Washington (1792), or between Decimus Burton's arch and screen at Hyde Park Corner and a street of early nineteenth-century mansions in the city of Ekaterinburg on the further side of the Urals is due to this international acceptance of a supra-national point of view; for certainly the social, political, and cultural situations in Russian, English, and American life between 1750 and 1830 are more conspicuous for their differences than for their similarities. Antiquity could serve a variety of purposes, so that superficial resemblances should not blind us to the fact that the same forms could be used as symbols of aristocratic romanticism in England, of democratic republicanism in the United States, and of authoritarian autocracy in Russia. Indeed, the latter interpretation of classical forms accounts both for their prevalence in Imperial Russia and for their revival in modern times. Peter and his successors established the tradition of an autocratic architecture which found its most perfect expression, after a century's experiment, in the buildings of Alexander I.

Peter's choice of a site is intelligible only as part of a short-term programme of military and commercial expediency. The islands at the mouth of the Neva were marshy, the waters scarcely deep enough to float vessels of the lightest draught, and frequent floods made transportation dangerous. The climate of these fog-bound wastes was unpleasant and unhealthy; at sixty degrees of latitude the winters were long and dark, the summers brief and hot, spring and autumn almost non-existent. Apart from the water route by way of Lake Ladoga, St Petersburg could only be approached through dense and relatively unexplored forests, whereas the roads to Novgorod and Moscow had been familiar for centuries. Wood was available in the neighbouring forests, but Peter wanted a fireproof city of brick and stone, which had to be manufactured in improvised kilns or transported at an inordinate cost in time and effort from other parts of Russia. Nor would such a situation seem congenial for the development of a typically national culture; for St Petersburg lay on the periphery of Russia close to the Swedish and German enclaves in Finland and the Baltic lands to the west. Yet just this accessibility to other cultures may have appealed to Peter.

In 1702 he had taken the Swedish fortress of Nöteburg on the point where the Neva issues from Lake Ladoga and had renamed it Schlüsselburg, an indication that he considered it a 'key' to the lower Neva and the Gulf. The following year he captured another Swedish fortress, Nienschanz, on the Neva a short distance from the estuary, and the island of Kotlin in the Gulf, where he built the fortress of Kronstadt. Finally, according to tradition on 16 May 1703, the foundations of a new fortress and maritime port were laid, when ground was broken with a sword on one of the larger islands in the delta. Work started at once on two buildings which in time came to symbolize the political and dynastic as well as the commercial and cultural aspects of St Petersburg. These were the Fortress on the large Peter Island, and the shipyards, soon to be called the Admiralty, opposite on the mainland.

For the first few years construction of these and other utilitarian structures was the principal activity; for Peter was still occupied with the Swedes and was also considering the possibility of another town, at the other end of Russia on the sea of Azov, as a warm-water port for trade with the countries of southern Europe and the Mediterranean. Only after his forced withdrawal from Azov and the overthrow of Charles XII of Sweden at the battle of Poltava in 1712 could he turn to his new city. From that year it consumed not only Peter's energies, but also those of his favourite, Prince Menshikov, who was often quite as much master of St Petersburg as the Tsar himself. During these years construction proceeded very slowly because of the difficulties of the site, where all buildings had to be placed on piles sunk in the marshes, and the lack of sufficient labour and materials.[4] Although there were enough houses for Peter's immediate family and relatives, who had moved there in 1710, and for the most essential Government services, much needed to be done even after the city was proclaimed the capital of the Empire in 1712. Forced measures were required, and through a series of ukases Peter conscripted labour, materials, tools, and even a population. Yet so scarce was the supply of stone that in 1714 masonry construction was prohibited elsewhere in Russia, while all vessels coming from Lake Ladoga were ordered to bring stone as ballast. Meanwhile the nobility and government officials were ordered to build houses at once, the size, plan, and materials regulated according to each man's wealth and the number in his family. Even the design of each house had to conform to plans provided by the chief architect. The population consisted either of labourers – little better than slaves – who died by the thousand of overwork, poor food, and disease, or of the upper classes, who had been brutally wrenched from their ancestral homes. But for all that the city was gradually taking shape. By 1717 a panorama engraved for foreign circulation showed a series of substantial buildings lining both banks of the Neva.[5]

Peter had first thought that the island (Plate 108) on which the fortress was constructed, later known as the Petersburg Side or Quarter, would become the administrative as well as military centre of the city.[6] Here were first built, in addition to the fortifications, the two Cathedrals of SS. Peter and Paul and of the Trinity, the Twelve Colleges for use as Government offices, and the markets. Later the colleges and customs were moved to the large Basil Island (Vasili Ostrov), so called from the Christian name of an officer of the public works. Neither of these locations was satisfactory in the long run, for the principal reason that transport to and from the mainland was always slow, usually difficult, and not infrequently dangerous, especially during the freezing and thawing of the Neva. Consequently the centre of the city gradually shifted to the mainland, where houses soon clustered around the Admiralty. Farther to the east a large park was laid out – the Summer Garden – where Peter had a small pavilion for his own use, while the palaces of the nobility stood along the embankment between the Garden and the Admiralty. Somewhat to the south some small streams were widened and straightened into a concentric system of canals, providing transport by water through the city from the Neva and confirming the impression that St Petersburg was built around and upon the water quite as much as Venice, Amsterdam, or Stockholm.

Peter's original idea had been to build a city like Amsterdam, which he had visited in 1697 and where he had been impressed by Dutch efficiency. His admiration for Holland appeared in the name he gave his new city: he called it Sankt Pieter Burkh, pronouncing it in the Dutch fashion. And the first important architect he summoned seems to have known something of Dutch building. This was the Swiss-Italian, Domenico Tressini (Andrei Petrovich Trezin, 1670–1734).[7] Soon after 1700 he was in Copenhagen at work on the palace of Frederick IV. The Russian ambassador, who had orders from Peter to recruit artists, offered him a contract on very generous terms. This was signed 1 April 1703, several weeks before the founding of St Petersburg. Tressini, with ten other master-builders, engineers, and artists, reached Moscow in August by way of Arkhangelsk, since the approaches to Russia from the sea were still held by the Swedes.

Through his experience in Copenhagen, Tressini was familiar with the small-scale late Baroque architecture of northern Europe, which at this time bore many marks of Dutch influence. His ability to design small, practical dwellings, and to construct them in wood and brick, plastered and painted in imitation of stone, was just what Peter and his gentry required in these first years, when more monumental building was beset with difficulties. This sensible, utilitarian style appeared in his designs for houses for the various classes of citizens who were permitted or commanded to settle in the new city. For the upper classes he provided a two-storey house with high-pitched roof, a dignified central doorway surmounted by an open-work balcony, and with the surface of the walls enlivened by quoins at the corners and panels between the windows. Although almost all traces of the earliest urban architecture have disappeared, the character of Tressini's design could still be seen in his Summer Palace (1711–14), built for Peter at the edge of the

Summer Garden. The Palace was distinguished from the residences of the nobility less by its size than by the allegorical scenes in relief in the panels between the first and second storeys. Wealthy merchants were provided with less elaborate one- or two-storeyed houses, while the lower classes had to be content with severely simple one-and-a-half-storey cottages.

Two aspects of this residential building are in striking contrast to previous Russian domestic architecture. The imposition of a definite plan which everyone was obliged to follow according to his means at once gave St Petersburg a uniformity and homogeneity quite unlike the earlier cities where the decorative character of later medieval masonry architecture had encouraged the greatest variety of forms. Secondly, this homogeneity was achieved by a negation of the qualities and peculiarities of materials, an appreciation of which had been one of the most distinctive aspects of older Russian architecture. Peter wished his city to look like those he had visited in Western Europe, which were almost entirely of brick and stone. As these were costly and unavailable in St Petersburg, recourse was had to substitutes. The first houses were of wood constructed according to traditional methods, but on the exterior the logs were shaped smooth and painted to resemble brick or stone; later brick buildings were covered with plaster and disguised the same way. Thus both brick and wood, materials with an ancient and honourable history in Russia, where their special qualities had been evoked for the characteristic styles of the sixteenth and seventeenth centuries, were suppressed in favour of a painted plaster imitation. But an older Russian tradition assumed new significance when these plaster surfaces were painted various colours. Colour had been seen in the painted and gilded churches of Vladimir, in the painting of the interior surfaces of the wooden churches of the North, and in the coloured and gilded tiles which enlivened the stone and brick architecture of the later Muscovite period.

Very little of Tressini's work remains untouched. The early houses quickly deteriorated and were soon replaced. Tressini's ability as a military engineer can be surmised from the Fortress which was of earth and wood, was faced with brick, on the pentagonal plan, with projecting angular bastions, popularized by Vauban and seventeenth-century military science. Within the court Tressini raised the Cathedral Church of SS. Peter and Paul (Plate 110), the first ecclesiastical structure in St Petersburg and one which, as the burial church of Peter and his successors, assumed a venerated position in the legend of St Petersburg as an imperial city. This gaunt and awkward structure does little for Tressini's reputation, but its present appearance is probably not very close to his original intention. When the wooden spire was struck by lightning in 1756, it fell and destroyed the roof and dome. For ten years the church lay in ruins, until it was restored by Catherine II. Although the architect then was the son of the Dutch engineer Harman van Boles (1683–after 1753), a 'master of spire and roof construction', who had built the tower for Tressini, a comparison of the present tower with that which appears in early engravings suggests that it must once have been more gracious and more Baroque. Taste in Catherine's time had turned so far towards the soberer effects of Neo-Classicism that Tressini's church was altogether stripped of its original exuberance and its surfaces flattened and peeled of their ornament. At present only the eastern façade preserves any vestiges of the once vigorous Corinthian pilasters, entablatures, and the papery volutes. The impression which we might thus have had of Tressini is borne out by the robust treatment of the Petrovski Gate in the Fortress (1717–18), the only untouched part of his design.

At best, however, the Cathedral of SS. Peter and Paul was not the most graceful building. The box-like shape and angular plan, with long nave and aisles broken in the centre by a tall iconostasis without relation to the proportions of the interior, show that Tressini either had not familiarized himself with Orthodox liturgy, or that he was following Peter's determination to remodel the Russian church edifice as well as church organization. In contrast to earlier and even later Russian churches, the interior was more like a Protestant 'temple' than an orthodox cathedral, for the wide windows admitted a flood of light.[8] Certainly the excessively tall spire – 394 feet high, as against a total length of 210 feet – more in proportion to the city than to the church itself, was an aggressive assertion of Peter's wish that the horizon of St Petersburg should be the antithesis of the rounded, bell-like aspect of Moscow. Such pointed spires were unknown in earlier Russian architecture and were certainly suggested to Peter during his travels abroad, possibly by his recollection of the forest of spires above London.

Tressini's chief usefulness to Peter lay in just that instinct for utility which militates against his success in the Cathedral. For the ministries he built the so-called Twelve Colleges on Vasili Ostrov (1722–32) (Plate 111B). This was a long row of twelve two-storey pavilions embraced within a colossal order of pilasters resting on a basement. Each pavilion was marked out from its neighbours by a high hipped roof and projecting portico crowned by an attic with volutes. The material was brick with white stone facing for the simple pilasters. The whole effect was practical, reticent, and efficient. Peter had a building which was proof of his intention that his Government was not to become so hopelessly enmeshed in confusion as had the old overlapping offices of the Kremlin. In the nineteenth century the Twelve Colleges were assigned to the new University of St Petersburg, and with the levelling of the roofs their appearance was spoiled.

Tressini's position during his first years in St Petersburg had been that of Master of Building, Construction, and Fortification, in a sense the chief architect responsible for all building activity. But as Peter and his Court became more familiar with European architecture, Tressini's style seemed too plain. He was eventually superseded as chief architect by newer arrivals, although throughout his long career until his death in 1734 he was a respected and busy builder, principally responsible for such public works as hospitals, city gates, and powder magazines, and the barracks at Kronstadt and Schlüsselburg. His most ambitious design was a plan for the Alexander Nevski Lavra (1715) but, because of his failure to orient the principal church towards the east, it was changed and reworked later by other architects. It is regrettable that his first scheme was not executed; for it would certainly have been Tressini's masterpiece and one of the most notable monuments of early Petersburg architecture. He had designed the conventual buildings as a series of staggered blocks around a large rectangular court, joined by pavilions like those of the Twelve Colleges. In the centre the monastery cathedral, resembling the Jesuit churches of the West, was to have been crowned with another exceptionally tall tower and spire. To judge from contemporary engravings, the whole conception would have had a more energetic and Baroque spirit than can now be seen in the altered and damaged works by Tressini which have survived.[9]

When more sophisticated architects were sought to give the city the character of a palatial, governmental centre, it is possible that Menshikov's tastes were more decisive than Peter's. The Tsar himself had liked plain buildings with small, low-ceilinged rooms, a curious preference considering his own great height. Nor did he care for any palace for his personal use. His Summer Palace in the Summer Garden and the wooden house built for his wife Catherine in 1703 were not more pretentious than those of the wealthy merchants and higher officials.[10] When he required a large house for entertaining or the reception of important dignitaries, Peter borrowed one from Menshikov or another friend – a habit he had carried over from his younger days in Moscow, where Lefort's palace had stood ready for his use. The second important architect to arrive in St Petersburg had been, like Tressini, summoned from the service of a European monarch. But Andreas Schlüter (1664–1714), the German sculptor and architect of the Royal Palace in Berlin, enjoyed a wider, even international reputation.[11] He had fallen on evil days after the disastrous collapse of his Mint Tower for the Royal Palace in Berlin, and in 1713 was looking to repair his fortunes when he was offered a contract as Russian 'Oberbau-direktor'. Peter and Menshikov undoubtedly hoped that their new architect would produce buildings rivalling those of the European Courts they hoped to emulate, but unfortunately very little came of Schlüter's residence in Russia. His energy seems to have been vitiated by his misfortunes, he spent most of his time on a perpetual-motion machine, and in any case he died the next year. The most that can be given to him are, apart from the bas-relief panels between the first and second storeys of the Summer Palace, parts of the interior decoration of the same palace, and a drawing for a grotto which was subsequently erected in the Summer Garden by Le Blond. He may also have had something to do with the design of Peter's Cabinet of Curiosities (Kunstkammer, 1718–25), later the library of the Academy of Sciences (Plate 111A). This was built from plans by Georg Johann Mattarnovi (Ivan Stepanovich Maternovi, died 1719), a German architect who came to Russia with Schlüter and who seems to have stood in a close relation to the older man, possibly inheriting his plans and models.[12] The central octagonal section with concave faces divided into panels by rusticated pilasters and surmounted by a stepped tower resembles Schlüter's Tower in Berlin. As it stands now the building has suffered through the removal of the upper storeys of the tower and alterations elsewhere. Whether or not the original conception was Schlüter's, its pedestrian appearance was typical of Mattarnovi, who seems to have devoted most of his short career to a customs house and dockyard. Little more can be said for his severely angular plan for the first Cathedral of St Isaac of Dalmatia (1717), later rebuilt by Herbel, nor for the second Winter Palace (1716), a simple two-storeyed house with a central projecting pediment supported on pilasters and with a rusticated basement; this replaced the earlier and more Dutch-looking residence of 1711. A few years later Tressini more than doubled the size of the Palace and reduced Mattarnovi's façade to the status of an end pavilion beside a monumental entrance motif in the style of a triumphal arch (Plate 113).

Menshikov's role in the development of St Petersburg was dramatically expressed by the two residences built for him by the German architect Gottfried Schädel (Shedel, died 1752), who arrived in St Petersburg in the same year as Schlüter. On the Vassili Ostrov opposite the Admiralty Schädel erected a palace which was the finest in St Petersburg at that time.[13] The general distribution of the plan and mass as a three-storeyed central block with projecting wings and pavilions, each with a separate high roof with each of the storeys carrying its own order of pilasters, may have lacked originality. It resembled a hundred late seventeenth-century noblemen's houses elsewhere in Europe, and for these reasons was probably exactly what was wanted at that time. After Menshikov's fall it passed to the favourites of other sovereigns, until in the later years of the century it was remodelled for the headquarters of the First Corps of Cadets. It then lost almost all its original character, especially when the triple range of pilasters on the main block was re-placed with a single giant order, and the shapes of the windows were changed. In spite of later alterations, the country residence of Menshikov at Oranienbaum (1713–25) (Plate 112), on the southern shore of the Gulf to the west of the city, kept more of its original appearance. The distribution of the various elements recalls the early engravings of the Vasili Ostrov Palace, and recaptures something of that unusual combination of ostentation and domesticity which was present in so many of the early buildings of the capital. The plan of a central block flanked by lower semi-circular wings ending in octa-gonal two-storeyed pavilions was a bold attempt to embrace with some sense of spacious-ness the wide panorama of land and water stretching below the house to the formal gar-dens and so down to the sea. As the first of the larger Petersburg country palaces, Ora-nienbaum had considerable influence on later estates, both imperial and noble.

The other German architects who are known to have worked in St Petersburg after 1715 left little to show for their activity, which may have been largely devoted to public works. The only one who approached the stature of Schädel was Theodor Schwertfeger (in Russia 1716–33), who worked for Menshikov at Oranienbaum and Kronstadt. Later he assisted Tressini in revising the plans for the Alexander Nevski Lavra and himself built the cathedral (1720–32, demolished 1755). From the wooden model (Plate 114A) which has been preserved it can be seen that the rectangular plan was not unlike that of the Peter and Paul Cathedral. Schwertfeger reversed Tressini's proportions by building a more powerful dome over a crossing which occupied almost half the length of the church. At the west he placed two tall five-storeyed towers. The vertical alternation of pilasters and engaged columns shows a lively instinct for the play of Baroque forms which one might almost think Italian, in the tradition of Borromini, were it not that the insistent verticality is closer to North German architecture.

From France came an architect as distinguished as Schlüter, Jean Baptiste Alexandre Le Blond (1679–1719). He was already well known in Paris when he was hired by the Tsar's agent in 1716 at the generous salary of 5000 roubles annually, on the condition that he would teach his art to young Russians.[14] Le Blond, whom Peter himself described as an 'active and intelligent man', had built hôtels in Paris and had edited works on architecture and gardening. But, as with Schlüter, death unexpectedly interrupted a career which held the greatest promise for the future of Russian architecture. As it turned out, French influence, which might with Le Blond have proved a counter-attraction to German and Italian styles, was carried on by the painters, wood-carvers, and decorators who accompanied him to Russia. Immediately upon his arrival in his capacity as superintendent of all architectural work, he organized an Office of Construction, to which all designs were to be submitted. The following year he published his plan for St Petersburg, drawn up at Peter's request, which shows the dangers of theory unsupported by practical considerations. Le Blond followed Peter's thoughts in placing the centre of the city on one of the islands, in this case moving it from the Petersburg side to Vasili Ostrov, which he laid out as a series of straight streets running at right angles between important squares which were also connected by diagonal avenues. An oval ring of fortifications with angular bastions tightly enclosed the city. Rigid and arbitrary as the scheme was, it had its progressive aspects. Such public services as schools, prisons, and hospitals were to be situated on the periphery of the residential areas surrounding the central core of Government buildings, while industries and commercial establishments were placed even further away. But the scheme failed to take account of certain practical and personal considerations. By planning the city on an island, Le Blond inhibited its natural and inevitable growth on the more accessible mainland south of the Neva, and he failed to understand the ambition of Menshikov whose palace was already well advanced and who had no intention of seeing his valuable properties on Vasili Ostrov turned into a municipal housing development. While Peter was abroad in 1717 the initial work was compromised by Menshikov; the canals were dug too narrow for shipping and so poorly that the earth fell back into them.

Le Blond's most important work was his design for the palace at Peterhof, Peter's country residence on the Gulf on the road to Menshikov's Oranienbaum. Like the latter, this consisted of a central two-storey block flanked by low wings terminating in pavilions. But the whole was marked by French restraint and sobriety in contrast to Schädel's Baroque exuberance. The wings were straight instead of curved, and for the fanciful high-pitched roofs surmounted with princely crowns were substituted flat roofs over the main block and a square hipped roof over the central pavilion. Rastrelli later enlarged the palace for Elizabeth and destroyed its original coherence by adding an additional storey and formidably increasing the length in the manner of Tsarskoe Selo.[15] Peterhof, with its formal gardens, terraces, fountains, and cascades, must once have been more nearly what Peter seems to have wanted: a Russian equivalent of the palace and gardens of Versailles which he had visited in 1717. The very names of the pavilions – Marly, Hermitage, Monplaisir – proclaimed that Peter, after having adopted Dutch and German names for his city and palace, was now moving in the wider orbit of French culture.

In addition to his general supervisory duties, Le Blond redesigned the Summer Garden. This park, once more extensive than it is now, was laid out as a series of ornamental and geometrical patterns like those in the separate parts of the park at Versailles. With the disappearance of all the buildings actually constructed or designed by Le Blond, this Summer Garden, even in its later mutilated condition, was a reminder of how successfully he had transported to the Neva the principles of French landscape architecture.

The premature deaths of Schlüter and Le Blond left Peter's remaining plans in competent if uninspired hands. The completion of Le Blond's second country residence for Peter, at Strelna near Peterhof, was carried forward and the palace changed into an Italian villa by Nicolo Michetti (Miketti, in Russia 1718–23), who had worked with Carlo Fontana and in the papal service. But Strelna was thrice rebuilt in the nineteenth century, so that it is of no interest for the Petrovian period. The third and last Italian among Peter's architects was Gaetano Chiaveri (1689–1770), who worked in St Petersburg during the 1720s, at first as an assistant to Michetti. He is best known for the library of the Academy of Science (Plate 114B) in Mattarnovi's Kunstkammer, completed by Catherine I in fulfilment of Peter's wishes. This solemn hall is an admirable expression of the serious side of Petrovian architecture. Practical straightforward arrangements for the storing of the books came first; the decorative adornments, the two orders of columns and the simple but effective design on the ceiling, second. Chiaveri's later works, which included the royal churches in Warsaw and Dresden, were so imbued with the ceremonial gaiety of Borromini's Roman Baroque that we can well believe the sober character of the Library to have been an apt reflexion of the spirit of Petrovian society.[16]

The last of Peter's architects was the first native-born Russian to work in the international style. Mikhail Grigorievich Zemtsov (1688–1743) was born in Moscow and educated in St Petersburg, where as a boy he learned Italian, Dutch, and German – necessary tools for communication with the foreigners in the capital.[17] In 1710 he was apprenticed to Tressini, and later served as his assistant. He also worked with Le Blond and Michetti on the grotto for the Summer Garden. In June 1720 Michetti certified that Zemtsov was capable of undertaking architectural work independently, whereupon he went to Reval to finish Michetti's Ekaterinental Palace, a country seat built by Peter for his wife. When Michetti failed to return from a trip to Italy in 1723, Zemtsov filled his place. In 1725 he designed a temporary 'Salon' in the Summer Garden for the wedding ceremonies of Peter's elder daughter, Anna Petrovna, with the Duke of Schleswig-Holstein. This was a single large hall appearing externally as a two-storeyed pavilion with a giant order of Corinthian pilasters and a low roof behind a balustrade. The taste was Italian, a consequence of his work with Michetti, but the gracious proportions suggest that Zemtsov had absorbed something of Le Blond's French manner. His more lasting contributions were two churches, SS. Simeon and Anna (1732–42) and the Nativity of the Virgin on the Nevski Prospekt (1733–7), the latter on the site of the present Kazan Cathedral. In each case he followed the system of Tressini's Peter–Paul Cathedral, a long, rectangular nave with an eastern dome and western belfry and spire. However, he varied the proportions, reducing the height of the spire and increasing the size of the dome so that the three elements were more in harmony with each other. The interior of the Nativity of the Virgin, as it appears in an eighteenth-century painting, in its spacious lightness and lack of pictorial embellishment far more resembles Wren's city churches than any previous Russian building.[18] Zemtsov's architecture is not very original. Yet if he was more an able eclectic than a creator of new forms, his career is important. It showed that a native-born architect could obtain some understanding and competence in the European manner, even without study abroad. Zemtsov maintained his position as the leading architect of the Court throughout Anna's reign and into the first years of Elizabeth's. Late in life he prepared a new plan for the reconstruction of the palace at Tsarskoe Selo, a work which was ultimately carried out by Rastrelli.

With the accession of Elizabeth an old order ended and a new began. Peter and his immediate successors had been chiefly interested in the architecture, arts, and sciences of the North of Europe. Peter's enthusiasm for German science and Dutch and English technology is seen in the choice of his first architects from among men working in Denmark, Germany, and Holland, although curiously the Dutch architects were the least numerous of all in early St Petersburg.[19] The presence and activity of Tressini, Schlüter, Schädel, and Schwertfeger gave to the first constructions a sober, utilitarian quality which was the visual expression of Peter's military science and political economy. Only with the appearance of Le Blond and the French craftsmen who accompanied him was this sense of practicality relaxed to permit the building of pleasure palaces and the development of extensive gardens, which also had for Peter a practical as well as an artistic interest.

At the time of his death Peter could have looked upon his city with a sense of accomplishment. Its monumental buildings – the Cathedral, the Fortress, the Twelve Colleges – were variations of a European style, to be sure, but they were also not quite like similar buildings in any other country.[20] As yet St Petersburg lacked a truly imperial residence and would have to wait until Elizabeth's Winter Palace came into being. But already fine private residences were standing along the river banks, and if there were only a thin line of flimsy wooden houses between them and the encroaching forests, there was time to grow and space to grow in. The sporadic distribution of its buildings, on the low plains bordering the broad, swift waters of the Neva, gave the capital a wide, if somewhat empty, grandeur. Unloved and unlovable though the city may have been at first, it would acquire in time a strange and oppressive beauty.

CHAPTER 20

ELIZABETH'S ROCOCO:
1741-1762

THE fourth of Peter the Great's successors was the closest to him in blood and most nearly resembled him in character. Elizabeth Petrovna was stubborn, sensual, hottempered, and wholeheartedly devoted to Russia. But she differed from her father in being blessed with great good nature, beauty, and an insatiable ability to enjoy herself. Elizabeth's attitude towards her inheritance can be seen in her affection for Moscow. She of course went there for her coronation in 1742, but she chose to stay a year, holding a gayer and more brilliant Court than the Muscovites had ever seen. And she continued to return to Moscow for lengthy visits throughout the twenty years of her reign, especially to worship at the holy shrines as a pilgrim during recurrent accesses of religious enthusiasm. In this way the old city recaptured some of its prestige which Peter had tried to destroy, and its new status is reflected in the considerable development of architecture in Moscow and its environs during the later eighteenth century.[1]

The combination of Elizabeth's love for her own country with her French tastes – she had once thought of marrying Louis XV, and all her life tried to maintain friendly relations with the French Court – proved extraordinarily beneficial for Russian culture. The influx of French diplomats, travellers who came to pay court to the fabulous Empress and to admire the sights – artists, adventurers, and odd-job men – stimulated an interest in international affairs on the part of the Russian upper classes which Peter had been unable to arouse with his peremptory reforms.[2] It is some measure of Elizabeth's accomplishment that however disinterested she may have been in political and territorial aggrandizement her reign saw the emergence of the first great modern Russian intellectual, the renowned chemist and man of letters, Mikhail Vasilievich Lomonosov (1708/15-65), and the foundation in Moscow of the first Russian university (1755). The spectacular achievements of Catherine II were based, far more than she ever cared to admit, on the cultural and spiritual foundations laid by her predecessor.

The character of the sovereign and of the environment which she wished to create for herself and for Russia appeared immediately in the first works of her chief architect. Count Bartolommeo Francesco Rastrelli (Bartholomei Bartholomeevich Rastrelli, 1700-71) was the son of an Italian sculptor, Count Carlo Bartolommeo Rastrelli (the title was a papal one), who had come to Russia with Le Blond in 1715.[3] As a boy he entered at once into the activity of those first Petersburg years, and soon showed such a talent for architecture that on two occasions, in 1719-21 and again about 1725, he was sent abroad to study. The first time he went to Paris to work under Robert de Cotte; during the second trip, which may have lasted five years, he probably visited Saxony, Bohemia, Austria, and Italy. His talents were recognized by Anna Ioannovna, from whom he received in 1752 the commission to reconstruct Tressini's and Michetti's

Winter Palace. For Anna's favourite, Johann Ernst Biron, Duke of Courland, he began a palace at Mitau. Neither of these works exhibits more than a competent handling of late Baroque forms, perhaps lighter in some respects than the architecture of Peter's time, but fundamentally simple, probably due to the German tastes of Anna and her courtiers. A more vigorous touch, hinting at things to come, possibly once distinguished the wooden palace Rastrelli built for Anna in the Kremlin on the occasion of her coronation in 1730. The Empress was so pleased that the following year she had it re-erected in the German Quarter on the edge of the river Yauza. This 'Summer Annenhof' was burned down in 1746, but was rebuilt for Elizabeth after new designs by Rastrelli.[4]

Rastrelli's real opportunities came with the accession of Elizabeth. For twenty years he not only designed all the larger Government buildings, but also supervised all other architectural activity in Russia. And since, as time passed, more and more of the younger generation became his pupils or followers, his genius is indelibly printed on Russian architecture of the middle years of the century. It was fortunate for Rastrelli that his imagination was matched by Elizabeth's taste. In this most autocratic of empires he survived what for a less talented man at the hands of a less generous sovereign would have meant exile and disgrace. It is little less than miraculous that he was in turn the architect of Anna Ioannovna, of her German favourites Biron and Münnich, and of the Regent Anna Leopoldovna, for whom in 1740 he began the 'third' Summer Palace. This work involved only the enlargement of the little cottage Peter had built at the bottom of the Summer Garden for Catherine. The plans were revised and considerably enlarged for Elizabeth, so that in the end the new Summer Palace (Plate 115B) was the most magnificent building in St Petersburg and the Empress's favourite city residence. It was built of wood, a material Rastrelli had already used in his vanished palaces in Moscow. Elizabeth's own spirit also began to work its spell; for the building, to judge from contemporary paintings and engravings, had a truly fairy-like character. In plan it was French. From the street a central two-storey block which contained a single large ballroom somewhat in the manner of Zemtsov's pavilion of 1725 was flanked by one-storey service wings forming a courtyard not unlike that of a Parisian *hôtel*. The central block carried two orders of pilasters, while the long expanse of the wings was broken only by pedimented windows and angle pilasters in the Italian manner. The flat roofs supported balustrades and a host of ornamental statuary. On the north the palace faced the Summer Garden across the Fontanka. Here, where the main storey stood upon a high basement and the gardens were reached by a double flight of curving steps, the effect was more Italian.

In this first building of the new reign the quality of Rastrelli's architecture is already clearly evident. In the best sense of the word he was an eclectic, with that rare ability to combine elements from other styles in something not wholly derivative nor entirely untraditional. Elizabeth and her Court wanted neither. It was well that the palace resembled those of the Courts of Western Europe, and yet that it was something which could only have been created in St Petersburg. The specifically Russian characteristics were undoubtedly due to scale and colour, two aspects which disappeared for ever when Paul I tore down the Summer Palace to make way for his Michael Castle.[5]

After the new Summer Palace, Rastrelli's next task was to finish the Anichkov Palace (Plate 115A), on the Nevski Prospekt by the Anichkov Bridge over the Fontanka. In 1742 Elizabeth had commissioned Zemtsov to design this residence for Alexis Razumovski, but the Russian architect died the next year. After 1744 Rastrelli finished the palace as a five-part structure, with central and end pavilions separated by lower wings. As in the Summer Palace, the details were Italian, but the exuberant, dome-like roofs over the pavilions are the first hints of Rastrelli's growing appreciation of older Russian forms. The Anichkov Palace was several times rebuilt and so thoroughly altered that only early engravings show its original character. In Makhaev's view of 1761 can be seen the contrast between the commanding height of the palace and the low, one-storey housing after Tressini's designs.

Within the next few years Rastrelli built many town residences for the nobility, but only two still preserved into the twentieth century their original exteriors. The Vorontsov Palace, later the Corps of Pages (1743–5), recalls the Summer Palace in the distribution of the pedimented windows and the arrangement of coupled pilasters and paired columns about the main entrance. Now the material is masonry and the forms have grown noticeably more sober and more assertive. If the relation to the Summer Palace could be considered a dynastic one – for Vice-Chancellor Vorontsov was related to the Empress by marriage – the building marks an important transitional stage between the caprice of the Summer Palace and the more august work Rastrelli would shortly create for Elizabeth. The projection of the paired columns, on the lower storey grouped with masterly freedom and all the more effective for their omission above, gives the central part of the façade an almost sculptural form. The second of Rastrelli's preserved palaces, for Baron Stroganov (1750–4), is closer to his imperial work. Here the earlier compartmented façade with two storeys of windows of equal size has been reorganized as a *piano nobile* on a basement with an attic above. The irregular windows are framed in the more playful style of the German or Austrian Rococo. The central element receives a more vigorous treatment, as the upper storeys are bound together by a giant order of coupled columns, the inner pairs supporting a curved, broken, and recessed pediment. The proportions of the whole have been somewhat spoiled by a rise in the level of the street, so that the windows in the rusticated basement have lost a third and more of their height. The Stroganov Palace, more than any of Rastrelli's work up to this time, shows his genius for combining the fancy of Rococo decorative devices with a powerful handling of aggressive Baroque forms.

Rastrelli's next task was the reconstruction of Peterhof. Elizabeth cherished this palace for its memories of her father, but his simple small rooms could no longer accommodate the crowd of pleasure-seekers who clustered around her. As early as 1741 she decided to enlarge the palace, but the revised plans were not accepted until 1747, and the palace was not finished until 1752. Elizabeth insisted that Rastrelli double the length yet retain the general *ordonnance* of the central block, to which he was obliged to add one storey in order to keep it the dominant element of his composition (Plate 116B). For this reason the central part of Peterhof is less Rastrellian, preserving as it did something of the early discretion of Le Blond. The interiors have been altered, but the Merchants' Hall (Plate

118C) and Staircase preserves much of the original brilliance of Rastrelli's inexhaustibly inventive decorations.

Rastrelli's flair appeared in the two square pavilions at the end of the wings, one containing the palace chapel and the other known as the Pavilion of the Coat of Arms. They are flanked by low wings and bear the familiar giant order of pilasters on a high basement. The roofs, in the form of rectangular flattened domes crowned with lanterns and bulbous cupolas, are among Rastrelli's most ingenious Rococo improvisations on a theme from older Russian architecture. Elizabeth herself suggested the study of the late seventeenth-century churches of Moscow. Examples of her interest in these are the two facts that in 1746 she unexpectedly ordered Rastrelli to change the original one-dome design for the palace chapel at Tsarskoe Selo to five domes, and in 1747 she commissioned another five-domed church in St Petersburg after an 'approved model' based on drawings and measurements which had been made from the cathedrals in the Kremlin.[6]

The church at Peterhof was the first of a series wherein Rastrelli recovered for Russia the older Orthodox form after its brief eclipse by the churches built for Peter the Great. In his Cathedrals of St Andrew in Kiev (1747–67) and of the Smolny Convent in St Petersburg (1748–55) Rastrelli united the most spontaneous enthusiasm with a sensitive understanding of the harmonious relation and distribution of the parts. Both churches were Rococo in the fullest sense of the term, if by that we can understand that a very personal attitude towards Baroque forms has been imbued with a gay, secular feeling. Each was extravagant, not so much in the sense of the cost or value of the materials, as in the prodigal expenditure of architectural devices, yet each was at the same time unmistakably a church. The now destroyed Church of St Andrew was erected by Prince Razumovski, Elizabeth's morganatic husband, on the highest point of land in the old city where St Andrew was said to have preached. The plan was a Greek cross, lengthened along the east–west axis by the projecting apse and western bay. The four subsidiary domes took the form of small lanterns above buttresses extending diagonally from the angles of the cross. Additional importance was given to these projections by the paired engaged columns, in contrast to the paired pilasters which adorned the walls of the church itself. In the design of the central dome and subsidiary cupolas Rastrelli devised a variety of forms which in plan, section, and profile composed an intricate counterpoint upon the principal theme. Nowhere else could his genius show to better advantage than in the contrast of this white-and-gold invention with the lumpy, provincial Baroque decoration with which the legendary early churches of Kiev had been smothered (Plate 5A).

For Elizabeth's Smolny Convent, an establishment for orphan girls to which Catherine II later added a school modelled after Mme de Maintenon's seminary at St Cyr, Rastrelli devised a vast plan of conventual structures arranged in a Greek cross with domed pavilions at the re-entrant angles repeating in diminished proportions the form of the Cathedral in the centre. The model, which is still in existence, shows how carefully he intended the general silhouette to resemble the great monastic establishments of medieval Russia. The many domes and lanterns would have recreated the impression of churches rising behind the fortified walls of some older monastery. Over the main entrance Rastrelli intended to place an exceptionally tall tower, even loftier than the belfries of the older monasteries. Here again he combined the old and the new, for if the lower portions were treated as a rather ponderous version of the typical Baroque many-storeyed tower complete with columns, pediments, and brackets, the upper part was planned as a vertiginously elongated version of the tower of Ivan Veliki in Moscow. The unusual height may have been due, however, quite as much to Rastrelli's desire to create a monument which would dominate both the city and the convent, as to the Russian taste for sheer size (Plate 118A).[7]

The magnificent Cathedral was only begun by Rastrelli, and the lack of all the ornament which he wished to use to enliven the façades cannot be blamed on him. The wooden model, cut away to show the interior, proves that Rastrelli did not intend to place the subsidiary turrets so close to the central dome, and that the white-and-gold interior of the church would have been one of his most generous decorative schemes. As it happened the work dragged on and was finished only in 1835 by the architect Stasov, who replaced Rastrelli's original designs with a chastely severe neo-classical interior in white and gold, and grey marble.

Rastrelli's last large works for Elizabeth were the two most important imperial palaces, and however much their Rococo style was scorned by later rulers, they fixed the forms and symbols of the residential architecture of the Russian autocracy.

In the rebuilding of the Great Palace (later called the Catherine Palace) at Tsarskoe Selo (1749–56),[8] and the Winter Palace in St Petersburg (1754–62), Rastrelli again had to deal with unusually extended façades, as had been the case before at Peterhof. The Great Palace of Tsarskoe Selo (Plate 116A) is 978 feet in length, and unlike Peterhof this tremendous range is unbroken by any significant projections or changes in height. As at Peterhof, Elizabeth insisted on preserving as much as possible of the original palace, built for her mother, Catherine I. Rastrelli's problem was to find some way of adding larger State apartments to this relatively modest core which he had inherited from the reconstruction of the palace by the Russian-born architect Kvasov.[9] The original element – a three-storey block with slightly projecting pavilions at the centre and ends separated by ranges of four windows' width – was in itself a more up-to-date version of Le Blond's central block at Peterhof. By enlarging the palace through the almost endless extension of the wings, Rastrelli could do little more than perform variations on the same theme. His effort was concerned with the parts rather than with the whole. For the long wings he adopted the powerful entrance motif of the Stroganov Palace: a series of alternate pairs of pilasters and boldly projecting engaged columns supporting broken pediments. The original colours may have enlivened the endless expanse of columns and windows; for the walls were painted yellow, the architectural ornament white, and the figure sculpture, caryatides, and garlands were gilded.

For the park at Tsarskoe Selo, Rastrelli designed three domed pavilions with one-storey wings ornamented with the familiar repertory of engaged columns and curved, angular, and broken pediments. The Hermitage (1748–52) and the Grotto (1755–62) were preserved to modern times, but suffered somewhat through the loss of much of their sculptural decoration. The finest of the three, Mon Bijou (Plate 119), familiarly called in Russian Monbezh, was allowed to deteriorate, and in the 1820s was demolished by Nicholas I to make way for a pseudo-Gothic 'Arsenal'. The disappearance of Monbezh is very regrettable, if the eighteenth-century engravings have correctly preserved the Rococo brilliance of this little pavilion. The multiple flights of steps were among Rastrelli's finest studies in Baroque space, and the dome, with its bulbous cupola, was yet another fantasy first evoked at Peterhof. Rastrelli's design for the park and gardens closely followed the irresistible example of Versailles. Near the palace were small geometrical *parterres*, in the distance wooded groves bisected by broad avenues.[10]

The fourth and final Winter Palace in St Petersburg presented once more the same problem of an interminable façade which had to be unified (Plate 122B). Rastrelli designed a tripartite treatment along the Neva first and a quintuple arrangement for the front on the Winter Palace Square. But the façades are yet too long; on the Neva the end pavilions consist of no less than nine bays, and the effect is that of an endless succession of identical parts, however skilful the alternation of window and column may be within the separate groups. For the *ordonnance* Rastrelli returned to a more Italian arrangement than he had used since his first work. Upon a low basement he placed three storeys, the upper two embraced by a giant Corinthian order, so fantastically elongated that they seem to crush the engaged columns on the lower storey. This depressed effect, however, has undoubtedly been exaggerated by the disappearance of the basement, when later on the ground level was raised. Since Elizabeth and Rastrelli preferred above all else the graces of the Rococo style, perhaps the pleasantest parts of the Winter Palace were the treatment of the windows and the host of statues and urns which once cavorted on the balustrade above the cornice. When the palace was new and painted turquoise blue with white trim, it must have shimmered in the waters of the Neva, the last and most exuberant of Elizabeth's creations. In the nineteenth century a uniform coat of dark red paint extinguished its gaiety, and the interior suffered even more grievously. In 1837, after a fire which raged three days, it was completely rebuilt and renovated according to the eclectic tastes of Nicholas I. Only the Jordan staircase, so called because the sovereign descended it for the annual Blessing of the Waters on the Feast of the Epiphany, kept its Rastrellian character, the character of the Merchants' Staircase at Peterhof.

A comparison of the three immense palaces – Peterhof, Tsarskoe Selo, and the Winter Palace – with the Smolny Cathedral and its belfry, St Andrew in Kiev, the pavilions of Monbezh and the Hermitage at Tsarskoe Selo, even with the oratory of the Holy Sepulchre in the New Jerusalem Monastery (1747–60),[11] shows that Rastrelli was not really a monumental architect. He excelled when the programme required a small unified structure. Like all true artists of the Baroque inheritance, he saw shapes sculpturally. Perhaps that is why his smaller buildings are so complete; Rastrelli visualized them from all sides, as three-dimensional objects. The large palaces offered no such opportunity, and his imagination flagged when faced with the design of a long and flat façade. His use of columns at Tsarskoe Selo and of a two-storey *ordonnance* of engaged columns and pilasters at the Winter Palace was an ineffectual attempt to escape from what he must have felt as a menace of formidable sterility.

The significance of Rastrelli's accomplishment for Russia lies in his creation of a consistent Russian version of the late Baroque, distinguished from its European counterparts by its scale, its plastic exuberance, and its colour. Had Smolny been completed as he designed it, the conventual city of towers and domes, painted blue and white with details picked out in silver, would have been one of the most sumptuous monuments of the style. Rastrelli's informed and tasteful eclecticism was undoubtedly drawn from many sources, a circumstance common at the time. Yet though his work shows many resemblances to contemporary architecture elsewhere, especially in Northern Italy and Austria, we may, in the absence of documentary information concerning his early life and travels, postulate his use of published sources.[12] The unmistakably theatrical quality of his architecture may even have a more direct relation to the theatre than has been suspected. The long façades of his palaces, the diagonal axes of his church towers, and of the wings of his garden pavilions, the unexpected and inexplicable vertical elongation of his orders, are expressions of a visual rather than of a structural or functional æsthetic, such as he could have studied in the engravings of Piranesi and in the theatrical designs of the Bibienas.[13] If this be so, then Rastrelli, perhaps more convincingly and certainly more grandiosely than any of his predecessors or contemporaries, made as imperceptible as possible the transition from the life of the stage to the life of the world. In this connexion we should not forget that his vivacious Empress was happiest in masquerade.

When Elizabeth died in January 1762 Rastrelli's influence passed immediately.[14] The new Tsar, Peter III, was more interested in drilling troops than in building palaces, and his wife, the Grand Duchess Catherine, had no more patience with his tastes than with those of her frivolous aunt. She was determined to alter matters drastically, and in a very short time she did.

CHAPTER 21

THE CLASSICISM OF CATHERINE II :
1762–1796

IT is a paradox of Russian history that the greatest sovereign of the Romanov dynasty should have been neither a Romanov nor a Russian. The Princess Sophia of Anhalt-Zerbst was a German by birth and education, but when she was married in 1744, at the age of fifteen, to the Grand Duke Peter, she entered the Orthodox Church, took the name of Catherine, and settled down to make a career for herself in Russia. Six months after Elizabeth's death Catherine won the support of the guard regiments in St Petersburg, swept her weak and spiteful husband aside, imprisoned him, and probably countenanced his assassination a few days later. When she had secured the throne, she immediately demonstrated that singular combination of intelligence, energy, and taste which marked the thirty-four years of her reign. Her character was a compound of moral purpose, calculation, and instinct. Her sensuality surprised even her contemporaries; her opinions were respected by Voltaire, Grimm, and Helvétius. In her political actions she alternated between conservative liberalism and traditional Russian autocracy. She abolished torture as a legal instrument, yet condemned the Metropolitan of Rostov to perpetual solitary confinement for opposing the sequestration of Church property. She undertook, unsuccessfully to be sure, the revision of Russian law, in the hope of providing equal justice for all classes, yet she participated as greedily as Prussia and Austria in the three partitions of Poland. In these opposed though complementary aspects of her character she does not differ essentially from other sovereigns of the eighteenth century whose concepts of enlightened despotism combined a cruelty which appals us with a theoretical liberalism we can admire to-day. For the history of Russian culture Catherine's enigmatic personality was of the greatest importance. She possessed both an informed interest in European thought and taste and a sincere affection for and knowledge of her adopted country. No other ruler, with the exception of Peter the Great, travelled so widely throughout the country, and it is probable that no other had so comprehensive an understanding of the history and traditions of Russia.[1] During her reign the art of architecture lost the last vestiges of provincialism and became if not a decisive at least a fully valid contribution to the history of European art. The other arts – literature, painting, and sculpture – were slower to develop, but the foundations for their future triumphs were laid during Catherine's reign, and largely through the institutions which she fostered and the climate of opinion which her lively intelligence induced. Those who consider a church by Rastrelli only a Russian variant of the European Rococo will be obliged to admit that the Admiralty of Zakharov (1806) and the poetry of Pushkin (1799–1837) are not only great works of Russian art but, in spite of all the difficulties of distance and translation, are important contributions to European classicism and romanticism. And neither is conceivable without the artistic preparation of Catherine's reign.

Catherine's taste was always a decisive factor.[2] Peter the Great and Elizabeth had both lived publicly, the father as a jack-of-all-trades and the daughter as the leader of a never-ending masquerade, and their buildings expressed their personalities. Catherine kept her public and private lives apart. For the first time in Russia the private and the official life of the sovereign were different in purpose and character. This situation, unimaginable in Muscovy, and unnecessary for Peter or Elizabeth, enabled Catherine to live as a European citizen, while outwardly maintaining the apparatus of an imperial state. Thus the buildings of her reign are of two different kinds; public buildings which surpassed in intention if not in execution anything hitherto proposed in Russia, and private buildings for her own use. Between the two a third class consisted of large palaces erected for her favourites, or by the wealthier gentry. They were less willing than Catherine to withdraw from the public eye and more anxious to attribute to themselves some of the magnificence which, as the owners of enormous estates and masters of thousands of serfs, they were able to afford.

The architecture of Catherine's reign represents not just one phase of later eighteenth-century classicism, but includes several interesting changes of direction and of emphasis. Through the 1760s Catherine's first task was to establish a new point of departure by dispersing or dissolving the traces of the Rococo inherited from her aunt.[3] From the later 1760s and through the 1770s a more energetic attitude of innovation appeared in the work of three architects of different nationalities: Velten, a German, Rinaldi, an Italian, and Bazhenov, a Russian. Each created at least one important building which, though still Baroque in plan or elevation, was at least more demonstrably classic in detail than any previous work. Bazhenov's designs were the culmination of the Russian Baroque in the hands of a master of plan and organization, but one whose very energy seems to have compromised him with the Empress. The third and last phase was marked by a thorough-going classicism based on the interaction of two influences: the study of antique architecture and the revival of Palladio. Again this was in the hands of an international triumvirate: the Scotsman Cameron, the Italian Quarenghi, and the Russian Starov. Starov came last; and he committed the architectural future of Russia for two decades or more to that strict classicism known abroad as the Empire Style. For another half-century Paul I, Alexander I, and Nicholas I, in a sense merely continued with modifications the fundamental elements of plan, structure, profile, and detail worked out by Catherine and her architects from 1780.

Catherine's preference for a simpler style than the Rococo was prompted as much by instinct as by her contempt for the antics of Elizabeth. Yet at the start she was obliged to look to the past for her first architectural projects. Even in the midst of Elizabeth's reign there had been agents at work ready to modify the Rococo. They would probably have done so even had Elizabeth herself lived longer. Such an agent was the young Count Ivan Ivanovich Shuvalov (1727–97), who of all his countrymen was probably the one most in sympathy with European civilization. He spoke several languages, had travelled extensively, and corresponded with several of the leading *philosophes*, including Voltaire and Helvétius. Under his patronage the young Russian architect Alexander Filippovich Kokorinov (1726–72), who had been trained in Moscow in Prince Ukhtomski's school, built a palace in St Petersburg (1753–4) where a precocious use of academic, even neo-classical, details was combined with a new sobriety in the plain walls relieved by the slightest of window-frames and panels. In the windows, too, he abandoned Rastrelli's aggressive plastic ornament for simple rectangular and oval shapes.[4]

Since it is unlikely that a Russian architect could have learned in Moscow, in a school saturated with Rastrellian influence, these decorative touches so thoroughly in the spirit of French classicism of the 1750s, it is probable that Shuvalov himself had discovered them in his travels. Shuvalov then commissioned the distinguished French architect, Jean François Blondel the Younger, to design a building for the Academy of Fine Arts which he proposed to establish as a branch of the University of Moscow, founded through his initiative in 1755. The Senate, in response to Shuvalov's eloquent memorandum, issued a ukase in 1758 for the establishment of an academy and the erection of a proper building in St Petersburg.

In 1759 Shuvalov summoned to Russia and appointed as a professor in the new Academy the French architect Jean Baptiste Michel Vallin de la Mothe (1729–1800, in Russia 1759–75).[5] Since the similarity between Blondel's design for the projected Academy in Moscow and the present building is striking, it may be that the younger architect was urged to make use of it, or perhaps even to enlarge and make more monumental a structure commenced by Kokorinov from Blondel's designs before the arrival of Vallin de la Mothe. At all events through Kokorinov's long association with the Academy as professor, vice-rector, and rector, the building may have gained much of its character, and Levitski's portrait (Plate 148) showing him pointing to the plan suggests that by his contemporaries he was considered largely responsible for the work, perhaps as a general superintendent.[6]

The French inclinations of Shuvalov and Kokorinov found a full and very beautiful expression in Vallin de la Mothe's design (Plate 123A). It is a square around a large circular court flanked by four smaller rectangular courts. For the time this was a practical as well as palatial solution. From the principal entrance a double flight of stairs leads up to a circular ceremonial hall. To the left and right are long galleries for exhibitions culminating in octagonal halls at the far ends. Along the sides and around the circular courtyard are the drawing- and painting-rooms, and a chapel for the students and faculty. On the exterior Vallin de la Mothe retained Blondel's two storeys above a rusticated basement embraced by a giant order and the central pavilion, but he replaced the awkward roof with a low dome. Even though his design suffered in execution through the substitution of pilasters for columns except on the pavilions, the suppression of the roof, and the elimination of some delicate detail around the base of the dome, the Academy takes a noble position among the institutional buildings along the Neva. The increasing experience and sophistication of architect and patron alike could be seen by comparing Mattarnovi's strenuous but clumsy Kunstkammer, a few hundred yards to the east, with this dignified structure.

The Academy of Fine Arts must have made a deep impression on Catherine; for shortly after its completion she commissioned Vallin de la Mothe to build the first Hermitage (1764–7), intended as a private residence whither she might withdraw from the draughty grandeur of the Winter Palace. The façade on the embankment shows Vallin de la Mothe working in a manner little removed from that of his Academy. Upon a high rusticated basement he placed two storeys embraced by a giant order of pilasters and accentuated by a projecting portico of six columns. The delicate details, the slightest sculptural treatment of the keystones of the round-headed windows, with a carved Greek key above them, are in the best French tradition. On the inner, street side he skilfully tied his building to Rastrelli's florid palace through the use of doubled columns on the lower storey, each supporting a section of an entablature. But at the upper storey he returned to his own scheme of pilasters, rounded windows, and swags and garlands in very low relief.[7]

For the city of St Petersburg, Vallin de la Mothe built the Markets (Gostinny Dvor) on the Nevski Prospekt, a huge two-storey arcade round a large open court.[8] In a nineteenth-century alteration the building lost much, including the bases of the capitals, but the stark forms demonstrate a workman-like approach to the problem of conferring upon a humble building something of civic dignity. This quality is even more apparent in the untouched portions of the brick-and-stone gateways and warehouses of New Holland (1765), originally the main port of St Petersburg to the west of the Admiralty. The arrangement of coupled columns flanking an arch with round-headed windows at the corners is so close to the Markets that New Holland must be attributed to Vallin de la Mothe in the absence of documentary evidence. Only he could have invented this combination of heavy mass with delicate detail, still to be seen in the profiles of the arches and windows. Since this warehouse was never plastered or painted, the frankly exposed materials have a majestic dignity more like the masonry imagined by Piranesi or Hubert Robert.

This ability to create a composition serene and dignified yet richly Baroque appears in the work of Catherine's second architect, who also had come to Russia during the reign of Elizabeth. Antonio Rinaldi (c. 1709–after 1790) had worked in Rome some time before the middle of the century, and had been brought to Russia by Cyril Razumovski, the younger brother of Elizabeth's lover and morganatic husband, Alexis Razumovski.[9] In 1755 Rinaldi helped Cyril Razumovski, now Grand Hetman of the Cossacks, to raise the village of Baturin to the position of a 'capital'. Little was built but the palace, subsequently entirely reconstructed. In 1755 Rinaldi was in St Petersburg, and the next year he was appointed Court architect to the Grand Duke. Peter put him to work at Oranienbaum to enlarge the pleasure pavilions of the old Menshikov Palace. His first works – a large hall for theatrical performances and the Chinese Pavilion – have not survived, but his later Chinese Palace (1762–8) revealed his knowledge of the more exotic aspects of the Rococo. Like many such structures elsewhere in Europe, the exterior was relatively sober: a low one-storeyed central portion with side pavilions connected by short wings. The decoration in the Chinese taste was limited to the interior, which consisted almost entirely of frescoes executed by Italian decorators.[10] The Chinese Palace proved that the Russian Court was aware of the latest trends in European architecture. This style, so thoroughly unoriental, which by a curious inverted process reached Russia not directly from the East but by the long way round from China through Europe, enjoyed an international currency in the 1750s and 1760s. The Oranienbaum pavilion is not far removed in spirit or date from Frederick the Great's tea-house at Potsdam (1754–6), or the similar structure at Drottningholm (1763), to mention only two of these eighteenth-century *chinoiseries*.

Rinaldi's own taste for simplicity had a better chance to appear in the two-storey pavilion which is all that is left of his 'Sliding Hill' (Katalnaya Gorka) at Oranienbaum. A 'Sliding Hill' is a helter-skelter, or a chute-the-chutes, that is an artificial slope down which people coasted in winter on sledges or in summer on small wheeled carts. In a country so flat as northern Russia even such a slight elevation provoked a sensation of height and speed, and the Hills were popular attractions at fairs and public parks. The actual mechanical apparatus has long since disappeared, but Rinaldi's two-storey pavilion was preserved as an example of the sobriety of later eighteenth-century pleasure architecture. The plan recalled the Baroque dispositions of an earlier age in the central circular hall with three square wings. Only the crowning element – a slender tapering dome somewhat like a Chinese hat – was at all fantastic. Otherwise the walls with their severe pilasters and the surrounding verandah with alternating paired and single columns were calm and dignified.

Rinaldi built two important private palaces for Catherine's favourite, Prince Grigori Grigorïevich Orlov. In the city the Marble Palace (1768–72), so called from the veneer of red granite and grey Siberian marble which covers the exterior, was the first building to be faced with such splendid materials (Plate 123B). The façade presents the familiar eighteenth-century ordonnance of two storeys framed by a giant order of pilasters resting upon a high rusticated base.[11] Yet this severe effect is lightened at intervals by the window niches inserted in the centre of each principal façade and by the interruption of the panelled attic by a large coat-of-arms in the centre of the roof over the niches. Above the main entrance, which was approached through an open court, Rinaldi placed a clock-tower with a broken pediment, a last Baroque intrusion in a design which was settling into the soberer mood of Neo-Classicism. The interior has been so extensively remodelled that little remains of Rinaldi's work except the marble staircase, the design of which complemented the exterior.

The second palace was at Gatchina (1766–72), in the country south-west of St Petersburg.[12] This was more severe than the Marble Palace, with a central block flanked by two square towers. From the sides projected two-storey galleries, the upper floors of which were treated as open loggias. The arrangement of coupled Doric and Ionic pilasters was carried through the central block and the galleries. Unhappily Gachtina was spoiled, when the Grand Duke Paul received it from his mother in 1783 after Orlov's death. The open loggias were walled and glazed and two immense service buildings were put up on either side of the court, completely destroying Rinaldi's original proportions. In the interior the marble staircase and 'White Hall' alone recalled Rinaldi's mastery of a solemn ceremonial scheme.

Rinaldi's most important church, and one of his least Russian works, the new Cathedral of St Isaac, was never completed. From the model and drawings it would seem that this would have been an impressive structure. In plan it was a Greek cross with rounded apse and transepts. It was extended to form a Latin cross by one bay to the west. The central cross was to have been surmounted by five domes, a large dome surrounded by four lanterns with cupolas. To the west a stepped tower supported a similar lantern with slight ornamental elements recalling Borromini's belfries in Rome. The treatment of the exterior as a single, monumental storey with an attic closely resembled St Peter's in Rome, and something of the majestic dignity of the Roman basilica might have been re-called by Rinaldi's lavish use of marble on the interior. But the church proceeded slowly, the costs were immense, and upon Paul's accession work was suspended, the marbles carted off to his new Michael Castle, and in 1801 the church was peremptorily finished by Brenna in brick.[13]

The third architect of the earlier years of Catherine's reign, and the only one of Ger-man origin which the German-born Empress regularly employed, was Yuri Matveevich Velten (1730–1801), whose father, Johann Velten, had come from Danzig in 1703 as a 'master-cook' for Peter the Great.[14] Velten was educated abroad; at the age of thirteen he had gone with a professor from the Academy of Sciences to study mathematics at Tübingen. Shortly afterwards he turned to architecture, and for a time worked on the castle at Stuttgart and in 1749 in Berlin. Upon his return to Russia he assisted Rastrelli at the Winter Palace in 1754, and by 1760 had attained the rank of an independent architect. Catherine valued Velten's engineering abilities, which were superior to his architectural imagination, and set him the task of facing the Neva quays with granite. These, with the exquisite iron grilles for the Summer Garden, were his most import-ant contributions to the development of St Petersburg. The granite embankments, superbly severe and simply yet boldly adapted to the curving entrances of the canals, and intersected by flights of steps to the water-gates, supplied a magnificent base for the palaces, a foundation more grandiose and coherent than any other European city could boast. The same ability to work in the simplest forms is seen in Velten's grilles for the Summer Garden, where plain granite posts, in the form of Roman Doric columns, alternate with wrought-iron panels of a severe rectilinear design.[15] Velten's mastery of granite and iron was a result of his engineering and mathematical instincts, for his archi-tectural works are much less unusual. His 'Second Hermitage' (1771–5) was a dignified addition to Vallin de la Mothe's 'Old Hermitage'. His most remarkable work – a palace for Catherine in commemoration of the naval victory of the Russians over the Turks at Tchesme – was designed in a neo-medieval style, and will be considered later with other structures of the same type.

A similar direction towards a stricter use of simple geometrical forms marked the work of two Russian architects, the first members of the younger generation to benefit by the new course of architectural training. The education of the elder, Vasili Ivanovich Bazhenov (1737–99), was in startling contrast to that which a Russian builder of pre-Petrine Russia would have received, and demonstrates how the systems devised by Peter and Elizabeth were immediately effective.[16] Bazhenov's father, a minor cleric from a country town near Yaroslavl on the Volga, had moved to Moscow, where he sent his son to the Slavonic-Greek-Latin Academy and, when he showed a talent for drawing, to Prince Ukhtomski's architectural school. In 1755 the Prince enrolled him in the recently established Moscow University to study foreign languages, and in 1758 sent him to the new Academy in St Petersburg. Until the complete programme was ready Bazhenov was put to work with S. I. Chevakinski (1713–83), Rastrelli's brilliant pupil, on the naval church of St Nicholas, then under construction.[17] When Vallin de la Mothe arrived, he quickly recognized Bazhenov's talent. In 1760 the young Russian was assigned to Rastrelli as his assistant, and a few months later was sent to Paris to study for two years with Charles de Wailly. He made such progress at the French Academy that he would have won the Prix de Rome in 1762 had he not been a foreigner. He then went to Italy, and in a short time became a member of both the Roman and Florentine Academies. When he returned to St Petersburg in 1765 his international reputation excited the jealousy of the members of the Academy, and it was some time before his talents were officially recognized. His first important commission, the new Arsenal (1769) (Plate 124A), is impregnated with French taste and is not far removed from Vallin de la Mothe's work at the Academy and the Hermitage. But close as this design was to contemporary French work a Russian taste for aggressive monumentality appears in the curious inverted proportions of the entrance, the elements of which increase in size as they mount upwards.

In his Kamenni Ostrov Palace (on 'Stone Island'), for Grand Duke Paul (1765–75), Bazhenov went a step further towards the definition of Russian classicism in his unbroken walls, marked only by a horizontal string course at the height of the second storey and a plain six-columned portico and pediment on the principal façade. This stern exterior, where the play of abstract architectural elements was unrelieved by any decoration, concealed a more informal plan which included a private theatre and a large oval salon across the garden front. Here Bazhenov gave the measure of his ability. Catherine at once appreciated the possibilities of such talent and awarded him two tremendous commissions. The first was for her 'Institute for Daughters of the Nobility', a school on the lines of Mme de Maintenon's seminary at St Cyr, which she proposed to add to Elizabeth's orphanage of Smolny. Bazhenov's designs were never executed, but even in the drawings it is apparent that this would have been one of the masterpieces of Russian, indeed of European, eighteenth-century architecture. The influence of French practice, which he had learned in Paris, can be seen in the plan, where a great variety of square, round, and polygonal rooms are disposed in rigid symmetry on either side of a large central hall. On the court side the building stretched in a great sweeping curve. Yet for all the Baroque magnitude of such a plan, on the exterior variety was subordinated to a massive unified *ordonnance*, the familiar scheme of a rusticated basement, here of two storeys, supporting the upper storeys within a giant order of coupled columns and punctuated at intervals by groups of columns.

Bazhenov's second *magnum opus* was not carried out either. It was nothing less than the reconstruction of the Kremlin as a gigantic triangular palace enclosing the existing buildings and churches. Bazhenov's design, known from drawings and a large wooden model, would have destroyed the character of the ancient Kremlin, and of Moscow as well, so that the failure to erect it can scarcely be regretted. But his genius can be seen in the scope of the project and the masterly control of an intricate plan with many disparate elements brought together in a single embracing unity. Russia was not yet economically or aesthetically prepared for works of such comprehensive character, and it is even possible that they might have eliminated too thoroughly any sense of human scale. But the plans must be included among the truly monumental conceptions of European architecture.

From the surviving fragments of the original wooden model (Plate 124B) it can be seen that the palace had much in common with the designs for Smolny.[18] Upon the

Figure 25. Moscow. New Kremlin Palace (Bazhenov)

same basement, here unusually high because the scheme ignored the irregularities of the site, Bazhenov placed two storeys bound together by a giant order of Ionic columns. Much sculptural decoration and a freer treatment of the projections at the corner pavilions make the Kremlin design even more Baroque than the Smolny project. Although the oldest and most important dynastic shrines were to be preserved, the construction of the palace would have required the demolition of a great deal within the Kremlin walls.

Along the southern side, facing the river, work had already begun by the time the inaugural ceremonies were held in the Empress's presence in 1772. But Catherine, who may have thought the project more important than its accomplishment, in the sense that it was a striking advertisement of the implied grandeur and stability of her reign, lost interest, after thousands of roubles had been poured into the plans and models.[19] She suddenly ordered the work to be suspended, and commissioned Bazhenov to design the Neo-Gothic Palace of Tsaritsyno. This she soon found too sombre, the half-finished palace was abandoned, and thus the third of Bazhenov's great undertakings came to nothing. In the later years of Catherine's reign Bazhenov became one of Paul's favourite architects, and participated after 1796 in his fantastic project for the Michael Castle.

During his long residence in Moscow, Bazhenov exerted considerable influence over the younger generation of Russian architects, and from this period, the 1780s, date many of the late Baroque and early Neo-Classical country houses around Moscow. His hand may possibly be seen in the Pashkov Palace, later the Rumyantsev Museum (1787) (Plate 125), attributed to the Moscow architect Kazakov, but in the bold distribution of the parts showing much of the spirit of the older man. It is less controlled and more delicate than Bazhenov's usual work, but also more powerful than other contemporary or later Moscow palaces.

The second Russian architect of the earlier years of the reign developed a style more in harmony with Catherine's own tastes. Ivan Yegorovich Starov (1743–1808) was born in Moscow and, like Bazhenov, was the son of a priest and enjoyed an identical education, studying first at the University of Moscow and subsequently in St Petersburg at the Academy of Sciences, and in 1758 at the newly opened Academy of Fine Arts.[20] In 1762 he was sent to Paris with Bazhenov to study under de Wailly. After travelling in Italy and a second sojourn in Paris he returned to St Petersburg in 1768, where his talents were soon put to use for the design of country houses. His first work was in the restrained French manner of Vallin de la Mothe, who was head of the department of architecture in the Academy, where Starov was appointed an associate professor in 1770. The façades of his house for Catherine's and Gregory Orlov's son, A. G. Bobrinski (1771–6), resembles the Old Hermitage, but in the country house for Prince Gagarin at Nikolskoe (1774–6), the superintendent of construction for the Bobrinski Palace, Starov introduced a freer treatment of the familiar Neo-Classical elements, more in the manner of Bazhenov's use of late Baroque forms. Starov's invention of a circular terrace above the semi-circular projection of the lower basement storey and a corresponding recession of the first storey is an ingenious use of space. His niches, columns, and angular corner projections are slighter and more sensitive versions of Bazhenov's designs for Smolny.

The delicacy and reduction of his forms to a small scale seem to have appealed particularly to Catherine; for in the later 1770s she turned more and more from an extravagant to a demure and purified conception of architecture. A possible connexion between the converging tastes of Catherine and Starov in these years may be found in the church, and more particularly in the belfry at Nikolskoe (1774–6) (Plate 127B). Here all traces of the Baroque were banished in favour of a full and successful Neo-Classicism, based on an appreciation of the geometrical beauty of classical forms. Starov's studies in Paris reinforced by his Italian travels had prepared him for this rejection of the Baroque. There is a feeling for French formal order in the lower cylindrical, rusticated mass, broken only by the geometrical circular and semi-circular niches, and surmounted by a colonnade topped by a rhythmical series of mouldings diminishing in size. The small Roman Doric porticoes show even more clearly Starov's affection for classicism. This belfry was indeed precocious, the forms far more suggestive of later Alexandrian classicism than of these still early decades of Catherine's reign.[21]

Since Catherine was in Moscow in 1775, and since she would probably have known Starov's work through the relationship between Gagarin and Bobrinski, it is not unlikely that her opinion of Nikolskoe prompted the appointment of Starov as chief architect for the new cathedral of the Alexander Nevski Lavra. The earlier structure by Tressini and Schwertfeger had fallen into decay and was threatening to collapse, but the competitive plans submitted by several architects failed to please the Empress, and she turned to Starov. His projects of 1776 are inscribed 'to be by himself', proving that he had obtained the exclusive right to construct the cathedral. The drawings and fine model (Plate 127A) indicate that Starov's work, unlike Rastrelli's for Smolny, was built as designed except for minor details which had to be changed because of adjacent structures. Catherine's choice of an architect was brilliant. The plan and mass of the cathedral have a noble simplicity characteristic of the full tide of Catherinian classicism. Starov continued the tradition of Tressini's Peter-Paul Cathedral, as modified by Tressini and Schwertfeger, retaining the Latin cross plan, central dome, and two western towers, but by reducing the verticality of Schwertfeger's design, he achieved a more powerful composition. He also suppressed the subsidiary turrets or lanterns at the corners of the dome, whereby Rastrelli and Schwertfeger, and even Rinaldi, had kept up the pretence of a five-domed Orthodox church. The plan is the most remarkable aspect of Starov's cathedral; for it shows a greater integration of the Orthodox central plan with the Latin cross than any previous church in St Petersburg. The relation of the nave and narrower aisles to the central space beneath the dome, flanked by side spaces to the north and south and a semi-circular apse, is complete and comprehensible as a single unity. For his ornament Starov developed and carried further the columnar harmony he had hinted at in the residence for Prince Gagarin. His surfaces are enlivened by pairs of columns supporting a projecting entablature, and the main altar is a columnar composition backed by six pairs of columns turning the semi-circular apse.

Catherine was so pleased with the Cathedral that she commissioned Starov to design a vast town house for her lover, Gregory Potemkin, ennobled as 'Prince of Tauris' after his conquest of the Crimea. The Tauride Palace (1783–8) was occupied by Potemkin for little more than a year. He sold it to the Treasury in 1790, but it remained a favourite residence of Catherine's. For this reason it was brutally desecrated by Paul, who turned it into barracks and stables for the Horse Guards. When Alexander I decided to restore the palace it was so defaced that his architect practically had to rebuild it. To counteract the dampness which had developed, Luigi Rusca (1758–1822) raised the floors two and a half feet, thus destroying the harmony and elegance of Starov's Ionic order. Later in the nineteenth century the splendid gardens between the main façade and the Neva were sold for industrial purposes, factories and water tanks began to obscure the river approach, and after 1905 the building was again remodelled for the Imperial Duma. All this is deeply regrettable; for the Tauride Palace was once one of the wonders of Europe.

Starov's design consisted of a central domed and porticoed block connected by narrow galleries to large wings containing the private living apartments and offices. The continuous low masses were broken only by the flattened dome over the main entrance. Nothing could more clearly exemplify the change in Catherine's conception of architecture. Her new taste appears in the severely plain walls, punctuated by unframed windows and surmounted by the simplest of entablatures with a frieze of metopes and triglyphs. Although the columns of the porticoes on the main entrance and wings of the garden façade are still Tuscan, the effect was undeniably more Greek than Roman. In the interior this impression was substantiated by the consistent use of a Greek Ionic order, closer to the Erechtheum than to any Roman version. And here Starov's instinctive sense for the 'poetry of columns' achieved its most successful expression. The central suite of reception rooms was entered from a square vestibule through which one passed to a high octagonal hall beneath the central dome. This hall, soon known to Potemkin's contemporaries as the 'Pantheon', resembled its antique prototype in the use of the dome, and to a certain extent in the treatment of the wall surfaces. Doors in the four long sides gave access to other parts of the palace, but the shorter sides were filled with tall blue-and-white tile stoves. Through the door opposite the entrance one passed into the 'Catherine Hall' (Plate 126), a gallery with rounded ends longer than the main block itself, from which opened, through a range of eighteen pairs of columns, an immense enclosed Winter Garden, in the centre of which a smaller circular colonnade resembled the little rotundas then in fashion in the parks of country houses.

The scale of the Tauride Palace may owe much to Starov's training in Paris, but nowhere except in Russia could the grandeur of his designs have found fulfilment in actual execution. If only for this, the Tauride Palace could be considered a distinctly Russian work, but its influence was even more important. It became the ambition of many a nobleman and country gentleman to emulate the design of the central block with plain walls, simple six-column portico, and low dome. For forty years many smaller versions throughout the Russian countryside, in wood as well as in stuccoed masonry, showed how directly Starov's masterpiece appealed to the cultivated Russian taste of the period.

The dignity of the Lavra Cathedral and the Tauride Palace makes it all the more difficult to understand Catherine's often expressed dissatisfaction with her native architects. It is true that she was so discouraged and disgusted with Bazhenov's extravagance and erratic behaviour that she exiled him to Moscow. But she had also been annoyed by the grandiose plans submitted from Paris by the French architect Charles-Louis Clérisseau (1722–1820), who had sent her a project for an enormous palace when she had asked for a small garden-house, apparently wishfully thinking that the Empress of Russia would stop at nothing.[22] The remaining architects in St Petersburg were either men of small matter, or were occupied with civil and utilitarian projects. Yet it is hard to understand why either Velten, at work on the Neva quays, or Starov, busy at the Lavra, deserved the reproach implied in Catherine's letter to Grimm of 16 April 1779. She asked him to

Figure 26. St Petersburg. Tauride Palace

direct her agent Reiffenstein to find her 'deux bons architectes, Italiens de nation et habiles de profession ... gens honnêtes et raisonnables, point de têtes de Falconet, marchant sur terre, point dans les airs,' because, as she continued, 'tous les miens sont devenus ou trop vieux, ou trop aveugles, ou trop lents, ou trop paresseux, ou trop jeunes, ou trop fainéants, ou trop grands seigneurs, ou trop riches, ou trop solides, ou trop éventés.'

Catherine exempted one single architect. In a letter of 23 August 1779 she advised Grimm that 'à présent je me suis emparée de mister Cameron, Ecossais de nation, jacobite de profession, grand dessinateur nourri d'antiquités, connu par un livre sur les bains anciens'. And she added that she and Cameron were devising a terraced garden and gallery with baths below. The presence in Russia of a Scottish architect is not so surprising as it might seem. Catherine had for long turned to England almost as much as to France for her cultural and political ideas. On 21 June 1778 she wrote to Grimm: 'Le mois de mai m'a été très fatal; j'ai perdu deux hommes que je n'ai jamais vus, qui m'aimaient et que j'honorais: Voltaire et milord Chatham,' and she admired Charles James Fox so much that his was the only bust of a contemporary in the row of antique philosophers and statesmen to adorn the Cameron Gallery she was soon to build at Tsarskoe Selo. Even her dogs had English names, and as early as 16 July 1772 she had written to Voltaire: 'J'aime à la folie présentement les jardins à l'anglaise'.[23]

How exactly 'mister Cameron' turned up in Russia is still a mystery. Of the scraps of information about Charles Cameron (c. 1740–1812/20), Catherine's letters supply as much as any source.[24] In addition to his Scottish birth, Jacobite sentiments, and classical proclivities, we learn that he was a nephew of Miss Jenny Cameron, had lived at Rome in the house of the Pretender, and was an admirer of Clérisseau, whose drawings he used for his work in Russia. Besides this it is only known that in London in 1767 and 1772 he exhibited drawings of the Roman baths which he published in 1772.[25] To his admiration of antiquity and the works of Palladio was added an interest in the European East. As early as 1773 he had stood for his portrait in a costume which can best be described as 'Russian'. Whether he had actually been to Russia or had merely picked up the clothes somewhere in Italy or England may never be known, but his predilection for the country may perhaps have been due to his realization that in England his work was bound to come in competition with the brothers Adam, and that as a Jacobite he stood a better chance of finding work on the continent. Of all the European courts only Catherine's offered a fair field for a British subject. His estimate was correct and he spent the remainder of his life in Russia, except for a brief visit to England about 1800. During this time he was employed, not without interruptions and misunderstandings, by Catherine and her successors, and a proof of the esteem in which he was held is seen in the fact that in 1820 Alexander I acquired in England 114 of his drawings to be used by Stasov in restoring the apartments at Tsarskoe Selo which had been damaged by fire.

Cameron's first work for Catherine at Tsarskoe Selo, after a few additions to the Chinese Village, was a series of rooms where she could live in absolute privacy and on a scale befitting a noble lady rather than a monarch (Plates 128 and 129). These apartments, with the adjacent Agate Pavilion and Cameron Gallery, which were added to the southwest wing of Elizabeth's palace, were the most classical environment achieved in Russia up to that time. Cameron's taste, shaped by Palladio, and refined by Clérisseau, was Roman in the manner made familiar in Europe and America by the epithet 'Adam'. Here was the same extensive knowledge of classical forms and motifs, similarly manipulated to provide the utmost in comfort. Here was the same intimate, human scale, which could also rise to a more austere vision of antique dignity when the occasion required. Yet here was also a new and unexpected sumptuousness. Catherine boasted to Voltaire that the marbles available in Russia would not have displeased the Italians, and her feeling for materials, even in these small apartments, was in startling contrast to the St Petersburg tradition of improvising architecture in brick and plaster. Cameron not only used the customary materials of Neo-Classicism, moulded plaster reliefs, marble columns and revetments, wood panelling and parquet floors, but went much further in his search for the precious and exotic. The Agate Pavilion was perhaps the most conspicuous example of this; for the columns and walls of two rooms were made of small pieces of agate and malachite cunningly pieced together. He also used bronze for the capitals and bases of his columns and a whole repertoire of decorative forms in ceramic and glass. He inserted small Wedgwood plaques with figures after Flaxman's designs around his chimney-pieces. As for glass, Cameron used moulded glass for columns and ornaments, and flat panes of coloured or clear glass set on coloured felt, to create shimmering surfaces. Once again a Russian patron had called for the best a European artist had to offer and the product was a new contribution to European art. Cameron also brought to Russia a sense of colour which became an inherent part of the new classicism. The brilliant blues and golds, the strong clear hues which had characterized Tsarskoe Selo in the time of Elizabeth, went out of fashion. Primaries were replaced by complementaries or by muted tones, bronze for gold, lavender for blue, olive and pistachio for bright green, and grey-blue for Elizabeth's favourite azure.

Cameron's success at Tsarskoe Selo led to his retention by the Grand Duke Paul as architect for the rebuilding of his country house at Pavlovsk (Plate 131B). He worked there for fifteen years (1781–96), although during this period his work was handicapped by controversies with Paul's favourite architect, V. F. Brenna, who subsequently altered Pavlovsk in a less refined spirit. Cameron's first work for Paul, as the Chinese Village had been for Catherine, was a series of small pavilions in the park, of which the circular Temple of Friendship (1780) was the first in Russia in the Greek Doric order. The palace itself was designed as a square main block facing an elliptical court surrounded by service wings. It was Cameron's largest commission, but it must be said that the whole is too small in scale to be truly palatial, and, however exquisite the Palladian details, it is obviously the work of a decorator rather than an architect. Brenna's additions after 1789 consisted of taller and more elaborate service wings which further spoiled Cameron's design by making it seem far too delicate for the huge courtyard upon which it faces. Only within could one see Cameron's true genius at work in the Italian and Grecian Halls. In the first of these he combined motifs from the Pantheon and Roman baths in a circular hall beneath the central dome. The spacious Grecian Hall beyond is certainly Cameron's most successful palatial interior. Here a richly ornamented stucco ceiling was supported on Corinthian columns of imitation marble which in turn framed niches in the walls in which were placed classical marbles. Catherine wrote to Grimm on 4 September 1794: 'J'ai tous les ouvrages des frères Adam', and Cameron may now have been obliged to use Adam engravings as he had earlier studied those of Clérisseau for inspiration for Tsarskoe Selo. The references to the work of Adam, especially to the Rotunda and Great Hall at Kedleston (1773), are unmistakable. But if Cameron was not the inventor of his Pompeian version of Neo-Classicism, and if his works differ more in degree than in kind from those of the brothers Adam, his work was important for the preparation of the later phase of Russian Neo-Classicism, that style which can be called Alexandrian or Empire, and which flourished during the reign of Alexander I. Cameron's immediate influence can be seen in Starov's 'Pantheon' in the Tauride Palace, where the painted and carved reliefs and the choice of ornaments against a plain ground owed much to the Scottish designer, especially to his Italian Hall at Pavlovsk.

Of his other work little remains. The palace at Baturin, commenced for Cyril Razumovski (1799), can be attributed to him, but when the Hetman died in 1803, work was suspended and for more than a century it lay in ruins. The devastated Ionic portico along the garden front had something of the majesty which Cameron had admired in Rome.[26] His church of Sancta Sophia for the village which Catherine established around Tsarskoe Selo, and which she so named in 1780 in anticipation of her conquest of Constantinople and the establishment of a Greek Empire, is strictly classical and belongs to the type of five-domed early nineteenth-century church more profitably studied in the work of Stasov. Cameron's first drawings, which were too expensive, were an attempt to suggest an Eastern, oriental character. His contemporaries, however, thought the church as built was an exact copy of Sancta Sophia in Constantinople. Upon Paul's accession Cameron was abruptly dismissed, only to be recalled in 1800. Alexander I appointed him chief architect to the Admiralty and he was set to work on buildings for Kronstadt, but was presently displaced by Zakharov. The sale of his library in St Petersburg in 1812 perhaps indicates that he had died, although the date of his death is unknown.

Giacomo Quarenghi (Dzhakomo Kvarengii or Gvarengii, 1744–1817), who arrived in Russia in 1780, was to prove not only the greatest architect of Catherine's reign but one of the most eminent European architects of the later eighteenth century.[27] Quarenghi had studied at the Academy in Bergamo, his birthplace, and later worked in Rome with Mengs. By 1779 his exquisite drawings had attracted the attention of collectors, and he was already in demand for architectural designs, although until then very few had actually been executed. Possibly his connexion with Mengs stood him in good stead with Grimm; for in the latter's reply of 17 July 1779 to Catherine's letter asking for two Italian architects, Grimm began by announcing Mengs's death, before he mentioned Trombara and Quarenghi, who, he said, would soon reach St Petersburg. Of Trombara little more has been heard; his talents were undistinguished and he left no mark in Russia. Quarenghi, on the other hand, immediately pleased Catherine, and she set him to work on the first of an endless series of projects, which increased in scope and expense until the end of her life. On 30 September 1782 she wrote to Grimm:

Je suis bien aise que cet habile architecte soit content; il ne manque pas d'exercice ici à son talent, car la bâtissomanie va un fort grand train. Il y a des endroits que vous ne reconnaîtriez pas si vous les revoyiez, comme par exemple les entours de la Fontanka, qu'on nettoie et dont les bords se bâtissent en pierre de quai.

Nor did her enthusiasm diminish; on 28 October 1785 she wrote:

Ce Quarenghi nous fait des choses charmantes: toute la ville est déjà farcie des ses bâtiments; il bâtit la Banque, la Bourse, des magasins en quantité, des boutiques et des maisons particulières, et ses bâtiments sont ce qu'il y a de mieux. Il m'a fait un théâtre à l'Hermitage, qui sera fini en quinze jours, qui intérieurement est charmant à l'œil; il peut y tenir deux à trois cents personnes, ma pas plus: c'est aussi le bout du monde pour l'Hermitage.

Catherine's constant use of the adjective 'charming' to describe Quarenghi's work seems scarcely consistent with her changing attitude towards classicism nor with

Quarenghi's style. Catherine, like the century in which she lived, was passing from a sentimental, imaginative, and literary attitude towards antiquity to a more serious understanding of the character of ancient art and of its supposed relations to the private life of the individual and the public life of the state. The tempered, moderate classicism in the works of Vallin de la Mothe, Rinaldi, and Velten, had found a very personal expression in the monuments she erected in her parks. The Egyptian pyramid near the graves of her favourite dogs is perhaps the most characteristic example of the sensitivity of this phase. Several years later she thought of a similar monument in a much more archaeological spirit. In the same letter of 1785 to Grimm she advised him that she had just had a long conference at the Hermitage with Quarenghi, who had been ordered to erect in the gardens at Pella, a country residence near Peterhof, 'les trois colonnes de marbre blanc, seul et remarquable reste du temple de Jupiter tonnant; voilà une fantaisie qui m'a prise depuis trois jours, ou j'ai comme une espèce de fièvre pour ces trois colonnes que je veux voir exécutées dans toute leur grandeur et beauté'. With his knowledge of Roman antiquity Quarenghi could quickly supply whatever she desired in the way of such reminiscences; for the gardens at Tsarskoe Selo he built an outdoor kitchen for the use of the Court on picnic days, cleverly disguised with bits of marble fragments and broken bricks as an antique ruin.

But there is much more to Quarenghi's work than the confection of artificial ruins like those in the paintings of Pannini and Hubert Robert. He was a great architect, a fact which Catherine realized. And he was the more remarkable in that he continued to create masterpieces in spite of the unending flood of commissions and projects with which Catherine overwhelmed him. His first important work, the English Palace, so called because it stood in the English Park at Peterhof, instantly gave the measure of the man and his taste. This uncompromisingly Palladian mansion demonstrated both the sources of Quarenghi's style and the use which he intended to make of them. His own words in this instance are important. In a communication addressed to a friend in Italy in 1785, enumerating the many commissions he had already received during his first five years in Russia, he confided his conception of architecture:

I tell you that the antique has been the fountain of all my observations. When I thought I had acquired a sufficient foundation of simplicity and antique grandeur, I studied the best things of the moderns and after having examined and drawn a little amidst the immensity of magnificent building at Rome, I twice undertook a tour of Italy to see, examine, and measure on the spot the best that our masters have left us. Florence, Vicenza, Verona, Mantua, and Venice were the places where I stopped longest; for there more than anywhere else abound the beautiful buildings of Palladio, the San Galli, Bramante, and others. I studied also the living masters, and I have pillaged the good wherever I could discover it, as I have sought as far as possible to make myself familiar with the distribution of rooms in the houses of the French, a skill which still appears to be entirely theirs, especially to-day when this nation can boast of a considerable number of artists in architecture.[28]

Such an eclectic programme could readily have led him to utter subjection to the past, whether of ancient Rome or of the Renaissance, but Quarenghi was aware of such dangers. He continued:

These studies and observations have made me adopt the principle that common sense and reason should not be the slaves of certain rules and examples, and in following servilely the theory and precepts of great masters, without studying their productions and without paying attention to their habits and the local circumstances, one will produce only mediocre things.

Here his programme emerges more clearly. On the basis of a searching and rigorous study of antiquity he conducted his analysis of great modern architecture which for him meant chiefly Palladio's. Only the first small churches he built in Russia suggest the influence of Bramante; for his noble conceptions of antiquity were soon made domestic by general reference to the works of Palladio, and to contemporary advances in residential planning developed in Paris. In this respect it is interesting to find that Catherine herself was less enthusiastic about French planning, and in her letter of 23 August 1779 had explained to Grimm that she wanted Italians: 'Parce que nous avons des Français qui en savent trop et font de vilaines maisons intérieurement et extérieurement, parce qu'ils savent trop'. Quarenghi's architecture, more than that of any other contemporary master in Russia, was antique without being archaeological, grandiose yet human in scale. Not otherwise could he so easily and for so long have caught the enthusiasm of the Empress, or have persuaded her that these massive and stern buildings were 'charming'.

The English Palace (1781–9) (Plate 130A) was the first and in many ways the most typical of Quarenghi's works. This was the first successful example of how he adapted his eclectic programme to Russian conditions. The quality of the palace is antique, the *ordonnance* Palladian, the scale Russian. The simple, symmetrical plan, which included his favourite rotunda in the manner of the Pantheon for the entrance hall, and a circular staircase at either end of the vestibule opening upon a loggia, had a clarity and unity which Cameron never attained, for all that he, too, was enamoured of Palladian and Roman architecture. Not less interesting was the manner by which he reversed the rhythm of his two façades; the projecting eight-column portico at the head of the majestic flight of steps leading up from the garden became on the opposite façade a columned loggia set back between the two wings. No superfluous decoration appears on the plain walls, broken only by ranges of windows without decorative frames and by the horizontal string courses. This was the essence of antiquity rather than a copy of its details. Quarenghi excelled in architectural abstractions. For him the circle, triangle, cylinder, and cube in the form of arch, pediment, column, and mass were the figures with which he composed his geometrical equations. The degree to which he achieved a personal expression within the general system of late eighteenth-century Palladianism can be seen by comparing his English Palace with Bazhenov's Kamenni Ostrov Palace of fifteen years before. Where Bazhenov hesitated, Quarenghi handled his forms with masterly confidence.

The formula of the English Palace, a cubical mass enlivened by a central portico, was one which he used many times, for the Academy of Sciences (1783–7), which preserves a haughty silence beside the pitiful remnants of Mattarnovi's Kunstkammer, and for the State Bank (1783–8) (Plate 130B). For the latter he placed his porticoed block in the centre of a two-storey semi-circular gallery which served as warehouse and storerooms and was connected with the central administrative block by two colonnaded wings. In plan and elevation the building was unequivocally an important governmental structure. The Bank no longer exists in its original condition, but the street façade of one of the wings of the semi-circular structure shows Quarenghi's geometry enlivened by an unexpected play of ornament.

The Hermitage Theatre (1782–5) (Plate 131A) was another example of his success in adapting his means to a specific end. On the exterior he expressed the function of the building by the high curved wall of the auditorium. For the façade along the Neva a range of giant Corinthian engaged columns upon a high rusticated basement, and the lively play of panels, niches, and statuary created a ceremonial atmosphere. Again his personality was seen in the insistent horizontal cornice and string-courses, and in the sharp accents of the pediments above the windows.

The last important building Quarenghi devised for the Empress was the palace at Tsarskoe Selo intended as a residence for her favourite grandson, the future Emperor Alexander I. Here again he designed a simple but low structure, tying the two wings with a majestic colonnade of coupled Corinthian columns. On the rear the rhythm of his arched Palladian windows and the projecting central pavilion with its dome was exquisitely just. The size was modest, the scale large yet restrained. A comparison with Cameron's Agate Pavilion indicates the distance between these two temperaments working within the same repertory of formal elements.

Cameron's Pavlovsk, too, serves as a useful point of comparison with Quarenghi's magnificent country residence at Lyalichi near Chernigov (1794–5) for Prince Zavadovski, who had been for a short time one of Catherine's favourites. Upon his retirement from Court, the Prince wished to surround himself with mementoes of his earlier days in St Petersburg. Quarenghi's design recaptured much of the dignity of the later buildings in the capital; for the formula was essentially that of the English Palace and the Academy of Sciences. Again he used a Palladian central mass, with a projecting portico and a central rotunda on an arcaded basement, and then added two sweeping semi-circular galleries connecting the palace with the service wings. Although the building stood for half a century in ruins, it lost little of the powerful and majestic unity which had been frittered away at Pavlovsk by Brenna's additions, but which it is doubtful whether Cameron himself could ever have attained. This comparison is not intended solely to the disadvantage of Cameron. His interiors at Tsarskoe Selo and Pavlovsk are unsurpassed in the skilful management of classical elements. Quarenghi's are in quite a different spirit, more sumptuous in the use of sculpture and painting, but perhaps not so inspired nor so properly the accompaniment of the splendidly severe exteriors.

The buildings mentioned here are only a small part of Quarenghi's work, for not only was he the designer of many other important structures, but he also served in an advisory capacity, so that the last two decades of the century belong more to him than to any other architect working in Russia. To a certain degree even his fellow-architects seem to have felt his influence, for there is a little of Quarenghi in Starov's Tauride Palace, just as there was a little of Cameron in the decorative treatment of Starov's central rotunda. Surprisingly enough, the Emperor Paul, who took such pains to wreck his mother's achievements, retained her chief architect in office. But during the five confused years of

Paul's reign Quarenghi's work was principally of a utilitarian character, such as the various designs for barracks and riding-halls. For the riding-stables of the Horse Guards (1800–04) his choice of a long rectangular mass ending in porticoes of eight Tuscan columns has the mark of his genius, but lacks the authority of his work for Catherine. Under Alexander I his fortunes declined. He endured his greatest chagrin when the Exchange, which he had begun for Catherine on the point of Vasili Ostrov looking towards the Fortress and the Winter Palace, was torn down to make way for a new design by the French architect, Thomas de Thomon (1803, 1805–16). Quarenghi's feelings could only partly be salved by the patronage of the Dowager Empress Marie, Paul's widow, who commissioned a huge new building at Smolny (1806–8). The work was competent, and thoroughly in the spirit of Quarenghi's Palladianism, but it added nothing to his prestige, which by this time had achieved international recognition. Alexander's indifference to the greatest architect of the older generation is the more regrettable in that Quarenghi's design for a church in Moscow commemorating the War of 1812, in the form of an immense Pantheon with boldly projecting porticoes to the east and west, would have been a triumph of the Alexandrian style, at once the boldest and most monumental transposition to Imperial Russia of the forms of Imperial Rome.

CHAPTER 22

THE ALEXANDRIAN EMPIRE:
1796–1850

SINCE under the autocratic system the selection of the chief architect and general superintendent of governmental building was in the hands of the sovereign, it was inevitable that even in a brief reign the Tsar's taste would affect the course of architectural history. The five years' rule of Paul I, the insane son of Catherine II, was a period of dread for his subjects, ending in his assassination in March 1801. Before this Paul had had time to impose his capricious tastes on Russian architecture. As a boy and young man he had been neglected by his mother, who disliked him and made no secret of her preference for Paul's eldest son, the future Alexander I. The grandson was admitted to the councils of state, while his father was obliged to remain apart at the 'Little Court' which he maintained in the palaces of Gatchina and Pavlovsk. Although the choice of Rinaldi and Cameron as the architects of these palaces had been Catherine's, in the course of time the interiors were redecorated by Paul and his gifted wife, the Grand Duchess Marie Feodorovna. Her taste was better than his, and was further refined by the visit she and Paul paid to Western Europe in 1782. Travelling as the Comte and Comtesse du Nord, they spent a month in Paris,[1] whence they shipped to Russia such enormous stores of furniture that their budget was depleted and Catherine herself not a little annoyed. Marie Feodorovna's affection for Pavlovsk appears in her detailed inventory, which lists the contents of the palace room by room.[2]

On their travels the young couple had encountered an Italian designer, Vincenzo Brenna (Vikenti Frantsevich, c. 1750–1814), whom they persuaded to come to Russia in 1780.[3] That he had been appointed for his ability as a decorator is seen from the fact that for the first five years or so after his arrival he was occupied with the completion of the interiors at Gatchina and at Pavlovsk, which Cameron had left unfinished. In Cameron's absence, and much to the annoyance of the Grand Duchess, Brenna was entrusted with architectural additions, so that in its final form Pavlovsk owed more to Brenna than to Cameron.

The interiors of Pavlovsk preserved much of Brenna's style, which was more robust and massive than Cameron's. For the delicate subtleties of Cameron's relief decoration, Brenna substituted a more naturalistic treatment which can be seen in the vigorous caryatids designed by Brenna and executed by the sculptor Kozlovski for the Throne Room (Plate 150). The prevalence of military motifs in the sculptural decoration was due to the Emperor, who, like his father Peter III, was devoted to his regiments. This martial aspect was a prominent feature of Brenna's most important undertaking, the Michael Castle (Mikhailovski Zamok), so called to distinguish it as a defensive fortress from the residential palaces of the previous sovereigns. Paul had a constant fear of assassination, and wanted a palace where he could feel his life was safe. Upon his accession he commissioned Bazhenov, whom he had befriended, when the elderly Russian architect had fallen out of favour with Catherine, to build him one. Since less than four months later, when Paul went to Moscow for his coronation in February 1797, Brenna in a Court order was named responsible for the construction of the Castle, Bazhenov may have had time only to work out the plan. This was in the form of a square enclosing an octagonal courtyard about which rooms of many different sizes and shapes opened out of loggia-like passages, and recalled Bazhenov's designs for Smolny and the Kremlin. The two separate entrance pavilions, which are all that is left of the extensive group of subsidiary structures, are also closer to Smolny than to Brenna's work.

The Castle itself looks more like the work of a decorator improvising as he went along than of an architect with as powerful an imagination as Bazhenov's. It has no unity of taste or style, within or without. The entrance façade is sombrely military, with heavy rustication and an abundance of trophies. Paul's haste is proved by the fact that much of the costlier material was pillaged from Catherine's still unfinished structures. The incongruous religious inscription above the entrance, for instance, came from Rinaldi's Cathedral of St Isaac. In the courtyard the ornamental rustication betrays Brenna's Italian descent in an order derived from the Palazzo Pitti in Florence. The garden façade on the Champ de Mars (Marsovoe Pole), the parade-ground of St Petersburg, has more the aspect of an Italian villa of the sixteenth century. The eclectic character of the building, so unlike the unified classicism of Catherine's architecture, probably pleased Paul, who desired nothing more than to eradicate the memories of his mother. It is an architectural irony that this capricious and ineffective castle should have been under construction in the very years when the Tauride Palace was defiled by the cavalry regiments of the guard. Three weeks after he had moved into his castle, Paul was slain in his bedroom. Soon the structure, which was detestable to Alexander, who sincerely loved his father and deplored his murder, was transferred to the School of Engineers, and in the course of time the reconstruction of the interiors spoiled Brenna's decorative work.

Unlike his father, Alexander I (1801-25) had great good taste and a clear understanding of what his grandmother had accomplished for Russian architecture. He had a profound affection for the city which his father had feared. During his long reign he continued the work of beautifying St Petersburg with buildings in a consistent and harmonious style. To Alexander as much as to any of his predecessors was due the final classical homogeneity of the city as a whole. As a contemporary historian wrote:

He wanted to make Petersburg more beautiful than any of the European capitals he had visited. For that purpose he decided to set up a special architectural committee under the chairmanship of [General] Béthencourt. Neither the legality of private ownership, nor the structural durability of public or private buildings were the affair of this committee: it was to be concerned only with examining designs for new façades, to accept, reject, or alter them, and also to attend to the plan of streets and squares, projects for canals, bridges, and the better construction of the outlying parts of the city, in a word, to [bring about] its uniform exterior beauty.[4]

Alexander's programme was consistent. At the lowest level of small private houses the designs published with the Emperor's approval called for structures of masonry or wood, wherein the minimum amount of classical motifs, plain wall, pediment, and portico, were handled with ease, if with no particular distinction.[5] Upon this foundation of private building Alexander's leading architects erected their monumental structures, buildings unmatched elsewhere in Europe.

The architectural activity of the reign can be divided into two parts, separated by the French invasion of 1812 and the burning of Moscow. The division, however, is due as much to accident as to the decline of Alexander's liberal idealism after the Napoleonic wars. It so happened that between 1811 and 1814 Voronikhin, Zakharov, and Thomas de Thomon, the three major architects of the first part of the reign, died. The three architects of the latter part, Stasov, Rossi, and Montferrand, lived on until the decade 1848–58, so that the principles of Alexandrian Classicism were continued, although with variations and modifications, until well towards the end of the reign of Alexander's successor, Nicholas I. There is in the architectural succession no growing bias towards native-born or foreign architects. During the earlier years two were Russian and one French; during the latter part one was Russian, one Italian, and one French.

Alexandrian Classicism can be interpreted as a Russian version of the Empire style so familiar in its original French decorative conceptions, and in the different national versions which spread throughout Europe. But it is only fair to say that nowhere, except possibly in the eastern United States during the 1820s and 30s, was the style used for so many public buildings. Even in France its proponents achieved only a limited success in the field of monumental architecture, and the few large buildings of the Napoleonic period – the Madeleine, the Bourse, and the Arc de Triomphe – are more Roman than Greek. Alexander's architects, on the other hand, thought more often in Greek forms, organized according to the rational and public conceptions of French planning. The reasons for the change in taste from Roman to Greek principles are many and well known, and are as consistent for Russian art as for European art in general. Greater familiarity with the history of ancient art, promulgated by Winckelmann and supported by archaeological research, established the superiority of the Greek original to the Roman 'copy'. To this were added other conceptions, literary, sentimental, and picturesque, as the Near East was discovered by more and more travellers in the later years of the eighteenth century and the early nineteenth.

This interest in what Winckelmann called the 'noble simplicity and quiet calm' of Greek art appeared soon after 1750 in drawings by travellers and in competitive architectural drawings, especially those produced by the students and prize-winners of the French Academy, which were executed in bold, geometrical masses with sharp contrasts of texture in smooth walls and rusticated masonry, and the opposition of strong, simple forms, cylinders, obelisks, cubes, and domes. But in this as in much else theory outran practice. Not until 1769, and the acceptance of Gondouin's designs for the École de Médecine in Paris (1769–86), was a building actually undertaken which incorporated some of these elements.[6] Gradually the movement became saturated with Greek detail, as architects became more familiar with Greek art, at first in the temples of Paestum and

Magna Graecia and later in Greece itself. Undoubtedly the most gifted architect of the geometrical phase was Claude-Nicolas Ledoux (1736–1806).[7] His designs for municipal buildings, theatres, factories, etc., and especially his plan for a complete city for the salt-works at Chaux, were uncompromisingly antique, yet strangely inventive. His gate-houses of Paris – the so-called Barrières, consisting of ingenious variations of temple forms – had immense influence. From 1782 until well along in the nineteenth century no visitor arriving in Paris could fail to be impressed by their classical and geometrical simplicity. Paul himself must have admired them; for after his return to Russia he purchased through an agent a collection of 273 drawings by Ledoux.[8] In 1804 Ledoux published a collection of his designs as *L'Architecture considérée sous le rapport de l'art, des mœurs, et de la législation*. The provocative title interested city planners and builders like Alexander who understood the large purposes of architecture and were impressed by Ledoux's logical conception of the relation between architecture and ethics. Their taste for geometrical forms was confirmed when they read that such were the proper expressions of the new moral attitude towards architecture. It thus followed that, where Catherine's classicism had been instinctively sentimental and personal, and where the typical buildings of her reign had been palaces, Alexander moved more widely in the public domain. The greatest works of his best architects were almost without exception governmental structures or city-planning projects.

The first use of pure Greek forms can be attributed to Cameron. For all his Palladian and Pompeian predilections, he built at Pavlovsk in 1780 a circular Temple of Friendship, in which a correct Doric column and entablature appeared for the first time in Russia. In the same year Catherine approved a project for a church at Mogilev (1781–98), commemorating her friendship with Joseph II of Austria, by the self-taught architect and man of letters, Nicholas Alexandrovich Lvov (1751–1803), in which he used a six-column Greek Doric portico.[9] Somewhat earlier the Tuscan Doric entrances and geometrical forms of Starov's belfry at Nikolskoe had shown that he was familiar with the latest Parisian developments. But all these efforts were slight, scattered, and remained largely unknown. Quarenghi's Palladianism had no room for such Greek forms so long as he remained the Court architect. But the Italian and Palladian hold was broken, at first tentatively by the discursive Italianism of Brenna, and then completely by the moral conceptions of Alexander.

Apart from the Michael Castle there is but one other monument which illustrates the transition between the declining but still gallant classicism of Catherine's reign and the stricter geometrical style of the early nineteenth century – a style which in a sense corresponded curiously with the personality of Paul I. One of the most startling signs of the Emperor's madness was his delusion that through his own efforts he could effect a union between Roman Catholicism and Eastern Orthodoxy. In this he was further persuaded by his unexpected election to the Grand Mastership of the Order of St John of Jerusalem, known as the Knights of Malta. This was the first time that a non-Catholic sovereign had ever occupied such a position, and to commemorate it Paul ordered Quarenghi to build a Catholic chapel dedicated to the Maltese Order in the Stroganov Palace, which then was occupied by the Corps des Pages. This was followed by his decision to revise the plans for the new cathedral in honour of the miraculous icon of the Virgin of Kazan, one of the most ancient relics of Moscow Orthodoxy, which had been brought to St Petersburg in 1710. It had first been placed in Zemtsov's Nativity of the Virgin, but towards the close of the century a new church was needed, for which Quarenghi prepared designs and selected massive columns of Finnish granite. When his star declined, Paul and his friend Count Alexander Sergeevich Stroganov (1733–84) decided that the new church should be an all-Russian creation. This arbitrary attitude towards the selection of architects, painters, and sculptors, contrary to Russian tradition, proved completely ineffectual as a nationalistic gesture; for the Kazan Cathedral is, if anything, the most thoroughly Catholic and Roman church in Russian classicism. This again was due to the Emperor's character; for after his elevation by the Knights of Malta Paul dreamed of being elected Pope.

Count Stroganov proposed and Paul accepted the appointment as architect of Andrei Nikiforovich Voronikhin (1760–1814), who had been born a serf on one of the Stroganov estates in Perm.[10] He showed such talent that his master sent him to Moscow to study painting, an art which he practised all his life. But his interest in architecture soon became paramount and attracted the attention of Bazhenov and Kazakov, who were working in Moscow in the mid 1770s. Count Stroganov responded by enrolling him in the St Petersburg Academy and then sending him as companion to his son, Count Paul Alexandrovich, on an extensive tour of Europe in 1784. Several years of study in Paris and Rome followed before Voronikhin returned to Russia in 1790. His first works in St Petersburg – the remodelling of a suite of State apartments in Stroganov's palace, originally built by Rastrelli, and the design of a dacha (country house) for Stroganov on the Neva – proved that the young architect was thoroughly conversant with the latest European versions of Neo-Classical design and decoration. The dacha particularly, where a light, open loggia floated above a rusticated lower storey, showed his ability to create that contrast of mass and void, of texture and colour, which would later become so prominent an aspect of Alexandrian Classicism.

Voronikhin's plan was influenced by St Peter's in Rome and the Piazza before it, but it would be unfair to think the new cathedral merely a copy of the old (Plate 132). Although the exterior order resembles Michelangelo's and Maderna's building as much as Rinaldi's Cathedral of St Isaac, which was still standing at this time, and the colonnade was obviously inspired by Bernini's, Voronikhin's conception was in its heroic character quite novel.[11] Since ritual orientation was obligatory, he set his church, on a Latin cross plan, parallel to the Nevski Prospekt, and devised two semi-circular colonnades to flank the north and south transept entrances. A third would have embraced a large square opposite the west façade, but unfortunately only the north colonnade was erected. In consequence the appearance of the church from the Nevski Prospekt is somewhat deceptive: the majestic portico and dome, flanked by the arms of the colonnade, appear to be the principal entrance.

Voronikhin, like Starov before him, understood the use of columns. In the interior double rows of brown granite shafts with gilt bronze bases and capitals support a powerful cornice upon which rests a richly coffered barrel vault. Without, the doubled ranks of the three porticoes and colonnade create a majestic rhythm held severely in time by the heavy attic and end pavilions, and by the balustrade between. The effect of the cathedral is complex, corresponding to the mixture of architectural currents which prevailed in Russia at this time. Although the order is Corinthian and the use of materials as luxurious as any in St Petersburg, the effect is austere and cold in the extreme. The exuberant panoply of the Baroque South seems caught and frozen in the far North. The answer most probably is that Voronikhin's vision of Rome at the end of the eighteenth century had been tempered by his studies of Greek art and the Neo-Classical influences of the Paris Academy. His emotions were not capable of Baroque display, for all that the plan, the order, and the material of the church were deliberately and intentionally Roman. Indeed, the influence of his studies in Paris can be seen in the fact that the general proportions and mass of the church, if the colonnades are removed, is far closer to Soufflot's St Geneviève (now the Panthéon), which was new when Voronikhin was in Paris, than it is to St Peter.

Although the Kazan Cathedral was begun and finished in the first decade of Alexander's reign, it had been planned for Paul, and his spirit pervades it, just as the great men it entombs – Kutuzov and Barclay de Tolly – were as much the military heroes of Paul's reign as of his son's. Voronikhin's first important work for Alexander immediately showed the Greek turn of his thoughts. For the Academy of Mines (Gorni Institut, 1806–11) on Vasili Ostrov he chose as a model the Temple of Poseidon at Paestum, placing a twelve-column portico with a rather thinly drawn pediment against a plain wall (Plate 133).[12] This was also his last important building. The Cathedral of Kazan absorbed so much of his energies that before his premature death in 1814 he had time for little more than a few small country houses.

The full measure of the Greek contribution to the classical revival was given St Petersburg by the French architect, Thomas de Thomon (1754–1813).[13] Born in Nancy and educated in Paris, he had travelled in Italy, where he was particularly influenced by the temples of Paestum and the engravings of Piranesi. Not wishing to return to France, since he was an ardent royalist, Thomon entered the service of the Comte d'Artois, later Charles X, and worked in Vienna for Prince Esterhazy before arriving in Russia in 1790. Alexander entrusted him with the reconstruction of two important public buildings – the Great Theatre (Bolshoi Teater) and the Exchange. The theatre had been built by the German theatrical painter, Ludwig Philipp Tischbein (1744–1806), and Quarenghi had completed the Exchange. Of the theatre, destroyed by fire in 1813, we can see from Thomon's drawings that it was derived from de Wailly's Odéon in Paris. A portico of eight Ionic columns adorned a two-storey block with Palladian windows, above which rose the pedimented roof of the stage. The plans also resembled French theatres of the later eighteenth century, a horseshoe-shaped auditorium surrounded by salons and offices to fill out an extended rectangle. Thomon's design for a theatre in Odessa, no longer preserved, is so much more antique that the Renaissance treatment of the façades may well have been due to the necessity of retaining part of the walls of Tischbein's first theatre.[14]

In Thomon's other municipal building, the Exchange, there was less compromise. On the plan of a peripteral temple he placed a large barrel-vaulted hall, covered with a gabled roof and illuminated with large arched windows appearing above the colonnade. The columns, although unfluted, were based upon those of the Temple of Poseidon at Paestum, and are one of the earliest examples, on such a scale, of the revival of the early, almost archaic Doric order. Thomon, however, was more than just a slavish imitator of antiquity; he gave these columns his personal signature by reducing the top of the shaft to less than the diameter of the capital, and he added low bases, scarcely visible from a distance. In addition to the Exchange, Thomon planned the whole area at the end of Vasilii Ostrov as a monumental setting for civic and commercial ceremonies with granite quays, ramps, and rostral columns for lighthouses with seated figures of marine divinities at their feet. Although his plans were not completely carried out, the intention and even the partial realization were an indication that for St Petersburg the new century, under the direction of the new sovereign, would be a period of planning on an unprecedented scale. His other works, whether commercial buildings such as the warehouses on the Salni Embankment (1804-5) or the memorial chapel to Paul I erected by his widow in the Park at Pavlovsk, show him equally at home in a utilitarian or monumental type of Neo-Classicism, but there is about them, as was the case in the Exchange, so much of the international character of the revival that they seem to belong to the general history of European architecture rather than to a specifically Russian version.

For a stronger Russian accent one can turn to the work of AdrianDmitrievich Zakharov (1761-1811).[15] He had entered the Academy at the age of six, was sent to Paris for four years (1782-6), where he worked under Chalgrin, and then travelled in Italy before returning to St Petersburg, where the remainder of his life was passed in the service of the Academy. Yet, stereotyped as the educational process had become by this time, and susceptible as Zakharov was to foreign influences, particularly those of the French Academy, his work was unmistakably and completely Russian. In it, and particularly in the one building on which his fame rests, the new Admiralty (1806-15), influences from the Western past were combined with certain persistent Russian factors: the colossal scale, the ability to manage a tremendous plan, and the typically Russian materials, brick and painted plaster.

By 1800 the century-old Admiralty of Peter the Great was no longer an appropriate monument for the centre of a great city which it had more or less accidentally become. Its fortifications, moats, embankments, and drawbridges were outmoded as well as in disrepair. Zakharov's task was severely limited. Not only was he obliged to retain the dimensions of the earlier group, for ship-building was still carried on, but he had to preserve something of the spirit of the old Admiralty, whose slender spire, the counterpart of the steeple of the Peter-Paul Cathedral across the Neva, had become a symbol of imperial St Petersburg. In the design of the new Admiralty, Zakharov kept the open plan of the earlier building as an extended rectangle, opening towards the river and enclosing the shipyards. Yet his design is also a superior example of the way traditional elements can be shaped into something new. The building was an interminable series of storerooms and offices, arranged in a double row separated by a narrow court. The total length is more than a quarter of a mile. To control this gigantic plan Zakharov devised

P

an alternating sequence of architectural forms, few in number and astonishingly simple, which nevertheless bound the whole into a single, integrated harmony. This is all the more remarkable since, so far as we can judge by his earliest drawings, Zakharov, like his contemporaries, had toyed with the fashionable archaeology of the day in all manner of fanciful projects. Thus his plan for a monument to Paul I took the form of a truncated pyramid with Doric porticoes flanked with crenellated Gothic pylons, the whole topped by a circular arcaded *aediculum* which might best be described as 'stripped Roman'. But for his executed work he eschewed the dangerous charms of eclecticism for a vocabulary of simplified antique and freely invented forms. He treated the central entrance of the Admiralty as a square pavilion, surmounted by a rectangular colonnade with statues supporting a square domed roof and slender spire. The design of this roof and dome echoes the earlier building and is a subtle reminder of the primitive boisterousness of the Petrovian era, and while it is possible that the proportions and spacing of the sculpture and reliefs on the first storey of the pavilion were derived from French academic projects of the 1780s, Zakharov's fusion of medieval, Baroque, and classical elements is inimitably his own, and Russian into the bargain (Plate 134).

The central pavilion could scarcely dominate the long façade were it not supported on either side by a wall of eleven bays treated with the utmost simplicity. The plain stuccoed walls on a rusticated base are relieved only by the sharp profiles of the window-frames. Farther on, the ends are designed as identical five-part compositions, with the middle portion enriched by porticoes of twelve columns on high bases, separated by ranges of six bays of wall from subsidiary pavilions with six columns. This treatment of the two ends of the main façade supplied the *ordonnance* for the sides. But Zakharov's most personal touch is seen in the side façades turned towards the river. Here the ends of the building become cubical pavilions, flanked by colonnades and supporting low cylindrical drums above which masts rise from twisted gilt dolphins (Plate 135). The combination of these simple cubes and cylinders of various sizes and proportions with the sparse sculptural embellishment, so knowingly placed and picked out in white against the bright yellow walls, created an effect which more than anything devised by Thomon or Voronikhin bore the accent of Alexandrian Classicism, related to, but not entirely like, similar designs elsewhere in Europe. In addition, Zakharov's genius in managing to achieve variety within the larger unity of his principal façade can be compared with other lengthy buildings, such as Rastrelli's Winter Palace and Tsarskoe Selo, where even the great Italian could not overcome the impression of restlessness and fragmentation.

In Zakharov's Admiralty, and other works, such as his designs for warehouses on the Neva and the executed Church of St Andrew at Kronstadt, the high-water-mark of Alexandrian Classicism was reached. In these, and in Stasov's belfry at Gruzino (1815) (Plate 137A) there is a distinction in the handling of geometrical forms which is unmistakably Russian. When this taste was applied to furniture, textiles, and decorative objects of all kinds, an environment was created which is, like the architecture, similar to the French Empire or German Biedermeier styles and yet not identical with either. The domestic application of the principles of the classical revival, and the creation of a peculiarly Russian environment, were perhaps best seen in and around Moscow, especially in the country houses of the nobility in the neighbourhood of the old capital. These houses were small and more intimate than their town houses in St Petersburg, which were often only reduced versions of the imperial palaces. Most Moscow architecture of the latter half of the eighteenth century was created by or under the influence of Matvei Feodorovich Kazakov (1733–1812), one of the most gifted Russian architects of the period.[16] He had studied at Prince Ukhtomski's unofficial academy with Bazhenov and Kokorinov, where he at first absorbed the Baroque manner of the Elizabethan period, but later, and largely on his own initiative, he passed through all phases of the classical revival, attaining in the end a style of remarkable serenity and purity. In this he was perhaps most assisted by his work with Quarenghi, for whom he supervised the construction of Count Sheremetev's residence at Ostankino. This modest country house, extensive only in the service buildings for the large number of serfs, may even owe something to Kazakov himself; for in comparison with Quarenghi's palace at Lyalich the Italian's aggressive Palladianisms have become more intimate and personal. Kazakov was more fortunate than Bazhenov in his dealings with the Empress. Catherine commissioned him to build the second palace at Tsaritsyno, when she grew tired of Bazhenov's Gothic pile, and it was Kazakov and not Bazhenov who in the end built a new palace in the Kremlin. His Senate (1771–85) is the most antique of all his buildings. Yet his natural exuberance appears in the extravagant forms of the later Pashkov Palace in Moscow (later the Rumyantsev Museum, 1782–84), which is also attributed to Bazhenov (Plate 125). Kazakov's characteristic treatment of classical forms for the solution of Russian problems can be seen in his Church of the Ascension on the Razumovski estate (1790–3) (Plate 136). Kazakov's architecture created for Moscow a classical environment as complete as Rastrelli's for Elizabeth's or Quarenghi's for Catherine's St Petersburg. Although many of his finest buildings, such as the University, were damaged in the fire of 1812 and rebuilt after his death by others, through his copious work he had substantially made over Moscow in the image of his classical dream. Kazakov died in 1812, but he left a host of pupils and followers, who rebuilt the ruined portions of the city with fine residences and public buildings in his simplified classical style, so that his tradition was continued in and around Moscow until well towards the middle of the century.

The Patriotic War, with the burning of Moscow and the triumphal progress of Russian arms across Europe to Paris itself, marked a turning point in the history of Alexander's reign, in politics as well as in architecture. The Emperor's decreasing interest in liberal reform, and his feeling that the security of the throne and of the empire rested upon a stricter interpretation of the principles of absolutism, can be seen in the change in the architectural scene, although this again was accidentally hastened by the simultaneous deaths of Voronikhin, Zakharov, and Thomon. After 1814 a new triumvirate appeared, composed of one Russian and two foreign architects, in this case an Italian and a Frenchman. The Russian, Vasili Petrovich Stasov (1769–1848), was born in Moscow, where he studied and first worked in the circles of Bazhenov and Kazakov.[17] Imperial recognition came in 1801, when Alexander admired his arrangements for the public festivities of the coronation, and in 1802 by imperial ukase Stasov was sent abroad to study. He spent six years in France, England, and Italy, where he was elected a member of the

Roman Academy of St Luke. In 1808 he returned to Russia, entered the imperial service, and was entrusted with renovations in the palaces of Oranienbaum, Peterhof, and Tsarskoe Selo, where he built the high school adjoining the Great Palace in 1811. In 1815 Arakcheev, Alexander's favourite adviser, commissioned Stasov to do some work for his country estate at Gruzino near Novgorod. The belfry he designed for the village church is perhaps his most famous creation (Plate 137A). Small in scale, of delicate proportions and refined details, it demonstrates, like Zakharov's pavilions at the Admiralty, the ability of the greater masters of Russian classicism to achieve an unexpected harmony in the union of classical and traditional forms.

Unfortunately he had also another manner, more suitable for official St Petersburg. In this he used whenever he could a simplified Doric system with large columns against severely plain walls, as in his Imperial Barracks (1817–23), which, notwithstanding the clever handling of the formal elements, already begins to show the implicit and eventually dominant conception of absolute power so characteristic of the later years of Alexander's reign. This sense of imperial authority received its fullest artistic expression in the Moscow Gate (Plate 137B), a triumphal arch erected on the outskirts of St Petersburg (1833–8) for Nicholas I to commemorate the campaigns of 1826–31. The weighty entablature, bearing eight military trophies and resting on twelve columns arranged in a double row, pushed the classical revival in its Greek Doric mode as far as it could go, a memorial to Nicholas's barren victories, as cold as the cast-iron of which it was made. Yet even here Stasov's architectural ingenuity is seen in the use of this relatively novel material and in the substitution of armed and winged victories (by the sculptor Orlovski) for the traditional triglyphs and metopes.

Stasov made a notable attempt to find for the early nineteenth century a solution to the problem of adapting the Orthodox church plan to modern architectural styles. Peter's first churches on the Latin cross plan had been amplified by Rinaldi and Vallin de la Mothe, possibly under the influence of the Moscow Baroque, with apses and richer detail, but in every case a single large dome over the crossing, with or without subsidiary cupolas, had been preceded by one or two tall west towers. Neither Starov nor Voronikhin had much modified this type, although their churches – the Nevski Lavra Cathedral and the Kazan Cathedral – carried farther the similarity of the plan and elevation with churches of the Western rite. Stasov returned to the central five-domed plan, most notably in his two large churches, the Trinity Cathedral for the Izmailovski Regiment (1828–35), and the Transfiguration for the Preobrazhenski Regiment (1826–8). For the latter he inscribed the cross in a square, and placed four small domes above the corners of a severely simple mass adorned with a four-column Ionic portico on the western façade. In the Izmailovski Church his solution was more ingenious. Although the plain walls, relieved only by a heavy frieze near the cornice, and the plan owe much to the Paris Panthéon, the plan is now quite literally a cross, emphasized externally by the projection of a six-column Corinthian portico on each façade. The smaller domes are placed over the arms of the cross, an arrangement which is more picturesque than the earlier Transfiguration and not as capricious as has been thought. At any rate, Stasov created a new silhouette for the traditional Orthodox elevation in the way the small domes, reductions of the greater one over the crossing, are related both to it and to the pediments below.[18]

Alexander's desire to make St Petersburg a city unrivalled in the world for its splendid public buildings found a perfect instrument in the personality and talents of an architect of Italian origin, Karl Ivanovich Rossi (1775–1849).[19] His imagination was as spacious as the Emperor's, and he was completely in sympathy with the exercise of authoritarian control over all new construction. Rossi was the son of an Italian ballerina, and as a child had lived with Brenna, who taught him the rudiments of architectural design. By 1796 he was accredited and was working as Brenna's assistant at Pavlovsk and Gatchina. This association with the older Italian, confirmed by a journey to Italy with Brenna, when the latter retired from Russia in 1802, determined the character of Rossi's own style. By-passing the Academy, as it were, Rossi, more than any other architect since the arrival of Vallin de la Mothe, was uninfluenced by the style of Paris and directly inspired by ancient and modern Rome. In this respect he put an end to the Greek Revival and re-covered for St Petersburg something of the earlier Roman grandeur it had known in the works of Rinaldi and Quarenghi. The scope of Rossi's imagination and his conception of his abilities were revealed in a memorandum to the Emperor describing his project for a granite quay in front of the Admiralty to provide continuous access along the Neva with-out interrupting the passage of ships from the ways to the river. His plan called for a new embankment pierced by twelve huge arches and ornamented with three rostral columns which, as Rossi boasted, would 'surpass those which the Romans considered sufficient for their monuments'.[20] After the War of Liberation such claims impressed Alexander, who felt it his duty to conduct the destinies of Europe. What better advertisement for the blessings of autocracy than that its architecture should surpass the moderns as well as the ancients? Rossi's assertions were not without foundation, for nowhere in Europe in the 1820s and 30s were projects on such a scale not only planned but also carried out.

Until 1816 Rossi had worked chiefly in Moscow, but after the disappearance of the earlier generation he was summoned to St Petersburg, where he joined Stasov on the Committee for Construction and Hydraulic Works under the chairmanship of a French military engineer, General Béthencourt. Alexander had created this committee to super-vise all private as well as public construction in St Petersburg. Soon the decisions of the Committee were effective for architecture throughout Russia. Alexander himself ex-amined the projects submitted to the Committee, and this practice of personal inter-vention was continued by his brother Nicholas. Rossi eventually became the dominant member of the Committee, but in the beginning the character of his own work was affected by the severe classicism of Stasov.

In his first work for Alexander Rossi was not a free agent. In the Yelagin Palace on the Kamenni Ostrov (1818–22) for the Emperor's mother he was handicapped by the pro-portions of an earlier building, and the result was somewhat heavy and old-fashioned.[21] Rossi's own taste prevailed only in the lavish interior decoration which is reminiscent of Brenna. Alexander was pleased with the palace, and in 1819 commissioned an even larger residence for his youngest brother, the Grand Duke Michael Pavlovich. The New Michael Palace (1819–23, later the Alexander III Museum and now the Russian Museum) was Rossi's most personal creation up to this time. Between two simple corner pavilions the central mass was faced with a noble Corinthian order and a prominent portico of eight Corinthian columns. The arrangement was clear, bold, and powerful. The Palace rose above low service wings with a Doric order which framed a courtyard separated from the street by a fine iron grille. The group of buildings was only comparable to Brenna's Michael Castle, and was unequalled by any previous palace ensemble in the city. Yet the plan is more impressive than the details, which have a feeling of repetition, of second-hand inspiration. Rossi, unlike Zakharov in his Admiralty or even Voronikhin in his Kazan Cathedral, could not re-work the familiar classical themes into a personal conception. Something of the heavy mediocrity of Brenna was present in this colonnade, the prototypes of which had been used for a century and a half in other countries. In the interior, only the splendid if somewhat pompous staircase was spared, when the palace was converted into a museum late in the nineteenth century.

Fortunately Alexander and his successor appreciated Rossi's talents in city planning and gave him ample opportunity to demonstrate his genius in this field. The last of Alexander's projects – the design of the Winter Palace Square – was solved by Rossi with the construction of a huge semi-circular building for the General Staff embracing two sides of the square (1819–29) (Plate 139). The sweep of this unadorned façade throw into relief the fanciful agitation of the Winter Palace and provide an admirably taciturn setting for Rastrelli's loquacious Rococo. In the centre of this hemi-cycle Rossi placed two large triumphal arches, the second behind and at an angle to the first, in order to accommodate the oblique entrance of the Morskaya Ulitsa which connects the Square with the Nevski Prospekt (Plate 140A). The view from beneath these arches proves how Rossi was more successful in creating enormous spatial perspectives than in inventing architectural details.

Before the Palace Square was finished, Nicholas I commissioned Rossi to design a new theatre. Once again the plan, which developed into a group of two new squares with a street between, was more remarkable than the actual buildings. The Alexandra Theatre placed between the Public Library and the Anichkov Palace is at the head of the one square (Plate 138A). Behind the Theatre a new street was cut through to the Fontanka, which it joined at the Chernuishevski Square. Rossi designed the façades of all the buildings on the squares and street as parts of a single monumental ensemble.[22] The yellow-and-white Theatre was a rectangular structure with corner pavilions, lofty porticoes on the longer sides, a second colonnade on the front and a range of pilasters on the rear, all of the Corinthian order. The block-like character typical of Rossi's work was emphasized by the strong horizontal cornices and the avoidance of a pediment, which he never used after the Michael Palace. But he knew how to make the best use of his few forms. Again the contrast between sober Doric and sumptuous Corinthian was reinforced by the paired columns between the bays of the continuous rows of houses facing Theatre Street which acted as a prelude to the monumental assertion of the theatre itself.

Rossi's fourth large municipal undertaking was his creation of buildings opposite the Admiralty and St Isaac for the Senate and Synod, the highest judicial and ecclesiastical bodies of the Government. His solution took the form of twin palaces joined by a triumphal arch embellished with paired columns supporting fragments of an entablature and an attic with a frieze (Plate 138B). Again Rossi's scheme embraced more than separate buildings; not only the arch, but the façades on the street behind were designed to bring the whole into a single architectural unity. This was his last important work. Worn out by a lifetime of pleasure as well as labour, he retired in 1832, and executed nothing more before his death.

Although structures more or less classical in design continued to be built in St Petersburg and Moscow and elsewhere in Russia, especially in the provincial capitals, where all governmental buildings had to be approved by the Committee in St Petersburg, the works of Rossi in several respects were the final triumphs of Petersburg classicism. Already, as we have seen, a certain sterility and mediocrity had begun to appear in some aspects of his design. The finesse and precision, the fertile invention of new combinations of forms, which had been so characteristic of the work of his immediate predecessors, and which had been present in the architecture of St Petersburg from its foundation, had grown less apparent. Other architects of the early years of Nicholas I's reign continued, with minor variations, the earlier solutions, so that, while the works of such men as Plavov, Briullov, and the Moscow architect Gigliardi are often noble and sometimes interesting, they add nothing to the development of Russian classicism.[23]

Only in the activity of the last important Petersburg architect was a specifically Russian characteristic present, and then perhaps not the most commendable. This was a passion for size so obsessive that the more important problems of scale and proportion were neglected to the disadvantage of the works concerned. In his own lifetime Alexander had decided to rebuild the Cathedral of St Isaac, left in a mournful condition after Brenna's hasty patchwork. In 1817 a competition was held by the Committee for Building under the chairmanship of General Béthencourt. The commission was awarded, not to any of the considerable number of well-known Russian architects who participated, but to a total stranger, an itinerant French draughtsman. Little is known of the early training of Auguste Ricard, who called himself Ricard de Montferrand (Avgust Avgustovich Monferran, 1786–1858),[24] but he seems to have worked as a youth on Vignon's church of the Madeleine in Paris before enlisting in the Imperial Guard. After the Battle of Leipzig he left the army and went to Russia, which he already may have known as a participant in the campaign of 1812. When he turned up in St Petersburg in 1816, he applied for a position as a draughtsman. In 1817 he submitted an album of sketches for the Cathedral competitions, presenting designs in the Chinese, Indian, Gothic, and Byzantine styles. Such eclectic tastes may have influenced the Committee, quite as much as the chairman's preference for a countryman. Or the choice of Montferrand may have been due to the Committee's thought that an unknown architect with no reputation to lose might bring some order into the plans and use the best elements of the competitive designs?[25] Certainly Montferrand's design for the cathedral which passed through a number of stages through the years – the final drawings for the interior were not completed until 1842 – brought together many of the important features found in the drawings submitted by Stasov, Mikhailov, Beretti, and others. In each the same solution was proposed: a huge church on a Greek cross plan bearing a large central and four subsidiary domes.[26] Most of the competition drawings had placed the Greek cross in a square with identical porticoes on each side. Montferrand's plans of 1825, which seem to have been based on a project of 1820–2 by Mikhailov, transformed the square internally into an aisled rectangle of three central bays, with slightly smaller entrance and altar bays. Externally the proportions of the square were retained by providing the porticoes on the long sides with a double row of columns. A sense of mathematical relationships prevailed in the elevation, which was designed as an almost equilateral triangle, or pyramid in three dimensions, evidence of Montferrand's interest in engineering (Plate 140B).

From the extant plans and wooden model it is apparent that the cathedral would originally have been more gracious than it gradually became; for with the passing of the years, especially after the death of Alexander, successive changes were introduced, all in the direction of greater size and heavier detail, so that, as it stands, the building has the authoritarian character demanded by Nicholas I. The decline of classical standards of taste and the growth of eclecticism can be read between the lines of Montferrand's own description of the cathedral:

Sa majesté voulut bien permettre que les quatres campaniles fussent placés sur un plan carré autour de la coupole, et que les deux côtés de l'est et de l'ouest, qui avaient été jugés trop simples dans leur composition, fussent augmenté chacun du portique que l'on y voit aujourd'hui. Ces notables additions … augmentèrent de beaucoup l'importance de l'édifice, et devaient lui imprimer un caractère de grandeur et de noblesse bien supérieur à celui des premiers plans.[27]

Montferrand's solution of the problem of designing an Orthodox church in the classical style was related to a certain extent to Stasov's Transfiguration. The large central dome, resembling Soufflot's Panthéon and Wren's St Paul's, has little relation to the small lanterns with cupolas. Montferrand himself felt the lack of connexion between these elements, but was unable to bring them together. The Cathedral creates its effect less through its rigid proportions than by the sheer size and unparalleled richness of the materials. The innumerable columns are monoliths of red Finnish granite, with gilt bronze capitals and bases. Neither money nor effort was spared to create the most splendid interior, although this is slightly spoiled in its final form by the light which enters only feebly through the windows of the drum. Externally the wealth of realistically sculptured figures, the agitated groups of the pediments, and the kneeling angels at the corners of the attic holding great bronze candlesticks, lighted on Easter Eve, create a curious contrast to the static, even inert, classical forms of wall and column. A telling sign that the reign of classicism was over could be seen by those who ventured to inspect the interior of the great dome. The masonry shell was supported by a forest of cast-iron girders, the first use of this material in Russia on such a scale.

Two other undertakings of Montferrand remain to be mentioned: his successful raising of the enormous 'Tsar Bell' in the Moscow Kremlin, which had been damaged by fire shortly after it was cast (1735) and had remained buried in a deep pit, and his erection of the Alexander Column in the Winter Palace Square (1829) (Plate 141).[28] This granite monolith, the largest in the world, was designed to surpass all other memorial columns, whether in Paris or Rome, the two cities from which Russian architectural history had continuously drawn its inspiration. And surpass them it did, though in size only, and not in beauty. Its transportation from the quarries on Lake Ladoga and its erection in the Square were accounted among the engineering triumphs of the century, but the huge column, apart from its impressive height, is ungracious in its proportions, another indication of Montferrand's fundamental lack of taste.

This confusion of scale and of artistic purpose is symptomatic of the imminent decline of all architectural standards in the following period of eclecticism which overwhelmed Russia as well as other European countries after the middle of the nineteenth century. St Isaac was the last great building erected under the supervision and control of Alexander's Committee. As time passed, such architectural censorship could no longer keep pace with the increasing exploitation of real estate by private capital. Even Nicholas himself, the most conscientious censor of all forms of popular expression, was obliged to yield, and in the 1840s Alexander's laws requiring all builders to conform to government designs were abrogated. Henceforth the classic architecture of St Petersburg was lost in a welter of eclecticism.

CHAPTER 23

THE MEDIEVAL REVIVAL: EIGHTEENTH-CENTURY ROMANTIC ARCHITECTURE

ALTHOUGH the public buildings of St Petersburg are the most conspicuous monuments of eighteenth-century Russian art, they were not the only significant structures, and perhaps were not even the most influential. The cathedrals and palaces on the broad squares and avenues were conceived as symbols of power and public purpose. In unexpected corners of town gardens and country parks there were smaller buildings, manifestations of architecture as the expression of personal feeling. Such sentimental, frequently literary, architecture appeared towards the middle of the century in Western Europe in the form of pleasure pavilions and monuments on the estates of the great landowners, and is familiar to us as part of the 'picturesque' and 'romantic' attitude towards nature.[1]

This attitude might not have reached Russia so quickly had Catherine II been less sensitive to changes of European taste. Not the least fascinating aspect of her personality is the way her passion for building encompassed an architecture of serious moral purpose as well as capricious schemes for the gratification of passing fancies.[2] Towards the end of the first decade of her reign, when such dignified public buildings as Vallin de la Mothe's Market, Rinaldi's Marble Palace, Velten's quays, and Bazhenov's Arsenal were already under construction, her plans for the park at Tsarskoe Selo had developed in quite another manner. Catherine detested the stiff avenues and neat hedges of Elizabeth's gardens, patterned after Le Nôtre's at Versailles, and preferred the new attitude towards nature which had been introduced by the English gardeners of the early eighteenth century. On 25 June 1772 she wrote to Voltaire:

J'aime à la folie présentement les jardins à l'anglaise, les lignes courbes, les pentes douces, les étangs en forme de lacs, les archipels en terre ferme, et j'ai un profond mépris pour les lignes droites, les allées jumelles. Je hais les fontaines qui donnent la torture à l'eau pour lui faire prendre un cours contraire à sa nature; les statues sont reléguées dans les galeries, les vestibules, etc.; en un mot, l'anglomanie domine dans ma plantomanie.[3]

Beside Elizabeth's prim patterns, Catherine laid out the undulating ground around the ponds at Tsarskoe Selo as an English park, with wooded slopes traversed by irregular paths, along which the meditative stroller might catch unexpected glimpses of the monuments which were to take the place of the banished Elizabethan statuary.[4]

In another letter to Voltaire, written 14 August 1771, during the first Turkish war, Catherine described some of these monuments:

Si cette guerre continue, mon jardin de Czarskozélo [sic] ressemblera bientôt à un jeu de quilles, car à chaque action d'éclat j'y fais élever quelque monument. La bataille de Kogul, où dix-sept mille combattants en battirent cent cinquante mille, y a produit un obélisque, avec une inscription que ne contient que le fait et le nom du général: la bataille navale de Tchesme a fait naître, dans une très grande pièce d'eau, une colonne rostrale: la prise de la Crimée y sera perpétuée par une grosse colonne; la descente dans la Morée et la prise de Sparte, par une autre. Tout cela est fait des plus beaux marbres qu'on puisse voir, et que les Italiens même admirent. Ces marbres se trouvent les uns sur les bords du lac Ladoga, les autres à Caterinimbourg [sic] en Sibérie, et nous les employons comme vous voyez: il y en a presque de toutes couleurs. Outre cela, derrière mon jardin, dans un bois, j'ai imaginé de faire bâtir un temple de mémoire, auquel on arrivera par un arc de triomphe. Tous les faits importants de la guerre présente y seront gravés sur des médaillons, avec des inscriptions simples et courtes en langue du pays, avec la date et les noms de ceux qui les ont effectués. J'ai un excellent architecte italien, qui fait les plans de ce bâtiment, qui, j'espère, sera beau, de bon goût, et fera l'histoire de cette guerre.

These rostral columns, obelisks, and arches are typical of the first phase of romantic architecture in Russia, as elsewhere in Europe. The elements are antique forms familiar for several centuries to educated Europeans, but used now as decorative objects for the expression of private feeling. The monuments of the 1760s and early 70s were followed in the next few years by more exotic structures. The Egyptian pyramid beside the graves of Catherine's dogs is the first hint. In 1774 Velten added a ruin in the form of a colossal column, half buried in the earth and supporting on its capital a small Gothic pavilion.[5] Even the most devoted adherents of classicism were pressed into service. One of Cameron's first tasks was to design a Chinese village, a collection of small pagoda-like pavilions far more 'oriental' than the earlier chinoiserie decorations of Rinaldi's Italian villa at Oranienbaum. By 1790 the park also contained Neelov's Chinese theatre, Admiralty, and kitchen for the Hermitage, the latter two in the Gothic taste.[6] Quarenghi contributed the 'Great Caprice' (Plate 143A), a pagoda on top of a huge artificial rock archway, a Turkish kiosk, and an outdoor kitchen for picnics disguised as an antique ruin. Tsarskoe Selo was not the only imperial park to be developed in this way. To the formal gardens at Peterhof was added an English Garden where stood Quarenghi's English Palace. At Pavlovsk the sloping banks of the meandering stream, the Slavyanka, were laid out as a wooded grove (Plate 145A). Even at Gatchina, where the terrain was less propitious, a series of pools was arranged, and at the head of one Paul built a little Gothic priory, theoretically an imitation of the headquarters of the Knights of St John at Malta. Throughout all these parks were distributed the usual obelisks, columns, arches, temples, Chinese bridges, and even, at Pavlovsk, an imitation rustic village like those Paul and his wife might have seen in France.[7]

Of all these, the Turkish and Gothic buildings provoke the most curiosity. Catherine's enthusiasm for Islamic architecture was a passing fad, prompted by Russian victories in the first Turkish war and unsupported by any serious study of Mohammedan art. The largest building in this style, Velten's Tchesme Palace outside St Petersburg (Chesmenskii Dvorets, 1770), built to commemorate the naval victory that year at Tchesme in the Black Sea, was a very uncertain fantasy.[8] The square block with circular corner pavilions was crowned with a series of flattened domes which were taken to be Turkish. The palace church, on a quatrefoil plan reminiscent of the late seventeenth-century churches of

Moscow, was striped and crested in a bizarre fashion, half old Russian and half western Gothic. Some years earlier a more serious attempt to recreate the forms of the past had been carried out by Bazhenov in the church at Cherkizov-Starak, near Moscow (1759). In this, his first independent production, he placed a storeyed cylindrical tower on a cubical mass reminiscent of the seventeenth-century churches of Moscow, and covered the surfaces with papery Baroque ornament. The slightly later church at Znamenki (1768–84), attributed to the same architect and usually considered the earliest strictly neo-Gothic structure in Russia, developed further a decorative scheme of old-Russian ornament combined with tall pointed spires, ogee and segmental arches.[9] The old Russian ornamental forms may have been demanded by Catherine, who was a serious student of Russian history. She knew that she had not the slightest legal claim to the throne and that, to maintain her position, she must identify herself as closely as possible with the past as well as the present of Russia. This had been brought home at her coronation in Moscow, when the people cheered more for her son, the legitimate heir, than for her. Catherine studied all the chronicles then known, using the actual documents and insisting on textual accuracy. As late as 1792 she declared: 'Je suis enterrée dans l'histoire ou plutôt dans les chroniques de la Russie que j'aime à la folie'. Her dynastic purpose can be read in her remark in 1784: 'Je crois qu'il est impossible de se délasser plus utilement pour l'empire qu'en débrouillant et arrangeant son histoire'.[10]

Her historical enthusiasm had immediate consequences for architecture. She had a genuine affection for Moscow, which she described to Voltaire as 'un monde, non une ville', and frequently visited. As early as 1762, when in Moscow for her coronation, she visited the old wooden palace at Kolomenskoe and regretfully conceded that it would have to be demolished (Plate 97A). But she insisted that drawings be made and a wooden model prepared, which are still our best sources for the study of old Russian wooden secular construction. And since Catherine chose to appear in the rôle of sponsor of ancient Russian buildings, her favourite architect Quarenghi also paid his respects to them. His drawings of the Moscow Kremlin are among the most sensitive interpretations of the Russian past and of an architecture which to most people in the eighteenth century seemed exotic and meaningless.

Nor were Catherine's interests limited to archaeological research and preservation. She thought to make a visible link between her new Europeanized Russia and the old by building in a medieval Russian style, thus ideologically reversing the course Peter had taken a century before. For her Kazakov constructed another monument commemorating her victories over the Turks. The Petrovski Palace (Plate 142) on the outskirts of Moscow (1775–82), of red brick with white stone trim, was strictly Palladian in plan; indeed, reminiscent of Pavlovsk, with its central rotunda covered with a flat dome, and large semicircular forecourt.[11] But the exterior walls were adorned with details very much like Velten's, although Kazakov undoubtedly had a more intimate acquaintance with medieval Russian architecture through his work in the Kremlin. Unfortunately the Palace was used by Napoleon and was wrecked when the French retreated. In the restoration of 1840 the proportions of the central block were slightly changed and more correct Neo-Russian detail was added which did not help its 'Gothic' aspect.

At the same time Catherine commissioned Bazhenov, whose work at the Kremlin had been suspended, to build another country palace at Tsaritsyno, a mile from Kolomenskoe. It is clear that her intention was to recapture something of the character of the vanished wooden palace, for Bazhenov was told to work in the medieval style. His grandiose palace, complete with an English park filled with pleasure buildings of all kinds (Plate 124B), was ready to receive the Empress when she visited Moscow in 1787. Unfortunately Catherine took an instant dislike to the rectangular palace, with tall pavilions which reminded her of a coffin surrounded by candles. She dismissed Bazhenov and ordered Kazakov to rebuild it. Even this was never finished and remained in a half-ruined condition vastly more picturesque in its dilapidation than it ever would have been if completed. The new palace included a central block with tower-like corner pavilions, framed with curiously classical colonnettes and topped by what might be taken for a tall mansard roof. Meanwhile Kazakov produced a third design for a country house for Count Vorontsov at Koukov. This was in plan a pentagon with projecting turrets at the five corners and two circular bastion-like pavilions connected by wings to the main structure. It was never built, but the presence of these neo-medieval elements in the work of an architect noted for his mastery of the purest classical style is sufficient indication that architectural taste in the later eighteenth century was no longer the uniform body of doctrine it had been before. Petrovski and Tsaritsyno, far more than the timid palace of Tschesme, may have seemed to Catherine valid contributions to Russian architecture. But neither she nor her architects were sufficiently versed in medieval techniques and forms to do more than use miscellaneous motifs plucked from seventeenth-century Russian architecture for the decoration of the surfaces of buildings planned and executed in a classical spirit.[12]

The medievalism of Catherine, Kazakov, Bazhenov, and Quarenghi remained without immediate issue. It was a personal affair between the sovereign and her servants, and lacked any broad popular support, as well as any real understanding of medieval principles of design. Only later, when the Russian past began to have a political use, would such forms be revived with greater accuracy but without the same charm. Meanwhile the search for exotic styles continued, passing from garden structures to more serious buildings, and soon threatening the whole framework of Neo-Classical idealism. If this was preserved in Russia well into the 1840s and even beyond, it was due more to the insistence of imperial authority than to the taste of the architects themselves.

This collection of curiosities is more important in the sum than in the parts. If an architect of Quarenghi's Palladian persuasion could work in so many manners, then the stately columnar façades of public architecture were bound to lose the power to convince, when the demand came for larger buildings in a variety of styles. Within the very heart of the classical revival the seeds of eclecticism had begun to germinate. The caprices of Quarenghi were the random thoughts of a great designer. Two decades later the eclectic spirit appeared more insidiously in the architectural conceptions of Luigi Rusca, who published in 1810 designs for the War College and a country villa in the Gothic manner, an Egyptian pavilion for a country house, and Moorish designs for Mohammedan mosques in St Petersburg.[13] In 1792 Adrian Zakharov indulged in a hodge-podge of

styles in his project for a triumphal decoration, the sort of student work which a generation before would have been unmitigatedly classical. Now Zakharov's lighthouses in the
form of monstrous Doric columns rested on crenellated medieval walls. In 1800 his designs for a monastery church at Gatchina showed a severely simple block, but with
pointed windows and Gothic rib vaults.[14] Even Carlo Rossi, whose monuments and
plans set the final classical seal on St Petersburg, had his romantic diversion. His two projects of before 1815 for a cathedral for the Nilus Hermitage on an island in Lake Seliger
bristle with tent-roofed belfries rising above a trefoil plan with smaller radiating
chapels.[15]

This curious interest, which was felt even by architects whose executed works were
thoroughly classical, lived on into the reign of Nicholas I, under whom the gardens of
Tsarskoe Selo received a complement of buildings marking the triumph of European
Romanticism in its most eclectic aspect. Here in the late 1820s an English architect, Adam
Menelaws (Menelas, died 1831), built a ruined 'Chapel' (1827), a Turkish elephant
house (1828), and several more habitable structures in a reasonably correct Gothic.
Rastrelli's effervescent Monbezh was destroyed to make way for a Gothic Arsenal containing a collection of old arms and armour.[16] Menelaws's most archaeological work was
the Egyptian Gate (1827–32) (Plate 167A), in the form of a double pylon, with bas-
reliefs forming one of the largest groups of Neo-Egyptian sculpture ever executed.

Inevitably the medieval revival affected church architecture, and by the end of Alexander's reign two currents were at work. In the first, as at Petrovski and Tsaritsyno,
medieval forms were fastened to buildings of traditional, even Neo-Classical, plan and
construction. Elsewhere another kind of design resulted from a study of Western European Neo-Gothic design. Such are the façades of the Synodal Printing Office (before
1773) (Plate 143B) and of the Church of St Catherine in the Convent of the Ascension in
the Moscow Kremlin (1817) (Plate 145B). The Western European sources for such a
design were explicit in the small Church of St Alexander Nevski at Peterhof by the German architect K. F. Schinkel (1832).

By 1842 Romanticism had become the passion for more than buildings. At a carnival
held at Peterhof the ladies and gentlemen of the Court, dressed in costumes which passed
for medieval, participated in hunts and tournaments in an environment made all the
more real for them by the medieval architecture of the Chapels and Arsenal in the park.[17]
While the last classical monument, the Cathedral of St Isaac, was nearing completion,
the Court of Nicholas I was thus unwittingly celebrating the end of a great architectural
tradition. Henceforward nothing more was possible but an unconditional surrender to
eclecticism.

Two of Nicholas's buildings, rather than St Isaac, which had been begun by his
brother, may serve to represent this turning point. A church in Moscow commemorating the victorious conclusion of the Wars of 1812–14 had long been contemplated. The
ageing Quarenghi had designed for it a majestic version of the Roman Pantheon. More
symptomatic of the times was the project of a Swedish architect, Alexander Vitberg,
who suggested a vast church on three levels, the lowest a rectangle, the second a cross,
and the third a circle, symbolizing progression from imperfect matter to perfect im-

materiality.[18] But the Church of the Redeemer (1839–83) as it was finally built by the German-Russian architect, Konstantin Andreevich Ton (1794–1881), was an ineffectual attempt to graft Byzantine detail on a classical form.[19] Ton's inability to resolve an important architectural problem with any personal conviction was further demonstrated in the Great Kremlin Palace (1838–49). This part-Renaissance, part-classical, and (in the treatment of the upper windows) even part-Russian, mixture was a sorry successor to the Kremlin palaces of Rastrelli, Bazhenov, and Kazakov. The decline of sovereign taste is all the more dismaying when we are told that the Emperor took a keen interest in the designs and allowed nothing to pass without the stamp of his approval.

PART FIVE

MODERN RUSSIAN ART

*

CHAPTER 24

EIGHTEENTH-CENTURY PAINTING AND
SCULPTURE

AN analysis of eighteenth-century painting in St Petersburg requires again a definition of the aims of criticism. To seek in it exclusively Russian values would be grossly to distort its purpose and the wishes of its patrons, while to compare it to its disfavour with contemporary painting in the West would be to disregard the peculiar historical conditions which determined its character. As with much colonial painting, its value is partly artistic and partly historical. Even when the degree of quality is lower than the average attained at the time elsewhere, such painting often has elements of rude vigour or unexpected psychological insight which have come to the surface in an environment where the social graces have worn a little thin. In the work of native-born artists trained abroad the same process of adapting a strange mode of expression to life at home can be full of surprise and charm.[1]

From the first not only new needs, as they were being supplied by the society of St Petersburg, but new educational methods were required. The Court had to be taught to want a new kind of art quite as much as artists had to be taught to produce it. From the first the demand was practical and secular. As in architecture, the useful took precedence over the decorative, and the first pictorial images were maps, topographical views, portraits of eminent men and women of the Court and upper classes, and prints of the victories by which Peter had won his empire.[2] The first group of itinerant artisans resembled the first generation of architects, headed by Tressini. They were often from the northern European countries which Peter had visited on his first trip abroad, and on the whole they were not men of much talent. It may be that Peter admired those who had a considerable knowledge of Europe and so had more experience to impart to their Russian pupils. As Tressini, an Italian Swiss, had worked in Denmark and possibly in Holland, so Peter's first portraitist, Gottfried Danhauer (c. 1690–1733/37), had been born in Bavaria, studied in Venice, and was painting in Holland when Peter met him in 1697.[3] He arrived in St Petersburg in 1710, and remained there for the rest of his life. His portraits for instance of the Tsar, his wife, and daughter are pedestrian and uninspired, at best adequate likenesses, and not above the standard for such painting elsewhere in Europe.

Peter was well aware that to promote Russian painting he must do two things: attract the best artists to Russia and send the most promising Russian pupils abroad. To this end he had issued in 1702 a manifesto inviting European artists to come to Russia and promising them special privileges. In 1711 the Government icon workshops in the Moscow Armoury were transferred to the new capital, and in 1718 a proclamation urged the merchants to allow their children to become trained as artists and craftsmen. At the same time schools had to be created to provide such education. A class in engraving and drawing in the Petersburg Printing Office was at best only a makeshift until more thorough training could be had, and for this Peter projected an art department in his proposed Academy of Sciences of 1724. His death the next year cut short these plans, and when Catherine I established the Academy in 1726, instruction in the arts was limited to the practical crafts of drawing and engraving. The character of the topographical work is represented in the prints of Mikhail Ivanovich Makhaev (1716–70), whose maps of St Petersburg (1753) and various engraved views of the city and environs are invaluable for the study of Petrovian and Elizabethan architecture (Plates 108, 112, 113, 115A, 115B, 116, and 119).

The first group of Peter's 'artist-pensioners' which left Russia in 1716 included five painters, among them the brothers Nikitin, who went to Italy. The painter Andrei Matveev and the architects Ustinov and Korobov went to Holland. Only one was sent to France – the engraver Stephan Korovin. Peter's earlier enthusiasms for northern European architecture and Italian painting can be seen in this distribution. Of all these young Russians, only Matveev (1701–39) made any particular contribution. In the last ten years of his life he painted portraits of the nobility and icons for the Peter–Paul Cathedral (later repainted). His unfinished self-portrait with his wife hints that in Holland he had learned something of the contemporary Court style. The brothers Nikitin fared no better. Little is known of their work, and the famous portrait of Peter on his deathbed, attributed to Ivan Nikitin (c. 1690–1741), may be by Danhauer.[4]

Peter realized that these first efforts would be long in producing results; so in 1715 he ordered his agent in Paris to discover whether any of the French king's artists might be persuaded to come to Russia. When Peter himself reached Paris in 1717 he met some of the men selected by Konon Zotov, including the architect Le Blond, whose personality delighted him. When Le Blond left for Russia he was accompanied by a group of artists, of whom the most prominent was Louis Caravacque (d. 1754), a portrait painter.[5] Caravacque's appointment was in the nature of a third choice. Nattier and Oudry, to whom Peter and his wife had sat for their portraits, had been approached, but both declined to enter the Russian service. Caravacque, born in Marseilles and educated in Paris, remained in St Petersburg until his death in 1754. He was a favourite of the Empress Anna, for whom he not only painted portraits and decorative ceilings in her Winter Palace, but also devised settings for Court ceremonies and theatrical performances. His talents were not above the ordinary, and his chief service to Russia was the instruction he offered in the art department of the Academy of Sciences. His portraits, especially the double portrait of Peter's daughters, indicate that he could handle the decorative French Rococo style, reminiscent of Largillierre, with modest competence.

Towards the middle of the century a brief revival of German influence, with the brothers Georg Christoph (1716–49) and Johann Friedrich Groot (1717–1801), preceded a new influx of Frenchmen and Italians. From Italy in 1756 came Pietro Rotari (1701–62), who painted the Gallery of Graces at Peterhof with three hundred portraits of the loveliest ladies of Elizabeth's court, and in 1762 Stefano Torelli (1712–84), a decorative painter who, with Rotari, had studied under the Neapolitan master Francesco Solimena. A third Italian, Giuseppe Valeriani (in Russia 1742–61), produced a quantity of theatrical decorations. The wave of French artists commenced with the arrival of Louis Joseph Le Lorrain (1715–59), who came to St Petersburg in 1758 as director of the new Academy, but died the next year. He was succeeded by Louis Jean François Lagrenée the Elder (1725–1805), who remained for two years. A stable arrangement was finally reached in 1759 with Nicolas Gillet (1709–91), a sculptor, who remained for twenty years. In addition, the portraitist Louis Tocqué (1696–1772) had a lively success when he visited St Petersburg (1756–8).[6]

Against this shifting background of resident and itinerant foreigners of varying degrees of ability, the work of the first generation of Russian-born painters, following such pioneers as Nikitin and Matveev, is perhaps not very startling. Alexei Petrovich Antropov (1716–95), a pupil of Matveev and Caravacque, at the age of forty-one turned to Rotari and worked with the Italian at Peterhof and on the decoration of the Anichkov Palace and the Opera. The polished oval surfaces and scrupulous detail in his portraits demonstrate his ability to absorb a mixture of manners. In his State portrait of Peter III (Plate 146A) for all the derivative pomp one's eye is immediately drawn to the mingled vanity and pathos in the tiny face. Antropov had studied icon-painting much earlier, but had so thoroughly absorbed the European style that his icons are indistinguishable from late Baroque Italian religious painting.[7]

Another portraitist, Ivan Petrovich Argunov (1727–97), who had been born a serf of the Counts Sheremetev, profited by the interest his owner's family had long taken in art. The details of his education are unknown, but his 'Ivan Lazarev as Amor' (Plate 146B) illustrates his superiority to Antropov in achieving movement. Where Antropov brought his figures close to the picture plane, as if to flatten them out, that he might the more easily examine all the details of face and costume, Argunov mastered a convincing *chiaroscuro*. The design of his State portrait of Paul I may be insistently angular, but in comparison with Antropov's Peter III, he stands solidly in a three-dimensional setting.

The origins of Feodor Stepanovich Rokotov (*c*. 1735–*c*. 1808), the third of this triumvirate of early portraitists, are also obscure, but it seems that he had worked with the first professor of painting in the Petersburg Academy, where he acquired a more fluent manner and a greater compositional ability than his predecessors. For ten years or more, after 1765, Rokotov worked in Moscow. The distance from Court helped the development of a more intimate and personal style to be seen in his delicate colouring and more direct treatment of character with a preference for bust-length portraits against a neutral background, as in the likeness of Count Peter Ivanovich Shuvalov (Plate 147A). Something of Rotari is still there in the smooth, rounded surfaces, but the characterization appears both more candid and more truthful.

With the organization of the Academy of Fine Arts in St Petersburg instruction was put on a permanent basis. The project, which had hung fire since Peter's death, was revived by Count Ivan Ivanovich Shuvalov, the brilliant and enthusiastic favourite of Elizabeth, who in 1755 had inaugurated the first Russian university in Moscow. Elizabeth approved his plans, and in 1757 the Senate published a ukase establishing the Academy in St Petersburg, although it remained an administrative department of the University of Moscow until 1763. Meanwhile, as we have seen, Shuvalov had commissioned the French architect J. F. Blondel to design the building which was finally erected by Vallin de la Mothe and Kokorinov. The Academy was not permanently organized until 1764, when Catherine II replaced Shuvalov as director with her own creature, the less imaginative and more disciplinarian Count Ivan Ivanovich Betskoi (c. 1703–95), who had lived in Paris during most of Elizabeth's reign. The regulations, like those for many academies elsewhere in Europe in the eighteenth century, were almost literally copied from the French Academy.[8] There was the same system of membership, rising through three grades from associate to academician and full professor. In the absence of any regular public schooling in Russia, there were added a secondary school which took pupils from the age of six, and trade schools which they might enter, if at the proper age they had failed to demonstrate sufficient aptitude for the fine arts. In contrast to France, where architecture, painting, sculpture, and the minor arts were taught in separate institutions, the Russian Academy brought all these under one roof. Provisions were also made to send the best students abroad in groups of twelve every three years. In 1760 the first two – the architect Bazhenov and the painter Losenko – went to Paris. Between 1760 and 1789, when the outbreak of the Revolution interrupted relations between France and Russia, more than forty young Russians studied in the French Academy and in the *ateliers* of Paris.[9]

The effects of this new institutional instruction soon appeared in the work of Anton Pavlovich Losenko (1731–73), one of the most gifted and neglected Russian painters of the early years of Catherine's reign. He had studied with Argunov and at the Academy under Le Lorrain before going to Paris as a pensioner for two years (1760–2). Whereas his predecessors had been pre-eminently portrait painters, Losenko attempted historical subjects, in the grand manner. In Paris he worked with Restout, and his 'Sacrifice of Abraham' showed that he had acquired the accepted academic manner, mixing equal doses of Poussin and Raphael with a measure of the antique. His historical paintings were much admired by his contemporaries, yet they add nothing to the common repertory of late Baroque painting. In his 'St Vladmir and Rogneda' (1770), he became the first modern Russian painter to interpret a national historical subject on so large a scale, and on the strength of this was appointed professor of history painting in the Academy.[10] In answer to the eloquent plea of Falconet, who recognized Losenko's talent in the beautiful drawing he had made of the sculptor's sketch for the monument to Peter the Great, Catherine acquired the 'St Vladimir' for the State, but imperial favour could not overcome the ill-will of the painter's colleagues. Losenko died three years later, a disappointed and discouraged man. Perhaps he had attempted too much, for certainly Russian history painting had to wait at least two generations until a man appeared who was equal to its challenge and difficulties.

This first generation had come of age artistically during the reign of Elizabeth, and their works in one way or another were imbued with the Rococo and ceremonial character of Elizabeth's French and Italian tastes. If we cannot point to this or that Russian element in their paintings, we can at least surmise that they supplied the Russian Court with the sensation of being European which the Empress and her courtiers wanted. It is worth observing, too, that these artists were predominantly portraitists. They established the costumes and make-up for the characters who began to act their roles in the works of the next group of painters.

Losenko, whose less formal works prove that he had a truly pictorial gift, was an Ukrainian, and also from Little Russia came the greatest portraitist Russia had yet known. Dmitri Grigorievich Levitski (1735/7–1822) [11] was the son of a priest who worked as an engraver in the Printing Office of the Pecherskaya Lavra in Kiev. The elder Levitski's prints show considerable familiarity with Western art, especially with Italian painting and engraving of the sixteenth and seventeenth centuries.[12] In 1752 the boy's talents were recognized by Antropov, when he came to Kiev to paint the iconostasis in the Church of St Andrew. When he was recalled to St Petersburg in 1756, he took Levitski with him. By 1762 he was a registered painter, and in 1769 became an associate of the Academy. Perhaps he was fundamentally an eclectic, but however much he absorbed from his contemporaries, the results were inimitably his own. It is not too much to say that Levitski invented the character of St Petersburg society for some time to come, much as Van Dyck earlier in England had created an image of an aristocracy which the members were from that time onwards obliged to emulate. More than that, his susceptibility to different personalities far surpassed that of his predecessors. He found a proper type of portrait and style of interpretation for each class and kind of person.

At the first exhibition of the reorganized Academy in 1770, to which seven artists contributed twenty paintings, Levitski became famous over-night with his five works. The spectators most admired his portrait of the architect A. F. Kokorinov (Plate 148). For the inauguration of the Academy Kokorinov had ordered a splendid new suit of lilac satin, which gave Levitski an opportunity to show his mastery of textiles. But his brilliant painting of materials was surpassed by the elegance of the three-quarter-length figure, turning easily towards the plans of the Academy spread out beside him on a fine French bureau. However numerous the influences of European Court portraiture may be, Levitski had absorbed them, made them his own, and was now prepared to offer his own contribution to European painting. This portrait of Kokorinov, for which Levitski was made an academician, was the clearest proof of the distance Russian society had come in the little more than a lifetime which had elapsed since the foundation of St Petersburg.

Levitski twice in the next few years repeated the general scheme of this Rococo design, somewhat less exuberantly for Prince A. M. Golitsyn (1772), and with a wealth of homely detail in the portrait of P. A. Demidov (1773), an eccentric philanthropist who had founded the School of Commerce. Demidov in informal dress stands by a table and points to two potted plants, symbols of the institutions which he nourished. In contrast to the *brio* and elegance of Kokorinov's lilac costume, the soberer hues of Demidov's clothes and the carefully distinguished textures of woods, fabrics, and metal, show Levitski's genius for creating a portrait in character.

The success of these paintings and his growing European reputation – his portrait of Prince A. M. Golitsyn was engraved in Vienna in 1773 – attracted the attention of the Empress, who commissioned Levitski to paint her favourite pupils in the Smolny Institute. Between 1773 and 1776 Levitski painted seven portraits of these young ladies, including some of the most beguiling delineations of childhood and adolescence which the eighteenth century has left us. Perhaps the best known is the double portrait of Princess Khovanski and Mlle Khrushchov (1773) acting their roles in a play given before the Empress. Levitski's mastery of textures can be seen in the contrast between the man's taffeta coat, so much too large for Mlle Khrushchov, and the silks and sheer muslins worn by the young Princess. The coquetry of this school performance, where the youthful pupils mimic their elders, is belied by something ineffably tender in the lingering traces of adolescent awkwardness. The double portrait of Mlle Rzhevski and Princess Nastasya Davydov (1776) (Plate 147B), combines technical brilliance, the grand manner, and an engaging pertness in the expressions of the little girls who are almost submerged by their elaborate costumes. In this suite of seven paintings the greatest variety prevails: Mlles Levshin and Nelidov are dancing, Mlle Alymov plays the harp, and Mlle Moltanov reads aloud. In the background of this last portrait there is a piece of electrical equipment, reminding us that this was the century when scientific experiment was the privilege of the upper classes.

Levitski's success with the Smolny portraits prompted Catherine to commission a series of full-length portraits of herself, although it seems unlikely that she posed for any of them. They are among the most majestic State portraits of the eighteenth century, but individually they tell us very little about the woman. Levitski dressed Catherine in flowing garments to conceal her increasing embonpoint and surrounded her with appropriate imperial symbols. The greatest contrast to these impressive but psychologically empty images is provided by his portraits of eminent men of letters. In 1773 he painted a bust portrait of Diderot, who was then visiting St Petersburg. The philosopher appears without a wig in a dressing-gown of green and white, Levitski's favourite colours. Possibly here he penetrated further than in any portrait up to this time into the sensibilities of a distinguished sitter.[13]

Towards the mid 1780s Levitski's style changed considerably. Inspiration from France which had been so strong in design, even in costume, and certainly in the search for expressive gesture, was replaced by the influence of English painting. There were many ways by which this could have reached Levitski, through the younger Falconet, who had studied in England under Reynolds, through the presence at Court of the English painter Richard Brompton, or through the numerous engravings after portraits by English masters which were circulated throughout Europe. The shift of interest from France to England is also understandable for other reasons at the close of this decade. Catherine had always liked English civilization, as we have seen in her enthusiasm for English landscape design, and when the French Revolution broke out, her fear of any threat to legitimacy caused her sympathies to turn towards England. Thus something of a simpler English manner appears in the late 1780s and first years of the 90s in Levitski's portraits of Catherine's grandchildren, the son and daughters of Paul I.[14]

These were the last evidence of Levitski's favour at Court. Ostensibly for reasons of health he had retired in 1788 from the Academy, where he was professor of portraiture. During Paul's reign his work was slighted, and the Emperor almost refused to pay for a series of portraits of the Knights of St Vladimir commissioned by his mother. After 1795, when the French portraitist Mme Vigée-Lebrun was in St Petersburg for eight years, his work takes on something of her sentimental and slightly Neo-Classical manner. In 1808 he returned to the Academy, but his powers declined, and after a few years he became religious, went blind, and finally died in 1822.

A last reflexion of eighteenth-century elegance persists through the reign of Alexander I in the work of Vladimir Lukich Borovikovski (1757–1825).[15] Of noble Cossack origin, he came of a family of icon-painters in the Ukraine. Among his earlier works are the iconostasis for the church built for Catherine II by Lvov at Mogilev to commemorate her meeting with Joseph II of Austria. The cold and limpid style of these paintings is so thoroughly Italian that Borovikovski's future reputation is all the more surprising. When Potemkin arranged Catherine's triumphal journey through the Crimea in 1787, Borovikovski was summoned to decorate a temporary palace at Kremenchug on the Dnieper. Catherine was so pleased with his allegories that she sent him to St Petersburg, where he seems to have first worked under Levitski and later as an assistant to the Austrian portraitist Johann Baptist Lampi (1751–1830; in Russia 1791–7). From the first he enjoyed the favour of the Court, even remaining in Paul's good graces after Catherine's death.

Borovikovski's first works were generally small, often miniature reductions of portraits by better-known painters, but after his service with Lampi he graduated to a larger scale, usually the life-size portrait. In addition to State portraits of the imperial family, which are not more distinguished than others of their kind, his principal works were portraits of women and young girls. These are very English, often introducing the informal dress and summary park-like background familiar in Reynolds and Gainsborough, but through all this appears Borovikovski's own personal sentiment, in the large eyes and languid postures which are a little reminiscent of Greuze. His women might be monotonous were it not for the fact that within this generalized *fin-de-siècle* mood of self-indulgent melancholy, Borovikovski was at heart a realist who never failed, so we feel, to create a likeness. His Russian women and young girls, for instance, seem really Slavic (Plate 149B). Somewhat apart from his usual production is a delightfully informal portrait of Catherine II in the last year of her life (1796). She is here not an empress but an elderly lady leaning on her stick in the Park at Tsarskoe Selo. Beside her is her favourite dog, and in the distance the rostral column she had raised so long ago to the glory of Count Orlov. Without Gainsborough the portrait could not be, and it is a precious document of late eighteenth-century sensibility in the relation of human personality to nature. After 1800 a new indication of French influence can be seen in the sturdy portrait of Catherine Alexandrovna Arkharov (Plate 149A). The frontal pose, crisp drawing, and precise detail prove that French Neo-Classicism had reached Russia, but Borovikovski leaves these David-like qualities behind in the sharp features and individual expression.

Although portraits and historical paintings occupied the major talents in eighteenth-century St Petersburg, other genres were not entirely neglected. In landscape the works of Russian masters, while not without charm and a certain historical interest, do not rise above the general European standard. Simon Feodorovich Shchedrin (1743–1804) and Mikhail Matveevich Ivanov (1748–1823) continued the topographical painting of Matveev, but enlarged it with a new feeling for the poetry of nature, for which the development of the imperial parks may be held responsible (Plate 145A).[16] Feodor Mikhailovich Matveev (1758–1826) and Vasili Petrovich Petrov (1770–1811) represented the more cosmopolitan tendency. After his studies in Italy, Matveev's landscapes were usually classical subjects based on the Roman Campagna; Petrov used a similar manner for pictures of Russian scenery. There was very little genre-painting, the lowest class in the academic hierarchy. The evidence of only one canvas, long attributed to Losenko, until the signature of a little-known painter, Ivan Firsov, appeared when it was cleaned, need cause no regrets. The rendering of a young artist seated at his easel sketching his younger sister is thoroughly French in design and technique, a testimony to Firsov's schooling in Paris (1748–56).[17]

Of the major arts, sculpture offers fewer surprises than painting or architecture. If in architecture Peter's task was to transform old traditions, in the case of sculpture he had practically to create a new art. The still effective prohibition by the Church limited the knowledge of three-dimensional forms to ecclesiastical furniture, and such rare sculptural embellishment as that which decorates the church at Dubrovitsi was entirely Western and without any specifically Russian characteristics. The scanty vestiges of folk sculpture are also to be explained by the influence of Western traditions, whether from Germany through Novgorod into the north-east, or through Poland and Lithuania to the Ukraine. In both regions from the middle of the sixteenth century there was a tradition of religious sculpture in wood, but the seated figures of Christ as the Man of Sorrows or the iconic images of the head of the Baptist are all in the manner of late medieval or Baroque European folk sculpture, and not essentially Russian.[18] Only rarely, as in some of the wooden standing figures of saints in the northern churches, where the flat, two-dimensional forms are derived from painted icons, or in the few Court sculptures such as the reliefs which decorate the so-called Throne of Ivan IV and which again are related to two-dimensional pictorial design, was there anything approaching the scale of Western sculpture. The three-dimensional instinct of the Russian people found its outlet in the bronze and silver-gilt religious vessels, in some of which the figure may attain a considerable size, or in carved wooden pulpits.[19] Under these circumstances the activity of foreign sculptors in Muscovy in the later seventeenth century was a prelude to the course which Peter followed. For the Petrovski Gate in the St Petersburg fortress the German sculptor Konrad Osner (1673–1747) carved a relief in wood representing the 'Fall of Simon Magus'. It is now so covered with paint that it is hard to judge its original condition, but it would certainly seem to have been much like, if no better than, the sculpture which may be attributed to him on the church at Dubrovitsi and which is thoroughly and unskilfully Baroque.

The first requirements for decorative sculpture were satisfied by the import of marbles from Europe, and casts of antique statues from Italy. Much of this was second-rate, like the allegorical figures in the Summer Garden ridiculed by Casanova. Soon recourse was had to artists summoned from abroad, such as Andreas Schlüter, the German architect and sculptor, to whom may be attributed the reliefs on Peter's diminutive Summer Palace, or Nicolas Pineau, who executed the ornamental woodwork for Peter's work rooms at Peterhof. A more monumental sculptor was Count Carlo Bartolommeo Rastrelli (c. 1675–1744, in Russia from 1716), the father of the great architect.[20] His bronze busts of Peter and Menshikov (1724 and 1729), as well as portrait medallions of Peter and other members of his family, are little more than competent exercises in the manner inaugurated three generations before by Bernini. Yet the confusion of his interpretation of the Baroque play of light and shade on costume and armour was made up by the strength of his likenesses. Rastrelli's major accomplishment was his equestrian portrait of Peter, finished after his death by Alexander Martelli, and erected much later by Paul I in front of his Michael Castle.[21] This is a chunky, ponderous group, in keeping with the practical character of Peter's art. A more commanding as well as more accomplished work was the bronze group of the Empress Anna Ioannovna and her little Negro page. Rastrelli's surfaces were still timid, more etched than modelled, but he introduced a little more light and shade, and thus lent the figure of the Empress a sense of movement and vitality lacking in his other sculpture.

Until the establishment of the Academy of Fine Arts in the later 1750s there was no further sculptural activity of much moment, except such trivial decorative schemes as the clumsy figures on the roof of the younger Rastrelli's Winter Palace.[22] The lack of any conspicuous talent obliged Catherine to summon the French sculptor, Étienne-Maurice Falconet (1716–91), when she decided to erect a monument to the memory of Peter the Great. Her choice was undoubtedly prompted by Diderot, who had an extravagant admiration for his work.[23] Falconet arrived in St Petersburg in 1767, and at once set to work on the equestrian statue which he envisaged as a figure of Peter in antique dress on a rearing horse, poised on a huge natural boulder. The lively action was intended to symbolize the Tsar's conquest of an unruly nation and his vision of the future. In 1770 the model was exhibited in the sculptor's studio, where a crowd of eager spectators studied it in silence, an indication that the sense of sculptural criticism was still undeveloped. Through the years the difficulty of finding properly trained workmen to do the casting and perennial squabbles with Count Betskoi over his salary embittered the sculptor, until he left Russia in 1778, before the work was finished. Meanwhile a colossal boulder was quarried in Finland and transported with enormous effort to St Petersburg, where the statue itself was finally cast and erected in 1782. This first and last truly Baroque monument of French art in Russia became a symbol of Peter's city.[24] The boulder was, as it were, a test of Russian ingenuity, a foretaste of the heroic exertion later undertaken to bring the columns for St Isaac and the monolith for the Alexander Column to St Petersburg. Upon the base the laconic inscription, 'Petro Primo Catharina Secunda' (and on the other side in Russian translation), summarized Catherine's attitude towards her predecessor and her conception of her place in the line of great Russian sovereigns.

At the Academy French influence was further confirmed by a succession of instructors, most notably by Nicolas-François Gillet (1709–91), professor of sculpture from 1757 until 1777. Although a mediocre sculptor, he was a good teacher, and through his encouragement a group of young Russians within a generation mastered the international style of the school of Paris.[25] The first and in some respects the ablest Russian sculptor was Fedot Ivanovich Shubin (1740–1805), whose work, like that of the best contemporary painters, was primarily in portraiture.[26] He had been born in the far north near Arkhangelsk, the son of a fisherman. In 1761 he entered the Academy, and by 1767 had won a scholarship to Paris, where he studied for six years with Pigalle. Later he visited Rome, Turin, and London, where he worked with Nollekens. Upon his return to Russia, Catherine and Potemkin commissioned their portraits, and his reputation was apparently secure. But his vivid and realistic busts failed to capture the interest of a nobility which did not yet understand sculpture as an art, and his career languished. His standing figure of 'Catherine, the Legislator', commissioned by Potemkin for the rotunda in the Tauride Palace, was completed in 1795 and may already have seemed old-fashioned.[27] The relaxed posture, tumbling draperies, and coquettish expression belong more to the waning Rococo than the nascent Neo-Classicism. To gratify Catherine's historical curiosity Shubin produced a series of forty-nine portrait reliefs of the sovereigns of Russia, from the Great Princes of Kiev through the Tsars and Emperors. Although these were executed in the realistic Baroque manner and have only the slightest pretensions to historical verisimilitude, they are interesting symptoms of the growing interest in the national past. In 1801 Shubin's studio was burned, with the loss of his life's work, and four years later he himself was dead. It is impossible to feel that his was a completely Russian talent. Without his training under Gillet and his experience in Paris, he perhaps could not have developed his gifts at all. The frequently made comparison of Shubin with Houdon works to his disadvantage, since, while he too possessed a gift for psychological characterization, his portraits lack the beauty and sensitivity of Houdon's.

A second pupil of Gillet, Mikhail Ivanovich Kozlovski (1753–1802), also studied in Paris on two occasions (1772–9, and again 1788–94). He liked ideal classical themes, and his 'Sleeping Cupid' (1792), 'Hymen' (1797), and 'Mounted Hercules' (1799) are competent essays in the familiar eighteenth-century manner, differing little from the earlier productions of Pigalle or Pajou. Slightly more energetic is the style of his caryatids in the throne room at Pavlovsk (1798) (Plate 150A). It hints that the coming Alexandrian classicism would be severely linear. For his monument to General Suvorov, whose rotund and commonplace appearance was unmanageable in monumental sculpture, Kozlovski awkwardly posed the hero as a youthful Mars. It is interesting that Suvorov is clad in a complete suit of plate armour and wears a plumed helmet – another indication that a more romantic and less realistic attitude towards history was approaching.

The last sculptor of this generation to rise above the level of mere competence was Fedos (Theodosius) Feodorovich Shchedrin (1751–1825). He studied in Rome, and from 1775 in Paris with Allegrain, where he developed a vigorous yet not ungraceful decorative manner, at its best in his groups of female figures supporting spheres (Plate 150B) before the principal entrance of Zakharov's Admiralty. In their mingled elegance and coldness they stand as a sign of the transition between the last bloom of Shubin's Rococo and the fully developed Neo-Classicism of Martos.

Ivan Petrovich Martos (1754–1835) studied like his predecessors under Gillet, but, when he went abroad in 1773, he set a precedent by remaining in Rome, which had already become an artistic Mecca for Russian architects in the 1770s and 80s.[28] There he studied with Anton Raphael Mengs, from whom he absorbed not only the doctrine but the manner of Neo-Classicism in a stricter sense than had yet been seen in Russia. Sentimental subjects requiring an emotional interpretation were executed on a broad scale in the coldest treatment of Neo-Classicism. The result is of an intensity which sets Martos apart from the ruck of his contemporaries. He excelled in funeral sculpture (Plate 151A), which he executed in quantity for the tombs of the nobility in the fashionable cemeteries of the Alexander Nevski Lavra in St Petersburg and of the Monastery of the Virgin of the Don in Moscow.[29] In these he surpassed the standardized mourning geniuses and sorrowing nymphs of Canova and Thorvaldsen by posing his figures in an excess of despair. But when his subject was other than classical, the result is less credible. At Odessa his standing figure of the Duc de Richelieu garbed as a Roman emperor lacks life, and in the famous group of 'Minin and Pozharski' (1804–18) (Plate 151B) he used antique garments for the prince and butcher who rallied the populace to the defence of the fatherland in 1611. They carry sword and shield, and display the most extravagant rhetorical gestures. The historical incongruity is all the more poignant since the monument was designed to be placed in the Red Square in Moscow opposite the walls of the Kremlin.[30]

After Martos, whose works have a certain irrational distinction, there is little more to be said for Russian sculpture of the nineteenth century than for that of any other academic national tradition. Boris Ivanovich Orlovski (1793–1837) continued the forms of Neo-Classicism in his angel for the Alexander Column and in his statues of Kutuzov (Plate 152A) and Barclay de Tolly for the square in front of Kazan Cathedral. His iron manner is the perfect complement to Voronikhin's linear architecture. The long life of Count Feodor Petrovich Tolstoi (1783–1873) enabled him to continue a tenuous classicism in his coins and portrait medallions until almost the middle of the century. After that the innumerable classical divinities and ideal figures, so popular in Europe through the 1830s and 40s, were gradually replaced by more naturalistic subjects and genre scenes. A last reminder of the earlier strength of the classical manner which had made St Petersburg an urban whole unique in the Western world was supplied by the works of Baron Peter Karlovich Klodt (1805–67).[31] His four horse-tamers on the Anichkov Bridge (1839) became one of the sculptural landmarks of the city, somewhat like the horses of Marly at the entrance to the Champs-Elysées in Paris. But the weak modelling and angular design prove that the classical vision of Martos had run out. Klodt's is a typical and pathetic instance of an artist of real talent, whose gifts were distorted by the fashions of the day and the official discipline of an Academy. His many studies from nature, especially his horses, show that he had a deep sympathy for animals and a not unselective eye for detail. At his best these small bronzes are not inferior to those of Barye. But the groups on the Anichkov Bridge are a disturbing blend of naturalism and idealism in subjects which required a consistent degree of abstraction. After this even the Academy was obliged to open its doors to naturalism.

CHAPTER 25

ROMANTICISM

RUSSIA's isolation from Western Europe at the close of the eighteenth century was a brief episode imposed by Paul's insane fear of revolution and his prohibition of foreign travel. In the following decade the Napoleonic Wars precipitated Russian intervention in European affairs to such an extent that henceforward Russian art history remained woven with the pattern of European expression as a whole. Therefore the examination of Russian art and architecture according to the standards of European criticism of comparable works during the same period does no violence to the intentions of Russian painters, sculptors, and architects through the middle years of the century. Just as they still continued to travel and study abroad, once their academic training had been completed, and visited the same cities as their Western colleagues, so they competed for the same honours at international exhibitions, and were respected at home so much the more, if their works resembled the types of European painting then in favour in St Petersburg and Moscow. And during the nineteenth century for the Russian, as for every artist, first Rome and then, after 1860, Paris were the centres of artistic research with Düsseldorf and Munich important for briefer periods, the first in the 1840s, the second towards the end of the 70s. With such an international scale of values we may also expect to find the same standards of technical competence which prevailed throughout Europe, the same selection and interpretation of academic and popular subjects, the same sequence of stylistic mannerisms from the polished Neo-Classicism of the early years through the romantic revival of the Baroque to the realist attitude to nature and then the development of naturalism culminating in the Impressionist movement of the 1870s.[1]

What, therefore, can we say is Russian in painting executed by Russians or in Russia during this period? If such qualities do not reside in technique, and after the disappearance of icon-painting Russia produced no notable technical discoveries, and was original only superficially in the choice of subject, where shall we seek it? It is perhaps to be found in what we may call the iconology of Russian painting – that is to say, in the meaning more than in the identification of the images which were used.[2] In this way we may hope to penetrate beneath the arbitrary distinctions of genre, portraiture, and history painting to discover what the Russian painter sought and what all too occasionally he found, in the course of the artistic experience of the nineteenth century.

A step towards understanding this point of view may be taken by comparing the last of the eighteenth-century portraitists with the first of the truly nineteenth-century painters. In Borovikovski's portraits sentiment is an additive element, something which colours or intensifies the forms, while the design remains eighteenth-century in the fullest sense of the word, derived from late Baroque spatial compositions, the individual shapes generalized or idealized, even when the details, as in much of Levitski's work, were deceptively realistic. And with it all there was ever present that eighteenth-century attitude towards society which saw men and women first as types, as members of a class, and only secondarily as individuals. With the portraits of Orest Adamovich Kiprenski (1773–1836) much more than the accent was shifted.[3] The sentiment was now directed towards a particular person as one individual with special psychological responsibilities to society and himself. Such comment was no longer added to a composition essentially generic, but was part of a compositional arrangement dictated by particular circumstances. The difference in the formal result quite as much as in the motivation can be compared with that which exists between an eighteenth-century garden pavilion in the Gothic taste, and the recreation of a Gothic environment in much European religious architecture of the 1830s and 40s.

Not only the work but the life of Kiprenski exemplifies this distinction. He had been born the illegitimate son of a nobleman, and brought up as a serf. His talent was recognized at an early age, and he was sent to the Petersburg Academy, where in 1805 he won the gold medal and a travelling scholarship for his thoroughly academic treatment of 'Dmitri Donskoi on the Field of Kulikovo'.[4] Some suggestion of a new and more introspective attitude towards a historical subject can be seen in the fact that the Prince is depicted reclining in an attitude of prayer rather than at the head of his victorious troops. But Kiprenski soon turned his back on academic instruction; as early as 1804 a portrait of his step-father reveals his study of the Baroque masters, especially van Dyck, Rubens, and Rembrandt, whose works he saw in the Hermitage. While waiting for the end of the wars in Europe, he moved to Moscow, where his pencil and oil portraits were appreciated by the nobility. Among many portraits of distinguished sitters, his handsome three-quarter length likeness of the poet and warrior Denis Davydov (1809) (Plate 152B), shows an early acquaintance with contemporary French painting. Even without presuming some as yet unexplained knowledge of Gros and Géricault, Kiprenski caught to the life the romantic yearning for heroic exploits which marked the generation absorbed in the Napoleonic Wars. Symptomatic, too, of romanticism were Kiprenski's many self-portraits (Plate 153), painted at short intervals throughout his life. In these he usually characterized himself as the artist he was, fixing his gaze irresistibly on the spectator and marking candidly the changing aspect of his countenance through the years.

After peace had been established, Kiprenski went to Italy, but this had a disastrous effect on his life and his art. He succumbed to the spell of the Italian mannerists and Raphael, and produced a series of sentimental, ideal heads of beggar boys and peasant girls. From the romantic tragedy of Géricault he passed to the pathos of Léopold Robert. In 1825 he returned to St Petersburg for four years, and during this period painted the portrait of Pushkin, one of his best known and most typical works. The mixed ingredients of early Romanticism, the searching details, and the classical reference of the statuette in the background, create that combination of the real and ideal which is found in Pushkin's poetry. The twist of the head and set of expression are romantic assertions of individual personality. After the accession of Nicholas I in 1825 even the limited Romanticism of such a portrait, like the poet's verses, was in disfavour. In 1827 Kiprenski returned to Italy for the remainder of his life, disturbed by ill health and an unhappy love affair, and achieved nothing which matched his earlier portraits.

Somewhat the same psychological dissatisfaction and artistic uncertainty marks the work of Karl Briullov (1799–1852), one of the most celebrated artists of his day, and the first Russian painter to enjoy an international reputation.[5] He had been born in Italy, and came to Russia as a child with his father, a sculptor of Huguenot descent named Briullo, whose name was later russified with imperial permission. By 1823 he had completed his academic education, won the necessary prizes, and reached Rome. There his first works were on the popular classical and sentimental themes, although for a series of ideal heads of Italian girls representing the times of the day, he did apparently much painting out of doors; for it is known that he was obliged to leave his study of evening unfinished because the sun set too soon. He would scarcely have distinguished himself from the host of painters from all countries working in Italy, had he not conceived the idea of a picture of the destruction of Pompeii. His imagination, fortified by a visit to the ruins, a performance of Pacini's opera, *L'ultimo giorno di Pompei* (1825), and Pliny's description of the catastrophe, soared until the result was an enormous canvas which became the wonder of the age. When 'The Last Day of Pompeii' (1828–30) (Plate 155A) was finished, the Italian press hailed it as a masterpiece, foreign visitors flocked to the studio, and Briullov himself became at once famous. Sir Walter Scott is said to have sat in front of the painting for an hour and then have remarked that it was not a painting but an epic.[6] Public enthusiasm for this huge 'machine' is easy to understand. In a period when artistic intuition had been systematized in the formulas of eclecticism, Briullov offered something for every taste. The melodramatic, even morbid treatment of a classical subject with a wealth of realistic detail appealed to all manners of intelligence, and even to-day surprises by its intensity. Artistically Briullov's sources were irreproachable; reminiscences of Raphael, Poussin, and David were cunningly mixed with the histrionic effects of Vernet, and the lurid brilliance of the colours outdid the later Bolognese.[7] When Briullov returned to Russia in 1841 he was hailed as the greatest master of the day, and was expected to repeat or even surpass his first work. But 'The Siege of Pskov by Stephen Batory in 1581' (1836–43), so large that it was never finished, was a disappointment. Confused, crowded, lacking the violent *chiaroscuro* of 'The Last Day of Pompeii', it concerns us only because of Briullov's conscientious attempt to recreate the historical past through careful attention to costumes and furnishings.

More interesting are the many portraits which he painted throughout his life. His women are often represented in fancy dress, to intensify their sentimental postures, or in out-of-door settings, sometimes on horseback as in the familiar portrait of a young lady of the Samoilov family, often called 'The Amazon'. In many of these his attitudinizing cannot quite conceal his fondness for the poetry of nature. His portraits of men are usually simpler and more penetrating. In the fine seated portrait of Prince A. N. Golitsyn (1838–40) (Plate 154), Briullov recreated not only the man but his surroundings. The trellis with growing plants, repeated in the distant room, is evidence of his feeling for nature, and the distribution of light throughout the space is in the tradition of the painting of interiors in which so many Russians excelled.

Briullov's Pompeii became a mark to be emulated by others of his generation. Feodor (Fidelio) Antonovich Bruni (1800–75), born in Moscow but of Italian parentage, reached Italy at an early age. In 1818 he was in Rome, where his bacchantes and ideal nudes matched those of Briullov and Kiprenski. But the renown of Briullov's famous painting stirred his ambition, and he proceeded to emulate its size, complication, and historical melodrama. His 'Moses and the Brazen Serpent' merely transposes to the Old Testament the pseudo-classical repertoire of agonized nude figures which had swarmed through the 'Last Day of Pompeii'. How much he hoped that it would become equally famous can be seen in the fact that he arranged his light to fall in a direction opposite that in Briullov's canvas. But public response was less enthusiastic, and Bruni's later works are scarcely distinguishable from the general run of academic art in these years. For much of his life he painted religious subjects for the Isaac Cathedral, but they are lost in the cold gloom of that church.

Neither of these enormous history paintings would be worth mentioning at such length, were it not that they provide an illuminating contrast with a third and last large canvas on a similar 'historical' theme, one wherein even more clearly than in the work of Briullov and Bruni the counter-currents of Classicism, Romanticism, and Realism can be seen at work, while an intensely personal conception of nature prepared the way for the future. Alexander Andreevich Ivanov (1806–58) was the son of a competent professor at the Academy, A. I. Ivanov, under whom he studied.[8] After winning the usual medals for exercises in the academic manner on classical and Old Testament themes, Ivanov went to Rome, where he remained for the next quarter-century. His first painting in Italy after his student days, a composition of 'Apollo, Hyacinthus, and Zephyrus', demonstrated his ability to handle the standard classical subject, not without some sensitivity for the nude figure.[9] After 1830, when Briullov's masterpiece excited so much attention, Ivanov's thoughts turned towards the creation of a similarly large work. A deeply religious man, he was taken with the subject of the first appearance of Christ to the people announced by St John the Baptist (Plate 155B). The theme was peculiarly suited to his mystical faith; for it combined certain traditional motifs with the opportunity to interpret them in a new manner. It was Ivanov's intention that his painting should surpass in spiritual profundity and natural truth all previous religious painting in the West. So he undertook the most extensive studies, and consulted every artist whose opinion he respected, especially the Nazarenes Cornelius and Overbeck, who influenced him considerably. The inevitable result was that his work took indefinitely long and that again and again he had to change his composition. Not only did he pursue the usual studies of earlier religious painting and investigate the historical aspects of the New Testament scene, although to his great regret he was unable to travel to Palestine, but he ransacked the storehouses of classical sculpture for types and expressions which he felt would best reveal his message. To the modern eye much of this seems academic rubbish, such as the derivation from classical sculptures of centaurs and fauns of the expressions of the young men who cynically mock the teaching of the Baptist. Of more interest was his search for truth to nature, which took him into the country. His landscape paintings, with their range of bright fresh colours, anticipated the naturalistic vision of the French Impressionists. And in his studies for the figures climbing from the river Ivanov's naturalistic treatment of the classical nude (Plate 156A) cannot fail to remind the Western eye of Degas's early work.[10] When the painting was finally exhibited in St Petersburg in 1858, after almost twenty-five years of painful effort, it failed to arouse the enthusiasm which had greeted Briullov's and even Bruni's canvases. In the later 1840s Ivanov himself had begun to doubt the effectiveness of his undertaking, especially when his social and religious convictions were disturbed by the revolutions of 1848–9 and by the new biblical criticism in France and Germany. Yet he did not shun sources dangerous to his faith, and visited D. F. Strauss in Germany, whose positivist *Life of Christ* had almost convinced him that his work had been in vain.

Ivanov's 'Appearance of the Messiah' must be called a noble failure. His figures are skilful, serious, and full of deep and varied feeling. The emotions of the listeners range from doubt and scepticism to sudden, overwhelmed conviction. But the contrast between the naturalistic background and the classically contrived groups is too abrupt to be bridged by spirituality alone. By the middle of the nineteenth century the conflicting claims of naturalism and idealism could no longer be reconciled; when the former took precedence it necessarily destroyed the latter. The reasons for Ivanov's failure are apparent in the curiously insignificant figure of Christ. There truth to naturalistic atmospheric and linear perspective vitiates the truth of spiritual experience.

Ivanov's message and legacy to Russian art are of another kind. His simpler studies of landscape, his sensitive nudes, and his provocative portraits of Roman women, in their casual design and brilliant effects of light and colour, opened the way for the understanding of Impressionism. In later years to allay his doubts he projected a series of religious scenes arranged according to a scheme which should reconcile ancient history and mythology with the Old and New Testaments.[11] At his death the series was incomplete, but he had already finished 257 drawings. Among them were many wherein his search for the purest revelation of the spirit took him into the then unexplored territory of Byzantine art. Already he had studied the Byzantine mosaics of Palermo and Monreale for the physical types and facial expressions of his Christ and St John. In these later drawings he often recovered, through the mysterious radiance which surrounded his allegorical figures signifying the great abstractions of the spiritual presence, the character of earlier icon-painting (Plate 156B). In this way his work, however much the more elaborate part of it failed to justify either his efforts or his intentions, ultimately was of great value. Under the impetus of the Slavophiles' enthusiasm for the recovery of the national artistic heritage, a younger generation found in these drawings justification for the Byzantine revival of the later nineteenth century.

While the conflicting demands of idealism and naturalism vitiated the work of Briullov, Bruni, and Ivanov, a less spectacular but ultimately more conclusive victory for the painting of Russian life was won by the emerging genre-painters of the 1830s and 40s. Until then the painting of everyday life had occupied the least part of Russia's pictorial talents. The members of the upper class, who were the only possible and consistent patrons of painting, did not care to be reminded that their national customs and costume were so different from those of Europe. Consequently, for the painters who were striving under considerable difficulties to learn European techniques and modes of expression, the treatment of Russian manners offered no particular advantages. Only with the rise of a nationalist spirit in the nineteenth century could genre-painting of this sort come into its own. Meanwhile in a handful of paintings of the later eighteenth century the gradual intrusion of such painting can be traced.

From the first years of the Academy subjects from Russian history had been proposed for the annual prize competitions, but this was no guarantee that the young painters' treatment of such themes would in any way reflect Russian customs.[12] The evidence of Losenko's 'Vladimir and Rogneda' shows that as late as 1770 a Russian painter could consider such a subject merely an excuse for devising a historical composition as a Late Baroque allegory, with the figures draped and undraped in the modish Roman manner.[13] This pseudo-historical tendency, which took no thought of archaeological discoveries or of existing folk arts and costumes, was continued by Grigori Ivanovich Ugriumov (1764–1823). He had studied under Levitski and for three years in Rome (1787–90), and possessed a certain technical facility, but the totally unhistorical character of his works belies his long-kept success as a Russian history painter. He first came to prominence with a canvas exhibited in 1787, 'Yan Usman's Feat of Strength', showing the mythical folk hero as he subdues a bull in the presence of Prince Vladimir of Kiev. The composition, costumes, and expression derive from Rubens and other Baroque masters, and effectively eliminate historical truth. His later works, especially the two historical canvases for Paul's Michael Castle, 'The Capture of Kazan' and 'The Coronation of the First Romanov Tsar, Mikhail Feodorovich', are not only theatrical but insipid and sentimental. With the coming of Neo-Classicism a stricter regard for historical appearances accompanied the closer scrutiny of the past. Something of this can be felt in two paintings of the turn of the century, the 'Minin and Pozharski' and the 'Meeting of Prince Igor and Olga' which have been attributed to a little-known painter, Vasili Kirillovich Malyshev (born 1782).[14] They show a more careful attempt to recreate the spirit of the past. The costumes bear some resemblance to traditional peasant dress, and in the background a wooden izba marks an improvement over the tents and draperies of Ugriumov's pictures.

The interest in native costume was a considerable step towards a more sympathetic understanding of the past. Even before Malyshev, Argunov in 1784 had painted a portrait of a girl in peasant costume and Levitski's portrait of his daughter of 1785 also introduced the national dress. Yet a decade earlier Mikhail Shibanov, a serf of Potemkin, had created the first purely Russian paintings of manners in his 'Betrothal' (1777) and 'Peasant Family at Table' (1774).[15] In spite of certain crudities of design and technique, and the general resemblance to the peasant scenes of Greuze, such paintings provide an unexpected glimpse of the appearance and habits of the wealthier peasant families of the eighteenth century, and more than anything executed under the supervision or influence of the Academy prepared the way for the true painting of peasant life early in the nineteenth century.

After the turn of the century interest in Russian life increased, as is proved by the work of Alexis Gavrilovich Venetsianov (1780–1847).[16] Of Greek origin, he had been brought up in the provinces, and had gone through the Academy, where he made a particular study of Dutch genre-paintings in the Hermitage. Like many at this time, he was influenced also by French painting, especially the works of Granet. After 1820 he withdrew to his country property, where he devoted himself to the study of peasant life, and out of suggestions from Vermeer, Le Nain, Chardin, and de Hooch created the most original Russian painting of manners of his time. His talents were mild; his drawing was sometimes insecure, his perspective often askew or exaggerated, and his composition frequently a collection of parts rather than an integrated whole. But for all that he had certain qualities which were as yet unknown in Russia and which set him apart even from his contemporaries in Western Europe. Above all else he understood the dignity of peasant life. His best pictures are devoid of that anecdotal preoccupation which distorts so much nineteenth-century genre-painting (Plate 157). They lack drama but not feeling, and in the best of them Venetsianov recaptures something of the grave serenity with which Louis Le Nain interpreted similar scenes in seventeenth-century France. We may add to this a very personal feeling for the quality of Russian light, for the long, low beams which fill the empty landscape.

The spiritual calm of Venetsianov's works distinguishes them from those of a young contemporary, Paul Andreevich Fedotov (1815–53), who had been born on the outskirts of Moscow and grown up amid the busy activity of the provincial capital.[17] He studied briefly at the Academy, but more important for the formation of his talents were the Dutch paintings in the Hermitage. Where Venetsianov saw light and space in such works, Fedotov was fascinated by anecdote, costume, gesture, and detail. It is even possible that he found the sources for his brisk little anecdotes in Hogarth's prints (Plate 158A). His works, small in dimensions and artistically unassuming, nevertheless are of some importance as indicating the emergence of both a new class, the wealthy urban bourgeoisie whose manners and tastes provided the source and demand for his paintings, and a new and more critical attitude towards Russian life. Fedotov's satire may seem to us bland enough, but in its time it risked official censure. His first popular success, 'A Newly Decorated Knight', showed the officer in dishevelled condition the morning after a hearty celebration. The Government refused to permit the publication of a lithograph after the painting, until the order had been removed and the title changed to 'The Morning After a Party'. It is typical that Nicholas I's zeal to suppress all criticism extended even to such good-natured raillery as Fedotov's mockery of the inordinate worship of the military caste. His most famous painting, 'The Major's Courtship', depicts the excitement of a rich merchant's family when a middle-aged and impecunious nobleman comes courting the daughter (Plate 158B). Although form and technique are typical of much nineteenth-century genre-painting, the description of the pretty, distraught young girl, her coarse and over-dressed mother, and the bewildered father in his old Russian caftan amounts to a sly criticism of the manners of the rising middle class. As Russian society became more sophisticated and more class-conscious, such episodes seemed more piquant, and suggested to young rebellious minds the innumerable contrasts between the appearances and realities of Russian life. In Fedotov's work there is more than a touch of Gogol, who with more brilliance and effect drew pictures of similar social conditions in *The Adventures of Chichikov* (*Dead Souls*, 1842) and *The Inspector General* (1836). In spite of the brevity of his career – his first paintings were exhibited only four years before his death – Fedotov's influence was considerable at the time. The accidental circumstance that he had come to art too late to enter the Academy, had the salutary effect of proving that an academic education was not essential for the development of true talent, and the restriction of his efforts to scenes from contemporary life breached the ramparts until then held by the idealists. Fedotov's satire was so gentle that with the passing of years it became almost imperceptible, and his pictures appeal now more as the painting of manners than as criticism of society. But in the stifling atmosphere of the later years of the reign of Nicholas I such subtleties were not lost on a younger generation which hoped to produce a new art for a new age.

Although Russia produced no unquestionably great master of romanticism – for even the indubitably earnest and prophetic labours of Ivanov cannot be compared with the production of a Delacroix or a Turner – in the less majestic fields of portraiture and conversation pieces a number of inconspicuous artists made their contributions in a style of painting which we can call romantic realism. In their painstaking but poetic interpretations of upper-class and bourgeois life they left a social record which is artistically and historically valid. The unfinished 'Portrait of Count Ya. I. Rostovtsev and his Family' by S. K. Zaryanko (1818–70) (Plate 159) can stand as an example. The study of detail is as searching as the later literary realism of the great Russian novelists, but the painting is not yet naturalistic; for all the details are subordinated to the general mood of affectionate concern for the persons depicted.

CHAPTER 26

IDEOLOGICAL REALISM

WITH the accession of Alexander II (1855–81) a period of limited liberalism commenced in Russian political and artistic life which culminated in the proclamation of the abolition of serfdom on 3 March 1861. Now the discreet satire of Fedotov was succeeded by bolder social criticism. In the freer atmosphere of Moscow, where the art school was less riddled with bureaucracy than the Petersburg Academy, there developed a number of interesting painters, the first of importance being Vasili Grigorevich Perov (1833–82).[1] Even before he received a travelling scholarship in 1861 and went to Paris, he had shown that, although his point of departure was the social satire of Fedotov, his own views were more critical of conditions in Russia. As early as 1857 he had caused a sensation with 'The Arrival of the Rural Police Inspector'. The edge of the moral was blunted by the slack and sentimental drawing of the peasant under interrogation, but the attack on the methods of the police was sharper than had been seen before. Four years later he exhibited two paintings critical of the Church. The 'Village Sermon' is something of a Hogarthian fable, with the local landlord asleep before the pulpit, while his wife listens to the whispers of her lover and an obsequious lackey keeps the peasants at a distance.[2] In 'The Easter Procession' (Plate 160B) he struck directly at the corruption and offensive manners of the rural clergy. This showed a group of priests in various stages of intoxication staggering out of a village tavern where they had been too well entertained in the course of their ceremonial visits. Such pictures were recognized for what they were, and even under the liberal regime, clerical authorities saw to it that they were withdrawn from exhibition.

Unfortunately the emergence of a new expressive point of view was not accompanied by a demand from artists or public for technical innovations. In this circumstance can be seen the persistent dilemma of much Russian nineteenth-century painting. To a large extent each of the radical artistic movements of the West had been based upon an examination of current technical resources and the invention of new means for new expressive purposes. In that way and in no other could a new kind of painting be created. One need only recall the technical discoveries of the Pre-Raphaelites or of the young naturalist painters in the circle of Courbet and Manet in Paris in the 1860s. In each case public disapproval was as much a matter of dismay at the unfamiliar appearance of a painting as at the new subject-matter.

The extent to which Russian painters of the middle years of the century were unaware of the necessity for such studies can be seen in the experience of Perov in Paris. He was there for only two years (1862–4), although his scholarship was for six, but after searching the boulevards for picturesque types and executing a few sentimental genre-paintings, he applied for permission to return home. He had been in Paris during the episode of the *Salon des refusés*, the first occasion since 1849 when the conflict between official approval and private investigation reached the proportions of a public scandal, yet in his work there was never a hint that he was aware of the position taken by Courbet, Manet, or Whistler.

When he returned to Moscow, the first liberal decade of the reign had ended, and government was hardening into the slow reaction of the later years. Perov's paintings also lost their bite. His 'Arrival of the Governess' (1866) was a return to Fedotov's satirical descriptions of the middle class, with a touch more attention to the vulgarity of the newly rich. More sentimental still was his attitude towards the poor, whose hardships and sorrows he presented in 'The Village Burial', 'The Drowned Girl', and 'Aged Parents at their Son's Grave' Although the titles suggest the aggravated pathos of such scenes, Perov's concern with the lower classes also contained an implied criticism of the existing social order which set him apart from such an impassive observer as Venetsianov, or even from Fedotov, who had never descended below the bourgeoisie. The religious and historical paintings of his later years, to be sure, were less accomplished than those by his contemporaries, but Perov retained his importance for the younger generation as a painter seriously concerned with the social order, whose earlier realistic studies had been honestly conceived and strongly executed.

While Perov had been abroad, a notable event had occurred in St Petersburg. In 1863 growing discontent with the reactionary attitude of the Academy in its artificial distinction between genre and historical painting burst into open revolt. A group of students competing for the annual gold medal objected to the attempt of the authorities to suppress the painting of contemporary life by imposing a specified subject for the competition. They demanded the right to choose their own; the Academy replied by stipulating 'The Banquet of the Gods in Valhalla'. Thirteen painters, joined by one sculptor, thereupon resigned from the Academy. This was a daring step in a place where, and at a time when, an artist's livelihood depended upon his successful completion of the academic programme. Yet it is interesting that their action was precipitated by the problem of freedom of expression more than of technique. The younger painters' insistence on their right to compose their own programmes can be seen as a result of the new criticism proclaimed by the social revolutionary, N. G. Chernyshevski, in his doctoral thesis, 'The Aesthetic Relations of Art to Reality' (1855). On the threshold of the age of reform he declared the superiority of reality to its imitation in art. From this it followed that subject and expression were more important than form, and that in the interests of the social order the choice of subject is all important. Soon after their withdrawal from the Academy the 'Thirteen Contestants', as they were called, and their associates formed an Artists' Co-operative Society (Artel Khudozhnikov) for the exhibition of their work. The results were encouraging, and eventually led to the formation in 1870 of the Society for Travelling Art Exhibitions (Tovarishchestvo peredvizhnykh khudozhestvennykh vystavok), whence the term 'peredvizhniki' ('travellers' or 'wanderers') for the members.[3] In the course of the next twenty years almost all the important contemporary painters contributed to the exhibitions, and many of the significant works of art created in Russia during the 1870s and 80s reached a wider audience than would have been the case had they been restricted to exhibitions in St Petersburg and Moscow. In their earlier struggles to obtain an audience the members of the Artel and the Peredvizhniki were given material assistance and encouragement by the Moscow collector, P.M. Tretyakov (1832–98). The collection given by Tretyakov and his brother to the city of Moscow in 1892 contained important paintings by most of the more significant Russian artists of the nineteenth century, with special emphasis on the work of the realists and 'wanderers'. Not all the works shown in the travelling exhibitions were of the first quality – they varied from revolutionary realism through historical painting to excessively sentimental genre – but in general the society can be credited with the propagation on a wide scale of a kind of art which we may describe as ideological realism.[4]

The leader of the Thirteen Contestants and one of the founders of the Society was the painter Ivan Nikolaevich Kramskoi (1837–87), whose sincere but limited artistic imagintion exercised a profound influence over the character of the works sponsored by the Society. Kramskoi had started life as a painter of religious pictures and had worked as a retoucher in photographers' studios in Kharkov and St Petersburg before entering the Academy in 1856. He was well on the way to academic distinction, having won the small gold medal in the competition of 1863, when he joined the Thirteen Contestants and resigned from the Academy. Kramskoi's art was created out of the tension between a deeply personal mysticism and the most desperately acute photographic vision. The results of his early photographic training can be seen in his numerous portraits – he left over 400 of them – which are striking likenesses as well as psychologically intense. Again and again he caught his subjects in characteristic poses and painted them with minute attention to detail against backgrounds severely unadorned. His pedestrian colour sense increased the similarity to photographs. But having conquered the veracity of natural appearances, Kramskoi knew some deep spiritual dissatisfaction, and dreamed of a religious painting on the theme of man's perpetual and painful search for moral truth. For this purpose he selected the 'Temptation of Christ' (1872–4) (Plate 160A) which he conceived as a figure crouched at daybreak in a stony waste. His desire was to portray not the outward man but the inner struggle between good and evil. The artist himself declared: 'This is no Christ, it is an image of the sorrows of humanity which are known to all of us.'[5] Certainly the painting has a strange and tragic fascination, although the conflict between the spiritual motivation and the accumulation of physical detail in the rocks, crumpled garments, and sombre figure invalidates the expression. The contrast between mysticism and accurate reporting suggests situations in the contemporary novels of Dostoevski, whom Kramskoi admired and whose portrait he painted.

Except for the 'Temptation', an unfinished 'Christ Mocked', and some undistinguished work in the Cathedral of the Redeemer in Moscow, Kramskoi's work consisted almost entirely of portraits, although there are indications that he had a gift for genre and sentimental subjects. Of his 'Inconsolable Grief', showing a mother who has just lost her only child standing beside the funeral flowers, he painted no less than three versions. The final one (1884) is another instance of the irreconcilable gulf between naturalism and symbollism, for certainly harrowing sorrow is more described than expressed in the figure, and strangely contradicted by the precise and exquisite flowers, the springtime freshness of the potted plants in the foreground, and the innumerable details of carpeting, furniture, and the like. As in so much narrative painting, the content fails to inform the design, and must be communicated through the title. The success or failure of such paintings – and success as well as failure must be considered apart from changes in taste – recalls the similar predicament of Ivanov, who hesitated between the real and the ideal. But there are in Kramskoi's work occasional revelations of higher imaginative faculties. In one of his rare genre-paintings – the unfinished 'Inspection of an Old House' – he treated a lighted, silent, shuttered room disturbed only by the passage of two figures in a mood so intense that it forecast the concluding moments of Chekhov's *Cherry Orchard*.

Kramskoi's 'Temptation', with its unresolved mixture of confidence in scientific truth and doubtful spiritual strength, is an important turning-point in the history of nineteenth-century religious painting. It finds its parallel in the political and social disillusion of the 1870s and 80s. Ivanov had been confused by biblical criticism, and his Messiah had dwindled into insignificance in the background of his painting.[6] The faith of Kramskoi's generation had been so shattered by scientific discovery that his man-Christ was powerless to act. Henceforward only two paths were open: to work out some compromise with official religion or to withdraw into oneself. The latter course was chosen by one of the most remarkable of Russian painters, Nicholas Nikolaevich Ge (or Gay, 1831–94), between whose early work of the 1860s and his last paintings there exists somewhat the same difference, and the same descent below the surface of literal description in the search for spiritual and psychic truth, which we can distinguish between the early realistic and the later symbolist novels of Dostoevski.[7] Ge, who was of French descent, entered the Academy in 1850, and by 1857 had won the first gold medal and the travelling scholarship. After desultory travel and landscape painting in southern Italy, he settled in Florence, where he lived, except for one brief visit to Russia, until 1869. In Rome he had met Ivanov, and had been deeply impressed by the faith and research which had gone into the creation of 'Christ's First Appearance'. Ge, too, read Strauss and Renan, but saved his faith in the determination to discover the historical Christ of the Gospels. His first large religious painting, 'The Last Supper' (1863), seemed to the academic circles of St Petersburg a startling departure from iconographical traditions, whether Byzantine or Baroque, although in the naturalistic composition there was little which was artistically novel. The general plan was reminiscent of Caravaggio, and the dramatic *chiaroscuro* and commonplace physical types could have been found in Rembrandt. Upon his return to St Petersburg he was attracted for a time to historical painting. The results enjoyed much attention, although they reveal the weakest side of his talents. Even the warm colours of his 'Peter the Great Interrogating the Tsarevich Alexis' (1871) or of 'Catherine II at the Bier of Elizabeth' fail to conceal awkward, even amateurish composition. Until then Ge would have been considered a very minor member of the large group of religious and historical painters, but at this point he renounced the career of an academic professor and withdrew for a period of ten years to his estate in the Ukraine. There the study of religious texts led him to Tolstoi, whose disciple he became in 1882.[8] Ge joined Tolstoi in his attempt to apply the principles of primitive Christianity to the realities of contemporary life. The first active result appeared in 'What is Truth' (1890), depicting a gross, contemptuous Pilate flinging his question at the mute, motionless Christ. The clumsy composition and naïve lighting were now the perfect means with which to express the irreconcilable conflict between the two protagonists. Although the painting was instinct with genuine religious feeling, the unconventional portrayal and the haggard, unprepossessing Christ offended the Church, already outraged by Tolstoi's teaching, and the painting was removed from exhibition.

Ge soon pushed his search for spiritual and historical truth even farther. In his unfinished 'Golgotha' (1892) (Plate 161B) a distraught almost frantic Christ clutches his head in horror as he waits for the dreadful preparations to be completed. The 'Crucifixion' (1891), which moved Tolstoi to tears, is an unforgettable demonstration of terror and agony. It is almost inconceivable that the imaginative reconstruction of historical actuality could be carried so far as this without loss of spirituality. Ge's paintings were more than exercises in shocking melodrama. The inexpressibly tragic figure of his wasted, wretched Christ forced the observer to reconsider the miraculous intervention in that pitiful being of the human and the divine, much as Tolstoi's intransigent insistence on the essentials of Christianity shocked a generation into a new examination of traditional Christian conduct.

In these last works Ge became the first important Russian painter to devise a new technique for his expressive needs. His crude compositions, simplified shapes, and abbreviated line were virtues rather than handicaps in the communication of this strange and poignant experience. It is difficult to think of any other religious painting of this period, when biblical criticism had shattered the comfortable familiarity of traditional iconography, which is such a combination of vision and faith. It is as if the religious emotion of medieval art had been recreated in modern terms. In Ge's work we can see the reasons for the failure of Ivanov and Kramskoi. Ge rejected Ivanov idealism, and at the same time, in choosing subjects which possessed an immediate communicative and dramatic content, avoided the weakness of Kramskoi's 'Christ', whose image was too deliberate to convey the conceptions with which he burdened it.

Through the 1860s and 70s Russian painters, in company with their contemporaries throughout the Western world, had mastered an increasingly realistic technique, and they were now faced with the problem of what to do with it. In France the attitude of Manet and the Impressionists to the painting of modern life without anecdote or comment was the expressive counterpart of their descriptive technique and objective vision. In Russia the lack of an audience so experienced, so critical, and so vocal prohibited the development of that kind of naturalistic painting, and we find instead, through the 1880s and the period of social and political reaction under Alexander III (1881–94), two more traditional types of pictures, the continuation of social criticism in a milder form in the works exhibited by the Peredvishniki and, on the other hand, the development of an energetic if less aesthetically gratifying school of historical painting.

Certainly there was nothing particularly novel about history painting as such. Nor was the specifically nationalist character of much of this painting new; the curious student will perhaps remember the political themes which inundated the Paris Salons in the years before the centennial celebration of the French Revolution in 1889. And certainly such subjects were the stock in trade of academic exhibitions everywhere in the nineteenth century. Yet for all that the Russian paintings are not without interest. They have long been the most familiar and most popular works of Russian art, both at home and abroad; and in technique and composition, if not in the implied attitude towards history, they have inspired much history painting under the Soviets.

In our present context they concern us for a new attitude towards the choice of subject which appeared soon after the middle of the century, when social criticism had become more dangerous. The works of a little-known painter, Valerian Ivanovich Yakobi (1834–1902), are a case in point. In 1861 his competition painting showing the momentary halt of a long convoy of chained prisoners bound for Siberia won him the Academy's gold medal, and was so enthusiastically received by the public that it was in some small measure held responsible for the alleviation of the conditions of political imprisonment. A trip abroad at this point distracted Yakobi from contemporary life; upon his return he treated historical subjects in a manner diluted by the French Rococo masters. His 'Marriage in the Ice Palace in the Reign of Anna Ioannovna' recounted the humiliation of Prince Golitsyn, who was obliged to marry an aged Kalmuk and spend his wedding night in an ice palace constructed on the frozen Neva for the sin of having embraced Roman Catholicism.[9] Before this Konstantin Dmitrievich Flavitsi (1830–66) had painted 'The Last Moments of Princess Tarakanov' (1866), showing the beautiful woman in the Peter Paul Fortress about to be drowned in her cell by the flooded Neva. Although neither of these pictures, in technique, design, or historical interpretation, differs to any extent from the standards for such sensational subjects elsewhere, taken together they could be understood as subtle attacks on the irresponsibility of autocratic power.[10]

In the work of Vasili Ivanovich Surikov (1848–1916), this tendency towards social criticism continued, although smothered in the trappings of nationalist pageantry.[11] His most famous works, 'The Morning of the Execution of the Streltsy' (1881) and 'The Boyarin Morosova' (1887) (Plate 161A), representing a fanatical Old Believer dragged off in chains to prison and death, were on the theme of personal opposition to the established Church and State. Surikov's compositions, so knowingly designed to bring the spectator into the painted space through the arrangement of circumstances which, if not always accurate, at least were drenched with the specific hues of old Muscovy, lulled the authorities into admiration. In addition, Surikov communicated a feeling for the Russian climate in the grey light of dawn which invests the Red Square, as the implacable Peter watches his enemies being prepared for their terrible fate, and in the gloomy winter skies above the Boyarin Morosova. In such atmospheric painting there was a faint reflexion of the general contemporary interest in nature which found its most conspicuous development in French Impressionism, and which is present to somewhat the same degree in the music of Moussorgsky, whose prelude to *Khovanshchina* (1872–80) suggests the dawn breaking over the Red Square in Moscow only a few years after the event illustrated by Surikov.[12]

A historical painter with a different purpose and very inferior ability, Vasili Vasilievich Vereshchagin (1842–1904) enjoyed during his life-time a wider international reputation than any Russian artist. This was largely the result of extensive self-advertisement and the appeal of his Tolstoian pacificism. He entered the Academy, but in 1863 forsook it to study in Paris with J. L. Gérôme, who developed his taste for meticulous detail, but could not improve his undeveloped sense of design and harsh colouring. Vereshchagin was fond of travel, and in the next few years executed a series of pictorial reports on the landscape of the Caucasus and Turkestan. More than any other Russian painter of the age he maintained constant contacts with Europe, residing in Munich and Paris for extended periods, and arranging one-man exhibitions of his work throughout Europe and America. The success of these exhibitions was due to the startling nature of his military paintings. These dealt, not with the usual triumphs of Russian arms and the pleasure of military life, but with the horrors of war which he had seen for himself as an artist-correspondent at the front during the campaigns in Turkestan (1867–8) and the Russo-Turkish War (1877–8).[13] From his recollection of his first experiences he painted three canvases dealing with the plight of soldiers surrounded and annihilated by the enemy or left dying to be devoured by vultures. Vereshchagin added a touch of sadism to the contemporary taste for painted bloodshed, but he also showed a genuine hatred of war in his lectures and pamphlets. In the intervals between battles he travelled in India (1875–6) and Palestine (1884), and covered numerous canvases with what he saw there (Plate 162B). He was at his best when he could display his startlingly photographic technique without at the same time trying to preach. At the beginning of the 90s, when there was a lull on the fighting fronts Vereshchagin painted his famous series of the French invasion of Russia in 1812. For all his industrious research into military records he had no real gift as a history painter; the compositions are clumsy, his colours crude, and the famous characters lack personality. As illustrations for Tolstoi's *War and Peace*, however, they are still the best-known Russian paintings of the period.

The course of late nineteenth-century Russian realism was epitomized in the long career of Ilya (Elias) Efimovich Repin (1844–1930).[14] Of humble stock, he had come from the southern provinces to the Academy in 1864, the year after the revolt of the Thirteen Contestants. In 1871 he was awarded the large gold medal and a six-year travelling scholarship for his 'Resurrection of the Daughter of Jairus', an exercise in the archaeologically realist manner of Ge's 'Last Supper' of 1863. Having satisfied the academic requirements, he immediately demonstrated his natural inclinations in a large group portrait representing an 'Assembly of Russian, Polish, and Czech Musicians (1871–2), and in his 'Bargemen', or 'Haulers' (Burlaki), often known as 'The Volga Boatmen' (1870–3). The 'Musicians', a competent if undistinguished essay in managing a variety of postures within an interior space, disappeared into the halls of a Slavic society in Moscow, but when the 'Bargemen' was exhibited in Vienna in 1873, it brought the young artist immediate European recognition as a realist. Between the two extremes represented by official, upper-class portraits, and the study of humbler social conditions Repin's long career developed, with occasional excursions into history painting. As a portraitist he made his reputation in St Petersburg, where he painted most of the prominent artists, writers, scientists, and statesmen of his day, and memorialized important public events for the Government. In a hundred portraits Repin satisfied his sitters and his public by his combination of a striking likeness with a traditional design, undisturbed by the psychological penetration of Kramskoi, and unalleviated by the elegance with which the younger portraitist, V. A. Serov (1865–1911), portrayed the fashionable men and women of the period (Plate 162A).

At the other extreme his 'Bargemen' (Plate 163), a study of the unfortunate wretches who hauled the heavy boats against the Volga current by sheer physical exertion, was the result of a trip along the river in 1870. The pathos and implied criticism of social conditions which permitted this brutal exploitation of human labour linked him at once with the Peredvizhniki whom he had joined, while his sensationally realistic presentation of these degraded creatures surpassed anything which had yet been seen in the Travelling Exhibitions, and still can so impress the spectator that he overlooks the artificial and not entirely integrated composition.[15] The combination of photographic detail, sentiment, and brilliant colour – for Repin had caught the broad white light of the Volga region – proved unfailingly successful in other historical paintings.

When Repin reached Paris, he was already an accomplished realist, who could learn from the French naturalists only how to brighten his palette, and how to put forward a more objective, less anecdotal point of view. But he was slow to take advantage of these opportunities, and they were only realized in his work much later. Thus his studies of Parisian men and women for his 'Paris Café' (1875) rival the oblique detachment of Degas's modified realism of those years, while the finished canvas is merely another example of overcrowded sentimental genre. And the same slow maturing is true of his experience of Impressionist colour. Gradually, after his second visit to Paris in 1883, his brush-stroke loosened and his light became more intense, and in such informal studies as his daughter 'Vera in the Sunlight' (1885) one can say that he had adopted the Impressionist palette, although he never went in for the broken colour of Monet. Perhaps his most truly naturalist painting, in colour, design, and expressive content, is the 'Surgeon E. V. Pavlov in the Operating Room' (1888), in which he grafted the non-committal attitude of Manet to that interest in human experience so earnestly championed at this time by Zola. The subtle whites and greys reveal Repin's sense of colour at its best.

Such painting, however, was too detached to suit either the sentimental moralizing of the Peredvizhniki or the sensational tastes of the public, both of which he tried to reach in his 'Religious Procession in Kursk' (1880–3). This was an enormous canvas of a huge crowd shepherded by the clergy and police following a portable shrine down a country road on a hot day. It was a stupendous demonstration of his ability to amass innumerable details, but it lacked the directness and pathos of the 'Bargemen' of a decade before. Even such incidents as the cripple hastening to keep up with the procession, the mounted police lashing at an upraised arm, or the stout *bourgeoise* carrying an icon had neither Fedotov's humour nor Perov's point. The government censorship as well as Alexander III's aggressive Orthodoxy may be held responsible for the failure of this uneasy attempt to combine a 'purpose' with an ostensible tribute to the Church.

Like so many others, Repin in the 80s turned to history painting. The subject of his 'Tsar Ivan IV with the Body of His Son' (1881–5) (Plate 164) was a favourite one at the time, and again can be taken as an implied criticism of autocratic rule. Repin had the courage to concentrate on the essential human tragedy of the situation. In the best tradition of historical horror painting he depicted Ivan's insane remorse as he slowly realizes the enormity of his crime and seeks to staunch the blood flowing from his son's shattered head. There is very little of the Muscovite bric-à-brac so dear to Surikov and other historical painters of the day. Something of the same directness is present in the broad humour of his seventeenth-century episode 'Zaporozh Cossacks Drafting a Reply to the Turkish Sultan' (1880–91), on which he spent years of ethnographical research until it became practically an anthology of the racial types of southern Russia. This, too, was critical of the regime; for the Cossacks, now the notorious bodyguard of the Emperor and whose name was synonymous with despotic brutality, had once been known throughout Russia as champions of the oppressed.

This interpretation of Repin's historical paintings might be thought fanciful were it not for the evidence that through the 1880s he was sincerely critical of tyranny and that his artistic sympathies were on the side of the social revolutionaries. In content, form, and expression these paintings provide a notable sequence in his artistic development. 'The Arrest of the Propagandist' was commenced in 1878, in the manner of Perov's anecdotal genre, but by the time the final version was finished in 1890 Repin had refined this portrayal of a young man in the hands of the police, who are ransacking his quarters for subversive literature and given it the simplified dramatic quality of his 'Ivan IV'. In the 'Rejected Confession' (1882) and 'Revolutionary Awaiting Execution' (1880s) he entered the darkness of the prisons to paint the proud and horrible last moments of men and women condemned to death for political offences. His most sensitive, intuitive, and in many ways most tragic political painting is also his most completely realized work, and one which ranks with the finest narrative painting of the nineteenth century. The comparison between the first and final versions of 'They Did Not Expect Him' (Ne Zhdali, 1883) also proves that when Repin's emotions were stirred, his pictorial imagination became more acute (Plate 165A). In the first version a young woman revolutionary, unexpectedly returned from exile, has just entered the living-room of a house where her appearance evokes varying responses from three other figures, two girls and a boy. The tone of the whole is one of sudden and dramatic surprise. In the second version Repin amplified the situation and endowed it with the overtones of tragedy. The political prisoner, now a man, uncertainly enters the room; the reactions of his family range from his mother's dawning recognition as she rises from her chair to the joy and fear on the faces of his three children, the youngest of whom is frightened by the appearance of this haggard and ragged figure.[16] What gives the picture true artistic quality is Repin's masterly balance of form and expression, especially in his oblique, asymmetrical composition. The right-to-left direction in space, opposed by the sharpened perspective drawing of the floorboards, is so suggestive of Degas that we can believe the lessons learned in Paris ten years before had at last come to fruition. At the same time Repin also revived the wonderful Russian painting of middle-class interiors which had been one of the triumphs of the romantics. In 'They Did Not Expect Him' tradition and innovation are marvellously combined. The picture must be regarded as the finest artistic achievement of the social point of view of the Peredvizhniki. With it Repin can be said to have crowned and closed the history of ideological realism in Russian painting.

In his later years Repin continued on the whole the vein of academic realism in which most of his work was composed. His history indicates the Russian painter's gradually growing awareness of contemporary developments in the West. In such works as 'They Did Not Expect Him' or the brilliant portrait of D. I. Mendeleev (1907) so reminiscent of Degas's portrait of Duranty, he could elevate the realist tendencies which had been such a fundamental part of Russian painting through the nineteenth century into something approaching the formal coherence of the European tradition. Repin's age – he was a contemporary of the major French Impressionists – undoubtedly prevented him from going further in the direction of Post-Impressionism, although in his eighties, after the October Revolution, when he had retired to his country house in Finland, a series of vivid Passion scenes proves his interest in the exacerbated expressionism of Munch and Nolde.[17] He had very considerable talent, an eye for character and situation, a sense of colour, and a gift for drama, all of which he spent perhaps too generously and too often in the service of the narrow aesthetic of the age.

Through the nineteenth century Russia produced many able and several distinguished painters, but it is difficult to say that there was a 'Russian School' of painting comparable to those in music and literature. The reason can be found in the absence of a traditional body of practice and opinion such as existed in Western European countries. Two hundred years is too short a time to develop a tradition, especially if the supervision exercised by an academy and the State discourages non-conformist talent. Nineteenth-century French painting is another example. Its least significant aspect is the work produced for or under the supervision of the Academy and the State. And Russia lacked what we might call a private public which, though small in numbers, through its encouragement made possible the experimental art of the West. While France had more than one Bruyas, Caillebotte, or Pellerin, men like Tretyakov were rare in Russia, and he, for all his interest, did not often depart from the prevailing standards of naturalism. The difficulty of the Russian painter's situation can be seen in 'The Prose of Life' (Zhiteiskaya proza, 1892–93) (Plate 165B), by Vasili Nikolaevich Baksheev (born 1892).[18] The content resembles the situations in the contemporary dramas of Chekhov, who also expressed the dissatisfaction of the Russian intelligentsia with a way of life which no longer had any relation to political or economic reality. And as Chekhov was a creative master of the dramatic form, so in this one painting Baksheev demonstrated his command of the resources of modern painting. The oblique right-to-left perspective and the subtle treatment of a lighted interior recall the works of the French Impressionists and prove that the Russians were aware of the formal qualities of modern art. Yet they could afford neither to renounce the advantages of subject-matter as the Impressionists had done, nor to wait for public approval to catch up with them. Their successful works were brilliant but isolated attempts to integrate the pictorial experience of modern times with the crumbling structure of their world.

CHAPTER 27

THE SLAVIC REVIVAL AND *MIR ISKUSSTVA*

DURING the last two decades of the nineteenth century the most progressive develop-ments in Russian art were closely related to the antithetical concepts of nationalism and internationalism. These tendencies were the further development of the controversy be-tween the Slavophiles and the Westernizers which had appeared in the 1840s under the police reign of Nicholas I; and they continued in a modified form until the end of the Empire in the social and political programmes of Pan-Slavism and the system of Western military alliances. As in the eighteenth century, so again, Moscow and St Petersburg were the centres from which emanated propaganda calling on the one hand for a return to the principles of ancient Russian life, summarized now in the formula of 'Orthodoxy, Autocracy, Nationality', and on the other urging that Russia's future lay in a closer political and cultural integration with the West. However antagonistic these systems might at first appear, the forms of their artistic expression had much in common.

The origins of the art of both programmes can be related to the aspirations of the Peredvizhniki. Although their intention through the 1870s and 80s had been the creation of a truly national art, and for that reason they had scorned too close associations with artistic movements abroad, their work had closer analogies with the technique and sub-ject-matter of contemporary European genre and historical painting than with any specifically Russian tradition. But while the Peredvizhniki tried, as did Tolstoi and Dos-toevski, to find the soul of Russia in the conditions of contemporary life, there arose simultaneously a tendency to exploit 'Old Russian' sources which eventually affected even the historical paintings of the Peredvizhniki and the arts of architecture, sculpture, interior decoration, book illustration, and stage design as well.

But it would be a falsification of cultural history to attribute the Slavic Revival of the later nineteenth century exclusively to political and philosophical causes. Just as it may be considered a continuation of Muscovite objections to Peter's reforms, so it was also assisted by the scholarly investigation of the Russian past, comparable to the archaeologi-cal and scientific investigations which were occurring in other European nations.[1] In-deed, changing conceptions and deepening knowledge of Russian archaeology and art history were soon reflected in contemporary creative work.

In 1839, when Count Anatol Nikolaevich Demidov travelled through Western Russia with the intention of compiling an illustrated account of Russian architecture, he was accompanied by a French draughtsman, André Durand (1807–67), whose hundred lithographs provided the most accurate visual account yet published of the more im-portant Russian monuments (Plates 110 and 166B).[2] While Durand was a man of his times and a westerner into the bargain, and his visual impressions of Russian buildings are romantically exaggerated in that he recorded what was strange to him rather than what was familiar to the Russians, on the whole he faithfully described the monuments as they appeared at his time. A significant advance towards determining the chronology and formal development of Russian architecture was made by A. A. Martynov (1820–95) and I. M. Snegirev (1793–1868), whose numerous publications in the 1850s and 60s contain much information still useful to-day.[3] Late in the reign of Nicholas I the Government became interested in these investigations and sponsored several folio volumes illustrating Russian antiquities, principally works of decorative art reproduced in coloured lithography.[4] Serious attempts to put these scattered studies on a sound basis began with the organization of the archaeological societies of St Petersburg (1846) and Moscow (1864). The latter, the Moskovskoe Arkhaeologicheskoe Obshchestvo, inaugurated in 1869 a series of triennial congresses in various Russian cities and towns. The publications of the papers and reports presented at these s'ezdy provide an invaluable store of information, not only for archaeological material (pre-historic and antique remains, principally in the South), but also for the earliest Russian architecture and painting in the Kievan and early Moscow periods.[5] In St Petersburg the Academy of Fine Arts also sponsored research, particularly the systematic examination of early Russian architecture by V. V. Suslov (Plate 73, A and B).[6] Meanwhile the study of painting kept pace with architectural research. As early as 1856 D. A. Rovinski (1824–95) laid the foundations for a systematic study of icon-painting, based on iconographical research and the correlation of chronicle texts.[7] This work was carried on in a series of scholarly studies by N. P. Kondakov (1844–1925) and N. P. Likhachev (1862–1935).[8] The latter, with I. S. Ostroukhov and S. P. Ryabushinski, established the principles of modern connoisseurship with their important collections of icons.

The Western student will recognize in this account the general outline of similar studies of national traditions in the West, which also progressed from a romantic interest in the picturesque aspects of medieval art, through the 'scientific' examination of monuments in the spirit of the positivist principles of nineteenth-century science and philosophy, to the gradual realization of the necessity for a synthesis. Such an inclusive history, incorporating the most recent discoveries and opinions, was begun under the editorship of Igor Grabar (born 1871) with the publication in 1909 of the first volume of a general history of Russian art, with contributions by the leading archaeologists and art historians of the day.[9] Unfortunately the progress of the work was interrupted by the outbreak of the First World War when only five volumes and a portion of a sixth had been published.

These studies also followed a pattern which had a parallel in Western European research. The gradual recovery of the past proceeded in reverse chronological order. The medieval revivals of the early nineteenth century in France and England started with the study of Late Gothic or Early Renaissance architecture, and slowly worked backward, so that it was only towards the end of the century that the qualities of Early Gothic and Romanesque, and finally of Early Christian and Byzantine art, were fully understood. The same principle applies in Russia. Sixteenth- and seventeenth-century art was appreciated and utilized from the first; the earlier medieval periods were exhaustively explored only towards the end of the century.[10]

A preliminary but not altogether satisfactory attempt to discover the characteristics of a Russian national style was instigated by Nicholas I, under whom, as we have seen, the solid front of Petersburg classicism was first breached by the forces of eclecticism. His predecessors had moved easily and with authority in the contemporary stylistic movements of Europe, and to each may be attributed the patronage of some more than ordinary master. Schlüter, Rastrelli, Quarenghi, and Rossi were choices of which any ruler and any nation might be proud. With the Tsars of the nineteenth century the story changes. Throughout this period a succession of German alliances (the wives of Nicholas I, Alexander II, and Nicholas II were German princesses; Alexander III married Dagmar of Denmark who was of German descent) strengthened German influence, which can be seen in the official domestic propriety and social dullness which pervaded the Russian Court. The result was an increasing separation between the sovereigns' artistic interests and those of the progressive artists of the day. At best they acquiesced in the popular bourgeois attitude towards art.[11]

Nicholas I's German propensities determined the choice of his favourite architects, A. Stakenschneider and K. A. Ton (1794–1881), to build the important palaces and churches of his reign. In addition, the German architect, Leo von Klenze (1784–1864), the architect of the Glyptothek and Alte Pinakothek in Munich, was called upon to design the new Hermitage Museum. Stakenschneider's large palaces for members of the imperial family in St Petersburg, skilful but dull variations on the styles of Rastrelli, Rossi, and Montferrand, at least maintained the city's tradition of massive dignity.[12] At Peterhof and Tsarskoe Selo, however, the Tsar and his architects indulged in a riot of eclecticism, the more surprising in that Nicholas was sincerely fond of Peterhof. The English architect Menelaws, in addition to his Egyptian and Oriental fantasies of the 1820s, designed a Gothic 'kottedzh' at Peterhof which became Nicholas's favourite country house. N. L. Benois (1813–79), the son of a French émigré, built the huge imperial stables in an English Tudor style, and Stakenschneider, in addition to several pavilions and a Belvedere in the classical manner, designed the 'Nikolski domik' (Nicholas Cottage) (Plate 167B), as a surprise for the Empress in 1834, in a style truly a surprise for its date. In contrast to Bazhenov's and Kazakov's fantasies on the theme of old Russian masonry architecture, this was a peasant farmhouse of horizontal timber construction with an unusual amount of appliqué ornament in the style of peasant carving.[13]

But this first attempt remained without issue for some time to come. The task of creating a new national style was assumed by Ton on the occasion of the erection of the colossal Church of the Redeemer in Moscow (Plate 168A), commemorating the victories of 1812–14 (1839–83). Although this structure might seem at first to upset the canons we have established for the chronologically reverse recovery of the Russian past, a glance assures us that only the horizontal arcades in the manner of the twelfth-century churches of Suzdalia revealed any archaeological investigation; the elevational system was taken from Montferrand's St Isaac. This timid compromise between archaeology and the clarity of Petersburg classicism was as much as the age could accept, and Nicholas approved Ton's general plan for churches throughout the Empire.[14]

Such a solution did not long satisfy the energetic Slavophiles, nor could it resist serious archaeological criticism. A more acute appreciation of old Russian architecture was inaugurated in the reign of Alexander II with the construction of the Historical Museum in Moscow (1874–83) (Plate 169) by an architect of English descent, V. O. Sherwood (1832–97). Here no doubt there was a certain justification for the revival of national forms; for the site lay beside the Kremlin walls and towers and opposite the Church of St Basil at the other end of the Square.[15] But Sherwood's building obeyed more the letter than the spirit of sixteenth-century buildings. Octagonal towers, tent-roofs, kokoshniki, were piled one on top of the other, but without any understanding of the constant contrast of masses which had been the essential formal principle of old Russian architecture. Sherwood's limitations can be seen in his symmetrical distribution of these elements on either side of a central axis. As a result the building is lifeless and flat. The same axial principles appeared in the design of the adjacent Retail Stores (Torgovye Ryadi, 1888–93), on the Red Square by A. H. Pomerantsev, and the Duma (the City Hall, 1892), by Chichagov.

In religious architecture the recovery of the sixteenth century was exhibited in an aggressive way in A. A. Parland's Church of the Resurrection (1883–1907), built in St Petersburg on the spot where Alexander II had been assassinated. The cluster of domes around the central pyramidal tower was an imitation of St Basil, although the treatment of the brick and marble walls imitated such seventeenth-century churches as Ostankino. This pastiche of bulbous brick forms, so out of keeping with the classical serenity of St Petersburg, is an unusually arrogant instance of Slavophilism.[16]

In domestic architecture an irresistible temptation was provided by the well-known model of the palace of Kolomenskoe. In Moscow in the 1890s two large private houses – the Igumnov house by N. I. Pozdeev and the private museum of P. I. Shchukin (Plate 168B), designed by B. V. Freidenberg to house the owner's collection of old Russian decorative arts – were curious combinations of the rusticated foundations and canopied staircases of the Kremlin Palace with the elaborate wooden roof shapes of Kolomenskoe. This phase of the Slavic Revival, which had its pictorial counterpart in such historical scenes as Surikov's 'Boyarin Morosova' and Repin's 'Ivan IV', cannot be without some relation to the work of the historians of the period, especially I. Ye. Zabelin (1820–1909), whose monumental studies of Russian life in the Muscovite period provided a mine of information.[17] The revised wooden style in the meantime had made a hesitant appearance abroad in the Russian Pavilion at the Paris Exhibition of 1878 (Plate 166A).

Sculpture, too, knew its exponents of the realistic interpretation of Slavic themes. The sardonic crouched figure of 'Mephistopheles' (1882) by Mark Matveevich Antokolski (1843–1902) may be his best-known work in the West, but Russian audiences admired 'Ivan IV' (1870), slumped on his throne remorsefully contemplating his crimes, or 'Peter the Great' (1872), boldly braving a gale.[18] Except for the subjects, nothing in Antokolski's technique or interpretation was exceptionally Russian. As with the work of so many of the ideological realists, the identification of their expressive content with the past and present history of Russia could not conceal their debt to European methods.

A second phase of the Slavic Revival can be identified with the programme of Pan-Slavism. This entailed lengthening the artistic and historical perspective to include the remote past of Kievan Russia, after the resources of Muscovy had been exploited.

The most conspicuous monument of this period was the Cathedral of St Vladimir at Kiev, commenced in 1862 on the occasion of the millennial celebration of the Russian nation.[19] The foundations were defective, and a considerable lapse of time intervened before the present structure was completed (1876–82) from designs by A. V. Beretti, the municipal architect of Kiev.[20] The plan was a compromise between an aisled basilica and a central cross with two more cupolas over the western bays making seven in all. The interior decoration, planned by the medieval archaeologist A. V. Prakhov (1846–1916) and executed by Viktor Mikhailovich Vasnetsov (1848–1927), was an elaborate attempt to create a national orthodox religious art on the basis of Byzantine painting and mosaics.[21] Vasnetsov was of humble birth, the son of a country priest, and had studied in a seminary before entering the Petersburg Academy in 1868. There he absorbed the realistic methods of the 'purpose painters' which he utilized for genre-paintings in the manner of the Peredvizhniki. A short stay in Paris (1876–7) did little to change either his technique or his expression; his boulevard scenes are indistinguishable from those of his contemporaries.[22] When ideological realism declined in official favour, after the accession of Alexander III, he turned to history painting, rejecting episodes from the political turmoil of the sixteenth and seventeenth centuries for scenes from the earlier 'heroic' history of Kievan Russia. His 'After Igor's Battle with the Polovtsi' (1890) (Plate 170A), where the field is strewn with corpses while vultures hover in the light of the rising moon, is an interesting contrast to Vereshchagin's gruesome battlefields of the same years inspired by the Russo-Turkish War. Where Vereshchagin's concern with actuality led to his aggressive pacifist statements, Vasnetsov's canvases evoked melancholy reveries of wars as remote as Charlemagne's.[23] Folk tales were another source of inspiration; his settings for Ostrovsky's drama *Snegorochka* ('Snow White') (Plate 170B), produced by the wealthy Moscow art patron Savva Ivanovich Mamontov in his private theatre in 1885 were the most accurate evocations of the Russian past which the stage had yet seen.

Through such work as this Vasnetsov's imagination was attuned to the programme for St Vladimir, and upon winning the competition he went to Italy and Sicily to study Byzantine painting at its source. His paintings in St Vladimir (1886–96) consist of fifteen large canvases, thirty single figures of saints, and numerous smaller portraits. His style is an uneasy combination of naturalism and symbolism, for although he appreciated the Byzantine two-dimensional treatment of the wall surface, he could not quite renounce the three-dimensional figural style he had learned in the Academy. In his larger compositions, such as the 'Baptism of St Vladimir' and the 'Conversion of the Kievans' he failed to subordinate his archaeological detail to spiritual abstraction. Even in the single figures of saints, where more of the two-dimensional effect of mosaic and icon-painting was present, the expressions of his figures are more mournful than majestic. Vasnetsov's younger brother, Apollinari (1856–1933), had first been a landscape painter, but in the 1880s he, too, began to investigate the Russian past. His scrupulous historical realism left no room for even the slight poetry which was present in his brother's work, but his reconstructions of medieval Russian life are at the least ingenious (Plate 171A).

A more successful modern religious style was devised by Mikhail Vasilievich Nesterov (1862–1942). A deeply religious man, like Vasnetsov, he had learned a realistic technique under Perov in the Moscow Art School, and his first works were in the vein of sentimental realism. But by 1887 his 'Bride of Christ', a study of a young novice in a nunnery, called attention to his special talent when it was exhibited by the Peredvizhniki. Nesterov had an instinctive sympathy for the saints and hermits of medieval Russia, and more than any other religious painter of the age he knew the conditions of their life; for it was his custom to withdraw for long periods to the monasteries and hermitages in the remotest parts of Russia, even as far as the Solovetski Monastery on the White Sea.[24] In contrast to Vasnetsov's strained academism Nesterov's paintings were built of the simplest elements. His figures were placed singly or in a row in the foreground, and behind them stretched an idyllically placid Russian landscape, emphasized as a flat background plane (Plate 171B). The combination of simplified contours, flat patterns, and naturalistic detail recalls the murals of Puvis de Chavannes which he had seen in Paris, although his backgrounds were never so idealized. More than any other master of these years he succeeded, by his substitution of symbolic line and colour for historical fact, in creating a truly artistic interpretation of Russian pietism and medieval faith.

The contrast between the religious paintings of Nesterov and those of Ge shows the gulf which separated the realists of the 70s and 80s from the new generation of the 90s. In Russia, as in France, the realist aesthetic fell into disrepute, when it became apparent that as a social force it could not alleviate injustice and as an artistic programme it hardly ever led to the production of true works of art. Nesterov's design, like his taste, was unmistakably refined and – a parallel to the discoveries of Gauguin and the Symbolist painters after 1889 – led him to the conclusion that formal elements were as artistically important as the ends they served. Just as the Symbolists destroyed the aesthetic of Impressionism, so Nesterov was one of the principal agents to prepare the artistic movement known as Mir Iskusstva ('World of Art').

The transition from the mystical idealism of Nesterov's religious pictures to the evaluation of art as symbol was accomplished by Mikhail Aleksandrovich Vrubel (1856–1911), a tragic yet typical exponent of the international Symbolist movement of the 1890s.[25] In a strange way his brief career seems symbolic of the impending doom of imperial Russia. It extended through the early part of the reign of Nicholas II and ended when in 1905, the year of the catastrophe of the Russo-Japanese War and the first fateful Revolution, Vrubel went mad. Yet from another point of view he also belonged to the international artistic generation of the *fin-de-siècle*, whose brilliant talents were so often allied with constitutional and psychological weaknesses, and whose artistic expression was permeated with a strange and melancholy sense of beauty. In his origin, too, Vrubel was an internationalist. To his mixed Polish and Danish ancestry he added a wide experience of Europe and of European art and literature. Before entering the Academy he had studied philosophy at the University of St Petersburg, and in 1876, and again in 1892 and 1894, he visited France and Italy. During his years at the Academy (1880–4) he subordinated academic proficiency to his interest in works of art which were then so esoteric as Greek vases and early Russian icons. His understanding of the artistic as well as archaeological significance of Russian art recommended him as a mural painter for the restoration of the ancient Church of St Cyril at Kiev. In preparation for this task he visited Venice, where he admired the deep brilliance of colour of the mosaics of St Mark and of the Venetian painters. But his St Cyril frescoes show far more his profound sympathy for old Russian painting. Where Vasnetsov, who two years later won from Vrubel the competition for St Vladimir, only collected archaeological facts, Vrubel possessed an uncanny ability to imbue the old religious iconography with his own disturbing conceptions.

After his work in Kiev he settled in Moscow as one of a group of young artists patronized by Mamontov, for whom he designed mural paintings, an addition to Mamontov's house (a house in a simplified Byzantine style) and made drawings for sculpture and decorative objects to be manufactured at Mamontov's art colony on his country estate of Abramtsevo. In all his work intense personal expression took precedence over any non-aesthetic programme. Form, colour, line, texture, and subject-matter were not merely instruments for the communication of meaning, but were meaningful in themselves. In colour he explored the strange harmonies of Persian carpets and oriental glass in an effort to clear up the muddy mixture of local hues which so afflicted contemporary Russian painting. With Vrubel, for the first time in the history of Russian art, the spectator is aware of art created for an essentially aesthetic purpose, or to use the much misunderstood term, it is 'art for art's sake'.

In the many versions of his 'Demon', Vrubel expressed not only the crisis which was present in so much late nineteenth-century art, its disgust with realism and the agonizing search to replace it with some truly artistic symbol, but he also made visible his tragic personal obsessions. He had treated the theme as early as 1890 as an exotic illustration to Lermontov's poem of a demon's love for a human being, but as time passed his vision changed, until his image of a Lucifer-like being, more than mortally beautiful, had become a half-female figure fallen to earth, the body contorted and crushed, its peacock-feather wings broken beneath it, and on its face an expression of unfathomable despair. The despair was Vrubel's, for through these years he was increasingly subject to the nervous attacks which culminated in his madness. The last five years of his life were spent in an asylum.

Vrubel's career has certain analogies with van Gogh's. As was the case with the Dutch painter, to his constitutional nervous disorder was added the wracking difficulty of finding himself in an impossible position between the old and the new. Contemporary taste was still shackled by conceptions of aesthetic meaning which demanded the externalization of experience at the price of sincerity, and the twentieth-century conviction that the aesthetic elements and their proper manipulation are what distinguish the work of art from any other form of expression had not yet been formulated. Unlike his French contemporaries, however, Vrubel was unable to find an entirely satisfying or successful technique for the expression of his ideas. The principles of Russian artistic life were too thoroughly saturated with the canons of academism, and Vrubel's work even at its best remained a decorative exercise on the meaning of colour and form rather than the creation of new colours and forms. The deeply personal and tragic spirit of Vrubel's art can be seen by comparing his unfinished water-colour of 'A Boyar' (Plate 172B) with the historical paintings which can be related to the Slavophile programme. Where Surikov or Apollinari Vasnetsov accumulated details like theatrical properties, Vrubel used a bold splash of colour in the costume to stress the tragic expression of the face. And though the abrupt margin at the top is a matter of accident, since the study was painted on the back of another composition, it serves to emphasize the expressive elements in the painting at the cost of the merely descriptive. In this respect Vrubel belongs to that group of masters who did so much, often with great pain and sacrifice, to create the conditions of much modern art, Munch in Norway, Klimt in Austria, Beardsley in England, Toorop in his early work in Holland, and Gauguin in France. How much Vrubel might have accomplished, had he lived longer to profit by the greatly expanded knowledge of European art which reached Russia after 1900, we can only conjecture, but the strange, unfinished decorative abstractions in his last portrait, of Valerian Briussov (1905) (Plate 173), suggest that in the discoveries of cubism he might have found formal satisfaction.

In cosmopolitan St Petersburg the search for modern expression led to a comparable revolution against academic traditions, but the forms which were discovered were very different from those favoured in Moscow. Once again Slavic Moscow and 'Western' St Petersburg were artistically opposed, although the essential problem remained the same. And in spite of the authority of the Academy, the revolt, when it came, occurred outside its walls and showed no concern for its standards or traditions. Indeed, the new artistic expressions in St Petersburg were not primarily concerned with the major arts of painting, sculpture, or architecture, but were developed in theatre design, book illustration, and antiquarian research.[26]

In the early 1890s a group of university students interested in discussing art and music gradually formulated a programme and created the circumstances for a new direction in Russian art in the movement eventually known as Mir Iskusstva ('The World of Art', from the title of their principal publication). The educational and cultural advantages enjoyed by the members of this group, several of whom soon achieved an international reputation, were in contrast to those of the Moscow artists or of their predecessors among the Peredvizhniki. Some of them were only partly or not at all of Russian blood, many of them belonged to the wealthier upper class; they had been educated at the University, and they travelled extensively abroad. Although their preferences were for French art and their greatest triumphs were to occur in Paris, it is well to remember that the leaders of the group – it is difficult to call it a movement – were not narrowly Francophile. It can be said of them more than of any comparable group of young artists of this period, that they had familiarized themselves with European culture as a whole. Situated geographically as they were on the eastern periphery of Europe, they saw its westernmost manifestations across the central European cultures. Consequently the flavour of their work is frequently eclectic, combining elements from various modern sources with reminiscences of the past, yet attaining an unmistakable quality of their own. Their style did not precipitate a final cleavage with the Peredvizhniki. When Serge Diaghilev (1872–1929) first began to collect pictures, he bought a quantity of sketches and drawings by Kramskoi; Alexander Benois (born 1870) admired the work of Repin and Isaak Levitan (1861–1900), the painter of idyllic Russian landscapes. The first issues of *Mir*

Iskusstva contained Repin's Memoirs and numerous illustrations of work by many of the painters who regularly exhibited with the 'Wanderers'. Benois, however, and his principal colleagues, Diaghilev, Léon Bakst (1868–1924), and V. A. Serov, realized that the artistic horizons of Russian cultural life had grown desperately restricted after so many years of social and political reaction. The museums of St Petersburg contained no examples of modern Western Art and exhibitions were few and inferior. In these circumstances it is all the more remarkable that these young men should have succeeded in familiarizing themselves with the most advanced currents in European art. In this they were assisted by the providential appearance in St Petersburg of a young French diplomatic official, Charles Birlé, who told them of Gauguin, van Gogh, and Seurat, and helped them to read Baudelaire, Verlaine, and Mallarmé. Their enthusiasm for French culture became so great that by 1895 Bakst and Benois had settled in France, where they were frequently visited by Diaghilev and other friends from St Petersburg.

For Benois and Diaghilev French art and architecture were decisive factors. Their determination to awaken an appreciation for the former splendours of St Petersburg, a city they deeply loved, recalls the enthusiasm, a generation earlier, of the de Goncourts for the eighteenth century. Similarly their efforts were at first more antiquarian than creative. Nostalgia accounts for much of the charm in the scenes of eighteenth-century St Petersburg by Benois and by his nephew Eugène Lanceray (E. E. Lansere, 1875–1946) (Plate 172A).[27] Diaghilev's enthusiasm for eighteenth-century painting led him to organize a huge exhibition of Russian portraiture, held in the Tauride Palace in 1905, which for the first time revealed to the Russian people the extent of their cultural resources.[28] In 1906 he arranged an exhibition of Russian art at the *Salon d'Automne* in Paris, the first occasion on which so many of the finest examples of Russian painting from the earliest times to the end of the nineteenth century were seen outside Russia.[29]

Meanwhile, in 1898, Diaghilev and his friends had founded the periodical *Mir Iskusstva*, which in its brief existence (1898–1904) became the organ for the most advanced artistic opinion in Russia. In its pages can be found a still exciting record of the enthusiasms of these young men. The early issues contained articles on Beardsley, the Pre-Raphaelites, and Whistler, and illustrations of works by Menzel, von Marées, and Böcklin whom they most admired. Before long these examples of weary realism and tarnished idealism were succeeded by accounts of important foreign exhibitions. French paintings began to appear in increasing quantity; works by Degas, Renoir, Gauguin, Vallotton. In architecture there were buildings by Olbrich and Mackintosh. They neglected little that was important or provocative in those years. This first of the important Russian art journals was soon followed by others. Benois, who had been absent in Paris, when *Mir Iskusstva* was founded and who regretted not occupying a more prominent position among the editors, secured funds for a publication of his own, *Khudozhestvennyya sokrovishcha Rossii (Artistic Treasures of Russia, 1901–7)*, a lavishly illustrated monthly composed of articles on public and private collections of Russian and European art, with special emphasis on aspects of St Petersburg and the imperial residences. This was followed by *Starye Gody (Past Years, 1907–16)*, another monthly with a series of important articles on Russian art and on the work of European artists in Russia. When *Mir*

Iskusstva ceased publication, its work was carried on by a comparable journal in Moscow, *Zolotoe Runo* (*The Golden Fleece*, 1906–9), and we may add to this extraordinary flowering of art publications the monthly *Apollon* (1909–17), which resembled *Starye Gody* although with more emphasis on modern developments.

From this record of editing and publishing one might think that the members of the group were dispersing their creative energies, but such was not the case. Since the talents of these young men consisted more in the formulation of a mood or tone in their approach to artistic problems than in the discovery of a new philosophy of art or the invention of a new technique, their greatest accomplishments appeared in the reorganization and renovation of an art which had grown shabby in recent years.[30] The enthusiasm of Benois and Diaghilev for the theatre, especially for the ballet, and their desire to rid the official productions of outworn conventions, and particularly to restore the tradition of pantomime combined with dance and to make the ballet once more an integrated whole, led to their experimenting with new ideas for librettos, music, and theatrical settings. The story of their relations with the imperial theatres is complicated, but in 1907 they scored a triumph with the performance of *Le Pavillon d'Armide* at the Mariinsky Theatre in St Petersburg. The book, stage-settings, and costumes were by Benois, the music by Nicholas Tcherepnin, and the choreography by Michel Fokine. Anna Pavlova was Armide, and the young Nijinsky danced the part of her slave. The following year Diaghilev presented Moussorgsky's *Boris Godunov* at the Paris *Opéra*.[31] The success of this brilliant production, with sets and costumes by Benois and the Moscow painter, Alexander Yakovlevich Golovin (1863–1930), persuaded him to arrange a season of ballet performances in Paris the following year.[32] The story of Diaghilev's *Ballets russes* is too well known to need recounting in detail, but it is worth observing that this first triumph of Russian art outside the boundaries of Russia united certain elements of the Slavic Revival of Moscow with the ideals of the Mir Iskusstva group in St Petersburg. Among the productions of the first years, Benois's *Pavillon d'Armide* and *Sylphides*, evoking the atmosphere of eighteenth-century France and of the earlier nineteenth-century classical Russian ballet, demonstrated the nostalgic tendencies of *Mir Iskusstva*. In contrast, there were ballets where Russian themes, set to new or unfamiliar music, provoked the greatest enthusiasm and were thought to be more typical of modern Russian art.[33] Such were the *Polovtsian Dances* from Borodin's *Prince Igor*, with scenery by Nicholas Roerich (1909), Stravinsky's *L'Oiseau de feu*, with settings and costumes by Golovin and Bakst (1910) (Plate 174B), and *Petrouchka*, with libretto, settings, and costumes by Benois (1911) (Plate 175). In *Petrouchka* Benois recreated the atmosphere of carnival week in St Petersburg in the 1830s, remembered from his childhood only a few decades later. Bakst's designs for Debussy's *L'Après-midi d'un Faune*, Ravel's *Daphnis et Chloë* and Tcherepnin's *Narcisse* (Plate 174A) recalled the earlier aestheticism of *Mir Iskusstva*, and especially his own predilection for classical themes; when he was a young man, one of his commissions had been the design of two classical tragedies for the theatre of the Hermitage.[34] But the more exclusively Russian elements reached a climax in Stravinsky's *Sacre du Printemps* (1913), with sets and costumes by Roerich. In this, the most complex and profound of all Stravinsky's ballets, a new chapter in the history of modern music was opened – paradoxically by a ballet described as 'Tableaux de la Russie paienne'.[35]

So far back into the past, to pagan Russia, the course of taste had reached. In this culmination of the Slavic Revival we encounter a number of artists from Moscow. Much of their work was done for the stage, and it is a sign of the times that the first production, and one of the most successful, by the Moscow Art Theatre (1898), was Count Alexei Tolstoi's tragedy on a sixteenth-century subject, *Tsar Feodor Ioannovich* (1868).[36] Although the sets by V. A. Simov were not distinguished, the presence in the repertory of this and subsequent productions of Tolstoi's *Death of Ivan the Terrible* (1899) and Pushkin's *Boris Godunov* (1907) kept the old Russian scene in the famous naturalistic style of the Moscow Art Theatre continually before the eyes of the Moscow public.[37] Golovin and Nicholas Konstantinovich Roerich (1874–1947) represented what we may call the expressionist period of the Slavic Revival.[38] For his subject-matter Roerich, like Vasnetsov, frequently explored remote periods in Russian history, as in his *Idols* (1901–10), representing a group of idols in a sanctuary such as Ibn Fadlan had described in the tenth century. But he treated such scenes in broad areas of flat bright colour analogous to the work of the early Expressionist and Fauve painters in Germany and France. Golovin's interest in Old Russia led him to study mosaics and icons, from which he developed his intricately patterned stage designs. This Moscow style was also used by Natalia Goncharova in her sets and costumes for Rimsky-Korsakov's *Le Coq d'or* (1914), and in her designs for the 1926 revival of *L'Oiseau de feu*, where the backdrop for the last act was a colourful synthesis of architectural scenes in medieval icons.

Much of the work inspired by the theories of *Mir Iskusstva* recalls the contemporary manifestations of *Art Nouveau*, which was the most progressive artistic movement in Europe during the decade 1895 to 1905, but the more characteristic Russian examples should not be confused with them.[39] At times there is the same interest in restrained colour schemes and two-dimensional patterns, and even the same attenuation of plant forms and other natural motifs. But the essential character of early modern Russian art was different. The productions of St Petersburg were more Rococo, influenced by Benois's and Diaghilev's admiration for the period of Elizabeth's and Rastrelli's Tsarskoe Selo, while those of Moscow were affected by the desire to revive older Russian traditions. In the Russian equivalent of the Arts and Crafts movement a connexion with certain aspects of the *Art Nouveau* episode can be found. Mamontov's colony at Abramtsevo was linked with the names of Vasnetsov and Vrubel, whose works were impregnated with Russian themes, although Vrubel in some of his designs, as for a series of jewelled combs, used natural forms in the manner of *Art Nouveau*. Closer to the ideals of the Moscow manner was Princess Tenisheva's self-supporting agricultural community at Talashkino, where instruction was offered not only in the popular crafts of the day, wood-carving, ceramics, weaving, and embroidery, but also in manuscript illumination and choral singing in an attempt to revive the ancient beauties of the Russian liturgical services.[40] Meanwhile a widespread movement to promote cottage industries and improve the standards of peasant arts and crafts, inaugurated by the Zemstvo, the rural administrative body, enlisted the services of many prominent artists, among them Maria

Vasilievna Yakunchikova (1870–1902), who produced a quantity of designs for textiles, embroideries, bookbindings, and the like. Pattern and line in her more independent productions, such as her coloured woodcuts (Plate 176A), are thoroughly in the spirit of the Russian version of *Art Nouveau*.[41]

With the exception of Vrubel's rare terra-cotta and majolica compositions and C. A. Somov's witty figurines, the *Mir Iskusstva* movement included little that was notable in sculpture. At the end of the century Prince Paul Petrovich Trubetskoi (1867–1938) achieved an international reputation with his contributions to the Paris Exposition of 1900 and the *Mir Iskusstva* exhibition in St Petersburg that year. Entirely self-taught, he had succumbed to the lure of impressionist light and shade and sought in his small portraits the movement of Rodin, and something of the atmospheric effects achieved by the Italian sculptor Medardo Rosso (Plate 180). His one large undertaking, the equestrian figure of Alexander III in St Petersburg, is a curious departure from his usual manner. While the composition is conceived more as an enlarged statuette than as a monumental design, the comparatively broad shapes indicate that Trubetskoi had studied the more narrowly national work of such men as Vasnetsov, with whose 'Bogatyri', depicting the warrior knights of Ancient Russia, the horse and rider have much in common.[42]

In architecture, too, the counter-currents of the Slavic Revival and *Mir Iskusstva* curiously combined to create some of the most interesting, but still little-known work of the period. In St Petersburg, as we might expect, the earlier years of the century saw a revival of classicism, urged in large part by the activities of *Mir Iskusstva*, especially for banks and Government structures. At times the mass and detail were so resolutely derivative that it is difficult to realize that such buildings were so recent.[43] To Moscow we may trace the tendency to revive the forms of the older Russian past. This could have been seen at the Paris Exposition of 1900, where the Russian pavilion, designed by the Moscow artists Golovin and Konstantin Alekseevich Korovin (born 1861), was a poetic yet accurate recreation of Russian wooden architecture.[44] A similar village, of great charm but little architectural novelty, was erected in Yaroslavl on the occasion of the tercentenary celebration of the Romanov dynasty. Masonry forms were also revived, often with startling fidelity. The Church of Our Saviour on the Waters (1910) in St Petersburg, commemorating the 12,000 sailors who perished in the Russo-Japanese War, was a replica of St Dmitri in Vladimir with the addition of Andrei Bogoliubovo's palace tower as a belfry. At Leipzig a memorial church commemorating the centenary of the allied victory over Napoleon closely followed the Ascension at Kolomenskoe (1913). Such scholarly inventions, like those elsewhere in the West, remained architectural curiosities without promise for the future.[45]

More interesting and potentially more influential were the attempts to rework old traditions in the spirit of a new age. At Abramtsevo and Talashkino there were churches in which older Russian forms were freely used to create an effect at once religious and new.[46]

Such religious architecture occasionally required decorative schemes of considerable character. Although in a memorial church at Abbas Tuman in the Caucasus Nesterov followed closely the style of medieval Caucasian frescoes, he was impelled to do so by the design of the church which was an obvious imitation of medieval Armenian architecture. On the other hand, at Talashkino and Schlüsselburg, Nicholas Roerich created murals and mosaics powerful in scale and bold in colour.[47] A further impetus towards such design was given in 1905 with the removal of restrictions against public worship for the Old Believers, who had suffered civil and religious disabilities from the middle of the seventeenth century. It was certainly not their intention to return to the Orthodox forms of the State religion, and for this reason their architects attempted to suggest in their churches not only the Orthodox character of the Old Believers' faith and its relation to Byzantine and Russian history, but also their long exile in the North. Thus an Old Believers' church in Moscow by I. Ye. Bondarenko (1909) (Plate 176B) contains elements reminiscent of wooden architecture. The exaggerated proportional relations also are a sophisticated comment on older Russian forms.

More romantic still, and certainly less successful as a solution to the problem of adapting older Russian forms to modern uses, were certain structures where pictorial effects took precedence over the expression of function. Such are the design of the Tretyakov Art Gallery by Viktor Vasnetsov (1900–2) (Plate 177), based on his study of medieval manuscript illuminations, and the Yaroslavl and Kazan stations in Kalantchevskaya Square in Moscow which taken together compose an extraordinary ensemble of architectural memories. In the Yaroslavl station, by F. O. Shekhtel (1906), the relaxed curves of the arches and the high crested roof with its metal ornament show the influence of *Art Nouveau* working upon a fantasy of Muscovite elements; the Kazan station (1914–40) (Plate 178A), by A. V. Shchusev, is such a conglomeration of souvenirs, including even a replica of the Siumbeki Tower at Kazan, that its purpose is completely disguised.[48] On the other hand the acceptance of a thoroughly Western version of the contemporary *Art Nouveau* manner can be seen in Shekhtel's Ryabushinski House in Moscow (Plate 174B).

That the future held the promise of Russia's increasing participation with Western Europe in the formulation of modern art as we have come to know it and in the development of a particularly Russian revision of that art, there can be no doubt. In Moscow itself the promise of that future could be seen. The outstanding examples of contemporary European painting, collected by S. I. Shchukin and I. A. Morozov, had already inspired members of the younger generation. Meanwhile the Russian artists stood at an important turning point.[49] They might, like D. S. Stelletski (born 1875) (Plate 179), attempt to adapt progressive techniques to older formal and iconographical programmes.[50] This was much like the position taken by Simon Ushakov in 1650, but it is difficult to see how it could have led to anything very expressive, since it was fettered by mannerisms. On the other hand they might seek, like their eighteenth-century predecessors, for the springs of modern experience in the European centres of artistic research. This was the path chosen by Kandinsky, Gabo and Pevsner, Chagall, and their many colleagues who were in school in Europe between 1900 and the outbreak of the War. After the brief but important triumph of the Constructivists in 1917–20, most of these distinguished artists went into exile. Their magnificent talents are indisputable proofs of the continuity of Russia's artistic heritage in the twentieth century.

NOTES

CHAPTER I

1. For the early history of Russia and of the Slavic peoples see G. Vernadsky, *Ancient Russia* (New Haven, 1943), and *Kievan Russia* (New Haven, 1948), *passim*.

2. M. I. Rostovtsev, *Iranians and Greeks in South Russia* (Oxford, 1922).

3. Under the presumptive date of 860–2 the *Russian Primary Chronicle* recorded the event. For the vexed question of the identity of the Varangians see G. Vernadsky, *Kievan Russia*, chapters vii–viii. Hereafter the texts of the chronicles will be cited for the appropriate year in the complete collection published by the Academy of Sciences (AN, Leningrad, 1843–1929), as *Polnoe sobranie russkikh letopisei* (PSRL), and in the English translations of the Laurentian Chronicle for the years 852–1116 by S. H. Cross as *The Russian Primary Chronicle* (Cambridge, Mass., 1930); and the First Novgorod Chronicle for the years 1016–1471 by R. Michell and N. Forbes, as *The Chronicle of Novgorod*, Royal Historical Society Camden Third Series, xxv (London, 1914). For a concise history of the various texts see N. de Baumgarten, 'Chronologie ecclésiastique des terres russes du Xᵉ au XIIIᵉ siècle', *Orientalia Christiana*, xvii (Rome, 1930), 17–21.

4. For the dynastic genealogies of the descendants of Rurik see N. de Baumgarten, 'Généalogies et mariages occidentaux des Rurikides russes du Xᵉ au XIIIᵉ siècle', *Orientalia Christiana*, ix (1927); S. H. Cross, 'Medieval Russian Contacts with the West', *Speculum*, x (1935), 137–44.

CHAPTER 2

1. For the most searching documentary and archaeological analysis in English of the early Kievan churches, see S. H. Cross, H. V. Morgilevski, and K. J. Conant, 'The Earliest Mediaeval Churches of Kiev', *Speculum*, xi (1936), 477–99. The most important Russian monumental inventory is E. E. Golubinski, *Istoriya russkoi tserkvi*, 2nd edition (Moscow, 1901–4), I, part 2, 1–161.

2. In Russian usage a cathedral, sobor, was not necessarily the seat of a bishop but might be a more important or venerable church, tserkov. See A. Grabar, 'Cathédrales multiples et groupement d'églises en Russie', *Revue des études slaves*, xx (1942), 91–120.

3. These and remains of later Christian burials have been published by M. K. Karger in his 'Knyazheskoe pogrebenie xiv v. Desyatinnoi tserkvi', AN., Institut istorii materialnoi kultury, *Kratkie soobshcheniya*, v (1940), 1219.

4. See K. J. Conant, 'Novgorod, Constantinople, and Kiev in Old Russian Church Architecture', *Slavonic and East European Review*, xxii (1944), no. 59, for the plan of St Irene, 87, and for a conjectural restoration of the Desyatinnaya, 79. — p. 9

5. The curious construction of the foundations, laid upon a bed of cement placed over crossed timbers which would quickly decay and produce uneven settling, suggests that the workmen were local artisans more familiar with wood than with masonry construction. See Cross, Morgilevski, and Conant, *op. cit.*, 484, 488. — p. 10

6. For an estimate of Yaroslav's reign see S. H. Cross, 'Yaroslav the Wise in Norse Tradition', *Speculum*, iv (1929), 177–97; N. K. Chadwick, *The Beginnings of Russian History, an Enquiry into Sources* (Cambridge, 1946).

7. The extensive literature on Sancta Sophia may be approached through the papers by Cross and Conant, and the bibliographies in D. Ainalov, *Geschichte der russischen Monumentalkunst der vormoskovitischen Zeit* (Berlin and Leipzig, 1932); and M. Alpatov and N. Brunov, *Geschichte der altrussischen Kunst* (Augsburg, 1932). See also G. G. Pavlutskii, 'Kievskie khramy domongolskago perioda', Moskovskoe Arkheologicheskoe Obshchestvo, *Trudy*, XIV S'ezd (Chernigov, 1908), II (1911), 29–36; N. Brunov, 'L'Église à croix à cinq nefs dans l'architecture byzantine', *Échos d'Orient*, xxvi (1927), 257–86.

8. Some leeway may be allowed the earlier dates in the chronicles. See Cross, *The Russian Primary Chronicle*, 109–15. — p. 11

9. See Cross, Morgilevski, and Conant, *op. cit.*, plates 2–7 for six conjectural reconstructions of Sancta Sophia by Professor Conant. — p. 12

10. Less expensive brick and mortar construction took the place of *opus mixtum* in the later eleventh century, in such buildings as the Golden Gate, St Irene, and the early twelfth-century Church of the Redeemer at Berestovo. For views of the ruins of the first two in 1848, see the paintings by M. M. Sajin, reproduced by A. Simsen-Sytchevsky, 'Un Peintre de la ville de Kiev', M. Hrushevski, ed., *Recueils d'histoire, d'archéologie, des mœurs, et des arts*

de Kiev, 1 (1930), 364–76 (in Ukrainian). The wall construction at Berestova is seen after the removal of later stucco in 1919 in G. K. Lukomski, *L'Architecture religieuse russe du XIᵉ siècle au XVIIᵉ siècle* (Paris, 1929), plate 3.

p. 12   11. K.J. Conant in 'Novgorod, Constantinople, and Kiev in Old Russian Church Architecture', *loc. cit.*, 79, has published a conjectural restoration of the wooden Sancta Sophia with octagon and tent roof, but the possibility of a Caucasian origin for such forms at this date is problematical.

p. 13   12. For plans of these churches see J. Strzygowski, *Die Baukunst der Armenier und Europa*, II (Vienna, 1918), 839, 848. N. Brunov has pointed out that Mokvi was not painted until 1089–1118 and may have been built only shortly before. His conclusions temper Strzygowski's enthusiasm for an Armenian origin for Kievan architecture: 'La croix inscrite à cinq nefs est originaire de Constantinople. Salonique, Mayafarquin, Mokvi, la Russie, ont imposé à ce type constantinopolitain des modifications plus ou moins profondes sous l'influence du style local', *Echos d'Orient, loc. cit.*, 286.

p. 14   13. Grabar, I, 148, n. 3.

14. Abraham van Westerveldt (d. 1692) accompanied Prince Janusz Radziwill as military draughtsman in the campaign of 1650–1 against the Cossacks of the Ukraine. His drawings were first published as views of unidentified structures by Y.I. Smirnov, 'Risunki Kieva 1651 goda po kopiyam ikh kontsa XVIII veka', MAO, *Trudy*, XIII S'ezd (Yekaterinoslav, 1905), Moscow, 1908, 197–512 (with excellent reproductions). Certain drawings were identified as representations of Sancta Sophia by I. (H.) V. Morgilevski, 'La Ste Sophie de Kiev, recherches nouvelles', in M. Hrushevski, ed., *Kiev et ses environs, histoire et monuments* (Kiev, 1926), 81–108 (in Ukrainian).

15. To this group may be added the rebuilt Cathedral of Sancta Sophia (1044–66) in Polotsk. It had five aisles, the outer ones ending in straight walls as in Sancta Sophia in Novgorod. The duplication of the three apses on the western façade may be due to German Romanesque influence in Western (White) Russia. The technique of unstuccoed brick without admixture of stone speaks for the Kievan source of the builders. The church has been analysed by N. Brunov in Alpatov-Brunov, 49–50. See also Ainalov, *Vormoskov.*, 67–8, and A. I. Nekrasov, *Ocherki po istorii drevnerusskogo zodchestva* (Moscow, 1936), 36–8.

p. 15   16. *The Russian Primary Chronicle, A.D. 1034–6.*

17. Strzygowski, *op. cit.*, II, 844.

18. Lavra, from the Greek *laure*, a passage, alley, avenue, or street, later a group of shops along a street, hence a bazaar. In ecclesiastical usage a lavra came to mean a series of hermitages around a monastery, and by association an important monastic foundation. Of the more than a thousand Russian monasteries (and convents) active before 1917, only four had the rank of lavra: the Kievan Pecherskaya, the Trinity-St Sergius near Moscow, the Alexander Nevski in St Petersburg, and the Pochaevskaya in Western Russia.

19. Reproduced respectively in Nekrasov, *Ocherki*, figures 19–22; Grabar, I, 153.

20. *The Russian Primary Chronicle, A.D. 945.* N. K. Chadwick has analysed the documentary evidence in *The Beginnings of Russian History*, 81–2. For plans and illustrations of objects found in the excavations of the palace area see I. A. Khoinonski, *Raskopki velikoknyazheskago drevnago grada Kieva*, (Kiev, 1893).

CHAPTER 3

1. G. Vernadsky, *Kievan Russia*, 121.

2. V. N. Lazarev, *Iskusstvo Novgoroda* (Moscow, 1947), a useful and well-illustrated history of Novgorod art and architecture, with extensive bibliographies, is the most recent authoritative study.

3. A convenient summary of ecclesiastical extracts from the chronicles, including those relating to church building before the Tartar conquest, is provided by N. de Baumgarten's 'Chronologie ecclésiastique des terres russes du Xᵉ au XIIIᵉ siècle', *Orientalia Christiana*, XVII (1930). Among the private citizens who built churches were Irozhnet (1135), Sedko Sitinits (1167), Mikhail Stepanits and Moisei Domanezhits (1176), Radko and his brother (1183), and the Volodarevitsi and Noseovitsi families (1207). Sedko Sitinits may have been the historical personage whose activity gave rise to the legend of Sadko, the merchant of Novgorod.

4. *The Chronicle of Novgorod*, 1179.

5. *The Chronicle of Novgorod*, 1015–16.

6. K. J. Conant, 'Novgorod, Constantinople, and Kiev in Old Russian Church Architecture', *Slavonic and East European Review*, XXII (1944), no. 59, 75–92, for a conjectural reconstruction of the wooden Sancta Sophia.

7. See the bibliographies in Ainalov, *Vormoskov.*, and Alpatov-Brunov. In 1893 Sancta Sophia was restored under the direction of V. V. Suslov. His report is described in 'Pervonachalnyi vid Sofii Novgorodskoi', MAO, *Trudy*, XI S'ezd (Kiev, 1899),

11 (Moscow), 82. See also Archbishop Arsenii, 'Nastoyashchee sostoyanie Sofiiskago sobora v Novgorode', MAO, *Trudy*, XV S'ezd (Novgorod, 1911), I (Moscow, 1914), 283–92. Suslov's work has been criticized by N. Brunov and N. Travin in their report of a thorough examination of the fabric in 1945, 'Sobor Sofii v Novgorode', *Soobshcheniya instituta i teorii arkhitektury* (Moscow, 1947), no. 7. They contend that Suslov concealed the picturesque quality of the building under too uniform a coat of plaster. In removing the subsidiary additions, however, Suslov disclosed for the first time the monumental mass of Sancta Sophia. During the Second World War the upper part suffered considerable damage when the roof and cupolas burned with the destruction of the frescoes on the vaults within. For photographs of the damage, see V. Lazarev, *op. cit.*, and I. Grabar, ed., *Pamyatniki iskusstva razrushennye nemetskimi zakhvatchikami v SSSR* (Moscow, 1948). The churches of Nereditsa, Nicholas na Lipne, and Volotovo were entirely destroyed.

8. Brunov and Travin, *op. cit.*, 16, believe that towers originally rose at the eastern corners. Presumably they were a defensive measure, to protect the princely and episcopal edifice from the towns-people.

9. For cross-sections of the cathedral see Imperatorskaya Arkheologicheskaya Kommissiya, *Materialy po arkheologii Rossii*, XXI (St Petersburg, 1897), 12, 17.

10. The origin of the bulbous dome and the means of its transmission to Russia must remain uncertain, but it seems probable that suggestions from oriental architecture, reaching Russia through innumerable contacts with the East, deserve equal consideration with the undeniable virtuosity of Russian carpenters. See the documented articles by A. P. Novitski, 'Lukovichnaya forma russkikh tserkovnykh glav', MAO, *Drevnosti*, *Trudy kommissii po sokhraneniiu drevnikh pamyatnikov*, III (1909), 349–62; W. Born, 'The Origin and Distribution of the Bulbous Dome', *Journal of the American Society of Architectural Historians*, III, No. 4 (Oct., 1943), 32–48. Dr Born concluded: 'The bulbous dome originated in a stratum of wooden architecture which extended through India, the Near East, and Russia. Its evolution is based on two elements of Indian architecture: the bulging but unpointed stone cupola of the *stupa*, and the ridged horseshoe vault of the wooden *chaitya* halls. ... Syria seems to have led the evolution. Russia followed probably in the thirteenth century'. The earliest representation of a bulbous Russian dome

appears in an illuminated manuscript, the Dobrilov Gospel of 1164. Throughout the fourteenth century bulbous domes frequently occur in such illustrations.

11. St Nicholas and the other churches discussed in this chapter are reproduced, Grabar, I, 171–222.

12. A recently discovered fresco in the stair-tower of the Nativity in the Anthony Monastery, crudely drawn and inscribed 'Petr' with an undecipherable date, may be a portrait of this early architect. See A. Vinner, 'Freski Novgoroda', *Arkhitektura SSSR* (1945), no. 10, 22–8; and M. Ilin, 'Master Petr', *idem* (1943), no. 2, 37–9; Grabar, I, 171.

13. The restoration is illustrated with measured drawings in P. P. Pokryshin, 'Otchet o kapitalnom remont Spaso-Nereditskoi tserkvi v 1903 i 1904 godakh', *Materialy po arkheologii Rossii*, XXX (St Petersburg, 1906).

14. For measured drawings of these two churches see V. V. Suslov, *Pamyatniki drevnerusskago iskusstva*, II (St Petersburg, 1909).

15. For the technique of these corbelled arches see P. P. Pokryshkin, 'Tserkvi pskovskogo tipa XV–XVI stol. po vostochnomy poberezhniiu Chudskago ozera i na r. Narove', *Izvestiya imperatorskoi arkheologicheskoi kommissii*, XXII (1907), 1–37; for theories of their origin see H. Weidhaas, *Formenwandlung in der russischen Baukunst* (Halle, 1935).

CHAPTER 4

1. The architecture of Suzdalia has been studied on the basis of recent archaeological investigations by N. N. Voronin in several publications of which the most convenient is *Pamyatniki Vladimiro-Suzdalskogo zodchestva XI–XIII vekov* (Moscow 1945). See also Nekrasov, *Ocherki*, chapter 5. For further illustrations see Grabar, I, 303–21; and D.R. Buxton, *Russian Mediaeval Architecture* (Cambridge, 1934), plates 8–15.

2. Voronin, *loc. cit.*, 13.

3. *Ibid.*

4. A. D. Varganov, 'Freski XI–XII vv. v Suzdalskom sobore', AN, *Kratkie soobshcheniya*, V (1940), 38–40.

5. Tipografskaya Chronicle, A.D. 1152.

6. Ainalov, *Vormoskov.*, 32–3.

7. The contemporary account of this fire is a vivid description of the destruction caused by these periodic conflagrations. According to the Hypatian

p. 24

p. 25

p. 26

p. 27

p. 29

p. 30

p. 31

p. 32

p. 34

. 22

. 23

Chronicle, A.D. 1183: 'Almost the whole city and the great princely palace were burned down, and the churches to the number of thirty-two; and the Cathedral of the Virgin (of the Dormition) with the golden domes was burned down, and all its golden domes with which the devout Prince Andrei had adorned it. And so the fire burned from the top to the bottom. ... And the silver censers and innumerable gold and silver objects and all the gold and pearl embroidered vestments and cloths ... were burned.'

p. 34 8. Photographs showing the condition of the remaining portions of Andrei's church, including evidence of fire damage, were taken during the restoration of 1891. See V. K. Trumovskii, 'Kratkii otchet o restavratsii Vladimirskago Uspenskago Sobora v 1891', MAO, *Drevnosti*, XVI (1900), 1–41.

9. Hypatian Chronicle, A.D. 1175.

10. For the history and iconography of the image of the Pokrov, see p. 91.

p. 35 11. For the plan see J. Strzygowski, *Die Baukunst der Armenier und Europa*, I (Vienna, 1918), 185.

12. The first modern Russian historian, V. N. Tatishchev (1686–1750), in his *Istoriya rossiiskaya*, III (Moscow, 1774), 487, n. 483, stated that in the absence of skilled architects in Vladimir, master builders were sent to Andrei by the Emperor Frederick Barbarossa 'with whom he was friendly'. Unfortunately Tatishchev failed to mention his source, which has never been discovered, but since he said that the texts he read were on parchment, he probably used an old and authentic manuscript.

p. 36 13. Yuri Dolgoruki married a Cuman princess, the daughter of Aëra II; his sons married Ossetian princesses. See N. de Baumgarten, 'Généalogies et mariages occidentaux des Rurikides russes du Xe au XIIIe siècle', *Orientalia Christiana*, IX (1927).

14. For photographs and conjectural reconstructions of the Bogoliubovo church and palace see N. N. Voronin, *Pamyatniki*, figures 15–19; N. N. Voronin and M. K. Karger, eds., *Istoriya kultury drevnei Rusi* (Moscow, 1948), 227–9.

p. 37 15. Laurentian Chronicle, A.D. 1194.

p. 38 16. See Voronin, *Pamyatniki*, figure 27, for an old view before restoration.

17. Laurentian Chronicle, A.D. 1222.

p. 39 18. For this little-known architect and sculptor, who also worked on the walls of the Moscow Kremlin, see N. N. Sobolev, 'Russkii zodchii XV veka, V. D. Yermolin', *Staraya Moskva* (1914), no. 2, 16–23.

CHAPTER 5

1. Laurentian Chronicle, A.D. 978–80. For the p. 4 importance of ornament in pre-Christian times see A. Guscin, 'L'Art indigène préchrétien de la Russie Kiévienne', *Revue des études slaves*, VIII (1928), 194–202.

2. L. Niederle, *Manuel de l'antiquité slave* (Paris, 1926), II, chapter 12. Brilliant primary colours remained for centuries characteristic of the Russian environment; see p. 274, ch. 10, n. 8.

3. Thus in Moscow the Krasnaya ploshchad, 'Red' or 'Beautiful Square', and in the Kremlin the *Krasnoe kryltso*, 'Red' or 'Grand Staircase'.

4. P. Muratov, *L'Ancienne peinture russe* (Rome and Prague, 1925), 29.

5. N. P. Sychev, 'Drevneishii fragment russko- p. 4 vizantiiskoi zhivopisi', Seminarium Kondakovianum, *Recueil d'études*, II (1928), 91–104, with colour plate and French summary.

6. For these patterns see D. V. Ainalov, 'Mramory i inkrustatsii Kievo-Sofiiskago sobora i Desyatinnoi tserkvi', MAO, *Trudy*, XII S'ezd (Kharkov, 1902), III (Moscow, 1905), 5–11.

7. For the relation of the Sancta Sophia mosaics to other Byzantine systems see C. Diehl, *Manuel d'art byzantin*, 2nd ed., II (Paris, 1926), 513–18.

8. Although the Sancta Sophia mosaics and frescoes have not been thoroughly restudied in recent times, the earlier publications are iconographically useful, such as the large lithographic plates in colour and line after drawings by F. G. Solntsev in *Drevnosti rossiiskago gosudarstva, Kievskii Sofiiskii sobor* (St Petersburg, 1871–87). See also V. Lazarev, 'Nouvelles découvertes dans la Cathédrale de Ste Sophie', *Arkhitektura SSSR* (1936), no. 5, 51–4 (in Russian).

9. The iconography of the Virgin in Byzantine p. 4 and Russian painting has been thoroughly examined by N. P. Kondakov in *Ikonografiya Bogomateri* (St Petersburg, 1914–15), 2 vols.

10. See p. 87; p. 275, ch. 11, n. 7.

11. See Alpatov-Brunov, plates 158–65, for p. 4 comparative details of the Sancta Sophia mosaics with other Russian and Greek examples.

12. A. Grabar, 'Les Fresques des escaliers à p. 4 Sainte-Sophie de Kiev et l'iconographie impériale byzantine,' Sem. Kond., *Recueil d'études*, VII (1935), 103–18.

13. Quoted by D. V. Ainalov, *Vormoskov.*, 26.

14. F. C. Belfour, tr., *The Travels of Macarius,* p. 4 *Patriarch of Antioch: Written by His Attendant,*

Archdeacon Paul of Aleppo, in Arabic (London, 1829), I, 231.

15. St Michael was demolished in the 1930s and the mosaics transferred to the Museum. For the stylistic analysis see D. V. Ainalov, 'Die Mosaiken des Michael-Klosters in Kiev', *Belvedere*, IX–X (1926), 201–16.

16. A. V. Prakhov, 'Kievskie pamyatniki', MAO, *Drevnosti*, XI (1887), part 3, plates 4–5.

CHAPTER 6

46   1. In the absence of any general or authoritative history of early Russian sculpture, see the summaries in L. Réau, *L'Art russe des origines à Pierre le Grand* (Paris, 1921); Ainalov, *Vormoskov.*; Alpatov-Brunov. For Perun and the other gods see L. Leger, *La Mythologie slave* (Paris, 1901); N. K. Chadwick, *The Beginnings of Russian History*, chapter 5.

2. A. S. Cook, 'Ibn Fadlan's Account of Scandinavian Merchants on the Volga in 922', *Journal of English and Germanic Philology*, XXII (1923), 58.

3. R. Holtzmann, *Die Chronik des Bischofs Thietmar von Merseburg* (Berlin, 1935), 302.

4. F. J. Tschan, *The Chronicle of the Slavs by Helmold* (New York, 1935), 219.

5. L.A. Magnus, ed. and tr., *The Tale of the Armament of Igor* (Oxford, 1915), 5, 6, 8.

6. Reproduced, Ainalov, *Vormoskov.*, plate 1b.

47   7. Now in the Academy, Cracow. See L. Niederle, *Manuel de l'antiquité slave*, II, 148, figure 48.

8. V. B. Antonovich, 'O skalnykh peshcherakh na beregu Dnestra v podolskoi gubernii', MAO, *Trudy*, VI (Odessa, 1884), I (Moscow, 1886), 86–102.

9. *The Russian Primary Chronicle*, A.D. 988.

10. Reproduced, Ainalov, *Vormoskov.*, plate 11. The Desyatinnaya fragments are published by M. K. Karger in 'Knyazheskoe pogrebenie XI veka v Desyatinnoi tserkvi', AN, *Kratkie soobshchenniya*, IV (1940), 12–20. For discussion and illustration of other fragments of early Kievan sculpture see N. Makarenko, 'La Statuaire et la sculpture de Kiev à l'époque prémongole', in M. Hrushevski, ed., *Recueils d'histoire, d'archéologie, des mœurs, et des arts à Kiev*, I (1930), 27–96 (in Ukrainian). The reliefs from St Michael's are now in the Museum, Kiev. See also A. I. Nekrasov, *Drevnerusskoe izobrazitelnoe iskusstvo* (Moscow, 1937), 65–6.

11. For the history and reproduction of this sculpture see the illustrated work by F. W. Halle,

Die Bauplastik von Wladimir-Ssusdal (Berlin, 1929); and A. A. Bobrinskoi, *Reznoi kamen v Rossii, Sobory Vladimiro-Suzdalskoi Oblasti, xii–xiii, xv.*, (Moscow, 1916), an album of 41 plates.

12. Halle, *op. cit.*, 62–3; Voronin, *Pamyatniki*   p. 48 (Moscow, 1945), 55, figure 26.

13. Alpatov-Brunov, 265–6, with quotations in   p. 49 German; A. Luther, *Geschichte der russischen Literatur* (Leipzig, 1924), 25.

14. Hypatian Chronicle, A.D. 1183.

15. *The Russian Primary Chronicle*, A.D. 1160.

16. C.R. Beazley, ed., *Texts and Versions of John de Plano Carpini and William de Rubruquis as Printed for the First Time by Hakluyt in 1598* (London, 1903), 141.

17. The sculptures have been carefully studied and put in a conjectural order by K. K. Romanov. Among his many publications are 'K voprosu o tekhnike vypolneniya reliefov sobora sv. Georgiya v g. Iurieve-Polskom', Sem. Kond., *Recueil d'études*, II (Prague, 1928), 149–60; and 'La Colonnade du pourtour de la cathédrale de Saint-Georges à Jurev-Polskij', in G. Millet, ed., *L'Art byzantin chez les slaves*, II (Paris, 1932), 54–67, with bibliography of his previous work.

18. Voskresensk Chronicle, A.D. 1234.   p. 50

19. On the so-called 'Gates of Sigtuna' of the Cathedral of Novgorod, a pair of bronze doors made in Magdeburg, Germany, towards the middle of the twelfth century, a small figure of a sculptor inscribed in Russian characters 'Master Avraham', may be a self-portrait of a Russian craftsman who helped to restore the doors when they were removed from Poland to Novgorod in the fourteenth century. See A. Goldschmidt, *Die Bronzetüren von Novgorod und Gnesen* (Marburg, 1922).

CHAPTER 7

1. For the restoration of Sancta Sophia see V.V.   p. 51 Suslov and others, 'Obsuzhdenie proekta stennoi rospisi Novgorodskago Sofiiskago sobora', *Materialy po arkheologii Rossii*, XXI (St Petersburg, 1897), 1–46.

2. Reproduced, P. Schweinfurth, *Geschichte der russischen Malerei im Mittelalter* (The Hague, 1930), figure 29.

3. I. Grabar, ed., *Voprosy restavratsii*, I (Moscow,   p. 52 1926), 25–6.

4. I. Grabar, *Die Freskomalerei der Dmitrikathedrale in Wladimir* (Berlin, 1925); summary by L. Réau, 'Les Fresques de la Cathédrale Saint-Dmitri

à Vladimir', *L'Art byzantin chez les slaves*, II, 68–76. Grabar dates the frescoes *c.* 1196.

p. 53   5. V. Myasoedov, *Freski Spasa-Nereditsy* (Leningrad, 1925); French edition, *Les Fresques byzantines de Spas-Nereditsa* (Paris, 1928). See also J. Ebersolt, 'Fresques byzantines de Nereditsa', Fondation Eugène Piot, *Monuments et mémoires*, XIII (1906), 35–55, Plates 4–5.

p. 54   6. V. Myasoedov, *Les Fresques byzantines*, 11, identified no less than ten different manners, but despite the presence of as many painters considered the ensemble entirely characteristic of Novgorod.

7. The dynastic character of the Spas-Nereditsa as a princely foundation explains the presence of SS. Boris and Gleb, and of Anna, St Vladimir's wife, in this procession. See N. P. Sychev, 'Sur l'histoire de l'église du Sauveur à Neredicy', *L'art byzantin chez les slaves*, II, 77–108.

p. 55   8. For the Caucasian influences at Nereditsa see C. Amiranachvili, 'Quelques remarques sur l'origine des procédés dans les fresques de Neredicy', *L'Art byzantin chez les slaves*, II, 102–20, and especially the comparison between figures at Nereditsa and early twelfth-century frescoes at Chio-Mghvime and Achtala.

p. 56   9. Novgorod Chronicle, A.D. 1338, 1353.

10. For the activity of Theognostus see G. V. Zhidkov, *Moskovskaya zhivopis sredinu XIV veka*, Moscow (1928), an important study of the documentary and critical bibliography up to that date. The chronicle excerpts are from the Patriarchal Chronicle, 216–7.

p. 57   11. V. V. Suslov, 'Tserkov Uspeniya Presvyatoi Bogoroditsy v sele Volotove, bliz Novgoroda, postroennaya v 1352', Moskovskago predvaritelnago komiteta, *Trudy*, XV S'ezd (Novgorod, 1911); II (Moscow, 1911), 5–65. For similarities between Volotovo and Palaeologos art compare especially the mosaic of the *Massacre of the Innocents* in the Kahrieh-Djami; reproduced, F. Schmidt, *Kakhrie-Dzhami* (Munich, 1906) (Albom, vol. XI, Izvestii russkago arkheologicheskago instituta v Konstantinopele), plate 37.

12. For the iconographical significance of the Mandilion portrait see p. 64.

13. The Volotovo frescoes are extensively reproduced in Grabar, VI, 158–67.

p. 58   14. I. Grabar, *Theophan (Feofan) Grek* (Kazan, 1922). Summary by P. Schweinfurth in Thieme-Becker, XXIII (1939), 2–3. See also A. Anisimov, 'La Peinture russe du XIVe siècle (Théophane le grec)', *Gazette des beaux-arts*, 6e pér., III (1930), 158–77. Grabar and Anisimov give most of the Novgorod frescoes to Theophanes.

15. The letter has been analysed by A. I. Nekra- p. sov in 'Les Frontispices architecturaux dans les manuscrits russes avant l'époque de l'imprimerie', *L'Art byzantin chez les slaves*, II, 253–81.

16. Reproduced, Alpatov-Brunov, plate 211.   p.

CHAPTER 8

1. The pioneer nineteenth-century studies of p. icon-painting culminated in such works as M. I. and V. I. Uspenski's *Materialy dlya istorii russkago ikonopisaniya* (St. Petersburg, 1899), 101 plates; and N. P. Likhachev's *Materialy dlya istorii russkago ikonopisaniya* (Leningrad and St Petersburg, 1906), 2 vols., 419 plates (text never published). The earliest works were iconographical rather than critical or historical. This archaeological attitude is also found in N. P. Kondakov's studies such as his monumental *Russkaya ikona* (Prague, 1928–33), 4 vols., with excellent reproductions. His *The Russian Icon* (Oxford, 1927), translated by Sir Ellis Minns, is a preliminary sampling of the *Russkaya Ikona*. Kondakov's stylistic conclusions are subject to revision, since they were based on colour notes made before many of the icons were cleaned.

2. A more critical and historical attitude appeared in the first decade of the twentieth century. See especially the synopses of lectures by A. I. Uspenski, *Ocherki po istorii russkago iskusstva* (Moscow, 1910); P. P. Muratov's catalogue of the Ostroukhov collection, *Drevne-russkaya ikonopis v sobranii I. S. Ostroukhova* (Moscow, 1914). His sections on icon-painting in Grabar's *Istoriya russkago iskusstva*, VI, chapters 1–11, have been translated as *L'Ancienne peinture russe* (Rome and Prague, 1925). See also his *Les Icones russes* (Paris, 1927).

3. The first discoveries of the State Restoration p. Workshops (*Tsentralnye gosudarstvennye restavratsionnye masterskie*) were published as *Voprosy restavratsii*, ed. by I. Grabar and A. Anisimov, 2 vols. (Moscow, 1926–8). For summaries in French of this work see A. Anisimov, 'Les Anciennes icones et leur contribution à l'histoire de la peinture russe', Fondation Eugène Piot, *Monuments et Mémoires*, XXX (1929), 151–65; and G. Millet, 'Les Ateliers de restauration', *L'Art byzantin chez les slaves*, II, 51–3. A collection of icons cleaned and restored by the Workshops was exhibited in Western Europe and America in 1929–31. For the catalogue see M. Farbman, ed., *Masterpieces of Russian Painting* (London, 1930) with good colour reproductions;

Metropolitan Museum of Art, New York, *A Catalogue of Russian Icons* (1931), with preface by I. Grabar. For an account of the travelling exhibition and a concise history of icon-painting see A. H. Barr, Jr. 'Russian Icons', *The Arts*, XVII (1931), 295–314 ff.

4. The most recent useful *résumés* of icon-painting are those by A. I. Nekrasov, *Drevne-russkoe izobrazitelnoe iskusstvo sredinu XIV veka* (Moscow, 1937), and V.N. Lazarev in his *Iskusstvo Novgoroda* (Moscow, 1947). See also O. Wulff and M. Alpatov, *Denkmäler der Ikonenmalerei* (Hellerau bei Dresden, 1925); reviewed by L. Bréhier, 'Les icones dans l'histoire de l'art byzance et la Russie', *L'Art byzantin chez les slaves*, II, 150–73.

5. A curious example of the distorted appearance of an icon much repainted can be seen in the *Annunciation* of the Anthony Monastery, Novgorod, reproduced, Kondakov, *Russkaya ikona*, III, 141 and figure 16. The twelfth-century subject is identical with the Ustiug *Annunciation* (Plate 41), but the forms have become grotesque caricatures of the originals.

6. For a detailed analysis and summary of the Byzantine prototypes of Russian iconography, see G. Millet, *Recherches sur l'iconographie de l'évangile aux XIVe, XVe et XVIe siècles* (Paris, 1916). Specific iconographical problems will be annotated as they appear below. A convenient summary of the principal iconographical themes appears in L. Réau, *L'Art russe des origines à Pierre le Grand* (Paris, 1921), 141–64; and Schweinfurth, 218–32. See also N. Scheffer, 'Symbolism of the Russian Icon', *Gazette des beaux-arts*, 6e pér., XXV (1944), 77–94.

7. See S. Runciman, 'Some Remarks on the Image of Edessa', *Cambridge Historical Journal*, III (1931), 238–52; L. Bréhier, 'Icones non faites de mains d'hommes', *Revue archéologique*, 5e sér., XXXV (1932), 68–77. An early Slavic (not identifiable as Russian) *Mandilion* is preserved in the Cathedral at Laon; A. Grabar, *La Sainte Face de Laon, le Mandylion dans l'art orthodoxe* (Prague, 1931). Icons treating scenes from the legend occur as late as the seventeenth century; I. Myslivets, 'Skazanie o perepiske Khrista s Avgorom na russkoi ikone XVII veka', Sem. Kond., *Recueil d'études*, v (1932), 185–90, with German *résumé*.

8. L. Réau, *op. cit.*, 153, publishes a convenient chart of the Russian examples and their Byzantine prototypes.

9. Copies of an icon of the Virgin miraculously discovered at Tikhvin in 1383 remained for several centuries the most purely Greek type of Russian painting. See N. Toll, 'Ikona tikhvinskoi Bozhiei Materi', Sem. Kond., *Recueil d'études*, v (1932), 181–4.

10. See p. 91.

11. See p. 79.

12. Comparative examples, illustrating the development of the iconostasis from the Byzantine altar rail, will be found in E. E. Golubinski, *Istoriya russkoi tserkvi*, Atlas (Moscow, 1906), plates 46–48, 50, and 51. Panels fixed on the chancel barrier appear in the frescoes at Assisi attributed to Giotto. *p. 66*

13. A complete iconostasis of the sixteenth and seventeenth centuries is illustrated in detail in D. K. Trenev, *Ikonostas Smolenskago sobora Moskovskago Novodevichyago monastyrya* (Moscow, 1902). *p. 67*

14. In addition to standard hagiographies see E. E. Golubinski, *Istoriya kanonizatsii svyatykh v russkoi tserkvi* (Moscow, 1903).

15. An eighteenth-century pattern book by Dionysius of Phourna was discovered on Mt Athos, translated, and published by A. Didron and P. Durand as *Manuel d'iconographie chrétienne grecque et latine* (Paris, 1845). *p. 68*

16. For the technique of icon-painting see N.P. Kondakov, *The Russian Icon*, chapter 3; Wulff and Alpatov, *Denkmäler der Ikonenmalerei*, 96–7; Schweinfurth, 209–16.

17. A late practice panel with heads of old and young men in various stages of completion, including one of each type drawn in outline on the gesso ground, is reproduced, N. P. Likhachev, *Materialy*, plate 311, no. 594.

18. P. Miliukov, *Outlines of Russian Culture*, III (Philadelphia, 1942), 44. *p. 69*

CHAPTER 9

1. For stylistic influences in the earliest icons see the 1937 Ilchester lecture by Prof. D. Talbot Rice, *The Beginnings of Icon Painting* (Oxford, 1938). *p. 70*

2. The Laurentian Chronicle, A.D. 1155: '... in the same year Andrei went from his father to Suzdal, whence he took the icon of the Blessed Virgin, which on the same ship had been brought from Tsargrad'.

3. For a detailed and illustrated analysis of the condition of the icon see A. Anisimov, *Our Lady of Vladimir* (Prague, 1928).

4. The attribution of the Yaroslavl Orans to Alimpi is discussed by D. V. Ainalov, *Geschichte der* *p. 72*

russischen Monumentalkunst zur Zeit des Grossfürsten-tums Moskau (Berlin and Leipzig, 1933), 59–60. The icon is reproduced in colour, A. I. Nekrasov, *Drevne-russkoe izobrazitelnoe iskusstvo*, opp. 122.

p. 73   5. Three icons were traditionally attributed to Alimpi: the *Virgin of Vladimir* in the Dormition in Rostov, *The Queen Did Stand* in the Moscow Dormition, and the Svenski Virgin in the Svenski Monastery in Briansk. The first two are now recognized as much later paintings; the third may be a thirteenth-century copy of an earlier Kievan original. All three are reproduced, M. and V. I. Uspenski, *Zametki o drevne-russkom ikonopisanii* (St Petersburg, 1901).

6. A colour reproduction of St Dmitri, showing various stages in the removal of old paint, will be found in M. Farbman, ed., *Masterpieces of Russian Painting*, 13.

7. A Mandilion on a pole is seen in the seventeenth-century icon of the *Battle between Novgorod and Suzdal*, reproduced, N. P. Likhachev, *Materialy*, plate cclxii, no. 486.

p. 74   8. Schweinfurth calls attention, 144, n. 1, to the gilded hair on late antique imperial portrait statues.

p. 75   9. Colour reproduction by Max Jaffe, Vienna. Another St Nicholas from Novgorod is signed and dated, in a later inscription, as the work of Alexander Petrov in 1294. The linear design is more emphatic and ornamental, so that a late thirteenth-century date is not improbable. See Wulff and Alpatov, *Denkmäler der Ikonenmalerei*, 266 and figure 31.

10. In rejoining the halves of the icon after they had split apart a small vertical section was lost down the centre.

CHAPTER 10

p. 77   1. Reproduced, Grabar, VI, 133. See also Kondakov, *The Russian Icon*, 68.

2. Anthony of Novgorod's *Pilgrim's Book*, translated by B. de Khitrovo, *Itinéraires russes en Orient* (Geneva, 1889), 95.

3. For enlarged details see P. Neradovski, 'Boris i Gleb iz sobraniya N. P. Likhacheva', *Russkaya ikona*, I (St. Petersburg, 1914), 62–78.

p. 79   4. L. Matsulevich, 'Dve ikony Rozhdestva Bogomateri iz sobraniya S. P. Ryabushinskago', *Russkaya ikona*, III (St Petersburg, 1914), 163–79.

p. 80   5. N. Scheffer, 'Religious Chants and the Russian Icon', *Gazette des beaux-arts*, 6ᵉ pér., XXVII (1945), 129–42. The icon is reproduced in colour,

M. Farbman, ed., *Masterpieces of Russian Painting*, 69.

6. I. Grabar, 'Ancient Russian Painting', *A Catalogue of Russian Icons* (Metropolitan Museum of Art, New York, 1931), xiii: 'The love of particular shades and combinations of colours which recur again and again in the icons produced in Novgorod, Pskov, or Ferapontov (Therapont) are borrowed from the landscape of those localities. ... The rosy, lilac, and light blue shades of the fresco paintings by Dionysius at Ferapontov are still to be seen on the shores of the neighbouring lake; but the marvellous green that predominates in the icons of Pskov was first discovered as recently as last summer on the banks of the river Velikaya'.

7. This contrast of bright primary colours occurred even in the landscape. An early nineteenth-century English traveller, describing a monastic settlement in Western Russia (the Iverski Monastery on Lake Valdai, see the seventeenth-century drawing, plate 91), wrote that: 'The whole scene around glows with that luxuriant interchange of white and red, and green and gold that enters so largely into the composition of a Russian view', J. T. James, *Journal of a Tour in Germany, Sweden, Russia, Poland, During the Years 1813 and 1814* (London, 1816), 349.

8. The *Four Saints Icon* may be compared with the admirable Byzantine painting of the *Twelve Apostles* in the Moscow Historical Museum, reproduced in colour, J. Myslivec, *Ikona* (Prague, 1947), plate 1.

CHAPTER 11

1. For the claims of Moscow see the argument p. by M. Alpatov in Alpatov-Brenov, 302 ff. The historical documentation for early icon painting in Moscow has been set forth by G. V. Zhidkov, *Moskovskaya zhivopis srediny XIV veka* (Moscow, 1928). See also V. N. Lazarev, *Iskusstvo Novgoroda* (Moscow, 1947), 65; Nekrasov, *Drevne-ruskoe izobrazitelnoe iskusstvo*, 149–50 and 223–4.

2. For the iconography of this image see H. (G.) p. Zhidkov, 'L'Icone du "Sauveur a l'œil courroucé" de la cathédrale de la Dormition à Moscou', *L'Art byzantin chez les slaves*, II, 174–94.

3. Grabar, *Voprosy restavratsii*, I, 83; summary in p. Schweinfurth, 303.

4. Although the type is Greek, the peculiarly p. Russian tenderness and the simplified treatment of the highlights preclude a Greek origin. Recent Soviet opinion considers the work Russian; V. N. Lazarev, *Iskusstvo Novgoroda* (Moscow, 1947), 84–5.

5. A. I. Uspenski, *Drevne-russkaya zhivopis XV–XVIII veka* (Moscow, 1906); N. P. Likhachev, *Manera Pisma A. Rubleva* (St Petersburg, 1907); I. Grabar, 'Andrei Rublev, ocherk tvorchestva khudozhnika po dannym restavratsionnykn rabot 1918–25 gg.,' *Voprosy restavratsii*, I, 7–12; Schweinfurth, 301–18.

7   6. In 1774, on the occasion of the visit of Catherine II to Vladimir, the frescoes were repainted in oil and the iconostasis replaced with a new one in the Baroque style. The old panels were sold to peasants in the nearby village of Vasilievskoe where twenty-seven were recovered by the Restoration Commission in 1922 and removed to Moscow.

7. M. Alpatov, 'La Trinité dans l'art byzantin et l'icone de Roublev, études comparatives', *Echos d'Orient*, XXVI (1927), 150–86; N. V. Malitski, 'K istorii kompozitsii vetkhozavetnoi Troitsy', Sem. Kond., *Recueil d'études*, II (1928), 33–46, with French résumé.

CHAPTER 12

9   1. Reproduced in colour, Kondakov, *Russkaya ikona*, I, plate 2.

0   2. A. Frolov, 'Le *Znamenie* de Novgorod, l'évolution de la légende', *Revue des études slaves*, XXIV (1948), 67–81; XXV (1949), 45–72; A. Anisimov, 'Etiudy o novgorodskoi ikonopisi', Part 2, *Sofiya* (1914), no. 5, 5–21; N. Scheffer, 'Historic Battles on Russian Icons', *Gazette des beaux-arts*, 6ᵉ pér., XXIX (1946), 193–206. The venerable *Znamenie* is reproduced, Kondakov, *Russkaya ikona*, n, Plate 8.

3. The identity of the fourth saint is obscure. Alexander Nevski's appearance would be chronologically impossible but spiritually appropriate. N. Scheffer, *loc. cit.*, has suggested the legendary Kievan hero, Ilya Muromets.

4. P. D. Lathoud, 'Le Thème iconographique du "Pokrov" de la Vierge', *L'Art byzantin chez les slaves*, II, 302–14.

5. Detail of central section reproduced in colour, *Russkaya ikona* (1914), 39.

6. This equestrian figure was one of the sights of Constantinople, especially for Russian travellers who had seen nothing like it since the bronze horses brought by Vladimir to Kiev from Kherson had disappeared during the Tartar invasion. See the descriptions by Stephen of Novgorod, who visited Byzantium about 1350, and by other Russian travellers, translated by B. de Khitrovo as *Itinéraires russes en Orient* (Geneva, 1889), 155 ff.

7. The inverted perspective of old Russian painting has been studied by A. I. Nekrasov, 'O yavleniyahk rakkursa v drevne-russkoi zhivopisi', Institut arkheologii i iskusstvoznianiya, *Trudy*, I (1926), 7–22.   p. 92

8. Reproduced, Grabar, VI, 301–11.   p. 93

9. Reproduced in colour, Grabar, VI, facing 241.

10. Reproduced in colour, *Russkaya ikona*, III (St Petersburg, 1914), 183.

CHAPTER 13

1. This concept first found literary expression in an epistle from the Monk Philotheus to the Great Prince Basil III (1505–33). N. Zernov, *Moscow the Third Rome* (London, 1937), 36. A pictorial expression of this concept can possibly be read in a curious sixteenth-century horizontal icon, variously interpreted as the Church Militant, or as a commemoration of the victory of Ivan IV over the Tartars at Kazan. It represents the Russian armies, led by holy tsars and saints and accompanied by a cloud of angels, approaching the Celestial City where the Virgin and Child are enthroned. See P. P. Muratov, 'Dva otkrytiya', *Sofiya* (1914), no. 2, 5–17; Ainalov, *Grossfürsten.*, 104–5, and figure 57.   p. 96

2. Reproduced, V. T. Georgievski, *Freski Therapontova Monastyrya* (St Petersburg, 1911).

3. E. Georgievskij-Druzinin, 'Les Fresques du monastère de Thérapon, étude de deux thèmes iconographiques', *L'Art byzantin chez les slaves*, II, 121–34. For the iconography of the Akathist see J. Myslivec, 'Ikonografie akathistu Panny Marie', Sem. Kond., *Recueil d'études*, V (1932), 97–131, with French résumé; N. Scheffer, 'Akathistos of the Holy Virgin in Russian Art', *Gazette des beaux-arts*, 6ᵉ pér., XXIX (1946), 5–16.   p. 97

4. The hand of Dionysius's son Theodosius, who is known to have worked in the Kremlin Annunciation in 1508, might possibly have been seen in the frescoes discovered in 1882 by V.D. Fartusov in the vestibule of the cathedral. The unmistakably Italian Renaissance character of the figures and the astonishingly life-like portrait heads might have been due to the influence of some Italian painter arrived in Moscow in the wake of his architectural colleagues. Unfortunately, the style of these frescoes was so little in accord with prevailing official conceptions of old Russian painting that Fartusov was accused of having too drastically restored them. A conservative icon painter who was hired to 're-store' them succeeded in destroying them by repaint. Fartusov's photographs, the only remaining   p. 99

record of these important and problematic works, seem to have been retouched, but the style as a whole was too remarkable a combination of Renaissance realism and Moscow idealism to have been entirely invented in 1882. For reproductions, A. I. Uspenski, *Drevne-russkaya zhivopis*, Moscow, 1906 (reprinted from *Zolotoe runo* (1906), nos. 7–9); A. I. Uspenski, 'Stenopis Blagoveshchenskago sobora v Moskve', MAO, *Drevnosti Trudy kom.*, III (1909), 153–77.

p. 99   5. See N. Scheffer, 'Days of the Week in Russian Religious Art', *Gazette des Beaux-arts*, 6ᵉ pér., XXVIII (1945), 321–34.

p. 100   6. Reproduced in colour, Grabar, VI, facing 336. The naturalistic atmosphere of such a scene as this may be related to actual ceremonial drama to somewhat the same extent that Western European painting derived from the mystery plays. In the Russian church the ritual on Palm Sunday became very elaborate, especially in Moscow where the Tsar and the Metropolitan (later the Patriarch) took part in a solemn procession between the Kremlin and the Church of the Pokrov (St Basil's) on Red Square. Olearius's description of the ceremony he witnessed in 1636 is substantiated by Meyerberg's illustration of 1662. In each case a prominent place is given 'a very large chariot, made of boards nailed together, but low, drawing after it a Tree, on which were hung abundance of Apples, Figs, and Grapes', In it were 'four Boys with surplisses who sung the Hosanna'.

p. 101   7. Such a subject was the representation of Sancta Sophia, the personification of Divine Wisdom. For this type of icon the most useful source is Kondakov, *The Russian Icon*, chapter 6.

8. Reproduced and described, Kondakov, *The Russian Icon*, 107.

9. E. Duchesne, *Le Stoglav ou les cent chapitres* (Paris, 1920); G. Ostrogorskij, 'Les Décisions du "Stoglav" concernant la peinture d'images et les principes de l'iconographie byzantine', *L'Art byzantin chez les slaves*, I (1930), 393–411.

p. 102   10. P. Miliukov, *Outlines of Russian Culture*, III, 37; N. E. Andreev, 'O "Dele dyaka Viskovatago",' Sem. Kond., *Recueil d'études*, V (1932), 191–242, with *résumé* in German.

11. Miliukov, *loc. cit.*, 39.

CHAPTER 14

p. 104   1. The most recent and best illustrated work on wooden architecture is S. Ya. Zabello, *et al.*, *Russkoe derevyannoe zodchestvo* (Moscow, 1942). Three important pioneer studies are A. S. Uvarov, 'Ob arkhitekture pervykh derevyannykh tserkvei na Rusi', MAO, *Trudy*, II S'ezd (St Petersburg, 1872), I, (Moscow, 1876), 1–24; V. V. Suslov, *Ocherki po istorii drevne-russkago zodchestva* (St Petersburg, 1889), 19–54, 85–108; B. Dunaev, 'Derevyannoe zodchestvo severo-vostoka Kostromskoi gubernii', MAO, *Drevnosti*, *Trudy*, *Kom.*, VI (1915), 313–32, with many illustrations.

2. The Hypatian Chronicle, A.D. 842, mentions two 'chambered' churches, but a stone building does not occur in the Laurentian Chronicle until A.D. 945. A tenth-century Arab traveller reported that the Russian traders 'come from their own country, anchor their ships in the Volga, which is a great river, and build large wooden houses on its banks'. See A. S. Cook, 'Ibn Fadlan's Account of Scandinavian Merchants on the Volga in 922', *Journal of English and Germanic Philology*, XXII (1923), 57.

3. Ainalov, *Grossfürsten.*, 15.

4. M. Alpatov, in Alpatov-Brunov, 117, 183, p emphatically rejects the theory that wooden forms influenced the sixteenth-century stone churches. But telling evidence for the contrary opinion is provided by the early sixteenth-century church of the Resurrection, if indeed it be so old, in the village of Gorodin. There the stone of the tent-roof is unmistakably copied from a wooden original. See M. Krasovski, *Kurs istorii russkoi arkhitektury* (Petrograd, 1916), 145, figure 72.

5. In Scandinavian wall construction the beams are usually upright; in Russian they are always laid horizontally.

6. Such logs in uniform lengths in orderly piles can be seen for example in the picture of St Petersburg in the middle of the eighteenth century (Plate IIIA).

7. Wooden buildings were notoriously unstable. p When Catherine was still a young grand duchess she had a narrow escape from death when a wooden house in which she was sleeping suddenly slid down a hill. Wooden supports had been removed during the winter; when the ground thawed in the spring the whole building slipped from its foundations. See *Memoirs of Catherine the Great*, translated by K. Anthony (New York and London, 1927), 138–41.

8. For the use of the axe in the eighteenth century see Archdeacon Coxe, *Travels in Poland, Russia, Sweden, and Denmark* (London, 1784), 270.

9. G. Fletcher, *Of the Russe Common Wealth* (London, 1591), in R. Hakluyt, *Collection of ...*

voyages ... A new edition (London, 1809), 542. Fletcher's assumption of the use of the plans by the Russians was erroneous.

07   10. G. Miege, *A Relation of Three Embassies from His Sacred Majestie Charles II to the Great Duke of Muscovie ... in the Years 1663 and 1664* (London, 1669), 135, 301.

11. A. Olearius, *The Voyages and Travels of the Ambassador from the Duke of Holstein, to the Great Duke of Muscovy, and the King of Persia, Begun in the Year m.dc.xxxiii and finish'd in m.dc.xxxix Rendred into English* (London, 1662), 57. The prefabricated houses were also observed by Miege, *op. cit.*, 301.

12. W. Coxe, *op. cit.*, I, 348.

13. The regular alignment of houses along the curving streets of a radial plan was more real than apparent. In spite of the comments of foreign visitors who frequently remarked on the lack of order, the evidence of existing maps and views (Plate 66A) proves the contrary. The necessity of leaving open spaces as fire-breaks, as well as the garden plots around each house, both made for and concealed the regular distribution of the houses. William Coxe, who found Moscow bewildering, nevertheless remarked that 'the streets are exceedingly long and broad', *op. cit.*, I, 265. For old maps and plans of Moscow, see Grabar, II, Chapter 14.

14. Olearius, *op. cit.*, 48.

15. Reproduced, Grabar, I, 498-500. See also N. V. Sultanov, 'Ostatki Yakutskago ostroga i nekotorye drugie pamyatniki derevyannago zodchestva v Sibirii', *Izvestiya, Imp. Arkh. Kom.*, XXIV (1907).

16. F. von Adelung, *Augustin Freiherr von Mayerburg und seine Reise nach Russland* (St Petersburg, 1827), 2 vols.; *Albom Meierberg* (St Petersburg, 1903).

08   17. See N. de Baumgarten, 'Chronologie ecclésiastique', 90.

09   18. The excavated plan of the temple is reproduced, L. Niederle, *Manuel de l'antiquité slave* (Paris, 1926), II, figure 47.

10   19. The first three churches are reproduced, Grabar, I, 359-63; Buxton, plates 68-9.

12   20. Grabar, I, 380-1; Zabello, 93. V. V. Suslov, who examined and measured the church in the 1880s, believed it had been built in the seventeenth century. In 1871 it was sheathed with planks, and in 1892 was destroyed by fire.

21. For this and other philological similarities see R. Wischnitzer, 'Orientalische Einflüsse in der russischen Architektur', *Osteuropa*, I (1925-6), 252-5.

22. For reproduction, Buxton, Part II, 'Transcausasia', and plates 92, 97, 100; N. V. Sultanov, 'Russkiya shatroviya tserkvi i ikh sootnoshenie k gruzino-armyanskim piramidalnym pokrytiyam', MAO, *Trudy*, V S'ezd (Tiflis, 1881) and (Moscow, 1887), 230-44.

23. Grabar, I, Chapter 21.   p. 113

CHAPTER 15

1. Despite the descent of the Russian Church p. 115 from the Greek, the Christianization of Russia was not accompanied by any thorough study of ancient authors. The early translation of the Greek service books into Church Slavonic discouraged the spread of learning among the priests who, unlike the Latin clergy, were not obliged to know any language other than the spoken vernacular. See G. P. Fedotov, *The Russian Religious Mind* (Cambridge, Mass., 1946).

2. Although succession from father to eldest son p. 116 was customary, the crown was considered the property of the sovereign who might bequeath it at his pleasure. The order of succession based on primogeniture was not regularized until the accession of Paul I in 1796.

3. The Redeemer and other churches of Moscow p. 118 and vicinity are carefully analysed and illustrated in M. V. Krasovski, *Ocherk istorii Moskovskago perioda drevne-russkago tserkovnago zodchestva* (Moscow, 1911).

4. Alpatov-Brunov, 83; Ainalov, *Grossfürsten.*, p. 119 1-4.

5. Reconstruction in Nekrasov, *Ocherki*, 197. The arches are called kokoshniki from their fancied resemblance to a kokoshnik, the arched head-dress worn by Russian women in the Middle Ages.

6. Reproduced, Grabar, II, 16.   p. 120

7. The Annunciation has been carefully studied and published by V. V. Suslov, *Pamyatniki drevne-russkago iskusstva*, I (St Petersburg, 1908), 11-20; II (1909), 6-14; III (1910), 11-26.

8. *The Travels of the Magnificent M. Ambrosio* p. 122 *Contarini, Ambassador of the Illustrious Signory of Venice to the Great Lord Ussuncassan, King of Persia, in the Year 1473*, in *Travels to Tana and Persia by Barbaro and Contarini* (London, Hakluyt Society, 1873), 107-73. Examples of metal-work made by foreign artists in Russia are the orb and sceptre of Tsar Mikhail Feodorovich in the Moscow Armoury, reproduced, *Khud. sokr.*, II (1902), nos. 9-10, plates 101-2.

p. 122   9. The rigid ceremonial and disconcerting aloofness of later Tsars and boyars are described by Herberstein, Olearius, Meyerberg, and other travellers.

10. Reconstruction of plan and section of the earlier Dormition in Nekrasov, *Ocherki*, 182–4, figures 117–8.

11. See the review of the latest Soviet monograph by V. Snegirev, *Aristotel Fioravanti i perestroika Moskovskogo kremlya* (Moscow, 1935), by P. Schweinfurth, 'Die italienische Forschung und das Buch von V. Snegirev', *Jahrbücher für die Geschichte Osteuropas*, II (1937), 413–32. See also N. Brunov, 'Due cattedrali del Kremlino costruiti da italiani', *Architettura e arti decorative*, VI (1926), 97–110.

12. V. Dorofeev, *Bolshoi Uspenskii sobor v Moskve* (Moscow, 1896), with 105 photographs of the exterior and interior of the cathedral taken during the restoration of 1894–5.

p. 125   13. Alpatov-Brunov, 97–8.

14. Nekrasov, *Ocherki*, 216. The articles in Thieme-Becker, I (1907), 331 and the *Enciclopedia italiana*, II (1929), 585, confuse him with the earlier Alevisio who had worked on the Kremlin Palace and fortifications from 1494.

p. 127   15. Paul of Aleppo's account contains a description of the sumptuous interior of the palace and church, as well as interesting reflections on the relations between Tsar and Patriarch, *Travels of Macarius*, I, 386–95, II, 224–34.

p. 129   16. See Alpatov-Brunov, 118, 229, and plates 61–3, 149, a–c, for comparisons of Russian tent churches with Persian and Indian architecture. See also R. Wischnitzer, 'Orientalische Einflüsse in der russischen Architektur', *Osteuropa*, I (1925–6), 252–5.

17. The tower church of St Sergius with a tall tent roof stood in the Moscow Kremlin from 1557 to 1807. It appears in a drawing of 1672, reproduced, Grabar, II, 71. It was very close to the still extant belfry of the Church of the Crucifixion in the Dormition Monastery in Alexandrov, *c.* 1565, reproduced, Grabar, I, 85.

p. 130   18. Nekrasov, *Ocherki*, 256–64. He proposes Italian influence on the massing of the five elements at Dyakovo, by analogy with such High Renaissance Italian churches as G. Alessi's S. Maria di Carignano in Genoa. More remarkable, however, is the similarity between the plan of St Basil in Moscow (1555, see below), and such a typical Renaissance plan as Sebastiano Serlio's design for a square domed church with circular chapels projecting from the centre of each façade, which appeared in the

fifth book of his treatise on architecture, published in Paris in 1547. Even the relation between the intermediate chapels at St Basil and the spaces in the corners of Serlio's square seems too close for coincidence. But if by some remarkable chance the architects of St Basil possessed a copy of Serlio's treatise, they scorned the Italian's elevation with dome and paired belfries.

19. The columnar buttresses also occur in the p. tower of the seventeenth-century Boris and Gleb Cathedral in Chernigov, reproduced, G. K. Lukomski, *O proiskhozhdanii form drevne-russkago zodchestva Chernigova* (St Petersburg, 1912), opp. 26.

20. V. V. Suslov, *Tserkov Vasiliya Blazhennago v Moskvie … istoriya, znachenie i sovremennoe sostoyanie pamyatnika* (St Petersburg, 1912). An interesting example of the technical primacy exercised by the sixteenth-century votive churches can be seen in the carved wooden altar canopy in the form of a cluster of tent roofs with kokoshniki, in imitation of St Basil reproduced, MAO, *Drevnosti, Trudy kom.*, I (1907), plate 6, 8.

21. J. Richard, *Tour from London to Petersburgh, and from thence to Moscow* (Dublin, 1781), 52.

22. The Tartars, being nomads, used temporary architectural forms such as tents and portable pavilions. Their chief contribution to Russian art was in the field of ornament. See A. I. Nekrasov, 'Tartarismen im russischen Ornament des XV.–XVI. Jahrhunderts', *Slavia*, IX (1930), 139–50.

CHAPTER 16

1. N. N. Voronin in his *Ocherki po istorii russkago* p. *zodchestva XVI–XVII vv.*, 129–30, lists twenty-nine foreign architects active in the seventeenth century. Among them were Thomas Bailey, a Scottish engineer (1658–60), and Christopher Galloway who installed the clock and built the upper part of the Spasski Tower of the Kremlin (1624–5). Other nationalities are Dutch, German, and Swedish. See also I. Lubimenko, 'Les Étrangers en Russie avant Pierre le Grand', *Revue des études slaves*, IV (1924), 264–81. The Yaroslavl churches have been published by N. G. Pervukhin, *Tserkov Ioanna predtechi* (Moscow, 1913); *Tserkov Ilii proroka* (Moscow, 1915); *Tserkov Bogoyavleniya* (Yaroslavl, 1916).

2. The unusual title of this chapel commemorates the presentation in 1624 of a relic of Christ's robe, which had been stolen from a church in Georgia, to the Patriarch Philaret and Tsar Mikhail Feodorovich by the Persian Ambassador as a gift from the Shah. The relic was ceremoniously de-

posited in the Moscow Dormition. An icon illustrating the event is reproduced, Grabar, VI, 389.

3. 'In observance of the rules of the Holy Apostles and the Fathers the Lord's church should have five cupolas and not resemble a tent. ... It should be built conforming to regulative and statutory law as prescribed by the rules and statutes of the church, and should be a one, or three, or five-domed, but never a tent-shaped church ... neither should the cupola have the shape of a tent', quoted by P. Miliukov, *Outlines of Russian Culture*, III, 13. See also M. Spinka, 'Patriarch Nikon and the Subjection of the Russian Church to the State', *Church History*, X (1941), 347–66.

4. Paul of Aleppo, who was present at the first reception in the new palace, described Nikon's taste for an almost oriental luxury. See *Travels of Macarius*, II, 224–34.

5. Russia, having come late to Christianity, possessed few actual relics of the early church and had to make do with replicas. Foreigners were often surprised at the matter-of-fact way in which venerated objects were pointed out to them, such as the Manger and the Pillar, when they knew for themselves that the originals were elsewhere.

6. Nikon and his builders certainly used contemporary illustrations of Jerusalem, especially those in Bernardino Amico da Gallipoli's *Trattato delle Piante e Immagini de Sacri Edifizi di Terra Santa disegnate in Ierusalemme* (Florence, 1620). Compare particularly plates 22 and 24 with Nikon's church and tower.

7. The Monastery of the New Jerusalem was mined and demolished on 10 December 1941. The roof of the rotunda was destroyed and the interior of the church reduced to ruins. With the collapse of the interior walls some remains of Nikon's majolica arcades, in a restrained Renaissance style, came to light. For the history and condition of the church, see I. Grabar and S. Toropov, 'Arkhitekturnye sokrovishcha Novogo Ierusalima', in I. Grabar, ed., *Pamyatniki iskusstva razrushennye nemetskimi zakhvatchikami v SSSR* (Moscow, 1948), 174–99. To explain the fact that Nikon condemned the tent roof after he had himself built the largest, Grabar advances the supposition that he was persuaded by the Latinized clergy from the Ukraine. A.I. Nekrasov has studied the origins of the church and has indicated its possible influence on the centralized plans of the Moscow Baroque churches of the second half of the century. See his 'Arkhitektura Istry i ee znachenie v obshchem razvitii russkogo zodchestva', *Ezhegodnik muzeya arkhitektury*, I (Moscow, 1937), 9–51.

8. For a recent examination of the church at Fili see *Pamyatniki russkoi arkhitektury* (Moscow, 1945). For other examples of the Naryshkin storeyed churches see I. E. Bondarenko, *Arkhitekturnye pamyatniki Moskvy* (Moscow, 1904–05), parts II–III, plates 1, 3, 4, and 7. p. 142

9. The Sukharev Gate and Tower (1692–5) were erected by Peter I in commemoration of the loyalty of the Sukharev Regiment during the Streltsi uprising of 1682. The architecture was of little interest, merely an accumulation of familiar decorative details on a six-storey tower rising from a rectangular base. Peter devoted the building to scientific purposes. Here the first Russian school of navigation was held, the first Russian naval maps prepared, and important astronomical observations performed. In the nineteenth century the tower was used as a reservoir and lately was demolished as an obstruction to traffic. See Bondarenko, *Arkhitekturnye pamyatniki*, 19–20, plate 9. p. 143

10. A conjectural reconstruction of the upper storeys has been published by A. Akselrod, 'Menshikova Bashnya v ee pervonáchalnom vide', *Arkhitektura SSSR* (1939), No. 10, 57–61. He adds a slender spire in the style of the Petrovian baroque. The elaborate stucco reliefs on the interior are reproduced, MAO, *Drevnosti, trudy kom.*, V (1914), plate 1.

11. Several hundred characteristic examples of Moscow church architecture from 1600 to *c.* 1850 are well reproduced in gravure in the publication *Moskva, sobory, monastyrie i tserkvi* (Moscow, 1882–3), 4 vols.

CHAPTER 17

1. The Pogankin House, restored in 1902, was severely damaged in 1941. For this and other secular buildings see the thoroughly documented study by A. Potapov, 'Ocherk drevnei russkoi grazhdanskoi arkhitektury', MAO, *Drevnosti*, XIX (1901–2), parts 1–3; XX (1904). p. 144

2. The standard work on the history and buildings of the Kremlin is S. P. Bartenev, *Moskovskii Kreml v starinu i teper* (Moscow, 1912–16), 2 vols. For recent opinion, see A. I. Nekrasov, 'Le Kremlin de Moscou, les murailles et les tours', *Arkhitektura SSSR* (1935), nos. 10–11, 90–3 (in Russian). The early sixteenth-century fortifications of Smolensk have been thoroughly examined by P.P. Pokryshkin, 'Smolenskaya krepostnaya stena', *Izvestiya imperatorskoi arkheologicheskoi kommissii*, XII (1904), 1–25.

p. 145   3. Temporary wooden structures of traditional horizontal log construction were erected within the Kremlin as late as 1894 for the coronation of Nicholas II. See the photograph of the procession in *Moskva*, x (1911), facing 66.

4. For an account of such an audience by Tsar Alexis Mikhailovich in 1661, see A. von Meyerberg, *Relation d'un voyage en Moscovie*, 1 (Paris, 1858), 99.

5. *Terem*, from the Greek, meaning an attic, garret, or chamber at the top of a house; in ancient Russia the rooms where the women lived.

p. 146   6. S. Bartenev, *Le Grand Palais du Kremlin et ses neuf églises* (Moscow, 1912). But scientific knowledge made slow progress. Olearius reported that in 1643 he showed the Muscovites a *camera obscura*: 'All that was done in the street and men walking upon their heads, wrought such an effect in them, that they could never after be otherwise persuaded than that I held a correspondence with the devil.'

7. S. Collins, *The Present State of Russia, in a Letter to a Friend at London* (London, 1671), 64. A seventeenth-century upholstered armchair covered with a Persian fabric, which is said to have belonged to Alexis Mikhailovich, was preserved in the Storozhevski Monastery near Zvenigorod, reproduced, MAO, *Drevnosti, Trudy kom.*, III (1909), plate G. (IV), figure 1.

8. See pp. 190–2.

9. W. Coxe, *Travels in Poland, Russia, Sweden, and Denmark*, I, 265, 'Moscow may be considered as a town built upon the Asiatic model, but gradually becoming more and more European; exhibiting a motley mixture of discordant architecture'.

p. 147   10. Catherine visited Kolomenskoe 4 October 1762. The historical sources have been published by I. Ye. Zabelin, *Domashnii byt russkikh tsarei v XVI i XVII st.* (Moscow, 1872), Part I, *materialy*, 3–38. Another important residence was the Stroganov mansion at Solvychegodsk which was in existence until the early nineteenth century. Old drawings and the historical data for it have been published by Zabelin.

p. 148   11. Olearius, *op. cit.*, 57.

12. For illustrations of these and other secular structures of the seventeenth century see Grabar, II, chapter 15.

13. A. von Meyerberg, *Relation d'un voyage en Moscovie*, I (Paris, 1858), 99: 'The building which was given us was large enough, and built of brick, which is rare in Moscow. For the houses of the Muscovites are ordinarily of wood. For some years

a considerable number of brick buildings have been built in Moscow, either for vanity, or for greater security against the fires which are very frequent there.' G. Miege, in his *Relation of Three Embassies* (1669), wrote that: 'The House we were lodged in in this Town, was a large building of Stone, no great distance from the Castle, and one of the most commodious to be found. The Chambers were all arched, every window had its shutters of iron, and every passage-door was also of iron, which gave one occasion to say, we were certainly in the iron age, though otherwise it be a mettle rare enough in that Country.'

14. *Travels of Macarius*, I, 397.   p.

15. Reproduced, Grabar, II, 274.

16. I. Mashkov, 'Drevnee zdanie kitaiskoi Apteki, Moskovskago Universiteta i staroi Dumy', *Drevnosti, Trudy kom.*, III (1909), lvi–lviii.

17. The other half of this engraving is reproduced, Grabar, IV, 29. The whole plate is reproduced in facsimile by D. A. Rovinski, *Materialy dlya russkoi ikonografii*, VIII (St Petersburg, 1884–91), plate 308.

18. Lefort's first house, built by himself *c.* 1690,   p. was entirely in the European manner; reproduced, Grabar, IV, 31. The palace built for him by Peter (1692–8), and occupied by the Tsar until he moved to St Petersburg, was a massive structure built around a rectangular court. See A. A. Kiparisova, 'Lefortovskii dvorets v Moskve', *Arkhitekturnye pamyatniki Moskvy XVII–XVIII vekov*, Moscow, Akademiya Arkhitektury SSSR (1948), 45–54, with a reconstruction by N. N. Sobolev in a picturesque old Russian manner, 56.

CHAPTER 18

1. For the problem of religious precedence be-   p tween Tsar and Patriarch see G. Vernadsky, 'Notes sur les vêtements saçerdotaux du patriarche Nikon', *L'Art byzantin chez les slaves*, I, 412–15.

2. A. I. Uspenski, *Tsarskie ikonopistsy i zhivo-   p pistsy XVII veka* (Moscow, 1910–16), 4 vols.

3. These frescoes and the later cycle in the p Faceted Palace were repainted in 1672 for Tsar Alexis by Simon Ushakov, whose written descriptions are the chief source of information for the subjects. Ushakov's restorations were destroyed in the fires of 1682 and 1812. See Grabar, VI, 320, 336; I. Ye. Zabelin, *Domashnii byt russkikh tsarei*, I (Moscow, 1895), 149, 151–78. Viskovati was shocked by these frescoes. He complained: 'The parables are

not painted according to the canonical rules. Near the figure of Our Saviour a woman is painted dancing nonchalantly, and the inscription on it is "lechery and jealousy"', Grabar, VI, 320.

4. D. Ainalov, 'Freskovaya rospis khrama Uspeniya Bogoroditsy v Sviyazhskom muzhskom Bogoroditskom monastyr', MAO, *Drevnosti*, XXI (1906); M.K. Karger, 'Les Portraits des fondateurs dans les peintures murales du monastère de Svijazsk', *L'Art byzantin chez les slaves*, II, 135–49.

5. The last large frescoes of the sixteenth century were painted in 1598 in the Cathedral of the Virgin of Smolensk, in the Novodevichi Monastery in Moscow. They were commissioned by Boris Godunov, who had been crowned Tsar in the church that same year. Four rows of icons were also added to the iconostasis in 1598, but like the frescoes they are in poor condition. See Grabar, VI, 337–46; D.K. Trenev, *Ikonostas smolenskago sobora moskovskago novodevichyago monastyrya* (Moscow, 1902).

6. For views of the architecture and church furniture in this city, see N. Makarenko, *Iskusstvo drevnei Rusi u soli Vychegodskoi* (St Petersburg, 1918).

7. For the 'Stroganov School' see Grabar, VI, chapter 10 (and the French translation in P. Muratov's *L'Ancienne Peinture russe*); N. P. Kondakov, *The Russian Icon*, chapter 9; Schweinfurth, 328–53.

56 8. See, for example, Archdeacon Paul's enthusiasm for a small picture with 'figures of the angels in it grouped as numerously as a swarm of flies' in *Travels of Macarius*, I, 401.

9. A.I. Uspenski, *Drevne-russkaya zhivopis* (Moscow, 1906); Grabar, VI, chapter 13; summary in Thieme-Becker, XXXIV, 5–6; for a recently discovered *Trinity* by Ushakov, N. Sychev, 'Novoe proizvedenie Simona Ushakova v gosudarstvennom russkom muzee', *Materialy po russkomu iskusstvu*, I, (Leningrad, 1928), 78–111. Rublev's type was repeated with more naturalistic modelling and Renaissance architectural details.

10. The icon has not been cleaned or adequately photographed. For an illustration of the whole panel see Kondakov, *The Russian Icon*, plate 59, and for details of the smaller scenes, Grabar, VI, 431–7.

57 11. Grabar, VI, 426; G. Lebedev, *Russkaya zhivopis pervoi poloviny XVIII veka* (Moscow, 1938).

12. P. Miliukov, *Outlines of Russian Culture*, III, 44.

58 13. *Travels of Macarius*, II, 49–50.

14. Olearius, *op. cit.*, 76.

15. Mikhail's father, Feodor Romanov (Patriarch Philaret), was a nephew of Anastasia Romanova, first wife of Ivan IV.

16. For reproduction, V. Dorofeev, *Bolshoi Uspenskii Sobor v Moskve* (Moscow, 1896). Certain frescoes are reproduced after cleaning, MAO, *Drevnosti, Trudy, kom.*, IV (1912), xii ff.

17. *Travels of Macarius*, I, 397. p. 159

18. Paulus Giovius (1483–1522) mentions a portrait of Basil III taken from Moscow to Rome by Dmitri Gerasimov. See G. Lebedev, *Russkaya zhivopis pervoi poloviny XVIII veka* (Moscow and Leningrad, 1938), 13–14. See also W. Troutowsky, 'Le Boyard Khitrowo à la tête de la Salle des armures à Moscou', *Starye gody* (July–Sept. 1909), 345–83; A. Novitsky, 'Le Portrait à la cour de Moscou', *loc. cit.*, 384–403; A. Mironoff, 'L'Authenticité des portraits du Tsar Michel', *Starye gody* (July–Sept. 1913), 7–24.

19. Lebedev, *op. cit.*, 15.

20. The painting was damaged in the destruction of the Monastery during the Second World War. Reproduced, Grabar, VI, 417. See also N. Romanov, 'Parsuna izobrazaiushchaya patriarkha Nikona proiznosyashchego pouchenie kliru', in I. Grabar, ed., *Pamyatniki iskusstva razrushennye nemetskimi zakhvatchikami v SSSR* (Moscow and Leningrad, 1948), 201–16.

21. The principal series are in Kostroma, Trinity p. 160 Cathedral (1685); Rostov, St John (after 1683), the Resurrection (1680), the Redeemer (1680); Vologda, Sancta Sophia (1868–88); for Yaroslavl, see the works of Pervukhin, p. 278, ch. 16, n. 1.

22. For the influence of Piscator's Bible see E.P. Sachavets-Feodorovich, 'Yaroslavskie stenopisi i bibliya Piskatora', *Russkoe iskusstvo XVII veka, sbornik statei* (Leningrad, 1929), 85–108. See also Grabar, VI, chapter 17.

23. There is little iconographical, technical, or formal evidence to support P. Miliukov's contention: 'It seems that Russian art, living in the atmosphere of general religious exaltation, stood at that moment on the threshold of another revival of Christian painting, similar to the one experienced in the West during the fourteenth and fifteenth centuries. Had it been left to its own devices, Russian art perhaps would have followed the same path as that of western art, and three or four centuries later would have attained its classical epoch', *Outlines of Russian Culture*, III, 47. The influence of Russian painting outside Russia, especially in the Balkan

countries, has been suggested by A. Grabar in 'L'Expansion de la peinture russe aux XVIᵉ et XVIIᵉ siècles', Sem. Kond., *Récueil d'études*, XI (1940), 65–93.

p. 161   24. In the late nineteenth century the revival of interest in the Russian past led to a search for the few surviving workshops. See A. V. Bakushinski, *Iskusstvo Palekha* (Moscow and Leningrad, 1934).

CHAPTER 19

p. 164   1. The titles of Great Prince and Great Princess (*Veliki Knyaz, Velikaya Knyaginya*) after 1700 are rendered as Grand Duke and Grand Duchess, according to European usage since the seventeenth century.

p. 166   2. For the illustrated architectural history of the city see L. Hautecœur, *L'Architecture classique à Saint-Pétersbourg à la fin du XVIIIᵉ siècle* (Paris, 1912); L. Réau, *Saint-Pétersbourg* (Paris, 1913); V. Ya. Kurbatov, *Peterburg, khudozhestvenno-istoricheskii ocherk* (St Petersburg, 1913).

3. The important research undertaken by the Petersburg Society of Artist-Architects culminated in the comprehensive architectural exhibition at the Academy of Fine Arts in 1911, with an illustrated catalogue by A. Benois and I. A. Fomin, *Istoricheskaya vystavka arkhitektury* (St Petersburg, 1911).

p. 168   4. Luigi Rusca, an architect of the later eighteenth century, published detailed information on the construction of damp-proof foundations in Russia. For his own buildings he preferred vaulted stone basements. L. Rusca, *Recueil des dessins de differens batimens construits à Saint-Pétersbourg et dans l'intérieur de Russie* (St Petersburg, 1810), 4 ff.

p. 169   5. For details of early panoramas and engraved views of St Petersburg see Grabar, III, *passim*.

6. *Peterburgskaya Chast*, hence the affectionate nickname, 'Peter', for the city as a whole.

7. Grabar, III, chapter 3; M. Korolkov, 'Les Architectes Trezzini', *Starye Gody* (April, 1911), 17–36 (in Russian).

p. 171   8. The character of this church, for all that it was a dynastic sepulchre, is suggested by Baedeker's remark (1914): 'The interior is adorned with military trophies, flowers, and growing plants, and makes a very light and cheerful impression'.

p. 172   9. Engravings of the 1715 design and of the later revised plans by Tressini and Schwertfeger are reproduced, Grabar, III, 58–9. Numerous wooden models for eighteenth-century buildings have been preserved and are invaluable for studying the architects' original conceptions. V. Linkovski, 'Les

Modèles d'architecture en Russie', *Starye Gody* (Dec. 1910), 3–19.

10. The 'Catherine Palace' (Ekaterinhof), of traditional horizontal timber construction with Corinthian pilasters and a balustrade, is reproduced, *Istoricheskaya panorama Sanktpeterburga i ego okrestnostei*, I (Moscow, 1911), plate 20.

11. Grabar, III, chapter 4.

12. Grabar, III, 75–82. The Kunstkammer was damaged by fire in 1747, and all the decorative sculpture destroyed. The early engravings reproduced in plates 111A and 114B are taken from *Palaty Sankt Peterburgskoi Akademii Nauk, Biblioteka i Kunstkamera* (St Petersburg, 1741), by the librarian J. D. Shumacher, brother of a German architect active at that time. In 1941 the building again suffered during the bombardment of Leningrad. See P. Kaplan-Ingel, 'Petrovskaya Kunstkamera k vosstanovleniiu zdaniya', *Arkhitektura SSSR* (1946), no. 13, 36–40.

13. Grabar, III, chapter VI; the first Menshikov p. Palace is reproduced, 98–9. Schädel later worked with Rastrelli in Moscow, and in Kiev, where he built the Theological Academy (1735) and additions to Sancta Sophia in a turgid Baroque style.

14. Grabar, III, chapter 8; the plan of 1716–17 is reproduced 123. See also B. Lossky, *J.-B. A. Le Blond, Architecte de Pierre le Grand, son œuvre en France* (Prague, 1936).

15. The palaces at Peterhof were shelled and p. burned during the siege of Leningrad, but are now being reconstructed. The ruins of the main palace and the English Palace, and those of Tsarskoe Selo, Pavlovsk, Gatchina, and the Yelagin Palace, are described and illustrated in I. Grabar, ed., *Pamyatniki iskusstva razrushennye nemetskimi zakhvatchikami v SSSR* (Moscow and Leningrad, 1948).

16. The 'Petersburg' appearance, especially the p. pronounced verticality, of the Dresden and Warsaw churches may be explained as a result of Chiaveri's admiration for Schwertfeger's Alexander Nevski Cathedral (1720–3). A Roman Baroque conception, transported to Russia by a German architect, was taken back to Germany by an Italian trained in Rome.

17. Grabar, III, chapter 10.

18. Reproduced, Grabar, III, 161.

19. The 'Dutch' aspect of St Petersburg is more p. apparent in the decorated gables of a few houses in the early engravings than in any monumental structures. The few Dutch architects who came to Russia worked in the current international style. See

Grabar, III, 19, and chapter 7. Algarotti's impression seems to have been based on the general effect of tree-lined streets and canals, more than on any specific buildings: '[Dutch architecture] is the most prevalent, and it is no wonder. The Czar's first studies were in Holland, and it was at Saardam that this new Prometheus took the fire with which he animated his nation. It seems likewise to have been solely in remembrance of Holland that he planted rows of trees along the streets, and intersected them with canals, which certainly are not the same here as at Amsterdam and Utrecht', *Letters from Count Algarotti to Lord Hervey*, I, (London, 1769), 76, letter of 30 June 1739.

20. Algarotti, *op. cit.*, 76. A curious indication of that mixture of the most modern European fashions with Russian provincialism which prevailed in early St Petersburg can be found in the carved panelling in Peter's study at Peterhof, executed before 1721 by Nicolas Pineau (1684-1754), who had accompanied Le Blond to Russia. The modishly Rococo designs contain in the over-door panels asymmetrical motifs as advanced as any in France at that date. See Fiske Kimball, *The Creation of the Rococo* (Philadelphia, 1943), 132-4.

CHAPTER 20

7 1. C. Marsden's *Palmyra of the North, the First Days of St Petersburg* (London, 1942), is an informed account of the social and artistic life of the Russian court, principally under Elizabeth.

2. See E. Haumant, *La Culture française en Russie (1700-1900)* (Paris, 1910).

3. There is as yet no monograph in a non-Russian language on this important architect. The Russian sources are summarized in Thieme-Becker, XXVIII (1934), 26-8. For reproductions, Grabar, III, chapter 13; A. Matveev, *Rastrelli* (Leningrad, 1938), with bibliography.

8 4. Contemporary engraved views of this palace are reproduced, I. Ye. Bondarenko, *Arkhitekturnye pamyatniki Moskvy* (Moscow, 1904-5), parts 2-3, plate 51. Foreign visitors were always astonished at the portability of wooden buildings. Archdeacon Coxe described the removal of a palace in Catherine II's time: 'Wooden structures of large dimensions and handsome appearance are occasionally formed in Russia, with an expedition almost inconceivable to the inhabitants of other countries. A remarkable instance of this dispatch was displayed during the last visit of the Empress to Moscow. Her Majesty proposed to reside in the mansion of Prince Galitzin, which is esteemed the completest edifice in this city; but as it was not sufficiently spacious for her reception, a temporary addition of wood, larger than the original house, and containing a magnificent suite of apartments, was finished within the space of six weeks. This meteor-like fabric was so handsome and commodious, that the materials were afterwards taken down and reconstructed upon an eminence near the city, as an imperial villa', W. Coxe, *Travels in Poland*, etc., I, 348.

5. The Summer Palace charmed visitors to the very end of the century, when Rastrelli's Winter Palace already seemed old-fashioned and ungainly. Andrew Swinton, in his *Travels into Norway, Denmark, and Russia, in the years 1788*, etc. (Dublin, 1792), wrote that 'the Summer Palace [is] built of timber, and yet the most regular and elegant. It is placed in the Summer Gardens, upon the banks of the river, and is truly a delightful residence'.

6. Grabar, III, 199-200. For the Palace see also A. p. 180 Benois and A. Uspenski, 'Petergof v 18 veke', *Khudozhestvenyya sokrovishcha Rossii*, II (1902), Nos 7-8, with many illustrations.

7. The Russian tradition of a tall belfry must be p. 181 considered the factor determining the height of Rastrelli's tower, but it is interesting to compare his model with the design for a combination belfry and fountain published by Paul Decker in 1713 (Plate 3 of the supplement to his *Fürstlicher Baumeister oder: Architectura Civilis* (Augsburg, 1711). Decker's tower corresponds in many respects to the first four storeys of Rastrelli's.

8. The name of the original Finnish settlement on the site, *Saari mos* ('High Place') was russianized as Sarskoe Selo ('Saari Village') and after Peter I offered it to his wife Catherine as a country estate soon became Tsarskoe Selo ('Tsarist, or Imperial Village').

9. Models and drawings for the successive alterations at Tsarskoe Selo are reproduced, A. Benois, *Tsarskoe Selo v tsarstvovanie imperatritsy Elisavety Petrovny* (St Petersburg, 1910).

10. The original drawing for the park is repro- p. 182 duced, Matveev, *op. cit.*, 35.

11. Reproduced, Grabar, III, 215.

12. There is scant evidence in Rastrelli's work for p. 183 the tradition that he studied in Paris and travelled widely in Central Europe. There are, however, indications that he may have known the architecture of Northern Italy and Austria more intimately. To cite but two instances, at Smolny the relation between the dome and the subsidiary cupolas recalls Juvara's dome and belfry at the Superga near Turin (1706-20), and the diagonal axes of the towers at

Smolny and St Andrew in Kiev resemble Lukas von Hildebrandt's treatment of the Peterskirche in Vienna. It is interesting to think that if Rastrelli visited Vienna before 1725 he could have seen the Bibienas' sets for the opera, and could have studied Hildebrandt's designs for the new Hofburg (unexecuted) as well as the recently finished Belvedere. Hildebrandt's palaces, more than any others in Europe, have points in common with Rastrelli's early work in St Petersburg, such as the Anichkov Palace.

p. 183   13. This theatrical manner can be seen in the Cathedral of St Nicholas of the Sea in St Petersburg (1753–62) by Rastrelli's pupil and assistant, S. I. Chevakinski (1713–83), reproduced, Grabar, III, 247–9. The arrangement at each of the projecting angles of a cluster of Corinthian columns on high bases and supporting sections of a powerful entablature is virtually a translation of the familiar Bibiena programme of identical elements set on an axis diagonal to the proscenium. See the drawings by Ferdinando and Giuseppe Galli Bibiena in C. Ricci, *I Bibiena* (Milan, 1915); and A. H. Mayor, *The Bibiena Family* (New York, 1945), *passim*. Rastrelli's peculiar cupolas, especially those at Peterhof, resemble far less those of Pöppelmann's Zwinger at Dresden (1711–22), with which they are usually compared, than those in such typical Bibiena stage sets as Giuseppe's design of 1723 for *Costanza e Fortezza*, an opera presented that year in Prague, reproduced, G. G. Bibiena, *Theaterdecorationen …, Entwürfe … von G. G. Bibiena* (Berlin, n.d.), plate 19. Another provocative comparison may be made between Rastrelli's Hermitage at Tsarskoe Selo (1748–52), and Piranesi's *Gruppo di scala*, Plate 11 of his *Prima parte di architettura* (1743), reproduced, Grabar, III, and A. M. Hind, *G. B. Piranesi* (London, 1922), plate 73. The arrangement of columns, bases, and curved pediments is almost identical, and Rastrelli's wings projecting diagonally from the central portion exemplify the principle of Ferdinando Bibiena's *scena veduta per angolo*. Rastrelli's energetic but inorganic decoration may have been suggested by the engravings in Ferdinando Bibiena's *L'Architettura civile* (Parma, 1711; enlarged edition, Bologna, 1731).

14. Elizabeth died 25 December 1761, Old Style (5 January 1762, New Style), hence the date 1761–2 for the six-months reign (January–June) of Peter III.

CHAPTER 21

p. 184   1. Catherine's dual conception of Russia's position can be seen in the contrast between her interest in Russian history (see below, 240 and n. 10), and the peremptory statement at the head of her *Instructions to the Commissioners for Composing a New Code of Laws* (1766), that the first 'natural situation' to be kept in mind was that 'Russia is a European State'. W. F. Reddaway, ed., *Documents of Catherine the Great* (Cambridge, 1931), 215.

2. A less favourable attitude towards Catherine's taste is presented by L. Réau and G. K. Lukomski in *Catherine la grande, inspiratrice d'art et mécène* (Paris, 1930). They insist upon her lack of understanding of the arts and believe that she was merely lucky in her choice of men of genius. Réau even deprecates her passion for collecting, since it deprived France of so many fine objects. However that may be, the works of art and architecture commissioned and collected by Catherine constitute the most remarkable artistic achievement of any eighteenth-century sovereign.

3. Her attitude towards Elizabeth's taste is summarized in Casanova's account of his meeting with her in the Summer Garden in 1764. The Italian adventurer had been examining the sculptures, 'all being made of the worst stone and executed in the worst possible taste', when the Empress appeared and asked 'smilingly' if he were interested in them. Casanova replied that he presumed 'they had been placed there to impose on fools or to excite the laughter of those acquainted with history'. Catherine replied: 'From what I can make out, the secret of the matter is that my worthy aunt was imposed on, and indeed she did not trouble herself much about such trifles. But I hope you have seen other things in Russia less ridiculous than these statues', *The Memoirs of Jacques Casanova de Seingalt*, translated by A. Machen, x (n.p., n.d.), 183–4.

4. Grabar III, chapter 16. Prince Shuvalov's residence is reproduced, 265.

5. L. Réau, 'Vallin de la Mothe, documents inédits', *L'Architecture*, xxxv (1922), 173–80. He was a cousin of J. F. Blondel, who may have suggested his appointment to Shuvalov.

6. Blondel's design is reproduced, Grabar, III, 267.

7. Both façades are reproduced, Grabar, III, 280–1.

8. Rastrelli had prepared the first design for the Markets as a two-storey Rococo building with a central clock-tower. Vallin de la Mothe's plan followed Rastrelli's but stripped it of its ornament. See A. Matveev, *Rastrelli*, 20–1.

9. Grabar, III, chapter 17.

10. The interiors are reproduced by A. Uspenski and A. Benois, 'Kitaiskii dvorets v Oranienbaum', *Khudozh. sokrov. Rossii*, I (1901), 183–210.

11. The similarity between this *ordonnance* and that of Juvara's Palazzo d'Ormea in Turin (1730) suggests that Rinaldi, like Rastrelli, may have spent some time in Northern Italy. See the comparative photographs in A. E. Brinckmann, *Die Baukunst des 17. und 18. Jahrhunderts in den romanischen Ländern* (Berlin, 1919), 124–5.

12. The palace, its interior, and furnishings, are extensively illustrated in a series of articles by N. Lanceray, P. P. Weiner, *et al.*, *Starye Gody* (July–Sept., 1914), 5 ff.

13. Something of the character of the lost St Isaac could be seen in the Cathedral in Yamburg, west of St Petersburg (1762–82). Here the belfry with its circular lantern and baluster finial is very Roman, and the lower storeys and rounded arms of the crossing are also derived from St Peter. Reproduced, Grabar, III, 309.

14. Grabar, III, chapter 18.

15. Velten's grille was the first of many such characteristic adornments of St Petersburg. See G. N. Germont, *Reshetki Leningrada i ego okrestnostei* (Moscow, 1938).

16. Grabar, III, chapter 19; various essays on Bazhenov, *Arkhitektura SSSR* (1936), No. 2, 2–27; V. L. Snegirev, *Arkhitektor V. I. Bazhenov* (Moscow, 1937); 'Vassily Bazhenov', *Architectural Review*, XCVII (1945), 15–20.

17. Grabar, III, 247–9.

18. The model was much admired in the later eighteenth century by those fortunate enough to see it. In 1800 the English scientist, Edward Daniel Clarke, Professor of Mineralogy at Cambridge, visited Moscow and wrote that having 'obtained the keys from the secretary's office we were admitted to see the famous Model of the Kremlin ... one of the most curious things in Moscow. ... Its fronts are ornamented with ranges of beautiful pillars, according to the different orders of architecture. Every part of it was finished in the most beautiful manner, even to the Fresco painting on the ceilings of the rooms, and the colouring of the various marble columns intended to decorate the interior. ... Had the work been completed, no edifice could ever have compared with it,' E. D. Clarke, *Travels in Russia, Tartary, and Turkey* (London, 1810) (ed. of 1839, p. 32).

19. At the head of her instructions to the Legislative Commission of 1766 Catherine declared that:

'The Intention and the End of Monarchy, is the Glory of the Citizens, of the State, and of the Sovereign', W. F. Reddaway, ed., *Documents of Catherine the Great* (Cambridge, 1931), 217.

20. Grabar, III, chapter 20.

21. This belfry was totally destroyed 20 December 1941. The ruins are reproduced, *Pamyatniki zodchestva razrushennye ili povrezhdennye nemetskimi zakhvatchikami*, part II (1944), 57–9. p. 193

22. The Clérisseau *contretemps* is discussed by Catherine and Grimm in letters exchanged 17 December 1778, 2 February, 26 April, 7 November, 1779. See L. Réau, 'Correspondance artistique de Grimm avec Catherine II', *Archives de l'art français*, nouv-pér., XVII (1932), 1–206. More quotations from this correspondence will be found under the corresponding dates. p. 194

23. *Documents of Catherine the Great*, 163, letter to Voltaire, 25 June 1772. p. 196

24. G. K. Lukomski, *Charles Cameron* (London, 1943). The portrait 'à la russe' is reproduced as the frontispiece. See also Grabar, III, chapter 20.

25. C. Cameron, *The Baths of the Romans Explained and Illustrated, with the Restorations of Palladio Corrected and Improved* (London, 1772). Cameron's debt to Palladio can be seen by comparing the plans and elevations of the Palace of Pavlovsk with Palladio's Villa Trissino at Meledo (best reproduced in the Hoepli facsimile text of the *Quattro Libri dell'Architettura* (Milan, 1945), 60).

26. G. K. Lukomski, *Baturinskii dvorets, ego istoriya, razrushenie, i restavratiya* (St Petersburg, 1912). p. 198

27. Grabar, III, chapter 22.

28. Published by F. M. Tassi, *Vite de' pittori, scultori e architetti bergamaschi* (Bergamo, 1793), 150. In addition to the works here described, Quarenghi listed designs for two-storey shops, churches, hospitals, and other public works, and added: 'Ho fatto moltissimi altri Progetti per S.M., che forse non avranno luogo per ora, e per cio non gli accenno'. p. 199

CHAPTER 22

1. See Grimm's letter to Catherine of 4 November 1782 recounting the amusing episode he witnessed in Paris, when at a reception for the Comte du Nord Clérisseau tried to make amends to Paul for his past difficulties with Catherine. p. 203

2. Marie Feodorovna's inventory in French has been published as 'Description du Grand Palais de

Pavlovsk, rédigée et écrite par la Grande-Duchesse Marie Feodorovna en 1795' (1903), 371–82, with many illustrations showing the French character of the interiors and furnishings at Pavlovsk.

p. 203   3. Grabar, III, chapter 23. Brenna's designs for the Michael Palace were gradually evolved from his first idea of imitating the Villa Farnese at Caprarola. See S. M. Zemtsov, 'Documents pour l'histoire du Château des Ingénieurs', *Arkhitektura SSSR* (1935), no. 9, 63–70 (in Russian).

p. 204   4. F. F. Vigel (1786–1856), *Zapiski*, I (Moscow, 1864–5), 180. See also Grabar, III, 406; T. Talbot Rice, 'The St Petersburg of Alexander I', *Architectural Review*, LXXVII (1935), 245–9.

p. 205   5. See the collections of designs by A. A Mikhailov, *Sobranie fasadov ... dlya chastnykh stroenii v gorodakh rossiiskoi imperii*, Parts I–II (1809), III–IV (1812), reproduced in V. M. Vladimirov, *Starye arkhittekurnye proekty* (St Petersburg, 1913), 2 vols.

6. W. Kurbatov, 'Le Classicisme et le style de l'Empire', *Starye gody* (July–Sept., 1912), 105–19 (in Russian).

p. 206   7. For Ledoux's influence on Russian architecture see I. Grabar, 'Les Débuts du classicisme sous Alexandre et ses sources françaises', *Starye gody* (July–Sept., 1912), 68–96.

8. L. Réau, *L'Art russe de Pierre le grand à nos jours* (Paris, 1922), 90.

9. Grabar, III, 469; reproduced, 470.

p. 207   10. Grabar, III, chapter 26; V. A. Panov, *Arkhitektor A. N. Voronikhin* (Moscow, 1937); A. Krusetski and E. Lundberg, *Zodchii A. N. Voronikhin* (Sverdlovsk, 1937).

11. A. P. Aplaksin, *Kazanskii Sobor* (St Petersburg, 1911). An obelisk which originally stood in the centre of the square increased the resemblance to St Peter's.

p. 208   12. N. Tarassoff, 'L'École des Mines, à St-Pétersbourg', *Starye gody* (March, 1909), 139–45 (in Russian).

13. Grabar, III, chapter 27.

14 Odessa was once an interesting example of an integrated Neo-Classical city. It was founded by Catherine II in 1794, and by 1814 the town plan had been developed on a geometrical scheme. A considerable number of buildings erected in these years gave it a prevailing classical character. See M. Sinyaver, *Arkhitektura staroi Odessy* (Leningrad, 1935).

p. 209   15. Grabar, III, chapter 28; N. Lancere, 'Adrien Zakharoff et l'Amirauté à St Pétersbourg', *Starye gody* (Dec., 1911), 3–64 (in Russian).

16. I. E. Bondarenko, *Arkhitektor M. F. Kazakov* (Moscow, 1912); idem, *Arkhitektor M. F. Kazakov, 1738–1813* (Moscow, 1938). For further examples of Neo-Classical architecture in Moscow see I. Fomin, 'Moskovskii klassisizm', *Mir Iskusstva* (1904), no. 7, 147–98.

17. Grabar, III, chapter 30; Akademiya arkhitektury SSSR, *Arkhitektor V. P. Stasov* (Moscow, 1950).

18. Stasov's church is no less original when account is taken of the fact that the plan is essentially a reproduction of the previous wooden church of 1754 which was burned in 1828. This was on the familiar cross plan of the wooden churches of the North, but had five domes and was painted in imitation of stone. See the water-colour drawings in A. S. Drenyakin, *Istoricheskoe opisanie tserkvei leibgvardii Izmailovskago polka, 1730–1850* (St Petersburg, 1851). The appearance of a wooden church of the early Petersburg period can be studied in photographs of the Cathedral of the Holy Trinity near the Peter-Paul Fortress. It was built in 1710, remodelled in 1756, and burned in 1913. See *Starye gody* (March, 1913), 48–9.

19. Grabar, III, chapter 32; V. A. Panov, *Arkhitektor Carlo Rossi* (Moscow, 1937).

20. Grabar, III, 544.

21. Société impériale des architectes de St Pétersbourg, *Le Palais Yélaguine* (St Petersburg, n.d.).

22. N. V. Veinert, 'La Rue de l'architecte Rossi', *Arkhitektura SSSR* (1935), no. 7, 44–50 (in Russian). The inaugural performance in the great classical theatre, on 31 August 1832, of Krukovski's patriotic tragedy, *Prince Pozharski*, could be taken to symbolize the approaching downfall of classical ideals before the forces of a romantic interest in the Russian past; C. Derzhavin, *A Century of the State Dramatic Theatre, 1832–1932* (Leningrad, 1932), 18.

23. Grabar, III, chapters 33–5.

24. Grabar, III, chapter 35; L. Réau, ed., 'Lettres inédites de l'architecte Ricard de Montferrand à son ami Favart (1834–1843)', *Archives de l'art français*, nouv. pér., XVII (1932), 207–33.

25. The complicated procedure of the competition, and many of the plans, as well as Montferrand's several revisions, are analysed and reproduced, N. P. Nikitin, *Ogiust Monferran* (Leningrad, 1939).

26. Montferrand's *L'Église cathédrale de Saint-Isaac, description architecturale, pittoresque, et historique* (St Petersburg, 1845), is illustrated with sixty imposing lithographs showing various stages of

construction. Montferrand preserved the four piers and vaults at the crossing of Rinaldi's church in compliance with Nicholas I's command that the three consecrated altars should not be disturbed.

27. As a result of these 'augmentations', and in spite of the thousands of piles driven for the foundations, the weight of the Cathedral proved too heavy for the gravelly soil. Within a few years large cracks appeared in the walls. The measurements published by N. P. Nikitin, *op. cit.*, indicate the serious and unequal settling of the fabric.

28. A.R. Montferrand, *Plans et détails du monument consacré à la mémoire de l'empereur Alexandre* (Paris, 1836); P. Hofer, 'Montferrand and the *Alexandrine Column* at Leningrad', *Gazette des beaux-arts*, 6ᵉ pér., XXVI (1944), 333–48.

CHAPTER 23

1. The origin and development of this attitude have been studied by C. Hussey, *The Picturesque* (London, 1927). Russian parks and gardens may be examined in relation to European landscape design in V. Ya. Kurbatov, *Sady i parki* (St Petersburg, 1916).

2. See pp. 198–9.

3. W.F. Reddaway, ed., *Documents of Catherine the Great*, 163. Catherine's alterations extended to Moscow. Archdeacon Coxe described the gardens at the Annenhof : 'In some parts the grounds were laid out in a pleasing and natural manner, but in general the old style of gardening prevailed, and presented rows of clipped yew-trees, long straight canals, and a profusion of preposterous statues ... The reign of these deities was however doomed to be short; under the auspices of Catherine, all these instances of grotesque taste will be removed, and give place to more natural ornaments.' He also commented on Prince Panin's park at Miakulka: 'We could not avoid feeling extreme satisfaction that the English style of gardening had penetrated into these distant regions. The English taste, indeed, can display itself in this country to great advantage, where the parks are extensive, and the verdure, during the short summer, uncommonly beautiful. Most of the Russian nobles have gardeners of our nations, and resign themselves implicitly to their direction', W. Coxe, *Travels*, I, 270, 287.

4. For illustrations of the buildings in the park of Tsarskoe Selo see A. Benois, *Tsarskoe Selo* (1910); S. N. Vilchkovski, *Tsarskoe Selo* (St Petersburg, 1911), German ed., (Berlin, 1911); S.S. Bronstein, *Arkhitektura goroda Pushkina* (Moscow, 1940). In the

last year of her life Catherine called these little buildings her 'caprices', *Souvenirs de Mme (M.L.E.) Vigée Le Brun*, I (Paris, 1869), 316.

5. This was the best-known Russian artificial p. 219 ruin of the time and was painted by Hubert Robert in 1783 after drawings made on the spot. Reproduced, L. Réau, 'L'Œuvre d'Hubert Robert en Russie', *Gazette des beaux-arts*, 1914, 4ᵉ pér. XI (1914), 185. In the early nineteenth century an artificial ruined gateway in the classical style was built at Arkhangelskoe, the estate of Prince Yusupov, near Moscow, reproduced, S. V. Bezsonov, *Arkhangelskoe podmoskovnaya usadba* (Moscow, 1937), with many illustrations.

6. Ilya Neelov (b. 1745) was the son of an architect and studied at the Petersburg Academy (1761–70). In 1771 he visited England where he may have acquired his appreciation of garden architecture. He worked almost exclusively at Tsarskoe Selo. Velten's, Neelov's, and Quarenghi's pavilions are reproduced in S. S. Bronstein, *Arkhitektura goroda Pushkina* (Moscow, 1940), plates 110–43.

7. A drawing of the farm at Pavlovsk by the poet V.A. Zhukovski (1783–1852) is reproduced by the Grand Duke Constantine Constantinovich in his *Pavlovsk : dvorets, park, zhivopis*, III (St Petersburg, 1899–1904), plate 5 d. Paul and his wife were entertained in the park at Versailles and supplied with a number of plans and engravings of the royal residences. But since they left France in June 1782 they could only have discussed with Marie Antoinette the project for the *Petit Hameau*, which was not undertaken until December of that year. Most probably they saw the earlier *Hameau* at Chantilly. The Grand Duchess professed considerable interest in Gothic architecture, preferring Notre Dame to St Peter's in Rome. See P. Morane, *Paul Ier de Russie avant l'avènement, 1754–96* (Paris, 1907), *passim*; L. de Montbrison, ed., *Mémoires de la baronne d'Oberkirch*, I (Paris, 1869), 213. Several of the rustic buildings at Pavlovsk are reproduced, *Khudozh. sokrov.*, V (1905), plates 38–9.

8. Reproduced, Grabar, III, 320–1.

9. See D. Arkin, 'Bazhenov i Kazakov', *Obrazy* p. 220 *arkhitektury* (Moscow, 1941), 169–216; N.A. Kozhin, *Osnovy russkoi psevdo-gotiki XVIII veka* (Leningrad, 1927). Recent Soviet attributions to Bazhenov of most of the early Gothic work at Znamenki, Krasnoe Selo and elsewhere are summarized in V. L. Snegirev, *Znamentii zodchii V.I. Bazhenov* (Moscow, 1950).

10. A. Mazon, 'Catherine II, historienne de la Russie médiévale', Académie des inscriptions et

belles-lettres, *Comptes-rendus* (Paris, 1944), 458–72. From 1783 to 1794 Catherine published regular instalments of her *Notes sur l'histoire de Russie* in the Petersburg *Interlocuteur*.

p. 220   11. See D. Arkin, *op. cit.*, p. 208.

p. 221   12. One may wonder whether Catherine's dissatisfaction with Bazhenov's Tsaritsyn, as well as her interest in medieval architecture, were not prompted by a study of the cream-ware dinner service made for her by Josiah Wedgwood in 1774. The 1,282 pieces were painted in mulberry-purple with views of English country-houses and historic sites, many of the latter Gothic monuments in various stages of decay. See G. C. Williamson, *The Imperial Russian Dinner Service* (London, 1909). For Bazhenov's original drawings of Tsaritsyn and good photographs of the ruins see E. G. Chernov and A. V. Shishko, *Bazhenov* (Moscow, 1949).

13. L. Rusca, *Recueil des dessins de differens batimens construits à Saint-Pétersbourg et dans l'intérieur de l'empire de Russie* (St Petersburg, 1810).

p. 222   14. Reproduced, G. G. Grimm, *Arkhitektor A. Zakharov* (Moscow, 1940), figures 1–4.

15. Reproduced, N. Veinert, *Rossi* (Moscow and Leningrad, 1939), figures 95–6.

16. The admiration which the Arsenal and the collections of arms and armour excited can be seen in the lavish photographs published by Théophile Gautier in the second part of his *Trésors d'art de la Russie ancienne et moderne* (Paris, 1859).

17. Horace Vernet who visited Russia in 1842 painted an episode from the Carnival. A mezzotint after his painting is reproduced *Pridvornaya zhizn, 1613-1913* (St Petersburg, 1913), facing 88.

p. 223   18. F. Vitberg, 'Alexander Vitberg et son projet d'église à Moscou', *Starye gody* (Feb., 1912), 3–19 (in Russian); V. Snegirev, 'A. L. Vitberg et ses travaux architecturaux', *Arkhitektura SSSR* (1939), no. 7, 79–82 (in Russian).

19. See p. 256.

CHAPTER 24

p. 225   1. In this connexion one can distinguish, as in the history of American painting, between work executed by foreigners of less than first-class talent, and work by gifted but uninstructed native painters attempting an alien mode. Examples of such primitive anonymous portraits, too little studied by Russian historians, are reproduced, G. Lebedev, *Russkaya zhivopis pervoi poloviny XVIII veka* (Leningrad and Moscow, 1938), 22.

2. For information on these and other early engravers see D. A. Rovinski, *Podrobnyi slovar russkikh graverov, XVI–XIX vv.* (St Petersburg, 1895), 2 vols.

3. For reproductions of works by Danhauer and other early eighteenth-century masters, see G. Lebedev, *op. cit.*

4. A. Savinov, *I. Nikitin, 1688–1741* (Moscow and Leningrad, 1945), the most recent essay on this painter, attributes to him a large *Battle of Kulikovo*. It is known that Nikitin executed a large painting of the genealogy of the Tsars for Anna Ioannovna, so it is possible that he also attempted battle scenes.

5. W. Weretennikoff, 'Le Peintre Louis Caravaque en Russie', *Starye gody* (June, 1908), 323–32 (in Russian).

6. L. Réau, *Histoire de l'expansion de l'art français moderne : le monde slave et l'orient* (Paris, 1924).

7. For reproductions of these icons see S. P. Yaremich, 'Zhivopis Andreevskoi tserkvi v Kiev', *Iskusstvo v iuzhnoi Rossii*, I (1912), 1–14.

8. See J. Hasselblatt, *Historischer Überblick der Entwicklung der kaiserlichen russischen Akademie der Künste in St Petersburg* (St Petersburg and Leipzig, 1886); S. N. Kondakov, *Iubileinyi spravochnik imperatorskoi akademii khudozhestv, 1764–1914* (St Petersburg, 1914–15), 2 vols, with valuable historical surveys by various contributors; N. Pevsner, *Academies of Art, Past and Present* (Cambridge, 1940), 181–3; *Russkaya akademicheskaya khudozhestvennaya shkola v XVIII veke* (Moscow and Leningrad, 1937); S. K. Isakov, ed., *Akademiya khudozhestv* (Leningrad and Moscow, 1940), a short historical survey.

9. L. Réau, 'Les artistes russes à Paris au XVIIIe siècle', *Revue des études slaves*, III (1923), 286–98. The obstreperous behaviour of young Russians in Paris was the subject of a *mémoire* from Diderot to Catherine II urging the establishment of a special hostel for them. See M. Tourneux, *Diderot et Catherine II* (Paris, 1899), 424–7.

10. Russian themes had appeared as early as 1766 as subjects for the annual competition in the painting classes of the Academy, but these were student programmes and not known to the general public, such as it was. Losenko's *Vladimir and Rogneda* is reproduced, M. Aptekar, *Russkaya istoricheskaya zhivopis* (Moscow and Leningrad, 1939), 22.

11. S. P. Diaghilev, *Russkaya zhivopis v XVIII veke, D. G. Levitskii* (St Petersburg, 1902); D. Roche, 'Un Portraitiste petit-russien au temps de Catherine II, D.-G. Levitski', *Gazette des Beaux-arts*, 3e pér., XXIX (1903), 494–507; XXX, 317–32.

12. Engravings by the elder Levitski are reproduced by K. Ladyzhenko, 'Zhizn i deyatelnost G. K. Levitskago', *Iskusstvo v iuzhnoi Rossii* (1914), nos. 5–6, 175–89.

13. This portrait now in the Public Library, Geneva, was the first important modern Russian painting to enter a public collection in the West.

14. Levitski may also have re-studied the portraits in the Hermitage. The only significant English painting was Reynolds's *Infant Hercules Strangling the Serpents* (1788), but influences from the several Van Dycks acquired by Catherine from the Walpole Collection, including portraits of Charles I and Henrietta Maria, can be seen in Levitski's portrait of F. P. Makerovski (1789), Diaghilev, *op. cit.*, No. 49. The artist may even have dressed the young man, then eighteen years of age, in seventeenth-century costume to disguise his extremely small stature.

15. D. Roche, 'Un peintre petit-russien à la fin du XVIIIe siècle et au commencement du XIXe siècle, V.-L. Borovikovski', *Gazette des beaux-arts*, 3e pér., XXXVI (1906), 367–81, 485–501.

16. Shchedrin's *View of the Park and Gardens at Gatchina* is reproduced, N. Kovalenskaya, *Istoriya russkago iskusstva XVIII veka* (Moscow and Leningrad, 1940), 217. For other eighteenth-century academic painters see the catalogue of the Academy of Fine Arts by S. K. Isakov, *Imperatorskaya akademiya khudozhestv muzei, russkaya zhivopis* (Petrograd, 1915).

17. Reproduced, Kovalenskaya, *op. cit.*, 215.

18. For reproductions of Russian wooden sculpture see B. Dunaev, 'Derevyannoe zodchestvo severo-vostoka Kostromskoi gubernii', MAO, *Drevnosti, Trudy kom.*, VI (1915), 313–32; N. N. Serebrennikov, *Permskaya dereviannaya skulptura* (Perm, 1928).

19. Reproduced, Grabar, V, chapters 4–5.

20. For Rastrelli's earlier work see D. Roche, 'Le Monument du marquis de Pomponne par Rastrelli', *Starye gody* (Dec., 1912), 37–40; for further reproductions, Grabar, V, chapter 6.

21. Paul's contempt for his mother's memory can be read in the inscription: 'From great-grandson to great-grandfather', mocking Catherine's haughty words on Falconet's statue.

22. Reproduced, Grabar, V, 212–13.

23. Catherine described the sculptor in a letter to Mme Geoffrin, 21 October 1766, as 'L'ami de l'âme de Diderot'. This, with Catherine's lively correspondence with Falconet on all manner of topics, has been published by L. Réau, *Correspondance de Falconet avec Catherine II, 1767–1778* (Paris, 1921).

24. The transport of the boulder was considered an engineering wonder. See Carburi de Ceffalonie, *Le Monument élevé à la gloire de Pierre le grand. ... Relation des moyens méchaniques qu'ont été employés pour transporter à Pétersbourg, un rocher*, etc. (Paris, 1777).

25. D. Roche, 'Les Sculpteurs russes élèves de N.-F. Gillet', *Revue de l'art ancien et moderne*, XXIX (1911), 33–48. p. 234

26. S. K. Isakov, *Fedot Shubin* (Moscow, 1938); S. A. Ukhtomski, 'F.I. Shubin', *Materialy po russkomu iskusstvu* (Leningrad, 1928), 185–208.

27. This and other works mentioned in this chapter are reproduced in Grabar, V, chapters 9–30. See also N. N. Vrangel, 'Katalog starrinykh proizvedenii iskusstva khranyashikhsya v Imperatorskoi akademii khudzhestv', *Starye gody*, special issue (1908); S. K. Isakov, *Imperatorskaya akademiya khudozhestv muzei, russkaya skulptura* (Petrograd, 1915).

28. N. Kovalenskaya, *I. P. Martos* (Moscow and Leningrad, 1938); G. Presnov, 'Antichnye reministsentsii v novom russkom iskusstve', *Materialy po russkom iskusstvom*, 221–33. p. 235

29. Moscow funeral sculpture is discussed and reproduced, Iu. Shamurim, 'Moskovskaya kladbishcha', *Moskva v eya proshlom i nastoyashchem*, VIII, 89–124.

30. The group has since been re-erected on an even less appropriate site, in front of St Basil on the Red Square (Plate 82).

31. Grabar, V, chapter 31.

CHAPTER 25

1. In this and the following chapters a distinction is to be understood between realism in the narrower sense, as the use of exact natural detail as a means of expression, and naturalism as the philosophical and stylistic interpretation of nature and contemporary life dominant in European art in the second half of the nineteenth century. p. 236

2. The distinction between *iconography*, the identification of the subject, and *iconology*, the meaning of the subject in a particular work of art, has been proposed and examined at length by E. Panofsky in his *Studies in Iconology* (New York, 1939).

3. N. N. Vrangel, *O. A. Kiprenski v chastnykh sobraniyakh* (St Petersburg, 1912), a catalogue of an exhibition of little-known works from private p. 237

collections; G. Lebedev, *Kiprenskii* (Moscow and Leningrad, 1937), a collection of plates.

p. 237   4. Reproduced in colour, M. Aptekar, *Russkaya istoricheskaya zhivopis* (Moscow and Leningrad, 1939), opp. 26.

p. 238   5. O. Lyaskovskaya's *Karl Briullov* (Moscow and Leningrad, 1940), is a well-documented study with many reproductions, catalogue, and bibliography.

6. Bulwer Lytton's *Last Days of Pompeii* (1834) was written under the influence of Briullov's picture.

7. The painting contains several references to Raphael's 'Fire in the Borgo'. One of Briullov's first tasks in Rome had been to copy 'The School of Athens' for the Petersburg Society for the Encouragement of Art, an organization founded in 1820 which supplemented the academic premiums and assisted many artists in the nineteenth century. See P. N. Stolpyanski, *Staryi Peterburg i obshchestvo pooshchreniya khudozhestv* (Leningrad, 1928).

p. 239   8. M. P. Botkin, *A. A. Ivanov, ego zhizn i perepiska* (St Petersburg, 1880).

9. For the origin of this painting, and preliminary drawings, see N. Romanoff, ' "Apollon, Hyacinthe, et Cyparisse", by A. Ivanoff', *Starye gody* (Jan.–Feb., 1916), 36–49 (in Russian).

p. 240   10. For reproductions see N. Romanov, 'Eskizy genr'a i etiudy A. Ivanova', *Apollon* (1912), no. 8, 5–19.

11. For charts of Ivanov's concordances see V. Zummer, 'Sistema bibleiskikh kompozitsii A. A. Ivanova', *Iskusstvo v iuzhnoi Rossii* (1914), no. 7–12, 1–111. Ivanov, like the contemporary New England Transcendentalists, read Iamblichus's and Porphyry's lives of Pythagoras.

p. 241   12. 'The Appearance of Rurik before the Walls of Novgorod' was the first Russian subject chosen for the painting competition in 1766. In 1763 the sculptors had worked on an episode from Peter's expedition to Azov in 1696. See *Russkaya akademicheskaya khudozhestvennaya shkola*, 110, 80.

13. Reproduced, N. Kovalenskaya, *Istoriya russkogo iskusstva XVIII veka* (Moscow and Leningrad, 1940), 214.

14. The paintings are in the State Tretyakov Gallery in Moscow; the second is reproduced, Kovalenskaya, *op. cit.*, 215.

15. Reproduced, Kovalenskaya, *op. cit.*, 216; O. Wulff, *Die neurussische Kunst*, figure 264. The difference between the cosmopolitan and native attitude towards Russian customs can be seen by comparing the drawings of J. B. Le Prince (1734–81), who travelled in Russia 1758–62, and idealized the peasants in the style of Boucher, with the truthful and unprepossessing drawings of Ivan Ermenev (act. after 1790), who portrayed rural and urban types in poverty and squalor. Reproductions, *Russkaya akademicheskaya khudozhestvennaya shkola*, 106–7; Kovalenskaya, *op. cit.*, 216. See also L. Réau, 'L'Exotisme russe dans l'œuvre de J. B. Le Prince', *Gazette des beaux-arts*, 5ᵉ pér., III (1921), 147–65.

16. N.N. Vrangel, *A.G. Venetsianov v chastnykh sobraniyakh* (St Petersburg, 1911), a catalogue of little-known works from private collections.

17. F.I. Bulgakov, *P.A. Fedotov i ego proizvedeniya* (St Petersburg, 1893); V. Dmitriev, 'P. A. Fedotov', *Apollon* (1916), nos 9–10, 1–36.

CHAPTER 26

1. For reproductions of nineteenth-century painting see G.K. Lukomski, *History of Modern Russian Painting, 1840–1940* (London, 1945); N. I. Sokolova, ed., *Russkoe iskusstvo, XVIII–XIX vv.* (Moscow and Leningrad, 1938). An interesting collection of essays on the ideological tendencies of nineteenth-century painting has been edited by V.M. Friche as *Russkaya zhivopis XIX veka* (Moscow, 1929). Perov's works are reproduced, by N. P. Sobko, *V. G. Perov, ego zhizn i proizvedeniya* (St Petersburg, 1892).

2. The point of the satire was sharpened by the fact that the landlord and his wife were seated, although in Russia it was customary to remain standing throughout the service. Perov's anticlericalism is closer to such Western symptoms as Vibert's malicious irony than to Courbet's forthright denunciation of ecclesiastical impropriety in his 'Retour de la conférence' (1863).

3. The exhibitions of the Society continued until 1920, although its artistic effectiveness diminished in the later 1890s with the emergence of *Mir Iskusstva*. See I. A. Sikorski, *Uspekhi russkago khudozhestvennago tvorchestva peredvizhnykh khudozhestvennykn vystavok, 1872–97* (Kiev, 1900); A. Novitski, *Peredvizhniki i vliyanie ikh na russkoe iskusstvo* (Moscow, 1897); L. R. Varshavski, *Peredvizhniki* (Moscow, 1937), with Kramskoi's account of the episode of 1863.

4. The extremes of such art extend from Repin's 'They Did Not Expect Him' (Plate 165A) to N. A. Yaroshenko's 'Everywhere there is Life', portraying convicts in a prison van throwing crumbs

to birds beyond their bars. More typical of the ideological realism at its best is G. G. Myasoedov's 'The Zemstvo Dines' (1872), showing the peasant delegates to the provincial assembly eating their few crusts outside the town hall, while the gentry dine in comfort within. Reproduced, Sokolova, *Russkoe Iskusstvo*, 118.

5. Sokolova, *op. cit.*, 126. See also Kramskoi's letter to F. A. Vasiliev, 10 October 1872, in the artist's *Pisma*, I (Moscow, 1937), 119-23.

6. It is significant that in the earliest versions, before doubt entered his mind, the Christ was placed much closer to the foreground of the composition.

7. As a painter of almost exclusively religious subjects Ge of all the nineteenth-century masters has been least studied by Soviet scholars. His correspondence with Tolstoi has been published, *L. N. Tolstoi i N. N. Ge* (Moscow and Leningrad, 1930). See V. Dmitriev, 'N. N. Ge', *Apollon* (1913), no. 10, 5-43, with catalogue.

8. E. J. Simmons, *Leo Tolstoy* (Boston, 1946), 362, 450-1, 493.

9. The episode is retold by C. Marsden in *Palmyra of the North*, 95-9.

10. Many others could be added to this list of pictures of implicit political comment, *e.g.* F. E. Burov's 'Peter III's Visit to Ivan VI' (recalling Elizabeth's and Catherine's cruel imprisonment of their legal predecessor), or K.V. Lebedev's 'Destruction of the Novgorod Veche' (now in the Joseph E. Davies Collection, University of Wisconsin).

11. Surikov's considerable talent can be gauged by his sensitive drawings, reproduced, Ya. Tepin, 'Surikov', *Apollon* (1916), nos. 4-5, 21-39.

12. Musicians matched painters in the exploitation of Russian history. To Moussorgsky's familiar *Boris Godunov* (1870) and *Khovanshchina* (1872) may be added Rimsky-Korsakov's *Sadko* (1867, revised 1891), and *Maid of Pskov* (1870-2); Borodin's *Prince Igor* (published posthumously, after 1887); and Serov's *Rogneda* (1865), to mention only the most important.

13. V. V. Vereshchagin, *Exhibition of the Works of V. Verestchagin* (New York, American Art Galleries, 1888), 6-8; 'These subjects I have treated in a fashion far from sentimental, for having myself killed many a poor fellow-creature in different wars, I have not the right to be sentimental. ... My intention was to examine war in its different aspects, and transmit these faithfully. Facts laid upon canvas without embellishment must speak for themselves.'

14. This and the other works by Repin discussed in this chapter are reproduced in the admirable biography by I. Grabar, *Repin* (Moscow, 1937), 2 vols, and in the interesting collection of documents edited by Grabar and I. S. Zilbershtein, *Repin* (Moscow and Leningrad, 1948), 2 vols.

15. The earlier drawings and studies from life p. 251 have a crude power which was lost to some extent in the artificially contrived final composition. For reproductions, Grabar, *Repin*, I, chapter 6, and I. Repin, *Burlaki na Volge* (*vospominaniya*) (Moscow and Leningrad, 1944).

16. In 1884 Repin repainted the face of the exile, p. 252 emphasizing his haunted and hesitant expression.

17. Among the curious paintings are a 'Noli Me p. 253 Tangere' (1922), and a 'Child Christ Preaching in the Temple' (of the 1920s), reproductions, Grabar and Zilbershtein, *op. cit.*, 299, 307. They are astonishing developments in the light of his only other important religious painting, the painfully realistic 'St Nicholas Staying an Execution' (1888).

18. *V. N. Baksheev* (Moscow, Sovetski khudozhnik, 1949).

CHAPTER 27

1. For further synopses of the history of this re- p. 254 search see L. Réau, *L'Art russe des origines à Pierre le g and*, chapter I; D. V. Ainalov, *Vormoskov.*, v-ix.

2. A. de Demidov, *Album du voyage pittoresque et archéologique en Russie* (Paris, *c.* 1845).

3. See especially *Russkaya starina v pamyatnikakh* p. 255 *tserkovnago i grazhdanskago zodchestva* (Moscow, 1851), folio, with text by Snegirev and lithographs by Martynov. There were several earlier and later collections by the same authors with illustrations on a smaller scale.

4. *Drevnosti rossiiskago gosudarstva* (Moscow, 1849-53), 6 vols.

5. The most useful publications of the Moscow Archaeological Society are its *Trudy* ('Works'), the reports of the fifteen congresses held between 1869 and 1915; *Drevnosti* ('Antiquities'), twenty-five volumes of reports issued between 1865 and 1916; and the publication, also entitled *Drevnosti*, of the *Komissii po sokhraneniiu drevnikh pamyatnikov* (Commission for the Preservation of Ancient Monuments), in six volumes (1907-15). Material on post-Kievan archaeology will also be found in the *Izvestiya* of the St Petersburg Imperial Archeological Commission, I-XXXII (1901-15).

p. 255   6. V. V. Suslov, *Pamyatniki drevnyago russkago zodchestva* (St Petersburg, 1895–1901), seven parts; *idem*, *Pamyatniki drevne-russkago iskusstva* (St Petersburg, 1908–12), four parts.

7. D. A. Rovinski, *Istoriya russkikh shkol ikonopisaniya do kontsa XVII veka* (St Petersburg, 1856).

8. See especially N. P. Likhachev, *Materialy dlya istorii russkago ikonopisaniya* (Leipzig and St Petersburg, 1906), 2 vols; N. P. Kondakov, *Russkaya ikona* (Prague, 1929), 4 vols.

9. I. Grabar, *Istoriya russkago iskusstva* (Moscow, 1909–1917), 6 vols. Among the contributors were A. Shchusev, V. Pokrovski, G. Pavlutski, V. V. Suslov, F. Gornostaev (architecture); N. N. Vrangel (sculpture); P. P. Muratov, A. I. Uspenski (painting). Grabar himself wrote many chapters, including the third volume on the eighteenth-century architecture of St Petersburg.

10. The changed attitude towards medieval art appears as early as 1824 in a popular guide to Moscow. G. Lecointe de Laveau remarked of St Basil: 'C'est sans contredit l'édifice le plus extraordinaire qu'ait pu produire l'imagination d'un architecte', *Putevoditel v Moskve* (Moscow, 1824), 187. In his earlier *Moscou avant et après l'incendie* (Paris, 1814), he had not mentioned the church.

p. 256   11. The art collection of Alexander III in the Anichkov Palace, his residence in St Petersburg, was indistinguishable from the accumulations of genre-painting, Italian antiques, and oriental bric-à-brac gathered by wealthy middle-class collectors throughout the Western world. It can be studied in A. Prakhov, 'Imperator Aleksandr tretii kak deyatel russkago khudozhestvennago prosveshcheniya', *Khudozh. sokrov.*, III (1903), nos. 4–8, plates 46 ff.

12. For illustrations of these and the work at Peterhof see A. Benois and N. Lanceray, 'Les Palais élevés par Nicolas I', *Starye Gody* (July–Sept., 1913), 173–95 (in Russian).

13. An earlier although less accurate reproduction of Russian wooden peasant architecture had occurred in the Alexandrovsky Colony at Potsdam, built after 1825 to house a group of Russian prisoners of war who had remained as singers at the Prussian Court. In 1827 each of the remaining twelve families had its own cottage in the Russian style. See M. Hürlimann, *Die Residenzstadt Potsdam* (Berlin, 1933), 293.

14. An example of Ton's formula modified only in detail is the Church of the Annunciation in St Petersburg, where the same imitation of the massing of St Isaac is topped by five octagonal lanterns with pyramidal cupolas.

15. For the architecture of the Slavic Revival see p. the brief accounts by Yu. I. Shamurin, 'Arkhitektura Moskva', *Moskva v eya proshlom i nastoyashchem*, XI (1912), 117–25; I. Anterov, 'Russkoe arkhitekturnoe nasledstvo i ego razvitie v novei-shei arkhitekture', *Arkhitektura SSSR* (1941), no. 2, 46–52. Among the curious water-colours by an obscure architect, Victor Hartmann, which inspired Moussorgsky's *Pictures at an Exhibition*, there was a project for a monumental gate at Kiev, which is an extreme example of the fantastic effects conceived in Slavic Revival architecture. See A. Frankenstein, 'Victor Hartmann and Modeste Musorgsky', *Musical Quarterly*, XXV (1939), 268–91.

16. Another imitation of seventeenth-century Moscow architecture in St Petersburg was the Church of the Kievan Lavra on Vasili Ostrov (1898), reproduced, E. Zabel, *St Petersburg* (Leipzig, 1905), 14.

17. I. Ye. Zabelin, *Domashnii byt russkago naroda v XVI i XVII st.* (Moscow, 1872), 2 vols.; *Istoriya russkoi zhizni s drevneishikh vremen* (Moscow, 1876–79), 2 vols.

18. Grabar, V, chapter 33.

19. The Slavic Revival was encouraged by such p. national occasions. The nine-hundredth anniversary of the conversion of Russia was celebrated in 1889, and the tercentenary of the Romanov dynasty in 1913.

20. This church was only the most publicized of the many examples of the Byzantine revival of the 1870s. See also the first prize designs by Schröter and Huhn for the colossal Garrison Cathedral in Tiflis, *Zodchii* (1878), plates 45–6.

21. The official character of the whole undertaking was marked by the dedication of the church in 1896 in the presence of the imperial family, and its commemoration in a *de luxe* folio of photographs, *Kievskii Vladimirskii Sobor* (Kiev, c. 1896). See also S.V. Kulzhenko, *Sobor Sv. Kn. Vladimira v Kiev* (Kiev, 1899).

22. The artist's work, except for his religious painting, is adequately reproduced, N. Morgunov, *V. Vasnetsov* (Moscow and Leningrad, 1941). The Kievan murals are described and reproduced by O. Wulff, *Neurussische Kunst* (Augsburg, 1932), chapter 28.

23. The revival of interest in early Russian poetry, particularly in the *Tale of the Armament of Igor*, had been marked a decade before by Borodin's posthumous opera, *Prince Igor*, and by Perov's 'Yaroslavna's Grief' showing the princess mourning for Igor.

24. E. Mahler, *Michail Nesterov, ein Maler des Gläubigen Russlands* (Lucerne, 1938), with good reproductions.

25. S. Yaremich, 'Vrubel', *Mir iskusstva*, X (1903), 143–90; idem, *M. A. Vrubel* (Moscow, 1911).

26. For the artistic conditions in St Petersburg and the formation of the *Mir iskusstva* group see A. Benois, *Reminiscences of the Russian Ballet* (London, 1941), Parts I–II; N. Sokolova, *Mir iskusstva* (Moscow and Leningrad, 1934); S. R. Ernst, *A. Benois* (Petrograd, 1942), with bibliography and catalogue; A. Benois, *Voznikiovenie 'Mira iskusstva'* (Leningrad, 1928). To the members discussed above may be added K. Somov, a painter of witty Rococo themes, and M. Dobuzhinski whose theatrical designs are well known.

27. The results of Benois's scrupulous historical research appeared in his book on Tsarskoe Selo, *Tsarskoe Selo v tsarstvovanie imperatritsy Elisavety Petrovny*, (St Petersburg, 1910). For Lanceray, who remained in Russia to become a 'social realist' painter, see M. V. Babenchikov, *E. E. Lancere* (Moscow, 1949).

28. V. Diaghilev, ed., *Katalog istoriko-khudozhestvennoi vystavki russkikh portretov v Tavricheskom dvortsie* (St Petersburg, 1905), 8 vols.

29. *Exposition d'art russe* (Paris, Salon d'automne, 1906). The bulk of the exhibition consisted of eighteenth and nineteenth-century painting; only thirty-six icons were exhibited, all but one from the Likhachev collection.

30. The *Mir iskusstva* 'tone' can be seen in the photographs of the Pskov Monastery (Plate 10B), one of several such views which appeared in early issues of *Mir iskusstva*. The oblique perspective and appreciation of contrast of textures are typical of this fresh point of view towards old Russian architecture.

31. Benois and Golovin were so determined that the production should be historically authentic that they scoured the Tartar junk-shops for antique materials, shawls, head-dresses, etc., although they were obliged to admit that on the stage these were less effective than other costumes which had been newly designed. See Benois, *Reminiscences*, 268.

32. V. N. Soloviev, 'A. Ya. Golovin, kak teatralnyi master', *Apollon* (1917), no. 1, 24–30.

33. *Ballets russes de Diaghilew, 1909–1929* (Paris, Musée des arts décoratifs, 1939). See also 'L'Art décoratif au théâtre', *Zolotoe Runo* (1909), nos. 7–9, 5–36; R. Fülöp-Miller and J. Gregor, *The Russian Theatre* (Philadelphia, n.d.), chapter 7 and figures 37–174.

34. V. Ya. Ivchenko, *Le Ballet contemporain* (St Petersburg, 1912); A. Ya. Levinson, *Bakst, the story of the artist's life* (London, 1923).

35. Historical retrospection was pushed even p. 264 further by S. Prokoviev in his *Scythian Suite*, originally commissioned by Diaghilev as a ballet in 1914, but produced only as an orchestral composition in 1916.

36. The historical trilogy by Alexei Tolstoi (1817–75) can be counted one of the prime movers of the Slavic Revival. It included *The Death of Ivan the Terrible* (1866), *Tsar Feodor* (1868), and *Tsar Boris* (1870). Only the second play enjoyed a lasting success.

37. C. Stanislavsky, co-founder of the Moscow Art Theatre, has described the opening performance of *Tsar Feodor* (14 Oct., 1898) in *My Life in Art* (Boston, 1924), 335. For photographs, a little dim, of these productions see *Moskovskii Khudozhestvennyi Teatr v illiustratsiyakh i dokumentakh, 1898–1938* (Moscow, 1938), 44–57, 76, 216–23.

38. A. Gidoni, 'Tvorcheskii put Rerikha', *Apollon* (1915), nos 4–5, 1–39; Iu. K. Baltrushaitis, et al., *Roerikh* (St Petersburg, 1916), with good colour plates. His sets for *Prince Igor* are reproduced, 140–3.

39. For the history of *Art Nouveau* see N. Pevsner, *Pioneers of Modern Design*, 2nd ed. (New York, 1949), chapter 4. A distinction must be made, however, between work executed in the spirit of *Mir iskusstva* and *Art Nouveau* objects or designs imported from abroad which of course were without any specifically Russian character. For architecture in this style see L. I. Rempel and T. V. Viaznikovtzeva, 'L'Époque du style moderne dans l'architecture de Moscou', *Arkhitektura SSSR* (1935), nos. 10–11, 90–3 (in Russian).

40. M. K. Tenisheva, *Khram svyatogo dukha v Talashkine* (Paris, 1938); idem, *Broderies des paysannes de Smolensk exécutées sous la direction de la princesse Marie Ténichev* (Paris and Chicago, n.d.). For illustrations of other work executed at Talashkino see S. Diaghilev, 'G. V. Maliutin i ego raboty v imenii kn. M. K. Tenishevoi "Talashkino"', *Mir Iskusstva*, IX (1903), 157–92.

41. Her work is reproduced, *Mir iskusstva*, XI p. 265 (1904). For the revival of peasant industries see *Russkoe narodnoe iskusstvo na vtoroi vserossiiskoi kustarnoi vystavke v Petrograde v 1913* (Petrograd,

1914); Réau, *L'Art russe des origines à Pierre le Grand*, chapter V.

p. 265   42. Grabar, v, Chapter 37; *Catalogue of Sculpture by Prince Paul Trubetzkoi* (New York, American Numismatic Society, 1911).

43. For the work of this revival see G. Lukomski, 'Novyi Peterburg', *Apollon* (1913), no. 2, 5–38. A. I. Nekrasov, in *Russkii ampir* (Moscow, 1935), 118–22, has interpreted the revival as part of a bourgeois reaction after the Revolution of 1905.

44. The pavilion is reproduced, *Mir iskusstva*, iv (1900), 98–109, and the *Art Journal* (supplement, 1901), 141.

45. The yearbooks of the St Petersburg society of Artist-Architects, *Ezhegodnik obshchestva arkhitektorov-khudozhnikov* (1906–15), contain numerous illustrations of projects and completed buildings in the Slavic and modern classical revival styles. Our Saviour on the Waters is reproduced, v (1910), 101–4; the Leipzig Church, vii (1912), 104–5, ix (1914), 111.

46. M. K. Tenishev, *op. cit.*, 5.

p. 266   47. The Schlüsselburg church in the style of the sixteenth-century tent churches, and Roerich's murals and mosaics are reproduced, *Ezhegodnik*, ii (1907), 94–124.

48. The Yaroslavl Station is reproduced, N. I. Sokolova, *Russkoe iskusstvo* (Moscow and Leningrad, 1938), 34. For Shchusev see M. Babenchikov, 'A.V. Shchusev', *Arkhitektura SSSR* (1941), no. 5, 17–28. Shchusev, who began as a follower of *Mir Iskusstva* in his Church of Martha and Mary in Moscow (1908–12), became one of the leading Soviet architects. He designed both the wooden (1924) and stone (1930) tombs for Lenin on the Red Square.

49. For these collections, the contents of which were subsequently incorporated into the Museum of Modern Western Art in Moscow, see S. Makovski, 'Frantsuzskie khudozhniki iz sobraniya I. A. Morozova', *Apollon* (1912), nos. 3–4, 5–16; Ya. Tugendkhold, 'Frantsuzskoe sobranie S. I. Shchukina', *Apollon* (1914), nos. 1–2, 5–46. The progress of French painting in Russia can also be traced in the pages of *Zolotoe runo* in the accounts of the exhibitions of 1908, which included most of the Post-Impressionists, and 1909 when contemporary paintings by Matisse and Braque were reproduced.

50. For Stelletski's clever but mannered parodies of older Russian painting see A. Benois, 'Iskusstvo Stelletskago', *Apollon* (1911), no. 4, 5–16. Stelletski also designed sets for A. Tolstoi's *Tsar Feodor*.

GENERAL BIBLIOGRAPHY

Since the annotation of the text contains references to the principal Russian sources, this bibliography includes works useful for the student who reads only Western European languages. The Russian works mentioned are valuable for their illustrations.

1. BIBLIOGRAPHIES OF RUSSIAN ART

Library of Congress, *Russia, a Check List Preliminary to a Basic Bibliography of Materials in the Russian Language, Part 3, Fine Arts.* Washington, D.C., 1944.

> Mimeographed list of 788 items.

BRUNOV, N. I., and ALPATOV, M. 'Altrussische Kunst in der wissenschaftlichen Forschung seit 1914,' *Zeitschrift für slavische Philologie*, II (1925), 474–505; III (1926), 387–408.

ETTLINGER, A., and GLADSTONE, J. M. *Russian Literature, Theatre, and Art; a Bibliography of Works in English, Published 1900–1945.* London, 1947.

EVDOKIMOV, I. *Sever v istorii russkago iskusstva.* Vologda, 1921.

> Extensive bibliography on northern Russian art, 164–76.

LAZAREV, V. N. *Iskusstvo Novgoroda.* Moscow, 1947, 143–51.

MILLET, G., ed. *L'Art byzantin chez les slaves,* Paris, II (1932), 'L'Ancienne Russie, les slaves catholiques.'

> Lists periodicals, publications of learned societies, catalogues of museums and private collections.

2. GENERAL HISTORIES OF RUSSIAN ART

AINALOV, D. V. *Geschichte der russischen Monumentalkunst der vormoskovitischen Zeit.* Berlin and Leipzig, 1932.

AINALOV, D. V. *Geschichte der russischen Monumentalkunst zur Zeit des Grossfürstentums Moskau.* Berlin and Leipzig, 1933.

ALPATOV, M. *Russian Impact on Art.* New York, 1950.

ALPATOV, M., and BRUNOV, N. *Geschichte der altrussischen Kunst.* Augsburg, 1932.

BUNT, C. G. E. *Russian Art from Scyths to Soviets.* London and New York, 1946.

GRABAR, I., ed. *Istoriya russkago iskusstva,* 6 vols. Moscow, from 1909.

HALLE, F. W. *Altrussische Kunst.* Berlin, 1920.

KOVALENSKAYA, N. N. *Istoriya russkago iskusstva XVIII veka.* Moscow, 1940.

> With bibliography.

LAZAREV, V. N. *Iskusstvo Novgoroda.* Moscow, 1947.

MATTHEY, W. von. *Russische Kunst.* Zurich, 1948.

> Short survey.

MILIUKOV, P. *Outlines of Russian Culture.* Philadelphia, 1942. Part III.

> Extracts from his comprehensive history.

NEWMARCH, R. *The Russian Arts.* New York, 1916.

> The first survey in English.

NIKOLSKI, V. A. *Istoriya russkago iskusstva.* Moscow, 1915.

NOVITZKI, A. *Istoriya russkago iskusstva s drevneishikh vremen,* 2 vols. Moscow, 1903.

> The first adequate Russian general history. Interesting illustrations.

RÉAU, L. *L'Art russe des origines à Pierre le Grand.* Paris, 1921.

> This and the following works by Réau are admirably ordered, but written with a pronounced French bias.

RÉAU, L. *L'Art russe de Pierre le Grand à nos jours.* Paris, 1922.

RÉAU, L. *L'Art russe.* Paris, 1945.

> A one-volume summary of his earlier work, brought up to date.

RICE, D. Talbot, ed. *Russian Art.* London, 1935.

> Short essays.

RICE, Tamara Talbot. *Russian Art.* West Drayton, 1949.

> An appreciation.

TOLSTOI, I. I., and KONDAKOV, N. P. *Russiya drevnosti v pamyatnikakh iskusstva,* 6 vols. St Petersburg, 1889–99.

> A monumental work of early archaeological scholarship. Many valuable illustrations.

VIOLLET-LE-DUC, E. E. *L'Art russe.* Paris, 1877.

> The first monograph in a Western European language. Concerned with the oriental derivation of Russian architecture and ornament.

VORONIN, N. N., and others. *Istoriya kultury drevnei Rusi do mongolskii period.* Moscow, 1948.

> The first volume of a popular survey, extensively illustrated.

WINKLER, M. 'Das Wesen der altrussischen Kunst,' *Osteuropa,* I (1926), 306–32.

> An interesting synthesis.

WULFF, O. *Die neurussische Kunst im Rahmen der Kulturentwicklung Russlands von Peter dem Grossen bis zur Revolution.* Augsburg, 1932.

> Art in relation to the history of the period. Many illustrations.

3. ARCHITECTURE, PRINCIPALLY BEFORE 1700

BUXTON, D. R. *Russian Mediaeval Architecture.* Cambridge, 1934.

> Illustrations from photographs by the author.

CROSS, S. H. *Mediaeval Russian Churches.* Cambridge, Mass., 1949.

EDING, B. von. *Rostov Velikii. Uglich. Pamyatniki khudozhestvennoi stariny.* Moscow, 1913.

ELIASBERG, A. *Russische Baukunst.* Munich, 1922.

GRABAR, I., ed. *Istoriya russkago iskusstva,* I–II. Moscow, from 1909.

Izvestiya, imperatorskoi arkheologicheskoi kommissii, Vols. I–LXIV (1908–17). Voprosy restavratsü, Parts 1–18.

> An inventory of architectural monuments and reports of restorations in progress. Many illustrations.

KRASOVSKI, M. V. *Kurs istorii russkoi arkhitektury.* Moscow, 1911.

> Wooden architecture.

KRASOVSKI, M. V. *Ocherk istorii moskovskago perioda drevnerusskago tserkovnago zodchestva.* Moscow, 1911.

> Admirable plans and sections.

LO GATTO, E. *Gli artisti italiani in Russia,* 2 vols. Rome, 1934–5.

NEKRASOV, A. I. *Ocherki po istorii drevnerusskago zodchestva XI–XVII veka.* Moscow, 1936.

> For recent Soviet theory.

RZYANIN, M. I. *Arkhitekturnye ansambli Moskvy i Podmoskoviya, XIV–XIX veka.* Moscow, 1950.

SERVINSKY, S. 'Über die Auffassungen der Wandfläche in der Entwicklung der altrussischen Steinbaukunst,' *Belvedere,* IX–X (1926), 257–68.

SUSLOV, V. V. *Pamyatniki drevne-russkago iskusstva.* St Petersburg, 1908–12, 4 parts.

> Drawings and water-colour renderings of architecture and painting.

SUSLOV, V. V. *Pamyatniki drevnyago russkago zodchestva.* St Petersburg, 1895–1901, 7 parts.

> Drawings of wooden and masonry architecture.

ZABELLO, S. Ya., and others. *Russkoe derevyannoe zodchestvo.* Moscow, 1942.

> The most recent comprehensive Soviet work on wooden architecture. Many illustrations.

4. ARCHITECTURE, PRINCIPALLY AFTER 1700

BONDARENKO, I. Ye. *Arkhitekturnye pamyatniki Moskvy,* Parts I, II–III. Moscow, 1904–5.

> Splendid gravure plates of 18th- and 19th-century buildings.

BUNIN, A. V. *Arkhitekturnaya kompozitsya gorodov.* Moscow, 1940.

> Chapters on Russian city-planning.

GRABAR, I., ed. *Istoriya russkago iskusstva,* III–IV. Moscow, from 1909.

HAUTECOEUR, L. *L'Architecture classique à Saint-Pétersbourg à la fin du XVIIIe siècle.* Paris, 1912.

Imperial Society of Architects, St Petersburg, *Ezhegodnik* (Yearbook), I– (1906–).

> With many illustrations of modern architectural projects.

Imperial Society of Architects, *Istoricheskaya vystavka arkhitektury.* St Petersburg, 1911.

> Illustrated catalogue, edited by A. Benois, of an important exhibition of old St Petersburg architecture.

USPENSKI, A. I., and others. *Istoricheskaya Panorama Sanktpeterburga i ego okrestnostei,* 10 vols. Moscow, 1911–14.

> With numerous illustrations.

5. PAINTING TO 1700

AVINOFF, A., ed. *Russian Icons and Objects of Ecclesiastical and Decorative Arts from the Collection of George R. Hann.* Carnegie Institute, Pittsburgh, Pa., 1944

> With an introduction.

FARBMAN, M., ed. *Masterpieces of Russian Painting.* London, 1930.

Catalogue of the exhibition of icons circulated by the Central State Restoration Workshop, Moscow. With contributions by A. J. Anisimov, R. Fry, and I. Grabar. Colour plates.

KONDAKOV, N. P. *The Russian Icon.* Oxford, 1927. Translated by E. H. Minns.

Summary of the following work.

KONDAKOV, N. P. *Russkaya ikona,* 4 vols. Prague, 1928–33.

The culminating study in the iconographical tradition. The first two volumes contain excellent plates in colour and black and white.

MURATOV, P. P. *L'Ancienne Peinture russe.* Rome and Prague, 1925.

A French translation of his chapters in Grabar's *Istoriya,* VI.

MURATOV, P. P. *Les Icones russes.* Paris, 1927.

NEKRASOV, A. I. *Drevne-russkoe izobrazitelnoe iskusstvo.* Moscow, 1937.

Summary of Soviet scholarship to that date, with bibliography.

RICE, D. Talbot. *Russian Icons.* London and New York, 1947.

Brief, with 16 colour plates.

SOBKO, N. P. *Slovar russkikh khudozhnikov,* 3 vols. St Petersburg, 1893–9.

A biographical dictionary, complete only for the letters A, I, P.

THEUNISSEN, W. P. *Ikonen.* The Hague, 1948.

Interesting illustrations.

USPENSKI, A. I. *Tsarskie ikonopissy i zhivopistsy XVII veka,* 4 vols. Moscow, 1910–16.

Monumental study of 17th-century Moscow painting, with numerous illustrations.

WULFF, O., and ALPATOV, M. *Denkmäler der Ikonenmalerei.* Hellerau bei Dresden, 1925.

With annotated catalogue of Byzantine and Russian icons.

ZOLOTNITZKY, J. *Trente-cinq primitifs russes.* Paris, 1931.

Preface by H. Focillon.

6. PAINTING FROM 1700

APTEKAR, M. *Russkaya istoricheskaya zhivopis.* Moscow, 1939.

BELYAVSKAYA, V. *Rospisi russkogo klassitsizma.* Leningrad and Moscow, 1940.

Interesting Neo-classic mural painting of the early 19th century.

BENOIS, A. *The Russian School of Painting.* New York, 1916.

An enlarged version of the author's earlier essay on 18th- and 19th-century painting written for R. Muther's *History of Modern Painting,* English tr. (London, 1895–6), III, Ch. xliii, with an interesting bibliography.

BENOIS, A. *Russkaya shkola zhivopisi.* St Petersburg, 1904.

10 folios of plates of 18th- and 19th- century painting.

BULGAKOV, F. I. *Nashi khudozhniki,* 2 vols. St Petersburg, 1890.

A biographical dictionary of later 19th-century painters, sculptors, engravers, etc. Numerous illustrations, poorly reproduced.

DIAGHILEV, V., ed. *Katalog istoriko-khudozhestvennoi vystavki russkikh portretov v Tavricheskom dvortse,* 8 vols. St Petersburg, 1905.

Catalogue of the large exhibition held in the Tauride Palace in 1905.

ISAKOV, S. K. *Russkaya zhivopis.* Petrograd, 1915.

Catalogue of paintings in the Academy of Fine Arts.

LUKOMSKI, G. K. *History of Modern Russian Painting.* London, 1945.

244 illustrations of painting from 1840 to 1940.

NICHOLAS MIKHAILOVICH, Grand Duke, ed. *Russkie portrety XVIII i XIX vekov,* 5 vols. St Petersburg, 1905–09.

Portraits by Russian and foreign artists, including miniatures.

NIKOLSKI, V. A. *Russkaya zhivopis, istoriko-kriticheskie ocherki.* St Petersburg, 1904.

Illustrated study of 19th-century academic painting.

USPENSKI, A. I. *Slovar khudozhnikov v XVIII Veke pisavshikh v imperatorskikh dvortsakh.* Moscow, 1913.

Dictionary of decorative artists working in the imperial palaces in the 18th century.

VRANGEL, N. N. *Katalog vystavki russkoi portretnoi zhivopisi za 150 let.* St Petersburg, 1902.

Biographical and bibliographical catalogue of an exhibition of portraits, 1700–1850.

7. SCULPTURE AND THE DECORATIVE ARTS

AINALOV, D. V. 'Trois manuscrits du XIVe siècle à l'exposition de l'ancienne laure de la Trinité à Sergiev,' *L'Art byzantin chez les slaves,* II, 244-52.

BARSHCHEVSKI, I. F. *Russkiya drevnosti*. Moscow, c. 1895.

150 plates of decorative arts.

BOBRINSKOI, A. A. *Narodnyya russkiya derevyannyya izdeliya*. Moscow, 1911.

200 plates of wood carving and furniture.

BOBRINSKOI, A. A. *Reznoi kamen v Rossii*. Moscow, 1916.

41 excellent photographs of Suzdalian architecture and sculpture.

BOUTOVSKY, V. de. *Histoire de l'ornement russe du Xe au XVIe siècle, d'après les manuscrits*, 2 vols. Paris, 1870–3.

BUNT, C. G. E. *Russian Art from Scyths to Soviets*. London, 1946.

Considerable information on the decorative arts.

Drevnosti rossiiskago gosudarstva, 6 vols. Moscow, 1849–53.

Coloured lithographs of objects of religious art.

GAGARIN, G. G. *Sobranie vizantiiskikh, gruzinskikh, i drevne-russkikh ornamentov*, 3 vols. St Petersburg, 1897–1903.

Byzantine, Georgian, and old Russian ornament.

GEORGIEVSKI, G. P. *Drevne-russkaya miniatiura*. Leningrad, 1933.

Medieval manuscript illumination. English ed., Moscow, 1934.

GUSHCHIN, A. S. *Pamyatniki khudozhestvennogo remesla drevnei Rusi X–XIII veka*. Moscow, 1936.

Industrial arts, old Russian.

HALLE, F. *Die Bauplastik von Wladimir-Ssusdal*. Berlin, 1929.

The best available account of medieval sculpture.

HOLME, C. *Peasant Art in Russia*. London, 1912.

ISAKOV, S. K. *Russkaya skulptura*. Petrograd, 1915.

Catalogue of sculpture in the Academy of Fine Arts, Leningrad.

LUKOMSKI, G. K. *Alt-Russland, Architektur und Kunstgewerbe*. Munich, 1923.

108 plates.

LUKOMSKI, G. K. *L'Art décoratif russe*. Paris, 1928.

192 plates.

LUKOMSKI, G. K. *Le Kreml de Moscou, ses cathédrales, ses palais et ses trésors d'art*, 3 vols. Paris, 1928.

120 plates, chiefly of the decorative arts.

LUKOMSKI, G. K. *Mobilier et décoration des anciens palais impériaux russes*. Paris, 1928.

84 plates, principally interiors of the Great Palace at Tsarskoe Selo.

LUKOMSKI, G. K. *Russisches Porzellan, 1744–1923*. Berlin, 1924.

62 plates.

NEKRASOV, A. I. *Russkoe narodnoe iskusstvo*. Moscow, 1924.

Peasant crafts.

NIKOLSKI, V. A. *Drevne-russkoe dekorativnoe iskusstvo*. Petrograd, 1923.

OLSUFIEV, I. A. *Opis drevnyago tserkovnogo serebra v. Troitso-Sergievskoi Lavre (do XVIII veka)*. Sergiev, 1926.

Ancient ecclesiastical silver.

ROVINSKI, D. A. *Podrobnyi slovar russkikh graverov*, 2 vols. St Petersburg, 1895.

Biographical dictionary of engravers.

ROVINSKI, D. A. *Materialy dlya russkoi ikonografii*, 13 vols. St Petersburg, 1884–91.

480 facsimile reproductions of early engravings.

SHCHEKOTOV, N. M. 'Drevne-russkoe shitie,' *Sofiya*, No. 1, 5–32.

Embroideries.

SHCHEKOTOV, N. M. *Russkaya krestyanskaya zhivopis*. Moscow, 1923.

Peasant painting.

SVIRIN, A. N. 'Une Broderie du XVe siècle de style pittoresque, représentant le "Cin",' *L'Art byzantin chez les slaves*, II, 282–91.

SYREISHCHIKOV, N. P., and TRENEV, D. K. *Ornamenty na pamyatnikakh drevne-russkago iskusstva*, 3 vols. Moscow, 1904–16.

Old Russian ornament.

TOLL, N. 'La Broderie populaire russe et les tissus du moyen age,' *L'Art byzantin chez les slaves*, I, 387–92.

8. HISTORY, LITERATURE, ETC.

BABEY, A. M. *Americans in Russia, 1776–1917*. New York, 1938.

BARING, M. *An Outline of Russian Literature*. New York, 1915.

BEAZLEY, R., FORBES, N., and BIRKETT, G. A. *Russia from the Varangians to the Bolsheviks*. Oxford, 1918.

CALVOCORESSI, M. D., and ABRAHAM, G. *Masters of Russian Music*. London, 1936.

CHADWICK, N. K. *Russian Heroic Poetry*. Cambridge, 1932.

CRANKSHAW, E. *Russia and Britain*. London and New York, c. 1943.

FORTESCUE, A. *The Orthodox Eastern Church*. London, c. 1911.

FÜLÖP-MILLER, R., and GREGOR, J. *The Russian Theatre, its Character and History*. Philadelphia, 1930.

GUDZII, N. K. *History of Early Russian Literature*. New York, 1949.

HRUSHEVSKY, M. *A History of Ukraine*. New Haven, 1941.

KERNER, R. J. *Slavic Europe, a Selected Bibliography in the Western European Languages*. Cambridge, 1918.

KLIUCHEVSKI, V. O. *A History of Russia*, 5 vols. London–New York, 1911–31.

KORNILOV, A. A. *Modern Russian History*. New York, 1943.

MAVOR, J. *An Economic History of Russia*, 2 vols. 2nd ed., London, 1925.

MAZOUR, A. G. *An Outline of Modern Russian Historiography*. Berkeley, 1939.

MILIUKOV, P. *Outlines of Russian Culture*, 3 vols. Philadelphia, 1942.

MIRSKY, D. S. *A History of Russian Literature*. New York, 1949.

MOHRENSCHILDT, D. S. von. *Russia in the Intellectual Life of 18th-century France*. New York, 1936.

PARES, B. *A History of Russia*. Rev. ed., New York, 1949.

PLATONOV, S. F. *History of Russia*. New York, 1929.

SALAVILLE, S. *An Introduction to the Study of Eastern Liturgies*. London, 1938.

SUMNER, B. H. *A Short History of Russia*. London and New York, 1943.

VERNADSKY, G. *Ancient Russia*. New Haven, 1943.

VERNADSKY, G. *A History of Russia*. 3rd rev. ed., New Haven, 1951.

VERNADSKY, G. *Kievan Russia*. New Haven 1948.

VERNADSKY, G., *The Mongols and Russia*. New Haven, 1953.

THE PLATES

NOTE BY THE EDITOR

It *has been singularly hard to collect illustrations for Professor Hamilton's volume. I sympathize with him in the worries which he must have had in preparing, as he did, a complete set of photographs from which our plates were to be made. Not all of them could be satisfactory. Many were re-photographed from existing older books. We tried to improve in a number of cases and are grateful to the late Sir Ellis Minns and Mr D. R. Buxton for their help; the Society for Cultural Relations with the U.S.S.R. also gave willing and valuable assistance in the search for illustrations, and were instrumental in providing a number of photographs otherwise unobtainable. But we would still have been much happier if quite a number of better photographs could have been obtained directly from Russia. The reader will, I hope, appreciate the author's and our own difficulties.*

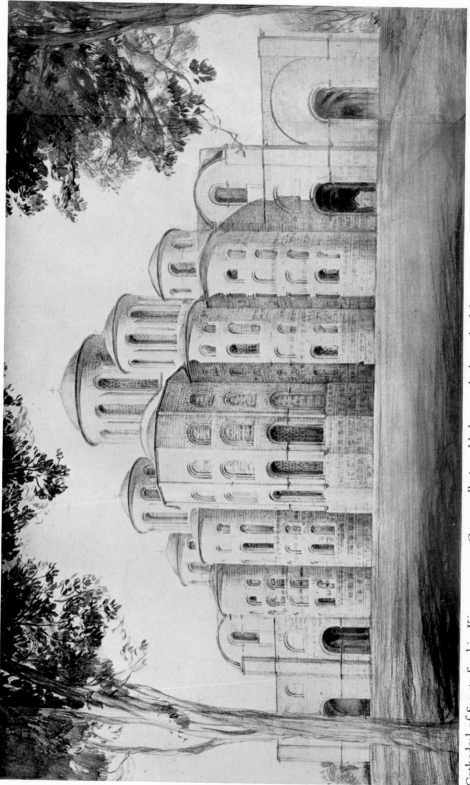

Cathedral of Sancta Sophia, Kiev. 1015–37. Outer galleries added towards the end of the century. Restored view from the east (K. J. Conant)

(A) Cathedral of Sancta Sophia, Kiev. The west façade in 1651.
From a drawing by A. van Westerveldt

(B) Cathedral of Sancta Sophia, Kiev. The outer south gallery in 1651.
From a drawing by A. van Westerveldt

Cathedral of the Transfiguration, Chernigov. Interior

Cathedral of the Transfiguration, Chernigov. Founded 1017. From the east

(B) Cathedral of Sancta Sophia, Novgorod. Interior

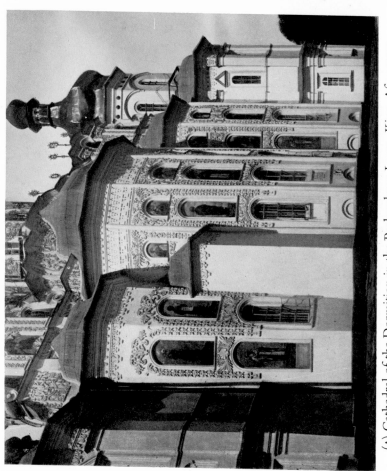

(A) Cathedral of the Dormition in the Pecherskaya Lavra, Kiev. After 1073.
Restored in the 18th century. From the west

5

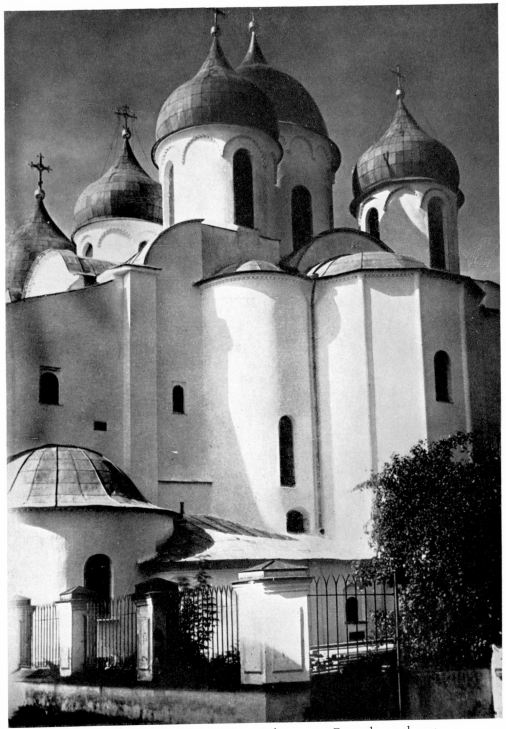

Cathedral of Sancta Sophia, Novgorod, 1045–52. From the south-east

6

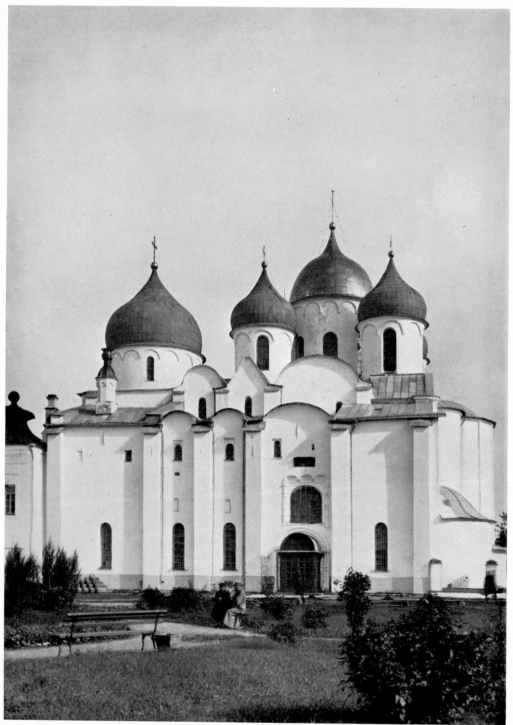

Cathedral of Sancta Sophia, Novgorod. South façade

Cathedral of St George in the Yuriev (George) Monastery, Novgorod, 1119–30

Church of the Saviour at Nereditsa, near Novgorod, 1198. Restored in 1904

9

(A) Cathedral of the Transfiguration, Novgorod, 1374

(B) Pecherski Monastery, Pskov. 14th–15th centuries

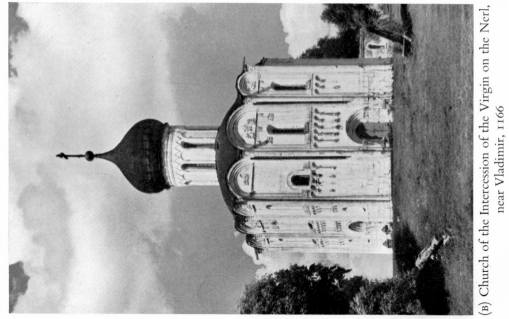

(B) Church of the Intercession of the Virgin on the Nerl,
near Vladimir, 1166

(A) Church of SS. Boris and Gleb at Kideksha, 1152

(B) Cathedral of the Dormition, Vladimir, 1158–61. Rebuilt 1185–9. From the north-east

(A) Prince Andrei Bogoliubski's Palace, Bogoliubovo. Remains of the tower, c. 1160

12

(B) Church of St Dmitri, Vladimir, relief sculpture in centre panel, west façade, c. 1195–1200. The figures and colonnettes at the bottom are 18th-century restorations

(A) St Dmitri, Vladimir. West Front

Church of St George, Yuriev-Polski, 1229–34. From the south-east

(B) Bogoliubovo. Tower. Detail of Plate 12 (A)

(A) St George, Yuriev-Polski. South Porch

Hunting and circus scenes. Fresco, from the staircase, Cathedral of Sancta Sophia, Kiev, late 11th century

16

Christ Pantokrator. Mosaic in the dome of the Cathedral of Sancta Sophia, Kiev, 11th century

(B) St Cyril Instructing the Emperor. Fresco. Church of St Cyril, Kiev, 12th century

(A) SS. Thomas, James, Simon, and Luke, from the Liturgical Eucharist. Mosaic. Church of St Michael, Kiev

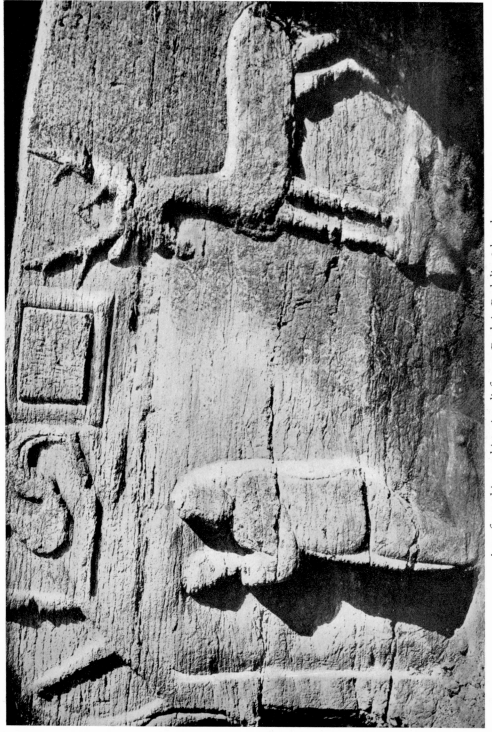

Act of worship, prehistoric relief, near Bush in Podolia, 8th–9th century

King David enthroned with birds and animals. Centre panel of the south façade.
Church of the Intercession on the Nerl, *c.* 1170

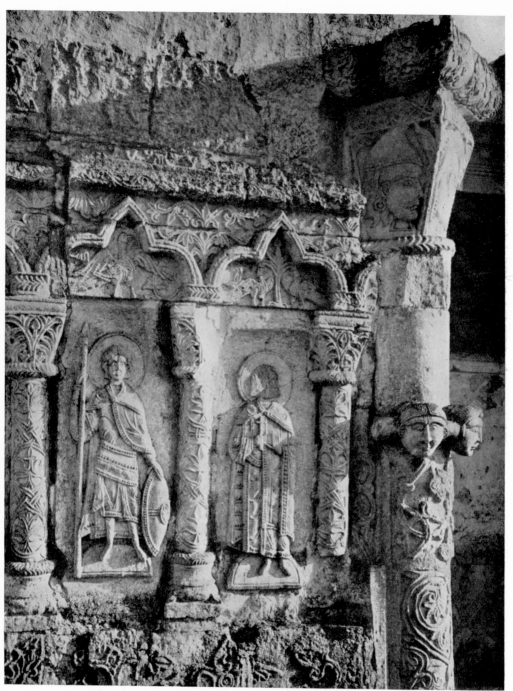

Church of St George, Yuriev-Polski. Relief Sculpture, 1230–4

(B) Head of an Angel. Detail of the Last Judgement. Fresco. Church of St Dmitri, Vladimir, late 12th century

(A) The Virgin. From a deesis. Church of St George, Yuriev-Polski, 1230–4

22

Head of an Apostle. Detail of the Last Judgement. Fresco. Church of St Dmitri, Vladimir,
late 12th century

Interior of the apse, Church of the Saviour, Nereditsa, 1199

(A) The Baptism. Fresco. Church of the Saviour, Nereditsa, 1199

(B) Head of St Phocas. Fresco. Church of the
Saviour, Nereditsa, 1199

(C) Head of St Peter. Fresco. Church of the
Saviour, Nereditsa, 1199

(B) Virgin Orans. Fresco. Church of the Saviour, Nereditsa, 1199

(A) Church of the Saviour, Nereditsa. Scheme of the frescoes within the dome. 1199

(B) Joachim's Dream. Fresco. Church of the Dormition. Volotovo, 1363

(A) The Transfiguration. Fresco. Church of the Dormition. Volotovo, 1363

An Archangel. Fresco. Church of the Dormition. Volotovo, 1363

The Patriarch Noah. Fresco. Church of the Transfiguration,
Novgorod. By Theophanes the Greek, 1378

The Patriarch Abel. Fresco. Detail of head. Church of the Transfiguration, Novgorod.
By Theophanes the Greek, 1378

St Macarius. Fresco. Detail of head. Church of the Transfiguration. Novgorod.
By Theophanes the Greek, 1378

The Virgin of Vladimir. Greek. Early 12th century. *Tretyakov Gallery, Moscow*

The Annunciation. Russian under Greek influence. 12th century. *Tretyakov Gallery, Moscow*

The Annunciation. Head of Gabriel. Detail from Plate 33

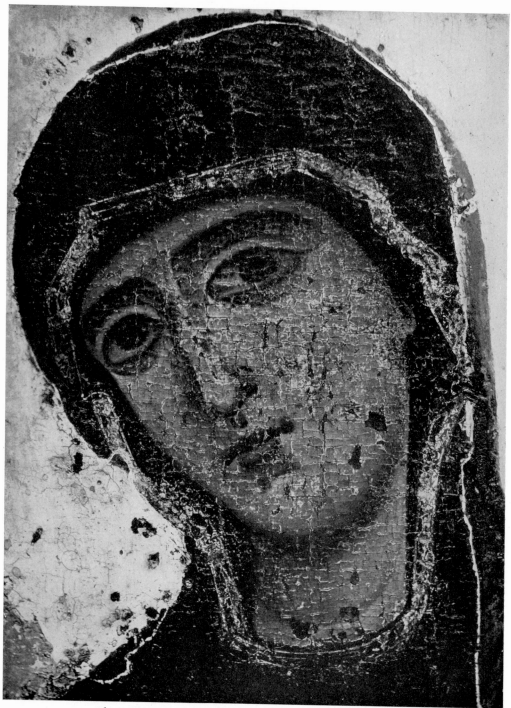

The Annunciation. Head of the Virgin. Detail from Plate 33

(B) The Virgin Orans. 12th century. *Tretyakov Gallery, Moscow*

(A) Head of an Archangel. 12th century. *Tretyakov Gallery, Moscow*

36

(B) Mandilion portrait of Christ, the 'Image not made with Hands'. 12th century. *Tretyakov Gallery, Moscow*

(A) The Virgin Orans. An Archangel. Detail from Plate 36B

(B) St Nicholas. From the Novodevichi Monastery, Moscow. *c.* 1200. *Tretyakov Gallery, Moscow*

(A) Reverse of the Mandilion. Angels adoring the Cross

38

(B) St Nicholas. From the Monastery of the Holy Ghost, Novgorod. *c.* 1200. *Museum of Russian Art, Novgorod*

(A) Christ with the Golden Hair. *c.* 1200, *Tretyakov Gallery, Moscow*

(B) St Dmitri, 14th century. *Russian Museum, Leningrad*

(A) SS. John, George, and Blaise, early 13th century. *Russian Museum, Leningrad*

(B) The Virgin's Assembly. Pskov School, 14th century.
Tretyakov Gallery, Moscow

(A) The Nativity of the Virgin, 14th century.
Tretyakov Gallery, Moscow

41

St George and the Dragon, with scenes from the saint's life, 14th century.
Russian Museum, Leningrad

SS. Boris and Gleb, 14th century. *Russian Museum, Leningrad*

(B) Head of Christ. From a deesis found in Zvenigorod, early 15th century. *Tretyakov Gallery, Moscow*

(A) The Four Saints Icon. Pskov School, *c.* 1400, *Tretyakov Gallery, Moscow*

44

(B) Head of Christ. Novgorod, 15th century.
Russian Museum, Leningrad

(A) The Virgin. Detail from the iconostasis in the Cathedral of the
Annunciation, Moscow. By Theophanes the Greek, 1405

(B) The Virgin of the Don. Russian under Greek influence, late 14th century. *Tretyakov Gallery, Moscow*

(A) The Dormition of the Virgin. Russian under Greek influence, late 14th century. *Tretyakov Gallery, Moscow*

St Peter. From the iconostasis in the
Cathedral of the Dormition, Vladimir.
By Andrei Rublev and Daniel Chorni,
1408

47

Old Testament Trinity. By Andrei Rublev, c. 1410–20. *Tretyakov Gallery, Moscow*

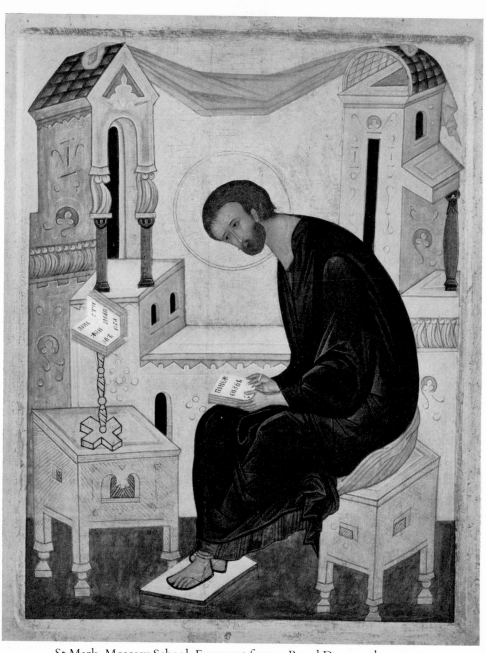

St Mark. Moscow School. Fragment from a Royal Door, 15th century.
Tretyakov Gallery, Moscow

(B) St Elias. Novgorod School, 1400. *Tretyakov Gallery, Moscow*

(A) The Archangel Michael. From a deesis found in Zvenigorod, Moscow School. Follower of Andrei Rublev, 15th century

(B) Head of St Dmitri. From the iconostasis of the Trinity-Sergius Monastery. By Andrei Rublev, 1425

(A) Head of St Michael. From the Zvenigorod deesis, 15th century. *Tretyakov Gallery, Moscow*

The Four-Part Icon. Novgorod School, *c.* 1400. *Russian Museum, Leningrad*

The Old Testament Trinity. Detail from the Four-Part Icon. Novgorod School, *c.* 1400.
Russian Museum, Leningrad

(B) The Battle between Novgorod and Suzdal. Novgorod School, late 15th century. *Museum of Russian Art, Novgorod*

(A) The Miracle of the Intercession of the Virgin. (Pokrov) Novgorod School, early 16th century. *Russian Museum, Leningrad*

54

(B) Christ enthroned with the Virgin and St John the Baptist. Central panel from a deesis. Novgorod School, 16th century.

Tretyakov Gallery, Moscow

(A) The Miracle of the Intercession of the Virgin. An Angel. Detail from Plate 54A

55

(B) The Deposition. From a range of the Twelve Feasts. Novgorod School, 16th century. *Tretyakov Gallery, Moscow*

(A) The Entry into Jerusalem. Mixed Style, early 16th century. *Tretyakov Gallery, Moscow*

(B) The Ascension. Moscow School, 15th century

(A) St Pyatnitsa (Good Friday) Novgorod School, 16th century.
Russian Museum, Leningrad

57

St Varlaam of Khutyn and Scenes from his Life. Moscow School, 16th century.
Tretyakov Gallery, Moscow

(A) The Parable of the Widow's Mite. Fresco. Church of the Dormition, Therapont Monastery. By Dionysius and his sons, 1500–1

(B) Christ Enthroned with the Virgin and St John the Baptist. From the Last Judgement. Fresco. Church of the Dormition, Therapont Monastery. By Dionysius and his sons, 1500–1

(B) The Incredulity of St Thomas. School of Dionysius, Moscow, 16th century. *Tretyakov Gallery, Moscow*

(A) The Vision of St Eulogius. Moscow School, 16th century. *Russian Museum, Leningrad*

60

(B) SS. Zosima and Savva at the Solovetski Monastery. Moscow School, 16th century. *Tretyakov Gallery, Moscow*

(A) The Entry into Jerusalem. Moscow School, Mixed Style, 16th century

SS. Florus and Laurus. Novgorod School, Mixed Style, 16th century

(A) Wooden storehouses. Northern Russia, 18th century

(B) Terentiev House. Northern Russia, 18th century

Tavern between Kostroma and Yaroslavl, 18th century. Lithograph by André Durand

(B) Tsaritsyn, on the Volga, in the 17th century

(A) Belfry. Tsivozero

(A) The outskirts of Moscow in 1682

(B) The Church of St Dmitri of Salonika, Staraya Ladoga, early 18th century

(A) The Iverski Monastery on an island in Lake Valdai, 1661–2

(B) The Village of Yadrovo, west of Moscow, 1661–2

67

The Church of St Nicholas, Panilovo, 1600

The Church of SS. Florus and Laurus, Rostovskoe, 1755

The Church of the Dormition, Kondopoga, 1774

The Church of the Trinity, Nenoksa, 1727

(B) The Church of SS. Florus and Laurus, Rostovskoe.
From the south-east

(A) The Church of the Dormition, Varzuga, 1674

(B) The Church of St Nicholas, Berezovets, early 18th century

(A) The Church of the Virgin of Vladimir,
Podporozhie, 1741

73

The Church of the Transfiguration, Kizhi, 1714

The Cathedral of the Annunciation in the Kremlin, Moscow, 1484–9

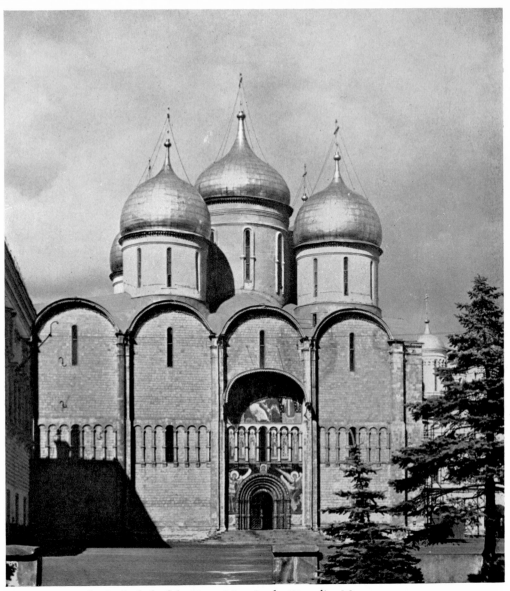

The Cathedral of the Dormition, in the Kremlin, Moscow, 1475–9

(A) The Church of the Dormition, Kondopoga. Interior

(B) The Cathedral of the Dormition, Moscow. Interior

(B) The Cathedral of St Michael the Archangel, in the Kremlin, Moscow, 1505–9

(A) The Cathedral of St Michael the Archangel, in the Kremlin, Moscow, 1505–9

78

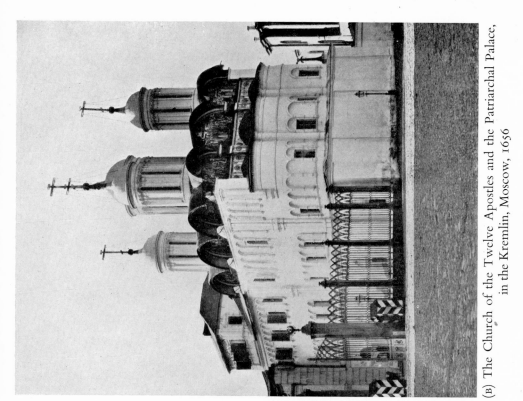

(B) The Church of the Twelve Apostles and the Patriarchal Palace, in the Kremlin, Moscow, 1656

(A) The Cathedral of the Dormition. Trinity-Sergius Monastery, 1585

79

(B) The Church of the Transfiguration, Ostrovo, before 1550

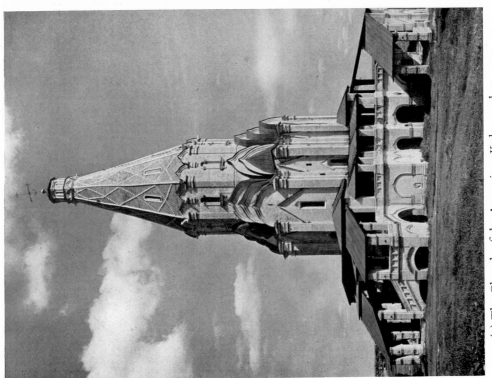

(A) The Church of the Ascension, Kolomenskoe, 1532

(A) The Church of the Decapitation of St John the Baptist, Dyakovo, before 1547

(B) The Cathedral of St Basil, Moscow, in the 17th century, before the addition of the covered gallery

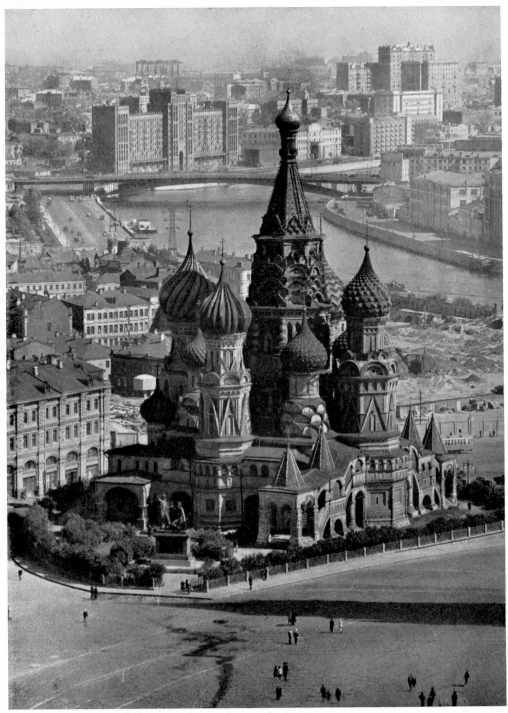

The Cathedral of St Basil, Moscow, 1555–60

(B) The Cathedral of St Basil, Moscow. Detail

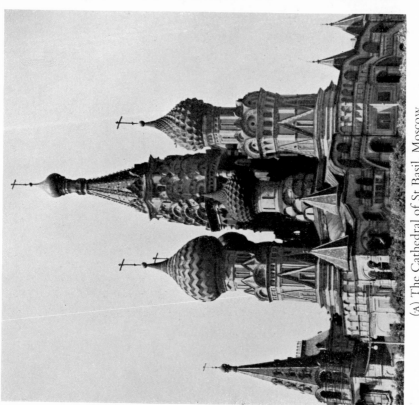

(A) The Cathedral of St Basil, Moscow

(B) The Church of the Nativity of the Virgin, in Putinki, Moscow, 1649–52

(A) The Old Cathedral in the Monastery of the Virgin of the Don, Moscow, 1593

(B) The Church of the Trinity, at Ostankino, near Moscow, 1668

(A) The Church of the Trinity and of the Georgian Virgin, Moscow, 1634–54

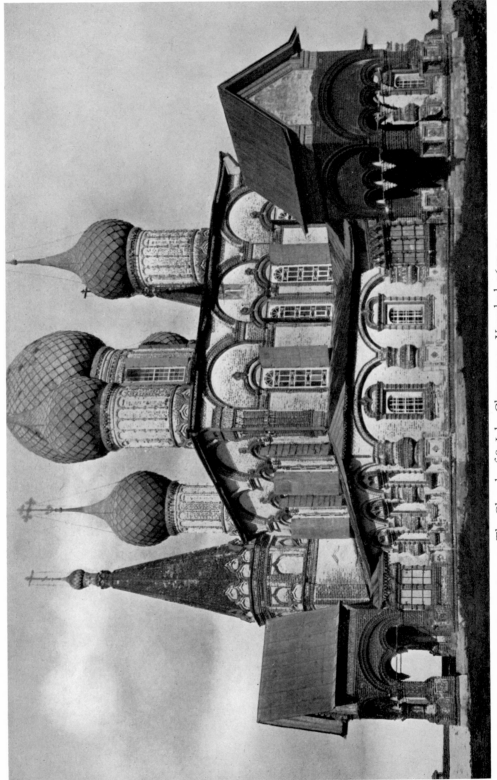

The Church of St John Chrysostom, Yaroslavl, 1649–54

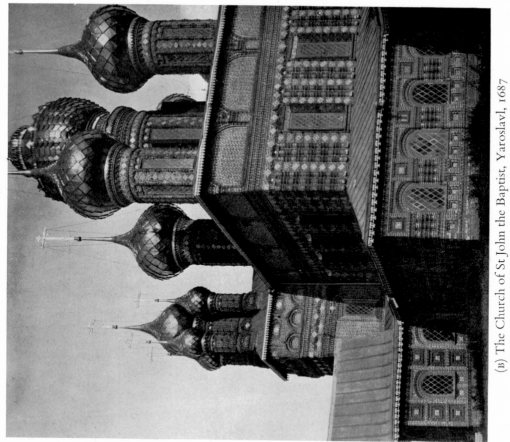

(B) The Church of St John the Baptist, Yaroslavl, 1687

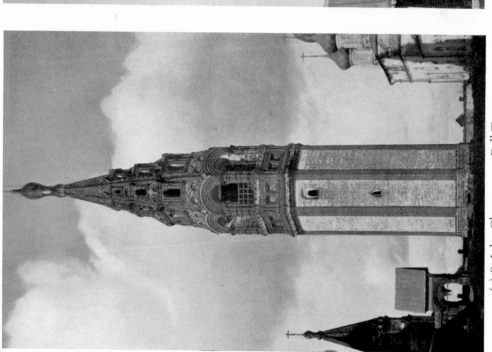

(A) St John Chrysostom. Bell Tower

87

(A) The Church of the Presentation, Borisoglebsk Monastery, near Rostov, 17th century

(B) The Church of St Nicholas of the Great Cross,
Moscow, late 17th century

(A) The Church of the Intercession of the Virgin, Fili, 1693

(B) The Church of the Vladimir Virgin, Moscow,
1691–4

The Church of the Virgin of the Sign (Znamenie), Dubrovitsi, 1690–1704

The Church of the Archangel Gabriel ('Menshikov Tower'), Moscow, 1704–7

(A) The Pogankin House, Pskov, 16th–17th centuries

(B) The fortifications of the Kremlin, Novgorod, 14th–16th centuries

(A) Moscow and the Kremlin in 1661–2

(B) The Palace Square in the Kremlin, Moscow, 1672

The Kremlin, Moscow

94

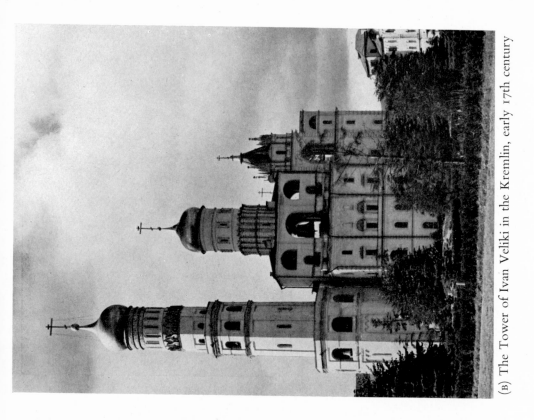

(B) The Tower of Ivan Veliki in the Kremlin, early 17th century

(A) The Borovitskaya and Vodovzvodnaya Towers of the
Kremlin Wall, Moscow. 17th century

(A) The Vaulted Hall in the Granovitaya Palata, early 17th century. From a painting in the Budapest Museum

(B) The Vaulted Hall in modern times

(A) The Wooden Palace at Kolomenskoe. From an 18th-century engraving

(B) Model of the Wooden Palace at Kolomenskoe, 1667–81

(C) The Ambassadors' Palace, Moscow, in 1661–2

97

(A) The State Pharmacy, Moscow, late 17th century

(B) The German District on the outskirts of Moscow, *c.* 1700. From an engraving by Hendrik de Witt, 1671–1716

(B) SS. Vasili Blazhenni and Artemius of Verkoli. Stroganov School,
early 17th century. *Tretyakov Gallery, Moscow*

(A) The Virgin, St Michael, and St Paul. Left wing of a small deesis.
Stroganov School. By Prokopi Chirin, *c.* 1620

99

SS. Boris and Gleb. Stroganov School. By a follower of Prokopi Chirin.
Stroganov School. 17th century. *Russian Museum, Leningrad*

St Alexis, Metropolitan of Moscow. Stroganov School, early 17th century.
Tretyakov Gallery, Moscow

Christ Enthroned. Yaroslavl School, later 17th century. *Museum, Yaroslavl*

The Lord's Prayer. Moscow School, late 17th century

Old Testament Trinity. Moscow School, 17th century. *Museum, Yaroslavl*

The Vernicle (Veronica's Veil). Moscow School. By Simon Ushakov, *c.* 1660

The Dormition of the Virgin. Moscow School. By Simon Ushakov, 1663. *Museum, Vladimir*

(A) The Church of St Elias, Yaroslavl. Interior showing frescoed wall

(B) Martin de Vos. Elias and the Shunammite Woman. Engraving from Piscator's *Theatrum Biblicum*, 1674

Central section of St Petersburg, showing the principal buildings in 1753. From an engraving by
M. I. Makhaev, 1753

108

St Petersburg in 1737

The Cathedral of SS. Peter and Paul in the Fortress, St Petersburg. By Tressini, 1714–25. From a lithograph by André Durand, 1839

(A) Peter the Great's Kunstkammer, St Petersburg. By Mattarnovi, 1718–25

(B) The Twelve Colleges on Vasili Ostrov, St Petersburg. By Tressini, 1722–32

III

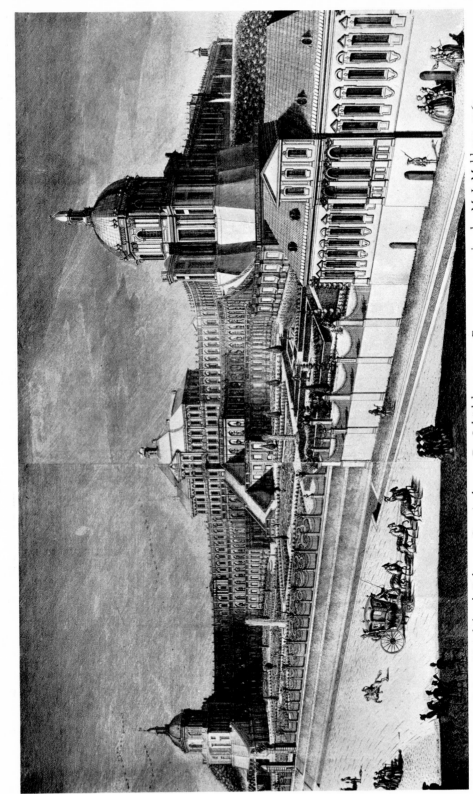

Prince Menshikov's Palace at Oranienbaum. By Schädel, 1713–25. From an engraving by M. I. Makhaev, 1761

The Winter Palace of Anna Ioannovna by Tressini and Rastrelli, and the Old Admiralty, St Petersburg. From an engraving by M. I. Makhaev, 1761

(A) Wooden model for the Cathedral of the Trinity in the Alexander Nevski Lavra, St Petersburg. By Tressini and Schwertfeger, 1720–3

(B) The Library of the Academy of Sciences, in the Kunstkammer, St Petersburg. By Chiaveri, 1725–6

(A) The Anichkov Palace on the Nevski Prospekt, St Petersburg. By Rastrelli.
From an engraving by M. I. Makhaev, 1761

(B) The Summer Palace, on the Fontanka, St Petersburg. By Rastrelli. 1741–4.
From an engraving by M. I. Makhaev, 1761

(A) The forecourt of the Great Palace at Tsarskoe Selo. By Rastrelli, 1749–56. From an engraving by M. I. Makhaev, 1761

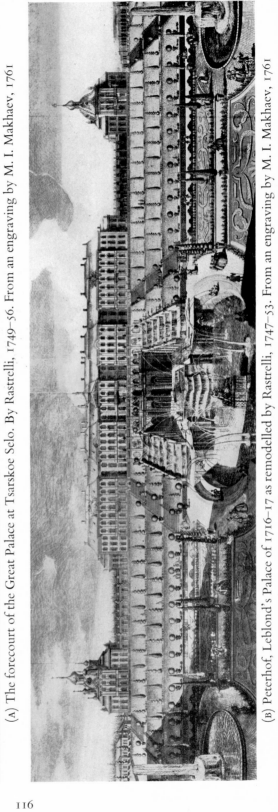

(B) Peterhof, Leblond's Palace of 1716–17 as remodelled by Rastrelli, 1747–53. From an engraving by M. I. Makhaev, 1761

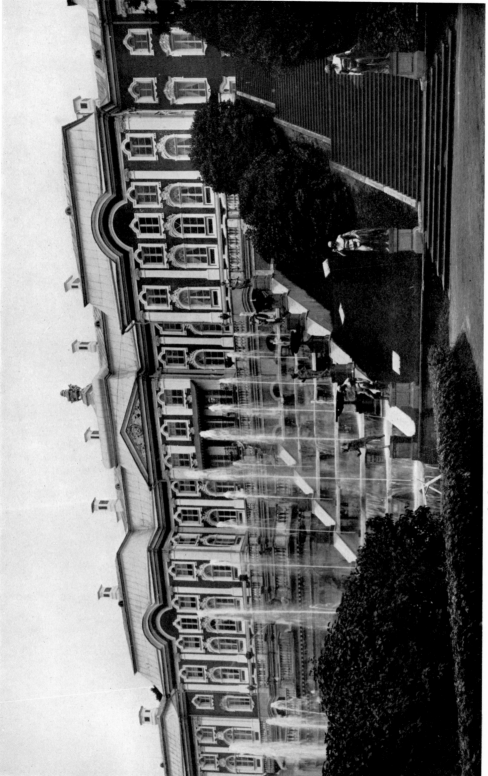

Peterhof. General view of the palace in modern times

(C) The Merchants' Staircase in the
Great Palace, Peterhof.
By Rastrelli, 1747–53

(B) The Smolny Cathedral, St Petersburg.
By Rastrelli, 1748–55

(A) Wooden model of the
proposed belfry for the Smolny
Institute, St Petersburg.
By Rastrelli, c. 1750

The Pavilion of Monbezh ('Mon Bijou') in the park at Tsarskoe Selo. By Rastrelli. 1750. From an engraving by M. I. Makhaev, 1761

Tsarskoe Selo. The Great Palace. Interior, the State Apartments

Tsarskoe Selo. The Great Palace. Interior, the Chapel

(A) The Winter Palace, St Petersburg. By Rastrelli, 1754–62

(B) The Winter Palace, St Petersburg. By Rastrelli

(A) The Academy of Fine Arts, St Petersburg. By Vallin de la Mothe and Kokorinov, 1765–72

(B) The Marble Palace. By Rinaldi, 1768–72

(B) Detail of the wooden model of the projected Great Kremlin Palace, Moscow. By Bazhenov, c. 1772

(A) The Arsenal, St Petersburg. Principal entrance. By Bazhenov, 1768–9

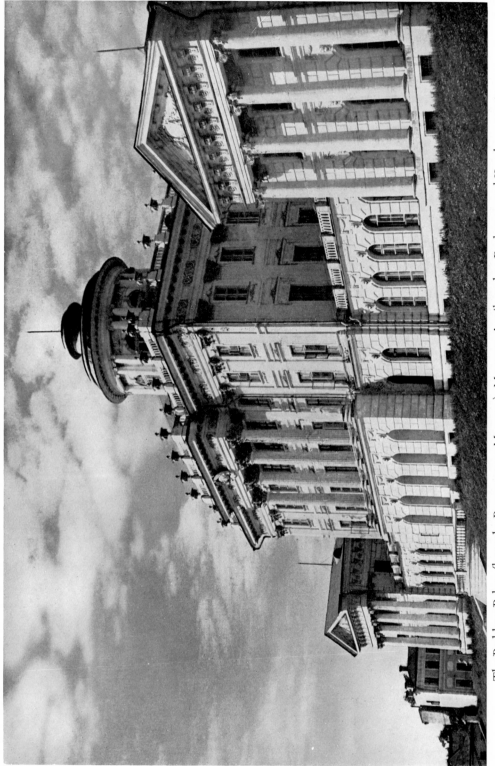

The Pashkov Palace (later the Rumyantsev Museum), Moscow. Attributed to Bazhenov and Kazakov, c. 1780

The Catherine Hall in the Tauride Palace. By Starov, 1783–8

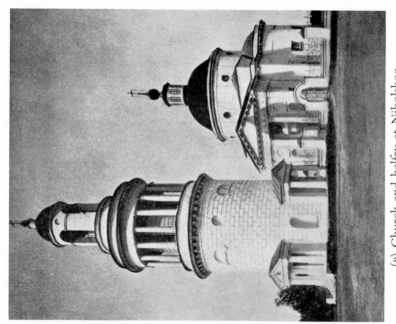

(B) Church and belfry at Nikolskoe. By Starov, 1774–6

(A) Wooden model for the Cathedral of the Trinity, Alexander Nevski Lavra, St Petersburg. By Starov, 1776

Tsarskoe Selo. Detail from the interior. By Cameron, 1782–5

Catherine II's bedroom at Tsarskoe Selo. By Cameron, 1782–5

(A) The English Palace at Peterhof. By Quarenghi, 1781–9

(B) The State Bank, St Petersburg. By Quarenghi, 1783–8

(A) The Hermitage, by Quarenghi, 1782–5, and the Neva Quay, by Velten, St Petersburg

(B) The Palace, Pavlovsk. By Cameron, 1781–96

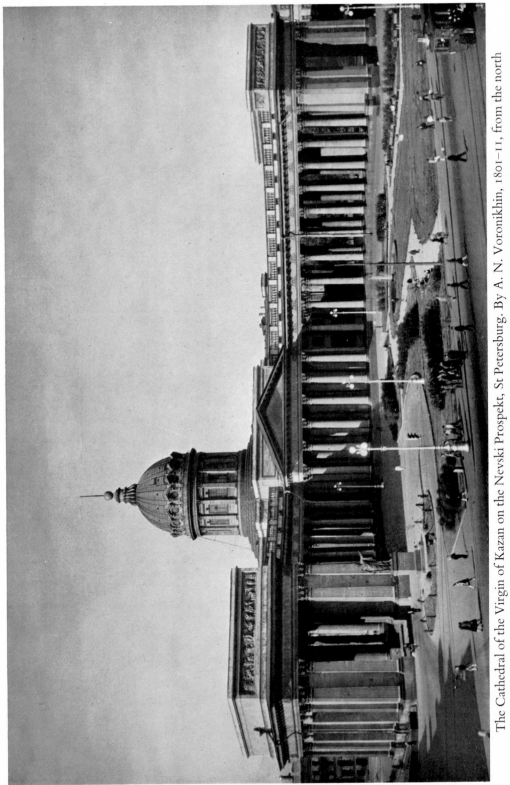

The Cathedral of the Virgin of Kazan on the Nevski Prospekt, St Petersburg. By A. N. Voronikhin, 1801–11, from the north

The Academy of Mines, St Petersburg. By A. Voronikhin, 1811

The New Admiralty, St Petersburg. By A. Zakharov, 1806–15

A Pavilion, the New Admiralty, St Petersburg. By A. Zakharov, 1806-15

The Church of the Ascension, Razumovski Estate near Moscow. By Kazakov, 1793

(B) The Moscow Triumphal Arch, St Petersburg. By Stasov, 1833–8

(A) The Alexandra Theatre, St Petersburg. By Rossi, 1827–32

(B) The Senate and Synod, St Petersburg. By Rossi, 1829–34

General Staff Arch, Palace Square, Leningrad. By Rossi, 1819–29

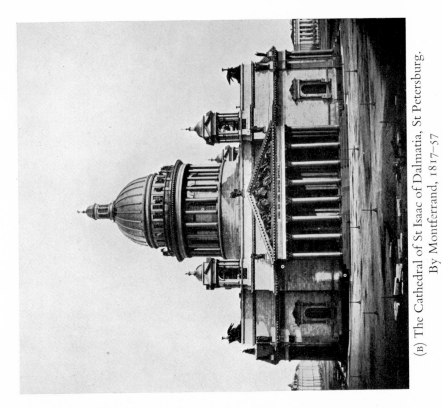

(B) The Cathedral of St Isaac of Dalmatia, St Petersburg. By Montferrand, 1817–57

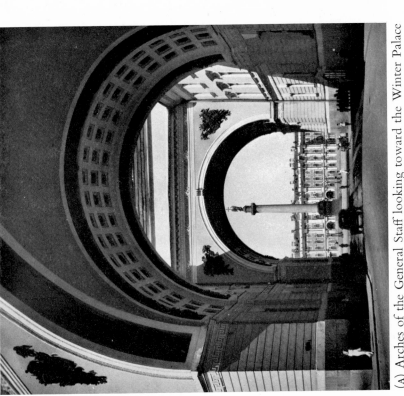

(A) Arches of the General Staff looking toward the Winter Palace Square, St Petersburg. By Rossi, 1819–29

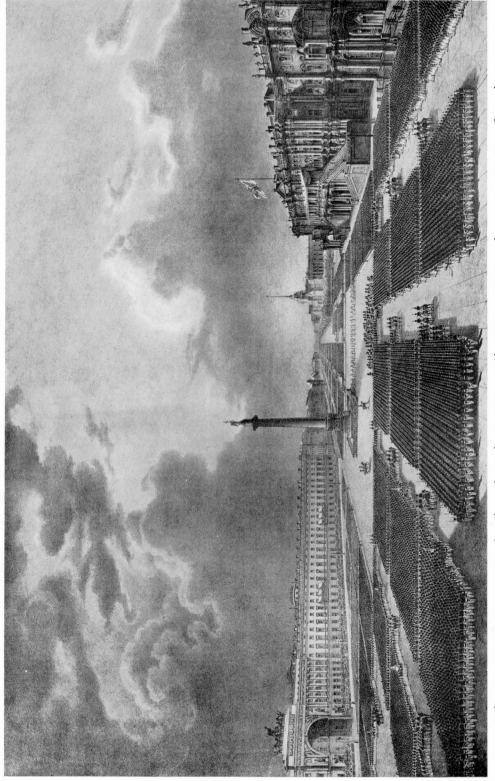

Military ceremony inaugurating the Alexander Column, Winter Palace Square, St Petersburg, 1829. By Montferrand, 1829

141

The Petrovski Palace, near Moscow. By Kazakov, 1775–82

(B) Synodal Printing Office, Moscow, before 1773

(A) The Great Caprice in the park at Tsarskoe Selo.
By Quarenghi and Neelov, c. 1785

143

Ruins of the Palace at Tsaritsyno. By Bazhenov and Kazahov, late 18th century

(A) View of the park at Pavlovsk, after S. F. Shchedrin, *c.* 1795

(B) The Church of St Catherine of the Monastery of the Ascension,
in the Kremlin, Moscow, 1817

(B) I. P. Argunov. Ivan Lazarev as Amor

(A) A. P. Antropov. Peter III, 1762

146

(B) D. G. Levitski. Princess Davydov and Mlle Rzhevski, 1776

(A) F. S. Rokotov. Count Peter Ivanovich Shuvalov

147

D. G. Levitski. The Architect Kokorinov, *c.* 1770

(B) V. L. Borovikovski. Mme Skoboev, c. 1795

(A) V. L. Borovikovski. Catherine Arkharov, c. 1810

(B) F. F. Shchedrin. Caryatids in front of the principal entrance of the New Admiralty, St Petersburg, 1812

(A) M. I. Kozlovski. Caryatids in the Throne Room, Pavlovsk. 1798

(B) I. P. Martos. Minin and Pozharski, 1804–18, Moscow

(A) School of Martos. Funeral Monument. Monastery of the
Virgin of the Don, c. 1810

(B) O. A. Kiprenski. Denis Davydov, 1809. *Russian Museum, Leningrad*

(A) B. I. Orlovski. Marshal Kutuzov. Kazan Cathedral, 1832

152

O. A. Kiprenski. Self-portrait. *Russian Museum, Leningrad*

K. P. Briullov. Prince A. N. Golitsyn, 1838–40

(A) K. P. Briullov. The Last Day of Pompeii, 1828–30. *Russian Museum, Leningrad*

(B) A. A. Ivanov. Christ's First Appearance to the People, 1833–55. *Russian Museum, Leningrad*

(A) A. A. Ivanov. Study, *c.* 1840

(B) A. A. Ivanov. The Annunciation

A. G. Venetsianov. Harvest

(A) P. A. Fedotov. Fido's Illness

(B) P. A. Fedotov, The Major's Courtship, 1848

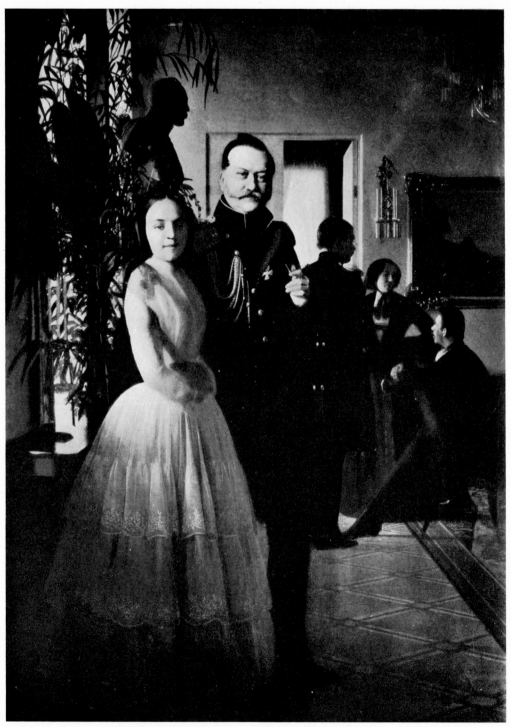

S. K. Zaryanko. Count Rostovtsev and Family

(A) I. N. Kramskoi. The Temptation of Christ, 1872. *Tretyakov Gallery, Moscow*

(B) V. G. Perov. Easter Procession, 1861. *Tretyakov Gallery, Moscow*

(A) V. I. Surikov. The Boyarin Morosova, 1887. *Tretyakov Gallery, Moscow*

(B) N. N. Ge. Golgotha, 1892. *Tretyakov Gallery, Moscow*

(B) V. V. Vereshchagin. Exterior of an Indian Tomb, *c.* 1880

(A) V. Serov. Portrait of Princess Yusupov, *c.* 1900

162

I. E. Repin. Bargemen, 1870–3. *Russian Museum, Leningrad*

I. E. Repin. Tsar Ivan IV with the Body of his Son, detail, 1881–5. *Tretyakov Gallery, Moscow*

(A) I. E. Repin. They Did Not Expect Him, 1884. *Tretyakov Gallery, Moscow*

(B) V. N. Baksheev. The Prose of Life, 1892–3. *Tretyakov Gallery, Moscow*

(A) The Russian Pavilion at the Paris Exposition of 1878

(B) A. Durand. The Kremlin, Moscow. Lithograph, 1843

(B) The Nicholas Cottage, Peterhof.
By Stakenschneider, 1834

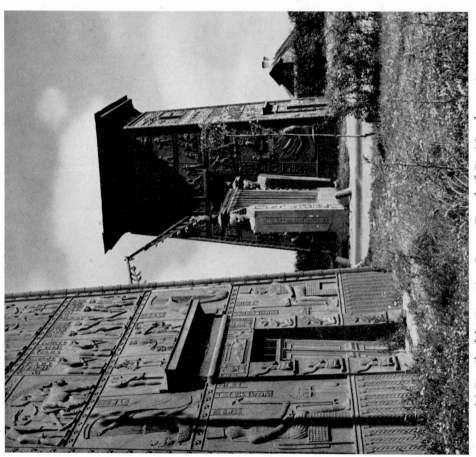

(A) Detail of the Egyptian Gate at Peterhof. By Menelaws, 1829

(A) The Cathedral of the Redeemer, Moscow. By Ton, 1839–83

(B) The Shchukin Museum, Moscow, c. 1890. By Freidenberg

The Historical Museum, Moscow. By Sherwood, 1874–83

(A) V. M. Vasnetsov. After Prince Igor's Battle with the Polovtsi, 1890

(B) V. M. Vasnetsov. Setting for the third act of Ostrovski's drama, *Snegurochka*, 1885

(A) A. M. Vasnetsov. Old Moscow

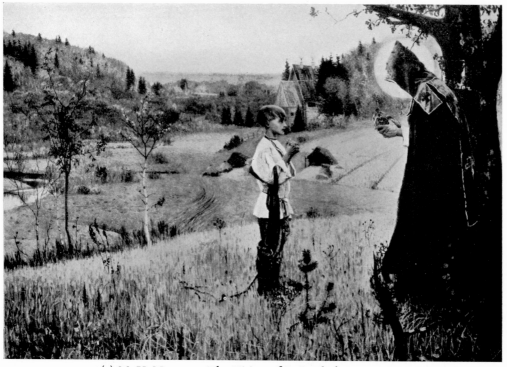

(B) M. V. Nesterov. The Vision of St Bartholomew, 1890

(A) E. E. Lansere. St Petersburg in the Days of Peter the Great

(B) M. A. Vrubel. A Boyar

M. A. Vrubel. Valerian Briussov (unfinished), 1905

(B) L. Bakst. Costume study for *L'Oiseau de feu*, 1910

(A) L. Bakst. Costume study for the ballet, *Narcisse*, 1911

174

A. N. Benois, Design for the first act of the ballet, *Petrouchka*, 1911

(B) Old Believers' Church, Moscow. By I. Y. Bondarenko, 1909

(A) M. V. Yakunchikova. The Cemetery. Coloured woodcut

176

V. M. Vasnetsov. Design for the Tretyakov Art Gallery, Moscow, 1900

177

(A) Kazan Railway Station, Moscow. By A. V. Shchusev, 1914–40

(B) Ryabushinski House, Moscow, by F. O. Shekhtel, *c.* 1905

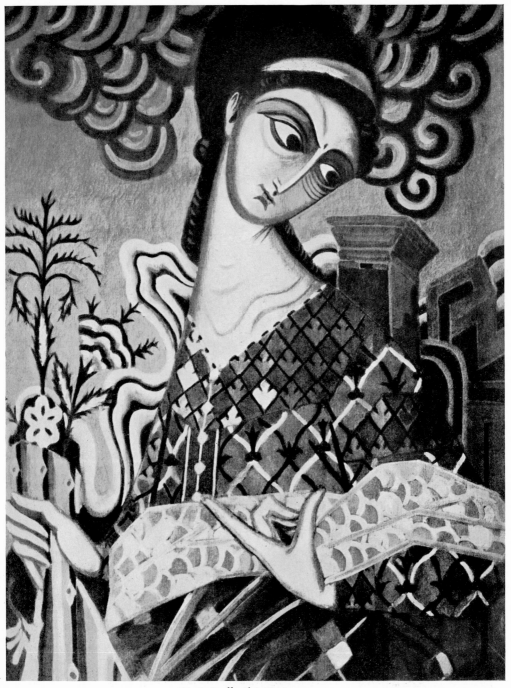

D. S. Stelletski. Dawn, 1910

P. P. Trubetskoi. S. Iu. Vitte. 1901, Bronze. *Russian Museum, Leningrad*

INDEX

Churches and other buildings will be found indexed under the name of the town or other place at which they are located : thus St Basil's Cathedral, Moscow, will be found under the heading Moscow. The dates given for Tsars and other rulers indicate their regnal years. References to notes are given to the page on which the note occurs, followed by the number of the Chapter to which it belongs and the number of the note. Thus 272(7)[8]. Numbers in *italics* refer to plates.

A

M